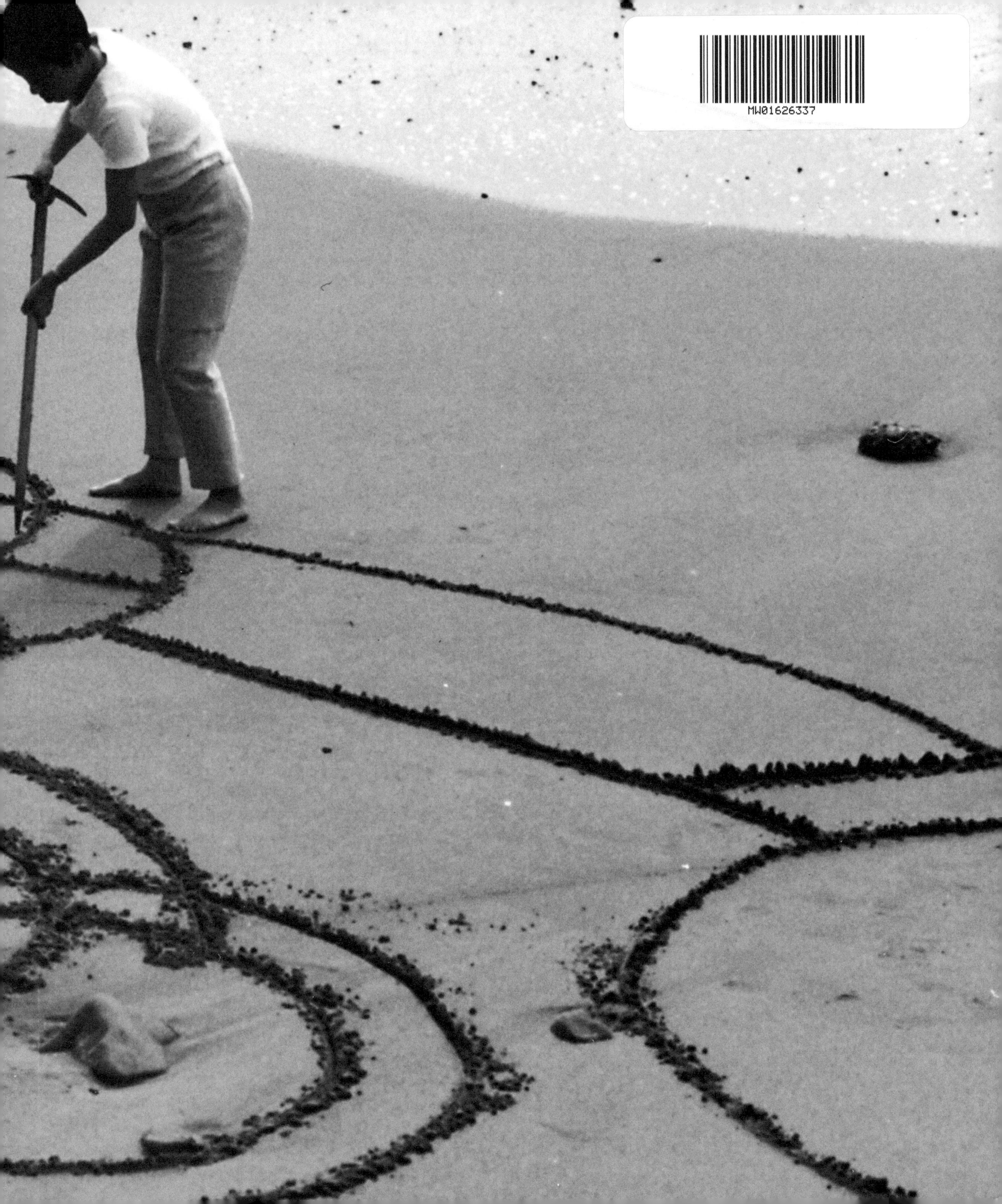
MW01626337

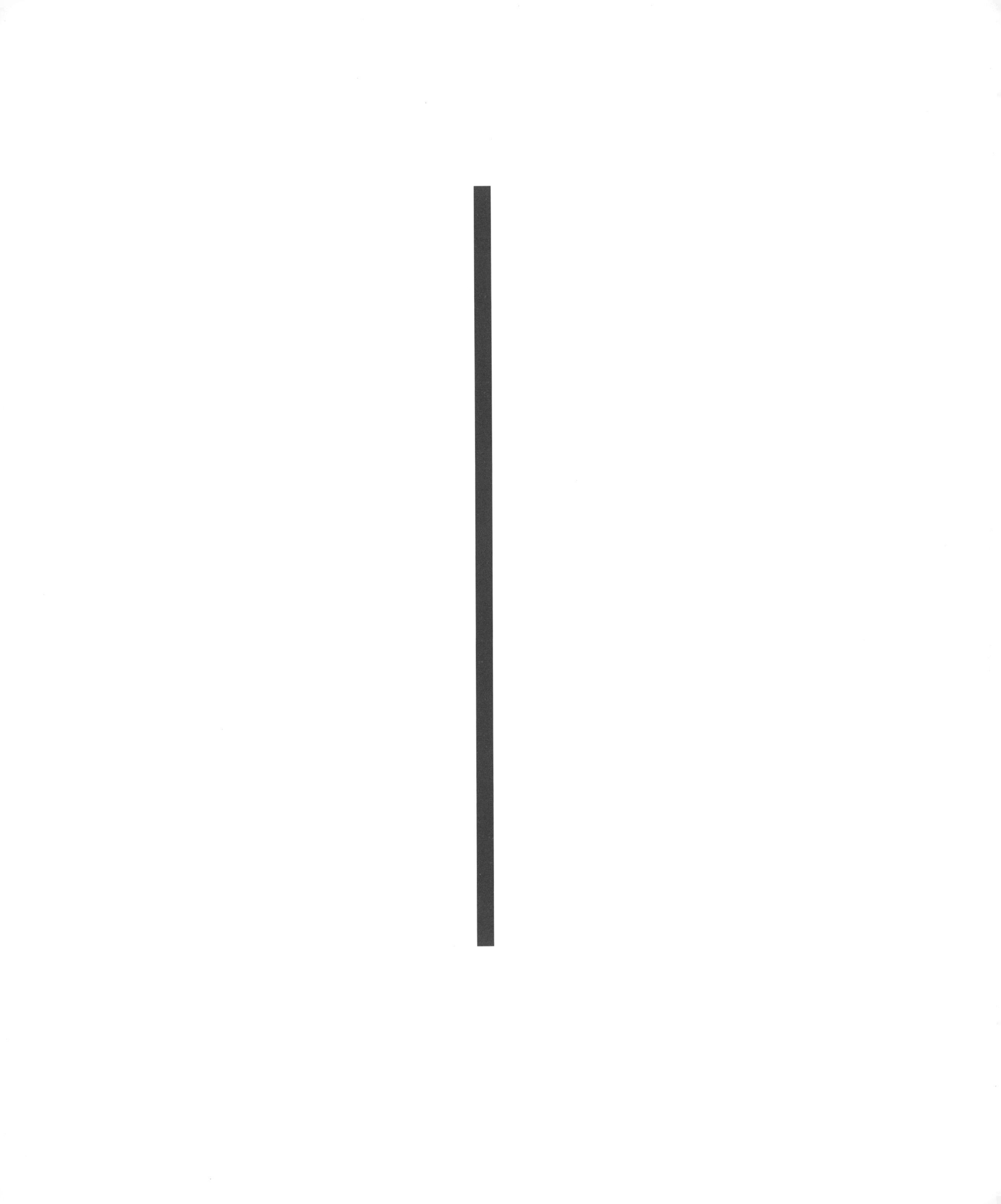

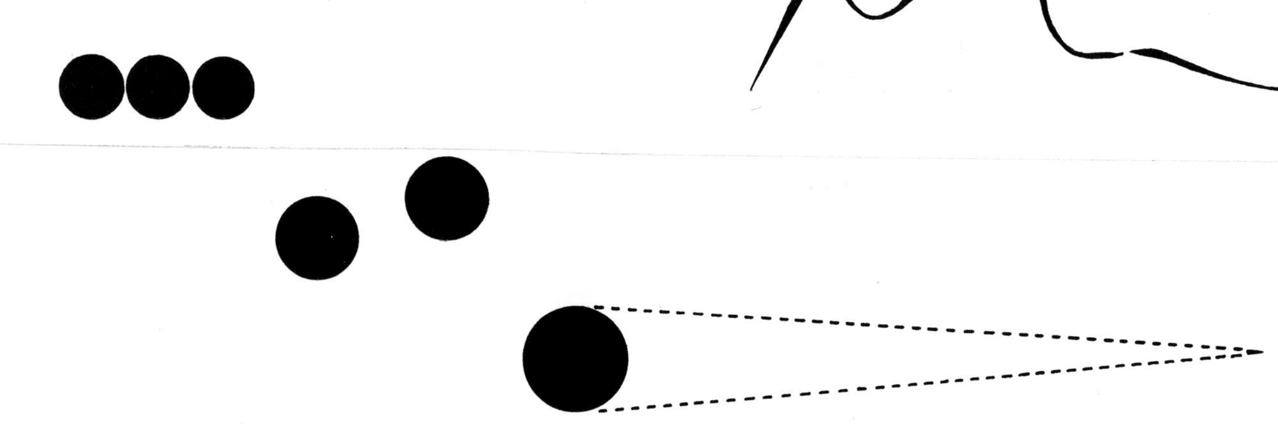
II Thema d. V Symphonie.
135

ON LINE

DRAWING THROUGH THE TWENTIETH CENTURY

Cornelia H. Butler | Catherine de Zegher

The Museum of Modern Art, New York

Published in conjunction with the exhibition
On Line: Drawing through the Twentieth Century,
at The Museum of Modern Art, New York
(November 21, 2010–February 7, 2011),
organized by Cornelia H. Butler, The Robert Lehman Foundation
Chief Curator of Drawings, and Catherine de Zegher, former
Director of The Drawing Center, New York

The exhibition is made possible by MoMA's Wallis Annenberg Fund
for Innovation in Contemporary Art through the Annenberg Foundation,
Maja Oeri and Hans Bodenmann, and by The Contemporary Arts
Council of The Museum of Modern Art.

Produced by the Department of Publications,
The Museum of Modern Art, New York

Edited by David Frankel
Designed by McCall Associates, New York
Production by Christina Grillo
Printed and bound by Trifolio s.r.l., Verona

This book is typeset in Kievit, AT Sackers Gothic,
and Freight Sans. The paper is Luxosamt Offset 150 gsm

Published by The Museum of Modern Art,
11 W. 53 Street, New York, New York 10019

Library of Congress Control Number: 2010936657
ISBN: 978-0-87070-782-7

Distributed in the United States and Canada
by D.A.P./Distributed Art Publishers, Inc., New York
Distributed outside the United States and Canada
by Thames & Hudson Ltd, London

Front cover: Julie Mehretu. *Rising Down* (detail). 2008.
Ink and synthetic polymer paint on canvas, 8 x 12′ (243.8 x 365.8 cm).
See plate 115

Back cover: Françoise Sullivan. *Danse dans la Neige* (Dance in the snow; detail)
no. 3. 1948. 1 of 17 gelatin silver prints (photographs: Maurice Perron)
mounted on Masonite mounted on wood. Each: 15 3/8 x 15 3/8″ (39 x 39 cm).
See plates 169–73

Front endpapers: Atsuko Tanaka. *Round on Sand*. 1968.
16mm film, color, silent, 9:50 min. See plate 179

Back endpapers: Michelle Stuart. *Nazca Lines Star Chart. Nazca Lines Southern Hemisphere Constellation Chart Correlation* (detail). 1981–82.
Earth from Nazca plateau, Peru, rubbed into paper. 10′ 1/4″ x 14′ 1/2″
(305.3 x 428 cm) and 17 x 22″ (43.2 x 55.9 cm). See p. 223

Frontispiece: Vasily Kandinsky. *II. Thema der V. Symphonie*
(Theme II of the Fifth Symphony). 1925. Illustration for Kandinsky's
book *Punkt und Linie zu Fläche* (Point and line to plane), 1926.
Pencil and ink on paper, 9 1/16″ x 14 9/16″ (23 x 37 cm)

Contents page, opposite: Sol LeWitt. Untitled. 1971. Folded colored paper.
10 3/4 x 21 3/4″ (27.3 x 55.2 cm)

Printed in Italy

CONTENTS

DIRECTOR'S FOREWORD

The story of MoMA's thematic exhibitions is one of both groundbreaking efforts and scholarly syntheses. The history-making shows in the era of Alfred H. Barr, Jr., and the periodic surveys organized by Dorothy Miller in the 1950s and '60s, when contemporary art history was forged almost as quickly as art was produced in the studio; the momentous '30s architecture exhibitions that established a field in American museums where there had been none; and shows such as the great *"Primitivism"* and *High & Low* in the '80s and early '90s, which stirred controversy as much as they were prescient in addressing significant directions in art — this is a remarkable context for our continuing work here. More recently *Eye on Europe*, organized by Deborah Wye, *In and Out of Amsterdam*, organized by Christophe Cherix, and *Color Chart*, organized by Ann Temkin, have maintained the Museum's tradition of speculative, historically grounded exhibitions that attempt to make sense of an impulse or movement in art, or to write a new chronology of a period.

On Line: Drawing through the Twentieth Century continues this lineage, and also a more specific tradition of synthetic shows including *Drawing Now: 1955–1975*, organized by Bernice Rose in 1976; *Drawing Now: Eight Propositions*, organized by Laura Hoptman in 2002; and many others organized in the drawings galleries from the museum's collection, such as *Transforming Chronologies: An Atlas of Drawings*, organized by Luis Pérez-Oramas in 2006. A collaboration between Connie Butler, the Museum's Robert Lehman Foundation Chief Curator of Drawings, and guest curator Catherine de Zegher, who initially brought the idea for the show to MoMA, *On Line* reflects both curators' desire to invigorate the discourse around drawing in the twentieth and twenty-first centuries through an investigation of line and its history, as traced both in artists' writings and in works of art. The endeavor has been an enriching one for the Museum, to whose extraordinary staff I am extremely grateful; the complexities of the exhibition, with its large number of objects and special artists' projects, have been orchestrated with the utmost professionalism and enthusiasm. I would like to acknowledge in particular the publications, installation, and curatorial teams for their sensitivity and grace in managing the intricacies of the project.

We are also extremely grateful to the committed individuals and foundations who have generously supported the exhibition, including the Wallis Annenberg Fund for Innovation in Contemporary Art through the Annenberg Foundation, Maja Oeri and Hans Bodenmann, and The Contemporary Arts Council of The Museum of Modern Art. We thank them for their support of this project and of the Museum's programming in general.

Many private individuals and museum colleagues have allowed us to borrow precious works in their collections for *On Line*. Their generosity has allowed us in many cases to exhibit art that has not yet been seen in the United States and in others to provide a new and revelatory context for more-familiar works. Many artists or their estates have lent extraordinary objects, some artists making works especially for the exhibition and all without exception giving freely of their time and of their thought. On behalf of the Trustees and staff of the Museum, I wish to thank them.

GLENN D. LOWRY
DIRECTOR, THE MUSEUM OF MODERN ART

ACKNOWLEDGMENTS

It has been our great pleasure and privilege to develop *On Line*, an exhibition with drawing at its core. We are indebted to the artists represented in the exhibition and in particular to those who so generously lent us their enthusiasm, intellectual support, and wonderful works. Their art and ideas have made this project richly rewarding for both curators and audience.

A project of this scale involves many individuals and we are deeply grateful to MoMA's extraordinary staff, whose skill and enthusiasm featured at every stage. In the Museum's Department of Drawings, the project's base, we first thank Curatorial Assistant Esther Adler, who did the work usually done by a team. Her organizational skills were monumental, her intellectual input was invaluable, and her research, insight, and feeling for the subject contributed immeasurably to both exhibition and book. Curatorial Assistants Samantha Friedman, Maura Lynch, and Alexandra Schwartz also contributed to the research. Curator Jodi Hauptman, Estrellita Brodsky Curator of Latin American Art Luis Pérez-Oramas, Harvey S. Shipley Miller Associate Curator of Drawings Christian Rattemeyer, Assistant Curator Kathy Curry, Curatorial Assistant Geaninne Gutiérrez Guimarães, Department Manager John Prochilo, Department Assistant Ji Hae Kim, and preparator David Moreno all contributed to the exhibition's success.

Deep thanks go to MoMA Director Glenn D. Lowry, whose encouragement and advice have been invaluable. Trustees Agnes Gund and Kathy Fuld were wells of inspiration and encouragement. Former Senior Deputy Director for Exhibitions, Collections and Programs Jennifer Russell and Associate Director Kathy Halbreich supported the project from its inception. Peter Reed, Senior Deputy Director for Curatorial Affairs, gave counsel on many occasions, while Deputy Director for Exhibitions and Collections Ramona Bannayan calmly oversaw all aspects of the exhibition's organization. We are grateful to MoMA's other Chief Curators — Klaus Biesenbach, Barry Bergdoll, Peter Galassi, Rajendra Roy, Ann Temkin, and Deborah Wye — for their suggestions and for the loans they provided from their departments. Additional input came from Gretchen Wagner, Assistant Curator of Prints and Illustrated Books, and Anne Umland, Curator of Painting and Sculpture. Interns Carmen Hermo, Samantha Conroy, Kristen Rudy, Anna Drozda, Anna Moser, Susan Carlson, Sara Griffin, and Betina Bethlem all provided critical research and clerical support.

An exhibition of over 300 works by over 100 artists requires complex orchestration. Head Registrar Stefanii Ruta-Atkins and Asssistant Registrars Corey Wyckoff and Sacha Eaton coordinated loans and insurance negotiations. The exhibitions staff, especially Coordinator of Exhibition Programs Maria DeMarco Beardsley and Associate Coordinator Jennifer Cohen, oversaw the budget and assisted with the complexities of the artists' projects. The exhibition's beautiful design was overseen by Director of Exhibition Design and Production Jerome Neuner and Production Manager Lana Hum. The show's public face was enhanced by Director of Interpretation and Research Sara Bodinson and Associate Educator Stephanie Pau, Assistant Editor Rebecca Roberts, and Graphic Design Manager Brigitta Bungard. We are proud of the exhibition's website and digital programming, for which we thank Creative Director of Digital Media Allegra Burnett and Media Developer Shannon Darrough. Chief Conservator Jim Coddington, Photography Conservator Lee Ann Daffner, Paintings Conservator Michael Duffy, Associate Paper Conservator Scott Gerson, and Sculpture Conservator Lynda Zycherman safeguarded the exhibition's large variety of objects. Audiovisual coordination was provided by Director of Audio/Visual Services K Mita and Manager Charlie Kalinowski.

Our work with living artists representing an international array of perspectives required assistance from MoMA's fantastic development team, including Senior Deputy Director of External Affairs Mike Margitich, Director of Exhibition Funding and Director of PS1 Development Todd Bishop, Assistant Director of Exhibition Funding Lauren Stakias, and Foundation Relationship Manager Elizabeth Burke. General Counsel Patty Lipshutz, Deputy General Counsel Nancy Adelson, and Associate General Counsel Henry Lanman handled the legal issues of bringing so many artists to work at the museum. The artists Francis Alÿs,

A. Balasubramaniam, Luis Camnitzer, Monika Grzymala, Arturo Herrera, Giuseppe Penone, and Ranjani Shettar created on-site projects for the exhibition, enhancing it tremendously.

Chief Communications Officer Kim Mitchell, Director of Communications Margaret Doyle, and Publicist Paul Jackson effectively disseminated word of the exhibition to the public. Deputy Director for Education Wendy Woon, Director of Adult and Academic Education Pablo Helguera, and Assistant Director of Adult Programs Laura Beiles were wonderful partners in communicating its themes. We also thank the speakers in the exhibition symposium: Benjamin Buchloh, Luis Camnitzer, Jean Fisher, Janet Kraynak, Ralph Lemon, Anna Maria Maiolino, and Julie Mehretu.

With the guidance and expertise of Publisher Christopher Hudson, Associate Publisher Kara Kirk, Editorial Director David Frankel, and Production Manager Christina Grillo, we have produced a publication that sensitively reflects the exhibition's themes. Mark Nelson of McCall Associates gave the book its beautiful design. We are deeply grateful to them and extremely proud of this publication.

The exhibition in the galleries is accompanied by a performance program in the Museum's Atrium and a film program in the theaters. The collaboration of Assistant Curator for Performance Jenny Schlenzka on the performance series has enormously enhanced it. The film program is organized by Associate Curator of Film Anne Morra and Esther Adler, whose selection reflects the diverse ways line has been used in film across the century.

The exhibition's objects are extraordinary, and we are vastly grateful to the institutional and private lenders who have temporarily parted with them. Colleagues who facilitated these loans and the commissioned projects include Livia Gonzaga Bertuzzi, James Caritey, Deborah Carruthers, Dominique Haim Chanin, Angelica Charistou, David Gray, Diana Howard, Bellatrix Hubert, Caroll Janis, Michael Jenkins, Finola Jones, Mizuho Kato, Walburga Krupp, Anne Lemonnier, Doris Leutgeb, Wolf Lieser, Dorotea Mendoza, David Moos, Ruggero Penone, Gabriel Pérez-Barreiro, Tricia Pierson, Julian Richter, Judith Ryan, Rocco Mussat Sartor, Hans-Michael Schäfer, Mathilde Simian, Margo Smith, Jen Stamps, Jonas Storsve, and Maria Tsantsanoglou.

Catherine de Zegher would like to thank Creative Capital, and its Consulting Director Margaret Sundell; The Andy Warhol Foundation, especially Program Director Pamela Clapp, whose Arts Writers Grant in 2007 gave her invaluable support for this book; The Bellagio Center of the Rockefeller Foundation, and Managing Director Pilar Palaciá and coordinator Linda Marston-Reid, for the 2007 residency that enabled the writing of her essay; Marian Goodman, who hosted the 2006 exhibition *Freeing the Line*, a predecessor of this exhibition; David Thomson, Avis Newman, Richard Tuttle, Giuseppe Penone, and Deepak Talwar, for our ongoing discussions on drawing; and last but not least Craigie Horsfield, for his inspirational companionship and thorough editing, and my children Samuel, Eva, and Marga De Jaegere.

Connie Butler thanks Maja Oeri, leader of the Drawings Committee, who, with her husband, Hans Bodenmann, provided critical support. David Shafer and Liam and Rainer Butler Schafer are an infinite source of support and inspiration.

Each of us would also like to express her appreciation for the other, and for the process of collaboration between us that has led to the range of artists and interests included in the show. That collaboration, we feel, amounts to more than the sum of its parts.

We are enormously grateful to MoMA's Wallis Annenberg Fund for Innovation in Contemporary Art through the Annenberg Foundation, Maja Oeri and Hans Bodenmann, and The Contemporary Arts Council of The Museum of Modern Art, who together have made the exhibition possible.

Finally we thank the Drawings Committee, whose commitment to the collection and activities of the Department of Drawings is remarkable, and MoMA's wonderful Board of Trustees. It is the Trustees' very personal engagement in the Museum's life, and the leadership of Chairman Jerry Speyer and President Marie-Josée Kravis, that makes possible such exhibitions as this.

CONNIE BUTLER   CATHERINE DE ZEGHER

SURFACE TENSION

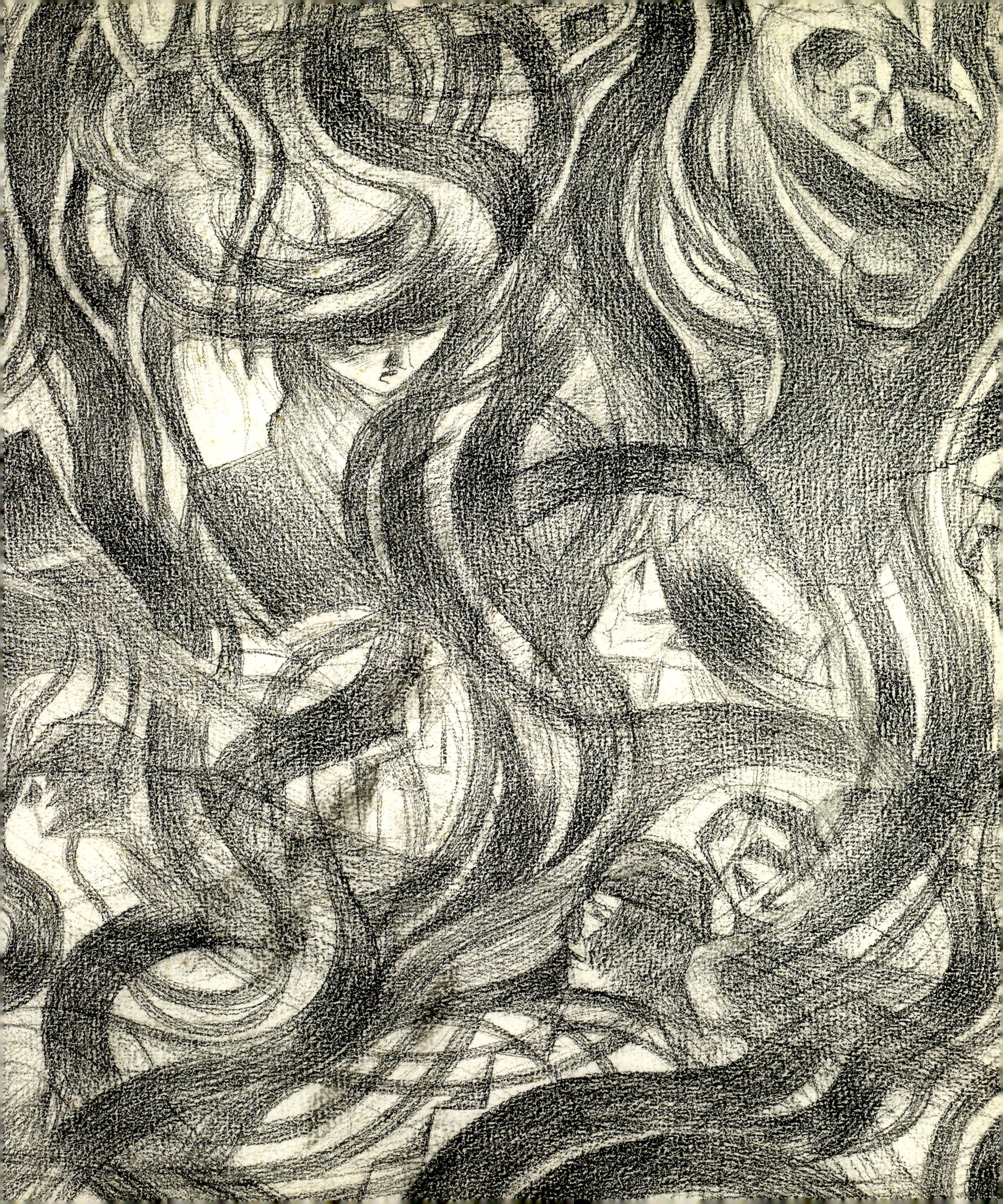

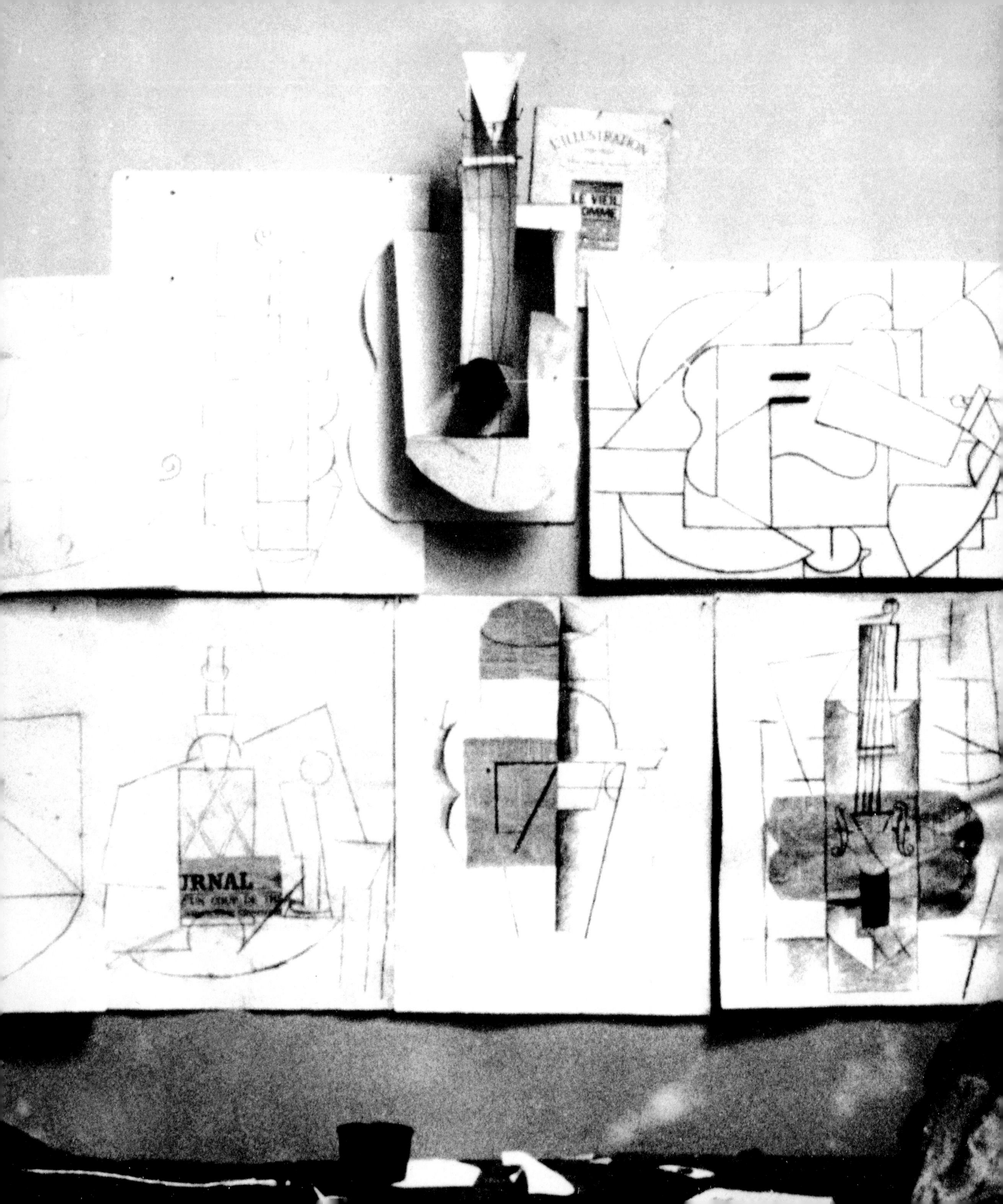
L'ILLUSTRATION
LE VIEIL
URNAL

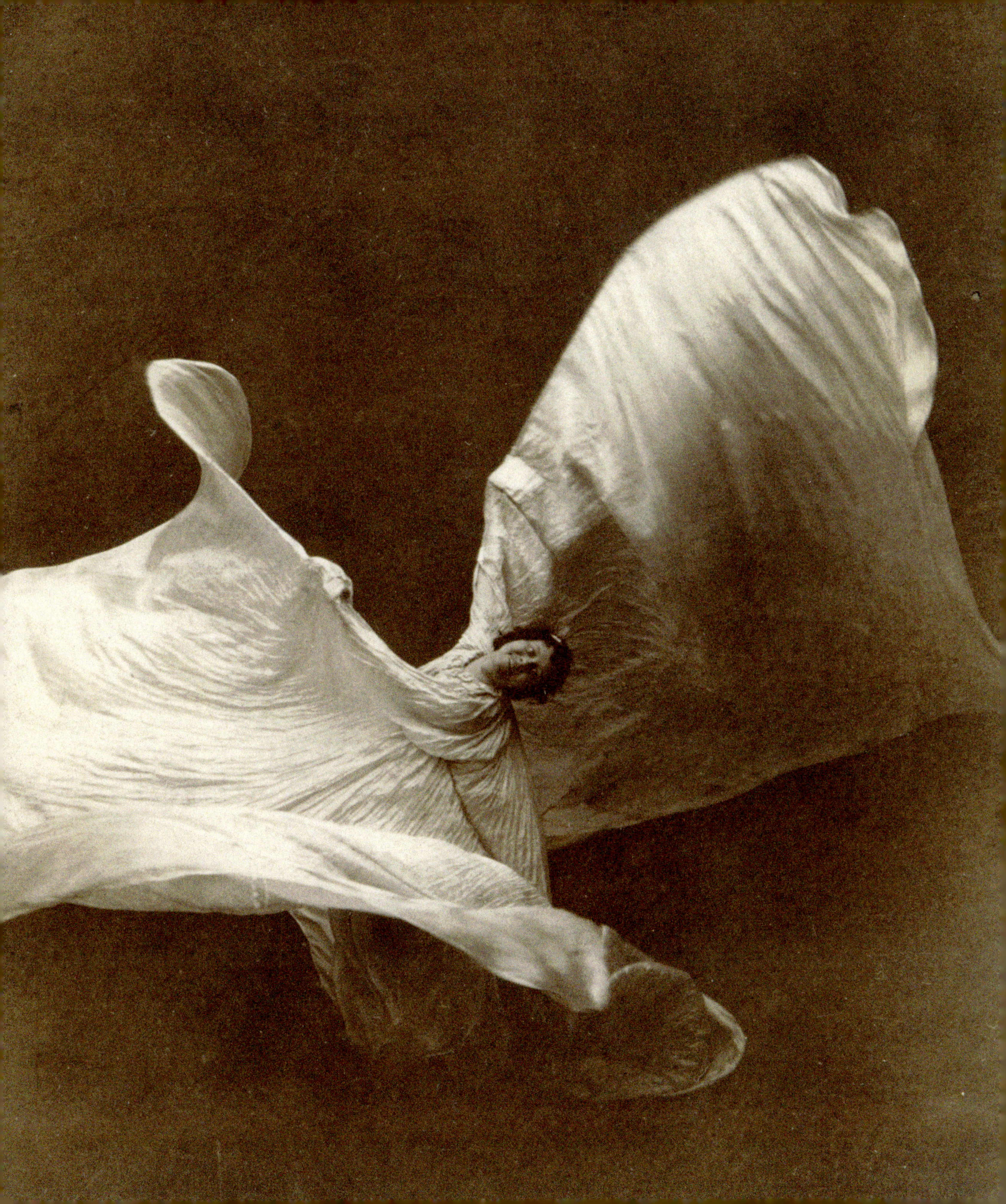

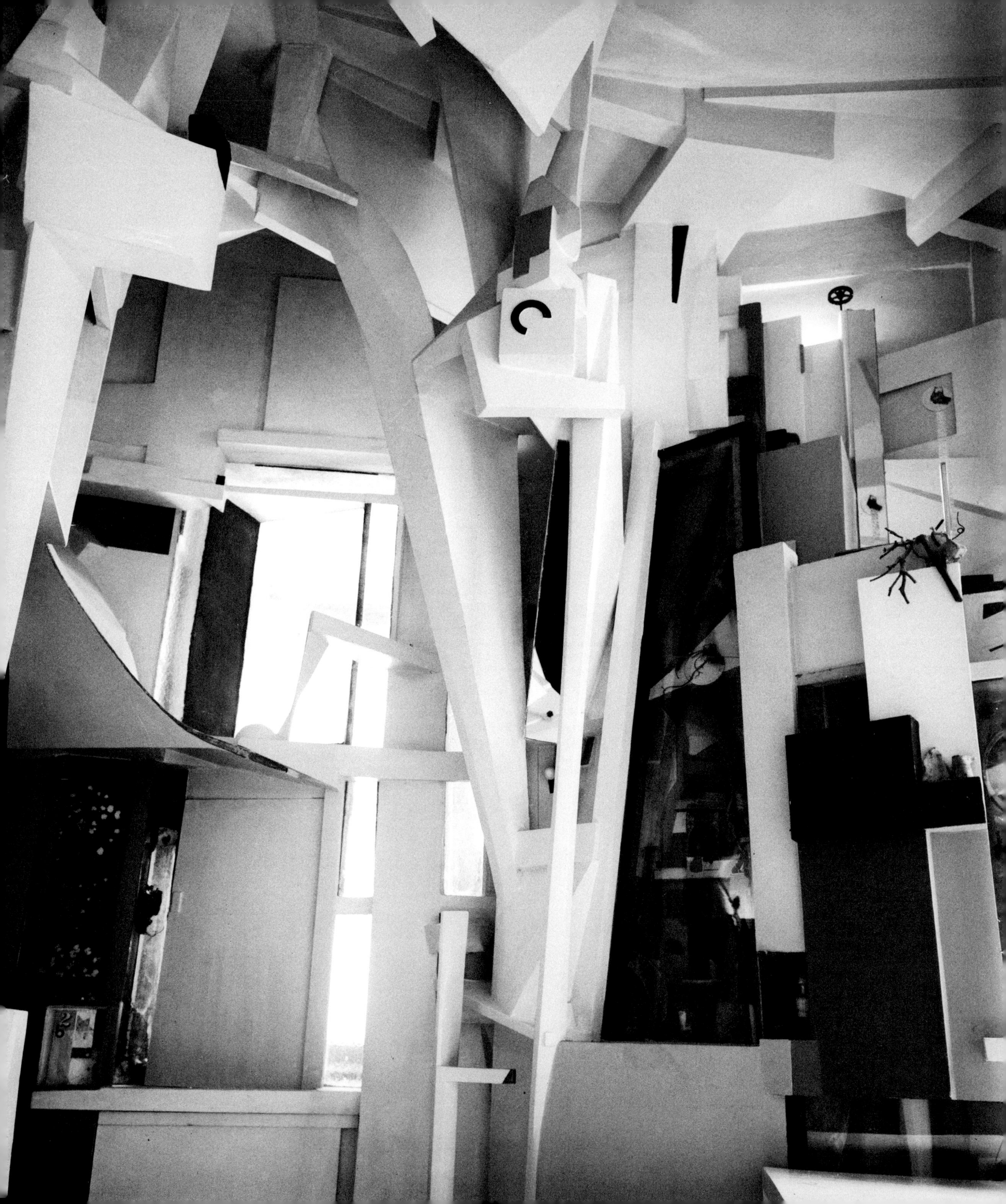

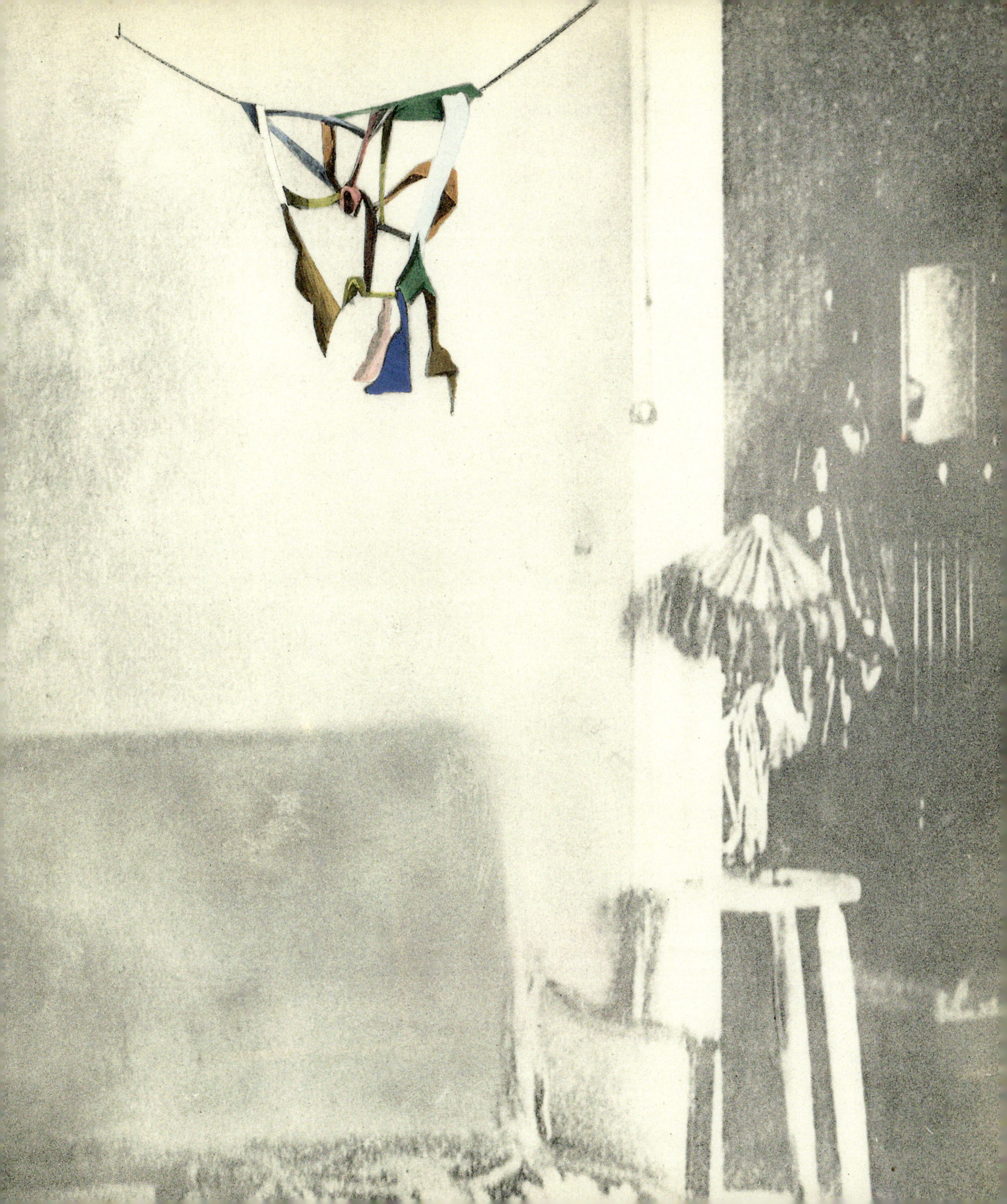

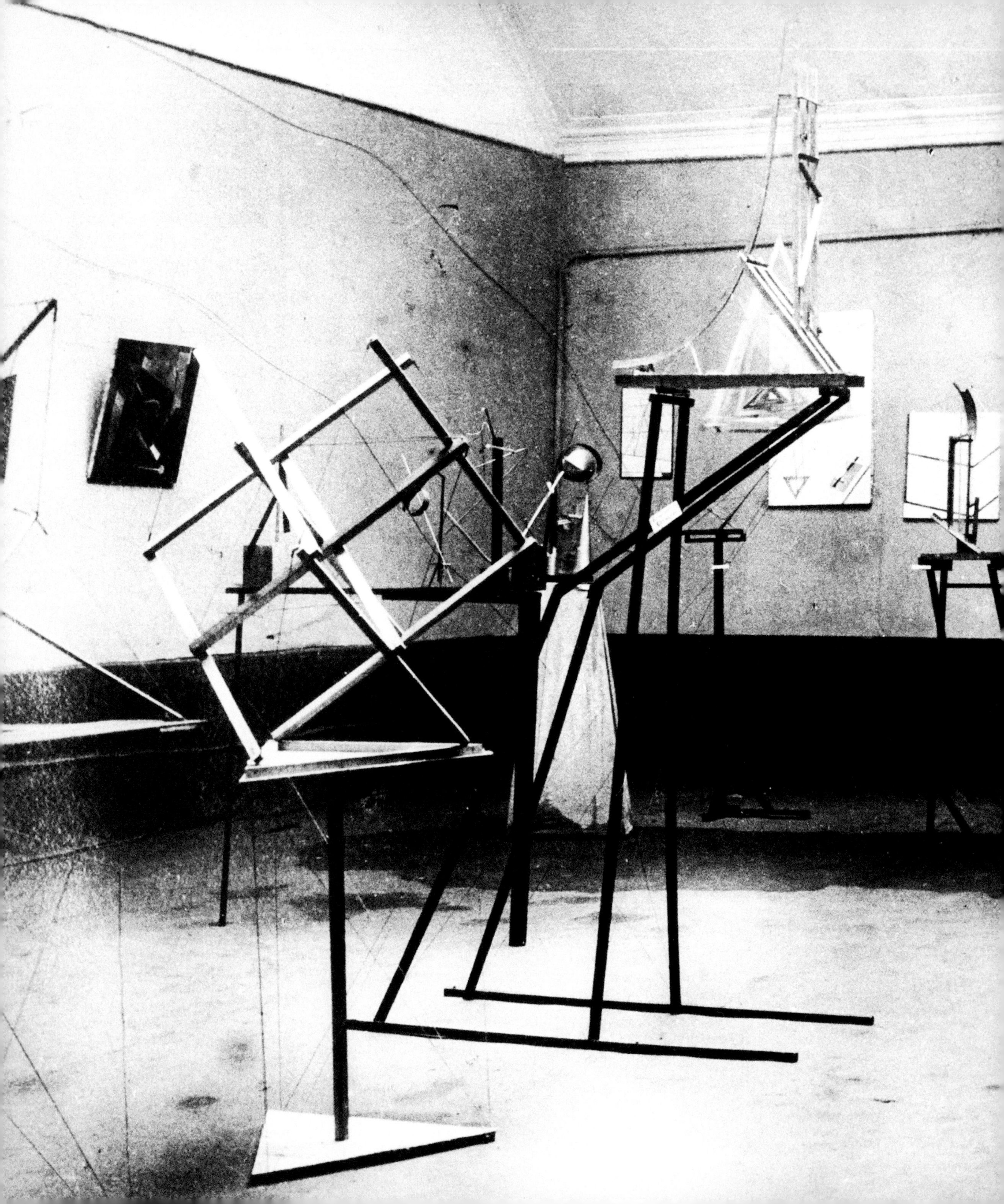

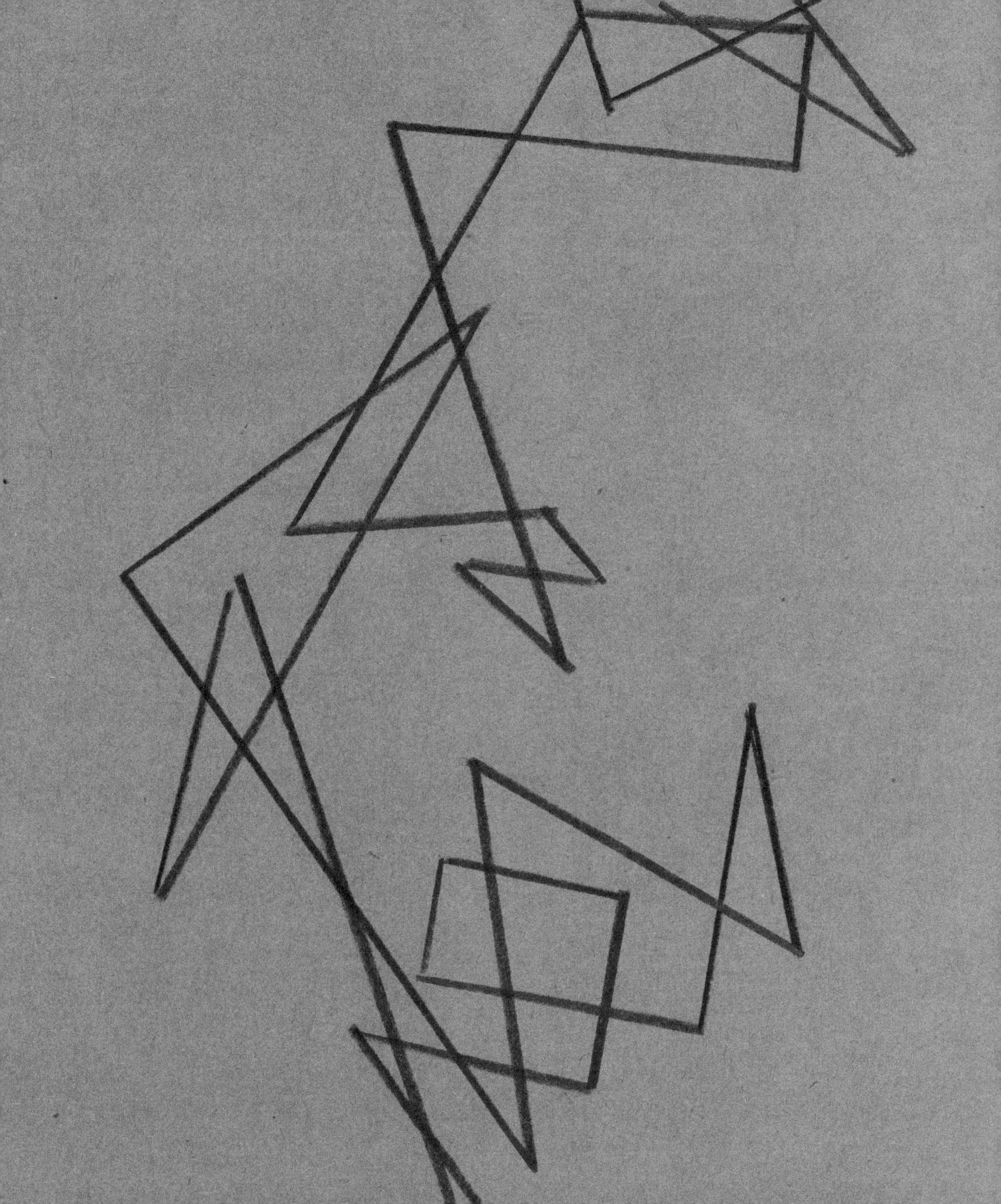

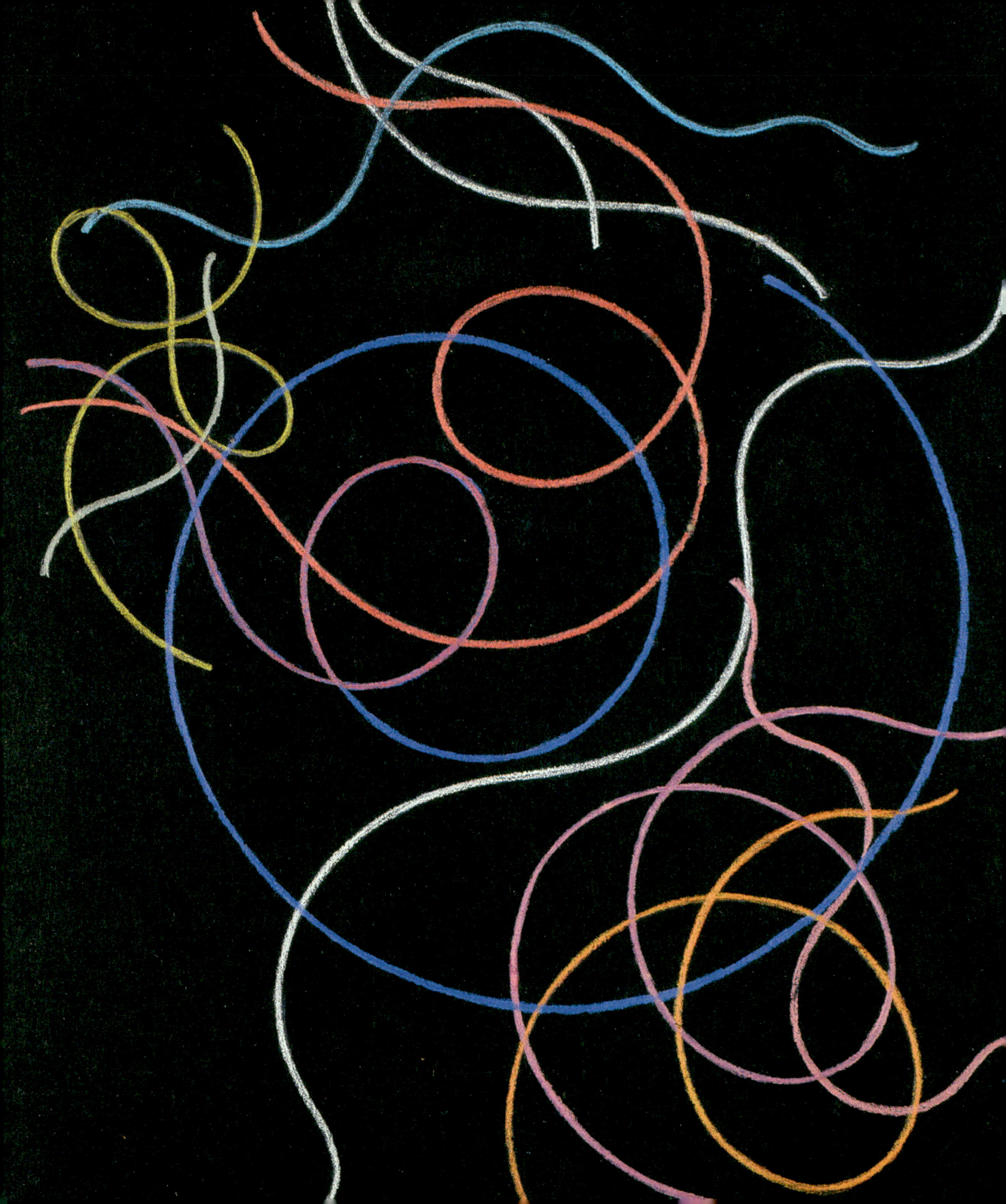

1. Umberto Boccioni
(Italian, 1882–1916)
Stati d'animo. Gli addii (States of mind: the farewells, detail; see plate 152). 1911
Charcoal and chalk on paper
23 x 34" (58.4 x 86.4 cm)

2. The wall of **Pablo Picasso**'s Paris studio in 1912 (detail; see plate 15)

3. Isaiah West Taber
(American, 1830–1912)
Loie Fuller dancing with her veil (detail; see plate 151). 1897
Gelatin silver printing-out paper print pasted on cardboard
4 7/16 x 6 1/2" (11.3 x 16.7 cm)

4. Kurt Schwitters
(German, 1887–1948)
Merzbau. Begun early 1920s, destroyed 1943
Paper, cardboard, plaster, glass, mirror, metal, wood, electric lighting, and materials on wood and stone
Installation view showing "Blue Window" section of the work, in Schwitters's house in Hannover, 1933

5. Marcel Duchamp
(American, born France, 1887–1968)
Sculpture de voyage (*Sculpture for Traveling*, 1918; detail; see plate 140) as reproduced in *Boîte-en-valise (de ou par Marcel Duchamp ou Rrose Sélavy (Box in a Valise [From or by Marcel Duchamp or Rrose Sélavy]).* 1935–41
Collotype with pochoir, from a leather valise containing 80 miniature replicas, color reproductions, and photographs of works by Duchamp
12 5/8 x 9 3/4" (32.1 x 24.8 cm)

6. *Second Spring Exhibition of the OBMOKhU* (Society of young artists), Moscow, 1921. Installation view (detail; see plate 33)

7. Aleksandr Rodchenko
(Russian, 1891–1956)
Untitled (detail; see p. 223). c. 1920
Pencil on colored paper
12 1/4 x 8 1/4" (31.1 x 21 cm)

8. Sophie Taeuber-Arp
(Swiss, 1889–1943)
Mouvement de lignes en couleurs (Movement of colored lines; detail; see plate 162). 1940
Colored pencil on cardboard
14 1/8 x 11" (35.9 x 28 cm)

9. A. Balasubramaniam
(Indian, born 1971)
Rest in Resistance. 2007
Fiberglass, acrylic, fishing hooks, and elastic
37 x 40 x 15˝ (94 x 101.6 x 38.1 cm)

A CENTURY UNDER THE SIGN OF LINE

DRAWING AND ITS EXTENSION (1910–2010)

Catherine de Zegher

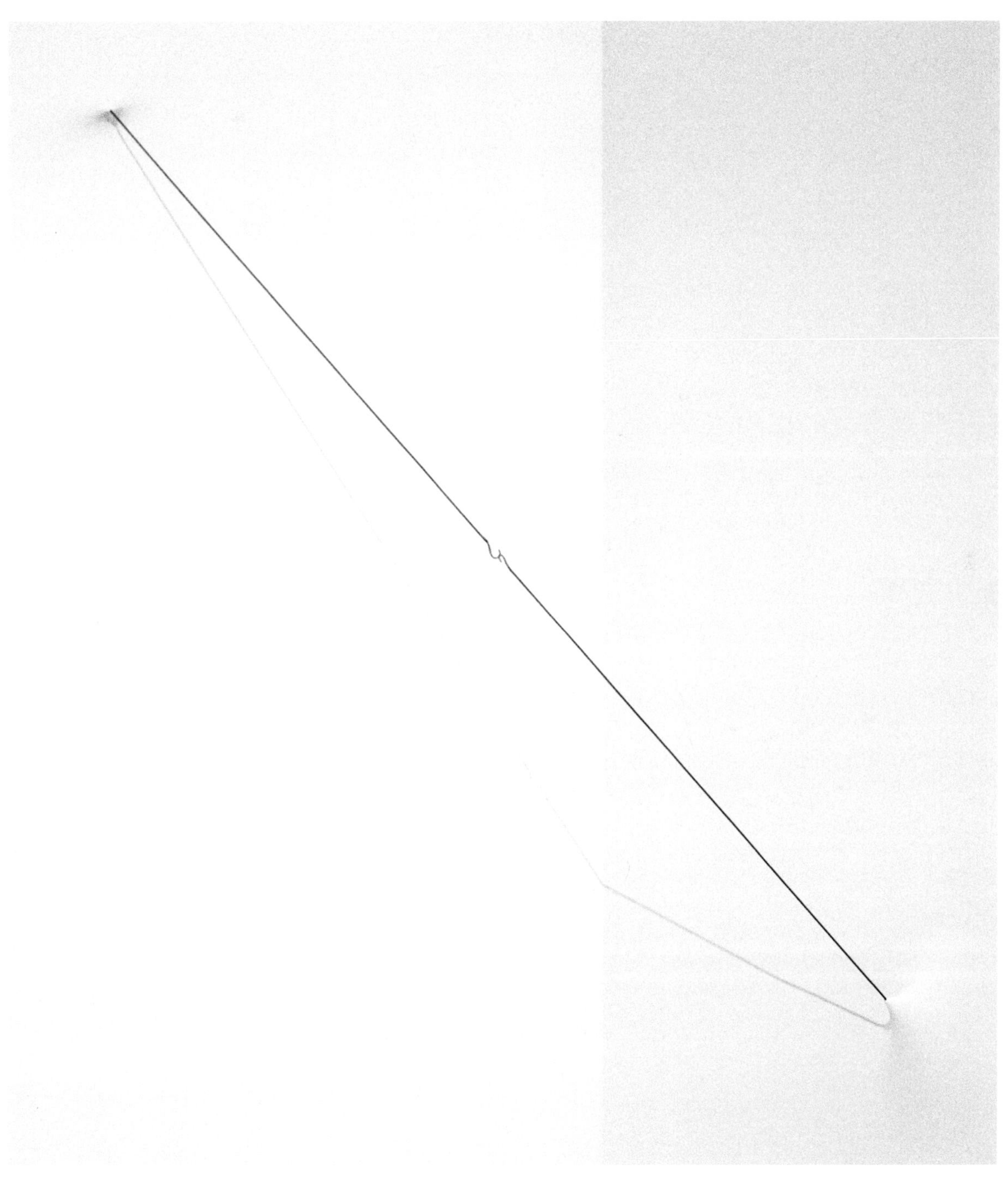

From these two graphic entities — point and line — derive the entire resources of a whole realm of art, graphics.

The point is now able to increase its size ad infinitum *and becomes the spot. Its subsequent and ultimate potential is that of changing its configuration, whereby it passes from the purely mathematical form of a bigger or smaller circle to forms of infinite flexibility and diversity, far removed from the diagrammatic.*

The fate of line is more complex and requires a special description.

The transference of line to a free environment produces a number of extremely important results. Its outer expediency turns into an inner one. Its practical meaning becomes abstract. As a result, the line discloses an inner sound of artistic significance.

A fundamental turning point is attained. Its fruit is the birth of the language of art.

Line experiences many fates. Each creates a particular, specific world, from schematic limitation to unlimited expressivity. These worlds liberate line more and more from the instrument, leading to complete freedom of expression.

— Vasily Kandinsky, "On Line," 1919

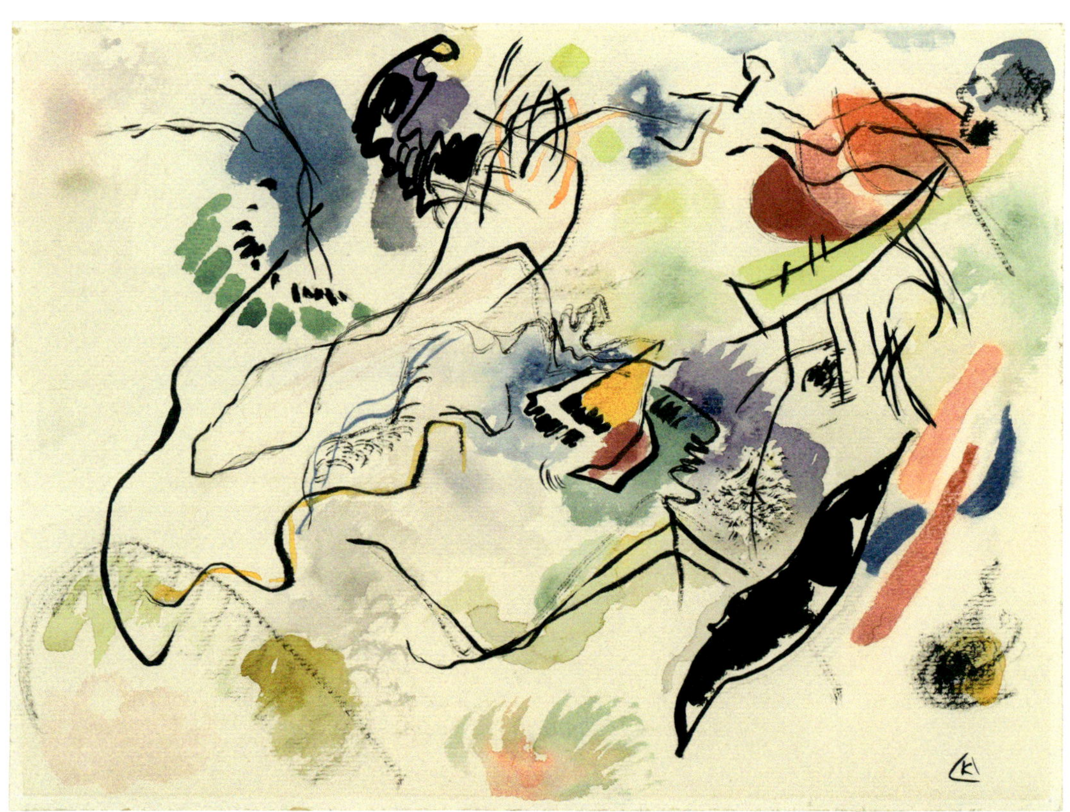

10. Vasily Kandinsky
(French, born Russia, 1866–1944)
Watercolor No. 14. 1913
Watercolor and ink on paper
9 3/8 x 12 3/8" (23.8 x 31.4 cm)

LIKE A TIGHTROPE DANCER

A kinesthetic practice of traction — attraction, extraction, protraction — drawing is born from an outward gesture linking inner impulses and thoughts to the other through the touching of a surface with repeated graphic marks and lines. Significantly, line draws on relation as much as relation draws on line. As a way of entering this large subject matter, let us begin with drawing as a matter of fact involving, according to the dictionary, "the formation of a line by moving some tracing tool from point to point on a surface," and the inscription of this gestural act, *a* drawing, being "any mode of representation by lines in which delineation of form predominates over consideration of color." Strictly taken, drawing includes "only the art of forming the resemblance of objects by means of outlines, where a single color, as india ink, is employed to produce shades."[1] The arrangement of lines to determine form — *delineation* — is much older than its companion, *perspective*. While perspective deals with the placement of objects in space, delineation deals primarily with analogy: the representation of objects as such, not as they appear in space. The combination of delineation and perspective allows objects in real space to be transcribed to the imaginary plane.

The principles of the kind of academic drawing that pertained at the end of the nineteenth century effectively constituted a highly conceptual system — a symbolic, philosophical system of convention and practice, pretending to something akin to scientific objectivity. With line as the prime element of a language concerned with the imitation of reality, drawing could be both a reliably accurate representation of objects as seen in reality and a poetically inspired representation conceived in the imagination.

A line *is breadthless length.*
A straight *line is a line that lies evenly with the points on itself.*

— Euclid, *Elements,* c. 300 B.C.

Line has in itself neither matter nor substance and may rather be called an imaginary idea than a real object.

— Leonardo da Vinci, "Definition of the Nature of Line," n.d.

Line may be broken or continuous, may comprise an extended sequence of single marks or an uninterrupted stripe. It is in the relation of one mark to another, in their shaping and shading, their tonal gradations, that a drawing acquires form, depth, volume. For centuries, a certain balance can be said to have been established between line and mark, in the sense that line, the leading principle, substantially defined the figure's contour, while modeling marks suggested a degree of spatiality and an impression of tactility. Together they induced a sense of movement and energy, with the mark as a means of nuance, vitality, and instability. The mental ideality of the contour line was complemented by the concrete staccato of small individual marks.

Seen as an open-ended activity, drawing is characterized by a line that is always unfolding, always becoming. And in the drawing's stages of becoming — mark becoming line, line becoming contour, contour becoming image — the first mark not only structures the blank page as an open field but also defines it temporally, as the drawing's marks follow one another in time. Their temporal sequence need not coincide with their spatial juxtaposition, however; they may overlap in space, and unlike painting, the act of drawing leaves it hard, after a while, to distinguish the first line from those that follow. The time of the drawing, as Dirk Lauwaert remarks, fades away as lines accrete, and soon the resulting image erases the sequence, whichever line came first disappearing into the rest.[2]

Thinking on drawing mostly excludes color. Line and color can of course be related in drawing, but pencil, graphite, ink, and charcoal have traditionally been considered the materials of the medium. Clarity and legibility may seem compromised by color, and lucidity of thought is exactly the aspect of drawing that is most valued. As in writing, this clarity seems to be linked directly to the fact that black tracing is easily discernible, in its contrast, against the presumed white background, while color is seen to confuse this perceptibility. A long-standing division between line and color accordingly persists in art history.

In the twentieth century, many artists made line the subject of intense exploration, including semiotic and phenomenological investigations. By line as such, they understood its pure existence in the world and the meaning that could be attributed to this existence as creative intention and interpretation. In fact, shaped as an "I," line is the first linguistic mark of differentiation, signifying the subject's entry into language. Much as poets and linguists were analyzing the line of speech or writing within the

larger, organized verbal whole, and were asserting the importance of laying bare its elements and devices before anything could be said of its meaning, artists were investigating the drawn and painted line as such. Unraveling its characteristics, they would go far in interpreting its form and function. Behind this parallel analysis was the belief of linguists and artists alike in the power of art to renew perception and to affect society, for the creation of a work of art was seen as the creation of the world. If, for the linguists, naming with the word was the act of consciousness through which we begin to know, for the artists the rendering of form in drawing transformed perception into naming, and so was the process through which they came to know. Cognition thus proceeds from creation, with line as indicator of a cognitive process.

From era to era and culture to culture, the support of drawing has varied: ground, wall, pottery, fabric, film, computer screen. With the commercial distribution of paper in Europe after the Middle Ages, however, it was with the sheet of paper that drawing conventionally became identified. And while the tools of drawing, similarly, have ranged from sticks to scrapers to pixels, graphite and ink have become inextricably linked with it. As exhibition and book, *On Line* describes a history of drawing that sheds the institutional reliance on paper as support by highlighting key shifts in artists' drawing practices since the start of the twentieth century. In considering this multivalent evolution, the exhibition necessarily involves a precarious balancing act between the definitions of drawing seen as canonical and what can be seen to be the extension of drawing.

Crucially, this project has been conceived with artist's marks and lines, their conversations and writings, at its core. In fact it derives its title from Vasily Kandinsky's essay "On Line," published in Moscow in 1919.[3] Beginning with the modern artist's idea of line as a point in movement, the exhibition chronicles the key shifts by juxtaposing avant-garde, neo-avant-garde, and contemporary drawings from diverse interrelated cultures. As such, and in the light of current practices, it charts the evolution of drawing in the twentieth and twenty-first centuries as a radical transformation of the medium, tracking its traverse from line as a moving of points, through the grid structure, to point as a crossing of lines, much as in online connection on the Internet and the World Wide Web. Indeed, by the end of the twentieth century, the terms "online" and "offline" had come to refer to a state of connectivity or disconnectivity with respect to computer technology and telecommunication. In analyzing this transformation, and a shift into virtual space, however, we also attend to the corporeal body itself as a point in motion, as in choreography, in which the dancer traces dynamic lines across the stage, or in land art, where the artist's wanderings leave traces on the earth.

Juxtaposing over 300 works, *On Line* examines different stages of the aesthetic exploration of line: the line in the plane (surface tension); the line broken free from that illusory surface into real space (line extension); and finally its apparent return to the relational space of the real and the imaginary, but with each now transformed in the process (confluence). In following the dilation of line's meaning, we also trace it in movement, across disciplines, and in its connectivity and continuity as it is drawn out and rewoven in time and space. Similarly, the history that informs the exhibition is interpreted here as an interweaving of materials, records, and the requirements of a changing present. This reading inevitably reflects notions of interconnection (as on the Web) and interdependency in a new globalized society. Where thought had been linear and progressive, it has evolved into a kind of network, something more fluid, open, simultaneous, and undefined.

11. Luis Camnitzer
(Uruguayan, born 1937)
Two Parallel Lines. 1976–2010
Mixed media and pencil on wall
Dimensions variable

LINE/PLANE/SPACE: IN TENSION (1910–1960)

Surface Tension (1910–1920)

At the beginning of the twentieth century, as drawing was increasingly defined by movement, the connection between the contour line and earlier modes of imitating reality was challenged by new methods of tracing and collage. In manifestos published in 1910–12, the Italian Futurists Umberto Boccioni (plates 1, 152), Giacomo Balla (plate 153), and Carlo Carrà criticized the stasis in what they saw as bourgeois aesthetics, instead emphasizing synesthesia and kinesthesia. These artists, however, pictured motion in a literal way, on a single plane, by repeating and blurring outlines. Their representations continued to be static, attaining neither a structural relation with the technology of speed nor the sensation of its lived experience, so that fluidity of perception remained stilled.

A true breakthrough was first achieved in the Cubist papier collés of Georges Braque (plate 180) and Pablo Picasso, in Paris in 1912. Cut paper had seen earlier uses, in the eighteenth-century "paper-mosaicks" of Mary Delany, for example, in the picture books of Hans Christian Andersen, and among the Victorian women who kept ornamented photo albums as a pastime. The motor behind the Cubist work with paper, however, was the obsession with velocity, energy, and change in real time and space — as it also was for the Futurists, but the Cubist move had more radical structural implications. The mere attachment of foreign matter to an otherwise unchanged pictorial conception in some Futurist work, such as the sequins applied to the dancers in Gino Severini's frenetic *Dynamic Hieroglyphic of the Bal Tabarin* (1912; plate 12), did not achieve what Picasso and Braque were developing in the papier collés.[4]

As Bernice Rose argues, among the inspirations for the Cubist drive to construct and experience movement within the flat picture plane were motion pictures and onstage dance, in particular the performances of Loie Fuller (plates 3, 13, 151). Fascinated by the novelty of film, both Braque and Picasso used its techniques of

> dissolves, close-ups, multiple exposures, parallel and crosscuts, and inserts to create different viewpoints in which one figure might be seen from the other's point of view as if from inside the frame — all kept the image changing. Cinema's movement was not just a series of stop-action photographs to analyze a succession of bodily movements, laying it out to the eye, frame by frozen frame, traced by Etienne-Jules Marey and Eadweard Muybridge, but the creation of an illusion of "real" movement: "the movement that was life." Here was a whole new illusionist representation of figure to ground, a whole new temporal and spatial simulation of reality. Film was at the same time both the flattest and most illusionistic of mediums; although it occupied only a thin membrane of its own creation, paradoxically, its dancing light suggested unlimited space and spilled over onto the audience, subverting the viewer into its sphere of experience.[5]

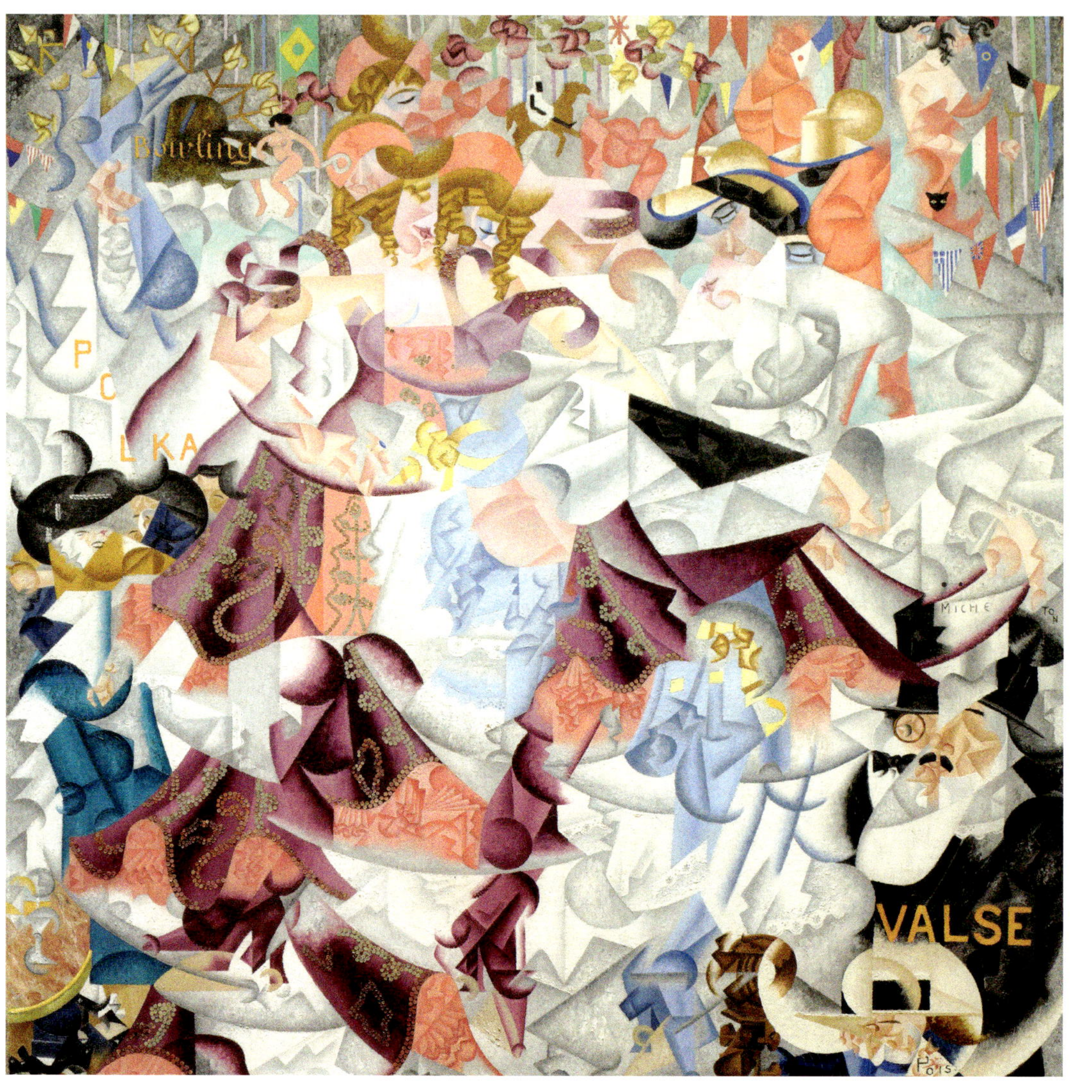

The invention of film had created a profound change in seeing, and its techniques had evolved with extraordinary rapidity since its first simple tableaux. In this context, film of Fuller's *Danse serpentine* appearing in 1896 and subsequently (plate 13) must have had an immediate impact. Based not just on the movement of the dancer, Fuller's art involved effects of light and color in constant transformation, notably in her *Fire Dance* (1896), in which she spun and twirled on glass illuminated from below. In a striking variation on the popular "skirt dance" of the day, Fuller experimented with the manipulation of lengths of silk and extended her skirts with bamboo rods, shining different-colored stage light on these moving panes and planes and giving the effect of an inspirational abstract art. Dance, film, and the flickering action of the projector can readily be imagined as influencing the nascent collage.

Braque's paper constructions of 1911–12, which led to the papier collés, included newspaper clippings, ribbons, bits of wallpaper, photographs, and other such, all glued to pieces of paper. These works depended on the literal treatment of reality, on actual material cuts and splices through space and time. The effects of cut-and-paste could also be equated with speed, as pieces slid past one another and zigzagged in disparate superimposed perspectives and ascending horizontal and vertical lines and angles. In the collages relating to Picasso's sheet metal *Guitar* of 1914, some of which the artist installed on his Paris studio wall in 1912 with drawings and the cardboard version of the work (plates 2, 14, 15), the cutting, folding, and retracing, both within each sheet and from sheet to juxtaposed sheet, rearranged

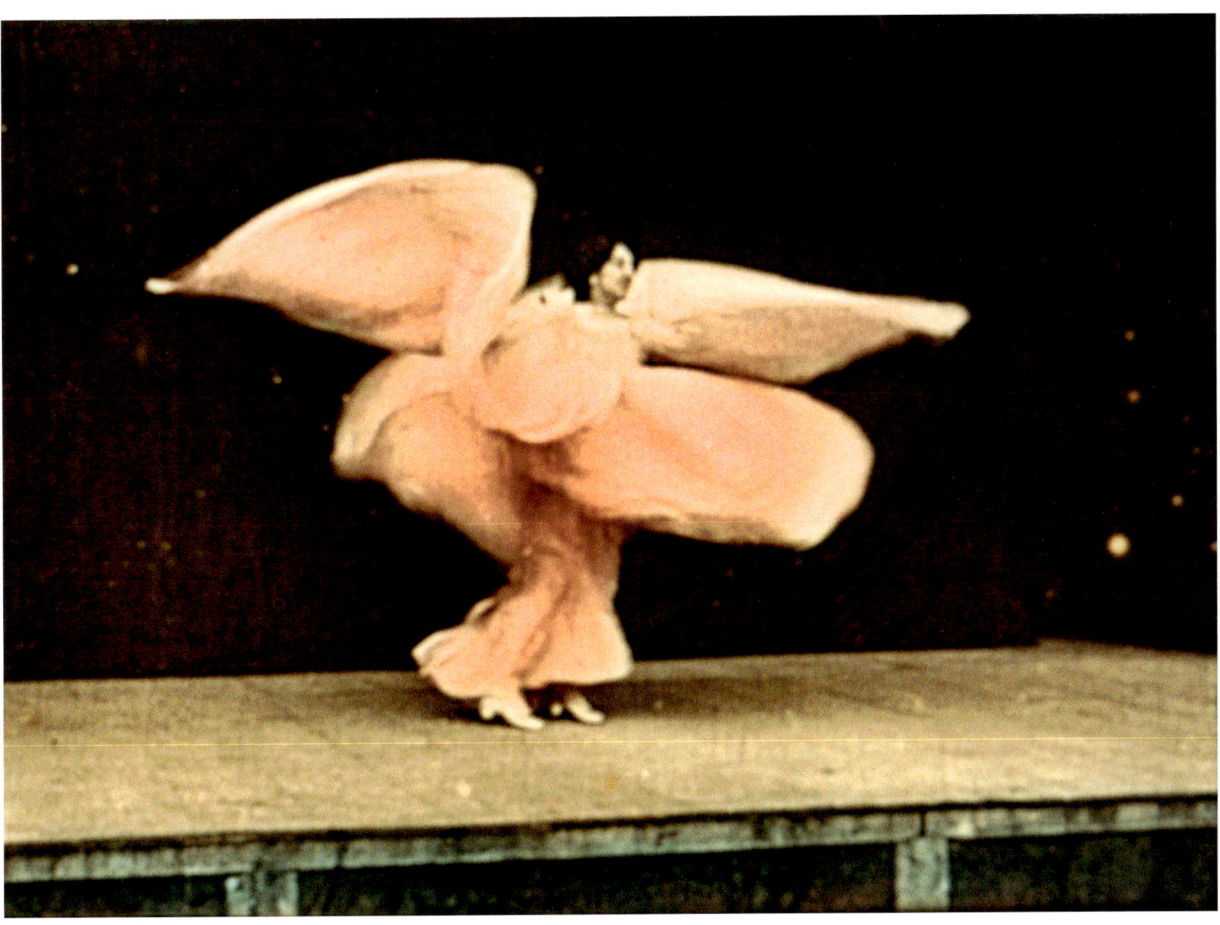

the metaphorical space of the drawing, extending into a new spatial dimension (plate 16). Breaking conventional pictorial perspective to show the guitar's sides and back simultaneously with the front, Picasso sought to apprehend the object from every angle at once, a composite of views constructed from an actual movement around it. For Rosalind Krauss, this simultaneity of distinct spatial positions as "a conflated time" posited a superiority of "conceptual knowledge" over merely perceptual realism.[6] Meanwhile, as assemblage, Cubist collage disrupted the planar surface of the picture to create a new composite whole. Becoming the seam between juxtaposed planes, line was both disjunctive, marking the edges of fragments of the fractured subject, and connective, delineating new relations.

As the cutouts of Braque and Picasso mostly perform on a stage of white, their positions are traced and retraced by outlines and marks drawn on the surface. Guided by the papers' cut edges, these linear markings are no longer a way of representing pictorial depth, aimed at producing an illusory space, but are coincident with the flat planes of the papers. Shading here is used against itself, creating the lowest possible relief, so that depicted volume is conflated with the flat surface. Cubist collage stresses both the flatness of the two-dimensional plane and the literal construction of reality, the several dimensions of the everyday (that is, the movement of life) introduced through actual material cuts in actual newspapers, advertisements, and other found papers. Gaps between the drawn and cut edges of the objects only emphasize the unbroken continuity of the plane.

Paradoxically, line was moving toward both a compression of pictorial space into flatness and an escape from it. As drawn outlines combined with the edges of cut papers, imaginary and real contours fused in a single plane, provoking a tension in the surface. Aligned with the frontality of the support, papers of various colors and shapes — wallpapers, newspapers, bottle labels, musical scores, pieces of old drawings, all taken from life, all overlaid like papers on a worktable — showed the work as paper

12. Gino Severini
(Italian, 1883–1966)
Dynamic Hieroglyphic of the Bal Tabarin. 1912
Oil on canvas with sequins
63 5/8 x 61 1/2" (161.6 x 156.2 cm)

13. Loie Fuller
(American, 1862–1928)
Danse serpentine (II)
(Serpentine dance [II]). 1897–99
Still from film by Société Lumière, color, silent

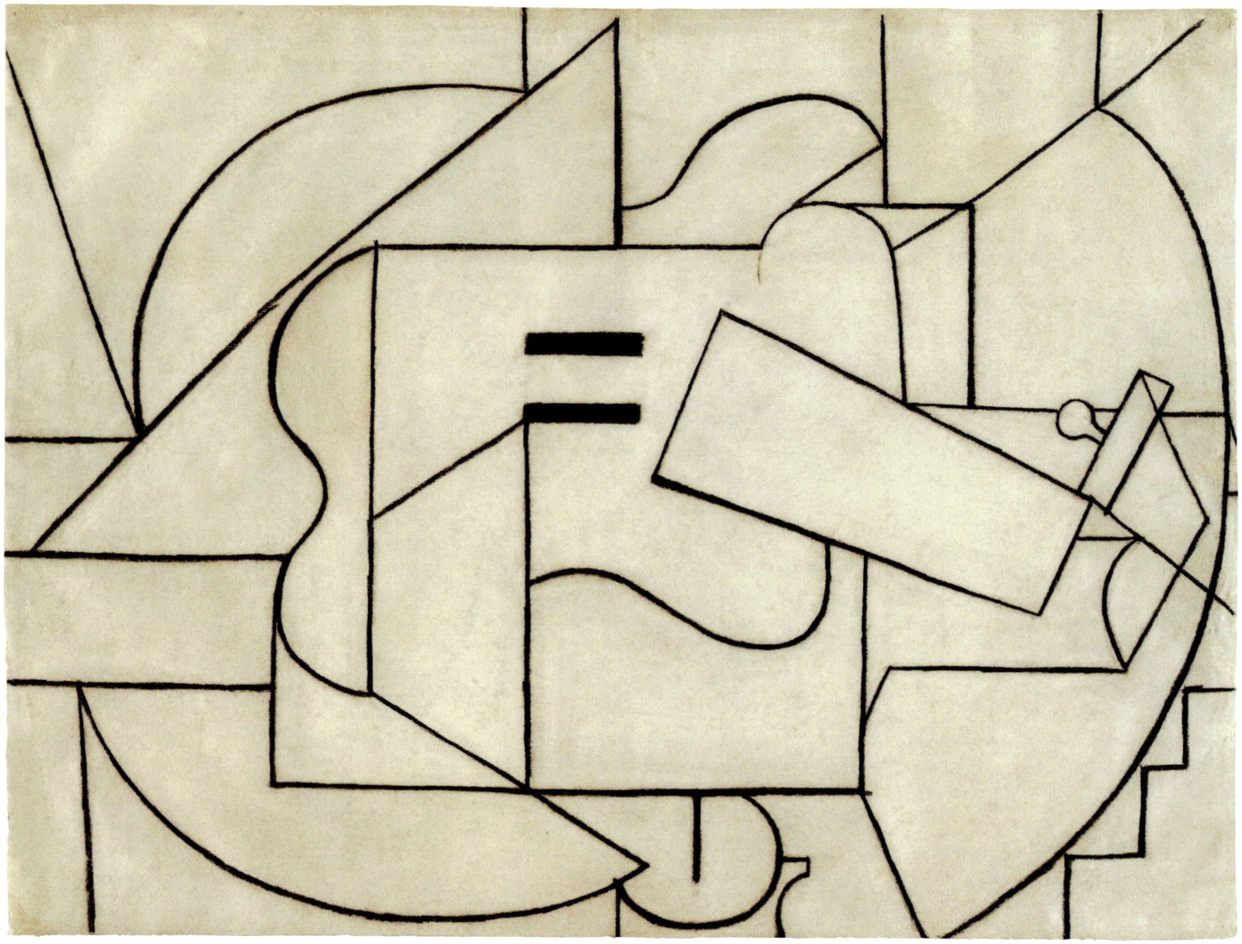

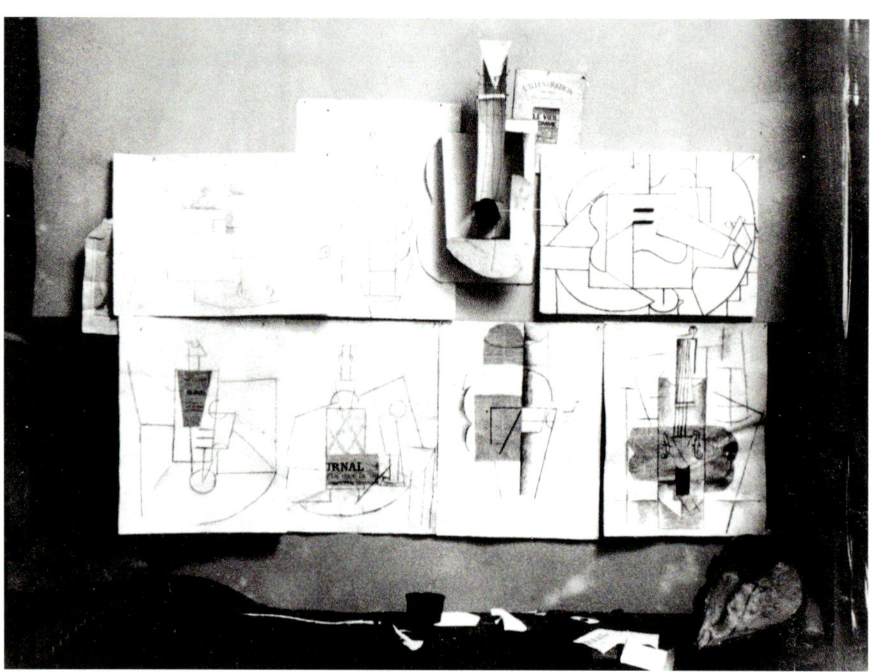

14. Pablo Picasso
(Spanish, 1881–1973)
Guitar. 1912
Charcoal on paper
$18\frac{1}{2} \times 24\frac{3}{8}$″ (47 x 61.9 cm)

15. Picasso's *Guitar* drawing (plate 14, above), cardboard *Guitar* (1912), and other drawings relating to the sheet metal *Guitar* of 1914 on the wall of his Paris studio in 1912

16. Pablo Picasso
(Spanish, 1881–1973)
Guitar. 1913
Cut-and-pasted paper and printed paper, charcoal, ink, and chalk on colored paper on board
$26\frac{1}{8} \times 19\frac{1}{2}$″ (66.4 x 49.6 cm)

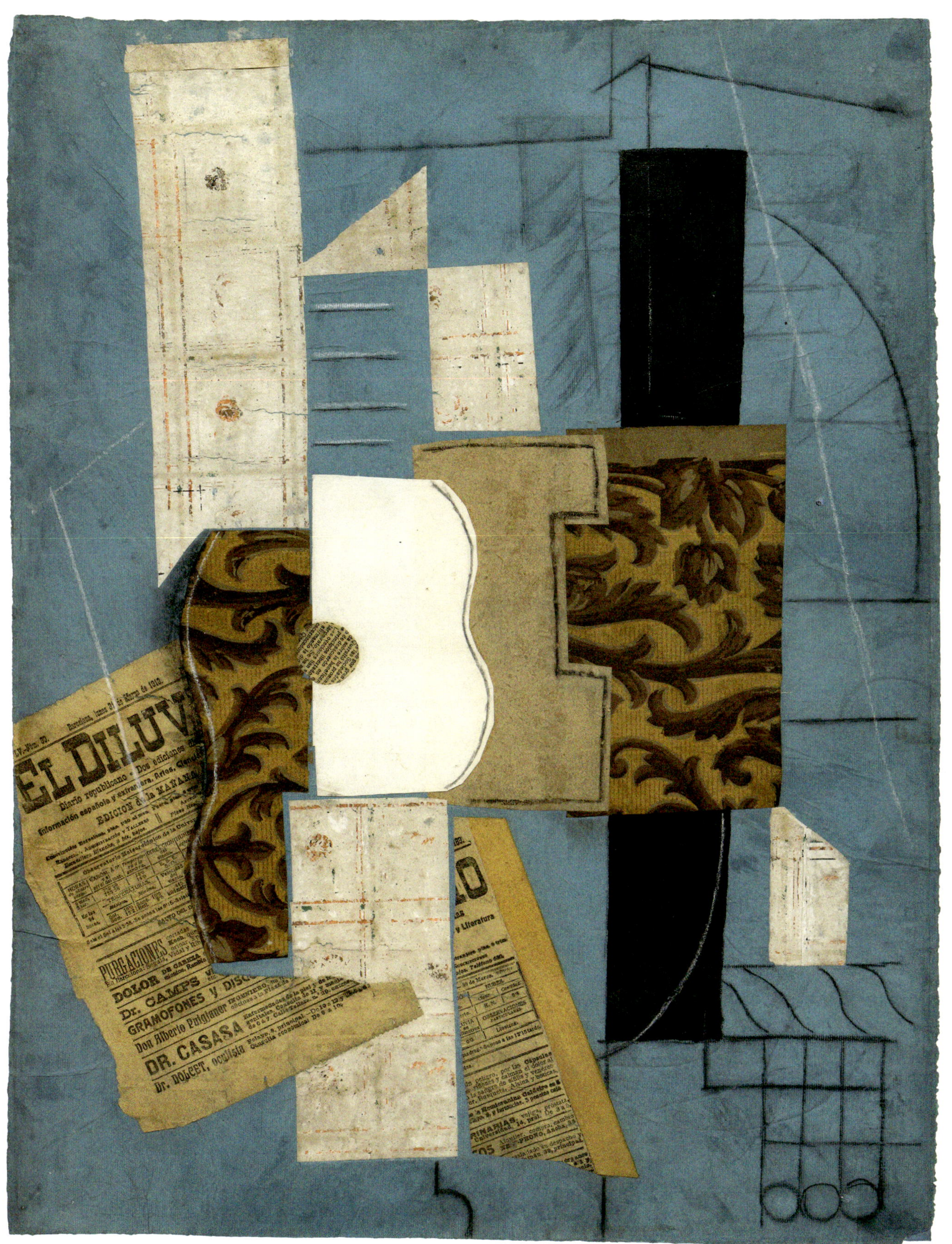
EL DILUV
Diario republicano
PURGACIONES
DOLOR
Dr. CAMPS
GRAMOFONES y DISCO
DR. CASASA
Dr. DOLCET, oculista

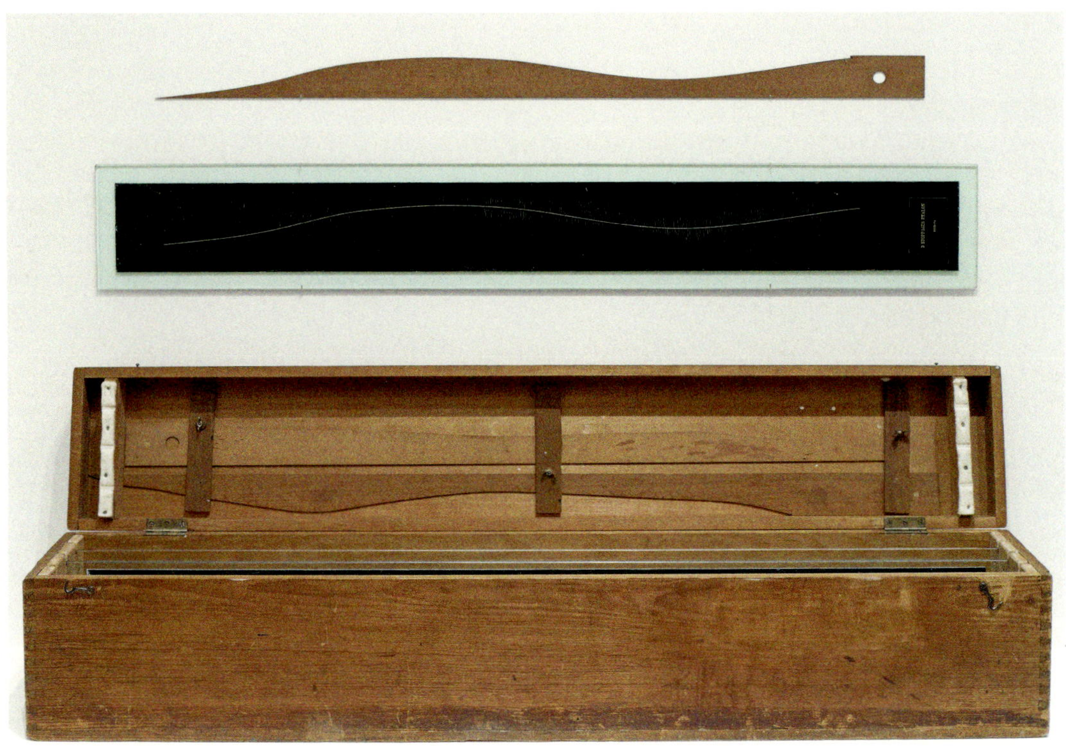

thin, its only depth being that of its accumulated physical layers.[7] At the same time, in its role, not as a descriptive contour delineating form, and so as subject to the creation of illusion, but as cut edge, line left the plane and gained an agency of its own. Instead of merely indicating movement, it became an initiator of movement in space.

In 1913–14, Marcel Duchamp picked up, as it were, one strand of the Cubist exploration of surface in his *3 Stoppages étalon* (*3 Standard Stoppages*; plate 17). Having dropped three meter-long threads from a height of a meter, he adhered them to three stretched canvases, preserving the random curves they had assumed upon landing. Cutting the canvases along the threads' profiles, he then translated these curves into wooden templates, new units of measure that retained the meter length but confused its rationale.[8] As in Cubist collage, Duchamp substituted readymade contour lines for handmade ones, but he reversed the Cubist principle, using line, its shape given arbitrarily by its fall, to determine form rather than allowing form to determine line through the cut at its edge. In the passage from collage to "stoppage," from artisanal to commercial modes of production (implied by the idea of the standard, and by the reference, through the French word *stoppage*, to the mending of woven fabric), we can imagine a tailor at work with measurements and patterns, "drawing with scissors," as Henri Matisse would later describe a method of his own. Similar tailored patterns, like pieces of a collage, appear in Man Ray's painting *The Rope Dancer Accompanies Herself with Her Shadows* (1916; plate 18). Inspired by a tightrope act he had seen in a vaudeville show, Man Ray cut pieces of colored paper into shapes corresponding to the tightrope dancer's acrobatic movements. Glancing down at the floor, however, he noticed that the discarded scraps of paper from which the shapes had been cut formed an abstract arrangement. Comparing this pattern, produced by chance, with the shadows a dancer might cast on the floor, he incorporated it into his composition.

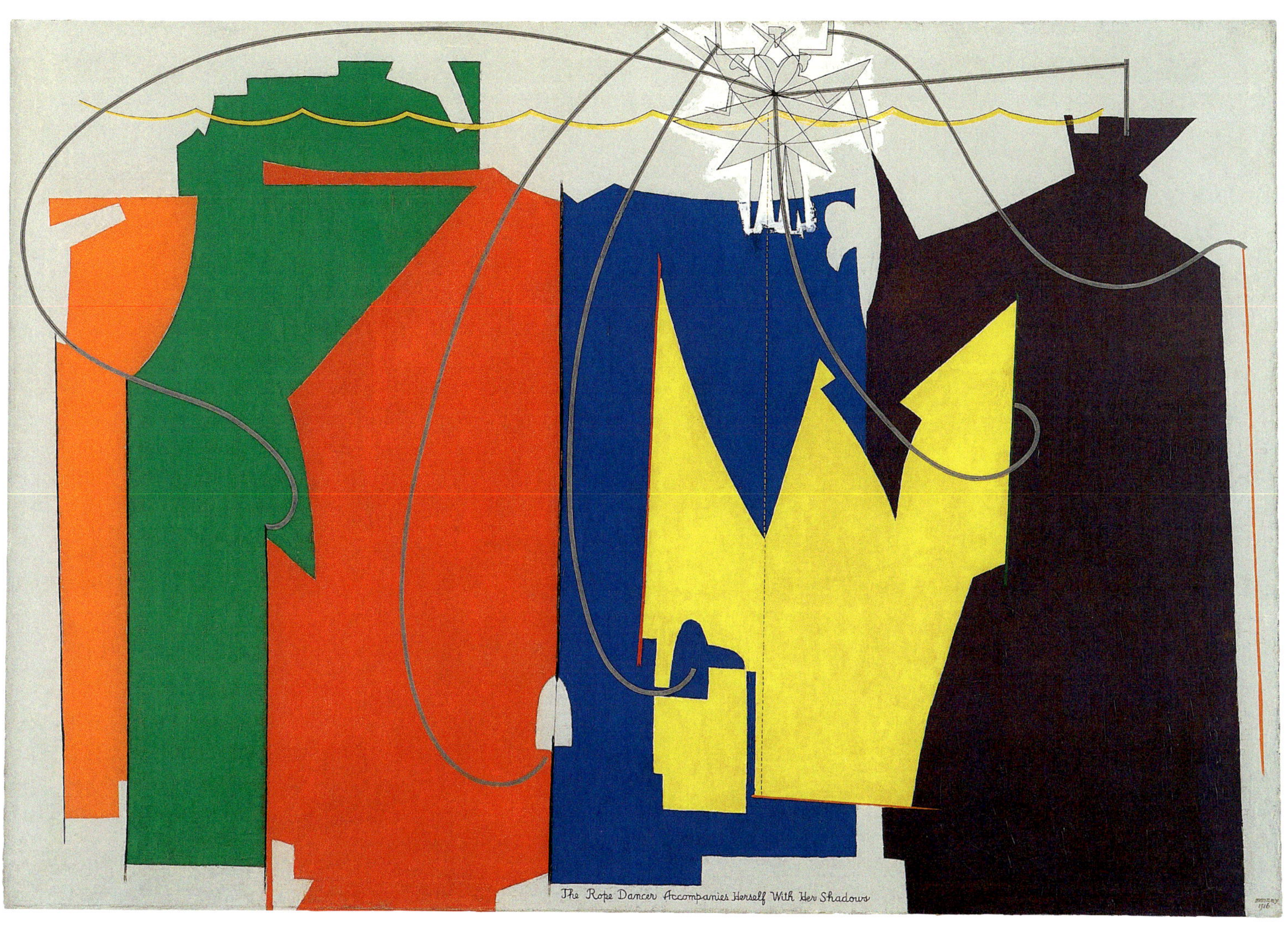

17. Marcel Duchamp
(American, born France, 1887–1968)
3 Stoppages étalon (3 Standard Stoppages). 1913–14
Wood box, 11 1/8 x 50 7/8 x 9″ (28.2 x 129.2 x 22.7 cm), holding three meter-long threads, each glued to a painted canvas strip, each strip mounted on a glass panel, 7 1/4 x 49 3/8 x 1/4″ (18.4 x 125.4 x 0.6 cm); and three wood slats 2 1/2 x 43 x 1/8″ (6.2 x 109.2 x 0.2 cm), each shaped along one edge to match the curves of the threads

18. Man Ray
(American, 1890–1976)
The Rope Dancer Accompanies Herself with Her Shadows. 1916
Oil on canvas
52″ x 6′ 1 3/8″ (132.1 x 186.4 cm)

String — a material ready to hand, and unencumbered by the illusionistic associations of traditional art materials — became a linear element in its own right in Duchamp's *With Hidden Noise* (1916; plate 19), a ball of twine contained by two screwed-together copper plates, and in Francis Picabia's *Tabac-Rat* (Rat tobacco, 1919/1949; plate 160). It was fully let loose in *Sculpture de voyage* (*Sculpture for Traveling*, 1918; plates 5, 140), a work today known only from a few documentary photographs and from a letter Duchamp sent to his friend Jean Crotti that same year before traveling on from New York to Buenos Aires after leaving wartime France: "Do you remember those rubber bathing caps that come in all colors? I bought some, cut them up into uneven little strips, stuck them together, not flat, in the middle of my studio (in the air) and attached them with string to the various walls and nails. . . . It looks like a kind of multicolored spider's web."[9]

With its strings pulling in different directions, *Sculpture for Traveling* may have induced a sense of dynamic change each time it was displayed. Here Duchamp set free not only line, in the lengths of string, but also shape, through the cut pieces of rubber, as if a bright-colored collage were afloat in space. T. J. Demos has argued that Duchamp's dedication to mobility — the mobility embodied in the shape-shifting *Sculpture for Traveling*, but also his own, in his various exiles — can be read as a loosening of the self from the grip of identity in an era of catastrophic world war. Demos notes that Roman Jakobson, a leader of the Moscow Linguistic Circle in the late teens and early '20s, situated an aesthetic of exile in an emerging culture of relativity (Hilma af Klint, for example, explored Albert Einstein's theory of relativity in her Atom Series of 1917 [plate 20]), arrived at through a confluence of developments in science, historiography, and Marxist concepts of value and intensified by advances in the technologies of travel and communication. Another model of interaction between self and other was implied, rooted not in the confidence of being but in the fluidity of becoming. This would allow the encounter with difference to change the self and thus dissolve the sense of identity that had ultimately led to polarization and war.[10]

Another artist exploring the transformative possibilities of becoming during these years was Kurt Schwitters, who started his *Merzbau* installation (plate 4) in the early 1920s by tying lines of string from one object, picture, or artwork in his Hannover studio to another, emphasizing and materializing their interrelations and interactions — a method of assemblage already apparent in his *Merzbilder* (*Merz* pictures), collages of found objects extracted from the physical reality of post–World War I Germany (plate 21). Eventually the strings were replaced by wires, and then by wooden structures joined together with plaster. These connected forms came to occupy several rooms on different floors of the artist's house. Schwitters's gesture must be seen in the context of the Dada movement, radical for what Jakobson called a "systemless aesthetic rebellion" leading to an art of relativity and ultimately to a destabilization of identity.[11]

Schwitters's abstract collages (plate 22) were influenced by the work of Jean Arp, who adapted Cubist collage to Dadaist ends. His *Untitled (Collage with Squares Arranged according to the Laws of Chance)* (1916–17; plate 23), in which rough squares torn from different-colored sheets of commercially available paper are glued to an empty page, seems to parallel such experiments with chance as Duchamp's *3 Standard Stoppages*, although any chance element may only have been ascribed to them or emphasized later on.[12] In any case Arp regarded his *papiers déchirés*, in their combination of chance, readymade, and the grid, as "a denial of human egotism," a displacement of the artist's "volition" in a move toward a condition of "anonymity."[13] He also explored this interest through so-called automatic drawing and in the gridded "duo-collages" that he made in 1915 with his wife, Sophie Taeuber-Arp, the collaboration itself a technique to loosen art from its traditional strictures of authorship and composition.[14] Eliminating the autographic, these works were made before the first modular abstractions of Piet Mondrian.

If Mondrian, in such paintings as *Tableau No. 2/Composition VII* (1913) and later works (plate 24), elucidated the grid "in a way that exceeded the faceted planes of Cubism," as Hal Foster writes, more strands from the exploration of surface in collage were picked up by other artists: "The flat shapes of

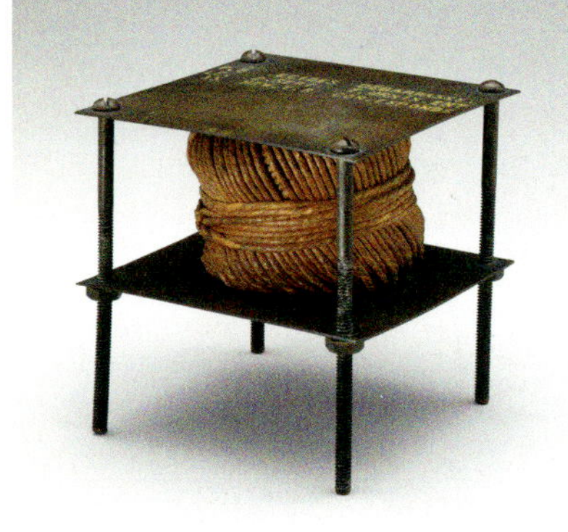

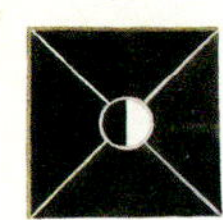

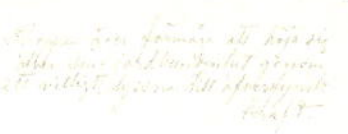

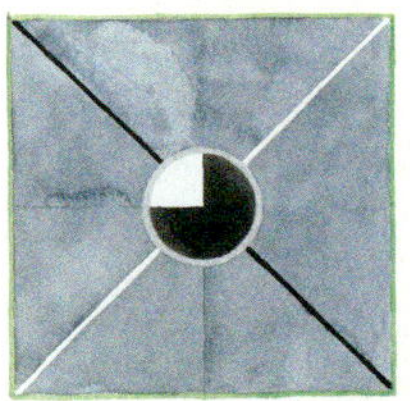

19. Marcel Duchamp
(American, born France, 1887–1968)
With Hidden Noise. 1916
Ball of twine between two brass plates, joined by four screws, containing unknown object
5 x 5 x 5 1/8˝ (12.7 x 12.7 x 13 cm)

20. Hilma af Klint
(Swedish, 1862–1944)
Atom Series, No. 5. 1917
Watercolor on paper
10 5/8 x 9 13/16˝ (27 x 25 cm)

21. Kurt Schwitters
(German, 1887–1948)
Revolving. 1919
Wood, metal, cord, cardboard, wool, wire, leather, and oil on canvas
48 3/8 x 35˝ (122.7 x 88.7 cm)

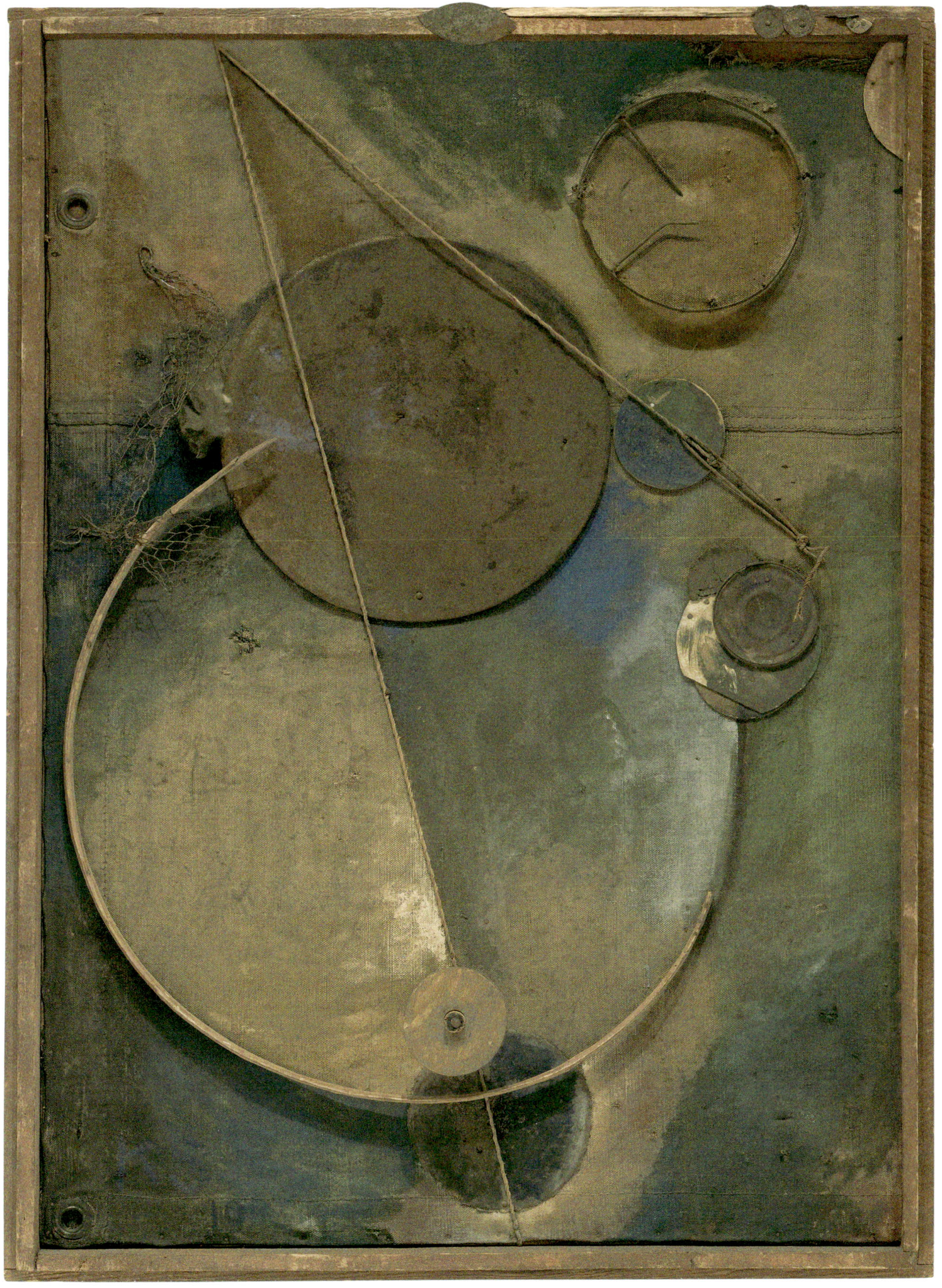

I call our world Flatland, not because we call it so, but to make its nature clearer to you, my happy audience, who are privileged to live in Space.

Imagine a vast sheet of paper on which straight Lines, Triangles, Squares, Pentagons, Hexagons, and other figures, instead of remaining fixed in their places, move freely about, on or in the surface, but without the power of rising above or sinking below it, very much like shadows — only hard and with luminous edges — and you will then have a pretty correct notion of my country and countrymen. Alas! a few years ago, I should have said "my universe": but now my mind has been opened to higher views of things.

In such a country, you will perceive at once that it is impossible that there should be anything of what you call a "solid" kind; but I dare say you will suppose that we could at least distinguish by sight the Triangles, Squares, and other figures, moving about as I have described them. On the contrary, we could see nothing of the kind, not at least so as to distinguish one figure from another. Nothing was visible, nor could be visible, to us, except straight Lines; and the necessity of this I will speedily demonstrate.

Place [...] a Triangle, or Square, or any other figure cut out of paste-board [on a table]. As soon as you look at it with your eye on the edge of the table, you will find that it ceases to appear to you a figure, and that it becomes in appearance a straight line.

— Edwin A. Abbott, *Flatland: A Romance of Many Dimensions*, 1884

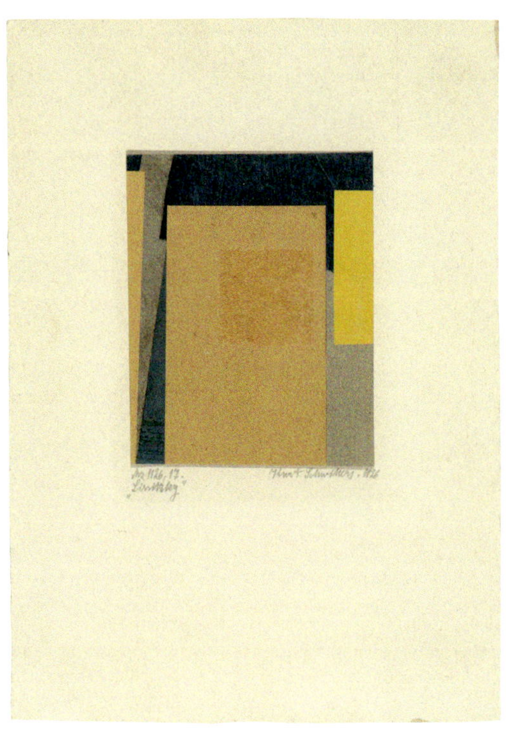

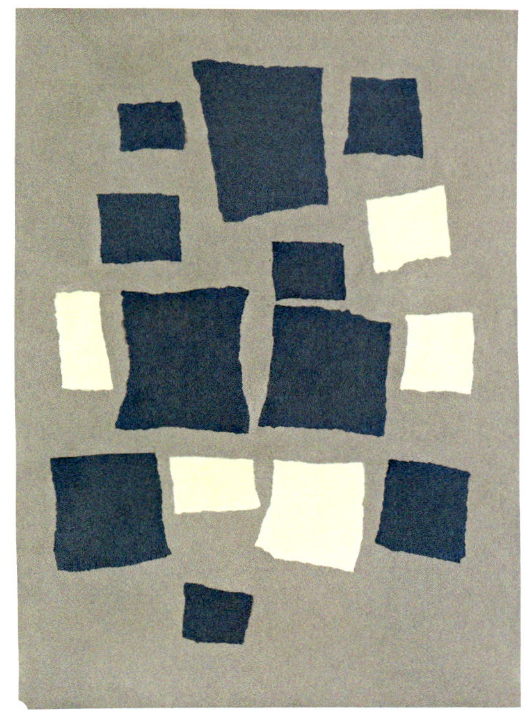

Cubist collage were the immediate precedent for the abstract color planes of Kazimir Malevich [plate 25], while the factual elements of Cubist construction, which Picasso showed Vladimir Tatlin in Paris in the spring of 1914, were one provocation of [the] Constructivist 'analysis of materials'" in Tatlin's *Counter-Reliefs*, which promoted an active rather than a contemplative engagement with art.[15] Believing in the power of art to renew perception, according to Yve-Alain Bois, Malevich endeavored to "de-automatize" vision "so as to confront the viewer with the fact that pictorial signs are not transparent to their referents but have an existence of their own, that they are 'palpable,' as Jakobson would say."[16] The inclusion in the work of either nominalist inscription or readymade objects produces a tautology: "the only purely transparent sign is that which refers to itself word for word, object for object."[17] Ivan Puni followed Malevich here (plate 28). But rather than venture into the aesthetic disjunctions of collage, Malevich isolated large, undivided, often square planes of color as flat and delimited, announcing Suprematism, his own version of abstraction.

By now it had become clear that tearing and cutting into patterned or colored papers withdrew the drawn line so that contour accrued instead to the paper's edge, and became increasingly coextensive with real space. This transference directed the viewer's attention to outlining new relations; collage opposed the simple literalism of figure against ground, allowing a visual play of discrepant scales and styles. Increasingly, the focus was on relation and on line. The marks once used to augment representational resemblance — shading and modeling, hatching and crosshatching — all these faded in importance. In collage, the "iconic" was displaced by what semiology named the "symbolic," the realm of arbitrary signs that make up language, signs — words — bearing no visible or audible connection to the objects or meanings to which they refer. By adopting this arbitrary form, collage declared a possible break with the whole system of analogic representation, based on "looking alike,"[18] that had long been the duty of line.

Extension, that is, ex-tension — leaving the surface and thus escaping surface tension — was line's next solution.

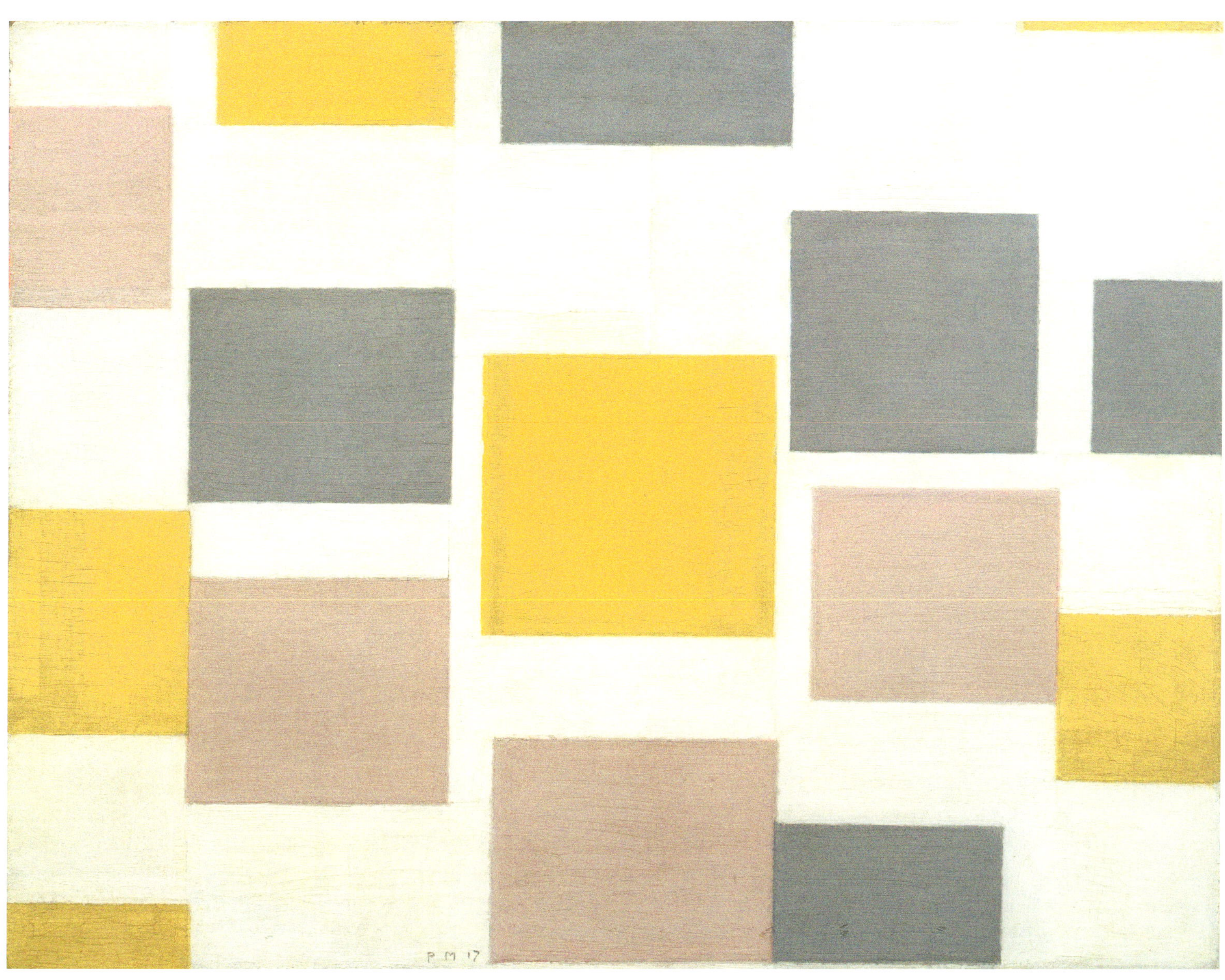

22. Kurt Schwitters
(German, 1887–1948)
Merz 1926 17. Lissitzky. 1926
Cut-and-pasted colored paper on cardstock
11 5/8 x 8 1/8″ (29.5 x 20.6 cm)

23. Jean (Hans) Arp
(French, born Germany [Alsace], 1886–1966)
Untitled (Collage with Squares Arranged according to the Laws of Chance). 1916–17
Torn-and-pasted paper and colored paper on colored paper
19 1/8 x 13 5/8″ (48.5 x 34.6 cm)

24. Piet Mondrian
(Dutch, 1872–1944)
Compositie No. 5, with color planes 5
(Composition no. 5, with color planes 5).
1917
Oil on canvas
19 3/8 x 24 1/8″ (49 x 61.2 cm)

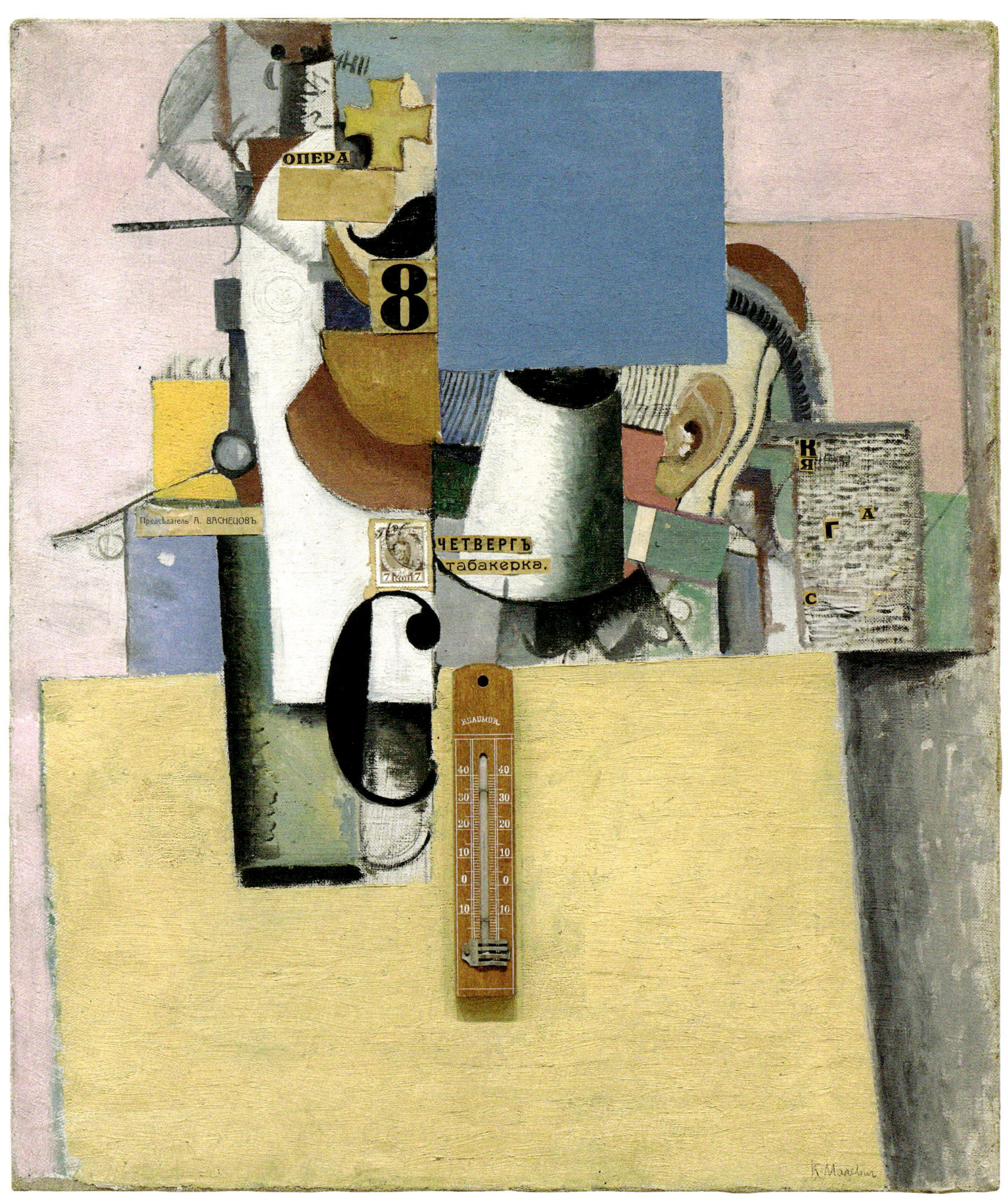
ОПЕРА
8
Председатель А. ВАСНЕЦОВЪ
ЧЕТВЕРГЪ
табакерка.
К
Я
Г
А
С
40 30 20 10 0 10

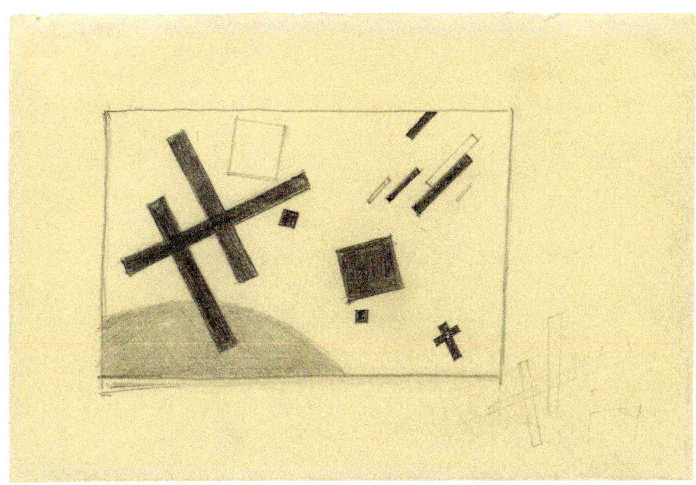

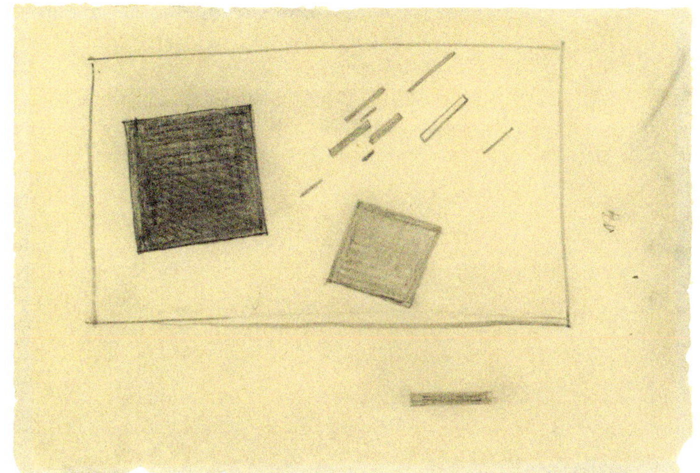

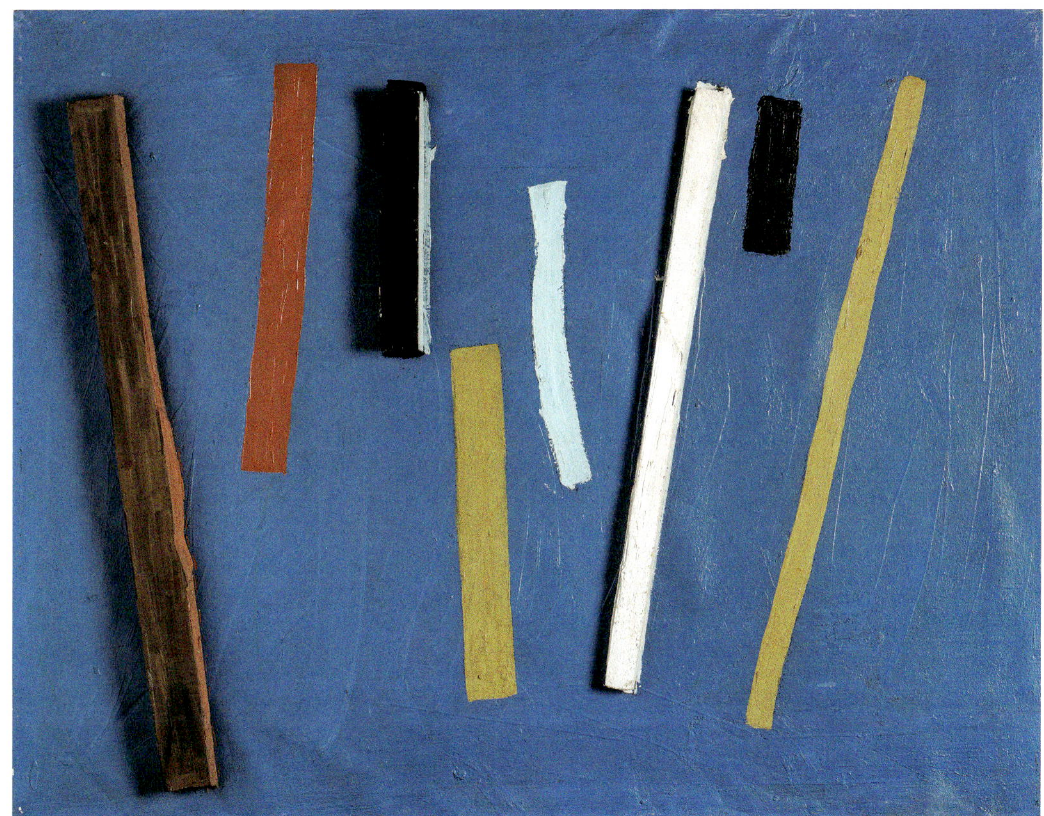

25. Kazimir Malevich
(Russian, born Ukraine, 1878–1935)
Reservist of the First Division. 1914
Oil on canvas with collage of printed paper, postage stamp, and thermometer
21 1/8 x 17 5/8″ (53.7 x 44.8 cm)

26 and **27. Kazimir Malevich**
(Russian, born Ukraine, 1878–1935)
Two drawings each titled *Suprematist Drawing*. Each: c. 1916–17
Each: pencil on paper
Each: 4 3/4 x 6 7/8″ (12 x 17.5 cm)

28. Jean Pougny (Ivan Puni; Russian, born Finland, 1892–1956)
Relief. 1915
Wood mounted on canvas, painted in oil
25 3/8 x 31 7/8″ (64.5 x 81 cm)

Plane and Line Extension (1910–1940)

In his *Pedagogical Sketchbook* (1925) and in lecture notes written at the Bauhaus, Paul Klee sought to define his fundamentally intuitive approach to artistic creation. His programmatic indirection is evoked in his credo "Art does not reproduce the visible; rather, it makes visible."[19] For Klee, every blot or puddle in a watercolor wash held a latent image, while line was "the most primitive of elements" and drawing was "taking a line for a walk."[20] He believed that the movement of a line in the process of its execution could be conveyed to the viewer, for whom the image would unfold in time more than in space. Beginning with line as an abstraction and gradually, apparently playfully outlining the material depiction of an idea, Klee elaborated many fine drawings: in *Die Zwitscher-Maschine* (Twittering machine, 1922; plate 29), the line as hand crank supposedly sets the birds in motion, and in *Artistenbildnis* (Portrait of an artiste, 1927; plate 159), the line features an elongated figure as tightrope walker. Singular and unexpected, Klee's line always ensued from the apparently free wandering of a point, the record of an action.

Klee was deeply concerned with the process by which a point becomes a line, a line becomes a plane, and a plane becomes a body. He shared this interest with Kandinsky, his friend and colleague on the faculty of the Bauhaus school in Germany. In 1919–20, Kandinsky had published a series of essays on aspects of modern art and design in the context of Soviet Russia, where the artist then lived. Of these, "On Point" and "On Line" demonstrate his interest in the elements of art — in analyzing the intrinsic constituents of the visual artwork. In June 1920, in his "Program for the Institute of Artistic Culture," Kandinsky wrote,

> Drawn form can be reduced to: 1. line and its moment of departure — the point, and 2. plane, produced by line. In turn, these two elements of drawn form fall into two groups: 1. A group of lines and planes of a schematic or mathematical character: the straight, the curved, the parabolic (zigzag) line, the plane — the triangle, the square, the circle, the parallelogram, etc. 2. A group of lines and planes possessing a free character, which cannot be accommodated by geometrical terms.[21]

Kandinsky elaborated on these essays in *Punkt und Linie zu Fläche* (Point and line to plane), published by the Bauhaus in 1926:

> The geometric line is an invisible thing. It is the track made by the moving point; that is, its product. It is created by movement — specifically through the destruction of the intense self-contained repose of the point. Here, the leap out of the static into the dynamic occurs. . . .
>
> When *a force coming from without* moves the point in any direction, [a] line results [whose] initial direction remains unchanged and the line has the tendency to run in a straight course to infinity.
>
> This is the *straight line* whose tension *represents the most concise form of the potentiality for endless movement.*[22]

This potential for movement ultimately led out into the third dimension. So it was that Kandinsky, arguing that the artist drew with point, line, and plane, also asserted that the dancer — for example the modern dancers Gret Palucca, on whom Kandinsky based a group of drawings (plates 30, 156), and Aleksandr Sakharov — did the same:

> Already in the classical ballet form existed "points" — a designated terminology which unquestionably is derived from "point." The rapid running on the toes leaves behind on the floor a trace of points.

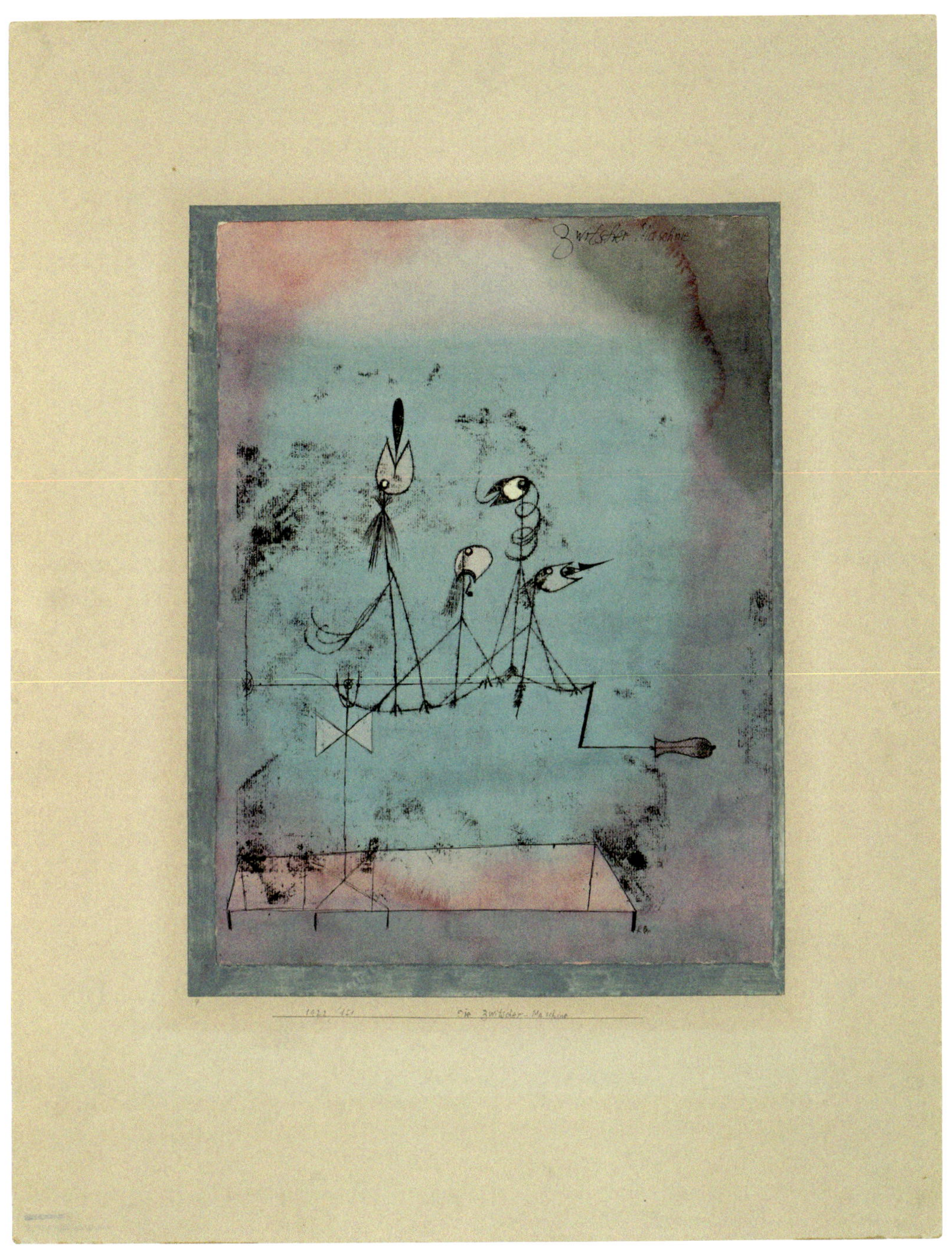

29. Paul Klee
(German, born Switzerland, 1879–1940)
Die Zwitscher-Maschine
(Twittering machine). 1922
Oil transfer drawing, watercolor, and ink on paper with gouache and ink borders on board
$25^{1/4}$ x 19˝ (64.1 x 48.3 cm)

Shortly after application of the pencil, or any other pointed tool, a (linear-active) line comes into being. The more freely it develops, the clearer will be its mobility. But if I apply a line, e.g. the edge of a black or colored crayon, a plane is produced (at first and when the freedom of movement is very limited).

If we had a medium that made it possible to move planes in a similar way, we should be able to inscribe an ideal three-dimensional piece of sculpture in space.

But I am afraid that is utopian.

For the present then let us content ourselves with the most primitive of elements, the line. At the dawn of civilization, when writing and drawing were the same thing, it was the basic element. And as a rule our children begin with it; one day they discover the phenomenon of the mobile point, with what enthusiasm it is hard for us grown-ups to imagine…

From point to line. The point is not dimensionless but an infinitely small planar element, an agent carrying out zero motion, i.e. resting. Mobility is the condition of change…. The primordial movement, the agent, is a point that sets itself in motion (genesis of form). A line comes into being…. In all these examples the principal and active line develops freely. It goes out for a walk, so to speak, aimlessly for the sake of the walk.

— Paul Klee, lecture notes, 1921

Where their extremities meet and where they delineate particular spaces, lines create new beings — planes.

— Vasily Kandinsky, "On Line," 1919

In general, the element of time can be recognized to a far greater extent in the case of line than in that of point — extension being a temporal concept.

— Vasily Kandinsky, *Point and Line to Plane*, 1926

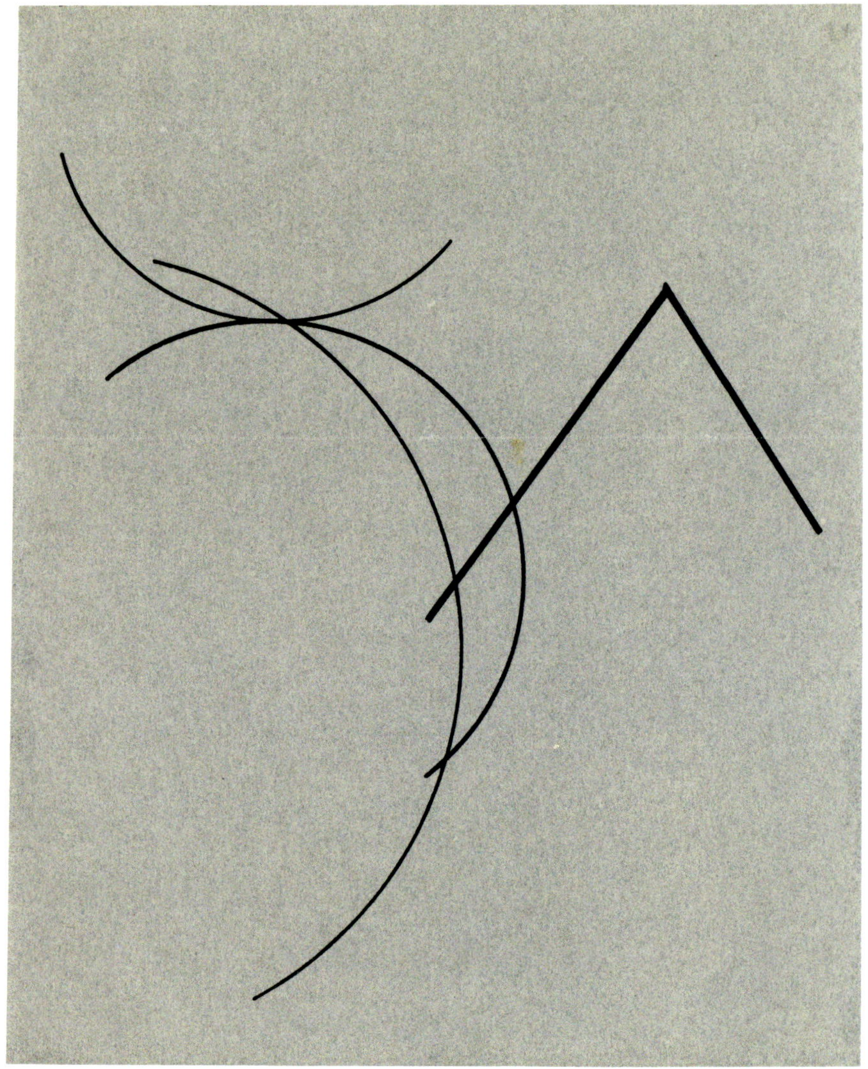

In the *dance*, the whole body — and in the new dance, every finger — draws lines with very clear expression. The "modern" dancer moves across the stage on exact lines, which he incorporates as an essential element into the composition of his dance (Sacharoff). The entire body of the dancer, right down to his finger tips, is at every moment an interrupted composition of lines (Palucca). The use of lines is, indeed, a new achievement but, of course, is no invention of the "modern" dance.[23]

In 1921 Kandinsky resigned from the Institute of Artistic Culture in Moscow and left Russia for Weimar, Germany, to join the faculty of the Bauhaus. He had become estranged from a Russian avant-garde oriented toward Constructivism and Formalism. For Kandinsky, "Every phenomenon of the external and of the inner world can be given linear expression — a kind of translation."[24] The line named the internal and became the external on the page, where it could be cognized and sensed by both artist and viewer (plate 31). The Constructivists took a more rational approach; as Kenneth Lindsay and Peter Vergo write, "While Kandinsky advocated the intuitive application of artistic elements such as the point and the line and declared that the 'clatter of the falling ruler speaks loudly of total revolution,' some of his colleagues, particularly El Lissitzky and [Aleksandr] Rodchenko, called for the rejection of caprice and intuition and the reliance on more scientific methods.... as if in response to Kandinsky, Lissitzky asserted

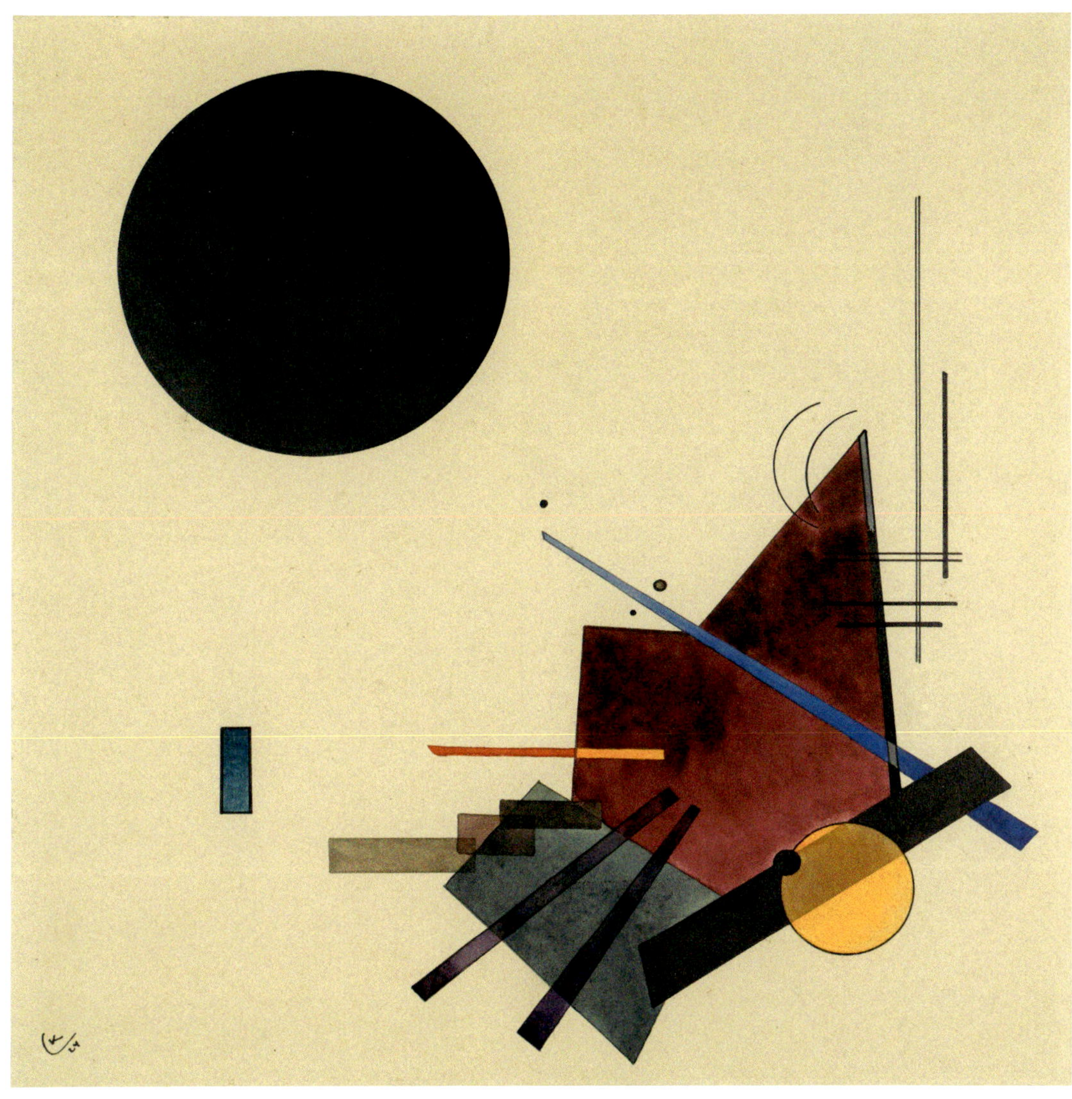

that 'those of us who have stepped out beyond the confines of the picture take ruler and compasses... in our hands.'"[25]

Following the line, the Constructivist comrades Rodchenko and Lyubov Popova, and their Suprematist colleague Malevich, were exploring the extension of the plane in space and time. In 1918, Rodchenko wrote, "Sending the plane into the depths, I leave a projection as its trace."[26] Or, if a plane, bounded by four lines, is projected into depth, that plane becomes so flat that it is readable along its edge as a single line. Here the Cubist line as cut edge of a real newspaper fragment becomes the line of a plane generated by other lines on an imaginary surface. Far from constituting a return to illusion, however, the cognitive line as the edge of a plane was to become the non-objective line of construction. Malevich's form-generating line — the line by which the human being names the world, its tension an inner creative force — was also the line as a factor of construction in society's transformation, the line as motion and module.

In 1920 Rodchenko went further:

> Recently, working exclusively on the building of forms and the system of their construction, I began to introduce the line into the plane as a new element of construction.
>
> The perfected significance of the line was finally clarified — on the one hand, its bordering and edge relationship, and on the other — as a factor of the main

30. Vasily Kandinsky
(French, born Russia, 1866–1944)
Drei Gebogene, die sich in einem Punkt treffen (Three curves meeting at a single point). Drawing after a photograph of the dancer Gret Palucca by Charlotte Rudolph. 1925
Ink on tracing paper
7 5/8 x 6 1/8" (19.3 x 15.5 cm)

31. Vasily Kandinsky
(French, born Russia, 1866–1944)
Schwarze Beziehung (Black relationship). 1924
Watercolor and ink on paper
14 1/2 x 14 1/4" (36.9 x 36.2 cm)

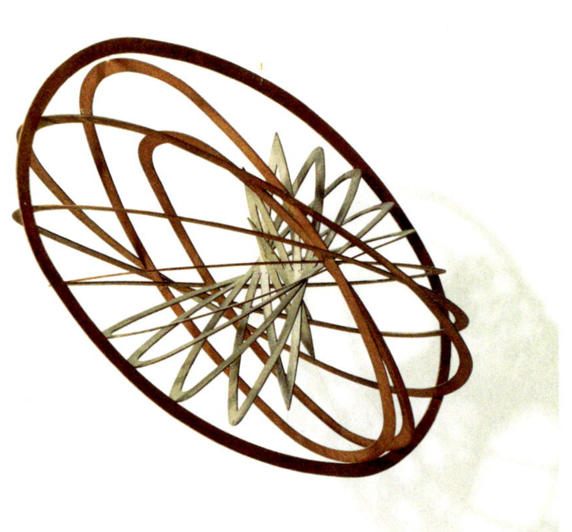

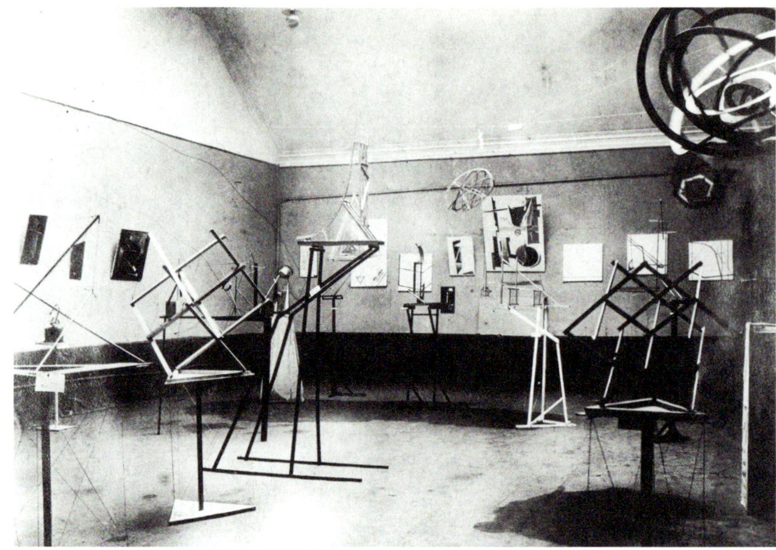

construction of every organism that exists in life, the skeleton, so to speak (or the foundation, carcass, system). The line is the first and last, both in painting and in any construction at all. The line is the path of passing through, movement, collision, edge, attachment, joining, sectioning.

Thus, the line conquered everything and destroyed the last citadels of painting—color, tone, texture, and surface.[27]

The importance of line for Constructivism was acknowledged in the *Second Spring Exhibition of the OBMOKhU* (plates 6, 33) and *5x5=25* exhibitions of 1921, where Rodchenko showed, first, "spatial constructions" made in wood and metal and then drawings on graph paper relating to them. For *Spatial Construction no. 12* (c. 1920; plate 32), for example, he cut concentric lines through the plane of a single sheet of aluminum-painted plywood, so that a series of rings could be unfolded and rotated to create a geometric volume. This three-dimensional shape could easily be folded back to its original planar condition. In the spatial constructions Rodchenko realized an idea he had introduced in his non-objective paintings of 1917–18, where lines were imagined as cuts into the surface plane, invoking extension beyond flatness into real space. Meanwhile, in the *5x5=25* exhibition, Popova presented drawings and paintings collectively called "Space-Force Construction" (plate 37). In a statement for the catalogue of this exhibition, she wrote, "All included structures are representational, and should be regarded only as a series of preparatory experiments leading to materialized constructions."[28] Both Rodchenko and Popova were following through on the Constructivist conviction that the artist's purpose was to transform the two-dimensional into the three-dimensional, not only in the viewer's imagination but also in reality. Having become construction, line now named and created a new world of objects and possibilities.

Popova's and Rodchenko's contributions to what the Constructivists dubbed "production art"—textile designs (plate 38), for example, of use to the proletarian masses—realized the prospect of spatial constructions entering and organizing actual social space. In 1921, in his essay "The Line," Rodchenko wrote, "In the line a new worldview became clear: to build in essence, and not depict (objectify or non-objectify); build new, expedient, constructive structures in life, and not from life and outside of life."[29] First extracted from everyday life in the Cubists' collages of clippings from newspapers, the line was now building, constructing, as part of a process of real-world sociopolitical and economic change, a movement toward a new world that in turn would be promoted in newspapers. Rodchenko continued,

The work of art ceased to be painted from nature, and began instead to derive its structure from the nature of the problems it treated.

32. Aleksandr Rodchenko
(Russian, 1891–1956)
Spatial Construction no. 12. c. 1920
Plywood, partly painted with aluminum paint, and wire
24 x 33 x 18 1/2" (61 x 83.7 x 47 cm)

33. *Second Spring Exhibition of the OBMOKhU* (Society of young artists), Moscow, 1921. Installation view, with Rodchenko's *Spatial Construction no. 12* (plate 32) at back

34. Aleksandr Rodchenko
(Russian, 1891–1956)
Construction no. 104. 1920
Oil on canvas
40 3/8 x 27 7/16" (102.5 x 69.7 cm)

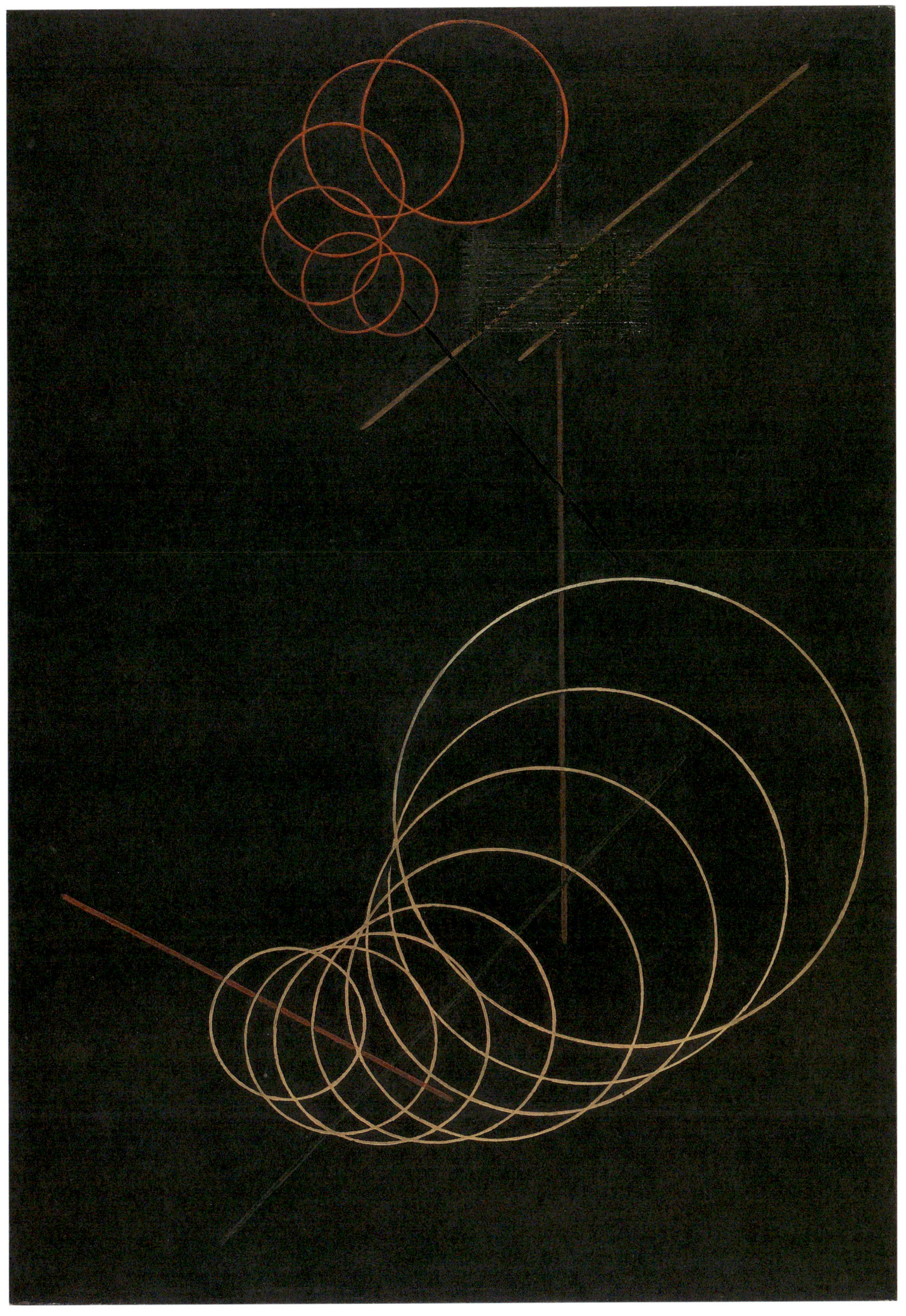

From an analysis of the volume and space of objects (Cubism) to the organization of the elements, not as a means of representation, but as integral constructions.

— Lyubov Popova, 1922

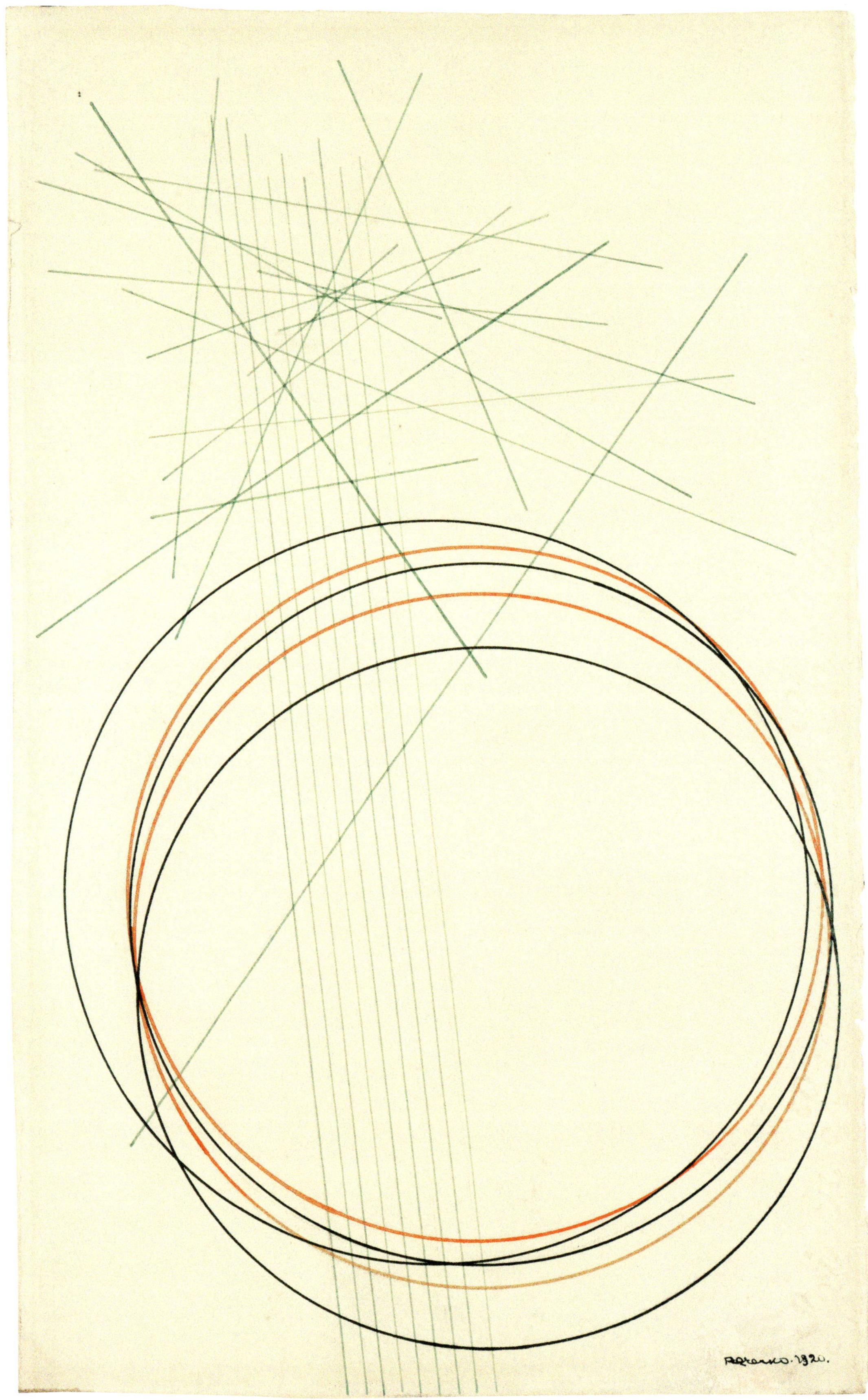

35. Aleksandr Rodchenko
(Russian, 1891–1956)
Construction. 1920
Ink and colored ink on paper
12 3/4 x 7 3/4″ (32.4 x 19.7 cm)

36. Lyubov Popova
(Russian, 1889–1924)
Study for Space-Force Construction. c. 1921
Crayon on paper
10 7/8 x 8 3/16″ (27.6 x 20.8 cm)

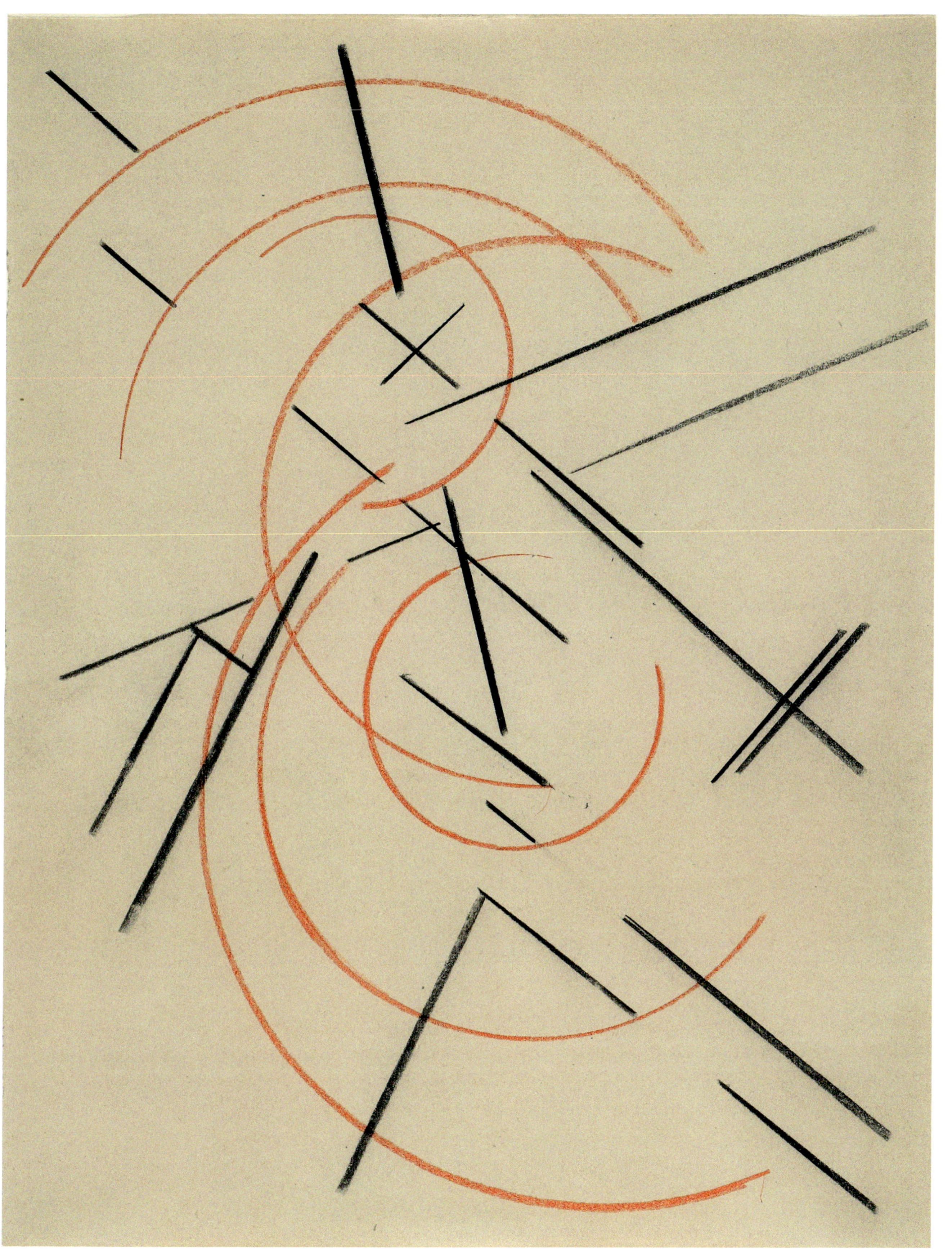

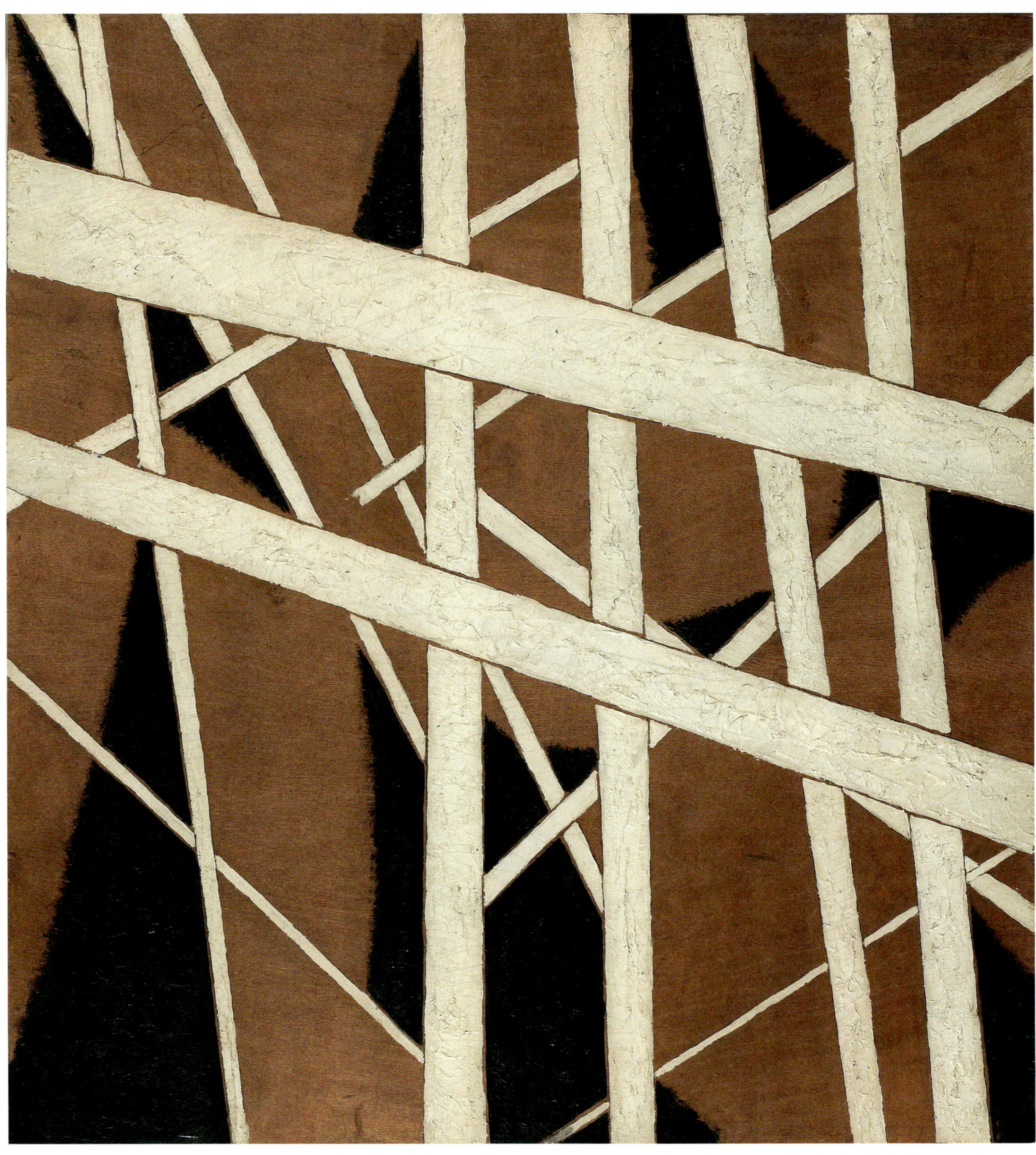

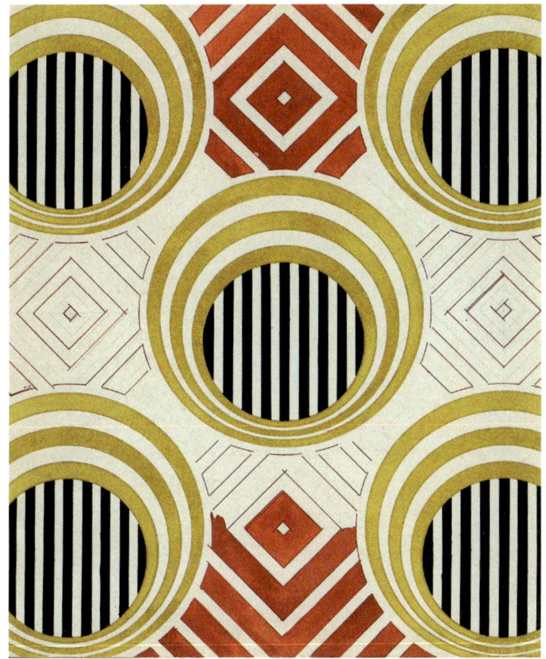

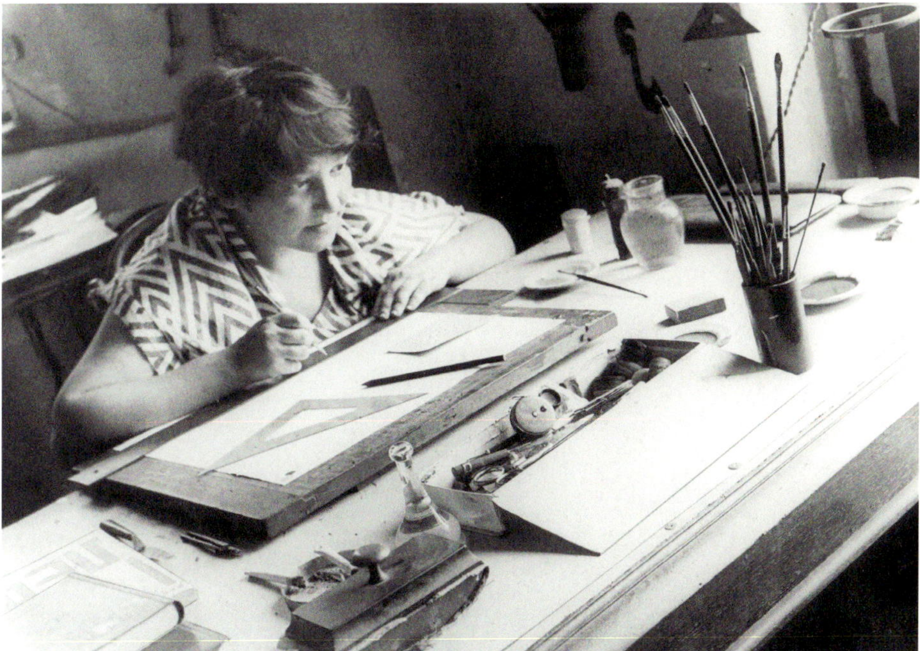

Thus the new form—the surface—required a new set of organizing principles.

The construction of the work of art became a separate concern, on which everything else depended, just as the elements of an organism are systematically subordinated to the whole.

Work on the creation of forms and a structural system for them gradually brought the line into the surface as structural element.[30]

The line of the new art was drawn not by hand but with a ruler and compasses (plates 34–36). Rodchenko wrote, "The craft of painting is striving to become more industrial. Drawing in the old sense is losing its value and giving way to the diagram or the engineering drawing."[31] Made with uniform tools, Constructivist works inevitably showed formal similarities, reflecting an emergent aesthetic grammar that emphasized the collective rather than the expression of an individual artistic self—a sense of self that the Constructivists saw as a product of capitalism. The lines on the paper are the traces not of an artist but of the implements of construction, and of the constructor as an element in a broad social dynamic. For Briony Fer, these metonymic attributes appear clearly in a photograph by Rodchenko, from 1924, of his partner Varvara Stepanova at her desk (plate 39): "The use of implements, such as ruler and set-square, enabled the works to appear as if untouched by human hands, as if the brush were the hand and the ruler its denial."[32] In Popova's work, Fer continues, "The use of straight lines, parts of circles and the broken line of the diagram...invoked the notation of engineers and technical drawing.... As Popova wrote in notes on the *5x5=25* exhibition in 1921,...'Our work on each of the elements (line, plane, volume, space, textural color, material, etc.) goes beyond the bounds of a mere abstract exercise in elements' to establish constructive principles in laboratory work."[33] Yet while the structures of Popova's compositions and constructions may be seen as *al*luding to a type of drawing, they also appear to *e*lude the proper purpose of technical drafting, which they continually undercut.

In *The Non-Objective World*, published as a Bauhaus book in 1927, Malevich called line the element that generates form and, as such, the determinant of a way of perceiving the world. "It was through the conscious line—through being conscious of the line before focusing consciousness on the object—that

37. Lyubov Popova
(Russian, 1889–1924)
Space-Force Construction. 1921
Oil with wood dust on plywood
28 x 25 5/16" (71.1 x 64.3 cm)

38. Lyubov Popova
(Russian, 1889–1924)
Textile design. 1923–24
Gouache, ink, and pencil on paper
13 3/4 x 11 1/8" (34.9 x 28.2 cm)

39. Aleksandr Rodchenko
(Russian, 1891–1956)
Two Portraits of Varvara Stepanova (detail). 1924
Gelatin silver print on paper
16 1/8 x 11 3/16" (41 x 28.4 cm)

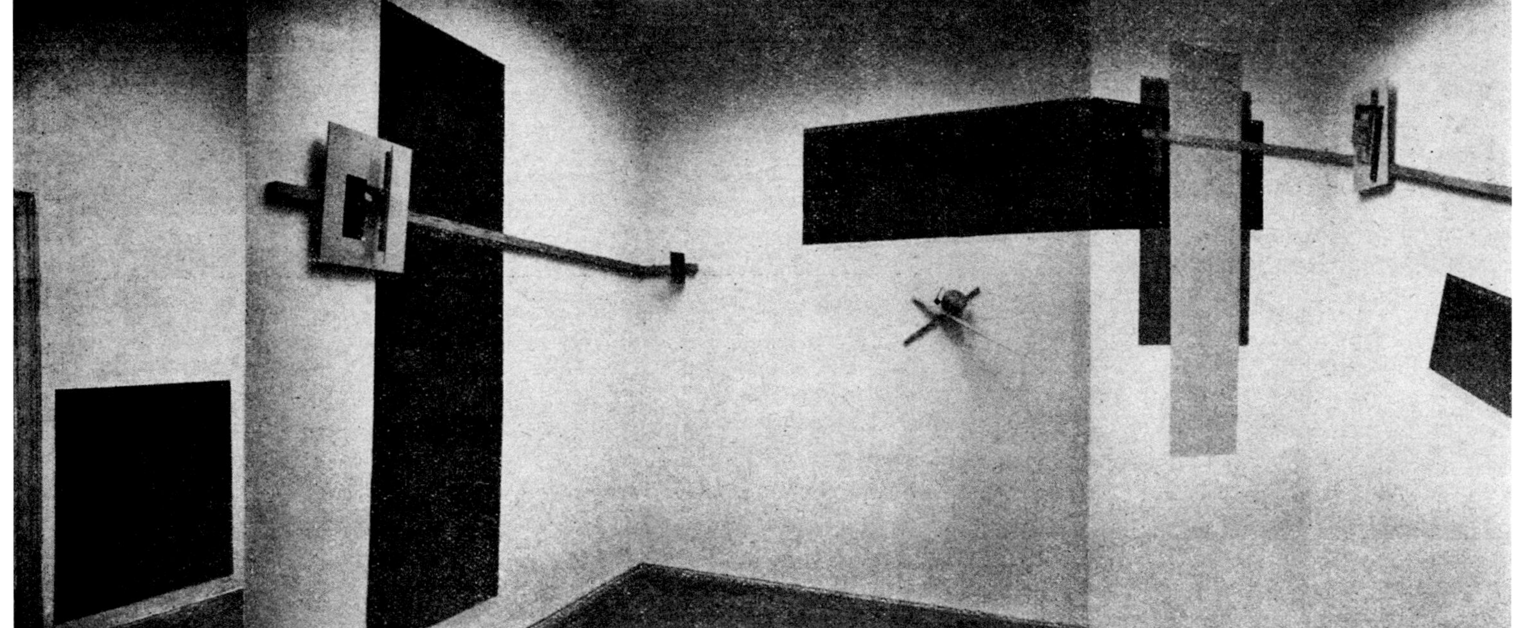

the artist could cognize not the object itself but what lay within that object: the non-objective forces that give structure and movement to it, to the world of space and time as such.... Art would express a perception, whether it was an intuitive thought or a sensation, and transform this non-objective sensation into knowing."[34] For Malevich, this integration of a sensation of space and movement in time was achieved through an understanding of line as giving unity to those disparate realities on a plane. That understanding had been realized for the first time in Cubism and Futurism, which, along with Suprematism, Malevich saw as reflecting the transrational consciousness of the non-objective world and its universe of forces. This new cognition engendered another experience of space-time, based on the principle of relativity and on a movement from a three-dimensional to a four-dimensional world. Malevich recognized an emerging awareness of a world in constant motion, and of a humanity with lives past, present, and future, never fixed or static. Rather than depicting the world of earthly objects, Suprematist art stimulated a universal experience of space-time.

From the beginning of the exploration of line in the twentieth century, hierarchies of drawing, painting, and sculpture, of architecture, typography, and environment, were broken down, as in Duchamp's *Sculpture for Traveling* and Schwitters's *Merzbau*. Malevich's collaborator Lissitzky was among those who blurred these disciplinary boundaries when he transformed his Prouns into "abstract rooms" (1923–28; plate 40), visualizing a new geometry of space and movement. Abstract images realized in a number of mediums, the Prouns (plate 41; "Proun" being an acronym for "Project for the Affirmation of the New" in Russian) were intended as prototypes for Lissitzky's visionary designs for inhabitable abstractions, in which the visitor could experience the gravity-defying sensation of geometric shapes and linear vectors wrapping around corners and launching to the ceiling. In 1922, Lissitzky and Schwitters became friends and collaborated on the "Nasci" ("being born" or "becoming") issue of Schwitters's magazine *Merz*, published in April 1924, an explicit, programmatic alliance of Constructivist and Dadaist ideas. The dynamic between these two apparently dialectical models found further expression in 1926–28, when Lissitzky's *Kabinett der Abstrakten* (Room of abstractions) was constructed in the Hannover Museum, in the home city of Schwitters's *Merzbau*.

40. El Lissitzky
(Russian, 1890–1941)
Prounenraum (Proun room). 1923
Installation, as reproduced in
G: Material zur elementaren Gestaltung
no. 1 (July 1923)

41. El Lissitzky
(Russian, 1890–1941)
Proun 19D. c. 1922
Gesso, oil, paper, and cardboard on plywood
38 3/8 x 38 1/4" (97.5 x 97.2 cm)

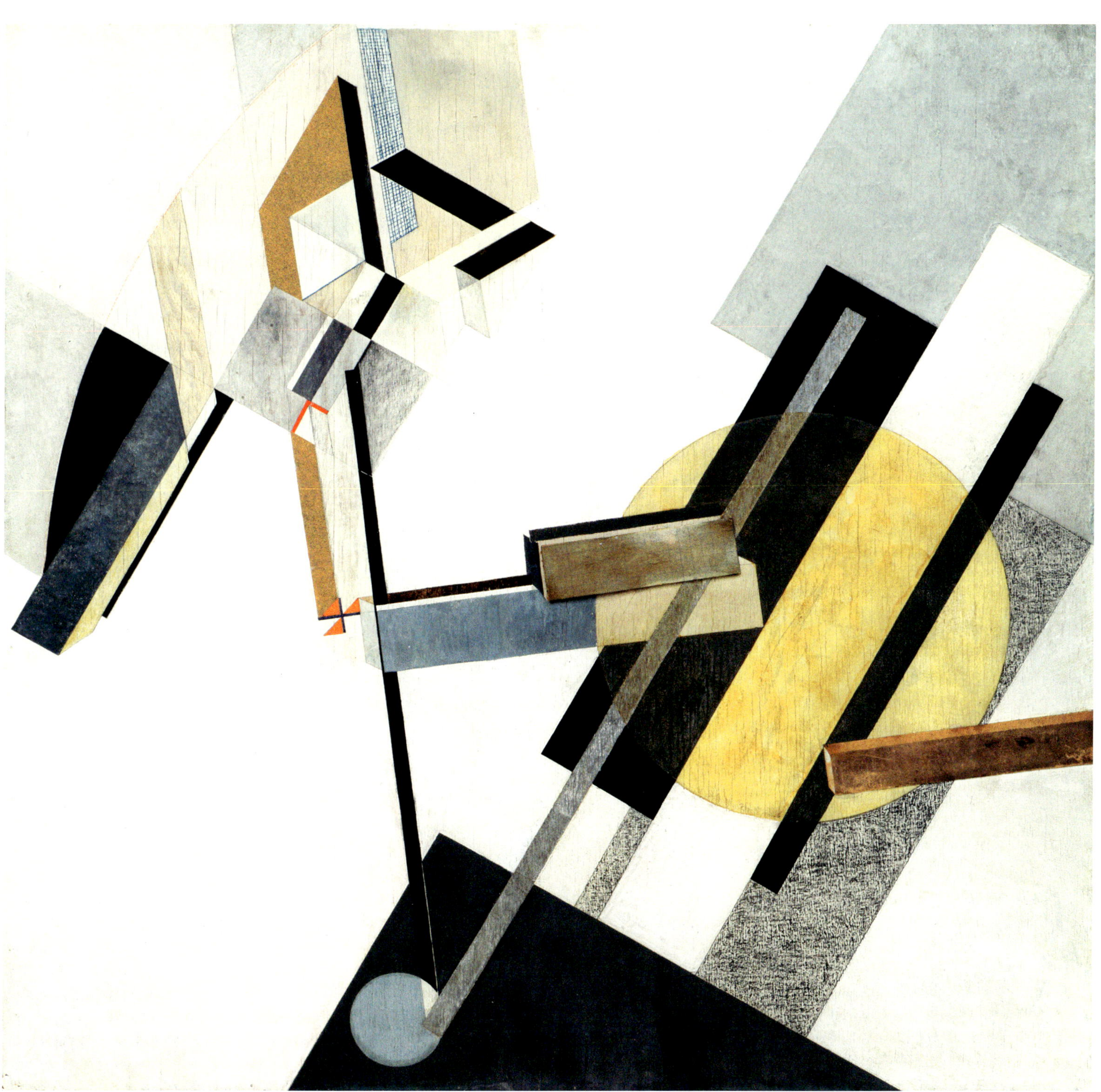

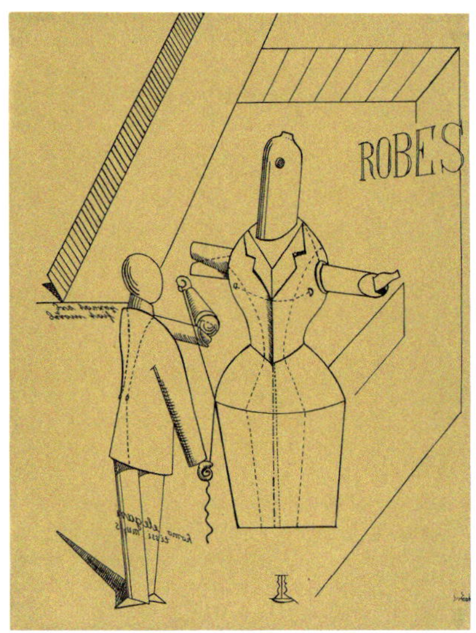

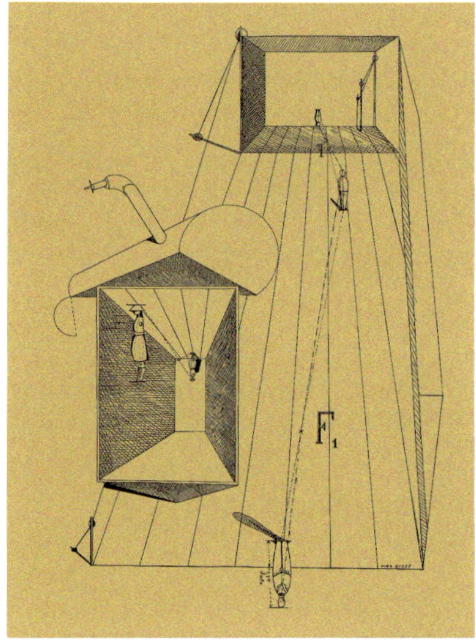

42 and **43. Max Ernst**
(French, born Germany, 1891–1976)
Plates I and VI from *Fiat modes pereat ars* (Let there be fashion, down with art). 1920
Two of eight lithographs on paper
Each: 17 3/16 x 12 9/16" (43.7 x 31.9 cm)

A Lineament in Space (1930–1960)

While Constructivists and Suprematists were advancing the cognitive line, Dadaists and Surrealists embraced the irrational. The title of Max Ernst's lithograph portfolio *Fiat modes pereat ars* (Let there be fashion, down with art, 1920; plates 42, 43), a witty inversion of the Futurists' slogan *Fiat ars, pereat mundus* (Let there be art, though the world perish), subordinated traditional art to commercial textile design, but the prints themselves, as if challenging the Constructivists, showed the rational world of industry gone awry. Although the tracing technique is diagrammatic and relatively orderly, the imagery includes nonsensical equations and ineffective measuring instruments, such as dysfunctional plumbs and weights.

Soon the Surrealists would set out the terms for a line reflecting, in André Breton's words, "psychic automatism in its pure state.... Dictated by thought, in the absence of any control exercised by reason, exempt from any aesthetic or moral concern."[35] Automatic and collective drawing had already emerged as ways of rendering what lies hidden behind reality, as in the sketchbooks used during the spiritualist séances of af Klint and "The Five" as early as 1896 (sometimes in the form of the *cadavre exquis*).[36] Now they were applied to the capture of the unconscious and the surreal.

The ensuing production of unrestrained line is exemplified in the automatic drawings of André Masson (plate 44) and in the "dream paintings" of Joan Miró, who by 1923 had joined Breton's circle in Paris. Letting the line loose to meander with the vagaries of erotic desire, Miró presented a space without limits. Bodies, objects, and words float in an infinite colored space, as if suspended in the narrative of progress — a modernist imperative embodied by the linear. Miró's engagement with the real and the corporeal, with movement and chance, is most apparent in tactile, sexually charged collage-objects such as *Spanish Dancer* (1928; plate 45), with its nails penetrating the support. While the Dadaists, as Anne Umland writes, advocated "the use of real objects as a means to reflect the post–World War I circumstances, Miró, a decade later, pushed his chosen objects and materials further to register not only as pictorial elements and as real-work objects but also as corporeal, carnal, and sexual signs."[37]

Miró himself remarked that he looked at "real things with increasing love — the carbide lamp, potatoes — in fact, I caress anything, it doesn't matter what, with my eyes."[38] His hand is evident in the shaping of the Spanish dancer's body, in part from materials of drawing — a drafting triangle or set square, a plumb line — but also from sandpaper, nails, plaster, cord, a cork, bits of crumpled paper, linoleum, thread, a tuft of hair, and flocked paper, all mounted on wooden boards. Miró's drafting triangle, Umland continues, is "forced into service as a sign for female genitalia, bawdily sporting (for those who care to get close enough) a small oval label advertising free entry: ENTRADA LIBRA."[39] How remote this is from the similar set square we have seen on Stepanova's desk, an instrument of tracing and building, used to efface human touch. Thus line is driven in diametrically opposite directions by the Constructivist and the Surrealist — opposite also in relation to women, phrased respectively as active subject and passive object of the gaze. In the developing ideology of modernism, it seems alternately charged by the logistic and the erotic. And as line comes to focus on the corporeal, it is increasingly corporealized or made physical as strings and wires in real space.

Alexander Calder would remember a visit to Miró's Montmartre studio in December 1928, when Miró showed him no paintings but instead a collage, "a big sheet of heavy gray cardboard with a feather, a cork, and a picture postcard glued to it. There were probably a few dotted lines.... I was nonplussed; it did not look like art to me."[40] Some time later, Miró attended a performance of the *Cirque Calder*, the miniature circus that Calder had created and operated between 1926 and 1931. Joan Simon writes,

> Calder's *Circus* figures were mobile, made of wire, wood, corks, bits of leather, and hand-sewn fabric, and had devices, springs and strings that launched acrobats in the air, and caused trapezists to fly from one rig to another or a cowboy to lasso a steer....

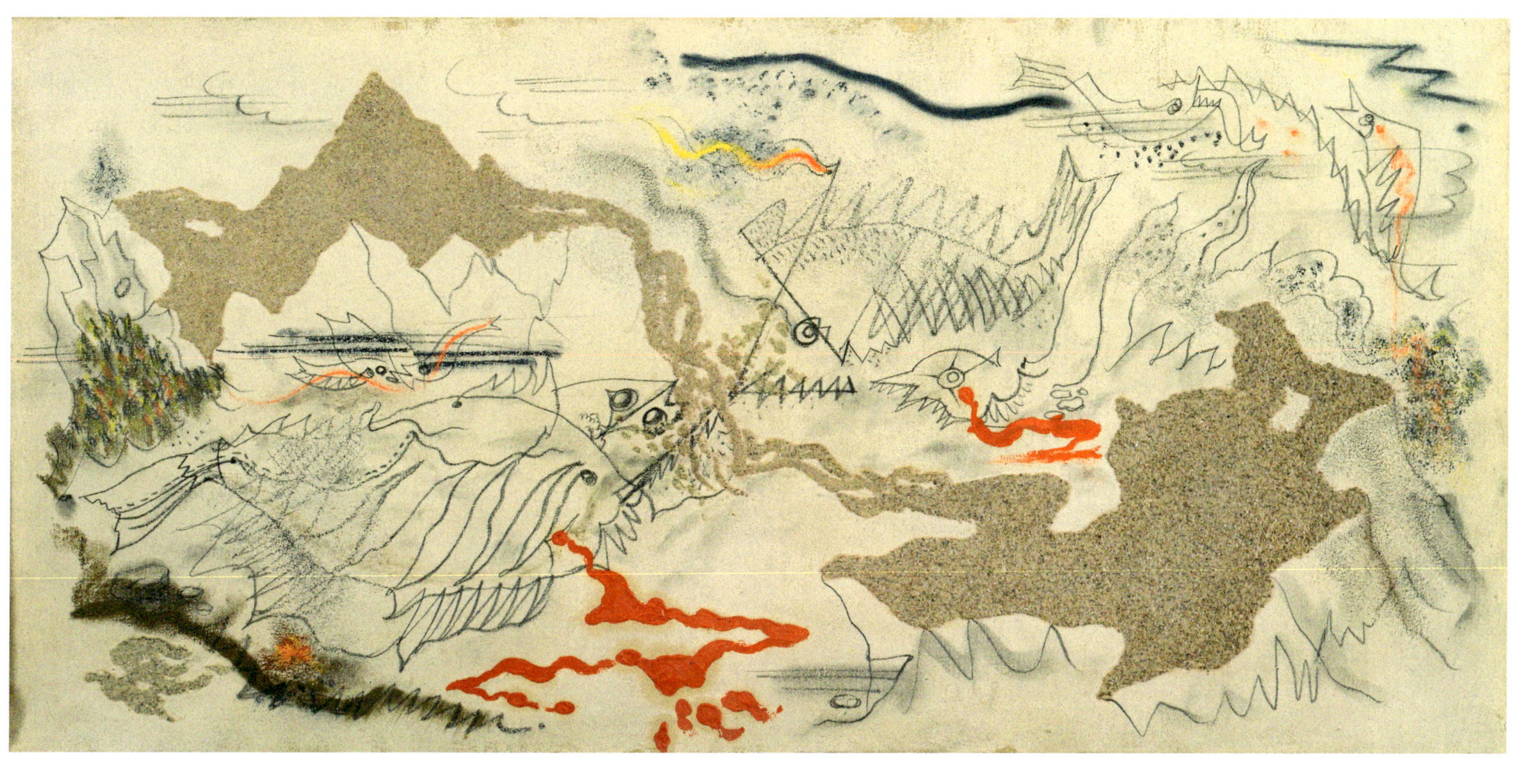

> Calder's first Paris-made three-dimensional objects were in many ways unclassifiable, in part because they were made with commonplace materials and because their mechanical workings gave some a gadgetlike appearance, but mainly because his works did not look like sculpture: they lacked mass, had the linearity of drawing outlining volumes, and often moved through space.[41]

Rather as the Constructivists were working with the opening of form, Calder was drawing three-dimensional forms in space with wire lines—"much as if the background paper of a drawing had been cut away leaving only the lines," as the curator James Johnson Sweeney would later write.[42]

In 1930, after a visit to Mondrian's studio in Paris, Calder painted a group of abstractions, precursors to his now-well-known "mobile sculptures," or "spatial drawings." A year later, while continuing to work figuratively, he joined the *Abstraction-Création* group, which also included Mondrian and Jean and Sophie Taeuber-Arp (plate 46, 47, 49, 50). He would soon start to make works that combined line with movement to varying degrees, whether by moving with air currents or the touch of a hand, such as *Sphérique I* (1931), or power-driven in some way, such as the hand-cranked *Two Spheres within a Sphere* (1931) and the motorized *A Universe* (1934; plate 48). The line that had indicated motion now actually initiated it, embodying it in time and in space. Interestingly, the line of Calder's moving-wire works recurs in his circus drawings on paper of 1931–32 (plates 165, 224), where it takes on airiness and even translucency, as if benefiting from his explorations in real space.

44. André Masson
(French, 1896–1987)
Combat de poissons (Battle of fishes). 1926
Sand, gesso, oil, pencil, and charcoal on canvas
14 1/4 x 28 3/4" (36.2 x 73 cm)

Leaving its phallic status of righteousness, line now oscillated between the geometric and the gestural, becoming unstable, wandering, seductive—the supposed attributes of the feminine. It was as though a congenital pulse drove it toward motion and, now, toward color. Until well into the twentieth

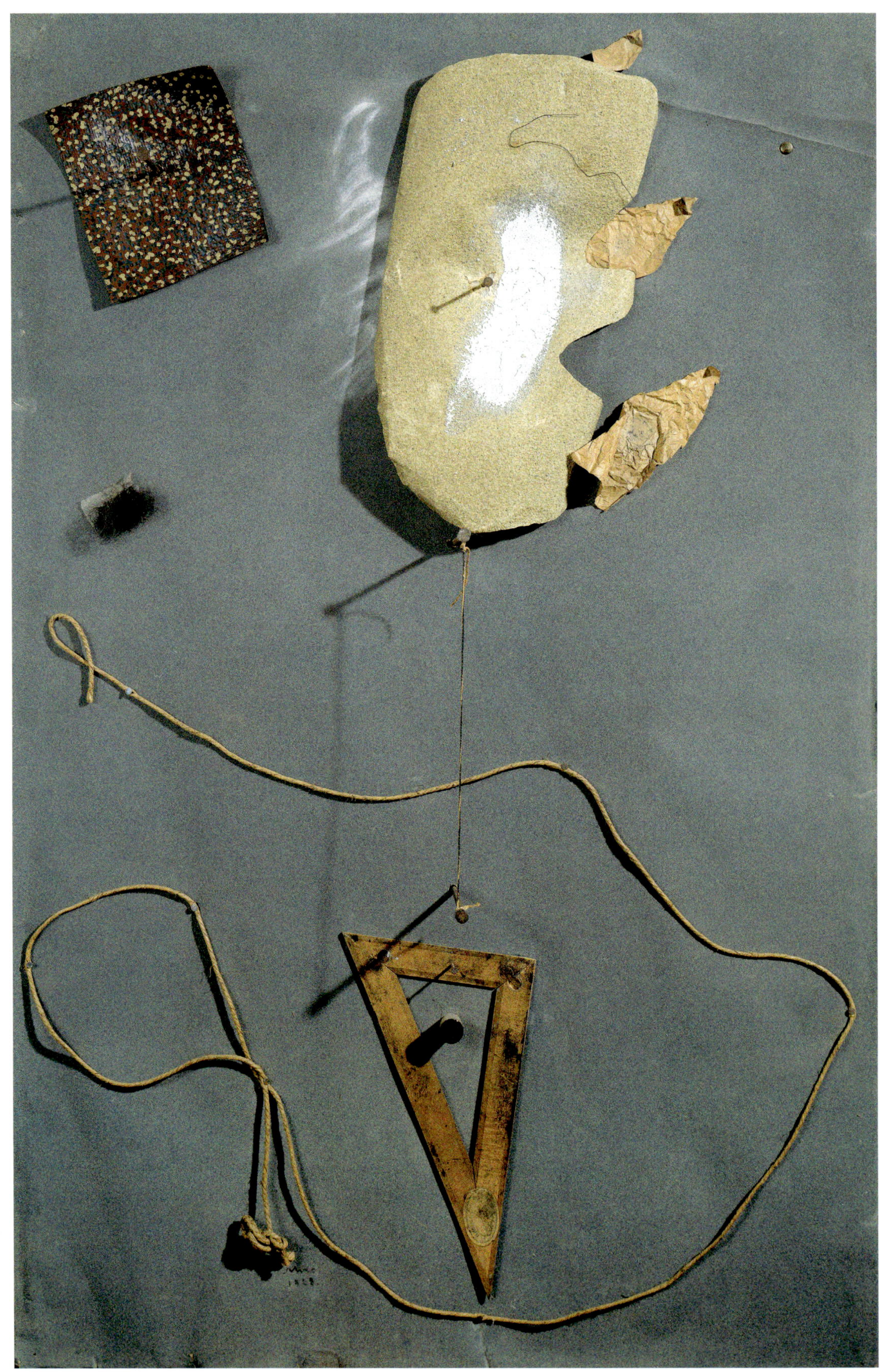

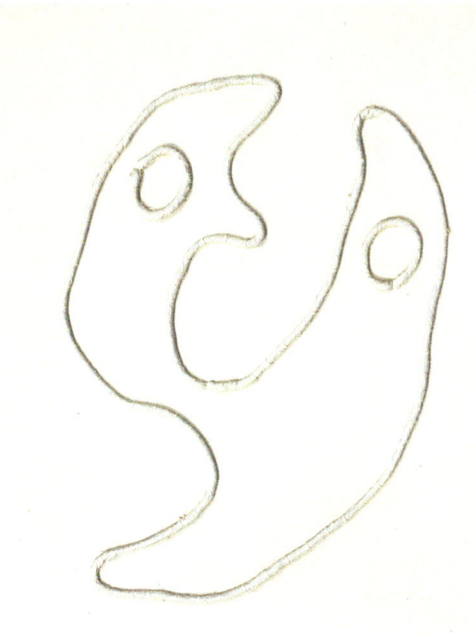

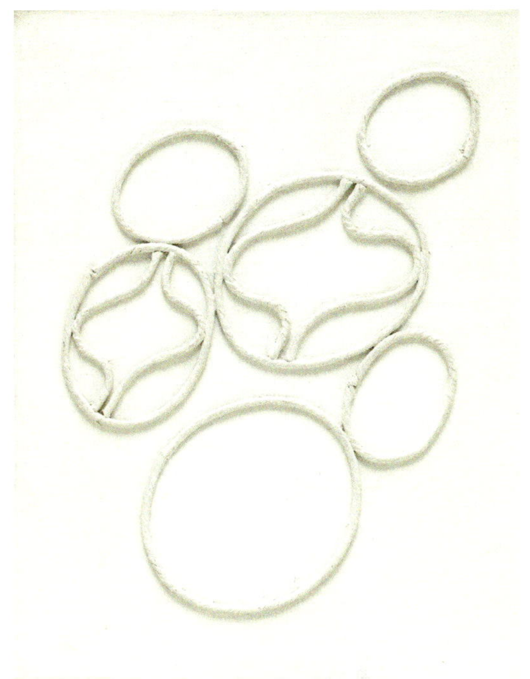

century, art historians and academic theorists had generally considered color sensual and "feminine." A certain truth of the hand, the stroke of pen or pencil manifest in the line — a certain honesty and discretion — had been favored over color's allure. Drawing itself, of course, was assigned an instrumental role, to which color appeared not to submit — yet color was seen as no more than a superfluous ornament, a supplement, embellishment, or enhancement to drawing. While line was to be dilated, color was still sublated — an instrument of an instrument. Color had to be kept in line! As did the emerging, unleashed line itself, sinuous, promiscuous, out of control.

As the century progressed, however, the antinomy between drawing and color began to wane, particularly in abstract art, as both liberated themselves, George Roque writes, "from the once-dominant instrumental-representational function, in order to stand on their own and assert their independent value."[43] In works such as Taeuber-Arp's *Mouvement de lignes en couleurs* (Movement of colored lines, 1940; plates 8, 162), a dance of colorful tracings seemingly alluding to her choreographic work or to the moving strings of her puppetry, or in the delicately painted lines of Georges Vantongerloo's *Relation of Lines and Colors* (1939), an attempt emerged to bridge the conventional division between line and color, motion and emotion. Again, the diagnostic charts that Emma Kunz made with a ruler and color crayon in a state of trance reflect an effort to merge gesture and geometric lucidity in an intuitive diagram. As Duchamp once remarked, "To all appearances, the artist acts like a mediumistic being who, from the labyrinth beyond time and space, seeks his way out to a clearing."[44]

At the brink of World War II, as a tragic period of dislocation, exile, and separation engulfed the lives of millions, an open-ended aesthetic model became apparent in which transformation and connection, asserted by the Surrealists through intimate relations of beings and things, were set against fixed definition and determination. The *Sixteen Miles of String* with which Duchamp filled a room at the *First Papers of Surrealism* exhibition in New York in 1942 (plate 167) — a show, organized by Breton, that featured a number of artists in flight from Europe — seems to epitomize such a model, rooted in responses and associations. In impeding walking, however, the twine of this immense "vintage cobweb? Indeed not!," as Duchamp remarked, effectively acted as an obstacle between the audience and the artworks in the room of the residential mansion in which the exhibition was installed.[45] While resembling the tinted tangle of Maria Helena Vieira da Silva's painting *Les Lignes* (The lines, 1936; plate 166), Duchamp's string lines rather established a perceptual and ideological mediation among objects, viewers, and what

45. Joan Miró
(Spanish, 1893–1983)
Spanish Dancer. 1928
Sandpaper, paper, string, nails, linoleum, drafting triangle, hair, cork, and paint on flocked paper mounted on wood boards
43 1/8 x 28″ (109.5 x 71.1 cm)

46. Jean (Hans) Arp
(French, born Germany [Alsace], 1886–1966)
Two Heads. 1927.
Oil and cord on canvas
13 3/4 x 10 5/8″ (35 x 27 cm)

47. Jean (Hans) Arp
(French, born Germany [Alsace], 1886–1966)
Leaves and Navels. 1929
Oil and cord on canvas
13 3/4 x 10 3/4″ (35 x 27.3 cm)

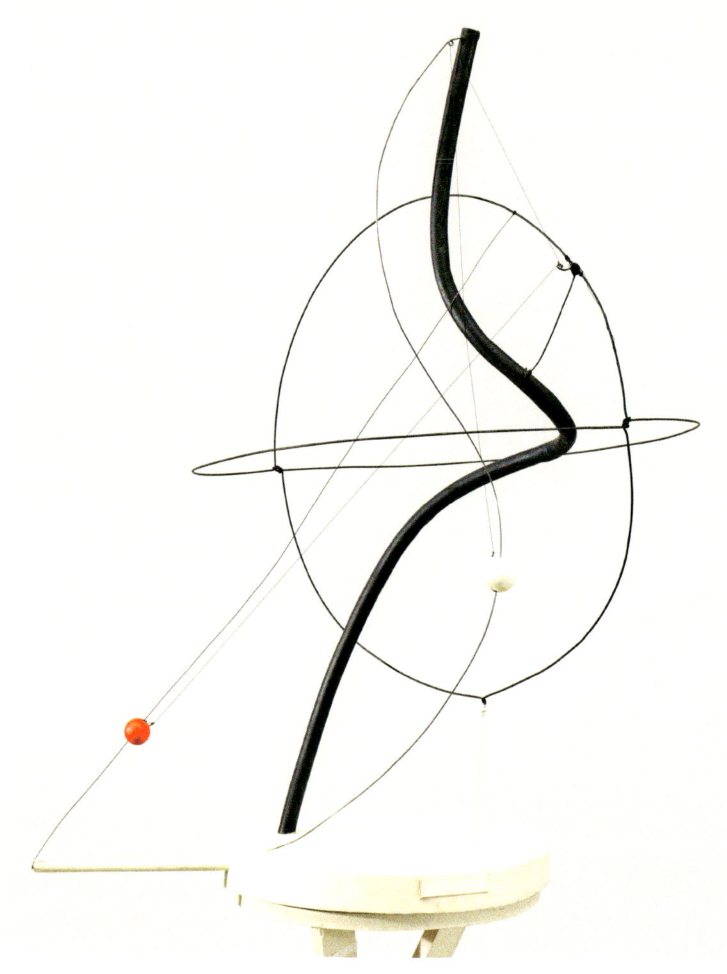

48. Alexander Calder
(American, 1898–1976)
A Universe. 1934
Painted iron pipe, steel wire, motor, and wood with string
$40\frac{1}{2}$ x 30˝ (102.9 x 76.2 cm)

was for many a "homeless" reality, addressing conditions of insecurity and exile. Embodying at once an insistence on the home as the locus of "the fantasy of fusion" and a resistance to "the 'home' as ideological site of nationalism,"[46] this confusing, aleatory cobweb seems to have had both the nurturing and the devouring traits of the spider. In fact *Sixteen Miles of String* replicated the condition of exile, refusing the potential of connectedness, of being in relation. Characterizing human existence as absurd, it reinforced separation in a solipsistic iteration of alienation. Ultimately the elaborate conceit of the web and, as Demos argues, "its promise of escape from ultimate arrest," only manifest the sour bad faith of frustrated exile. Over thirty years later, when Cildo Meireles realized his weblike *La Bruja* (The witch, 1979–81; plate 125) for the Bienal de São Paulo, he, like Duchamp, accepted the preexisting matrix of language, architecture, and institutional determination as inevitable preconditions for his work's reception and similarly elicited forces of disorientation from within the work itself.

With the radical extension of line into the spatial dimensions of sculpture and architecture, its connectedness to space and time brought a dilation of its meaning. Freed from the support, becoming itself in space, it no longer figured as merely the outline or delineation of form, so that its meanings were liberated from the task of depiction. Line's liberation from the two-dimensional surface over the course of the twentieth century found parallels not only in sculpture's similar break from containment into real space but in the reinvention of social space, first as a fragmented dimension of modernity and then as contiguous with self. In avant-garde practice, these impulses anticipated the material and spatial experimentation with drawing that preoccupied neo-avant-garde practice in the postwar era in disparate societies across the globe.

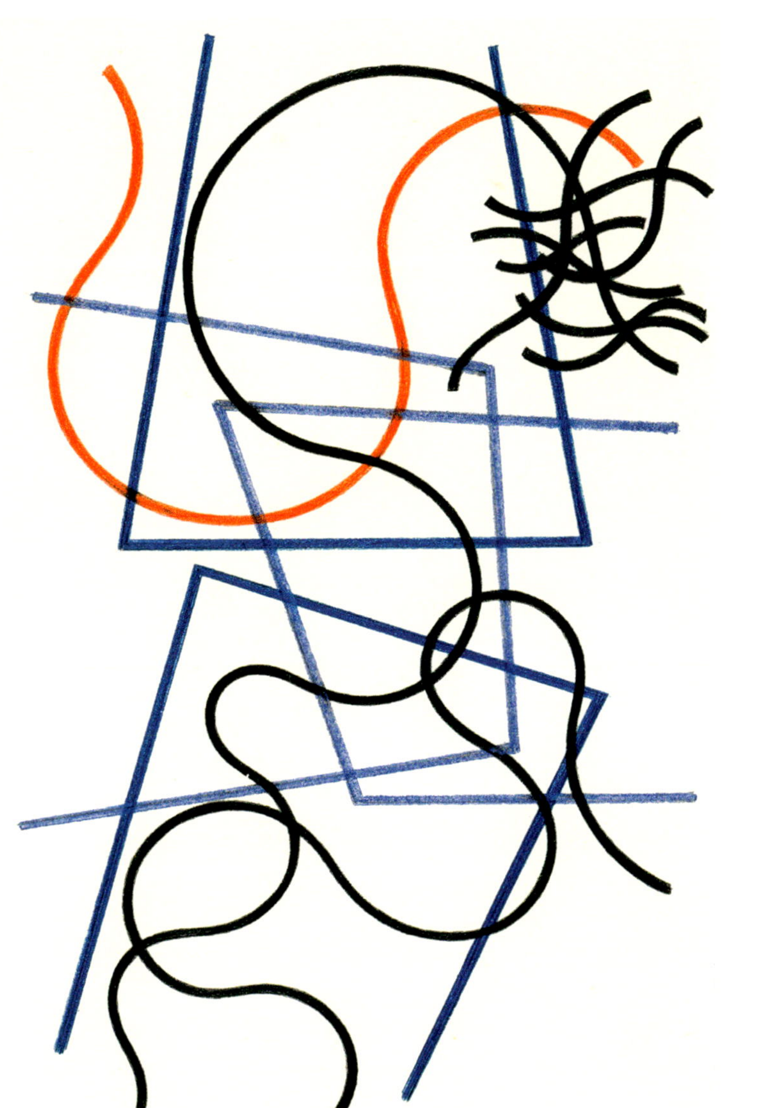

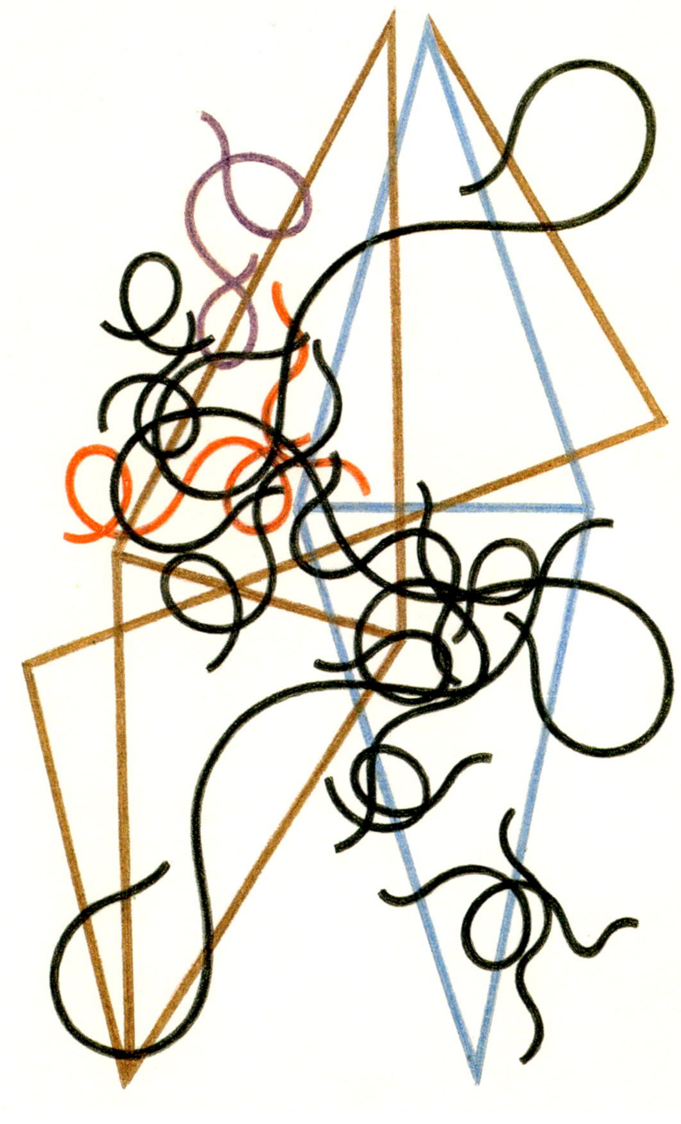

49. Sophie Taeuber-Arp
(Swiss, 1889–1943)
Lignes géométriques et ondoyantes
(Geometric and undulating lines). 1941
Colored pencil on paper
8 3/4 x 5 1/2″ (22.2 x 13.9 cm)

50. Sophie Taeuber-Arp
(Swiss, 1889–1943)
Lignes géométriques et ondoyantes
(Geometric and undulating lines). 1941
Colored pencil on paper
8 7/16 x 5 1/4″ (21.5 x 13.4 cm)

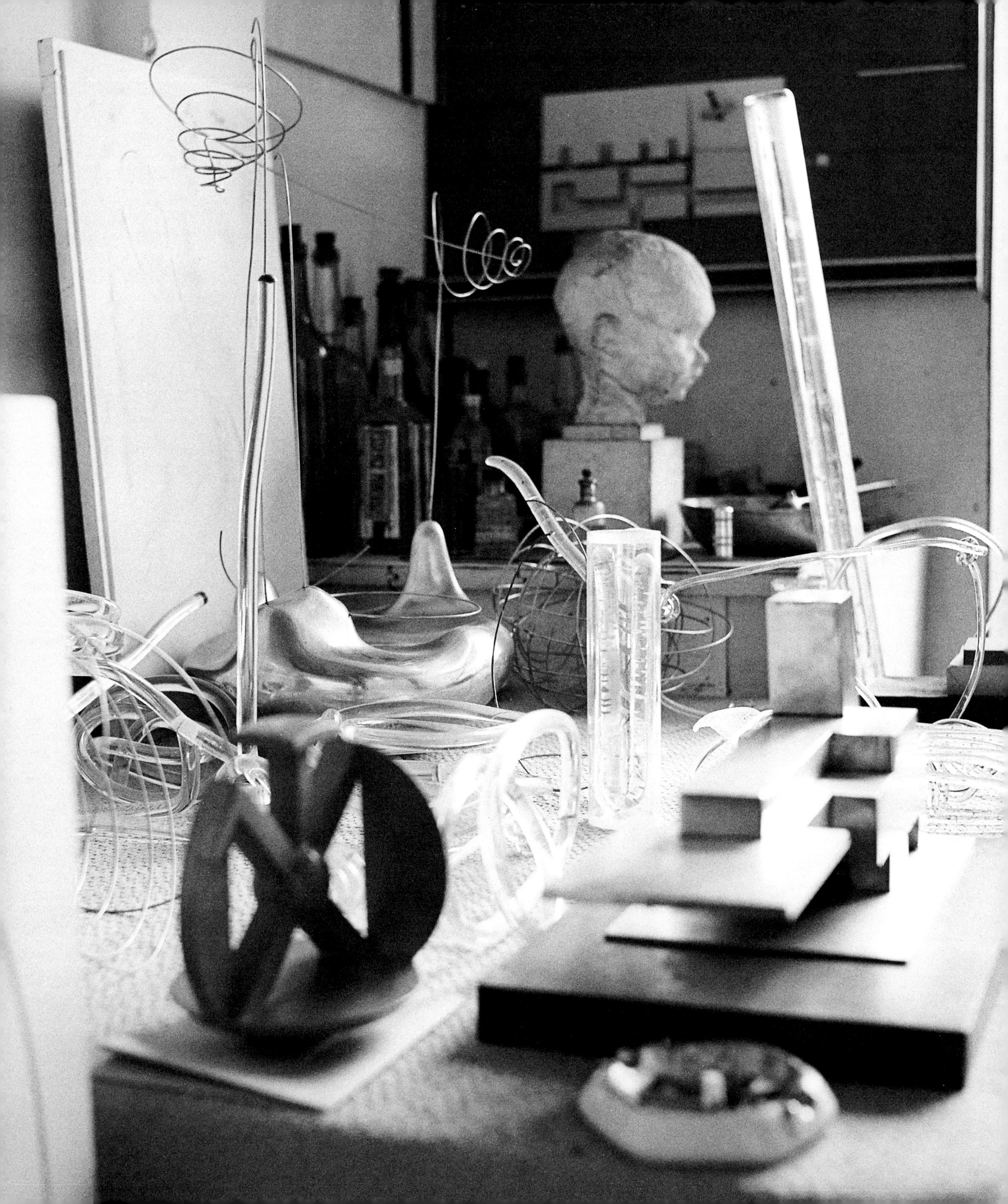

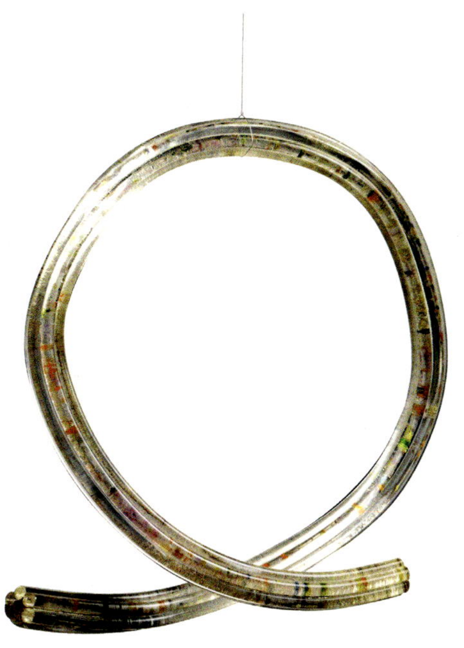

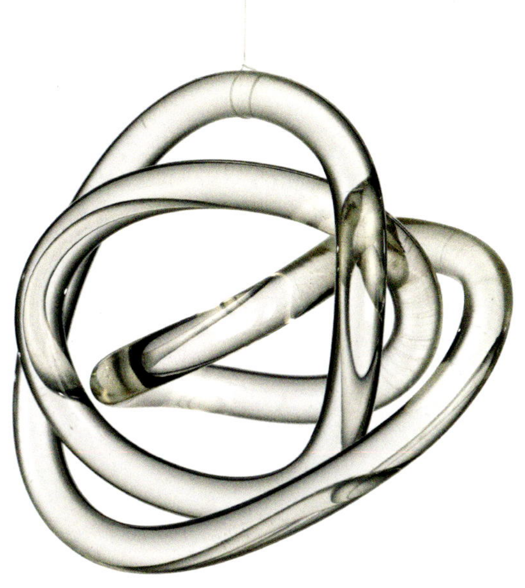

Longing for a space "without dimensions,"[47] Vantongerloo, who in 1917 had cofounded the de Stijl group with Mondrian and Theo van Doesburg, created his first linear sculptures in the 1940s: *Etendue (ligne dans l'espace) un point en mouvement engendre un volume* (Extended [line in space] a moving point engenders a volume), *Espace infini* (Infinite space), and *Vecteur* (Vector, all 1945), to which he would later add color paint. In a letter to Max Bill that same year, he wrote, "A point in movement traces a line which is not necessarily straight and evenly wide over its full length. On no. 163 there are two lines, emerging from a point that follows its own course without asking for my advice."[48] Vantongerloo was fascinated by Suprematism and Constructivism; his suspended linear *Revolution* (1946) could almost be a materialization of the line cut into the planar surface of Rodchenko's *Spatial Construction no. 12*. The titles of his works refer to geometry and astrophysics, the lines and vectors being those of cosmic energy. In 1947, to suggest infinity while using a material ground, he began to work with transparent Plexiglas, so that, in sculptures such as *Des éléments (ligne fermée)* (Elements [closed line], 1954), *Espace et couleur* (Space and color, 1956), and others (plate 51–53), line and colored dots appear to float free, mobile in space. Reflecting, in part, a common longing for liberation in Europe during and after World War II, the drive to elude confinement was an important motive for Vantongerloo, who wrote, "From 1938 until 1946, I have increasingly freed myself from labels. I am thus free. That is my right, and also yours. Art expresses itself in freedom, and I hope nobody will apply a new label for my view with the excuse that it is a new form of art — like film."[49] He increasingly saw his work as an attempt "to express space — the immensity of space — the universe, not scientifically nor philosophically nor allegorically, but through the comprehension of the immeasurable itself. I just made a work in which the colors are no more material but are present by radiation."[50] Following the credo "the volume + the void constitute space,"[51] he wanted his Plexiglas sculptures and white monochrome paintings to dissolve in infinity, to become one with the immeasurable cosmos. To capture space in light, he fused the color of painting, the spatiality of sculpture, and the linearity of drawing, seeking a result that was none of the above: line made transparent void, line devoid of contour — "no longer painting," Vantongerloo wrote, "nor sculpture or what they call plasticity, nor existence according to the laws of chance, but creations within creation."[52]

Across the Atlantic in Buenos Aires, Carmelo Arden Quin, Gyula Kosice, and Rhod Rothfuss, founders, in 1946, of the Madí group, were similarly aiming to transcend the formal limits of concrete art.

51. Studio of **Georges Vantongerloo** (Belgian, 1886–1965), Paris, 1960

52. Georges Vantongerloo
(Belgian, 1886–1965)
Espace et couleur (Space and color). 1956
Plastic
9 13/16 x 11 7/16 x 3 15/16" (25 x 29 x 10 cm)

53. Georges Vantongerloo
(Belgian, 1886–1965)
Cocon, chrysalide, embryonnaire
(Cocoon, chrysalis, embryonic). 1950
Plexiglas
3 15/16 x 5 1/8 x 3 1/8" (10 x 13 x 8 cm)

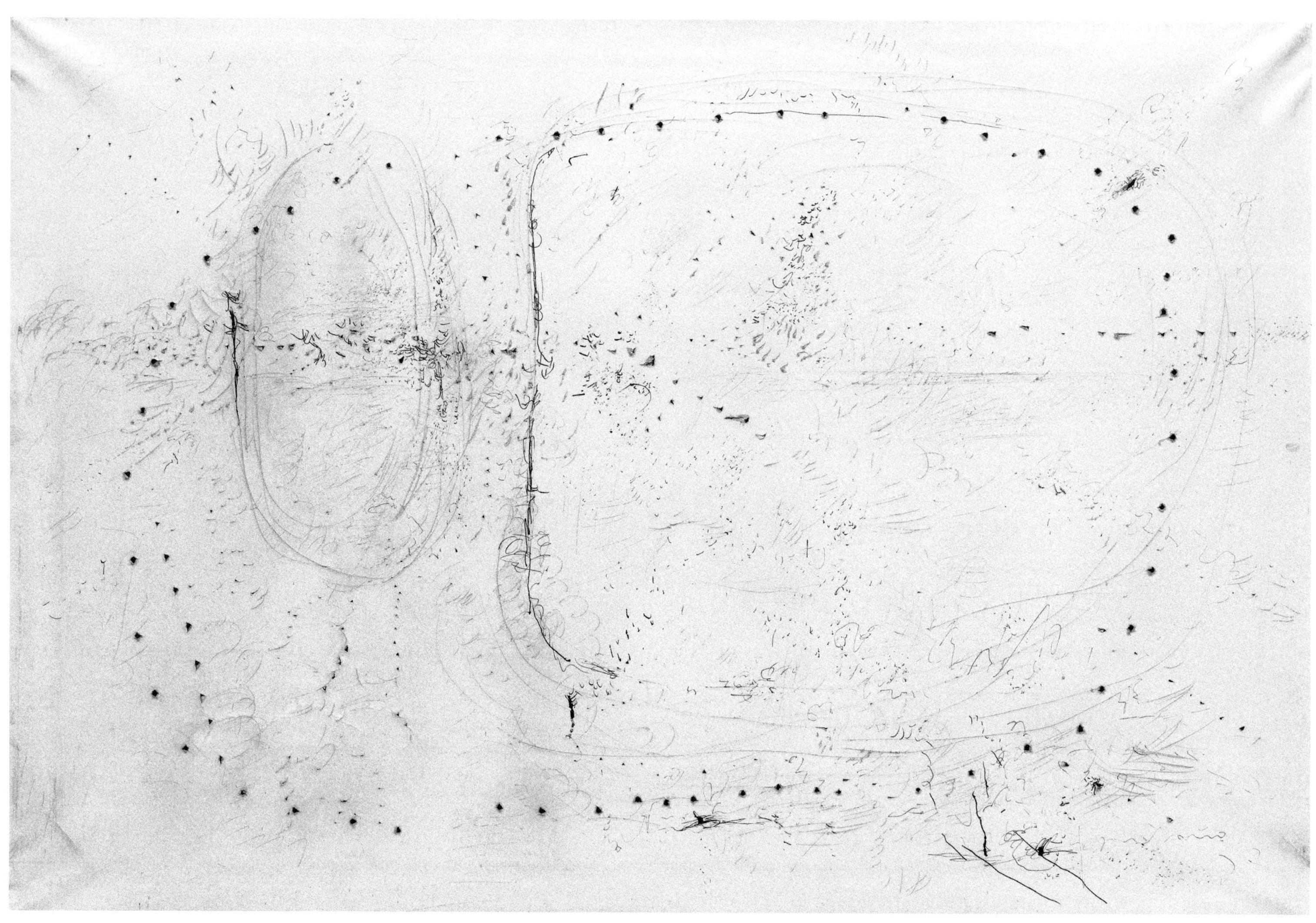

Their experiments with materials paralleled those of Vantongerloo, whom Arden Quin and Kosice would meet when they moved to Paris, at the end of the 1940s, and whose aesthetic of dematerialization strongly influenced Arden Quin's idea of "*plastique blanche*" (white plasticity). Also in 1946 in Buenos Aires, Lucio Fontana and his students published their *Manifesto Blanco*, which introduced the concept of "Spatialism." In an embrace of celestial dynamism recalling Vantongerloo's, and ultimately inspired by Futurism, Fontana sought escape from the imprisoning flat surface to explore movement, time, and space. In 1949, having returned to Italy, he began to develop his *Concetti spaziale* (Spatial concepts; plates 54, 55), puncturing and piercing the surfaces of sheets of paper to reach into the space behind, beyond, the illusionistic plane — in other words into the real, into what he called "a free space."[53] Rips, tears, and holes made in the page with an old-fashioned steel-nib pen were imagined as opening onto a space without physical boundaries. In 1958, as if realizing the potential of Rodchenko's linear "incisions" — lines traced as "cuts" into the surface plane — Fontana began to slash linear cuts in stretched canvases. He completed these works, giving them body, by easing open the edges of the cut with, effectively, an erotic gesture of the hand. The opening thus obtained onto the real, onto space, indeed onto the universe, was to allow for a sensation of boundlessness, a vertiginous ecstasy of dilation. Shedding its materiality, line became both orgiastic and cosmic, coextensive with infinite space, with creation itself. More literally, the works were intended as an art for the "space age" — an age of new technologies of science and transmission.

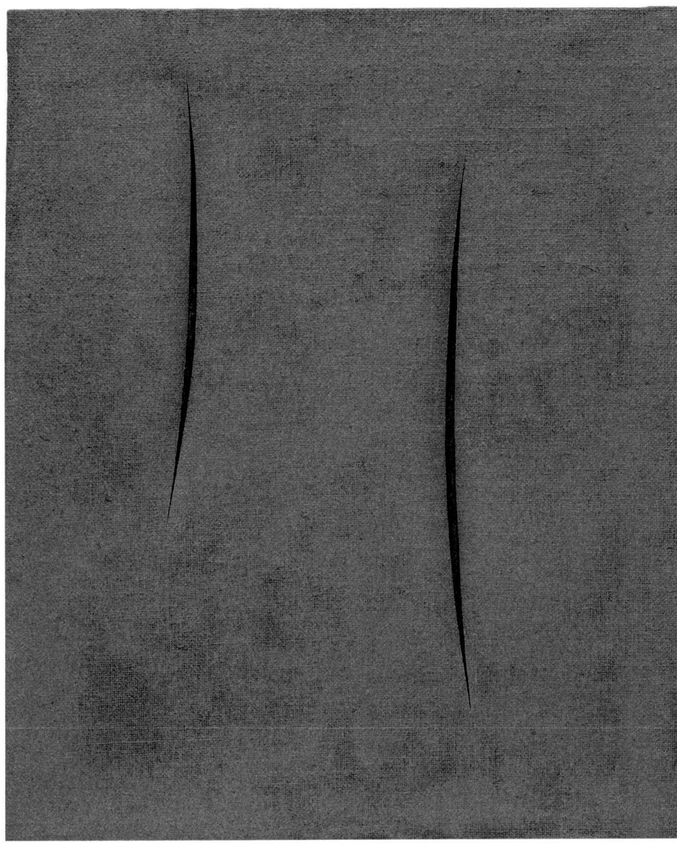

Infinity passes through [the cut lines of the Concetti spaziale*], light passes through them, there is no need to paint.*

—Lucio Fontana, n.d.

These artists' fascination with the white ground is striking not only in its reference to the pure, virginal state of the empty page (related to drawing) but also because of white's potential to fuse with the space around it, with the void. This artistic construct was conceived in the aftermath of World War II, when, in the face of destruction and annihilation, the idea of the tabula rasa was prompted by the wish for a new beginning, relieved of the burden of memory: an emerging model of creativity seen as universal, outside history, outside language, but inside space. Two decades earlier, Mondrian had pursued a utopian desire for the "dissolution of art into the environment" in his grid paintings (plate 61).[54] In his work of the late 1930s, however, line, previously subservient to structures of planes, had become the most active element, breaking down the particularity of the planes by its profusion. As line multiplied, it could no longer be fundamentally different from plane, and the one dissolved into the other.

In the 1940s and '50s, with Vantongerloo using unframed, white-painted canvas and Fontana slashing linear cuts through the canvas, line passed from bodily existence to a metaphorical zone of energy and light, released from physical containment. In Vantongerloo's suspended Plexiglas works, line was apparent only as transparency; in the *Concetti spaziale*, line was the absence between the lips of Fontana's cuts. Even when still material, in the "drip" paintings of Jackson Pollock (plate 56), line had a new volatility. Krauss writes that while Pollock's skeins or tightly woven webs of paint are

> constituted of pure line, the very stuff of drawing, they manage to undermine the goal of drawing, which is to bound an object by describing its contour. Constantly looping back on themselves, they not only disallowed the formation of anything like a stable contour but they also dispersed any sense of a focal point or compositional center within the optical field. In this sense, line was put to the service of the creation of a kind of luminous atmosphere, formerly the province of color, and...cancelling or suspending the distinction between line and color.[55]

54. Lucio Fontana
(Italian, born Argentina, 1899–1968)
Concetto spaziale (Spatial concept). 1957
Ink and pencil on paper on canvas
55˝ x 6´ 6 7/8˝ (139.7 x 200.4 cm)

55. Lucio Fontana
(Italian, born Argentina, 1899–1968)
Concetto spaziale. Attese
(Spatial concept: expectations). 1959
Synthetic polymer paint on
slashed burlap
39 3/8 x 32˝ (100 x 81.5 cm)

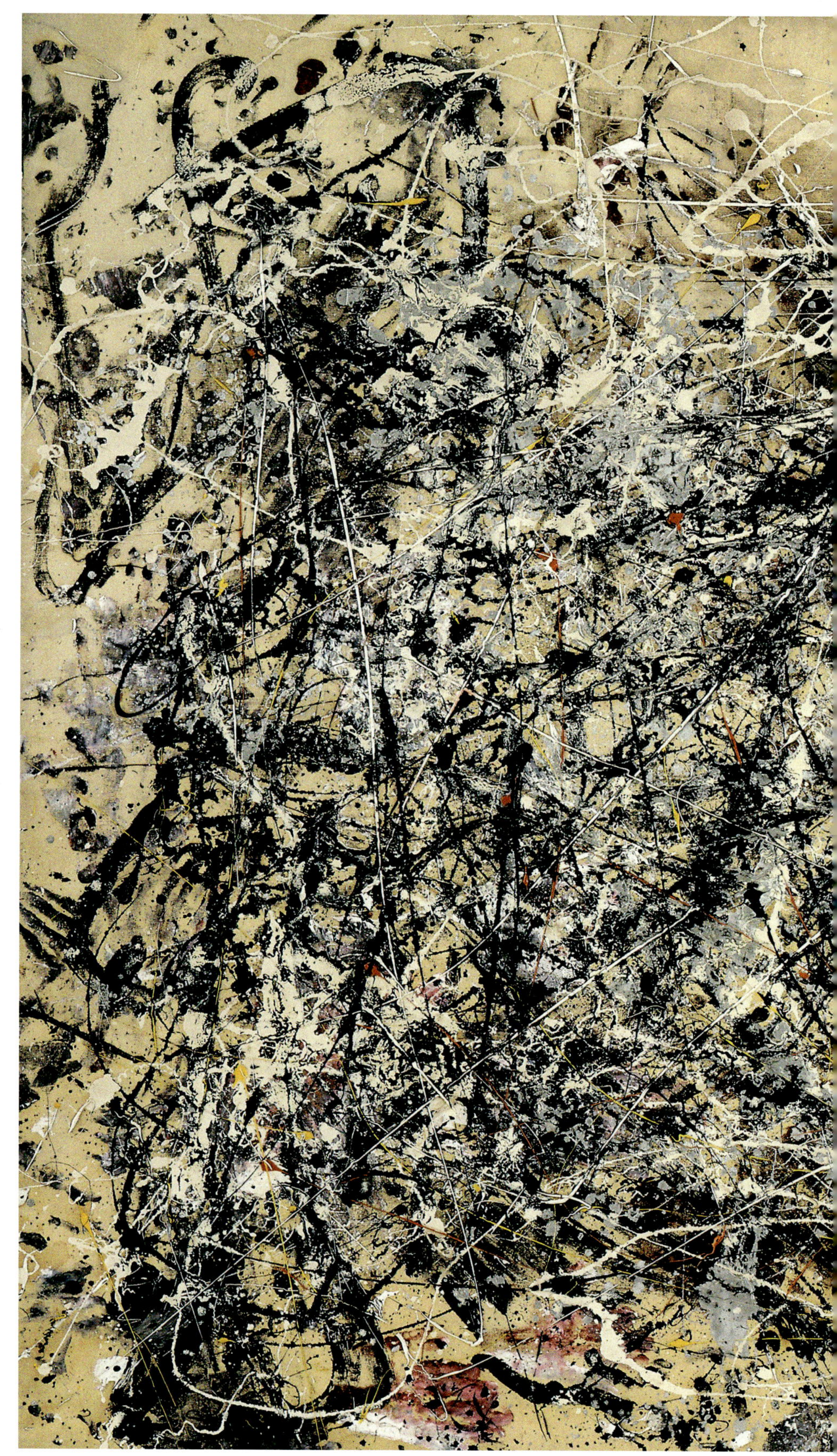

56. Jackson Pollock
(American, 1912–1956)
Number 1A, 1948. 1948
Oil and enamel paint on canvas
68″ x 8′ 8″ (172.7 x 264.2 cm)

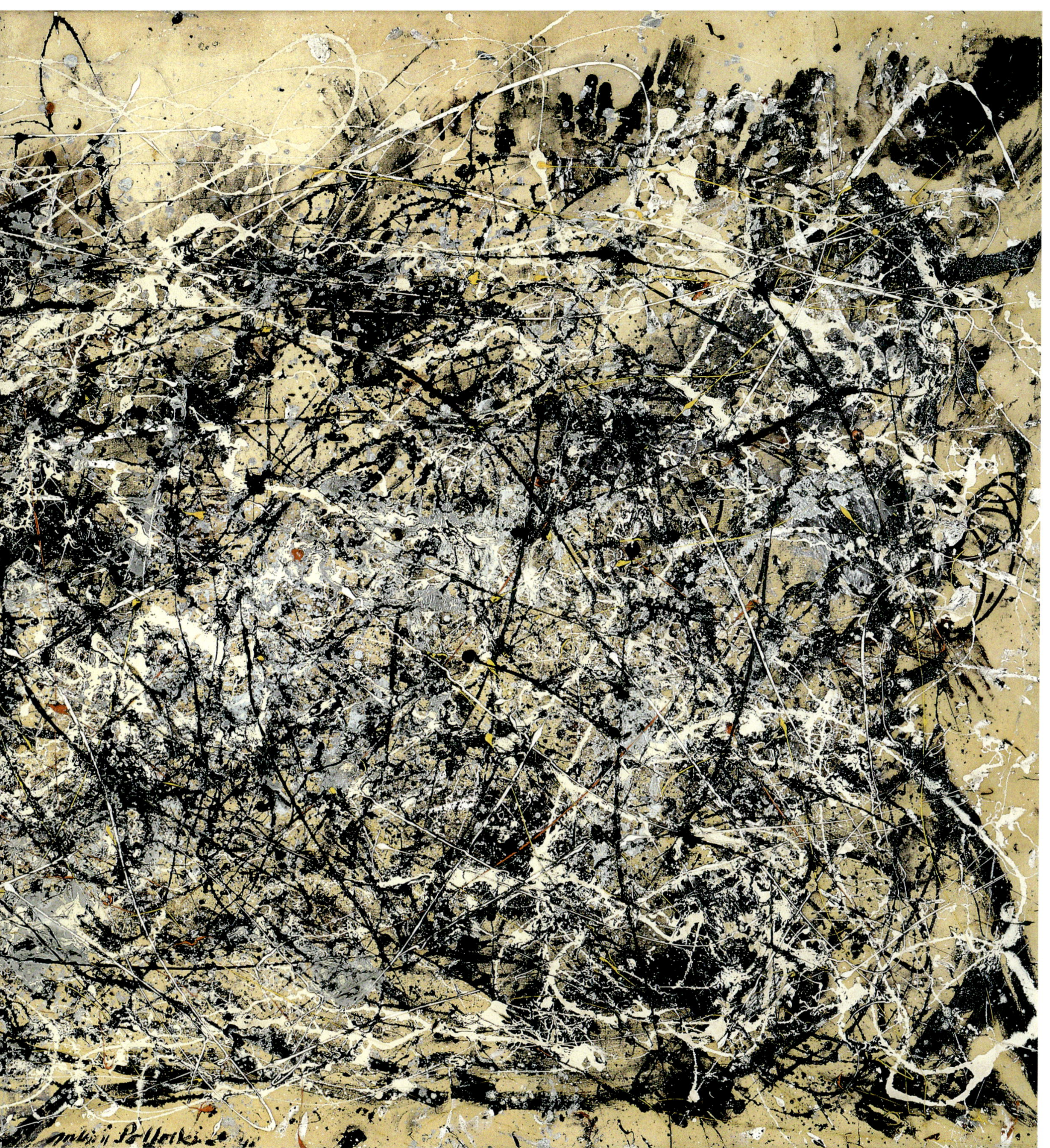

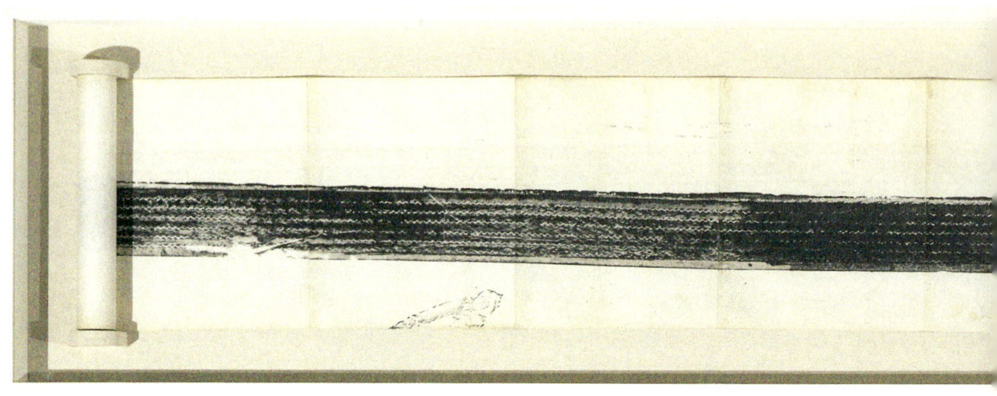

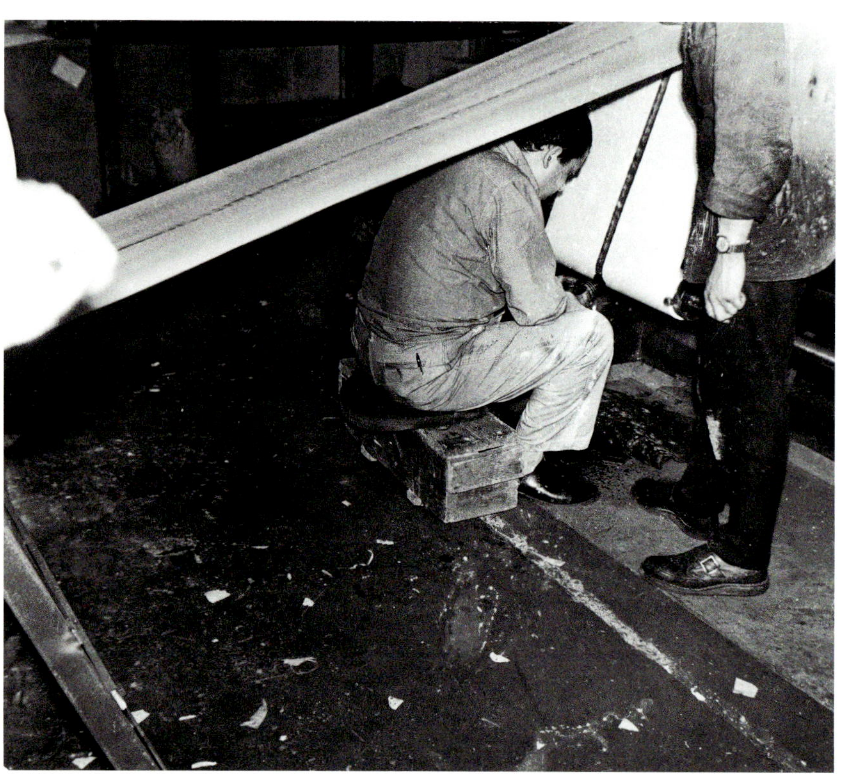

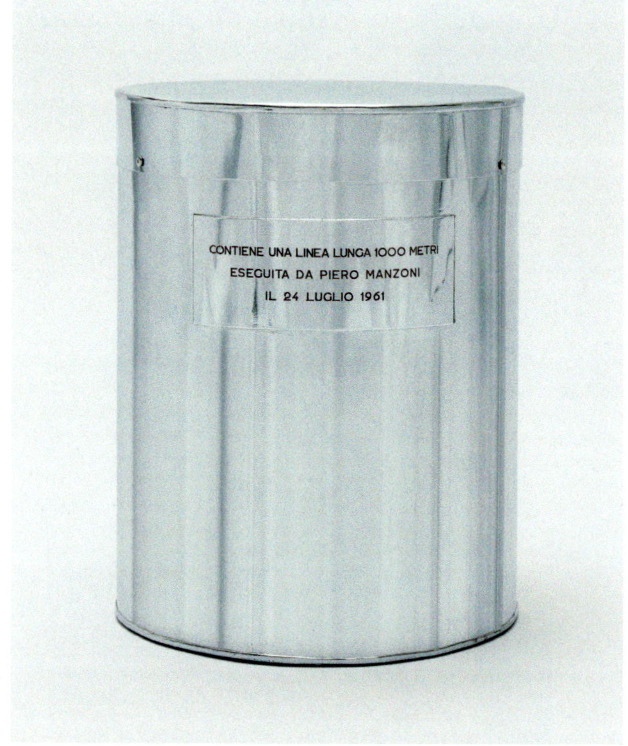
CONTIENE UNA LINEA LUNGA 1000 METRI
ESEGUITA DA PIERO MANZONI
IL 24 LUGLIO 1961

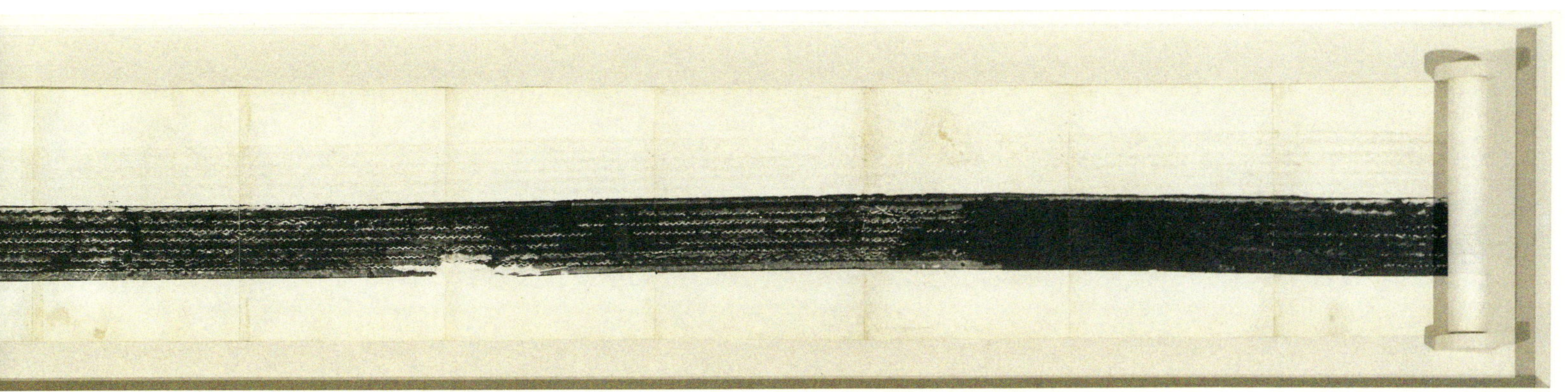

The wild, untamed line of Pollock and other American Abstract Expressionists began to be coded as a form of freedom — "a liberated sensibility increasingly deemed as setting a good example for the cause of democracy in Cold War–torn Europe."[56] Yet while many artists of this period let line loose into an ultimately metaphysical space, Pollock — famously laying canvases on the floor and dribbling paint onto them — regrounded it in the conditions of the earth, its gravity and reality. With no verticality, no contour, and no form, line was brought back from space to the surface, creating what would come to be called "antiform." Pollock's performative gestures recalled the movements of a dancer — perhaps those of Françoise Sullivan, a member of the Automatist group of Montreal, in her *Danse dans la neige* (Dance in the Snow) of 1948 (plates 169–73), both artists similarly leaving a picture of chance, choice, and chaos in kinesthetic traces on the white plane/plain.[57]

The painting and drawing of the Gutai group, founded in Japan in 1954 (plates 177–79), and the mechanically generated, meter-long lines boxed in containers by Piero Manzoni in 1959–61 (plates 57, 58) explored related concepts of gestural performativity in their different actions with line. This development would continue in the process and performance art of the 1960s. Yet Pollock's expressive line would soon be countered in works by Barnett Newman, Robert Rauschenberg, Ellsworth Kelly (plates 149, 150), and even Cy Twombly (plate 127, p. 225). Against the unique trace of the individual, against notions of spontaneity and authenticity, were posited the indexical imprint of a shadow, a tire print, or a graffiti mark, suppressing the autographic and the compositional. Though also created on the ground, and no less rooted in the real than Pollock's work, the readymade line in *Automobile Tire Print* (plate 59), made by Rauschenberg with John Cage in 1953, was conceived as being as unspontaneous, as devoid of the maker's character, as a line could be.[58]

The use of the index as a counter to action painting's sense of authorial presence coincided with the autonomous movement of the line in European and South American kinetic art. Jesús Rafael Soto, who moved from Caracas to Paris in 1950, made reliefs that featured a vibrating line (plate 84) recalling Duchamp's *Rotary Demisphere (Precision Optics)* (1925) and Calder's first mobiles. These works steadily grew in scale, to the point where, in the *Penetrables* (Penetrables, 1969), they became environments enveloping the viewer. Back in Venezuela, Gego, a contemporary of Soto's who had made the reverse journey from Europe to South America, developed modular three-dimensional systems, disembodying gesture and rematerializing line. Her *Reticuláreas* ("Reticulareas" [a coinage of the artist's], 1969; plate 85) use lines, or the distance between them, to produce transparency and interpenetration, as if she were studying their behavior in multidimensional space. She pointedly called one group of works *Dibujos sin papel y sin marco* (Drawings without paper, 1976–89; plate 207, p. 219), believing, as Robert Ryman later would, that the presence of line defined these works as drawings.[59] Like Vantongerloo, Gego experimented with space as a unity of volume and void, making art from an absence of substance as nonobstruction, in what was, in part, a critique of conventional sculpture.

In the late 1950s and early 1960s, Lygia Clark and Hélio Oiticica, cofounders of the Neo-Concretist movement in Rio de Janeiro in 1959, seemed to share an endeavor with Italian *arte povera* artists such as Giovanni Anselmo, Luciano Fabro, and Pier Paolo Calzolari in what was to follow on from the relation

57 (far left). **Piero Manzoni** making *Linea m 7200* (7200-meter line) at the paper mill of Herning Avis Printers House, Herning, Denmark, July 4, 1960

58 (near left). **Piero Manzoni** (Italian, 1933–1963)
Linea m 1000 (1000-meter line). 1961
Chrome-plated metal drum containing a roll of paper with an ink line drawn along its 1000-meter length
20 1/4 x 15 3/8" diam. (51.2 x 38.8 cm diam.)

59 (above). **Robert Rauschenberg** (American, 1925–2008)
Automobile Tire Print. 1953
Black paint on twenty sheets of paper, mounted on fabric
16 1/2" x 22' 1/2" (41.9 x 671.8 cm)

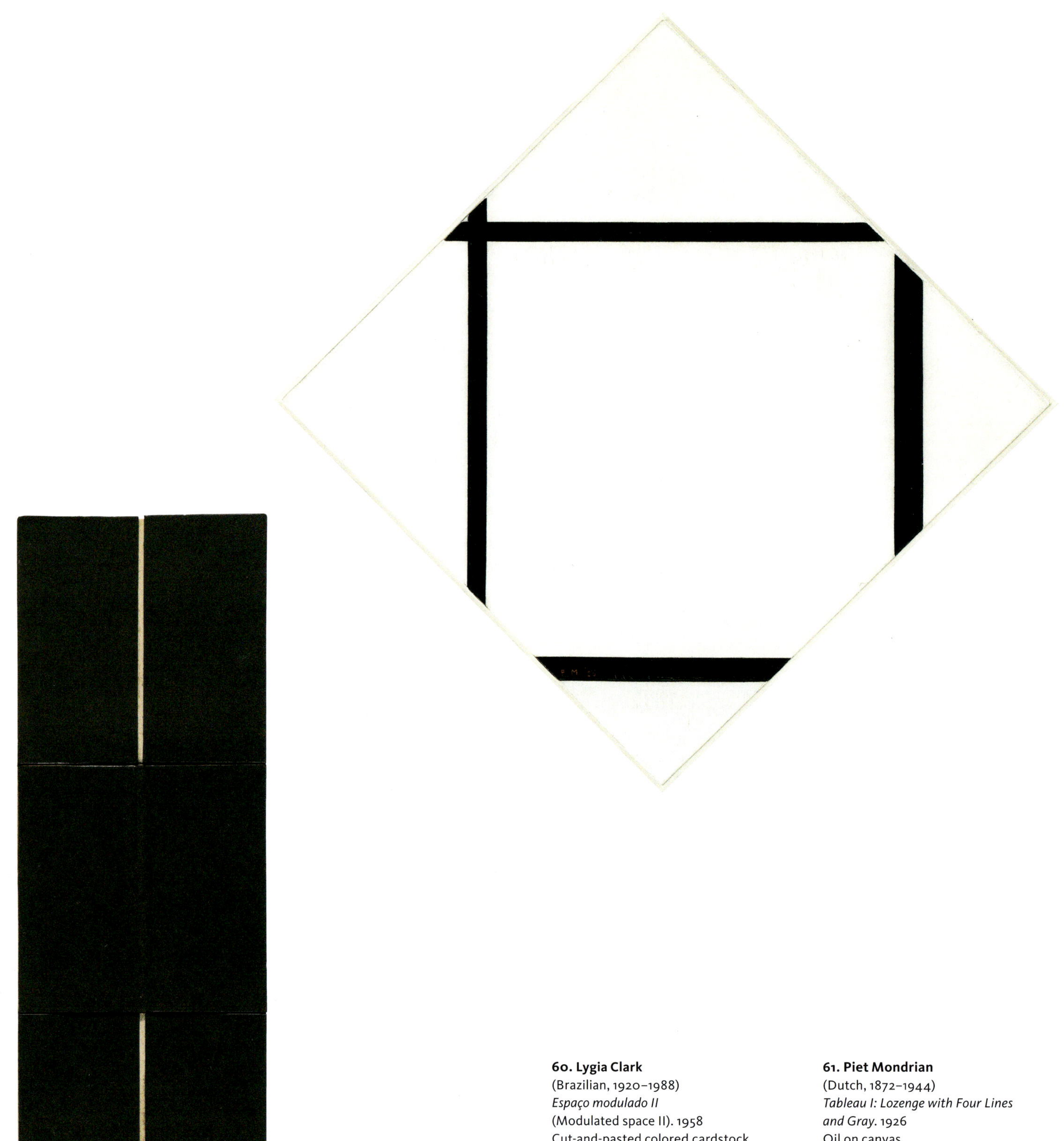

60. Lygia Clark
(Brazilian, 1920–1988)
Espaço modulado II
(Modulated space II). 1958
Cut-and-pasted colored cardstock
on cardstock
$11\ 3/4 \times 3\ 7/8''$ (29.9 x 9.9 cm)

61. Piet Mondrian
(Dutch, 1872–1944)
Tableau I: Lozenge with Four Lines and Gray. 1926
Oil on canvas
$44\ 3/4 \times 44''$ (113.7 x 111.8 cm)

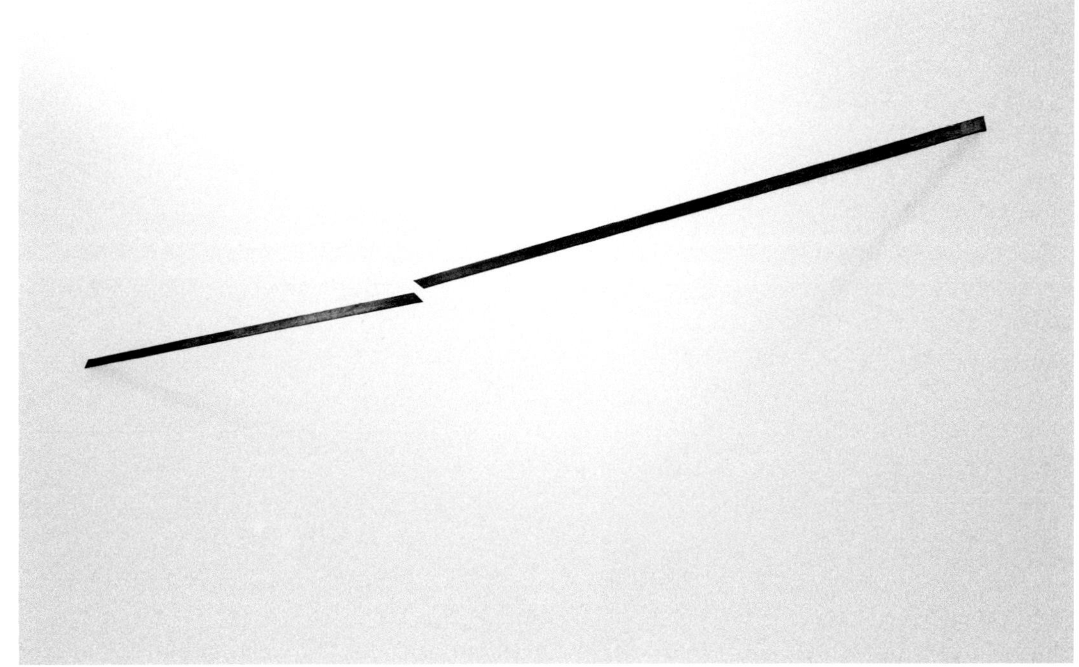

There is only one type of duration: the act.

— Lygia Clark, "Walking," 1964

To my mind, looking at [Mondrian's] verticals and horizontals, he divided up the picture simply into its own lines of construction. My own problem is tied up with this, that is to say when I am virtually turning the surface sideway, working with its peripheral "edge of space," as I called it. . . . The great importance of Mondrian, to me, was that he "cleaned" the canvas of representative space, and from this came the contemporary questioning of this space.

— Lygia Clark, "Mondrian"

between matter and space posited by Fontana's empty line. And while the two groups differed widely in their approach to the legacy of earlier avant-gardes — Oiticica explicitly emphasized their different uses of "poor" materials — they had a common concern with art as environment and process to be experienced rather than as object to be consumed. Each sought a revolutionary art, freed both from aesthetic convention and from the power of the corporation and the marketplace. They aimed to reconnect art with daily life, to liberate the art object from its formalist inertia by creating "living objects" in which could be glimpsed the primary energy, the endless process, the vital forces that stir in all things, thus engaging viewers and freeing them from their own inertia. When Anselmo, in 1967, bent a large sheet of transparent acrylic into a curve and connected its vertical edges with an iron wire (plate 63) — the line as sign of tension — he not only made energy apparent but reconfigured the relation of plane and void, inverting Fontana's "absent" vertical line into a horizontal solid, suspended over a transparent surface that appears to become one with space. Fabro's *Contatto-Tautologia* (Contact-tautology, 1967; plate 62), a metal beam running high in the air between one wall and another — but cut in the middle, the two parts unable to meet — similarly asks the viewer to reflect on relation in a state of tension. Fabro's many experiments with mechanisms of suspension demonstrate a constant concern with questioning the relationship between the artwork, the viewer, and the environment.

Meanwhile, Clark's and Oiticica's Neo-Concrete line led into the empty interstices or joints between planes that touch. Clark tried to reveal the "processuality" of geometry by "freeing the line in the plane" from its supposedly inanimate condition.[60] The emptiness of the seam between the planes in *Espaço modulado I* and *II* (Modulated space I and II, 1958; plate 60), for example, becomes a "line-space," which Clark called the "organic line": "The planes are juxtaposed with lines and gaps that make the surface dynamic," Suely Rolnik writes, "as if irrigating it with life-giving sap, causing the work to spill over and contaminate space. . . . The plane thus recovers its poetic pulse."[61] Eventually Clark translated her geometric paintings, with their perceptually unstable planes, into freestanding constructions, the *Bichos* (Animals, 1960–64), hinged planes of metal that could be unfolded (much like Rodchenko's Spatial Constructions) and manipulated into various shapes, acquiring volume in real space. The two-dimensional plane, "pregnant from its fertilization by space" and revealing "the virtual presence of relief," spread into three dimensions.[62] The fusing of opposites — inside and outside, subjective and objective, erotic and ascetic — in *O dentro é o fora* (The inside is the outside, 1963; plate 185) reflects Clark's desire to undo the binary, on which, in her

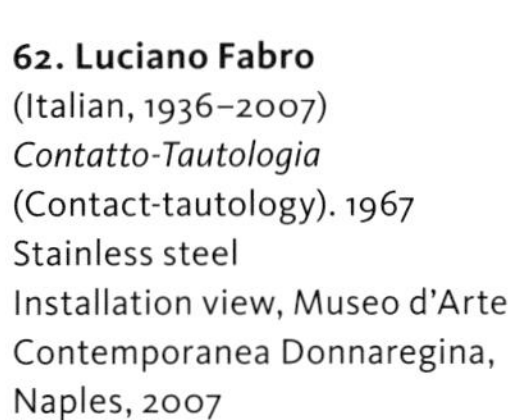

62. Luciano Fabro
(Italian, 1936–2007)
Contatto-Tautologia
(Contact-tautology). 1967
Stainless steel
Installation view, Museo d'Arte Contemporanea Donnaregina, Naples, 2007

Space has fun between the straight line and the curve.

—Luciano Fabro, *Attaccapanni*, 1978

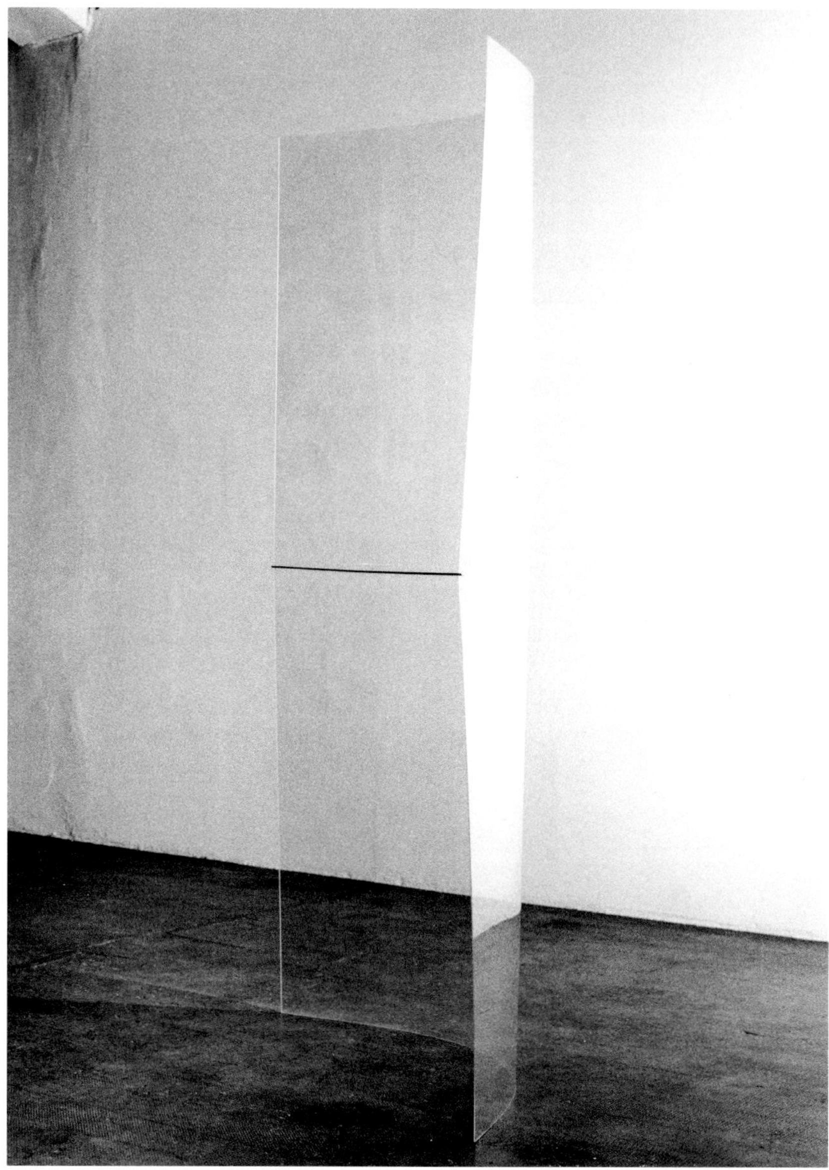

view, planar geometry and indeed the rational structures of society were based, and instead to develop the in-between, the relational, in order to counter the dissociating experience of what she called the "empty-full" in subjectivity. These conversations between line and plane, subject and object, in time led both Clark and Oiticica to collective, interactive performances intended to announce not only the fluidity of relation but also a beginning of the gradual disappearance of the authorial subject, and indeed of the art object as such. Convinced of the therapeutic potential of her artistic proposition of relation, Clark continued to treat individuals with "relational objects" in her studio until the end of her life (plate 186).

The wearable *Indumenti* (Garments) Fabro made in 1966 reflect a similar relational dynamic. Intimate items, these clothes include a *Posaseni* (Breast rest); a *Bandoliera* (Bandolier), a double ribbon passed between the legs and over the shoulder to support the male organ; and two pairs of cotton-wool *Calzari* (Footwear), one for a man, one for a woman. Fabro claimed, "These are garments which have no need to be understood but are simply worn." They represent the "shadow line," the subtle boundary between inner space (here understood as the body) and outer space, between the private sphere of existence and its public dimension.[63]

63. Giovanni Anselmo
(Italian, born 1934)
Untitled. 1967
Transparent acrylic and iron wire
6′ 5 11/16″ x 47 3/8″ (197.3 x 120.3 cm)

64. Luciano Fabro
(Italian, 1936–2007)
Asta (Pole). 1965
Stainless steel
Installation view, Museo d'Arte Contemporanea Donnaregina, Naples, 2007

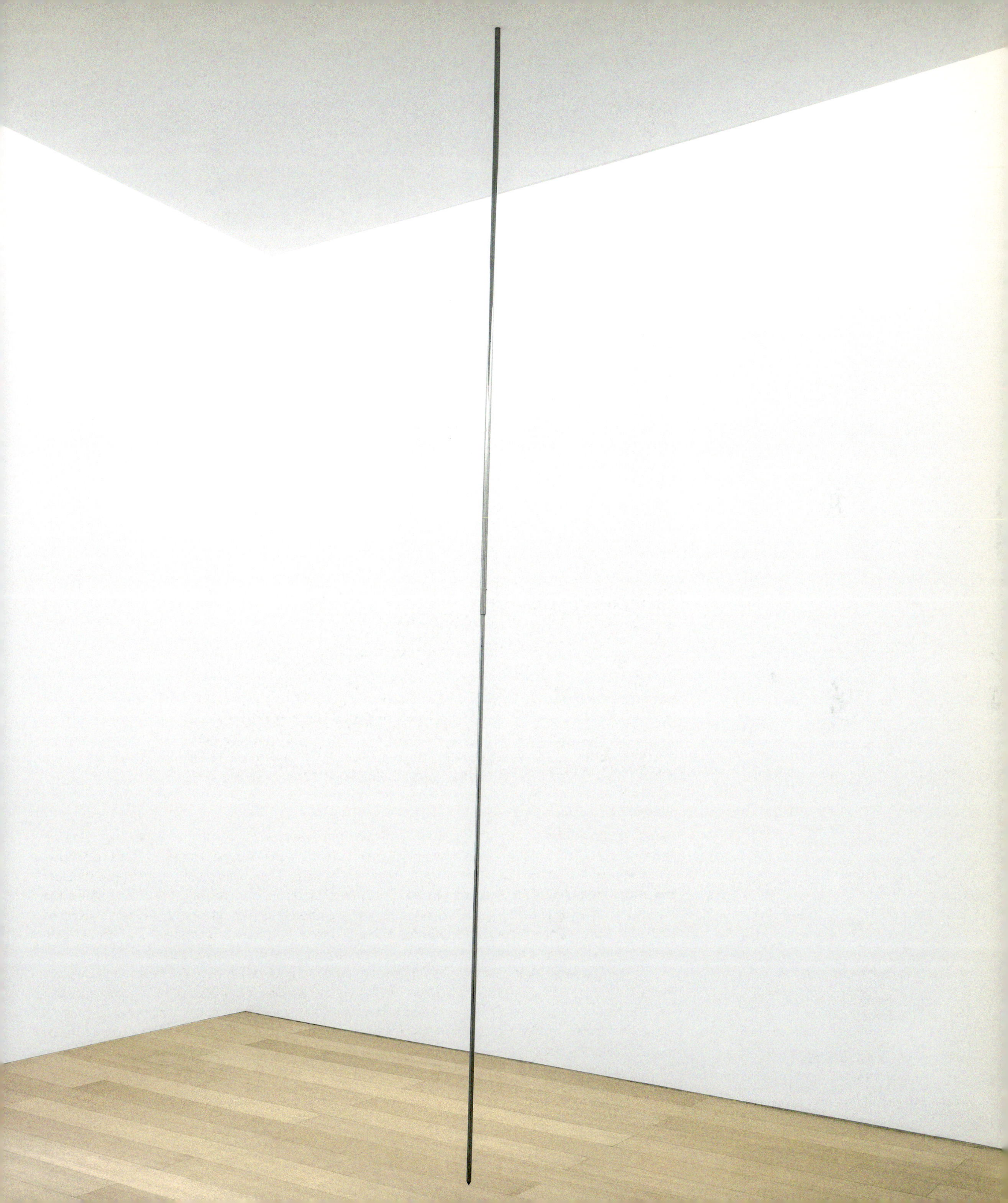

SPACE/LINE/PLANE: IN RELATION (1960–2010)

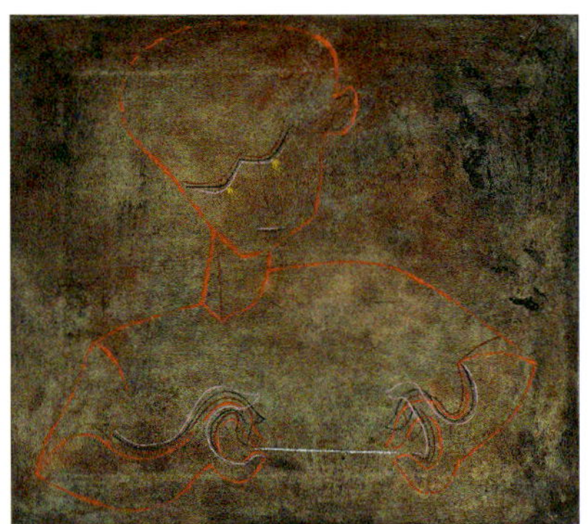

With line becoming a physical presence or absence, detached from the plane and independent of representation, drawing emerged from the first half of the twentieth century as a field coextensive with real space, no longer outlining an illusion marked off from the world. As art moved between two and three dimensions, drawing — and its basic mark, a newly dynamic line — subtly hybridized, becoming inextricably entangled with other mediums and materials. In the second half of the century, drawing became both independent and interdependent. Its differences from painting, printing, and sculpture blurred; the support no longer served as a separation between disciplines. A new visual language was developing, based on an expanded field for each aesthetic discipline, on new relations among them, and on the use of technological and eventually digital means.

In *Drawing Now*, the book accompanying an exhibition she organized at The Museum of Modern Art in 1976, Rose summarized the history of drawing since the mid-1950s as "the story of a gradual disengagement of drawing as autography or graphological confession and an emotive cooling of the basic mark, the line itself."[64] Attention increasingly focused on the dynamics of line itself, removed from authorship; and conversely, as line became independent, it came to signify drawing as an increasingly independent medium. Inextricably coupled, the story of line came to be the story of drawing. Following the assertions of artists on line, then, this exhibition and book must address not only drawing but its extended field, not only sketching or tracing with ink, pencil, crayon, or charcoal but works involving painting, sculpture, performance, and dance; winding, wrapping, and binding with wire and cloth; etching through film or photographic transfer; suspended webs of lines; and movement through actual or virtual space. *On Line* thus chronicles drawing as it became transdisciplinary, making the case for a discursive history of mark-making. It also examines not only the radical experimentation of postwar North American and Western European artists but concurrent drawing practices in South America, Asia, and Eastern Europe.

In the late 1960s, artists in many parts of the world, inspired by revolutionary social thinking, attacked the values of the established institutions of government, industry, and culture, questioning whether art, as private, individual expression, could still lay claim to authority, authenticity, or even an ethical reason to exist. In the traditional canons of art history and in the collections of the museums, distinct boundaries were (and still are) recognized between artistic mediums, but artists, elaborating on the avant-garde legacies of the first half of the century, opened up new spaces in which practices converged — now crossing the line, and making the line explicit. Coming from diverse cultural positions and moving in different directions, they often worked to occupy "real" social space. Line was apparent in every discipline. At the same time, drawing emerged from the 1960s as a medium of and on its own.

Drawing = Line = Drawing (1960–1980)

"Line in its pure state describes only itself," Rose wrote in *Drawing Now*,

> It is the relationship of one line to another that makes line function descriptively. As drawing moves away from description of contour it defines itself in terms of its primary unit, the nondescriptive line. For Cézanne, Pollock, and [Willem] de Kooning, line operates always in the most tenuous and delicate balance between two functions — and for a brief time it breaks free of contour in Pollock's paintings. In contemporary drawing, the generation of autonomous line, the use of nondescriptive lines as modular units, and the compression of gesture are all formal devices inherent in these prior uses of gesture and line.[65]

65. Michael Snow
(Canadian, born 1929)
A Man with a Line. 1953–54
Mixed media on canvas
16 x 18" (40.6 x 45.7 cm)

66. Robert Ryman
(American, born 1930)
Impex. 1968
Oil on unstretched linen canvas, and blue chalk line on wall
Canvas: 8′1″ x 8′1″ (246.4 x 246.4 cm); overall dimensions variable

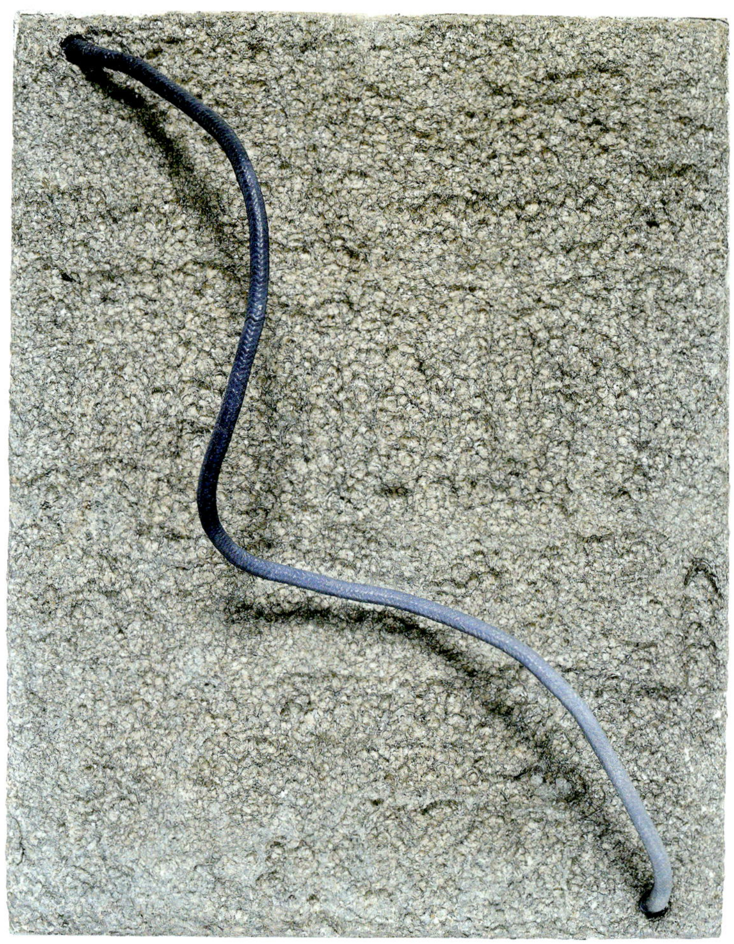

I had a great deal of difficulty with painting but never with drawing. The drawings were never very simplistic. They ranged from linear to complicated washes and collages. The translation or transference to a large scale and in painting was always tedious. It was not natural and I thought to translate it in some other way. So I started working in relief and with line — using the cords and ropes that are now so commonly used. I literally translated the line.

— Eva Hesse, 1970

It's kind of a basic theory of thinking about drawing that it has to do with line. I don't work with line in that way with my painting at all. When I draw, I am usually thinking about line, and what kind of line it can be. Really, that's how I look at drawings. It's more involved than that, too. As with any painting, you do have a surface to put the line on — what is that? How's the light going to work on it? And so on, so forth. So the approach is very similar to painting, but the focus is on line.

— Robert Ryman, 1992

Ryman defines any of his works that include a line as a drawing, notwithstanding the support, be it canvas, Plexiglas, cardboard, polyester, glassine, or aluminum.[66] Since the early 1960s, his interest in line has stemmed from its place at the core of the drawing medium. Through the use of paint and canvas, many of his drawings fuse with painting, but for him the linear element defines them as drawing, thus stretching the boundaries between mediums. Even the artist's signature is a linear element; in a number of works he turns the letters of his initials on their sides, making them as abstract as line itself.

Ryman has used a considerable array of materials and tools, from the traditional graphite, charcoal, and pastel to blue chalk applied with a snap-line (plate 66), a standard construction tool sold in hardware stores. By refining the conception of the artwork to its physical presence, and to the tools and mediums with which it is constituted, Ryman illuminates elements shared among aesthetic disciplines: line, surface, support. With this practical approach he exposes the material nature of art, yet the effect on the viewer may be an experience of the sublime. Throughout his career, Ryman has sustained this interest in the real, physical properties of materials, in their interaction with each other and in their response to the actions of the artist. He has shunned all forms of illusion, allusion, and reference, his art being characterized by a stark economy of materials and means. Like the work of Agnes Martin, it is a self-determined world of reductive principles, in which the artist has found endless variations to investigate. In the 1960s, Minimalist aesthetics were deeply engaged with the condition of the literal and with the purging of illusionism from the work by addressing the external.

Ryman's friend Eva Hesse had always felt more invested in drawing than in painting, and from the very beginning used what Lucy Lippard describes as "a wandering, tentative, string-like line."[67] Together with notions of space, connectivity, and progression, and a highly tactile sensibility for materials,

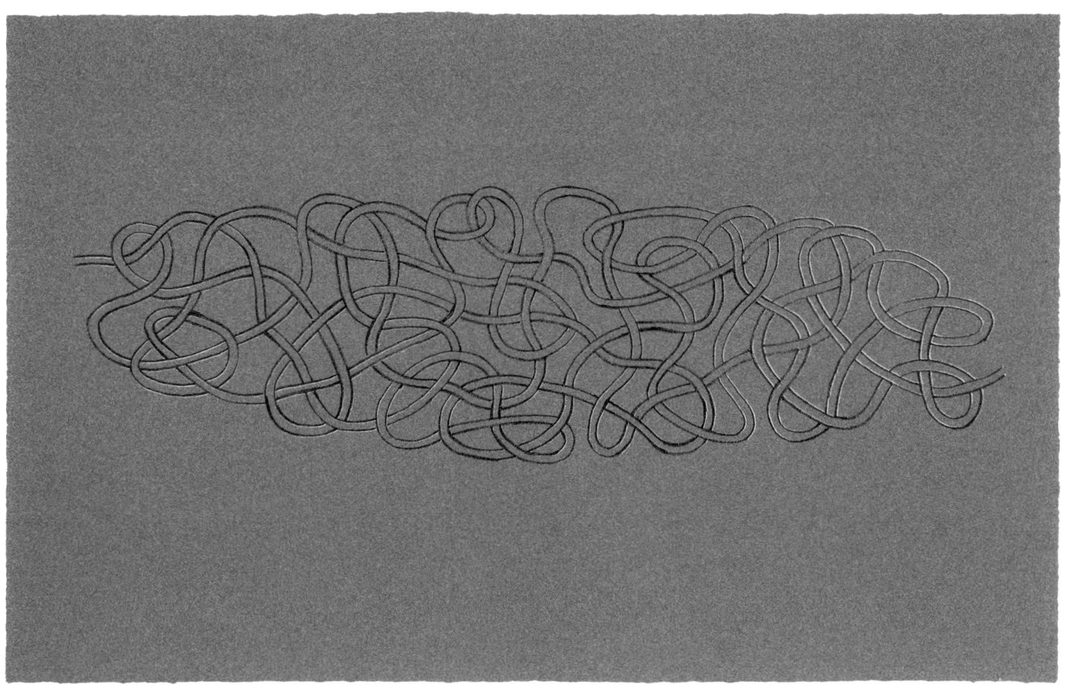

the vitality of this line was ultimately the thread in her work, leading from drawing in pen and ink to winding with string. By late 1965, Hesse's experiments had led her to wall-based constructions of cloth-covered wire and papier mâché. These cords — tangible lines — literally pulled her drawing into real space. She painted them with different tones of color, showing a preoccupation with color gradation, often from dark to light gray or vice versa, that recalled the work of Anni Albers (plate 68) and is in fact a characteristic of weaving.[68] These progressively accumulating tones intensified a sense of transformation and ultimately of light. Later, in works using fiberglass, latex, and resin, Hesse would convey light not by adding paint to her materials but through the materials themselves. As she explained, "Color is whatever comes out of the material and keeps it what it is. The light — I'm not too concerned with it, because if you use reinforced fiberglass clear and thin the light is there by its nature and the light does beautiful things to it. It is there as part of its anatomy."[69] Neither the remark nor the procedure is dissimilar from those of Vantongerloo.

In their subtle hybridization of drawing and sculpture, line and color, Hesse's reliefs anticipate her later works. The thin, protruding line of color in *Up the Down Road* (1965; plate 67) foreshadows the subversion of the conventional relationship between the plane, space, and frame of the picture in *Hang Up* (1966; plate 182) — a work the artist finally considered both "challenging" and "absurd."[70] Paradoxically, nonsense translated into a desire for sense, for meaning, for communication: the unstructured, free-falling cords in works such as *Ennead* (1966) and *Ditto* (1967), recalling breasts and nipples, and the umbilical-like cord in *One More Than One* (1967), can be read as reaching out to another, establishing connections with another. Indeed we find written in Hesse's notes, "Link, that which binds; bond, tie, connecting medium."[71] Using materials as various as wire, strips of fabric, surgical hose, and steel tubing, she moved toward interrelational, restorative aspects of art and life.

As in weaving, Hesse's graded cords and circle drawings address the connection or encounter of separate qualities — black and white — in tonal gradations of gray. In her color spectrum, as Cecilia Vicuña remarks, "One color dissolves to let the other be."[72] These unions of opposites in soft gradations, then, can be seen as a model of reciprocal subjectivity, one not rooted in binary thought, in oppositions of self and other, love and hate, incorporation and rejection. More than merely transgressing the boundaries between disciplines, Hesse's subversions move into the social, as her art's emphasis on interstitial space interrogates limits and raises basic questions of subjectivity.

67. Eva Hesse
(American, born Germany, 1936–1970)
Up the Down Road. 1965
Tempera, enamel, rope, Styrofoam, Masonite, and wood
25 3/4 x 19 3/4 x 7 1/2"
(65.4 x 50.2 x 19.1 cm)

68. Anni Albers
(American, born Germany, 1899–1994)
Enmeshed II. 1963
Lithograph
16 15/16 x 26 15/16" (43.1 x 68.5 cm)

To the eye of the viewer, the Drawing Objects, with their torn surfaces and empty spaces, crossed by lines and threads, are traces of a journey that point to the possibility of the existence of other planes. They suggest the existence of fullness in the empty.

— Anna Maria Maiolino

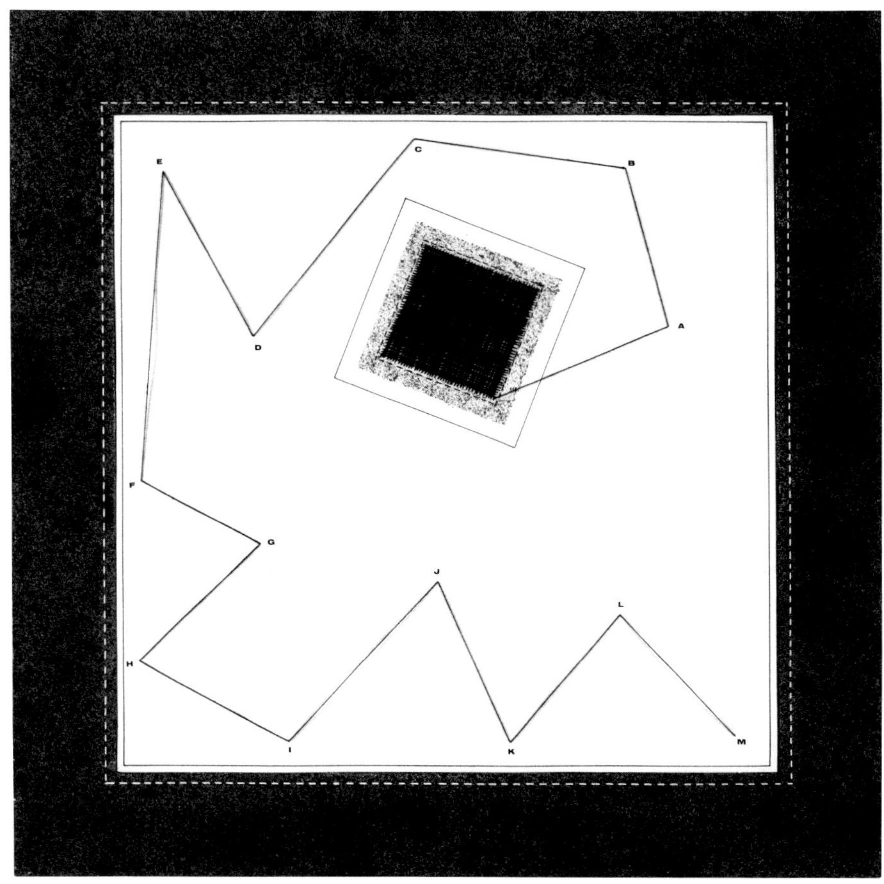

Hesse's attempt to fuse dichotomies while exploring the corporeality of her materials in both two- and three-dimensional space situates her work close to the practices of Latin American artists such as Vicuña and Anna Maria Maiolino in the 1970s. Where Clark, for example, was interested in line as an absence, a gap, that made the surface dynamic — "causing the work to spill over and contaminate space," as Rolnik writes — Maiolino's concern was with line as material presence in real space. Using sewing thread to mend gaps and materialize intertexture, she constantly questioned dialectics of division, the separation of inside from outside, positive from negative, black from white, for between these diametrical oppositions lies alienation, the hostility and aggression that may inflect antipodes of form. Maiolino's inquiry began with prints and drawings on paper, such as the etching *Escape Point* (1971), in which horizontal lines find their way out of an enclosing square. In *Desde A até M* (From A to M, 1972; plate 69), that line becomes solid: a zigzagging black thread is sewn into the paper, emerging from a grid of the same material in the center. Each point in this jagged, graphlike line bears a letter, so that the drawing runs through the alphabet until it has arrived at the artist's initials. The use of thread brings about a meeting between two-dimensional plane and three-dimensional space.

Maiolino was now experimenting with paper as more than a surface for drawing, whether figurative or abstract; for her it became "space and body."[73] She was trying to justify the uses of different mediums conceptually, giving more attention to the process of constructing than to what was constructed. In both prints and drawings, the front and the back of the paper became equally important:

> The matrix or plate used in the engraving process necessarily brings about our intimacy with the outside and the inside of the space of the impression. I was intrigued by the space at the reverse side of the paper: what is behind it, what is out of sight — the other space of the absent, the latent, the concealed. I began to print both the front

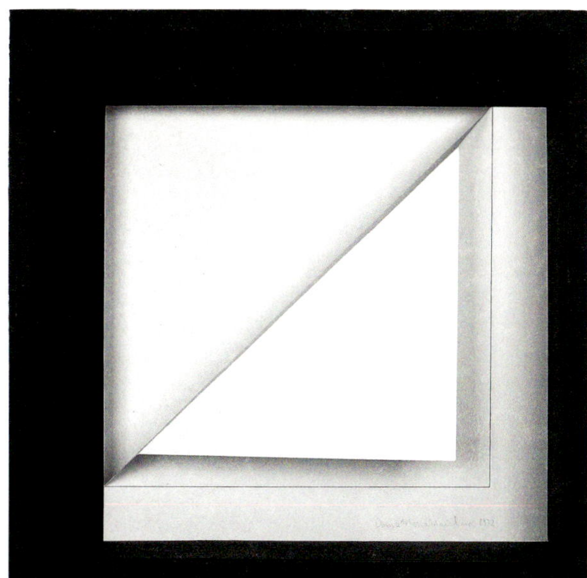

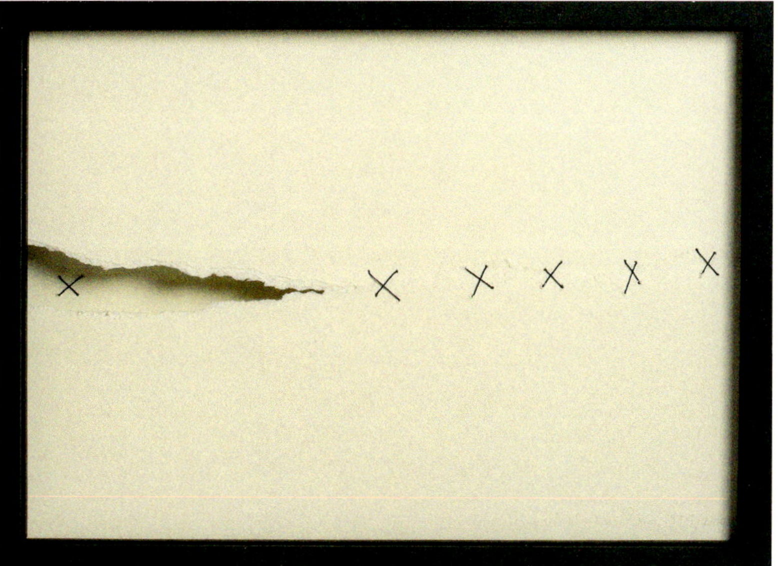

and back sides of the paper. Then, through cutting and folding, I was able to discover what was printed on the reverse and to incorporate it in the work together with the void left by the removal of the paper cut from it. Now the print did not only reside in the plane of the sheet, but by adding other dimensions became a graphic object. I entitled these works "Print Objects" (1971–72). This very same constructed spatiality came to dominate my drawing in the "Drawing Objects" (1971–76). If in the prints it was the sharp-cutting knife that revealed the other space and made it present, it is now the aggressive and spontaneous gesture of tearing that unveils the mystery of the void. The tear will then be suddenly sewn up... out of repentance.[74]

As for line, it now passed freely between frontal plane and encompassing structure, moving beyond the limits of ink to appear in thread, or in the seam of a fold, the edge of a cut, the cast of a shadow (plates 70–72, 131, p. 221). Conflating space, thought, and body, challenging the determining dichotomies in which limits become barriers, Maiolino evinced a connective activity on either side of what might otherwise be considered a binary division, sensitizing the viewer to possibilities beyond conventional, commonplace reality. In some works her line suggests an alimentary canal flowing between mouth and sphincter, evoking vital processes of transformation. Rather than describing life as constituted in organic form, it incarnates life as creating impulse — as permanent genesis, in the world and in art.[75]

To move beyond the modernist need to express the effects of bodily alienation in twentieth-century society, Clark, Hesse, and Maiolino used connective, curative materials, summoning line as string and as a link within the sensual realms of touch and gaze. Confusing the disciplines of drawing, sculpture, and painting, these women shaped a radically different dynamic in art, promoting a model of transsubjectivity — a reciprocal attitude that anticipated the concept of the "matrixial," theorized in the 1990s by the artist and psychoanalyst Bracha Ettinger. A new symbolic signifier in culture alongside the phallic, the matrixial allows for the coexistence of two subjectivities whose encounter does not involve a binary either/or. To formulate the concept, Ettinger drew on the image of the intrauterine encounter, during the late stages of pregnancy, where I and non-I both differ and share in subjectivity. Brought to bear on the practice of art, Ettinger's concept, along with the parallel work of other artists, has implications for ideas of what art can be and also for a redefinition of the feminine.[76]

Richard Tuttle was as much invested as Hesse and Maiolino in fusing drawing and sculpture. Each work in his Wire Pieces series of 1972 (plate 184), all made with florist's wire, nails, and graphite, comprises three elements: a line drawn on the wall in pencil; a wire strung along the length of this line,

69. Anna Maria Maiolino
(Brazilian, born Italy 1942)
Desde A até M (From A to M) from the series *Mapas mentais* (Mental maps). 1972–99
Thread, synthetic polymer paint, ink, transfer type, and pencil on paper
19 5/8 x 19 1/2" (49.8 x 49.5 cm)

70. Anna Maria Maiolino
(Brazilian, born Italy 1942)
Untitled from the series *Projetos construídos* (Constructed projects). 1972
Acrylic and transfer letters on paper in wooden box, with Styrofoam backing
17 11/16 x 17 11/16 x 4 15/16" (45 x 45 x 12.5 cm)

71. Anna Maria Maiolino
(Brazilian, born Italy 1942)
Untitled, from the series *Desenhos objetos* (Drawing objects). 1975–2001
Thread on paper in wooden box
9 13/16 x 13 3/8 x 2 9/16" (25 x 34 x 6.5 cm)

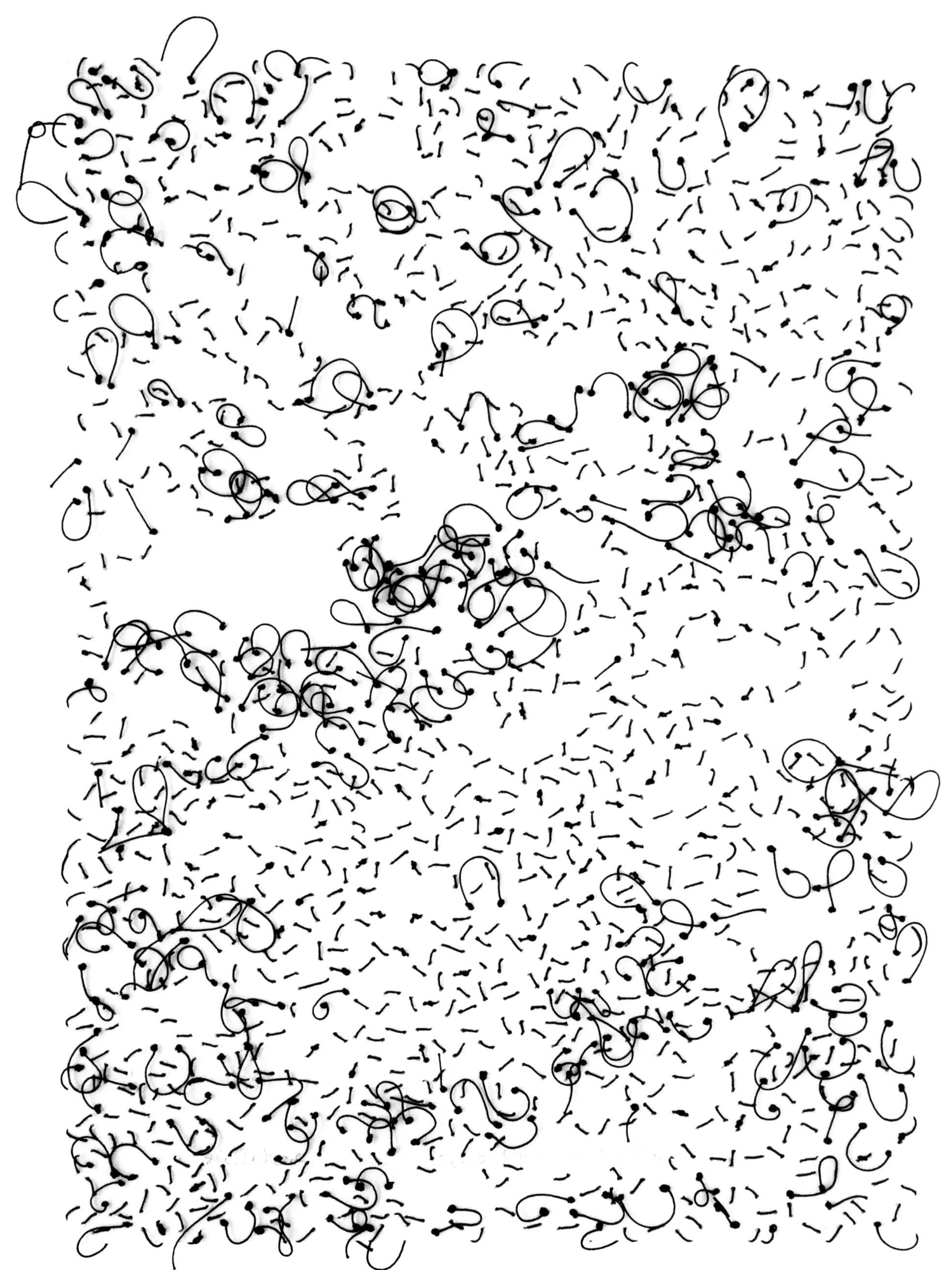

72. Anna Maria Maiolino
(Brazilian, born Italy 1942)
Untitled, from the series *Indícios*
(Indices). 2005
Thread on paper
13 3/4 x 10 1/16″ (35 x 25.5 cm)

73. Pierrette Bloch
(French, born 1928)
Five sculptures each titled *Fil de crin* (Horsehair line), each horsehair and nylon, ranging in date from 1988 to 1997
From 7′ 1 7/16″ (217 cm) to 10′ 8″ (325 cm) long. Installation view

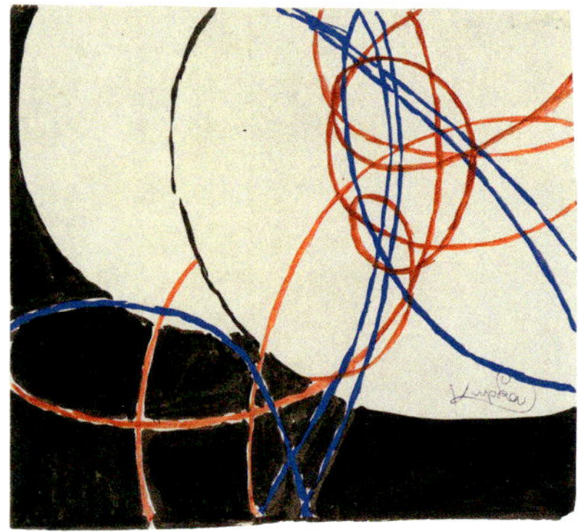

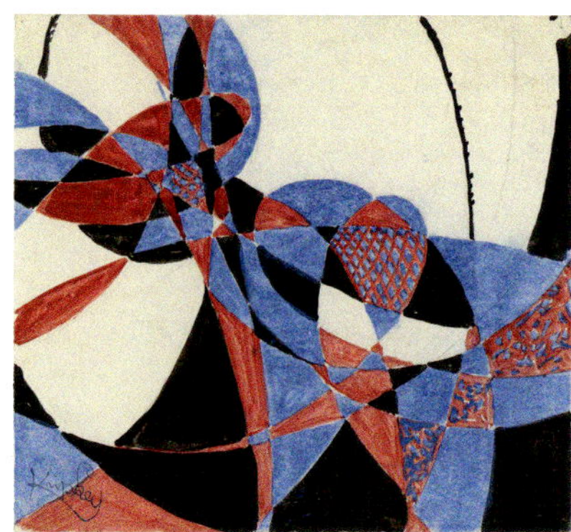

fastened to the wall at its terminal points by nails; and the shadow cast by the wire on the wall. Richard Shiff's description is precise:

> Although a pencil line is for all practical purposes unlimited in flexibility and a wire is itself entirely linear, Tuttle's wire cannot follow the lead of his pencil because, as a result of having been coiled, it retains a certain stiffness and springiness; this, coupled with its weight (however slight), causes it to project out from the wall, rather unpredictably. The shadow then follows the wire, not the pencil, but its own linear configuration is equally determined by the position of the source of light.[77]

Shadow was also a significant element in the horsehair drawings of Pierrette Bloch (plate 73), though her tracings relate more to writing. As she said of her drawing material, "I chose horsehair for its linearity, sharpness, and shadow."[78]

Tuttle has described the Wire Pieces as initiating a kind of liberation through drawing: to "make something that I'm the least part of, that I have the least to do with, that makes for a freer art."[79] He elaborates,

> At the beginning of the Wire Pieces, the question for me was "how can I keep myself out of my work?"... Drawing for the Wire Pieces is intended to empty every capacity I have. I have a configuration in mind and try to draw it "perfectly," by hand.... I can know exactly what the pencil will be, but I never know what the wire will do, that's conditioned by many things. And then, I have really no idea of what the shadow will do, none at all.[80]

In 2004, Tuttle would summarize this line of thought: "If I can free a humble material from itself, perhaps I can free myself from myself.... I think [my work] knows, is smarter than I am, better than I am." He accordingly asserts, "My work is an effort to overcome identity."[81]

Just as Hesse emphasized the ability of her "non-work" to find "its way beyond my preconceptions," Tuttle tried to "empty" his capacities by freeing his materials from themselves.[82] According to Shiff,

> With his wall drawing effort, often quite a physical performance, he renders his capabilities — intellectual and emotional as well as manual — "empty." He (his identity) vanishes. Because of this, whatever sensibility he possesses, as a mere living being, remains free, clear, without direction; in his drained state, he becomes receptive to whatever may show. "The passage from individuality based on control and direction to an individuality which is time" — that is, change, movement, immediacy — "is one of the greatest sagas of our times, and the Wire Pieces chronicle this."... Having emptied himself by drawing, Tuttle became free to let the wire and nails perform outside his human-culture intervention.[83]

Serving as a means of (de)liberation, in other words, Tuttle's line drawing "loosens him from himself and his formation rather than asserting an individually formed personality and the general character of a culture — both his own."[84] He recognizes that if one "listens" to the material, drawing can lead experience elsewhere: he "asks it to tell [him] what it knows and then [he] humbly listens — the payoff is greater than the humiliation."[85] While cultural identity is believed to be fixed and stable, then, drawing linked to materiality offered Hesse and Tuttle a way to abandon mastery, control, fixity, and permanence and to express an individual "self" released from the kind of social identity formed by cultural

74. František Kupka
(Czech, 1871–1957)
Amorpha. Fugue à deux couleurs
(Amorpha: Fugue in two colors). 1912
Gouache and ink on paper
8 1/4 x 8 7/8" (21 x 22.5 cm)

75. František Kupka
(Czech, 1871–1957)
Amorpha. Fugue à deux couleurs
(Amorpha: Fugue in two colors). 1912
Gouache, ink, and pencil on paper
8 1/2 x 9" (21.6 x 22.9 cm)

76. Karel Malich
(Czech, born 1924)
Odpoutaná krajina IV (a)
(Untitled landscape IV [a]). 1973–74
Galvanized iron wire, thread, and paint
6' 2 3/8" x 59" x 40 1/8"
(188.9 x 149.9 x 101.9 cm)

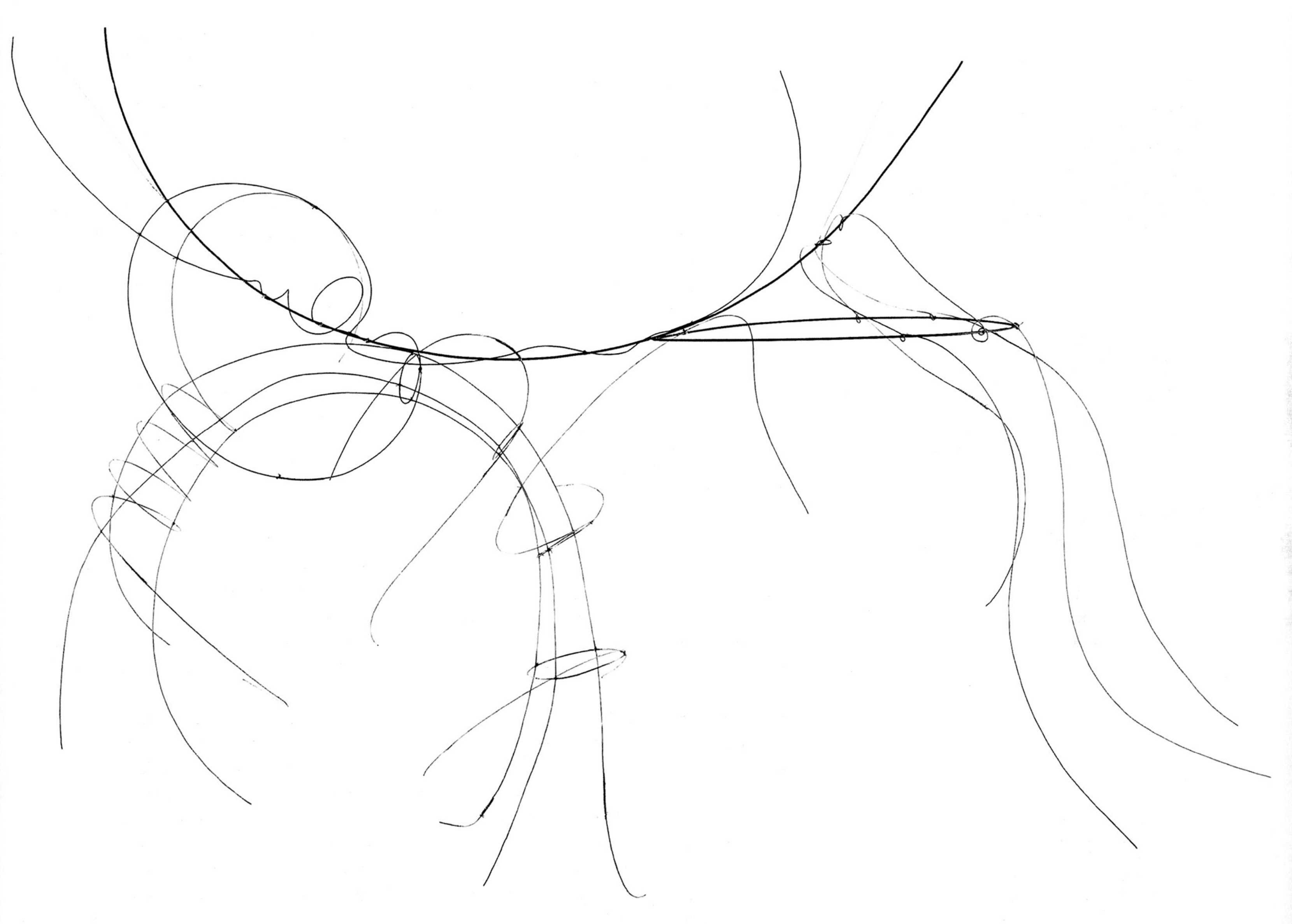

templates. It allowed them to counter the existing institutional culture, its norms, categorizations, and ideological clichés.

Karel Malich expressed a related attitude when he said, "I became everything, all the phenomena, all the signs that turned my attention to the same fate and I became nature," "breathing together with the cosmos."[86] Malich's works are conceived as events of pure energy in a differently imagined time-space. One hears echoes in his language of Frantisek Kupka, who believed his drawings could reflect the forces of the cosmos (plates 74, 75), and of the Russian Suprematists, who foresaw the liberation of a universal sensibility involving such energies. Malich has described his wire sculptures as "the expression of a new space and the investigation of it, which is yet to come."[87] Although he has never realized any of these sculptures on an architectural scale, that aim was part of his project: proposals at once cosmic and utilitarian, his sculptures of the 1960s were conceived as designs for cities in some revolutionary future, and he continued to think of his later tied-wire constructions as temporary models for large-scale projects.[88]

In works he began in the early 1970s, Malich suspended wires in space to function as the equivalent of an energy current (plate 76). These constructions paradoxically embody both kinetic *potential* — conveying a sense of the passage of time, of the mutable, ephemeral quality of their own duration — and kinetic *permanence*, in the form and substance of their aluminum, zinc, and stainless steel materials. In these dimensional drawings, then, contradictorily materializing and dematerializing forces seem to be at work. As Jirí Ševcík writes,

> Malich's linear depiction of energy (reminiscent of drawing) can be seen as one of the artist's obsessions — to draw the lines of the universe that seem to activate a universal sensibility in the spectator. The impact that they have is notably reminiscent of a description by Rudolf Steiner: "There are certain linear forms that we experience. However, we do not experience them as we would see them drawn in some space before us, but rather as if in the constant movement of the self we were to mimic each linear movement ourselves. We feel them the same way the person who drew them did and at the same time as the material with which they were drawn. And the drawing of each line, each change of place, is simultaneously an experience of the self. We learn to recognize that with each movement, the self is involved in the creative forces of the world. The laws of the universe are not something perceived from the outside, but rather a mesh, which we weave upon."[89]

Artists of the 1960s and '70s returned line to its essence, releasing it into space and effectively liberating the line of thought itself. Though characterized as pursuing the dematerialization of the art object, this generation, perhaps paradoxically, made process-based works that can be seen as materializing line. While "deskilling" — the downgrading of traditional artistic skills — had led to the disembodiment of gestural and linear mark-making, for example in the Minimalists' use of the grid, this disembodiment was simultaneously counteracted by an intensified materialization of linear structures. Embodied in unconventional materials — ready-made, discarded, taken from the daily environment — line now ranged widely in space and in the present. Favoring senses other than sight, artists renewed their commitment to materiality and tactility, while also challenging the anonymous, systematic, mechanical technology of what Benjamin Buchloh has called the "order of the diagrammatic."[90] The "depersonalization" of drawing, its withdrawal from figurative reference, found its counterpart in a reversal of parameters from private to public, from two- to three-dimensionality, and from mediated to unmediated presence. These oppositions would ultimately intersect in a newly acknowledged relational space of experience. The ability to respond to the other, a sense of responsibility and reciprocity, became paramount in the use of line to trace connective links within a space imagined as interstitial.

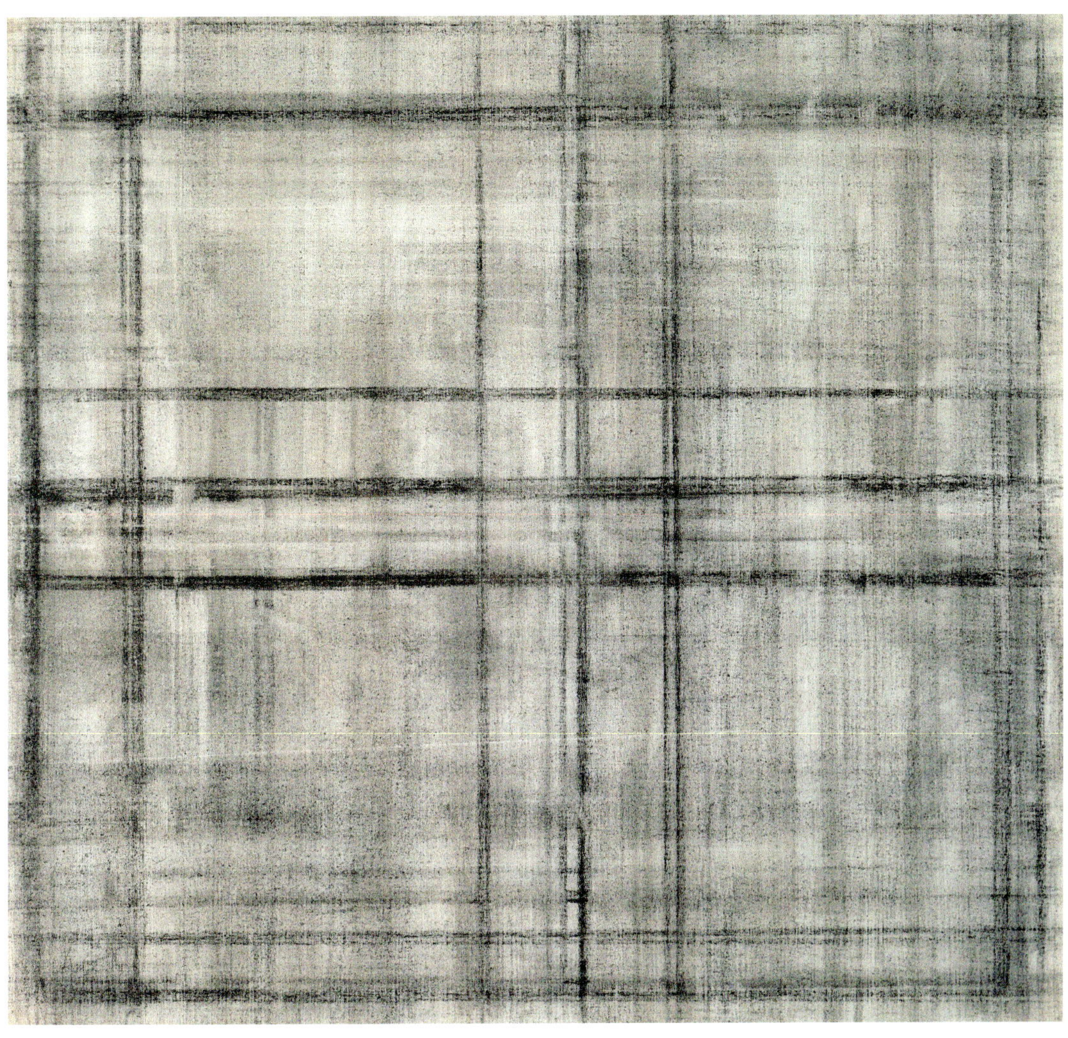

Lines over Lines: From Grid toward Web (1965–1995)

Early in the century, while some artists, through line, were seeking real space beyond the illusory plane of the page or canvas, Malevich and Mondrian were using the square and the grid to map this space as the physical surface of the drawing or painting itself in all its materiality — a kind of ultimate real, at once empirical and transcendental (plate 77). Using the grid to undo the traditional oppositions of figure and ground, motif and frame, they instead explored relations between horizontal and vertical, line and color, within its structure. For artists throughout the twentieth century, the grid, along with the monochrome, would become a paradigm of abstraction.

The grid had been used in earlier centuries as a perspectival lattice inscribed onto the depicted world as an organizing armature. As Krauss notes, however,

> Perspective studies are not really early instances of grids.... Unlike perspective, the grid does not map the space of a room or a landscape or a group of figures onto the surface of a painting. Indeed, if it maps anything, it maps the surface of the painting itself. It is a transfer in which nothing changes place. The physical qualities of the surface, we could say, are mapped onto the aesthetic dimensions of the same surface. And those two planes — the physical and the aesthetic — are demonstrated to be the same plane: coextensive, and, through the abscissas and ordinates of the grid, coordinate. Considered in this way, the bottom line of the grid is a naked and determined materialism.[91]

77. Piet Mondrian
(Dutch, 1872–1944)
Composition (Unfinished). 1938 or 1939
Charcoal on canvas
27 5/8 x 28 3/8″ (70 x 72 cm)

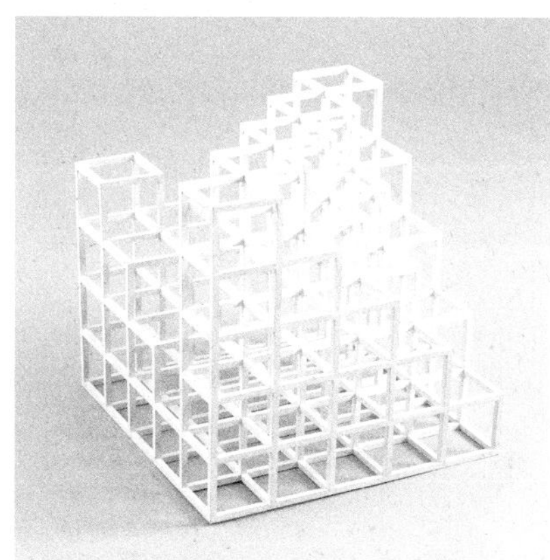

In their obsession with the real, artists such as Fabro, Hesse, Sol LeWitt, Martin, Ryman, and Michael Snow (plate 65) adapted the grid, in the 1960s and '70s, to convey the actual space of a plane or volume. By extrapolating line to shape a grid in space, some artists actually combined two ways of mapping the real: the materialization of the line, and the use of the grid as a physical presence in itself. Though referring to the Renaissance and the Baroque, Fabro's *Habitat "1962"* (1981), an environment with gilded wooden grid and brass rings, asks viewers to refocus on human qualities in the here and now, in a space divested of classical perspective but imbued with heightened attention. Informed by Fontana, Fabro also engages with Malevich and Mondrian, repeating the orthogonality of the square, rigid and abstract, only to deny it, and with it any sense of static, finite space. The space he develops is instead hyperbolic, constantly yet unpredictably mobile. *Davanti, dietro, destra, sinistra, cielo. Tautologia* (In front, behind, right, left, sky. Tautology, 1967–68; plate 79), a photographic enlargement of a gridded star chart, sets the infinite universe in front of the viewer and his or her own reality, emphasizing less the relativity of space than the fact that, as Fabro writes, "there is no such thing as absolute space, only space in relationship, personal space, insofar as it is related to a person. The movement of this person in space, even this space, the space of the sky, is more important than all the movement of the sky. After making the sky, I prefer to use a photograph of the sky with the person in front of it, which stands for the sky."[92]

For Krauss, "The grid's mythic power is that it makes us able to think we are dealing with materialism (or sometimes science, or logic) while at the same time it provides us with a release into belief (or illusion, or fiction)."[93] Is the grid connected to matter or to spirit? Does it mask or reveal? It is in this indecision, this ambivalence, that its peculiar potential resides. Another ambivalence lies in its ability to be understood as working both centrifugally and centripetally. In the centrifugal reading, "The given work of art is presented as a mere fragment, a tiny piece arbitrarily cropped from an infinitely larger fabric. Thus the grid operates from the work of art outward, compelling our acknowledgment of a world beyond the frame."[94] Here the gridded artwork is theoretically continuous with the world, and as such may be used to order aspects of reality, which is itself further abstracted through photography in Snow's *8 x 10* (1969), or through being treated as an architectural model as in LeWitt's modular lattice work *Cubic Construction* (1971; plate 78). Interestingly, the beyond-the-frame grid often entails a dematerialization of surface. The centripetal reading works, Krauss continues, "from the outer limits of the aesthetic object inward. The grid is, in relation to this reading, a re-presentation of everything that separates the work of art from the world, from ambient space, and from other objects. The grid is an introjection of the boundaries of the world into the interior of the work; it is a mapping of the space inside the frame onto itself."[95]

While the grid, as a ruled set of lines, is considered resistant to change, a number of women artists have questioned its rigid form, as we see in moving between two large floor structures, LeWitt's *Serial Project 1 (ABCD)* (1966) and the set for Trisha Brown's dance *Floor of the Forest* from 1970 (plates 133, 142) — as we move, that is, from an evacuation of meaning toward a connection of meanings. This kind of floor structure would be taken up thirty years later by Ellen Gallagher, in her *Preserve (Jungle Gym)* of 2001. In the 1990s, Gallagher began to make grid-based paintings influenced by those of Martin, whose paintings, read phenomenologically, reveal illusions of texture that change with the viewer's distance from the work. The paintings move from the materiality of canvas, gesso, and penciled or painted grids and bands to the point where, for Krauss, they "go atmospheric, or, rather they feel like mist. They seem to dissolve or dematerialize."[96] Inspired by Taoism and Buddhism, Martin seemed to understand the grid as part of something infinitely larger, for within the all-encompassing woven net is nothing less than the entire world and the universe. Although many of her works are untitled, when she does use titles they often refer to nature — *The Tree* (plate 80), *Cloud, Mountain, Milk River, Leaf, Wood, Stone*. Evoking the interpenetration, the mutual dependence, of disparate entities, her works concern notions of interreliance that are much at stake in current social and ecological debate.

78. Sol LeWitt
(American, 1928–2007)
Cubic Construction: Diagonal 4, Opposite Corners 1 and 4 Units. 1971
Painted wood
24 1/4 x 24 1/4 x 24 1/4″
(61.6 x 61.6 x 61.6 cm)

79. Luciano Fabro
(Italian, 1936–2007)
Davanti, dietro, destra, sinistra, cielo. Tautologia (In front, behind, right, left, sky. Tautology). 1967–68
Enamel on iron
11′ 7 3/8″ x 8′ 2 7/16″ (354 x 250 cm).
Installation view, with viewer

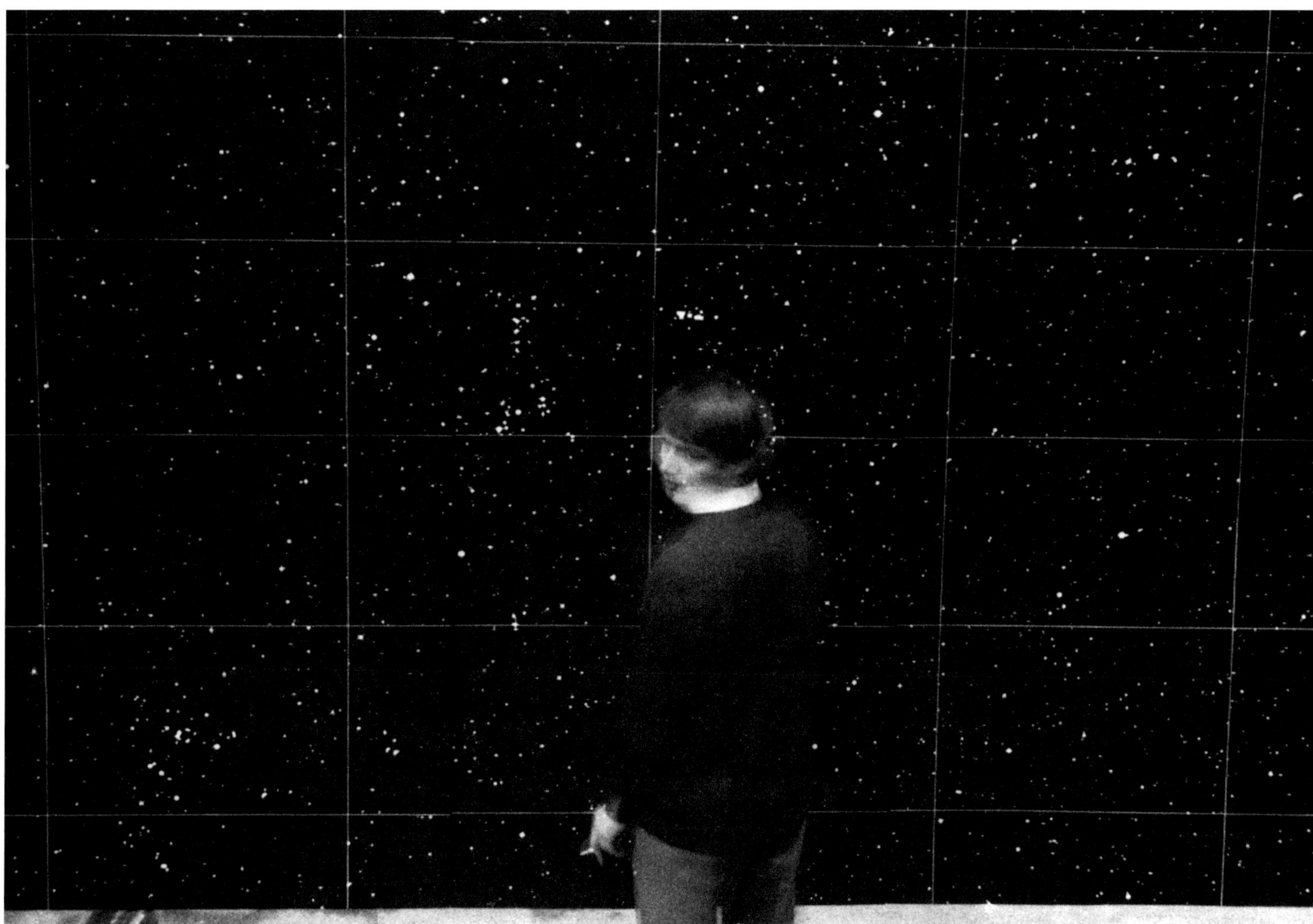

A drawing — each straight line ending with a different end.
Pick out drawings from the paper itself.
All the forces of nature are interlinked.
Pull with a direction.
Examine and reexamine each contour, each dot, where rhythm meets in space and continuous changes occur.
Develop form through intuition from point to point.
Each line, texture (form), are born of effort, history + pain.
Lines strengthening from Form to Form.

— Nasreen Mohamedi, 1968–71

Gallagher's drawn paintings similarly seem to go watery. Picking up on the structure of the painting's canvas-covered stretcher, she pastes patches of blue-lined paper onto the surface in such a way as to recover that grid's pattern — while also liquefying it, dissembling it, blurring it, dematerializing it with watercolor (plate 81). Among the papers' blue lines are small marks, repeated signs of race and gender — beady eyes, flipped wigs, unleashed tongues and lips. These details urge the viewer to move forward, pressing close to the surface to make them out, then to be taken aback to grasp the overall, dissolving pattern. If the grid offers a way to master space in an instrumental, clear, objective optical way, Gallagher's version, as subfloor or collage, is irregular, elongated, and distorted. Shifting and fracturing, much like the work of Vieira da Silva before her (plate 86), the painting leaves viewers without the unitary vantage point that would give them a sense of security and mastery.

In India in the 1960s and '70s, Nasreen Mohamedi used a nonrepresentational line to create what Martin called "a plane of attention and awareness" (plate 83).[97] In the West, her methodically linear work has often been aligned with Martin's, but the underpinning artistic content is different in its relation to the real: where Martin's hand-drawn, atemporal grids and horizontal lines, and her sensuous use of dilute primary colors, are avenues toward an ideal space, a space beyond the world, Mohamedi looks within the world, embracing the real and the social, both the peaceful environment of nature and its synthetic counterpart, the megalopolis. Rather than seeking refuge, or solitude, in a quiet place at a distance from the social world, Mohamedi often gravitated toward the harsh and tumultuous center. Yet her "lines among lines," in her phrase, share with Martin's a sense of fluency and of the fleeting — the nondual nature of all.[98]

80. Agnes Martin
(American, born Canada, 1912–2004)
The Tree. 1964
Oil and pencil on canvas
6 x 6´ (182.8 x 182.8 cm)

81. Ellen Gallagher
(American, born 1965)
They Could Still Serve. 2001
Pigment and synthetic polymer
on paper mounted on canvas
10 x 8´ (304.8 x 243.8 cm)

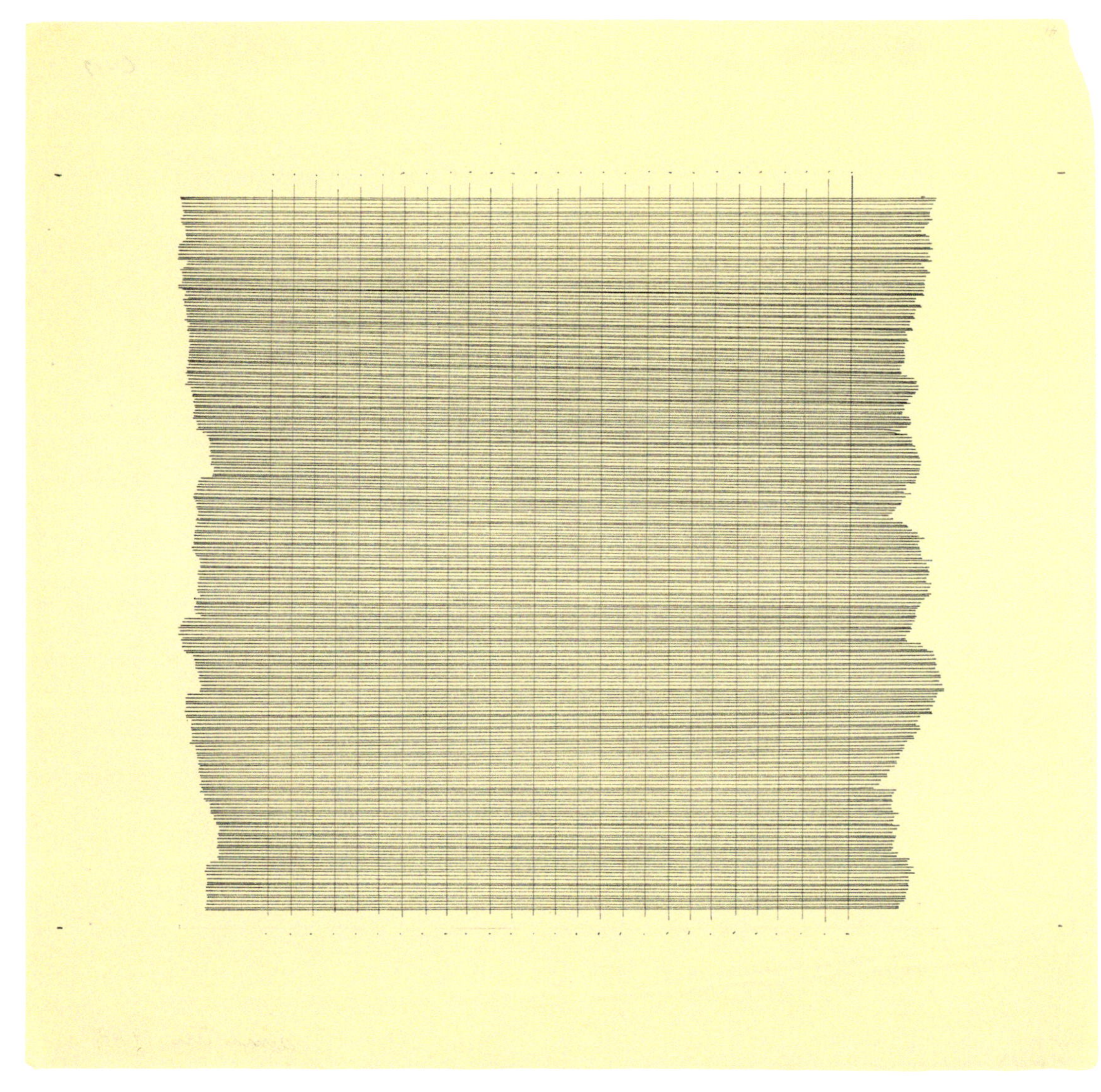

82. Agnes Martin
(American, born Canada, 1912–2004)
Untitled. 1960
Ink on paper
$11\,^{7}/_{8}$ x $12\,^{1}/_{8}$″ (30.2 x 30.6 cm)

83. Nasreen Mohamedi
(Indian, 1937–1990)
Untitled. c. 1970
Graphite and ink on paper
$18\,^{11}/_{16}$ x $18\,^{11}/_{16}$″ (47.5 x 47.5 cm)

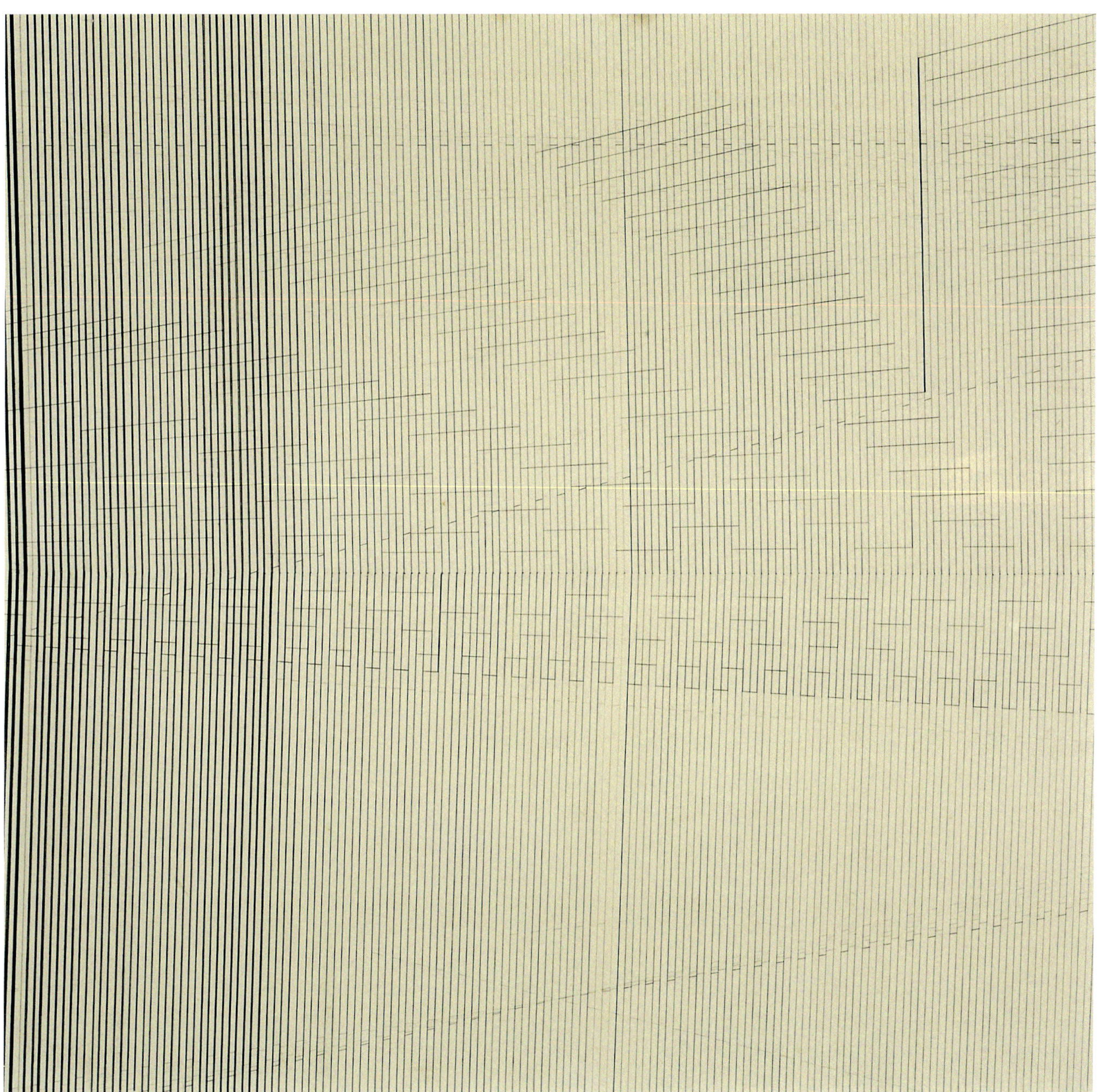

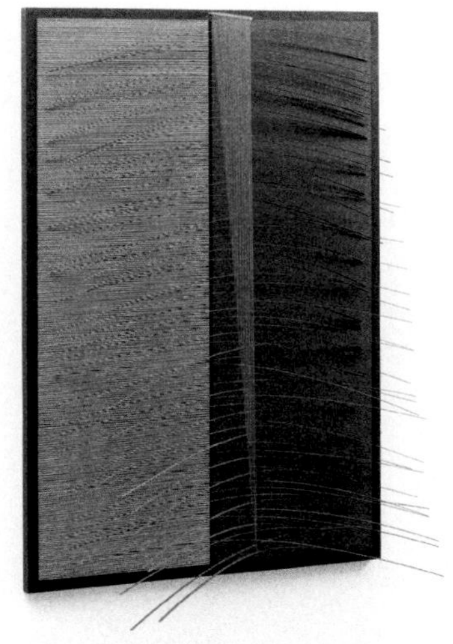

Gego used line to draw with or without paper, her practice culminating in the environmentally scaled *Reticulárea* of 1969 (plate 85). With their crisscrossing wire lines in space, the *Reticuláreas* increasingly liberated themselves from the structural system of parallel and vertical lines through the act of assembly itself: different types of joint, different modular configurations based on the triangle as well as the square, allowed for variables and changes in size, useful in adapting the work to the site as it progressed. The occurrence of nodal points — subtle twists of wire, modest pieces of plastic tubing — asked the viewer to experience the work not only sensorially but as a deliberate construction whose making could be rationally understood. "Delineating volume without confining it," Lourdes Blanco writes, Gego's drawings in space ultimately constituted a modeling of the human milieu.[99] As Roberto Guevara wrote of the large *Reticulárea*, "The drawing of lines has jumped to real space, the environment, to surround the spectator in a new and effective experience. It is as if we walked inside one of Gego's drawings [which] suddenly materialized making real space its own."[100] If the dispersed body of the *Reticulárea* seems woven in space, so the viewer seems woven into the *Reticulárea*.

As Gego's *Reticuláreas* appear to fulfill some of the objectives of the Futurists and the Constructivists, they also recall the Buddhist concept of Indra's Net, beautifully described in the ancient Avatamsaka Sutra:

> Far away in the heavenly abode of the great god Indra, there is a wonderful net which has been hung by some cunning artificer in such a manner that it stretches out infinitely in all directions. In accordance with the extravagant tastes of deities, the artificer has hung a single glittering jewel in each "eye" of the net, and since the net itself is infinite in dimension, the jewels are infinite in number. There hang the jewels, glittering like stars of the first magnitude, a wonderful sight to behold. If we now arbitrarily select one of these jewels for inspection and look closely at it, we will discover that in its polished surface there are reflected *all* the other jewels in the net, infinite in number. Not only that, but each of the jewels reflected in this one jewel is also reflecting all the other jewels, so that there is an infinite reflecting process occurring.[101]

Indra's net bears ready comparison with Gego's in its pronouncement of universal interconnectedness and interdependency: when any node in the net is touched, every other node is also affected, since not only does each jewel reflect all of the others but its very existence is dependent on that reflection in all others. It is a metaphor not only for a model of subjectivity-as-encounter but also for all that is interwoven. As the Vietnamese Zen teacher and poet Thich Nhat Hanh writes,

> There is a cloud floating in this sheet of paper. Without a cloud, there will be no rain; without rain, the trees cannot grow; and without trees, we cannot make paper. The cloud is essential for the paper to exist.... You cannot point out one thing that is not here — time, space, the earth, the rain, the mineral in the soil, the sunshine, the cloud, the river, the heat.... As thin as this sheet of paper is it contains everything in the universe in it.[102]

In this understanding, what appears to have independent, permanent existence is actually the consequence of many interacting forces; reality only takes form to the extent that it arises from an interdependent matrix of parts. Through this web of relation comes the realization that I am not merely grounded in this world, I *am* the world. In works like the *Reticuláreas*, the sense of the individual's separation from the world disappears. In the end, there is no-thing there to grasp.[103]

Marisa Merz's knitted networks of copper wire also upset conventions of unity and stability and reflect on the relation between the object and the experience of space and time, each of her wall

84. Jesús Rafael Soto
(Venezuelan, 1923–2005)
Oliva y negro (Olive and black). 1966
Flexible mobile of metal strips suspended in front of two plywood panels painted with synthetic polymer paint and mounted on composition board
61 1/2 x 42 1/4 x 12 1/2″
(156.1 x 107.1 x 31.7 cm)

85. Gego
(Gertrud Goldschmidt. Venezuelan, born Germany, 1912–1994)
Reticulárea (Ambientación) (Reticularea [Ambience]). 1969. Site-specific environment at Galería de Arte Nacional, Caracas
Iron and steel wires
Installation view, Galería de Arte Nacional, Caracas, 1997

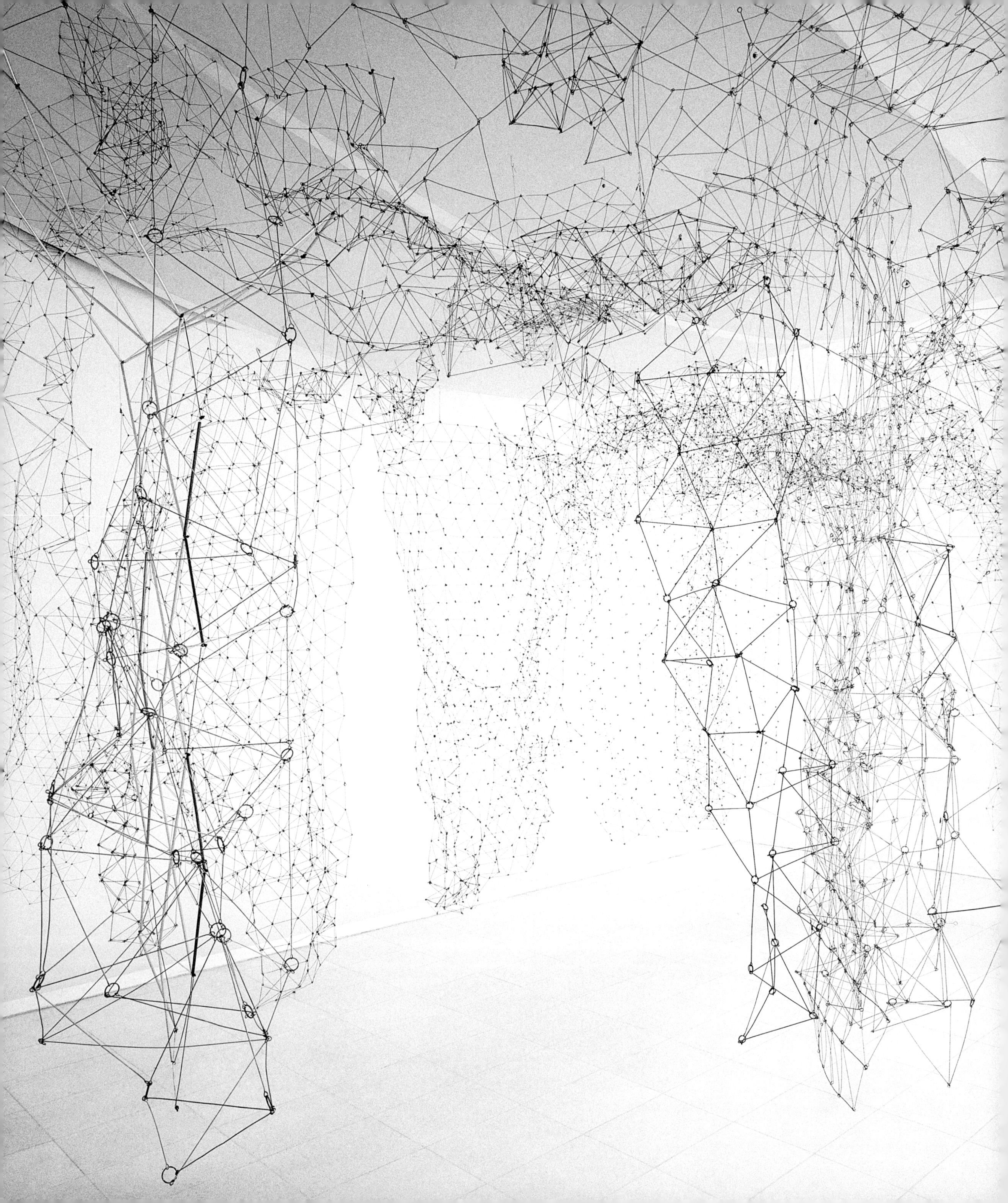

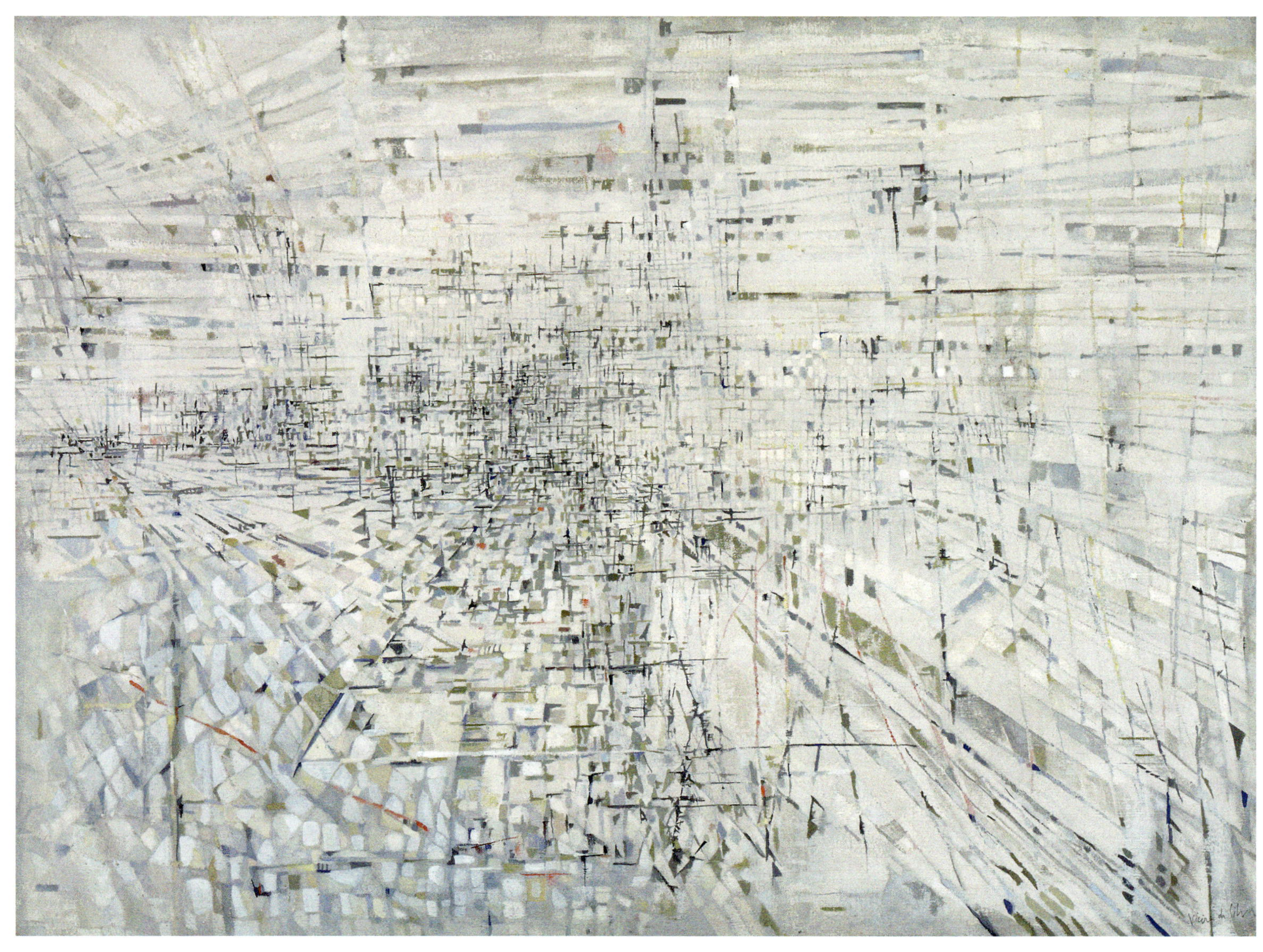

86. Maria Helena Vieira da Silva
(French, born Portugal, 1908–1992)
La Ville (The city). 1950–51
Oil on canvas
38 3/8 x 51″ (97.3 x 129.4 cm)

87. Marisa Merz
(Italian, born 1931)
Untitled (Stave). 1993
Copper wire, gold leaf on clay, and steel
Dimensions variable, here:
10′ 5 3/4″ x 22′ 8″
(322.5 x 690.8 cm), with clay element,
6 1/4 x 5 1/2 x 7 1/2″ (15.6 x 14 x 19 cm)

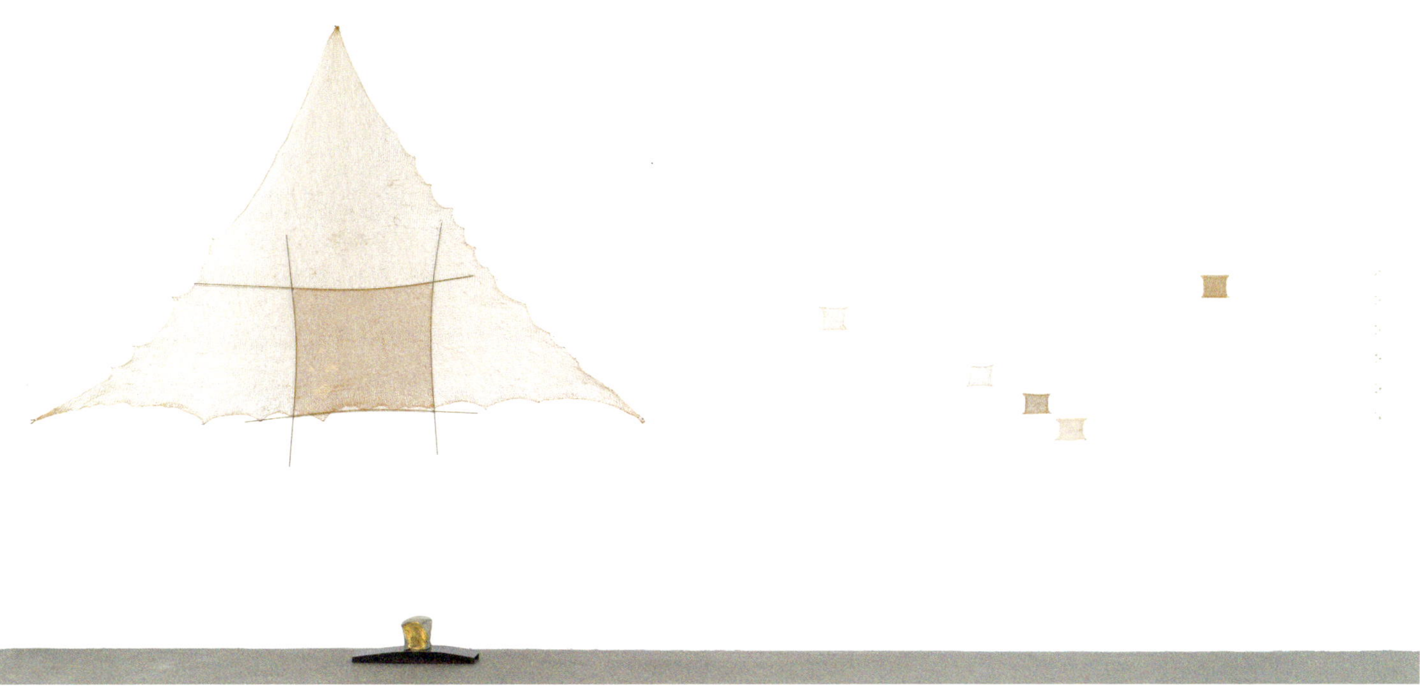

Our experience of the world is less of a long life developing through time than that of a network that connects points and intersects with its own skein.

—Michel Foucault, "*Des Espaces Autres*," 1984

I tend to think of things as ensembles of lines to unravel, but also to overlap. I don't like points; faire le point *[summing up] seems stupid to me. It is not that the line goes between points, but that the point lies at the crossing of several lines.*

—Gilles Deleuze, *Pourparlers*, 1990

pieces emerging through attention to the spatial realities of its site (plate 87). In a gesture oscillating between irony and assertion, the artist renders a *détournement* of knitting as an instrument of the oppression of women. Merz's knitted networks evolved in similar ways to Bloch's horsehair drawings from the same period.

In the work of all of these women it becomes clear that even where line breaks down in apparent chaos, there are forms of order—though not an authoritarian order. Instead there is an acceptance of the crossing of lines as points in an order yet to be understood, points and lines in a dimension of connection and relation: the matrixial. Extending their attention to others, the artists bring them inside what Ettinger calls "a matrixial web," an affirmative flow, refusing separation and alienation. Their work takes the individual not as a central point of reference but in relation, implying an openness to the other and the possibility of connection in mutually shared realities. All of these artists may work and live in very different contexts, but they have tried to escape the confining orthodoxies of modernity and of our time and they imagine art as reciprocity, as a compassionate witnessing of the lives of others and a form of empathically shared presence. Their work has much to offer the shaping of thought within the interdependencies of twenty-first-century society. In *On Line*, the idea of "a line as a point in movement" as it was conceived in the early twentieth century by Kandinsky, Klee, and others evolves in mid-century toward thinking of "a point as a crossing of lines," and beyond this, into the web of the present.[104]

The artists of the 1980s and '90s continued to shift and transform the grid, increasingly upsetting its regularity. In the choreographic work of Anne Teresa De Keersmaeker, the grid onto which lines of force are traced is always the basic structure to be both used and undermined (plates 88–93). Most of her dances, including *Drumming* (1998; plate 94) and *Rain* (2001), superimpose several grids and spirals. She has said,

> It all starts with one point, from which a line is drawn, from which a square is traced, and more squares are traced until you obtain a grid on which you posit several spirals—all drawn within the golden section proportions. The choreography anchors itself on the focal points of these elements in a very rigorous or loose way depending on the attitude toward the grid: both with reverence or with an urge for erasure,

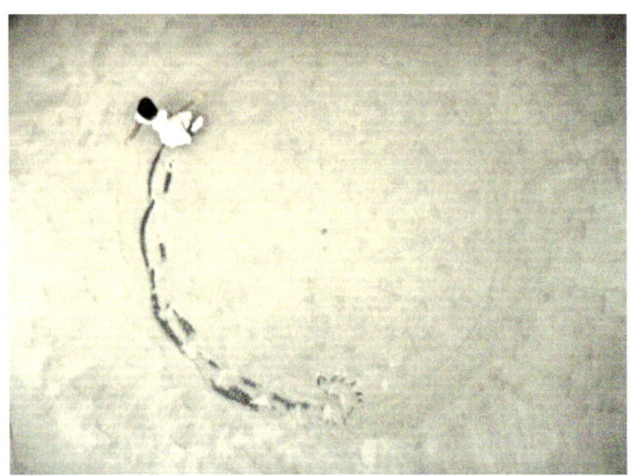

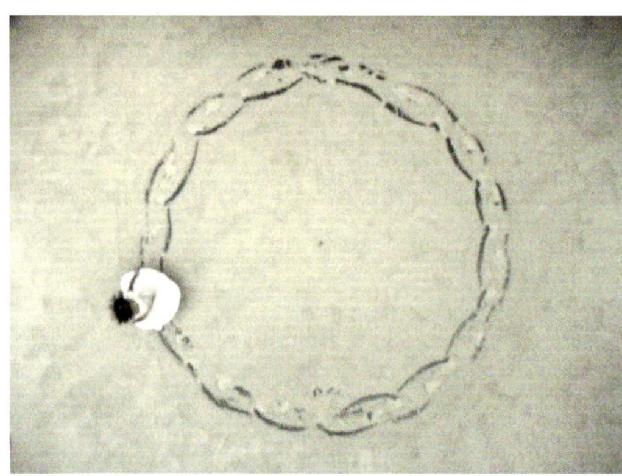

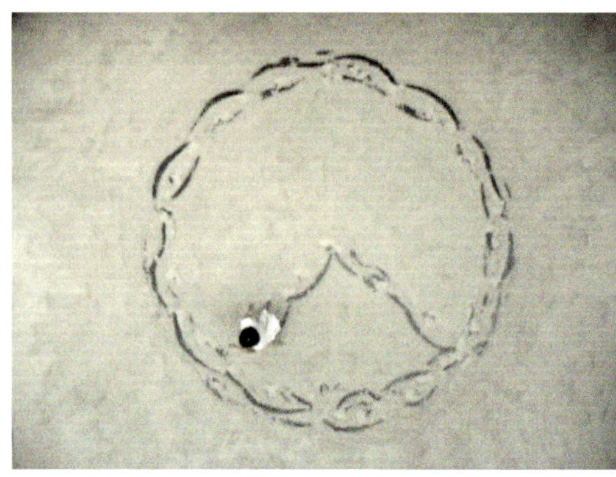

The bodies of the dancers are fixed and moving energetic points tracing lines. Between two dancers you have a line; between three dancers you have a surface, a territory that can enlarge. Dance is moving points in space, while remaining connected to the earth, because dancing is breaking out of the plane, emphasizing verticality against the laws of gravity. I like to dance with the grid, literally and smoothly... It appears as if structure creates freedom: there is no freedom, and freedom is only freedom in structure. I like the idea of the grid coming to the surface and then sinking back. Fuck the grid! And then suddenly in the most chaotic situation you can use it strategically to organize the space. The art is to let it go and use it to organize simultaneously.... Spirals are basic natural forms, present in many natural phenomena. While grids tend to be angular, giving a sensation of the binary, of inside or outside, of a kind of finity, a spiral has this sense of continuous unending. So I find the combination of spirals and grids very dynamic—though a spiral is anchored on a grid.

— Anne Teresa de Keersmaeker, conversation with the author, 2010

> in other words, forgetting it and returning to it. The grid is a kind of home which makes simultaneous, complex spatial organization possible with each dancer moving as a point in space.... As the grids are superimposed, they are continuously shifted around a fixed focal point. The opening and closing spirals dismantle the spatial grid. In this way, the grid can come to the surface in a very designed or articulated way, or it can simply be wiped out.[105]

In the work of a number of artists around the world, grids, remarkably, are slowly changing into webs, with their meaning of interaction and interdependency. Drawing itself, and its line, has become an interdependent medium. In a sense, this has allowed the grid to take on another political dimension, a relation to social reality. Of the grid in his *Malhas da Liberdade* (Meshes of freedom), also called *A Traves* (Through, 1983–89; plates 95, 201), Cildo Meireles has said,

> In the 1960s I was always doodling, like anyone who is bored. First, I'd draw a line, then another that intersects it, and so on, until I'd made a grid. In 1976 I decided to do the same with more rigid materials. Then it was no longer a matter of lines over lines; the second line was on an altogether different plane. This is the origin of *Meshes of Freedom*, of which the grid is just one manifestation. The work consists of a module and a law of formation: how the module intersects the previous one determines how it is then intersected by a third, and so on. The composition creates a grid, which spreads over a plane, but it also starts to grow in space, to create a volume. Theoretically, this structural principle could be used to make an endless variety of forms, from cubical, to spherical, to random structures. It has no formal limitations, but allows rather the passage from one part of the structure to another, at any point of the structure.[106]

If Meireles's grids, besides their political implications (a critique of the imprisonments and disappearances under the dictatorship in Brazil), deal with phenomenology (a long-term concern in Brazilian art), Mona Hatoum and Cornelia Parker's take up typical mannerisms of late formalism but load them with signs and symbols of political engagement, overwhelming the residual formal statement. While depending in part on formalism's presumed indifference to politics, its attempt to strip art of meanings to become pure form, Parker and Hatoum return formal tropes, now inevitably saturated with associative connotations, to referentiality. When line becomes a thread hammered out from a bullet, in Parker's work, or barbed wire in Hatoum's, it points to a world of barbarism and cruelty, barring its viewers from stepping aside into the disembodied, ideal formal realm that some might seek in art. Overwhelmed by the power of the sign, by the exorbitance of the meanings attaching to them, these works deploy a rhetoric of excess value. Hatoum's *Cube (9x9x9)* (2008; plate 96), a three-dimensional grid made of black steel shaped into barbed wire, asks a formalist structure to refer to the reality of war, violence, and imprisonment. Of her earlier cagelike structures relating to dislocation, migration, and exile, such as *Light Sentence* (1992),

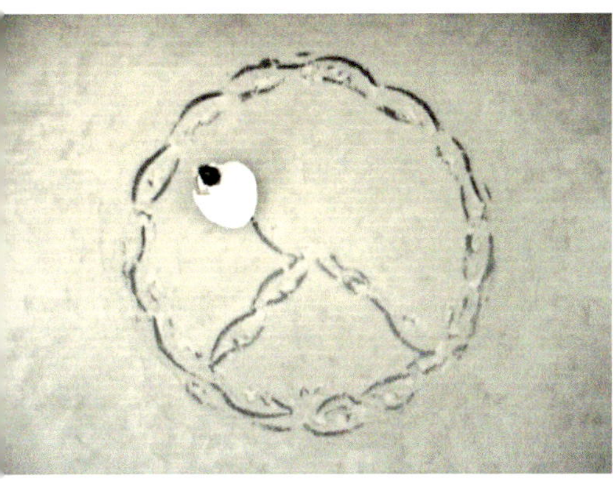

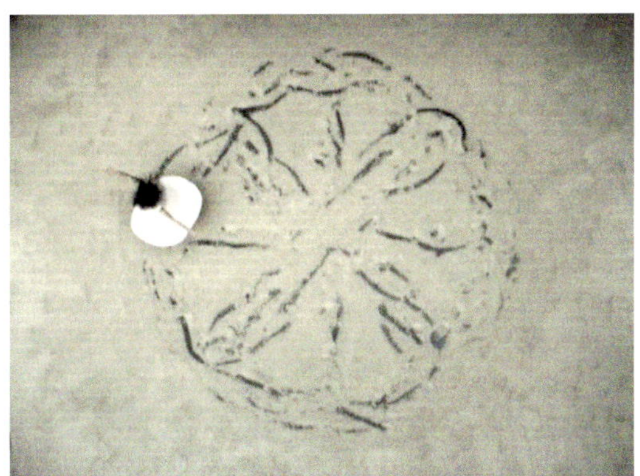

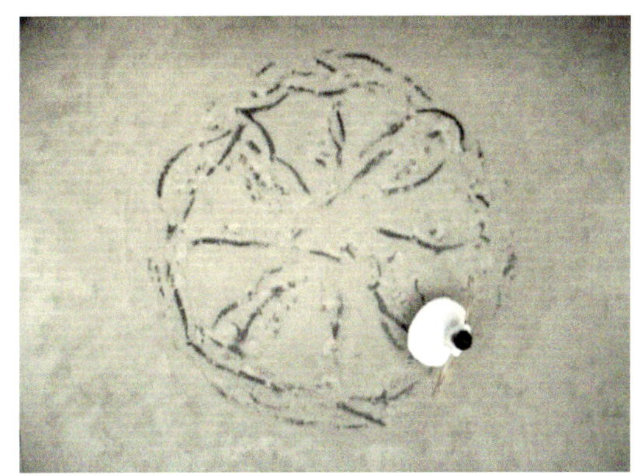

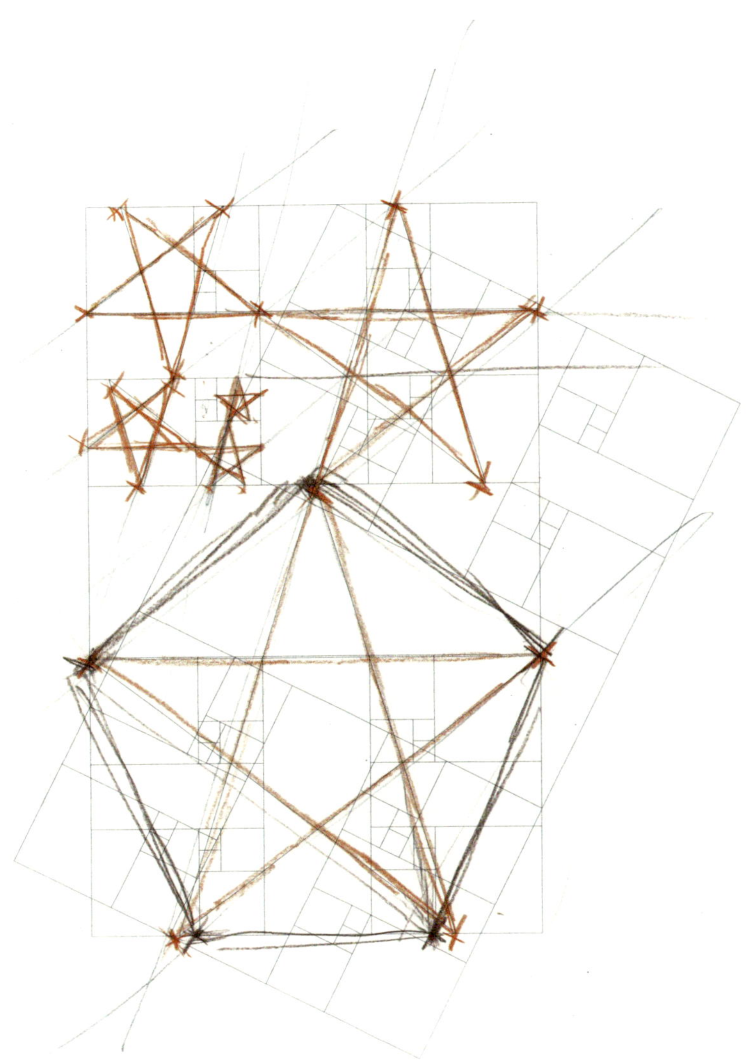

88–93. Anne Teresa De Keersmaeker (Belgian, born 1960) and **Thierry De Mey** (Belgian, born 1956).
Top Shot. 2002
Stills from film, color, sound, 16:04 min.
Choreography and performance: De Keersmaeker. Director: De Mey. Music: Steve Reich. Violin: George Alexander van Dam

94. Anne Teresa De Keersmaeker (Belgian, born 1960)
Drumming. Star and pentagon — basic patterns. 1998
Colored pencil on paper
16 1/2 x 11 7/16″ (42 x 29 cm)

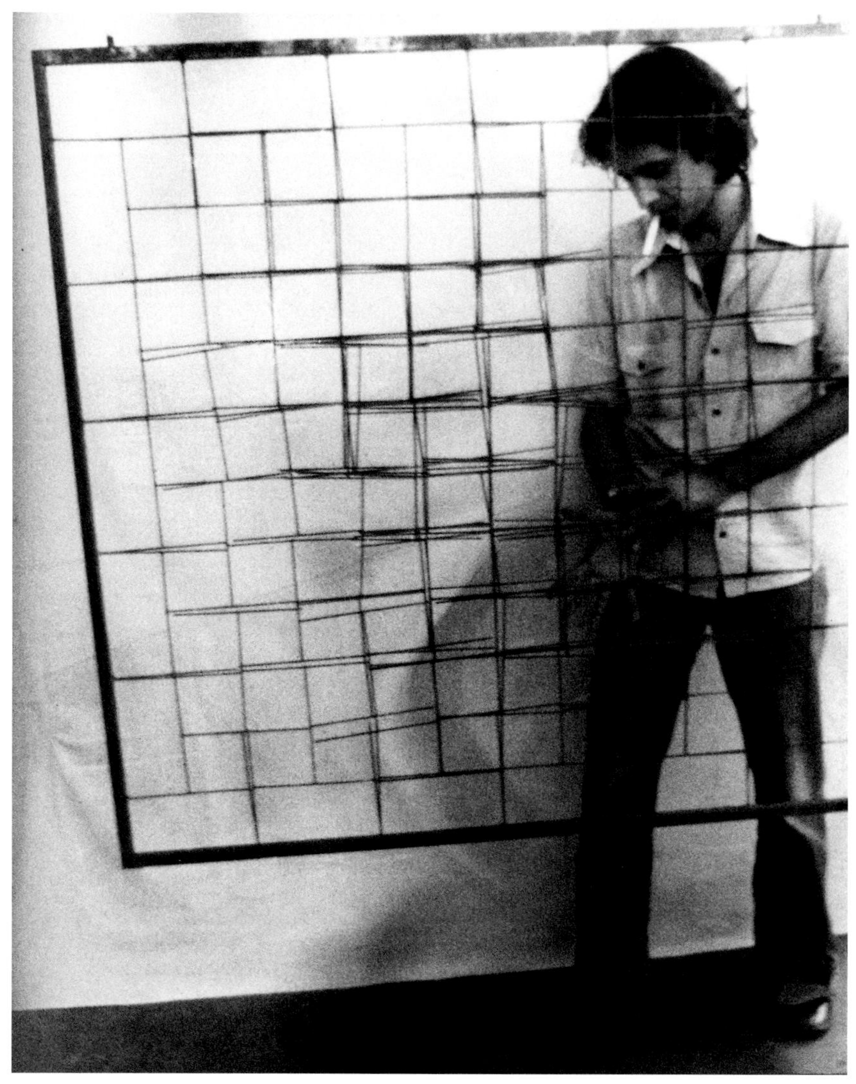

Quarters (1996), and *Current Disturbance* (1996), Hatoum has said, "I am speaking of encountering architectural and institutional structures in Western urban environments that are about the regimentation of individuals, fixing them in space and putting them under surveillance."[107] In the same vein, Parker's Bullet Drawings of 2008–9 (plate 97) are grids drawn in linear filaments made with the lead from bullets. In losing their possibility of function, the original objects are translated into an associative antinomy: the bullet, its direct velocity and power of rupture, versus the fine, fraying, unstable woven thread.

A risk in using line in this way is a loss of the meanings inherent either in the formal organization of a conceptually based artwork or in the actual experience of the real, with the result being a token of refined sentiment, removed from reality in the museum. In facing this challenge Gallagher simultaneously takes up and reverses the modes of a former generation of Minimalist and Conceptualist artists: evading the antinarrative aspect of the grid, her ruled fields of rectangular paper patches invite a marking, a writing, a telling of a story that was supposed to lack history, reference, or inscription. "In each canvas," Gallagher asserts, "the narrative comes from the legacy of marks."[108] Merging the nonreferential marks of the preceding generation of artists with socioculturally embedded signs and marks arising from her process of putting the story together, she embraces the risk of stepping beyond existing thresholds. As Judith Wilson points out, the color she uses is often meant "to evoke skin — i.e., the various skin colors associated with racial hybridity as a mode of transgression."[109] Under the applied color always lies

95. Cildo Meireles with his work
Malhas da Liberdade III (Meshes of freedom III). 1977
Iron, glass sheet
47 1/4 x 47 1/4" (120 x 120 cm)

96. Mona Hatoum
(British of Palestinian origin, born Beirut, Lebanon, 1952)
Cube (9 x 9 x 9). 2008
Black finished steel
71 x 71 1/2 x 71 1/2" (180.3 x 181.6 x 181.6 cm)

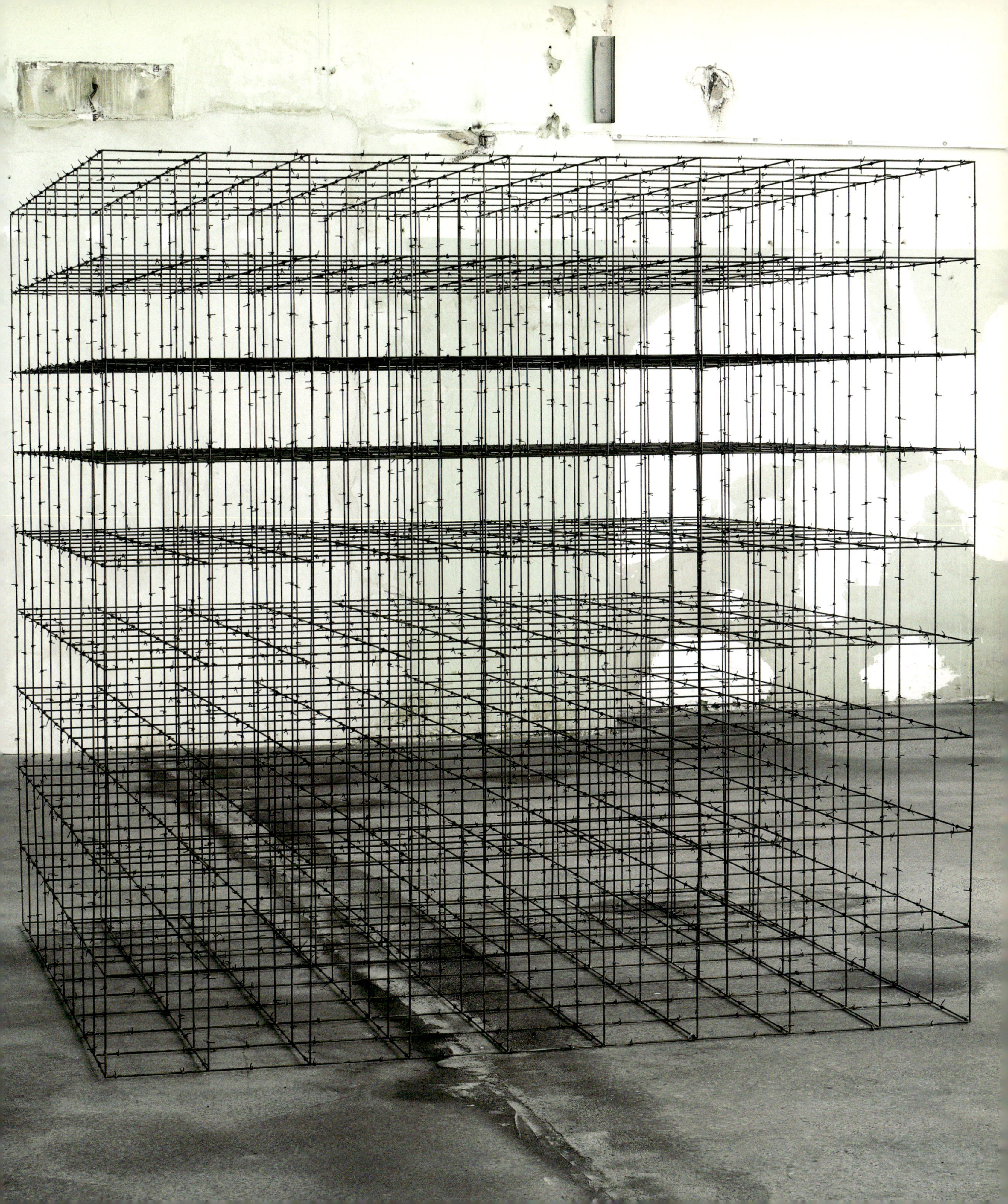

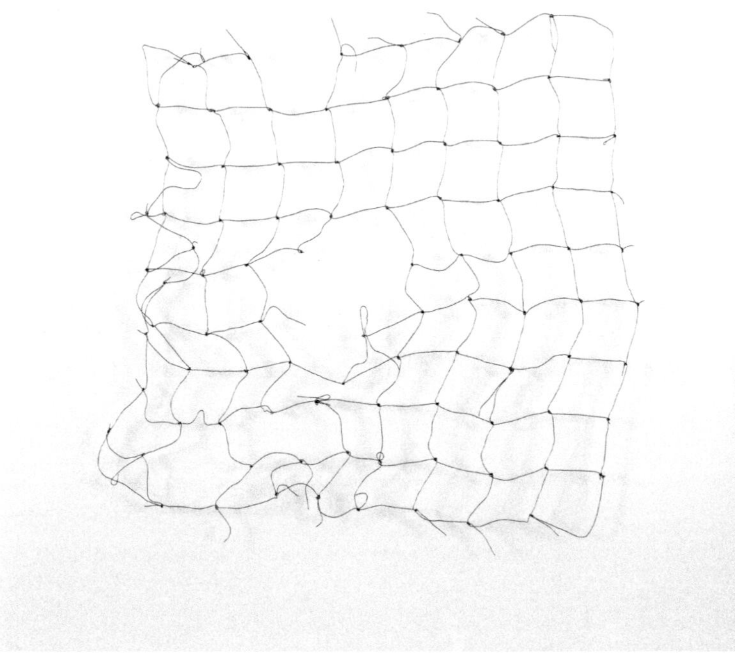

the blue-lined penmanship paper, figuring as the culturally regulatory grid of intelligibility in which a social space for and of the body is defined. In culture, a diffuse but active structuring of the social field results in a marking of the contours of the body as the surface upon which race and gender significations are inscribed, a marking that seeks to establish specific codes of cultural coherence. Gallagher's art extracts these signs of race that produce identity, and that, disembodied, are paradoxically at once free-floating and mapped in her grid structures.

Facing the same challenge, Hatoum and Parker defeat it, and overcome the separation between the museum and the world, through the insistence and brute force of the symbols they turn to use. Depending on traumatic effect, the works are understood not through the recognition gained from lived experience, at least for most viewers, but from knowledge of the events to which they allude, gathered from television and other news media and from the Internet, the artists reinvesting this material with symbolism. Hatoum's grid is conceived as a sign of authority and limitation, of a containment from which the feminine, as a void in the work, is always trying to escape. What besets the feminine, however, remains present, and in making visible the instruments of violence and confinement that circumscribe and threaten the feminine, Hatoum makes that absence powerfully underscore the theme of repression, and thus brings it within reach of perception. The strength of Parker's line, its power and force, lie in the *détournement* of the phallic bullet, its appropriation for another use. Stretched into a thin, fragile wire line, it becomes not a weapon but a link, an entanglement, a breaking down of the grid, a way for new patterns to emerge. From the bullet is drawn out the feminine, woven together with references to embroidery and lace. But the fine line also traces the becoming thin of late Conceptualism, the mannerisms and tropes of its increasingly enervated endgame.

To understand how the sophisticated intellectual structures of a very different world had come to this point, it is imperative to retrace the Conceptual line of the 1960s and '70s, when many artists gave critical examination to drawing. Dismantling the medium's institutional definition, and its reliance on paper as a support, they instead used the line in space as a tool with which to interrogate the status of the art object in relation to the body. We should return to the artists of this period, artists who redefined the parameters of drawing through a thorough investigation of line itself.

97. Cornelia Parker
(British, born 1956)
Bullet Drawing. 2009
Lead from a bullet drawn into wire
24 7/8 x 24 7/8" (63.2 x 63.2 cm)

98. Jacques de la Villeglé
(French, born 1926)
bleu O noir (blue O black). 1955
Torn-and-pasted paper on canvas
12 x 20 7/8" (30.5 x 53 cm)

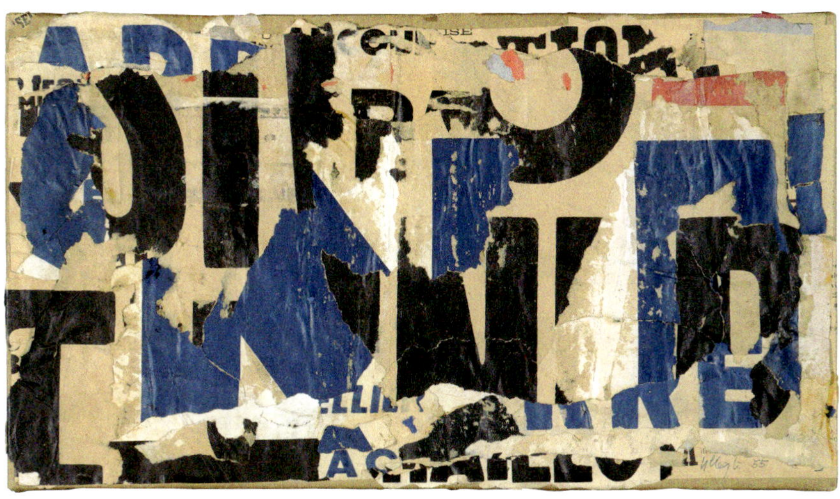

The Conceptual Line in the Plane / Plain (1960–2000)

In postwar Europe, a number of artists sought ways to expose the emerging forms of capitalism and mass consumerism centered on the image. Anticipating British and American Pop art, they analyzed this "society of the spectacle," as Guy Debord would call it. Their strategies would be theorized by the Situationist International (1957–72), a movement of the political neo-avant-garde that promoted a "critique of everyday life" through the construction of subversive "situations" arrived at through the techniques of the *dérive* and the *détournement*. The *dérive*, or "drift," evoked the idea of "psychogeography" and was defined as "a technique of transient passage through various ambiances." *Détournement* was "the integration of present or past artistic production into a superior construction of a milieu."[110] In aimless strolling through the city, the Situationists might find materials that could be "*détourned*," recombined or rearranged to give a different meaning from the one intended. Advancing the "class struggle" through the "battle of leisure," they sought to transform both art and politics.[111] Their key techniques of diverting images and texts into subversive viewings and readings were anticipated in France by the *décollagistes* such as Jacques de la Villeglé (plate 98) and Raymond Hains.

The collage of the future will be executed without scissors and razor or glue, etc., in short: without any of the utensils that were necessary until now. It will leave behind the work-table and the artist's cardboard surfaces and it will take its place on the walls of the big city, the unlimited field of poetic achievements.

— Léo Malet, 1936

As Buchloh writes,

> Rather than representing urban spaces iconically in the indirect trace of the found images of advertisement, newsprint, or photographic representation, the *décollagistes* shifted their operation from the space of the studio to that of immediate intervention. If in Schwitters's and the Dadaists' work the found materials from the street had ultimately only invaded the space of painting, in the work of the *décollage* artists the street is the site where the artistic intervention actually takes place.... rather than merely engaging in the elaboration of a new aesthetic of anticontemplative tactility—as Walter Benjamin had discerned it in the work of the Dadaists—tactility in *décollage* achieved the level of an actual collaborative act.... Rather than constructing a new pictorial universe from the affluence of industrial detritus and the languages and signs of consumer culture, it limits its choices to the images and messages of urban advertisement, the *affiches* found on billboards or dispersed on the walls lining city streets.[112]

Often large-scale friezes of scattered layers of torn and shredded paper, found on billboards in peeling accretions of fly-posters, ads, and graffiti, the *décollages* were created in the space of the real and in the present time of the life of the street. They were in effect collaborations with the vandals who had scratched and scarred the brazen propaganda sheets of corporate marketing, subjecting them to anonymous, lacerating defacements and mockingly reassembling them. "The *décollagistes* redefined notions of the collective unconscious," Buchloh continues, "expressly resuscitating these, not within

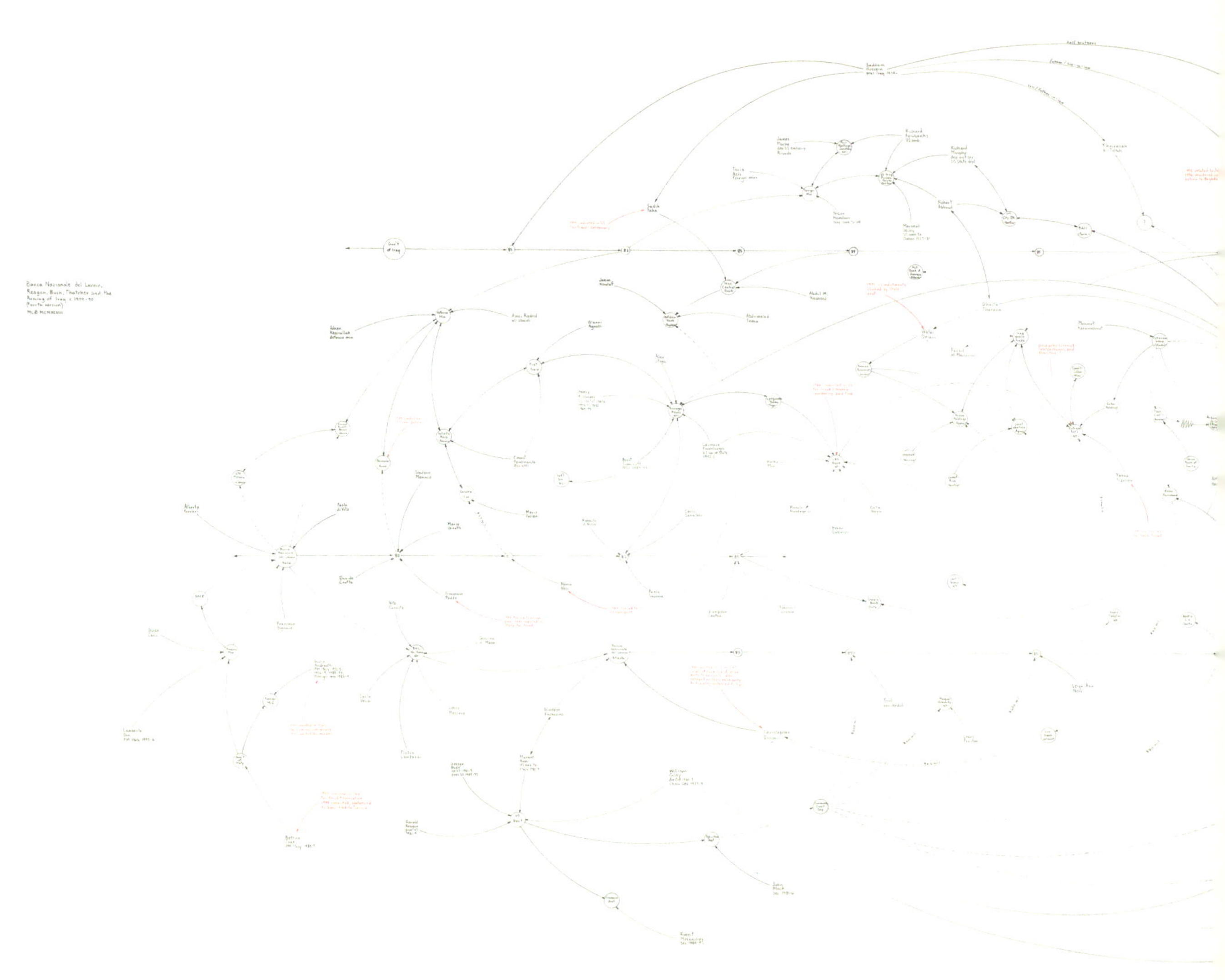

99. Mark Lombardi
(American, 1951–2000)
Banco Nazionale del Lavoro, Reagan, Bush, Thatcher, and the Arming of Iraq, c. 1979–90 (4th version). 1998
Colored pencil and pencil on paper
50″ x 10′ (127 x 304.8 cm)

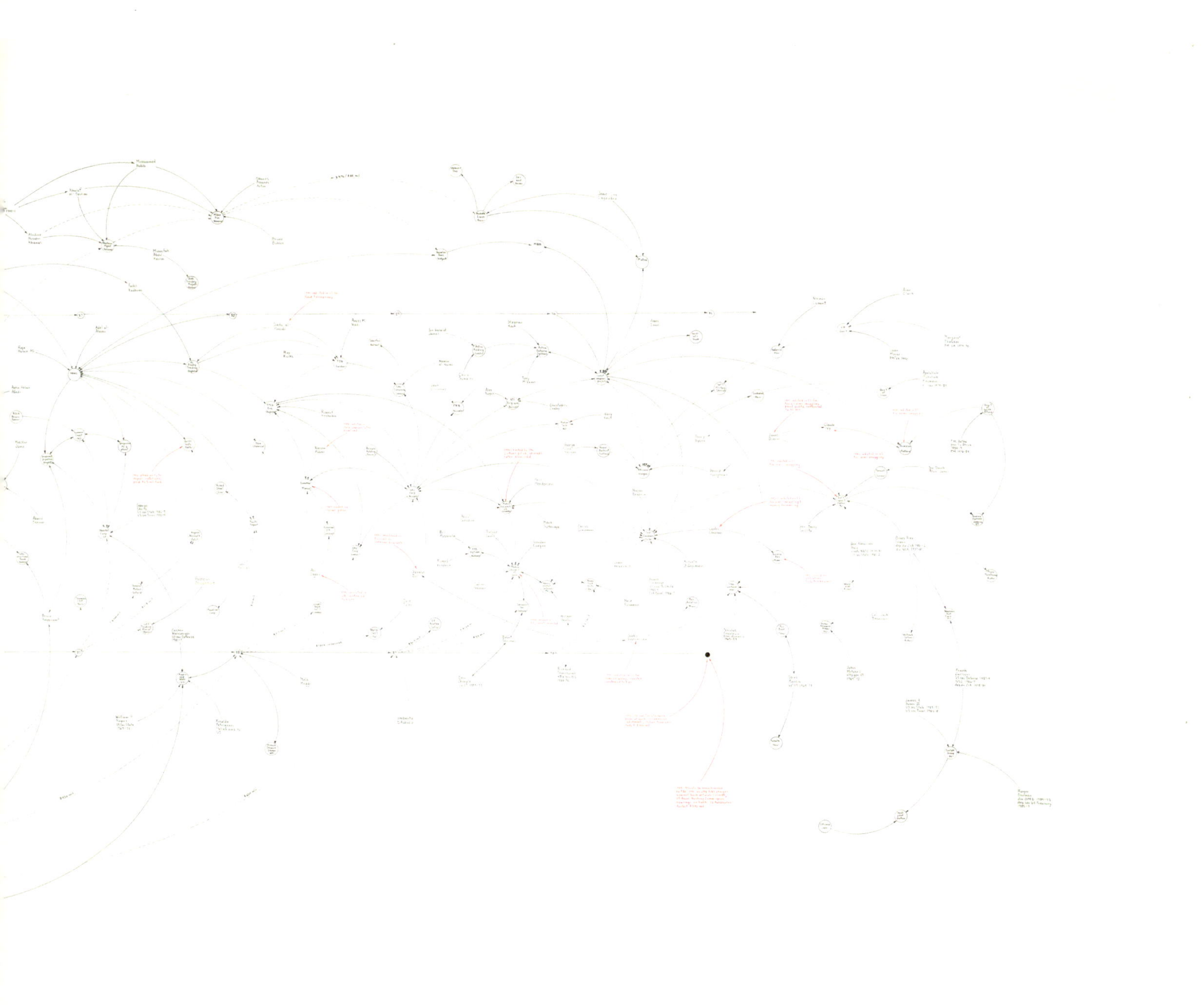

Because of the way in which a huge amount of data is presented, it's ultimately impenetrable to all but the most knowledgeable. The drawings represent only the bare bones of an intricate narrative, indicating "some type of influence or control" but not what type of influence or control.... I originally intended to use the sketches solely as a guide to my writing and research but soon decided that this method of combining text and image in a single field (called a drawing, diagram or flow chart, whichever you prefer)... tended to support the same goals as the writing — to convey socially — and politically use information; and confirmed 100% to my aesthetic inclinations — minimal, understated and somewhat iconoclastic.

— Mark Lombardi, "Proposal for Over the Line," 2000

mythical or archetypal models, but as inextricably and exclusively constituted within the urban space of commodity consumption and spectacle culture."[113] If Pollock and others extended Surrealism's automatist line into action painting, the *décollagistes* countered with an extension of the line from the studio into the real of the city street and of the newsreel. In their attention to subjectivity, these artists considered not only the line of the torn posters, simultaneously handmade and readymade, but also the drifting line of the flaneur, walking the city streets to experience chance encounters.

The relation of the *décollagistes* to this line in the real was very different from either Schwitters's or Rodchenko's, who, Buchloh writes,

> imagined the necessity of designing consumer products and product propaganda on avantgarde terms.... By contrast, the rebellious subject enacting postwar *décollage* is not only an anonymous vandal of product propaganda, but also an artistic agent whose aspirations to intervene in public space have diminished drastically. Neither the anonymous vandal nor the artist...can associate his or her activities with the utopian hopes of the prewar artist-designers, who were aiming at a successful collaboration between avant-garde artists and product propaganda in order to achieve a democratic distribution of the amenities of consumption. This mounting pessimism on the part of the most radical of the postwar artists recognizes for the first time the extreme reduction of public experience and self-determination to which advertising culture would subject its audiences. The pessimistic radicals would also understand how the deprivation of public social space would affect the definition of avantgarde practices themselves.[114]

There is an inherent melancholy to this account as there is to this work, a sense of loss, a separation from the possibilities of history as a progressive dialectic. This changed perception was in itself to become a limit on the possibilities of the engaged artist.

The line tracings of Stanley Brouwn echo the strategy of the drift or *dérive*. For *This Way Brouwn* (1960–64), the artist would approach passersby on city streets and ask them to sketch for him on a piece of paper the route to some destination he named. He would then appropriate their drawing by adding his stamp: "This Way Brouwn." Fascinated with location, direction, distance, and dimension, Brouwn has made many works dealing with his own meanderings as well as with short walks he proposed to others. As recently as 2005, drawing white lines on the floor of the Van Abbemuseum in Eindhoven, the artist added a sign inviting the visitor to "walk 4 m in the direction of Havana, distance: 7396584.7166m, measured from the very spot where you are standing in the museum." Holding meticulous recordings — the artist often kept a counter and measuring stick close at hand — Brouwn's idiosyncratic archive, with its filing system filled with index cards and its precise records of steps taken in various cities, is very much like the archive Mark Lombardi was to compile thirty years later, in the obsessiveness of its attentions, its order, but also in its lacunae, its partiality, and finally in its recognition of an impossibility, that of a utopia. Both artists' acceptance of omissions and absences implicitly acknowledges the limits of human endeavor — for Brouwn, the difference between a four-meter walk and the distance to Havana, for Lombardi, the knowledge that beyond the networks of influence and connection that he can trace lie still others, constantly mutating, unchartable.

Between Brouwn's collations of index cards and those from which Lombardi derived his diagram-like drawings, between a '60s and a '90s practice, line evolved from marking an artist's physical wandering — an early embodiment of Conceptual art's "aesthetic of administration," in Buchloh's phrase — to the mapping of late-twentieth-century corruption that Lombardi discovered by "connecting the dots" of seemingly disparate points of information available in the public domain (plate 99). "Implicit in Lombardi's drawings," Robert Carleton Hobbs writes, "is the concept of extension, so that ideas are literally drawn

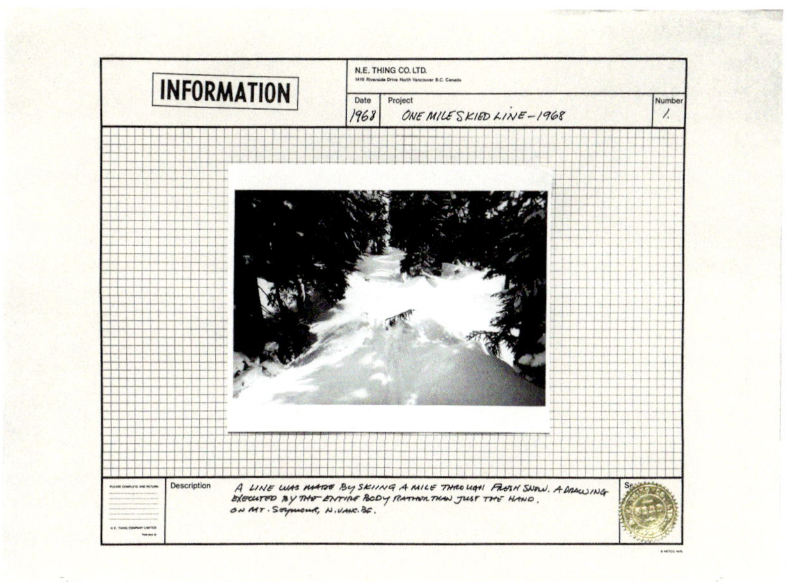

100. N.E. Thing Co. Ltd.
(Iain Baxter&, Canadian, born England 1936, and Ingrid Baxter, Canadian, born the United States 1938)
One Mile Skied Line—1968. 1968
Gelatin silver print collaged on paper with seal and felt-pen handwriting
18 x 24˝ (45.7 x 61 cm)

out in space by the artist, who recommends them as one of a number of possible ways to configure a given topic." A kind of intrigue here replaces the thrill of dry measurement. "Instead of enumerating tightly woven conspiracies," Hobbs continues,

> Lombardi opted for a structuralist paradigm: dramatizing information in terms of sets of imbricated networks so that individual players would be defined by the overall governing structures in which their names appear.... [The drawings] delineate the free flow of money characteristic of a postimperial world when multinational or consumer capitalism supplanted the monopoly stage, which in turn replaced an initial market form of capitalism. To convey this, Lombardi created subtle traceries of information pertaining to global financial deals and offshore banking that often resemble spider webs or portions of them.[115]

Conceptual art's line can be understood as congruent with "the notion of line [as] intellectual, a prime conceptualization, which in itself describes nothing," that Rose attributes to Leonardo.[116] This perception of line as describing nothing—nothing, that is, except itself—in fact remained crucial to the Conceptual line, which can be seen as following two principal tendencies in its pursuit of the real.

In the first, line left the plane of the page as a fully physical element—an existent within the world—to find a place on something that shared this quality of external space. Line was taken for a walk into the "real" world—onto the floor, the walls of buildings, into the plains and mountains, close to the earth, high in the sky.[117] Related to the dematerialization of the art object, this development can also, however, be seen as a loss of the imaginary space of the page.

In the 1960s and '70s, a number of artists in the Americas devised outdoor works with line, as if furthering the meanings of drawing as simple traction, the movement of a tracing instrument across paper transferring into the movement of one's body over the land: drawing as the marking of a landscape, an unlimited plane or plain. But every drawing is also a landscape of its own, an unframed, open space—a form of land art in response to the surrounding world. This approach is embodied in the linear tracings of Emily Kam Kngwarray, a "Utopia artist" from the Australian Northern Territory, who charted the desert as dreaming place (plates 198, 200, 225).[118] It was also literalized in land art, which was sometimes inspired by native traditions.

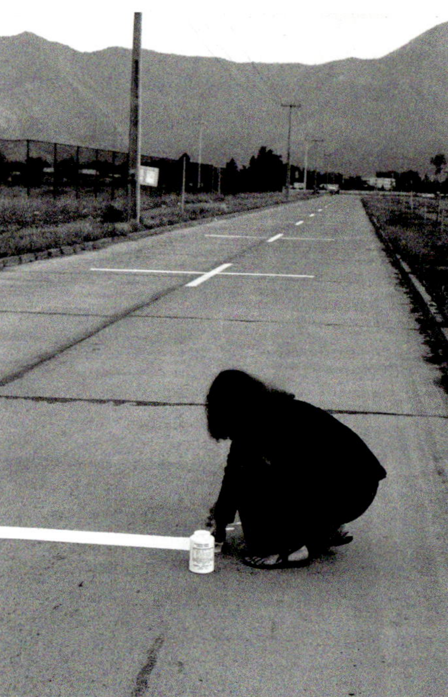

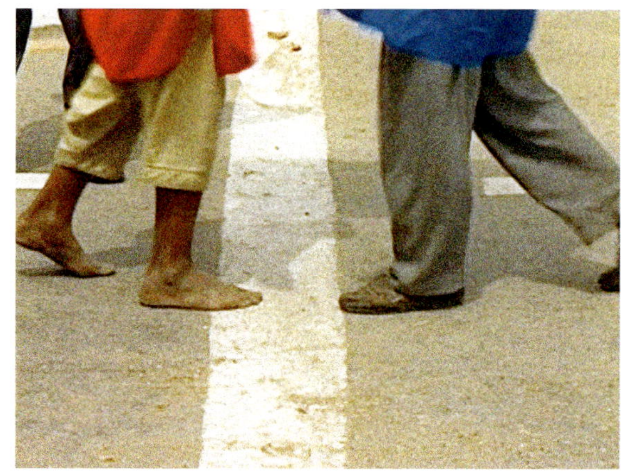

This stream of thought and action has informed the work of a wide range of artists, such as, in 1968 alone, Walter de Maria, whose *Mile-Long Drawing* was a pair of parallel chalk lines, twelve feet apart, drawn in the Mohave Desert; Dennis Oppenheim, whose *Time Line* was a three-mile-long drawing in the snow along the frozen St. John River, near Fort Kent, Maine; and Iain Baxter& and the collective N. E. Thing Co. Ltd., who also made lines in the snow, this time on Canada's west coast (plate 100).[119] In 1970, Michael Heizer laid out *Circular Surface Planar Displacement Drawing* (plates 104, 194, 195) as a series of circles, the largest one 400 feet in diameter, on a dry lake bed in Nevada, his medium being used tires that he dropped as he walked the perimeter of each circle holding a taut string fixed to its center, a human compass. Once the rings were in place, two motorcyclists raced around them, tracing the drawing's lines with their tires. The work both recalled the large-scale drawings made on the land in ancient times—along the lower Colorado River, for example, and in the Ica Valley in Peru—and looked forward to the phenomenon of crop circles.[120] Michelle Stuart would explicitly cite the Ica drawings in her *Nazca Lines Star Chart. Nazca Lines Southern Hemisphere Constellation Chart Correlation* of 1981–82, a drawing made by rubbing earth from Nazca onto paper. For *Niagara Gorge Path Relocated* (1975; plate 132) Stuart unrolled a 460-foot-long scroll of paper down the steep bank of the Niagara River, on the U.S./Canadian border.

Meanwhile, in South America, Lotty Rosenfeld and others in the Colectivo Acciones de Arte (CADA), an art collective formed after the military coup in Chile in 1973, made various public interventions and actions both as protests and as proposals for sociopolitical change. For one of Rosenfeld's projects with CADA, they wrote the word "no" next to a white traffic-line on the road, then gave the line a crossbar, so that it read "no +"—or "*no mas*" (no more). The project was documented as *Una milla de cruces sobre el pavimento* (A mile of crosses on the pavement; plate 101). The sign, which directly challenged the dictatorship of Augusto Pinochet, became public property, appearing everywhere on streets and walls and winning a place in popular discourse. Living in exile during the 1970s, Vicuña too participated in outdoor projects as political interventions against totalitarian regimes in her native Chile and throughout South America. Between 1966 and 2009, when she was able to return from exile, she repeatedly made the work *Kon Kon Pi*, named after the ancient site of Con Con on the Chilean coast, drawing it in sand and sea, sometimes with a stick, sometimes in lines of red wool evoking menstrual blood (plate 226). The performance found sequels in recent videos denouncing ecological disasters along Chile's Pacific coast, the results of their exploitation by international fishing corporations and oil refineries.

101. Lotty Rosenfeld
(Chilean, born 1943)
Una milla de cruces sobre el pavimento
(A mile of crosses on the pavement). 1979
Art action, Santiago, Chile

102. Amar Kanwar
(Indian, born 1964)
A Season Outside. 1997
Still from video, color, sound, 30 min.

103. Harun Farocki
(German, born Czechoslovakia [present-day Czech Republic] 1944)
Wie Man Sieht (As you see). 1986
Still from 16mm film, black and white and color, sound, 72 min.

104. Michael Heizer
(American, born 1944)
Circular Surface Planar Displacement Drawing (deteriorated; detail). 1970
Tire markings on playa surface
900 x 500´ area, Jean Dry Lake, Nevada

105. Steven Yazzie
(American, born 1970)
Draw Me a Picture. 2006
Performance view, Monument Valley, Arizona/Utah

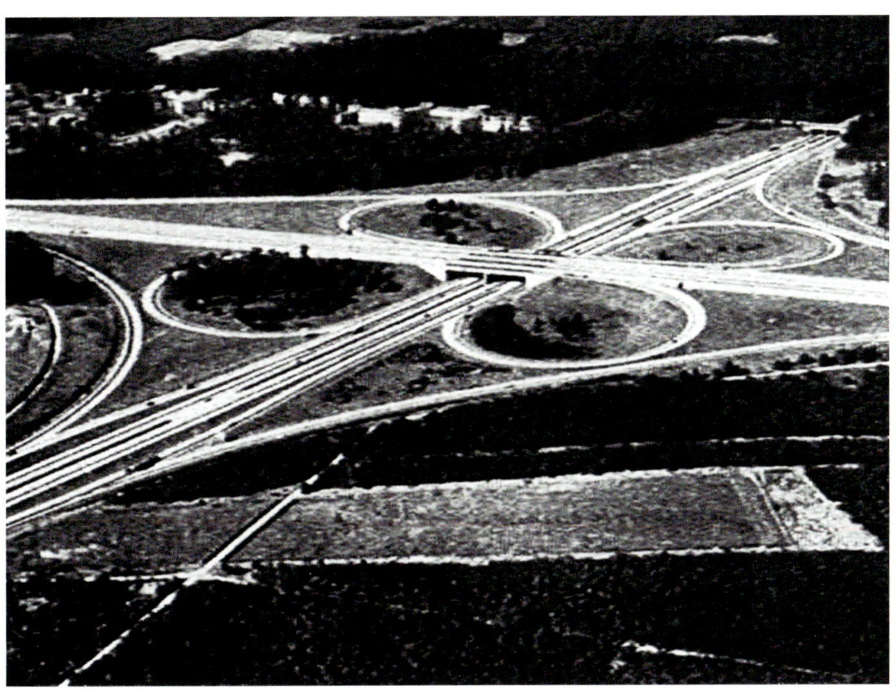

The line in these site-specific works is at once intellectual, as the conceptualization of an idea, and corporeal, in that it is drawn by the movements of the artist's body. Both conceptual and embodied, this line has continued to serve artists up to the present day, and its overtones are often explicitly political. In the 1970s, it often seemed to have no end in sight—to be without end and without purpose, specifically in North America. Soon, though, multiculturalism would open the art world to a larger and more diverse community that sees line as purposeful, in fact loaded with meaning. Works in this vein such as Amar Kanwar's *A Season Outside* (1997; plate 102), Harun Farocki's film *Wie Man Sieht* (As you see, 1986; plate 103), Francis Alÿs's *Green Line* (2007; plate 231), Steven Yazzie's *Draw Me a Picture* (2006; plate 105), and Mimi Gellman's *Between the Dreamtime and the GPS* (2009; plates 209, 228) do not rely solely on performance but also take into account existing lines in the city and landscape.

Alÿs's lines on the land are part of an ongoing series of projects he calls *paseos*, or strolls, which he has carried out worldwide, with various props in tow. He has strolled the avenues of Havana in magnetic shoes; he has crossed São Paulo's Pinheiros neighborhood carrying a punctured can of paint that marked his path with a fine line of color; he has walked the so-called "Green Line" between Israel and Palestine, again carrying a leaking can of paint; and he has walked across Stockholm dressed in a sweater that unraveled with every step, leaving a thread behind.

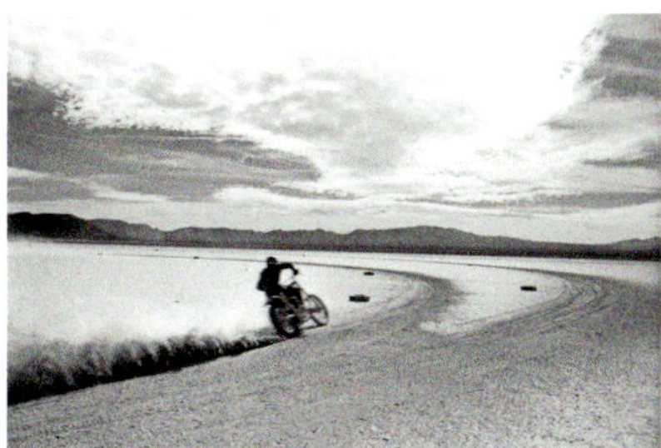

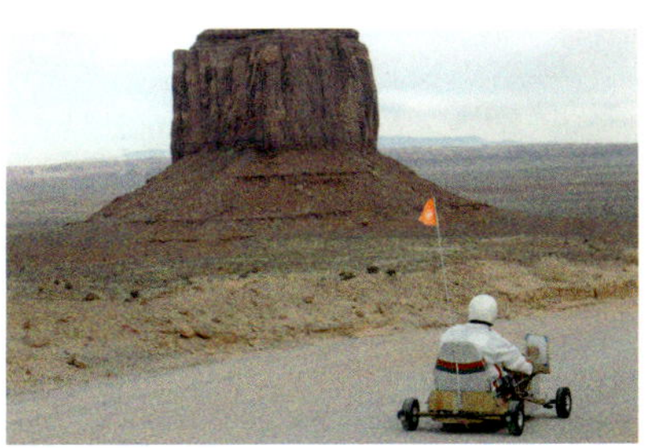

Yazzie describes his drawing project in Monument Valley as a reclaiming of his Navajo homeland:

> *Drawing and Driving* is a continuing project about landscape, travel, velocity, and the journey of that experience. I chose Monument Valley as the place to explore because I wanted to re-examine the perspective of this iconic landscape in the Southwest and challenge the dominant perspective of beauty and romanticism.... An interesting point to be made about this location is its accessibility only through a vehicle. Not only does a visitor need a vehicle to get to Monument Valley, but a vehicle is the preferred way to experience the canyon's eight-mile scenic loop.[121]

The vehicle Yazzie used to make his circuit, however, was essentially a one-person soapbox cart powered only by gravity and his feet. A fixed easel allowed the artist to draw the landscape as he was moving through it, a way of retrieving the land appropriated by conquest, by possession, by the Western gaze of movies and paintings. In one sense, Yazzie's drawing-and-driving without the use of fuel is a vivid and informed response to Heizer's motorcycle drawings, with the land (in every bump and pebble along the way) now inscribing itself in the work rather than the artist inscribing the land. The surface of this land is that of an ecology, and the history marked in it is that of the dependence on it of its people and of their separation from it.

Gellman's nightdrawing series combines a skeptical view of the rational yet illusory mapping systems of conventional cartography and its objective coordinates with a more intuitive response to the terrain. Taking as her cue the dislocation that these cerebral Western constructions often paradoxically entail, she turns to her Ojibway sources for their intimate connections to the land and the mind that travels it. As Gellman explains,

> A number of my original "Dreamwalk" drawings were input into a GPS handheld tracker as a "map" and given GPS coordinates, which were then attributed to a specific field near my home. Over a number of blustery winter nights, I was able to enact this series of walk/drawings through the interface of my GPS tracking system that led me to move from place to place according to the map-drawing within. Photographed from a great height, these photos exemplify the marriage of psychogeography and the physical re-tracing of the walk, with their powerful impact resonating from the disorienting orientation of their location and position in space. Like the Peruvian Nazca lines, the "nightdrawings" position the walker in an in-between place, floating between the dreamtime and the GPS.[122]

Each Dreamwalk drawing, then, as Ian Carr-Harris writes, is "a kind of palimpsest [in which] the formal vertical and horizontal axes of the standard European map [are] rendered as a fragmentary intersection that encloses and supports a photographic trace of the land they calculate. Across this construction, however, weaves the dreamwalk, a roughly drawn elliptical mass of fluid lines whose dense thicket of paths appears oblivious to the axes of calculation. Imagined, rather, as a record of the terrain itself, a tracing or caress of the earth, the dreamwalk offers another form of traveling, one that seeks not to define but only to encounter, if only through a dream, that longed-for elision of being and place."[123] And it was through work on the ground, in the horizontal plane, that the interrogative came from which artists like Gellman have challenged the work as vertical, permanent, nontransitive.

The second of the two tendencies of the Conceptual line involved a removal of line from its role as authorial gesture. By the late 1960s, ideas of the death or disappearance of the author were widespread, and artmaking had been reimagined as a more impersonal and deskilled practice. This transformation was both engendered and analyzed by artists who, as part of the same drift of thought, advanced the liberation of drawing from other disciplines and used a radically altered kind of mark-making to generate it. Here line consisted solely of the material residue of its own production. Typified by process-based works, made with or without paper, it gained importance in opposition to the ground — an unfolding that may be compared to the early-modern conception of progress itself as linear.

Looking at both the multiple meanings of the word "drawing" and the diversity of the drawings made in recent decades, one sees a parallel between linguistics and semiotics, on the one hand, and artists' explorations of drawing, on the other, both fields having reached new apogees of accomplishment in the twentieth century. Drawing today, in all the prolix variety of interpretation and method to which those artists' experiments in the medium led, is neither consequent upon nor directly inspired by the sciences of language, yet a connection exists as a subterranean, perhaps fortuitous, perhaps intuitive interchange. It is no coincidence that the boundaries of drawing were most widely expanded in the 1960s and

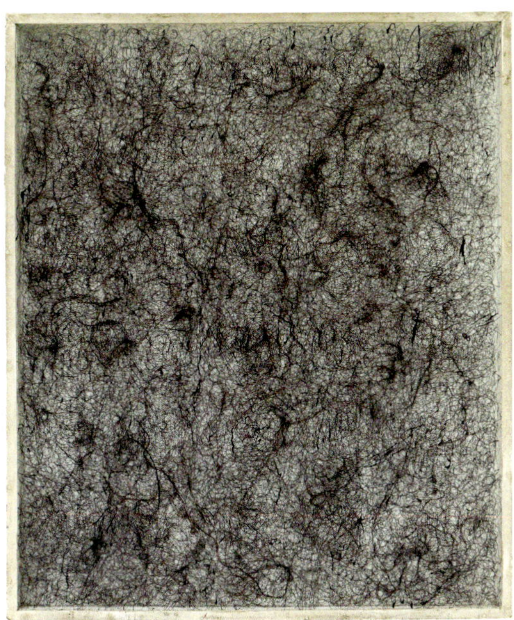

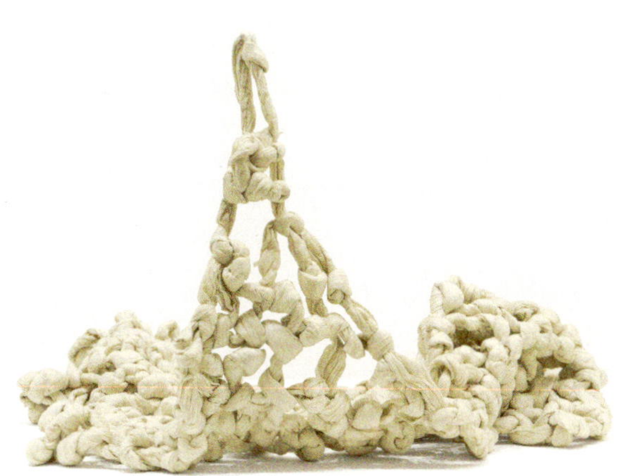

'70s, the period of liberation movements of all kinds, of the broad development of Structuralism, and of the so-called dematerialization of the art object in Neo-Concretism, *arte povera*, Conceptual art, Land and Process art, and their many variants. Ideas in linguistics spread into many other disciplines during those years, and the arts in turn influenced linguistics, particularly as the education and apprenticeship of artists was widely turned over to the academy. Given the basic conceptual belief that the knowledge and thought processes of artistic production mattered more than the finished object, writing and drawing, as both instrumental and intellectual tools, played steadily more powerful roles, while the conventions, methods, and orthodoxies of artmaking were increasingly challenged. Promoting the idea of art's slow working — of an artwork — artists who had come to see drawing as a core medium of exploration and conceptualization ultimately began to pull it farther toward a radically reimagined status of its own.

In South America — respectively in Argentina and Brazil — Léon Ferrari and Mira Schendel, both deeply involved with the graphic gesture, were equally fascinated with the word, even while denouncing the limitations of language. (Both, incidentally, maintained social connections with poets.) Ferrari was working with text well before the public emergence of Conceptual art in the United States. His work with line, both drawn and written, hovers between poetics and activist politics (plate 106).[124] Schendel began to make art as a painter, but after 1964 devoted herself to language-infused works on paper, often semitransparent rice paper hung in space between Plexiglas sheets, as in the *Objetos graficos* (Graphic objects, 1967). In the *Monotipias* (Monotypes, 1964–69), Luis Pérez-Oramas writes, "The drawing in fact *shines through*. Its body precisely inhabits the paper's transparency; its traits lie in the trace, the physical gesture, the muscular weight that produced it, as well as in the paper's intensified presence. It is as if the darkness of the drawn line grew integrally from the paper's white clarity without compromising either value. . . . the drawing seem[s] to emerge from within the support, rather than being imposed upon it from outside."[125] Meanwhile, in the *Droguinhas* (Little nothings, 1964–66; plate 107), the same luminescent paper becomes solid, being turned into three-dimensional coils and scrawls of line.

Western thought of this period was critically shaped by a concern with language, which became a paradigm for understanding human existence and daily reality. The emergence of textually and linguistically informed Conceptual art was just one aspect of this concern, also manifest in the writings of Claude Lévi-Strauss, Jacques Derrida, and many others. In art, the interest in the artwork as the residue of its own creation, exemplified in works such as Luis Camnitzer's *The Instrument and Its Work* (1976; plate 108) and Dorothea Rockburne's *Drawing Which Makes Itself* (1972) and *Neighborhood* (1973; plate 109), was integral to this body of thought. The drawn line had always corresponded in some way to the line of thought,

106. León Ferrari
(Argentine, born 1920)
Reflexiones (Reflections). 1963
Ink on gessoed wood, copper wire, and ink on glass, in artist's painted wood frame
34 1/8 x 28 x 2" (86.7 x 71.1 x 5.1 cm)

107. Mira Schendel
(Brazilian, born Switzerland, 1919–1988)
Untitled from the series *Droguinhas* (Little nothings). c. 1964–66
Paper
Dimensions variable,
c. 35 1/2" (90 cm) long fully extended

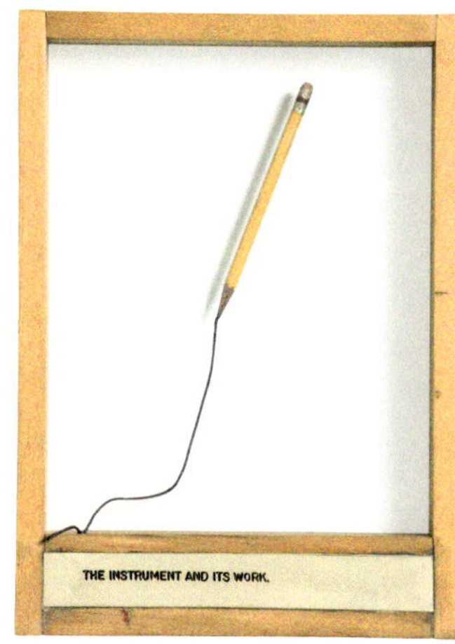

In [Rockburne's] Drawing Which Makes Itself, *... The act of drawing is ... conceived as different from the traditional procedure in which a set of objects (lines) is superimposed on another, foreign object (paper). Instead, one confronts works in which the lines arise from information that is "in" the paper. And the logic of the works states the self-evidence of the fact that this information, although it could be transferred to different situations (on the wall), could not be dislodged from the mediating body of the paper that is the source of the information.*

— Rosalind Krauss, *Line as Language*, 1976

but now, in a challenge to formalist self-reflexiveness, the literal line, the line embodied in the processes and materials of the work's production, was becoming equally definitive.

Generated in a process that flows from an exchange of responses between making and material, Tuttle's Wire Pieces share in the period's undoing of authorial signature. Even earlier, Vera Molnar (plate 110) had fully realized this idea of overcoming one's identity, in drawings she made by computer. She once candidly remarked, "I situate myself between the three 'cons': the conceptualists, the constructivists, and the computers."[126] Molnar wrote,

> I use the computer to combine forms, hoping that this tool will enable me to distance myself from what I have learned, from my cultural heritage and everything else that surrounds me; in brief, from the influences of civilization that define us. Thanks to its many possibilities of combination the computer helps to systematically research the visual realm, helps the painter to free himself from cultural "readymades" and find combinations in forms never seen before, neither in nature nor at the museum: it helps to create inconceivable images. The computer helps, but it does not "do," does not "design" or "invent" anything.[127]

What remained crucial was the distinction between drawing as an illusory projection, pointing to something beyond itself, and drawing as a kind of direct marking on the world, that is, on the floor and on the wall. The line does not project itself out of this world into another, into the world of an imaginary space. According to Krauss, LeWitt thought of his wall drawings as having "properties of material and surface that are untransformed by the agency of line, or rather of a kind of line that has been stripped of the powers of metaphor. The lines are simply elements that coexist with the surface onto which they are drawn."[128] For Tuttle, similarly, and for Hans Haacke, the floor proper — like the wall, like the world — is simply extended, oblivious of aesthetically defined boundaries, becoming the site of drawings such as Haacke's *Circulation* (1969; plate 233), an arrangement of long vinyl tubes circulating water, and Tuttle's *Ten Kinds of Memory and Memory Itself* (1973; plate 147). Here, in place of graphic lines, Tuttle simply throws varying lengths of cotton string onto the floor — a gesture recalling Duchamp's *3 Standard Stoppages* — in an attempt to literalize and thereby undercut the imaginary space of the sheet. The performative quality of this conceptual gesture coincides with the dance of the 1960s and '70s, another kind of drawing in space. In their reinvention of dance in those years, artists such as Pina Bausch, Trisha Brown (plate 111), Simone Forti, Anna Halprin, and Yvonne Rainer were working to disassociate the body from representation and narrative structures, just as artists were doing with line.

In developing conceptual and process art in its various forms, many artists chose the walls or floors of buildings as loci of interaction, creating site-specific work in a new relation with the viewer. In the 1970s, Gordon Matta-Clark made collages of stacked cuttings of paper and cardboard (plate 112), then, in his "anarchitectural" pieces, began to cut through the walls and floors of abandoned or derelict buildings (plate 113). In proceeding from collage to *coupage*, his working method recalls that of Schwitters, in the collages and *Merzbau* project. To turn again to Krauss, "With these wall- and floor-based works we have moved very far indeed from the private space of intention and meaning that operated throughout an earlier convention of drawing. Instead, we find ourselves engaged by a projection or emptying of meaning outwards — precipitating it onto the physical space of the world."[129]

Even when line came to be considered conceptual, devoid of corporeality, sensual bodily motion inescapably remained a trait of drawing. Some artists, Krauss continues, share "the need to explore the externality of a propositional space and therefore of meaning. But at the same time this need has a parallel project in the work of other artists: the discovery of the body proper as an externalization of the space of the self."[130] This was apparent in Carolee Schneeman's drawing performances *Up To And Including Her*

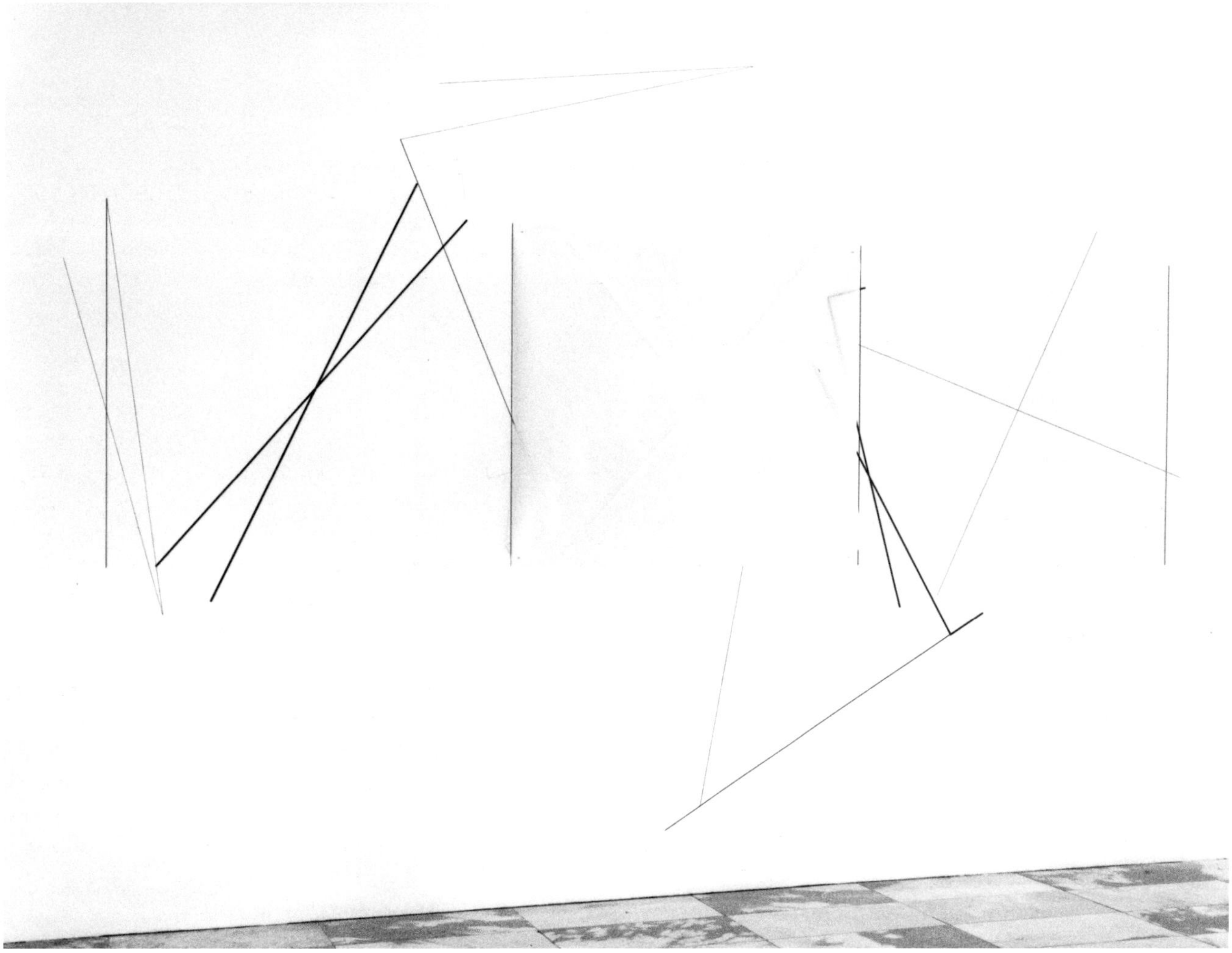

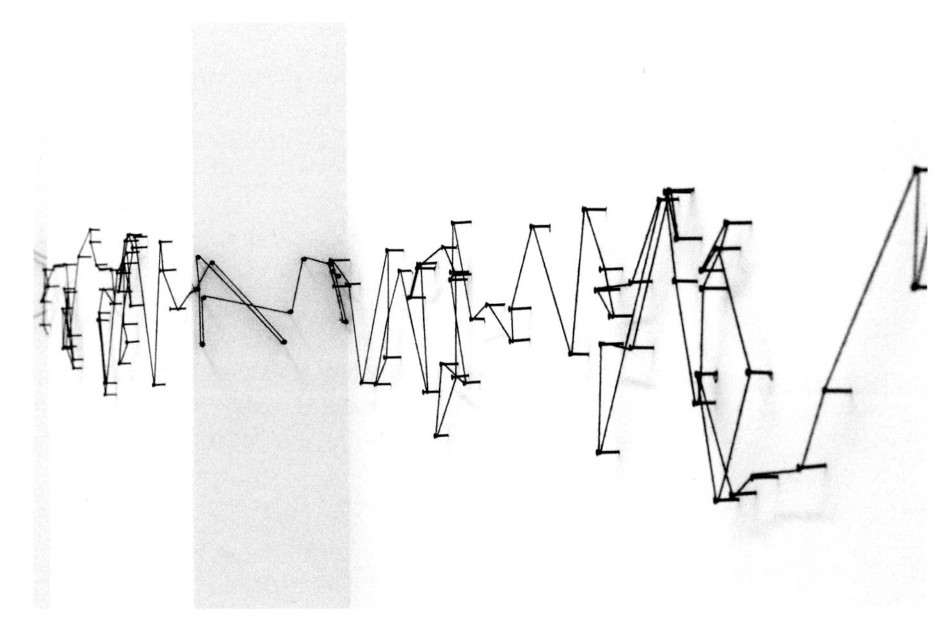

108. Luis Camnitzer
(Uruguayan, born 1937)
The Instrument and Its Work. 1976
Wood, glass, and metal
11 13/16 x 10 1/16 x 1 15/16˝ (30 x 25.5 x 5 cm)

109. Dorothea Rockburne
(American, born Canada 1932)
Neighborhood. 1973
Transparentized paper, pencil, and colored pencil on wall
13´ 4˝ x 7´ 6˝ (406.4 x 228.6 cm)

110. Vera Molnar
(French, born Hungary 1924)
Promenade (presque) aléatoire
(Walk [nearly] random). 1998–99
Black wire and nails
Dimensions variable

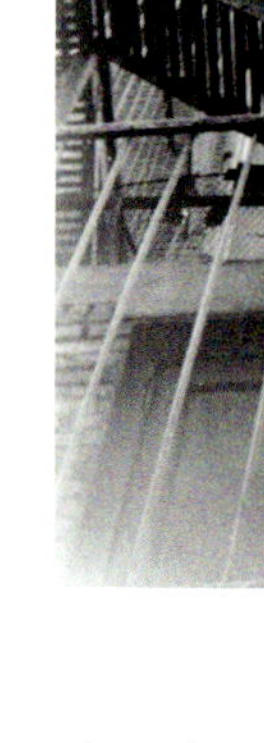

Limits (1973–76; plates 128, 211), in which the artist, suspended in the air in a harness, drew on the walls and floor, which were covered with paper, as she maneuvered around the space. The action of Tom Marioni's *Drawing a Line As Far As I Can Reach* (1972) is summarized by its title. Both titles cite the idea of the bodily limit — "as far as I can reach" — but simultaneously convey the sense of externalization and extension of line as liberating, even, in the case of Schneeman, ecstatic.

In this particular extension of line, line and body appear to fuse, to collapse, a move that returns the authorial mark of the artist to the picture. In another gesture of this kind, Giuseppe Penone would often begin his large-scale wall drawings of the 1970s by blackening small areas of his skin with charcoal, then laying adhesive tape on the surface to pick up its delicate texture and pattern. Next he would transfer the imprint on the tape to a glass surface, conserving a trace of human presence and at the same time recording a pressure on the surface of the skin, the limit, the boundary or rather the point of contact between the inner and outer worlds. Enlarging the skin print by projecting it on the wall, Penone traced wall drawings of its lines that seem to waver before the eye, turning microcosm into macrocosm, as if we were enveloped in the tiniest cracks of our own sensory surface as well as of the earth's rhizomatically ramified one. Penone's *Propagazione* (Propagation; plate 227) of the early 1990s similarly begin with his fingerprint, recorded in pencil lines that start out on paper, then spill over onto the walls of the space, as though they were the ring lines of a steadily growing tree, as though they were limitless.

This fusion of skin, wall, and world corresponds closely to the principles and the methods of A. Balasubramaniam. Attempting to undo the line between private and public in *Rest and Resistance* (2007; plate 9), Balasubramaniam shows the surface of a wall pulled outward by a fishing hook on a wire, as though the room were a second skin — the bodily skin being one layer of separation between inside and outside and the wall a second layer, and so on through the house, the city, and beyond, the planet, the universe. Balasubramaniam is interested, he says, "in how the skin creates the meaning for the space. . . . people are so comfortable with the feeling of being inside the room as being protected or being safe. . . . I am interested in a place where the mind is not able to make a decision."[131] His attempt to fuse private and public also recalls the work of Fabro, in particular the *Indumenti*.

Although most of these works use the wall and floor as the arena of action (as the Gutai artists do also), paper never completely disappeared as the support and was often reintegrated in the process (prominently, for example, in Penone's *Propagazione*). And this is exactly where the next generation picked up. In fact, in the last decades, both the wall as real space and the page as imaginary space have increasingly been juxtaposed and seen as interrelated by the movement of line itself. Over time, this relation, this interaction generated in the work, is becoming more mobile and confluent.

111. Trisha Brown
(American, born 1936)
Man Walking Down the Side of a Building. 1970
Performance view, 80 Wooster Street, New York

112. Gordon Matta-Clark
(American, 1945–1978)
Untitled (Cut Drawing). 1976–77
Pencil on layers of cut paper
22 1/2 x 29 1/2 x 1/2" (57 x 74 x 1.3 cm)

113. Gordon Matta-Clark
(American, 1945–1978)
Circus — The Caribbean Orange. 1978
Silver dye bleach print
39 1/2 x 29 7/8" (100.3 x 75.9 cm)

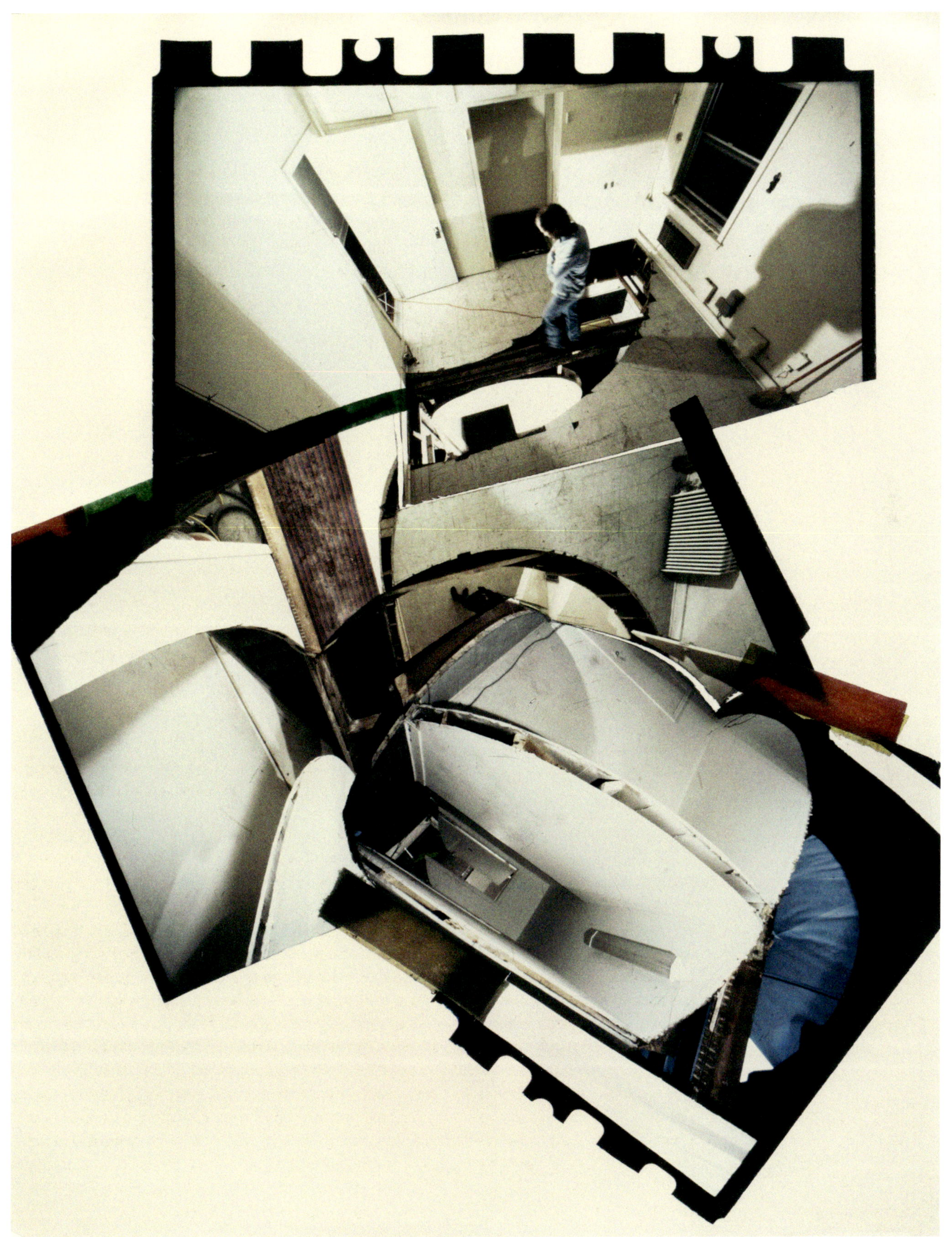

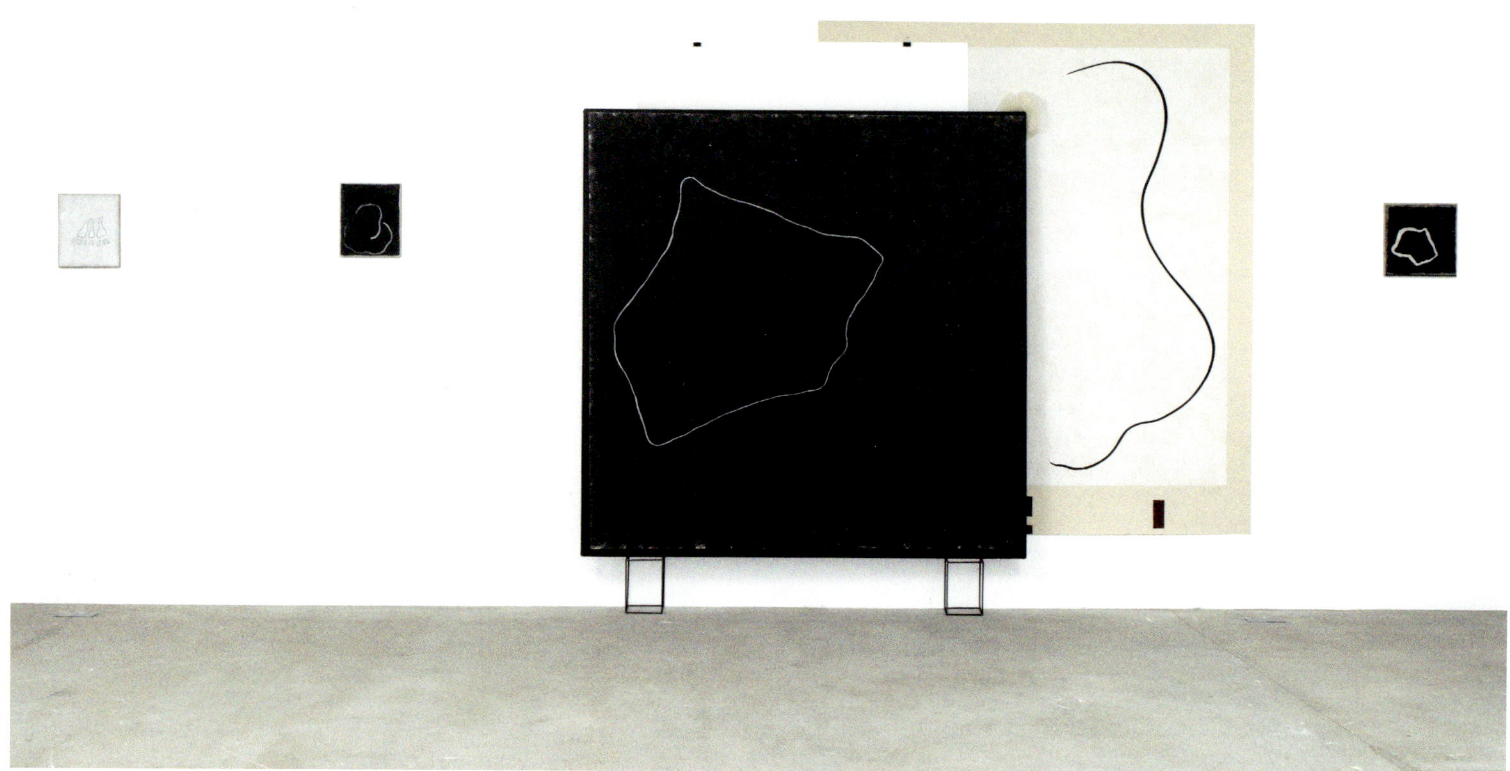

PLANE/SPACE/LINE: A MOBILE SET OF RELATIONS (1990–2010)

Artists today thrive on the interdependency of drawing, printing, painting, sculpture, and performance, of surface and space, and mostly of line and support, whether paper, floor, or wall. Drawing indeed goes beyond the sheet of the paper, a process that continues to be materialized by extrapolating lines into space. Postmodernism, multiculturalism, and feminism affected this development. The contemporary conception of drawing, however, emphatically stresses reciprocity and empowerment, acknowledging that a single line can challenge and change the understanding of the ground itself. Line and ground, in fact, may now become interchangeable and confluent. The work of many contemporary artists situates itself in a generative in-between, connecting wall and paper, vertical and horizontal, abstract and concrete, imaginary and real, in a peripatetic set of lines and relations.

Avis Newman, for example, has described the working process of her painted drawings as neither a "construction" nor a "composition" (as in the Constructivist debate) but "a configuration allowing for the work not to have an absolute fixity."[132] Provisional in arrangement, Newman's *Configuration of no-thing* (2007–9; plate 114), part of a cycle of works, suggests an ambivalent body of relations with the perpetual potential for reconfiguration. As Newman states,

114. Avis Newman
(British, born 1946)
Configuration of no-thing. 2007–9
Acrylic and chalk on linen and cotton duck, paper, and metal
Six parts:
11 13/16 x 9 13/16" (30 x 25 cm),
11 13/16 x 9 13/16" (30 x 25 cm),
6' 1/16" x 6' 1/16" (183 x 183 cm),
39 3/8 x 55 1/8" (100 x 140 cm),
6' 10 11/16" x 68 7/8" (210 x 175 cm),
11 13/16 x 11 13/16" (30 x 30 cm)

> The assemblage of elements proposes a series of mobile relations in which images do not suggest a correspondence to things in the world but are things in themselves. I am attracted to ideas of paradox and inconsistency where a plurality of form, which promises ceaseless elaboration, is contained by the "rational" of its elements or parts. These thoughts are grounded in my fascination with the conceptual space of drawing, which I understand to be in essence an encounter with the materialization of the continually mutable process, the movements, rhythms and partially comprehended ruminations of the mind: the operations of thought. In that domain the work becomes a process of enunciation. The edge, layered, extended, unframed, becomes a series of operations which interferes with any anticipation we might have of completion. The line manifests a division that conjures the "this" and the "that" and in so doing is symbolically the mark of language.[133]

Speaking of exceeding boundaries in "a mobile set of relations that can thus change in space and time," Newman seems to address new possibilities for the condition of the unstable subject in the present world. Instead of continuing to insist on common fragmentation, such mobility proposes a series of variables. If in the real conditions of life it may refer to paradox, change, even chaos, it is embedded in the work through interleaving, layering, and suspension.

Interleaving and Internetting

Twentieth-century modernism replaced the narrative and communicative functions of drawing with an almost exclusive consideration of its notational and self-referential dimensions. Drawing has since evolved from gestural expression to matrixial design informed by the modernist doctrines of objectivity and of deskilling (as in the drawings of the Minimalists and Conceptuals), from an intimate statement to a structural model in which lines and marks are organized in a matrix determined by the space of the paper sheet. As soon as representation came to be defined by the process of its own generation, drawing became the exploration of marks and lines left by the process itself. Paradoxically, as this occurred, the autographic and the conceptual—and with them the present and the past, the local and the global—again fused, a development of line most visible in the drawings of a younger generation of artists.

To understand how Julie Mehretu collapses the autographic and the structural matrix, the narrative with the antinarrative, is to unfold the complexity of the layering process in her images (plate 115). Change is embedded in the material stratification of these drawn paintings or painted drawings. Mehretu starts work by stapling raw canvas to the wall, then covering it with gesso to produce a smooth surface. Using an overhead projector and technical pens and rulers—the use of rulers much in the spirit of Rodchenko, who, refusing to draw without a set-square or a compass, created unexpected perspectives to "educate man to a new longing," he said[134]—she next draws in parts of urban-planning grids, architectural imagery, the city plans of economic, financial, and political capitals, and her own sketches made by computer. Some tracings are masked with tape, then painted or airbrushed with clear acrylic paint, applied flatly to avoid visible brushstrokes. Being ultimately the base of the painting, the drawing could be seen as subservient to it, fulfilling the medium's old preparatory role, but it actually confounds that conventional progression, fusing different disciplines. Once this stage is complete, the canvas is sprayed with an acrylic-and-silica mixture, then sanded to a polished surface resembling chalk paper—and now the whole process is repeated, as more images of urban and architectural plans are projected and copied. Mehretu has said, "The language of mapmaking, specific architectural plans, and then eventually the symbolic sampling of visual traditions in art history slipped into the layers of the paintings. Different types of visual language symbolized and referenced various social and political ideas and attitudes. . . .

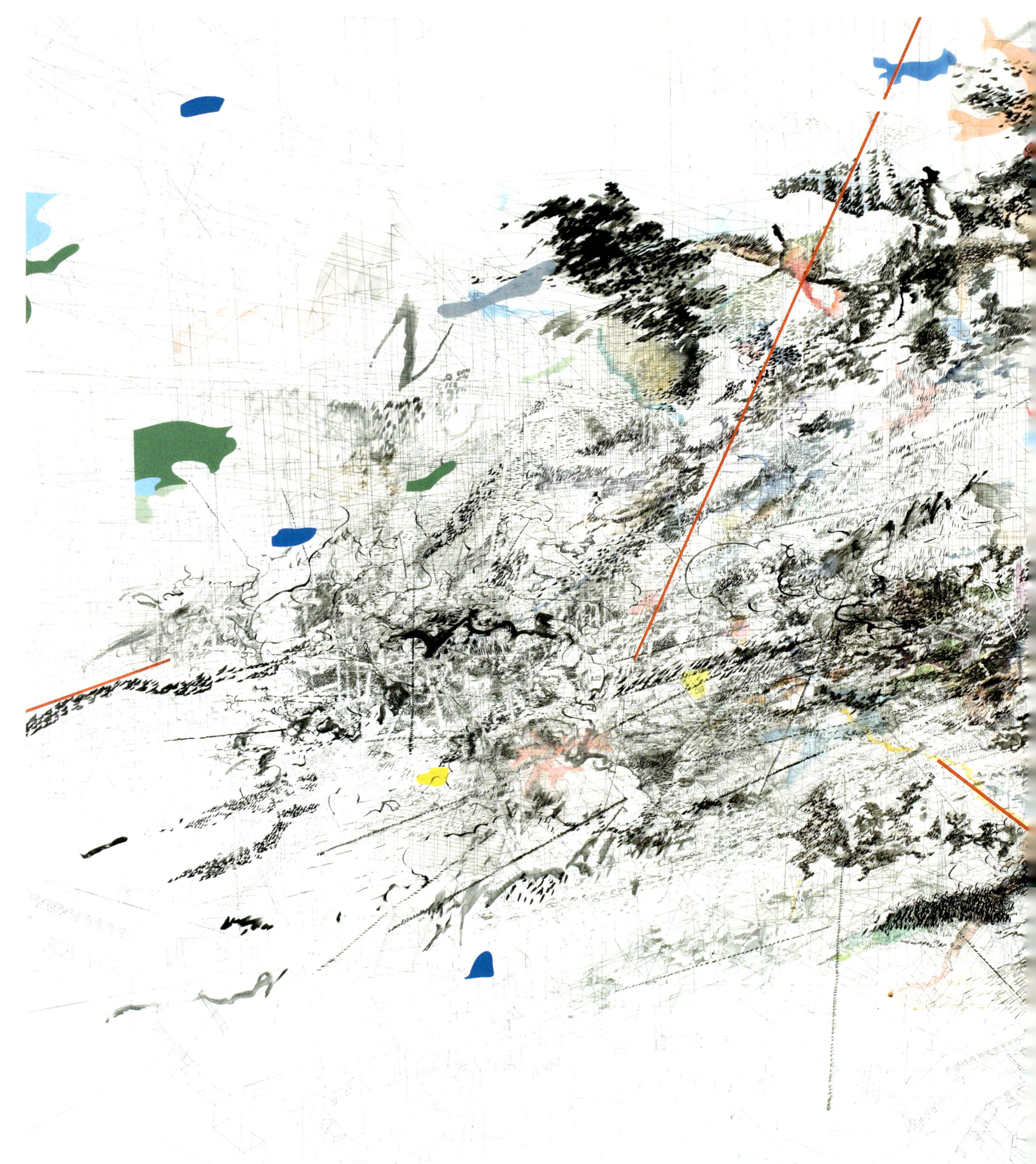

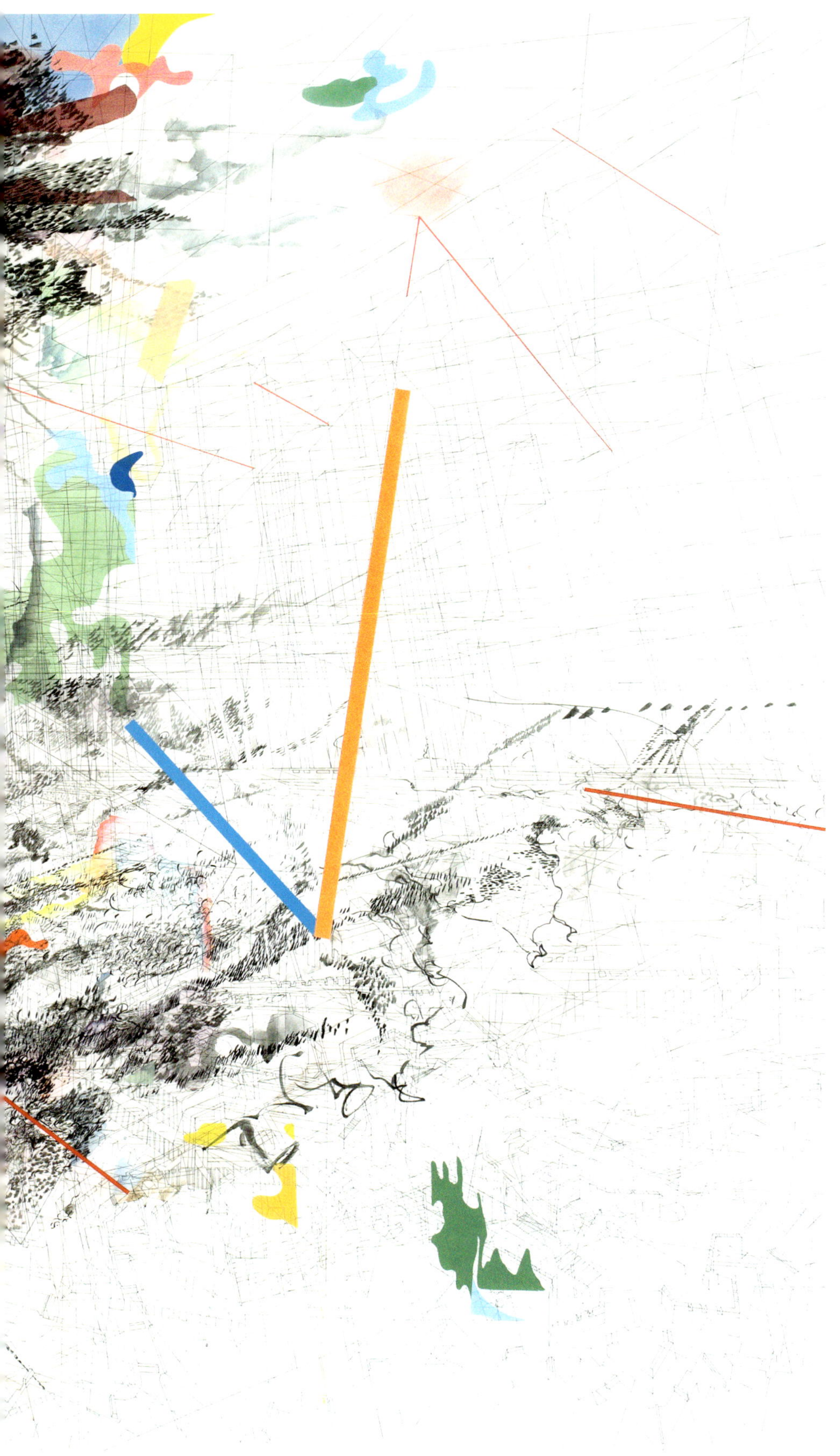

The layering process in my work really developed with the investigation of the characters. At first, the paintings were just composed of layers of drawing. There were a few characters that huddled together and created a community. As they migrated and mixed with other characters, they made new cities. Eventually, a whole terrain would be drawn upon and entangled with a narrative. When that was saturated with drawing, I would pour the acrylic-and-silica mixture of paint over the entire surface. It would dry into a smooth transparent ground that I could draw on, with the previous drawing embedded underneath. This created a stratified, tectonic geology in the paintings, with the characters themselves buried — as if they were fossils.

— Julie Mehretu,
"Looking Back," 2003

115. Julie Mehretu
(American, born Ethiopia 1970)
Rising Down. 2008
Ink and synthetic polymer paint on canvas
8 x 12´ (243.8 x 365.8 cm)

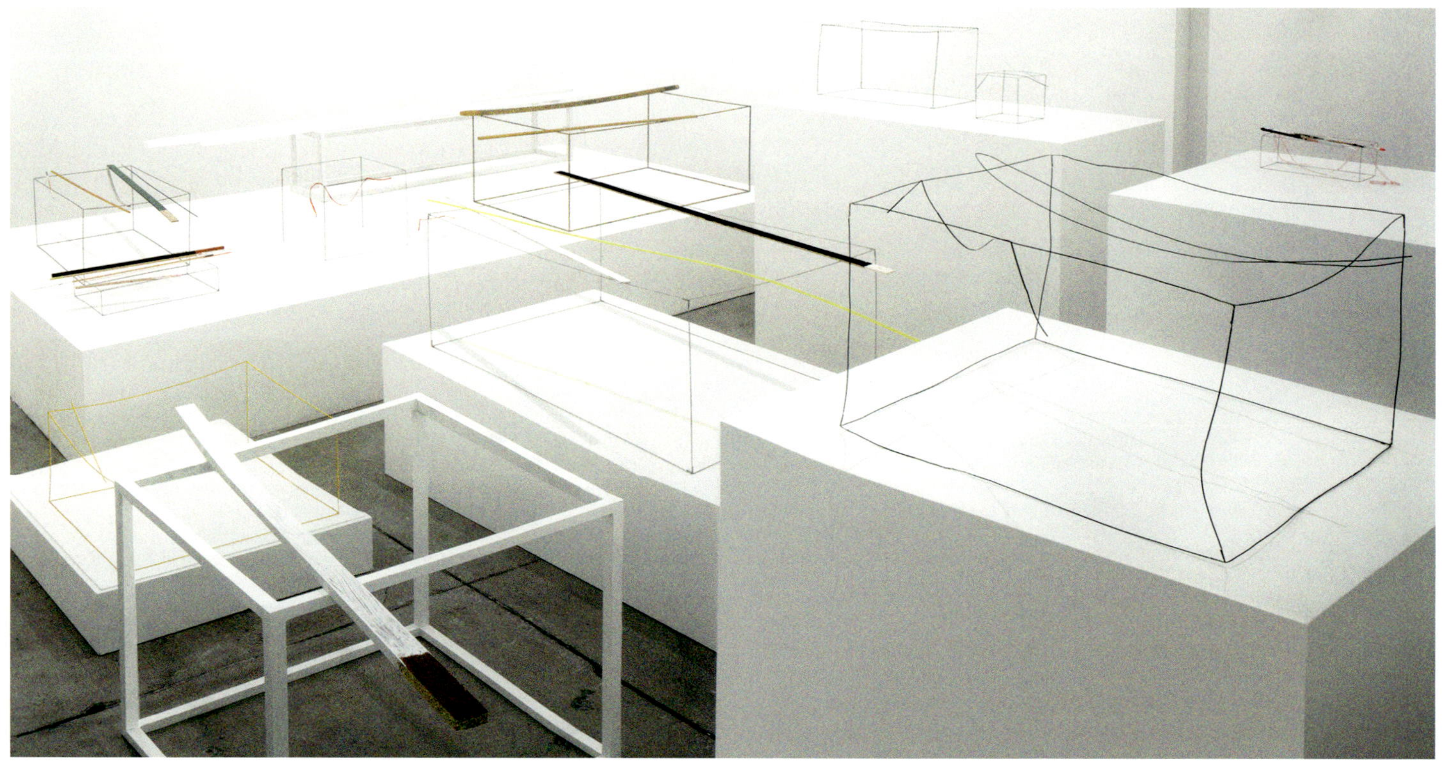

When I just sit on a chair in front of a house or a public building, the reactions of people in every culture are different. Recorded in my videowork, it is clear that this performative act always changes the movement of people around me; and as I observe, I can discern different patterns. It proves how somehow all people are connected. It is a real situation but at the same time totally abstract: Their movement is like a drawing, like dancing.

—Susan Hefuna, conversation with the author, 2010

They acted as a metaphoric bridge...into the more tangible, monumental, and recognizable world we inhabit, historicize, and politicize."[135]

Mehretu's interleaving thrives on repetition and, within the layers, combines decontextualized matrices and highly structured schematics with her own compulsively and expressively brushed marks in ink. Embodying the purely corporeal grapheme, these gestural lines of flight and curves of energy are imagined by the artist as her "characters' responses to the megastructure of the previous layers. They inherently resist order due to their gesture."[136] Drawing on the double meaning of the word "character," Mehretu inscribes her own individual narrative into the folds of (art) history by mobilizing small anthropomorphic pictographs as social agents in communities that overthrow "rulers" and systems to make change possible: "The underlying conceptual framework of my paintings lies in the relationship between the individual and the community, the whole. Each mark represents individual agency, an active social character."[137] The result being a structured cityscape inhabited by these "characters," her epic canvases come to incorporate sociality and history.

Susan Hefuna sees the layering of tracing paper in her drawings as embodying a conversation among traces, a conversation with what lies behind each translucent sheet, with what cannot yet be understood. Her drawn nets (plate 118), at times delicately sewn together, containing this kind of multidimensional space are inspired by the Egyptian *mashrabiya*, a window screen, both functional and ornamental, common in Islamic architecture.[138] Hefuna always draws in a state of high concentration, a meditation between interior and exterior worlds, the latter often epitomized in gridlike building structures. As she says, "These lines of thought are beyond control but always in motion, starting with a point yet without a plan in mind."[139]

Ranjani Shettar's *Just a bit more* (2005–6; plate 232) takes the notion of interdependency further. An arrangement of spiraling webs suspended from the ceiling, with strings connecting hundreds of "buds" colored in slight gradations of blue, it recalls Gego's *Reticuláreas* in structure, but where those works were

116. Joëlle Tuerlinckx
(Belgian, born 1958)
Room of Volume of Air—13 Elements.
1993–2004
Iron, copper, wood, and found floor materials
Dimensions variable. Installation view

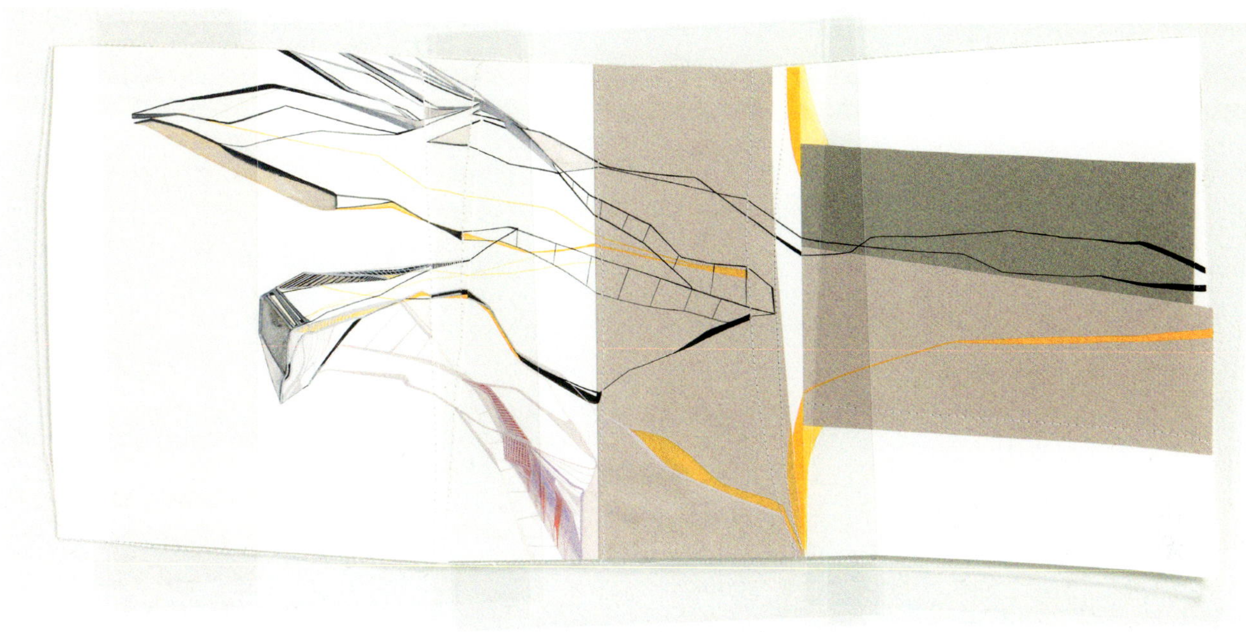

[My lines] realize that maybe it is better to be a little tame and a little wild. With that they may reach a harmonious balance… and manage to create their own world. A world which has no boundaries barring them from going on the other side… a world which is full of happiness and joy… so they try, but, that is real hard so they try again, and again… and life goes on… maybe one day they will arrive somewhere.

— Sheila Makhijani, 2005

117. Sheila Makhijani
(Indian, born 1962)
Take a leap ⟶. 2009
Gouache and thread on paper and plastic sheets
12 1/2 x 25" (31.8 x 63.5 cm)

in metal, *Just a bit more* is made of cotton thread, dyed in tea, and nodules of pigmented hand-rolled beewax. As in Hesse's work, the color gradation invokes a principle of soft transition, of malleability, promoting connection and flexibility in defiance of fixity and definitive order, in form and by extension in society. Shettar's "internetting" alludes both to contemporary computer technologies, with their vast powers of communication and information delivery, and to biology, to the structure and growth of living organisms, to nature. Despite its subtlety and abstraction, the work readily connects with an ever more urgent need for sociopolitical action on a global scale against the "background" of the widely feared possibility of environmental catastrophe.

That possibility, of course, is not a background against which our actions constitute the forefront figure; the distinction between figure and ground is a false one here. In the same way, once line was let loose into space in the modern period, and free to speak beyond convention, the accumulation of human marks that made up a drawing often undid that distinction, as it appeared more clearly to be without a ground. Rather than the support being the precondition of the drawing, drawing now can be seen as what Alain Badiou calls "a constructive deconstruction," its marks and lines articulating and indeed constituting the ground itself. As Badiou writes, "In a true drawing, a creative one, the marks, the traces, the lines, are not included or closeted in the background. On the contrary, the marks, the lines—the forms, if you will—create the background as an open space.… In the drawing, some marks create an inexistent place. As a result, we have a description without place."[140] In this way, freed from both support and the task of representation, drawing has created a space for becoming that did not previously exist. If line can articulate and alter the background—which is to say, the order of our social reality, potentially—then drawing allows a rare open space for the conscious formation and critical development of subjectivity and so for social change. For Tuttle, "Drawing is 'inside' the person; not on the paper. The appreciation, development of drawing is one of the great characteristics of a human well-being. The drawing gives the human the full possibility of exploring their possibility."[141]

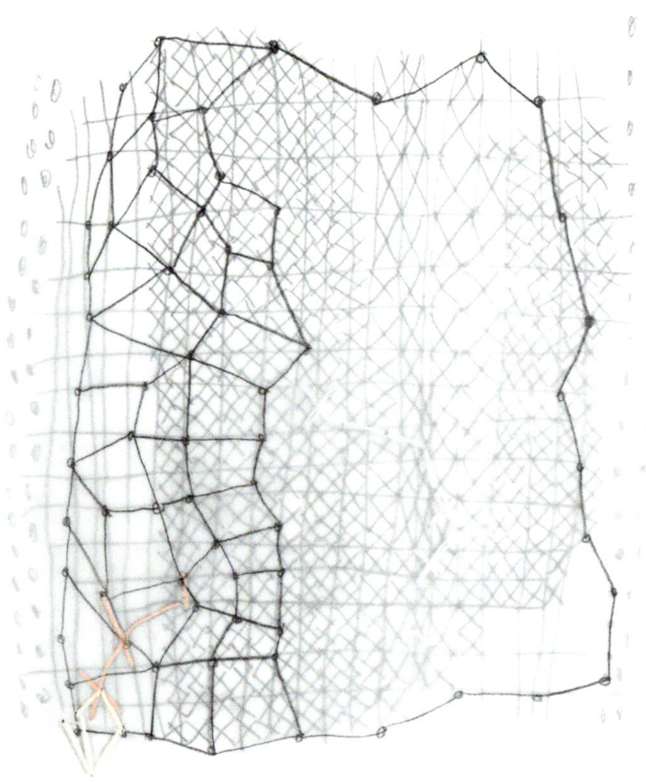

118. Susan Hefuna
(German, born 1962)
Building. 2008
Pencil and embroidery on tracing paper
$21^{1}/_{16}$ x $27^{3}/_{16}$″ (53.5 x 69 cm)

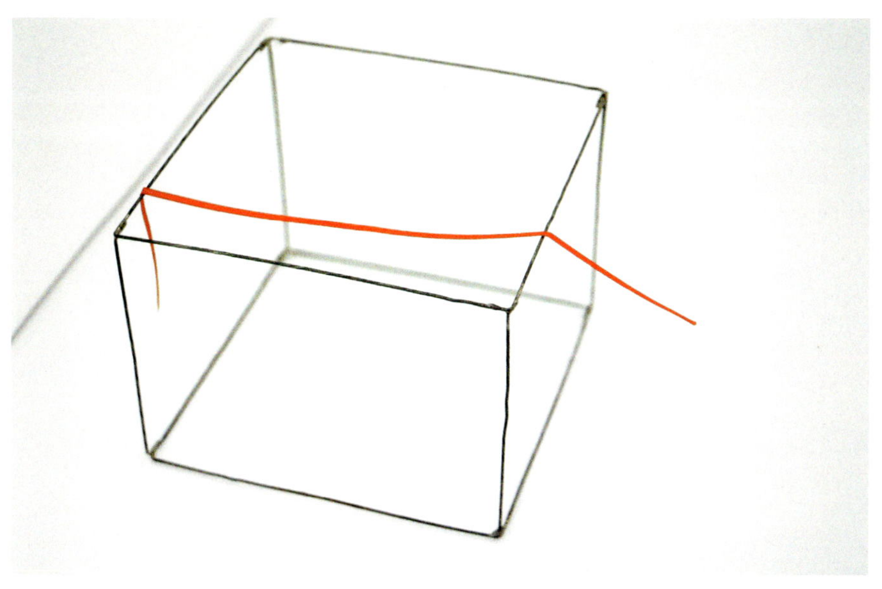

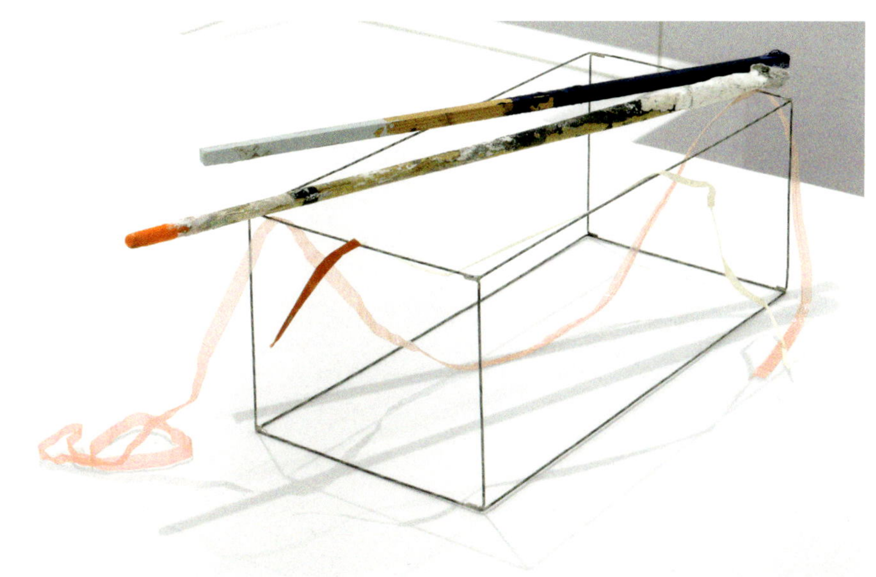

119–20. Joëlle Tuerlinckx
(Belgian, born 1958)
Room of Volume of Air—13 Elements.
1993–2004
Iron, copper, wood, and found
floor materials
Dimensions variable. Installation views

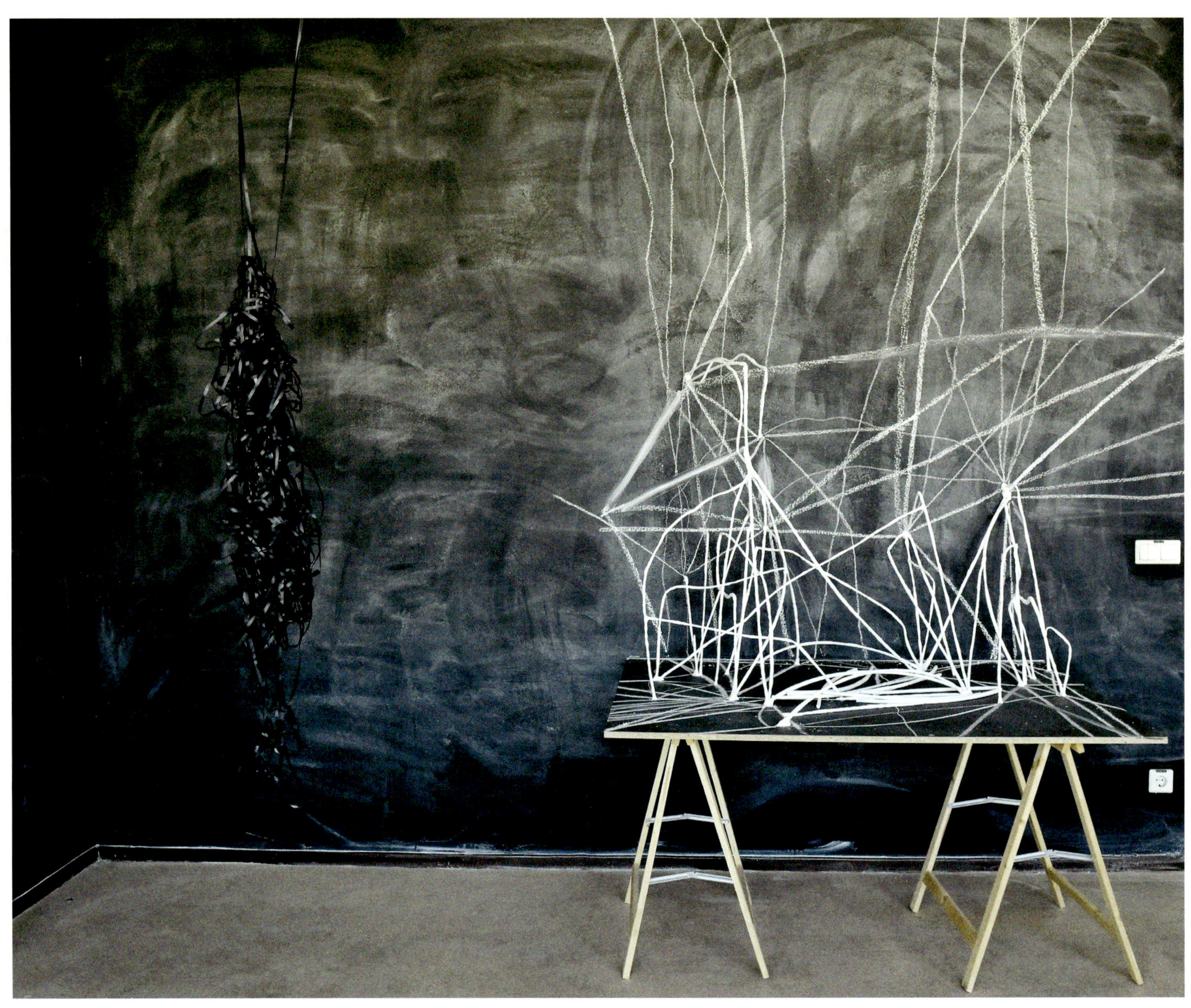

The image carrier (the wall) and image (the drawing) become one. The lines are elements that coexist with the surface onto which or into which they are drawn. They create their own topological space.

— Monika Grzymala, 2010

It is an essential feature of contemporary drawing to make this open space visible as a new possibility. Joëlle Tuerlinckx's *Room of Volume of Air — 13 Elements* (1993–2004; plates 116, 119, 120) and *Floating Lines* (2003–6), her systematic marking and measuring of emptiness, can be seen as circumscribing, bringing distinctness to, the open void. The layered deconstruction of linear modernist structures is crucial to the filmy surfaces of Mehretu's psychogeographies, to Hefuna's translucent gridlike Cityscape and Building drawings, to Sheila Makhijani's interleaved and stitched collages (plates 117, 230), and to Monika Grzymala's temporary three-dimensional drawings, with their miles of adhesive tape (plate 121). While Grzymala extends a physical line as a form of drawing space and time onto the walls and columns of the museum or gallery, Mehretu reverses that operation, using space and time to project the line onto the flat surface, but both artists stress the interdependency of line and support, and the necessity for a coexistence of real and imaginary space in order to rethink the world. Makhijani's stitching meanwhile seems to gather parallel moments of time and sequential fragments of space, creating tangible borders crossed by delicate yet purposeful lines of colored thread and paint.

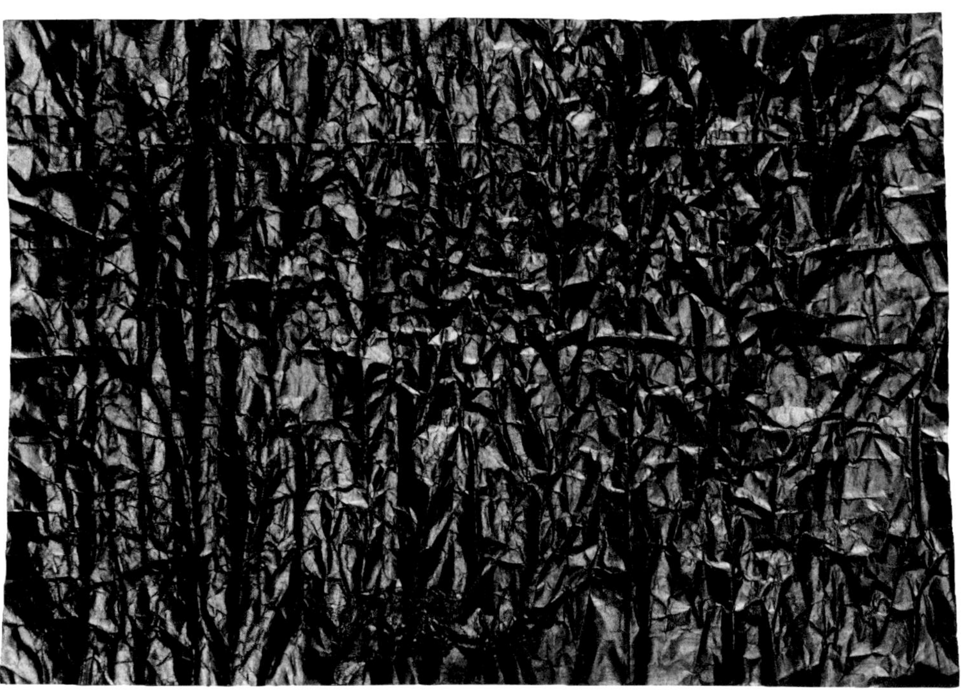

These works point further to the fact that not only is the background drawn as much as the line is, but that when we draw the ground, we tend to forget that it also draws us. This spells out the precarious and complex reciprocal relationship between the human and natural worlds. As self-assured as we have become in imposing ourselves on the encompassing earth, leaving the erroneous impression that we are in charge, it often escapes us how interdependent we are with one another, with the many-voiced landscape, with the tangible background, which remakes us as much as we remake it. We are human only in relation, in conviviality.

Confluence and Suspension

In recent drawing, the ground has become as important as the line to the point where there is a confluence, the line becoming ground and the ground becoming line, in an ongoing confusion. (It is to be noted that this was already a feature of the work of Kngwarray and other Aboriginal artists.) In Balasubramaniam's *Rest and Resistance* the wall is a full protagonist, not ground but effectively skin. The artist has said,

> Two hooks are pulling each other with equal power and it looks so still, like nothing happens; but if she is pulling from that side and I am pulling from this side with an equal energy, what happens is that as a viewer you may not see the energy, the tension, or the friction in the line. It is a moment in really high speed but the moment becomes no moment at all. So in order to give that sense of actually pulling each other I have to pull the wall. This adds the meaning to the place where the two hooks are meeting. Otherwise, it just looks static.... to show that tension in suspension I pulled the wall.[142]

Grzymala's *Up There Up Here* (2006–10) operates similarly: the walls of a room are covered with Japanese washi paper, out of which thin lines of paper are pulled into space, shaping the room as though enveloping the viewer within the drawing itself. As if tracing an ecological awareness, this skinlike ground and the lines drawn out of it seem to address the viewer's slowly growing understanding of the fact that the environment draws and shapes us as much as we draw and shape the environment. In short, the world and I reciprocate one another.

121. Studio of **Monika Grzymala** (German, born Poland 1970), Berlin, 2010. Left: *Clump*, black tape; right: *Untitled (skeleton of a drawing)*, paperclay and chalk

122. Edith Dekyndt (Belgian, born 1960) *Drawing 003*. 2009 Graphite on paper $18\frac{1}{2} \times 25\frac{5}{8}$" (47 x 65 cm)

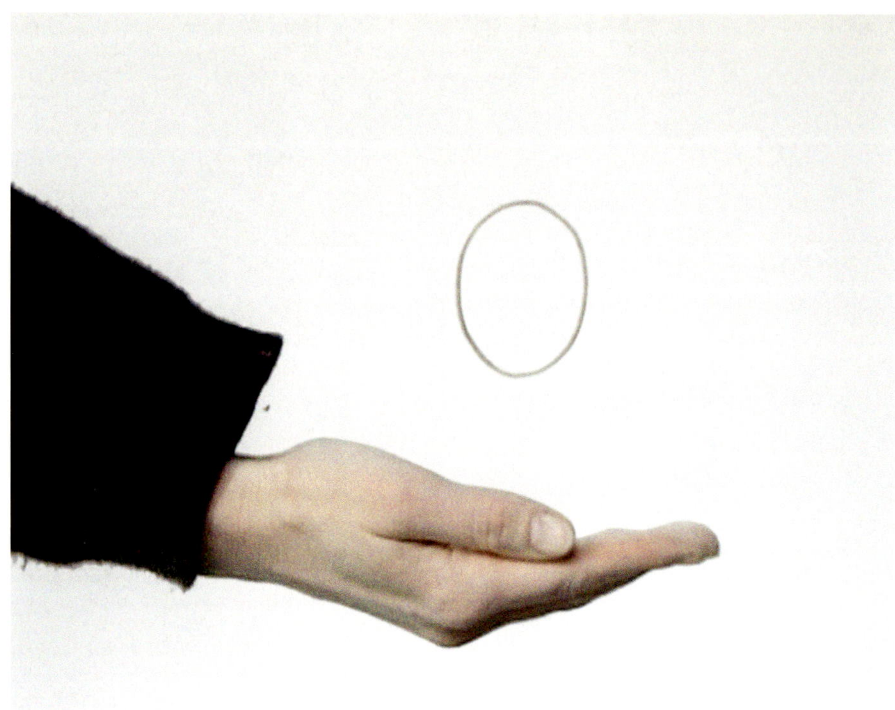

Alia Syed's experimental film *Priya* (2008), on the Kathak dancer Priya Pawar,[143] is in the same vein: Syed buried the film stock in her backyard compost, accepting the traces left on the emulsion by the earth, and by the chinagraph editing pencil, as part of the filmmaking process. The work in this way acquired a sense of extreme fluidity between the subject matter of ecstatic dance and the physical interactions that had gone into the filmmaking. The use of aerial perspective augments this confluence of subject and support. The moving picture of Pawar corresponds in subtle yet mesmerizing ways to the earlier one of Loie Fuller, both dancers swirling away in a long lineage, spiraling and inspiring.

In Edith Dekyndt's videos *Slow Object 04* (1997; plate 123), *A Is Hotter Than B* (2005), and *XY 02* (2008), and in the works of Zilvinas Kempinas that float magnetic tape over fans (plate 217), the suspension of line becomes literal. Dekyndt's lines consist of volatile substances, without fixed contour and therefore aligned with nonform. They point to notions of the indeterminate, the impermanent, the dissolving. In the work on paper *Drawing 003* (2009; plate 122), line is extended to its own extinction, being layered obsessively until the whole page is filled, confusing line and support. Kempinas's use of unspooled videotape as a hovering line that blowing fans keep in constant movement, the alternation between the thin edge and the wide edge of the tape creating a vibrant, disorienting flicker and dancing, Kandinsky-like silhouettes, seems to evoke the early-twentieth-century notion of "on line" as well as the late-twentieth-century "on line."

The practices of these artists allow us to formulate a vision of art as an experience premised not on a perpetuation of alienation and violence in twenty-first century society but on reciprocity and transitivity. Their drawing is rooted in the idea of working through traces coming from others to whom the artist is linked. We could describe it as a kind of intersubjective encounter, with line as the connector confirming the interdependency of all. Line, however, does not of itself constitute this kind of relation. It may have come to stand for the dynamically streaming activities of the Internet — for what is a web but line? — but it does so just metaphorically. As Gego wrote of the play of lines (which she called *un trabajo meditativo*, a meditative work), "I discovered the charm of the line in and of itself—the line in space as well as the line drawn on a surface, and the nothing between the lines and the sparkling when they cross, when they are interrupted, when they are of different colors or different types. I discovered that sometimes the in-between-lines is as important as the line by itself."[144] Relation is indeed about the

123. Edith Dekyndt
(Belgian, born 1960)
Slow Object 04. 1997
DVD projection, color, silent, 9:15-minute loop

124. A. Balasubramaniam
(Indian, born 1971)
Link. 2009
String, hook, and magnet
71 x 71 x 52˝ (180.3 x 180.3 x 132), dimensions variable

spaces between the lines, the "in-between-lines" — the background, which, more than line, constitutes our being and becoming, our relation to each other. As Craigie Horsfield insists, "The background is not the void but is the coming into being and the dynamics of relation."[145]

The path of line through the twentieth century was instrumental in tracing these shifts of understanding, both interpersonally and in terms of a wider cultural behavior. The line's venture into space, into the real, allowed it to break with convention and speak freely, but also brought a separation from the background, the support, and at the same time from imaginary space, without which it is impossible to think the world anew. The return to the support as relational brought a return to imaginary space as coexistent with real space. In the words of Badiou,

The paper is just as much drawn as mark is drawn.

— Richard Tuttle, 1990

> That is exactly the problem of drawing. In one sense, the paper exists, as a material support, as a closed totality; and the marks, or the lines, do not exist by themselves; they have to compose something inside the paper. But in another and more crucial sense, the paper as background does not exist, because it is created as such, as an open surface, by the marks. It is that sort of movable reciprocity between existence and inexistence, which constitutes the very essence of drawing. The question of drawing is very different from the question in Hamlet. It is not "to be or not to be," it is "to be and not to be." And that is the reason for the fundamental fragility (and femininity) of drawing: not a clear alternative, to be or not to be, but an obscure and paradoxical conjunction, to be and not to be. Or, as Deleuze would say: a disjunctive synthesis.[146]

Once the relation of line and support is reconfigured, once they are seen as constituting a space of interdependency, line that had been separated and independent recovers its reciprocity. For some contemporary artists it is the computer (as in Arturo Herrera's *Walk/14 Parts*, 2009; plate 215), with its enormous possibilities for connection and interrelation over the Web, that now has become a primary medium. The emotive cooling of line itself in the 1960s and '70s has now transformed: line has become a moving trace in time and space, stressing interreliance and transsubjectivity. The Timeline of the twentieth century has morphed into the Web lines of the twenty-first.

FROM SURFACE TENSION TO LINE EXTENSION TO CONFLUENCE

On Line focuses on convergences in drawing practices over the course of the twentieth century and draws on the interconnections between those works across cultures and geographies. It is not a linear chronology, suggesting a retrospectively inevitable continuity, but rather evokes a spiraling sense of concurrent thought, understanding, exploration, and invention.

Although this intertwining of conversations is informed by not only the past but the contemporary, it cannot be considered an encyclopedia of the present moment; some lines are inevitably missing. Yet *On Line* seeks to represent varied impulses by being inclusive, by enlarging the expected scope of its project as widely as possible. It neither embraces the model of the individual genius, nor attempts to establish a new canon different only by being more heterogeneous, nor presents an overview of those necessary inclusions without which it would be radically incomplete. Instead, it follows lines of sympathy, confluence, and sometimes common goals within a dynamic history. By inference, the exhibition and book index the possibility of opening other lines of inquiry that might illumine the present — work from the past that would take new meaning in a changing world.

To think through the remarkable convergences in the exploration of line across time and space, we have traced dialogic connections among artists on both a generational and an intergenerational basis. These connecting tissues are the project's guiding principle. They are clearly sustained in part through actual relationships, whether of friendship, acquaintance, shared purpose, or chance encounter, but they are also graphically apparent in the artists' materials, in *our* material: the line, the grid, the web. The project may be imagined as a skein of threads to be woven together; and from this coming web, some threads are drawn out to find new meaning while others remain loose, their meanings fugitive, still to be formed. The reweaving of these lines constitutes a shaping and interpreting of history. The meanings we seek concern an understanding of the world through relation and connection, and the new patterns we discern belong to the past, certainly, but most of all to the present. We cannot attach ourselves to ossified, fixed structures that confirm only established reputations, condemning the significance of others to obscurity, when relationships are always, necessarily, in flux.

Coincident with this thinking of the world and its history as an interweaving is the work of many women artists. This is no essentialist claim for women's work but an acknowledgment of a profound shift, reflected in the exhibition through the predominance of work by men at the show's chronological beginning and of work by women at the end, their activities in fact giving rise to the very notions that structure the entire project. Indeed, contemporary women's work, in fascinating and various ways, often corresponds to a contemporary sense of weaving or knitting together materials, ideas, conceptions, sensibilities. Our attention to the role of women's work in the transformation of drawing opens up to many forms of expression, in terms not just of materials, or of the use of the body in dance and other forms of action, but of a sense of fluency, physicality, collision, of ideas and creation in their coinciding. Many women work with line not as separation but as connection. In turn, this approach ties in with ideas about networks, interconnections, interdependencies — notions currently ever more prominent as we try to take account of changes in society at large. In following this move of line to grid and then to web, our ultimate interest in this project is present perception. When Kandinsky wrote "On Line," in the early twentieth century, he and his contemporaries believed in the power of line to transform society. They could hardly have imagined how line would indeed bring this change about, empowering and constructing the new reality of an online society at the end of the century.

Like all curatorial practice, *On Line* has involved the exercise of judgment, but the aim in doing so has not been to take a definitive position but to build a nexus of attention and to be conscious of potential consequence. A survey like this one can never be exhaustive and should not attempt an authoritative, determining voice. Following no single line across the century, it instead examines the interconnections of numerous lines and their constitution of networks of meaning. We hope that it encourages others to develop alternative connections and readings. In this, we as viewers advance meanings into a new web of attention, sharing in the making of consequence together with the artists whose work is shown here.

NOTES

1. The definition of the verb "to draw" in its various senses is taken from the *Oxford English Dictionary.*

2. See Dirk Lauwaert, "The Mark and the Void," in *De betekenis van het tekenen* (Bussum: Uitgeverij Thoth/Rijksakademie van beeldende kunsten, 1995), p. 63.

3. Vasily Kandinsky, "Little Articles on Big Questions: On Line," 1919, reprinted and trans. in *Kandinsky: Complete Writings on Art*, ed. Kenneth C. Lindsay and Peter Vergo, 1982 (reprint ed. Cambridge, Mass.: Da Capo Press, 1994), pp. 424–27.

4. Within two years, however, in *Interventionist Demonstration* (1914), Carlo Carrà would apply the Cubist fragmentation of traditional perceptual space to the suggestion of kinesthesia, through "a visual dynamic set up by the collage's construction as both a vortex and a matrix of crisscrossing power lines set as mutually counter-active diagonals." Benjamin H. D. Buchloh and Rosalind Krauss, in Hal Foster, Krauss, Yve-Alain Bois, and Buchloh, *Art since 1900* (London: Thames & Hudson, 2004), p. 95.

5. Bernice Rose, *Picasso, Braque and Early Film in Cubism* (New York: Pace Wildenstein, 2007), p. 41.

6. Krauss, in Foster, Krauss, Bois, and Buchloh, *Art since 1900*, p. 107.

7. See ibid., p. 112.

8. In 1914, Marcel Duchamp realized *Network of Stoppages* (plate 143), taking up an earlier painting of his and overlaying its surface with diagrammatic lines using the templates from *3 Standard Stoppages*.

9. Duchamp, quoted in T. J. Demos, *The Exiles of Marcel Duchamp* (Cambridge, Mass.: The MIT Press, 2007), p. 68.

10. See Demos, in ibid., pp. 76–77.

11. Roman Jakobson, quoted in ibid., p. 78.

12. Conservation studies show clear traces of Arp adjusting the placement of the squares. Beginning in 1930, however, the Surrealists embraced the idea that he had made his works of this kind by chance, as later did Alfred H. Barr, Jr., who seems to have supplied the title phrase "squares arranged according to the laws of chance" when he showed the work at The Museum of Modern Art in 1936; there is no earlier record of it. Anne Umland writes of this work that it "may be as much a visual sign, a carefully composed representation, of the aleatory as the product of chance itself." See her entry on this and a related work in Umland and Adrian Sudhalter, *Dada in the Collection of The Museum of Modern Art* (New York: The Museum of Modern Art, 2008), pp. 44–49, and Scott Gerson's "Conservation Notes" in the same entry. In an email during the production of the present volume, Umland adds that she has no reason to believe Arp knew Duchamp's *3 Standard Stoppages* when he made the "chance" collages in 1916–17.

13. Arp, quoted by Foster and Krauss, in Foster, Krauss, Bois, and Buchloh, *Art since 1900*, p. 137.

14. See ibid.

15. Foster, in ibid., p. 121.

16. Bois, in ibid., p. 131. Jakobson underlined the fact that the sign and the object it signifies are not coidentical, "because without contradiction there is no mobility of concepts, no mobility of signs, and the relationship between concept and sign becomes automatized."

17. Ibid.

18. Krauss, in ibid., p. 112.

19. Paul Klee, "Creative Credo," reprinted in *Paul Klee Notebooks*, vol. 1, *The Thinking Eye*, ed. Jurg Spiller (London: Lund Humphries, 1961), p. 79.

20. Klee, "Contributions to a theory of pictorial form: lecture notes from the Bauhaus at Weimar and at Dessau," 1921, reprinted in ibid., p. 103.

21. Kandinsky, "Program for the Institute of Artistic Culture," in *Kandinsky: Complete Writings on Art*, p. 459.

22. Kandinsky, *Point and Line to Plane*, trans. Howard Dearstyne and Hilla Rebay, ed. Rebay (New York: Solomon R. Guggenheim Foundation for the Museum of Non-Objective Painting, 1947, reprint ed. New York: Dover, 1979), pp. 57–58. First published in the Bauhausbücher series as *Punkt und Linie zu Fläche* (Munich: Albert Langen, 1926).

23. Ibid., pp. 42, 100. Closer to our own time, Merce Cunningham titled one of his performances *Points in Space* (1986).

24. Ibid., p. 68.

25. Lindsay and Vergo, headnote to Kandinsky, "Little Articles on Big Questions," in *Kandinsky: Complete Writings on Art*, p. 422.

26. Aleksandr Rodchenko, "The Dynamism of Planes," 1918, in *Aleksandr Rodchenko. Experiments for the Future: Diaries, Essays, Letters, and Other Writings*, ed. and with a preface by Alexander N. Lavrentiev. trans. Jamey Gambrell (New York: The Museum of Modern Art, 2005), p. 83.

27. Rodchenko, "The Line," 1921, in ibid., p. 113.

28. Lyubov Popova, quoted in Margarita Tupitsyn, "Being-in-Production: The Constructivist Code," in Tupitsyn, ed., *Rodchenko & Popova: Defining Constructivism* (London: Tate Publishing, 2009), p. 19.

29. Rodchenko, "The Line," p. 114.

30. Rodchenko, "The Line," 1921, in Richard Andrews and Milena Kalinovska, eds., *Art into Life: Russian Constructivism 1914–1932*, trans. James West (Seattle: Henry Art Gallery, University of Washington, and New York: Rizzoli, 1990), p. 72.

31. Ibid., p. 73.

32. Briony Fer, "What's in a Line? Gender and Modernity," in *Oxford Art Journal* 13, no 1 (1990):80.

33. Ibid., p. 81.

34. Kazimir Malevich, quoted in Patricia Railing, "The Cognitive Line in Russian Avant-Garde Art," in *Leonardo* 31, no 1 (1998):69–70.

35. André Breton, "The First Surrealist Manifesto," 1924, in, e.g., Charles Harrison and Paul Wood, eds., *Art in*

Theory 1900–2000: An Anthology of Changing Ideas (Oxford: Blackwell Publishing, 1992), p. 452.
36. See Catherine de Zegher, "Abstract," in *3 x Abstraction. New Methods of Drawing: Hilma af Klint, Emma Kunz, and Agnes Martin* (New York: The Drawing Center, and New Haven: Yale University Press, 2005), p. 26.
37. Umland, *Joan Miró: Painting Anti-Painting (1927–1937)* (New York: The Museum of Modern Art, 2008), p. 44.
38. Miró, quoted in ibid.
39. Umland, in ibid., p. 47.
40. Alexander Calder, quoted in Alexander S. C. Rower, "Chronology," in Joan Simon and Brigitte Leal, *Alexander Calder: The Paris Years (1926–1933)* (New York: Whitney Museum of American Art, and Paris: Centre Pompidou, 2009), p. 270.
41. Simon, "Alexander Calder: The Paris Years," in ibid., p. 26.
42. James Johnson Sweeney, *Alexander Calder* (New York: The Museum of Modern Art, 1951), p. 120.
43. Georges Roque, "Writing/Drawing/Color," in *Yale French Studies* no. 84, *Boundaries: Writing and Drawing*, ed. Martine Reid (December 1993):60.
44. Duchamp, "The Creative Act," 1957, in, e.g., Kristine Stiles and Peter Selz, eds., *Theories and Documents of Contemporary Art: A Sourcebook of Artists' Writings* (Berkeley, Los Angeles, and London: University of California Press, 1996), p. 818.
45. Duchamp, quoted in Demos, *The Exiles of Marcel Duchamp*, p. 226.
46. See Demos, *The Exiles of Marcel Duchamp*, pp. 198, 218, 241.
47. Georges Vantongerloo, letter to Max Bill, April 12, 1945, quoted in Jan Ceuleers, *Georges Vantongerloo 1886–1965* (Antwerp: Pandora and Ronny Van de Velde, 1996), p. 156.
48. Ibid.
49. Vantongerloo, "Paintings," 1948, quoted in ibid., pp. 163–64.
50. Vantongerloo, letter to Bill, July 11, 1958, in ibid., p. 172.
51. Vantongerloo, "Reflections," *De Stijl* 1, no. 9 (1918):97–98, as reprinted in Bois, Guy Brett, Guitemie Maldonado, et al., *Georges Vantongerloo: A Longing for Infinity* (Madrid: Museo Nacional Centro de Arte Reina Sofía, 2009), p. 73.
52. Vantongerloo, letter to Bill, July 17, 1951, in Ceuleers, *Georges Vantongerloo 1886–1965*, p. 178.
53. Lucio Fontana, quoted in Sarah Whitfield, *Lucio Fontana* (London: Hayward Gallery Publishing, 1999), p. 14.
54. Mondrian, quoted in Bois, in Foster, Krauss, Bois, and Buchloh, *Art since 1900*, p. 308.
55. Krauss, in ibid., p. 357.
56. Ibid., p. 356.
57. In 1948, acting on a spur-of-the-moment invitation from Jean-Paul Riopelle, Françoise Sullivan created an improvisational dance performance on the slopes of Mont Saint-Hilaire, Quebec, recorded in a now-lost film by Riopelle and in surviving still photographs by Maurice Perron.
58. See Krauss, in Foster, Krauss, Bois, and Buchloh, *Art since 1900*, pp. 368–72.
59. See Hanni Ossott, *Gego* (Caracas: Museo de Arte Contemporaneo, 1977).
60. Lygia Clark, quoted in Guy Brett, "Lygia Clark: The Borderline between Art and Life," in *Third Text* 1 (Autumn 1987):67.
61. Suely Rolnik, "Molding a Contemporary Soul: The Empty-Full of Lygia Clark," in Rina Carvajal and Alma Ruiz, *The Experimental Exercise of Freedom: Lygia Clark, Gego, Mathias Goeritz, Hélio Oiticica, Mira Schendel* (Los Angeles: Museum of Contemporary Art, 1999), p. 72.
62. Ibid.
63. Luciano Fabro, quoted on the Web site of the Museo d'Arte Contemporanea Donna Regina (MADRE), Naples: http://www.museomadre.it/opere.cfm?id=46.
64. Rose, *Drawing Now* (New York: The Museum of Modern Art, 1976), p. 14.
65. Ibid., p. 13.
66. Robert Ryman, conversation with the author, 2005.
67. Lucy R. Lippard, *Eva Hesse*, 1976 (reprint ed. Cambridge, Mass.: Da Capo Press, 1992), p. 9.
68. See de Zegher, "Drawing as Binding/Bandage/Bondage or Eva Hesse Caught in the Triangle of Process/Content/Materiality," in *Eva Hesse Drawing* (New York: The Drawing Center, and New Haven: Yale University Press, 2006).
69. Eva Hesse, in an interview with Cindy Nemser, in Ellen H. Johnson, ed., *American Artists on Art from 1940 to 1980* (Boulder: Westview, 1982), p. 193.
70. See de Zegher, "Drawing as Binding/Bandage/Bondage," p. 91.
71. Hesse, quoted in Lippard, *Eva Hesse*, p. 148.
72. Cecilia Vicuña, conversation with the author, 1998.
73. Anna Maria Maiolino, conversation with the author, 1999.
74. Maiolino, quoted in de Zegher, "Ciao Bella: The Ins and Outs of a Migrant," in *Anna Maria Maiolino, Vida Afora/A Life Line* (New York: The Drawing Center, 2002), p. 84.
75. See ibid., p. 98.
76. See Bracha Ettinger, *The Matrixial Gaze* (Leeds: University of Leeds, 1995), *Artworking: 1985–1999* (Brussels: Ludion/Palais des Beaux Arts, 2000), and *Bracha Lichtenberg Ettinger: The Eurydice Series*, Drawing Papers 24 (New York: The Drawing Center, 2000).
77. Richard Shiff, "It Shows," in Madeleine Grynsztejn, *The Art of Richard Tuttle* (San Francisco: San Francisco Museum of Modern Art, 2005), p. 265.
78. "J'ai choisi le fil de crin pour son côté linéaire, son acuité, son ombre." Pierrette Bloch, quoted in Philippe Chabert, "Pierrette Bloch, de fil en fil," *Pierrette Bloch. Mailles, collages et fils de crin* (Troyes: Musée d'art moderne de Troyes, 1987), n.p.
79. Richard Tuttle, quoted in Cornelia H. Butler, "Kinesthetic Drawing," in Grynsztejn, *The Art of Richard Tuttle*, p. 176.
80. Tuttle, quoted in Shiff, "It Shows," p. 265. See also Shiff's note 46, referring to an interview with Tuttle by Sylvie Coudrec (October 1986) in Jean-Louis Froment, ed., *Richard Tuttle: Wire Pieces* (Bordeaux: CAPC Musée d'art contemporain de Bordeaux, 1987), p. 39.
81. Tuttle, quoted in ibid., p. 263.
82. Hesse, quoted in Lippard, *Eva Hesse*, p. 131.
83. Shiff, "It Shows," p. 265.
84. Ibid., p. 255.
85. Tuttle, quoted in ibid., p. 263.
86. Karel Malich, quoted in Jirí Ševcík, "Turbulence," in *Karel Malich: Wires* (Prague: The Research Center of the Academy of Fine Arts, 2005), pp. 8, 13.
87. Ibid., p. 15.
88. See Ševcík, in ibid., pp. 8–15.
89. Ibid., p. 12.
90. Buchloh, "Hesse's Endgame: Facing the Diagram," in *Eva Hesse Drawing*, ed. de Zegher (New York: The Drawing Center, and New Haven: Yale University Press, 2006), p. 117.
91. Krauss, *The Originality of the Avant-Garde and Other Modernist Myths* (Cambridge, Mass.: The MIT Press, 1986), p. 10.
92. Luciano Fabro, quoted on the Web site of the Museo d'Arte Contemporanea Donna Regina (MADRE), Naples: http://www.museomadre.it/opere.cfm?id=143.
93. Krauss, *The Originality of the Avant-Garde*, p. 12.
94. Ibid., p. 18.
95. Ibid., pp. 18–19.
96. Krauss, "The /Cloud/," in Barbara Haskell, Anna Chave, and Krauss, *Agnes Martin* (New York: Whitney Museum of American Art, 1992), p. 159.
97. Martin, quoted in Haskell, "Agnes Martin: The Awareness of Perfection," in ibid., p. 102.
98. Nasreen Mohamedi, quoted in Susette Min, "Nasreen Mohamedi: Lines among Lines," *Drawing Papers* no. 52 (New York: The Drawing Center, 2005).
99. Lourdes Blanco, *Gego: Reticulárea* (Caracas: Ediciones de la Galeria Conkright, 1969), quoted in Mónica Amor, "Another Geometry: Gego's

Reticulárea, 1969–1982," *October* 113 (Summer 2005):107.
100. Roberto Guevara, "Reticulárea de Gego," *El Nacional* (Caracas), June 10, 1969, quoted in ibid., p. 114.
101. The Avatamsaka Sutra, in Francis H. Cook, *Hua-yen Buddhism: The Jewel Net of Indra* (University Park: The Pennsylvania State University Press, 1977), p. 2.
102. Thich Nhat Hanh, *The Heart of Understanding: Commentaries on the Prajnaparamita Heart Sutra* (Berkeley: Parallax Press, 1988), p. 3.
103. See David Loy, "Indra's Postmodern Net," *Philosophy East and West* 43, no. 3 (July 1993):489–90.
104. See Gilles Deleuze, *Pourparlers* (Paris: Les Editions de Minuit, 1997), p. 219. Translated from the French by the author. The text was originally a conversation between Deleuze and Robert Maggiori, published in the French newspaper *Libération* in 1990.
105. Anne Teresa De Keersmaeker, conversation with the author, 2009.
106. Cildo Meireles, in Guy Brett, ed., *Cildo Meireles* (London: Tate Publishing, 2008), p. 90.
107. Mona Hatoum, in Chiara Bertola, ed., *Interior Landscape* (Milan: Edizioni Charta, 2009), p. 25.
108. Ellen Gallagher, quoted in Judith Wilson, "Elephant Bones: The Poetics of Race in the Art of Ellen Gallagher," in *Callaloo* 19, no. 2 (Spring 1996):337.
109. Wilson, in ibid., p. 339.
110. "Situationist International: Definitions," 1958, reprinted in, e.g., Stiles and Selz, eds., *Theories and Documents of Contemporary Art*, p. 703.
111. See Foster, in Foster, Krauss, Bois, and Buchloh, *Art since 1900*, p. 393.
112. Buchloh, "Villeglé: From Fragment to Detail," 1991, in *Neo-Avantgarde and Culture Industry: Essays on European and American Art from 1955 to 1975* (Cambridge, Mass.: The MIT Press, 2000), pp. 451, 454.
113. Ibid., p. 453.
114. Ibid., p. 446.
115. Robert Carleton Hobbs, *Mark Lombardi. Global Networks* (New York: Independent Curators International, 2003), pp. 14, 19.
116. Rose, *Drawing Now*, p. 10.
117. John Knight, for example, has planned a work mapping the lines of aircraft flights in the sky above San Diego and Los Angeles.
118. See Rex Butler, "Emily Kame Kngwarreye and the Undeconstructible Space of Justice," in Jason Gaiger and Paul Wood, eds., *Art of the Twentieth Century: A Reader* (New Haven: Yale University Press, in association with The Open University, 2003), pp. 304–18, and Vivien Johnson, "Desert Art," in Sylvia Kleinert, Margo Neale, and Robyne Bancroft, eds., *The Oxford Companion to Aboriginal Art and Culture* (Melbourne: Oxford University Press, 2000), pp. 211–20.
119. See Lippard, *Six Years: The Dematerialization of the Art Object from 1966 to 1972*, 1973 (reprint ed. Berkeley: University of California Press, 1997), pp. 65–66.
120. See Julia Brown with Barbara Heizer, eds., *Michael Heizer. Sculpture in Reverse* (Los Angeles: The Museum of Contemporary Art, 1984), pp. 82–83.
121. Steven Yazzie, conversation with the author, 2009. See also the artist's website, www.stevenyazzie.com/yazzie/Drawing_and_Driving_2006.html.
122. Gellman, speaking from notes in conversation with the author, 2009.
123. Ian Carr-Harris, in notes in the possession of the artist.
124. For Luis Pérez-Oramas, Léon Ferrari's *Cuadro escrito* (Written painting, 1964) "followed a period of intense focus on drawing that led him from abstraction to deformed, illegible writing, and then to the sophisticated but no less hermetic calligraphy of his written drawings." Pérez-Oramas, *Léon Ferrari and Mira Schendel: Tangled Alphabets* (New York: The Museum of Modern Art, 2009), p. 14.
125. Ibid., p. 27.
126. Vera Molnar, quoted in Vincent Baby, "Lignes et Méandres," *Vera Molnar et Julije Knifer. Lignes et méandres* (Alex, France: Fondation pour l'art contemporain Claudine et Jean-Marc Salomon, 2004), p. 14.
127. Molnar, "Inconceivable Images," in Wulf Herzogenrath and Barbara Nierhoff, eds., *Vera Molnar. Monotonie, Symétrie, Surprise* (Bremen: Der Kunstverein in Bremen, 2006), p. 31.
128. Krauss, *Line as Language: Six Artists Draw* (Princeton: The Art Museum, Princeton University, 1974), p. 6.
129. Krauss, ibid., p. 27.
130. Krauss, ibid.
131. A. Balasubramaniam, conversation with the author, November 2009.
132. Avis Newman, conversation with the author, 2008.
133. Ibid.
134. Rodchenko, "The Paths of Contemporary Photography," in *Aleksandr Rodchenko. Experiments for the Future*, p. 211, where, however, Rodchenko's Russian is translated, "In order to teach man to see from new viewpoints, it is necessary to photograph ordinary, well-known objects from completely unexpected viewpoints and in unexpected positions."
135. Julie Mehretu, "Looking Back," in *Julie Mehretu: Drawing into Painting* (Minneapolis: Walker Art Center, 2003), p. 12. "Looking Back" is an interview conducted by e-mail between Mehretu and Olukemi Ilesanmi.
136. Ibid., p. 15.
137. Ibid., p. 13.
138. See Negar Azimi, "A Deception of Sorts," in Hans Gercke and Ernest W. Uthemann, eds., *Susan Hefuna: xcultural codes* (Heidelberg: Kehrer Verlag, 2004), pp. 106–11.
139. Susan Hefuna, conversation with the author, 2010.
140. Alain Badiou, "Drawing," in *Lacanian Ink* 28 (Fall 2006):43.
141. Tuttle, statement, in *40 Tage: Zeichnunger Richard Tuttle* (Bonn: Galerie Erhard Klein, 1989), n.p.
142. Balasubramaniam, conversation with the author, November 2009.
143. "Kathak is not an exclusively Indian classical dance; instead, Muslims took a religious Hindu dance form and transformed it into a secular entertainment. It's a mix of different cultures — very syncretic." Alia Syed, in "Alia Syed: Materials for a Film," *Art Asia Pacific*, September/October 2008, p. 127.
144. Gego, "Testimony 4: You Invited Me," in *Sabiduras and Other Texts by Gego*, ed. Maria Elena Huizi and Josefina Manrique Cabrera (Houston: International Center for the Arts of the Americas, and Caracas: Fundación Gego, 2005), p. 167.
145. Craigie Horsfield, "The Translation of Souls," lecture at the symposium "Performance, Art and Anthropology," Musée du Quai Branly, Paris, March 2009.
146. Badiou, "Drawing," p. 44.

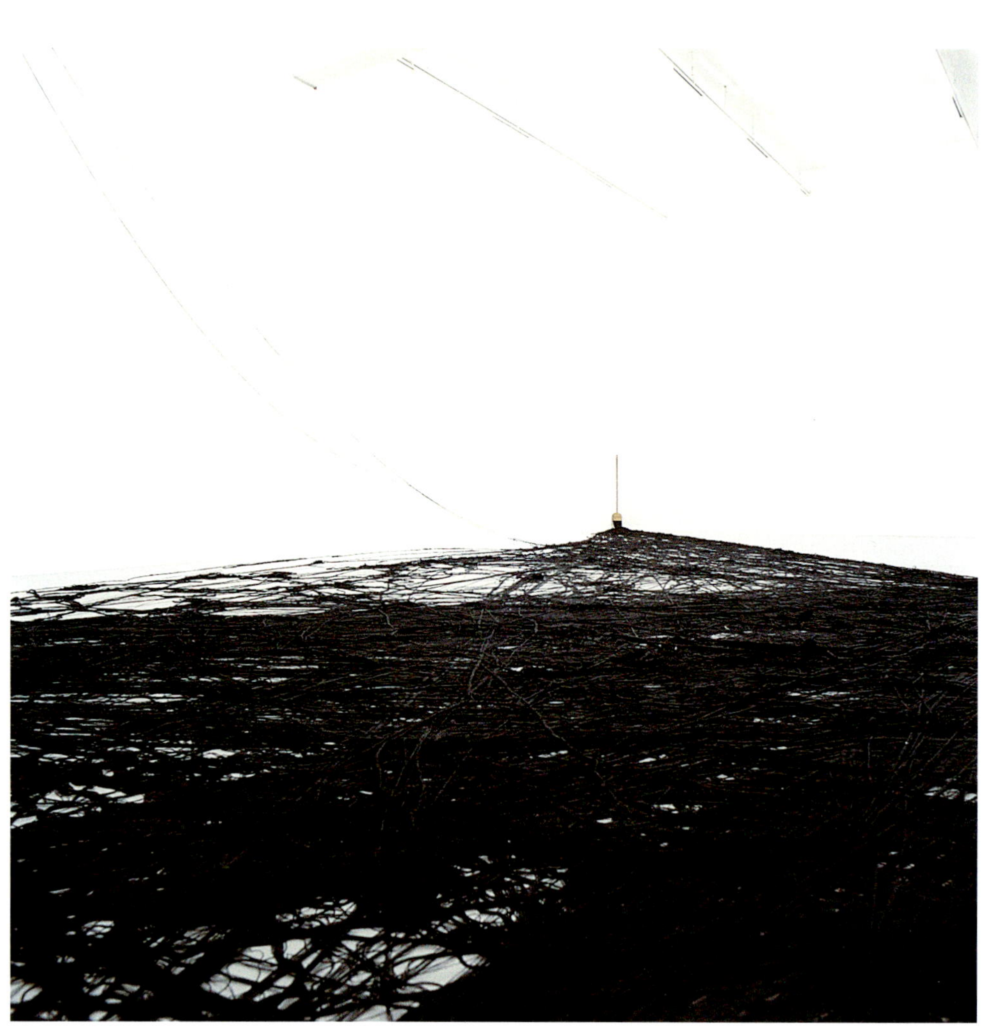

125. Cildo Meireles
(Brazilian, born 1948)
La Bruja (The witch). 1979–81
Wooden broom handle and head, cotton thread
Dimensions variable. Installation view, Kunstverein, Hamburg, 2004

LINE EXTENSION

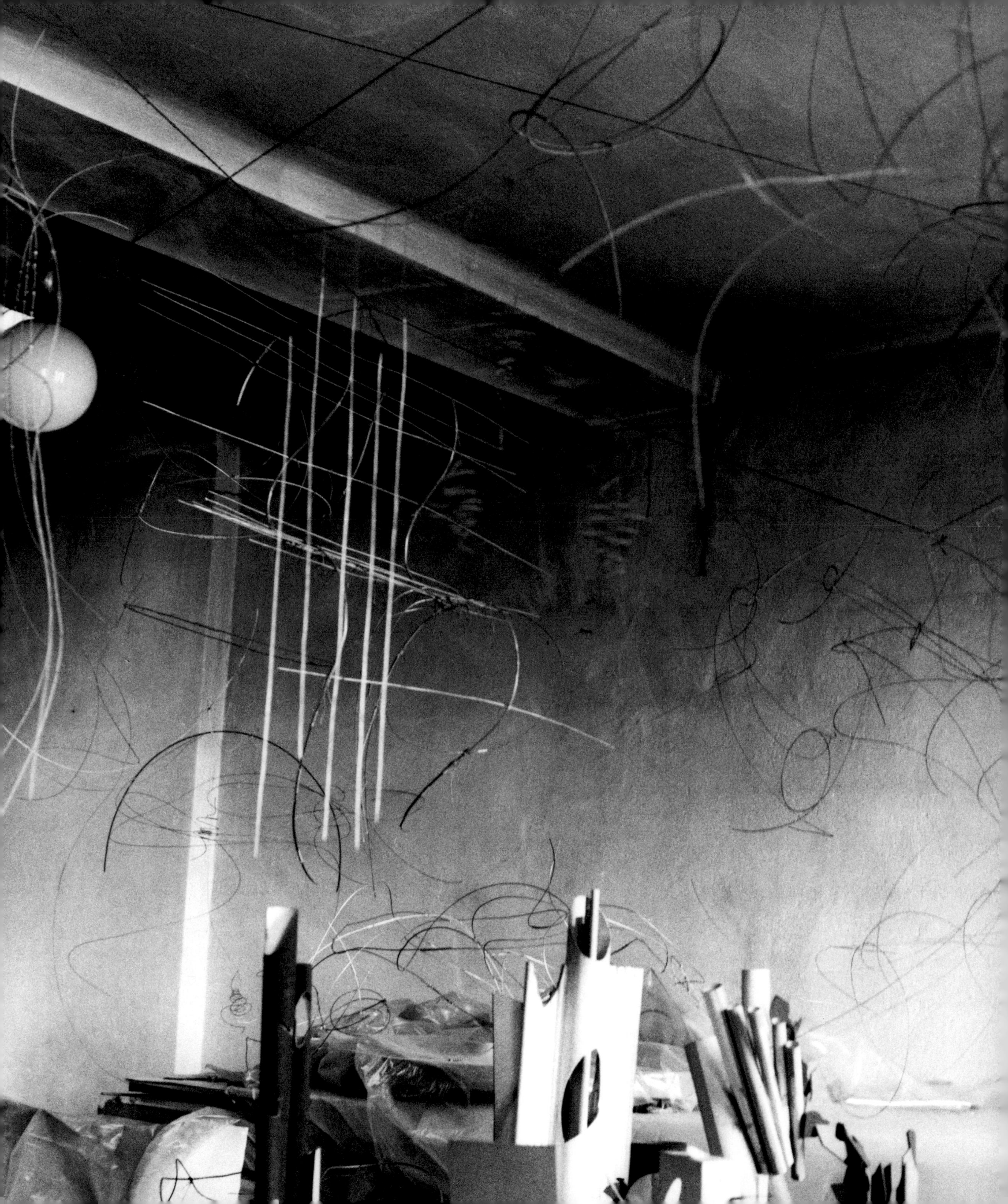

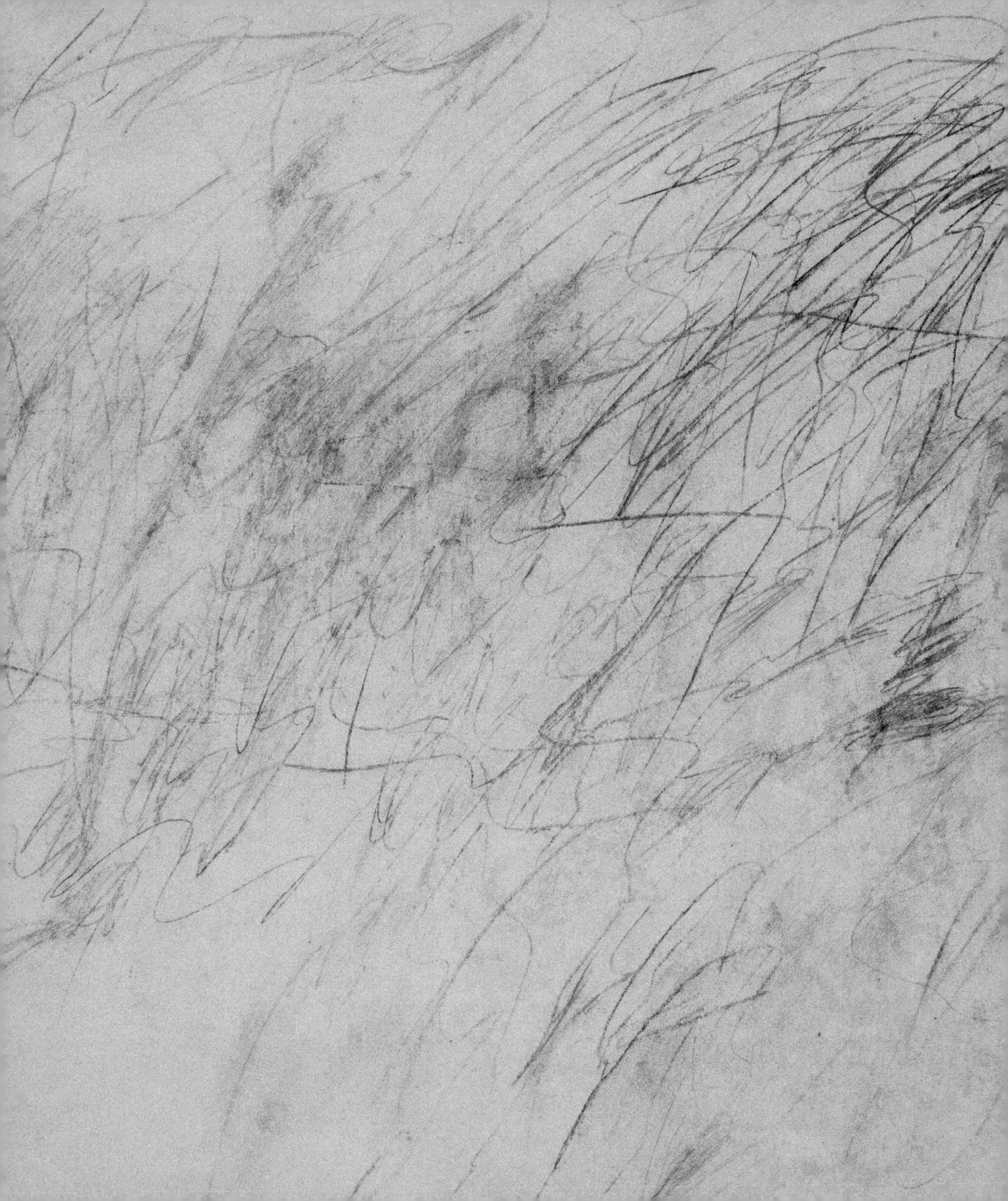

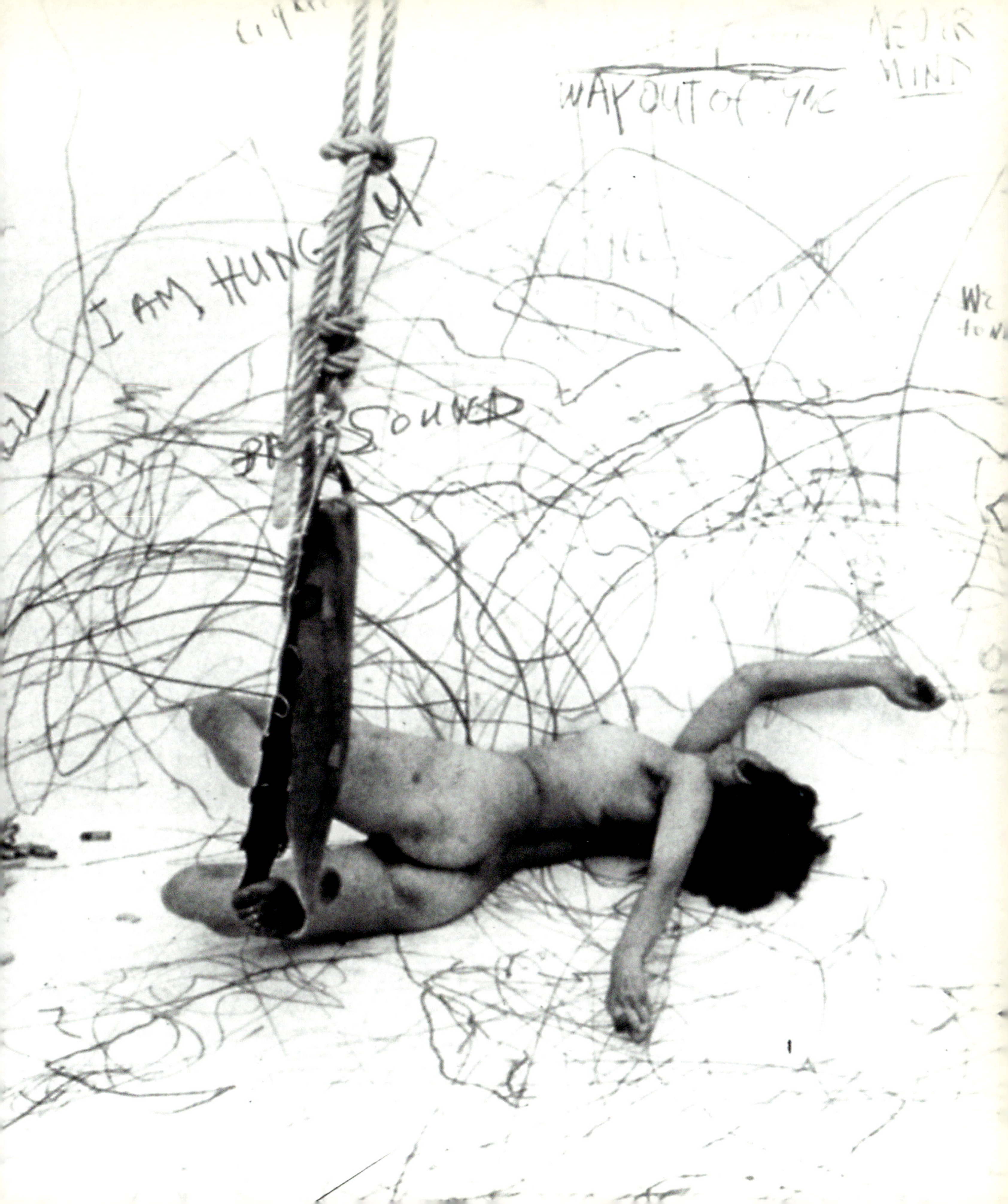
WAY OUT OF
I AM HUNG

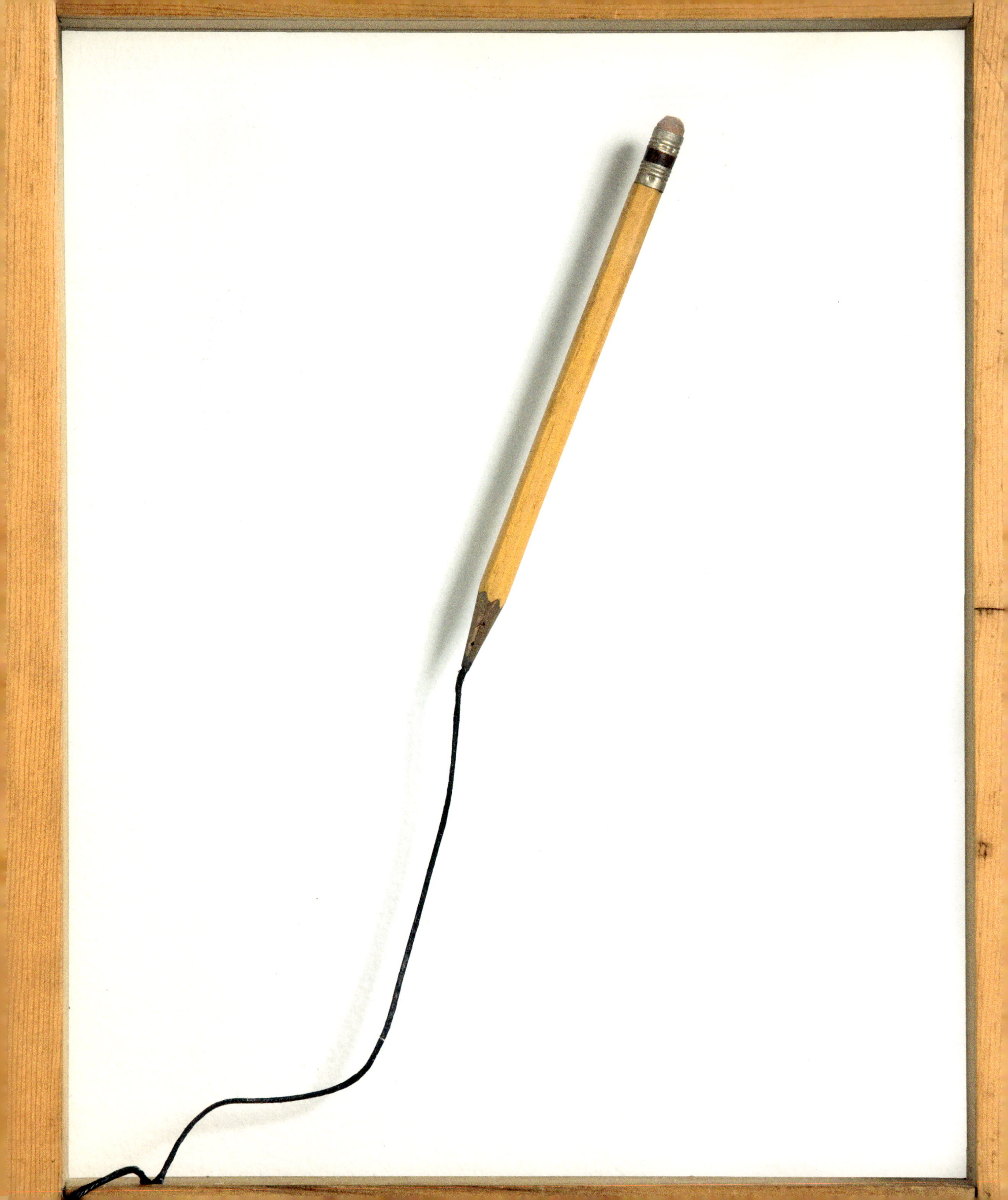

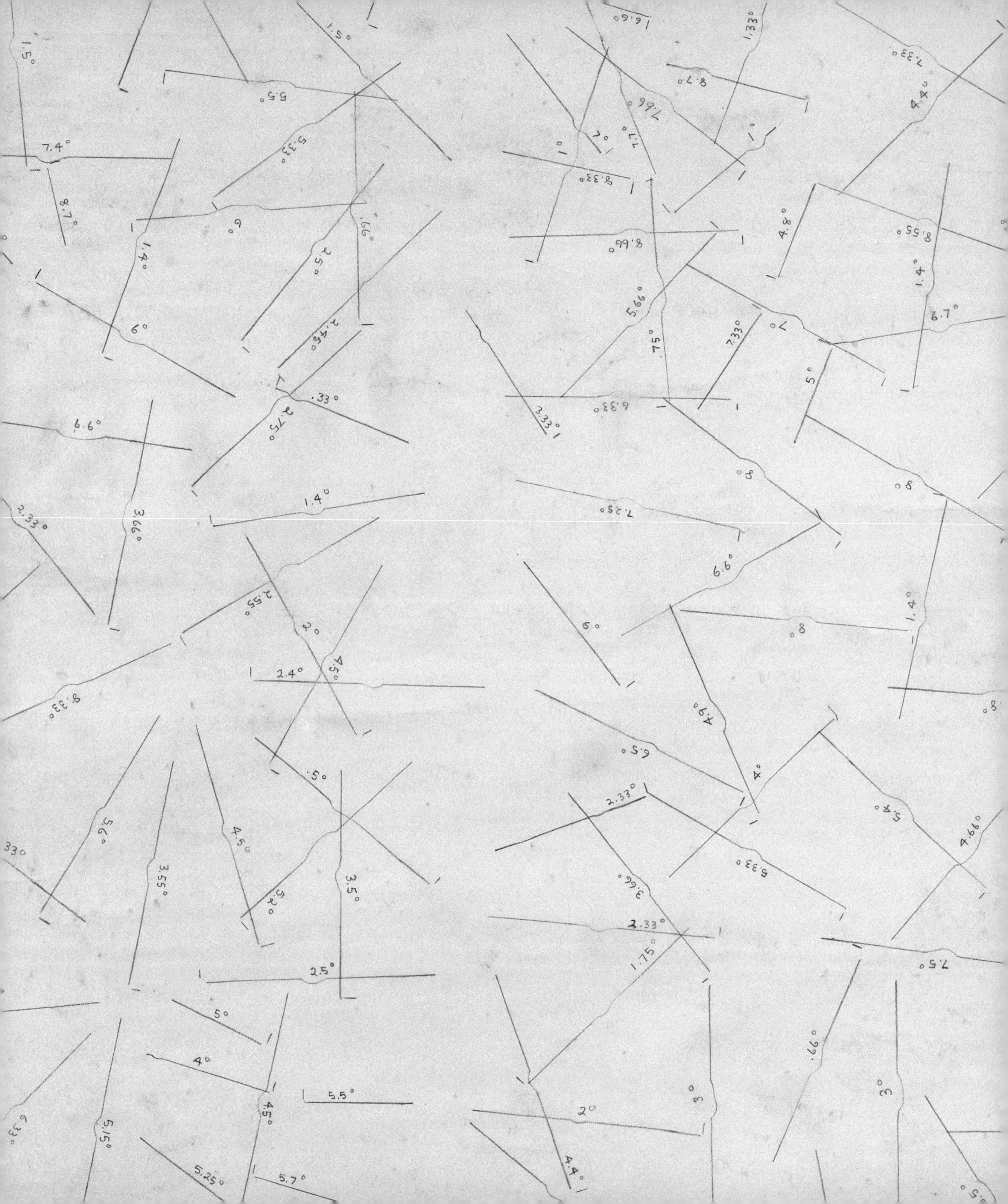

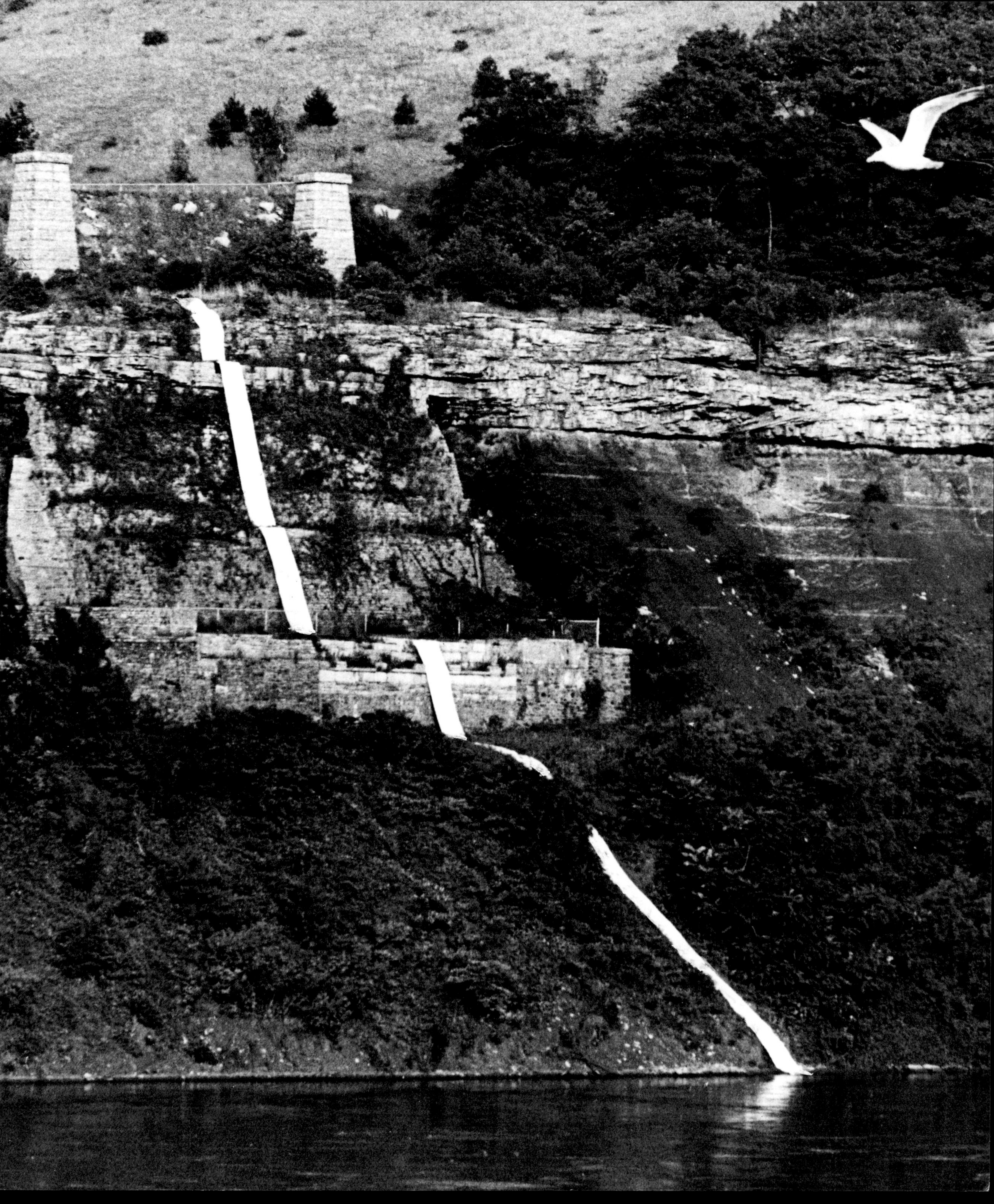

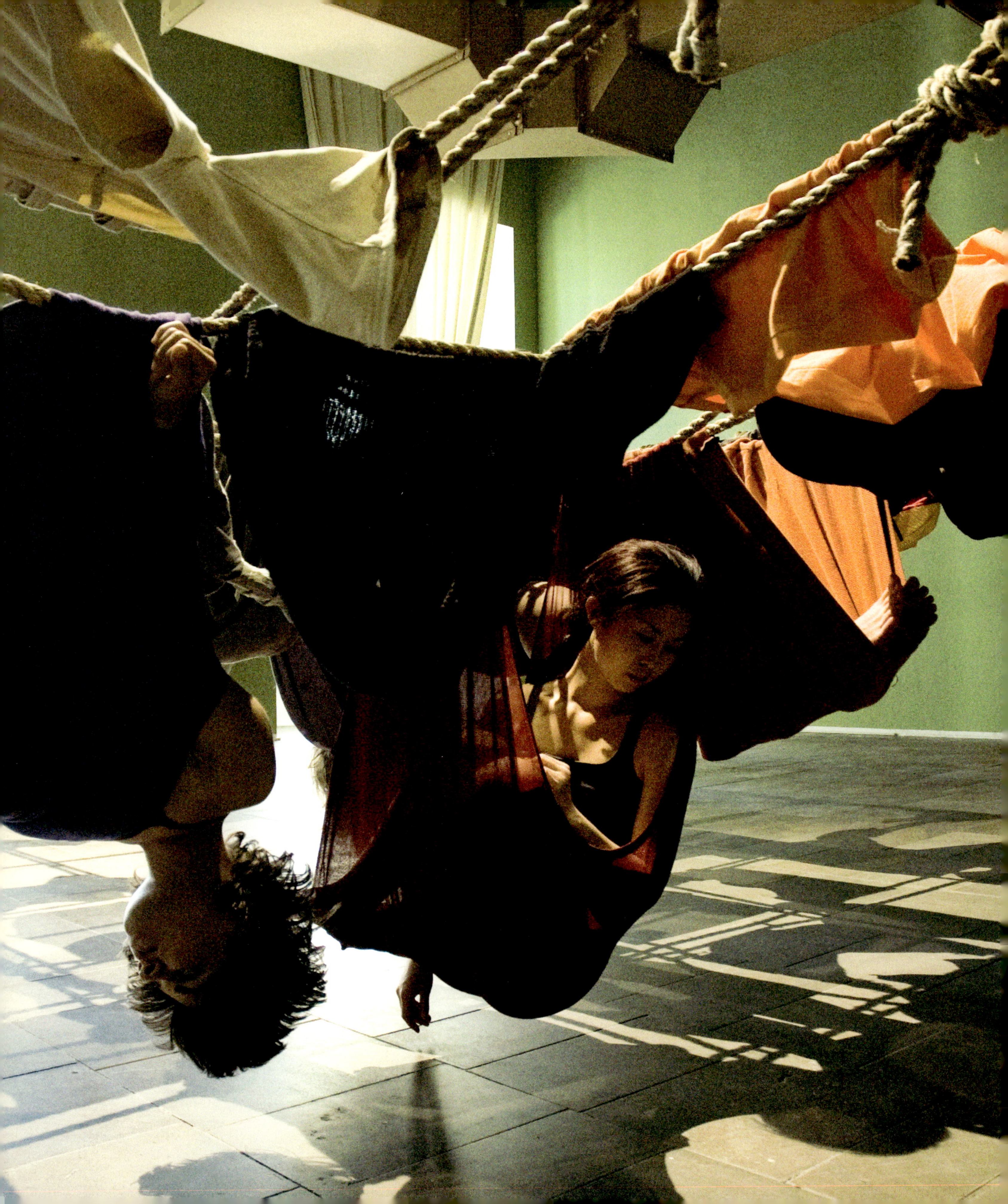

126. Studio of **Karel Malich**
(Czech, born 1924), Prague, late 1980s

127. Cy Twombly
(American, born 1928)
Untitled (detail; see p. 224). 1955
Pencil on paper
24 3/8 x 36 1/8˝ (62 x 91.7 cm)

128. Carolee Schneemann
(American, born 1939)
Up To And Including Her Limits
(see plate 211). 1973–76
Performance, with crayon on paper
and rope and harness suspended
from ceiling

129. Luis Camnitzer
(Uruguayan, born 1937)
The Instrument and Its Work
(detail; see plate 108). 1976
Wood, glass, and metal
11 13/16 x 10 1/16 x 1 15/16˝
(30 x 25.5 x 5 cm)

130. Alex Hay
(American, born 1930)
Ground Drawing (detail; see plate 141).
1968
Pencil on paper
68 1/4 x 38˝ (173.4 x 96.5 cm)

131. Anna Maria Maiolino
(Brazilian, born Italy 1942)
Entre os dois (Between the two; detail;
see p. 221) from the series *Projetos
construídos* (Constructed projects). 1972
Paper in wooden box with glass
18 7/8 x 11 13/16 x 2 3/8˝ (48 x 30 x 6 cm)

132. Michelle Stuart
(American, born 1938)
Niagara Gorge Path Relocated. 1975
Earth work on the Niagara River,
Lewiston, New York. Red Queenston
shale from gorge site rubbed on
muslin laminate
460´ x 62˝ (140.2 m x 157.5 cm)

133. Trisha Brown
(American, born 1936)
Floor of the Forest. 1970
Performance, with installation.
Shown here at Documenta XII,
Kassel, 2007

134–39. Lygia Clark
(Brazilian, 1920–1988)
Caminhando (Walking). 1963–64
Performance views

WALKAROUND TIME

DANCE AND DRAWING IN THE TWENTIETH CENTURY

Cornelia H. Butler

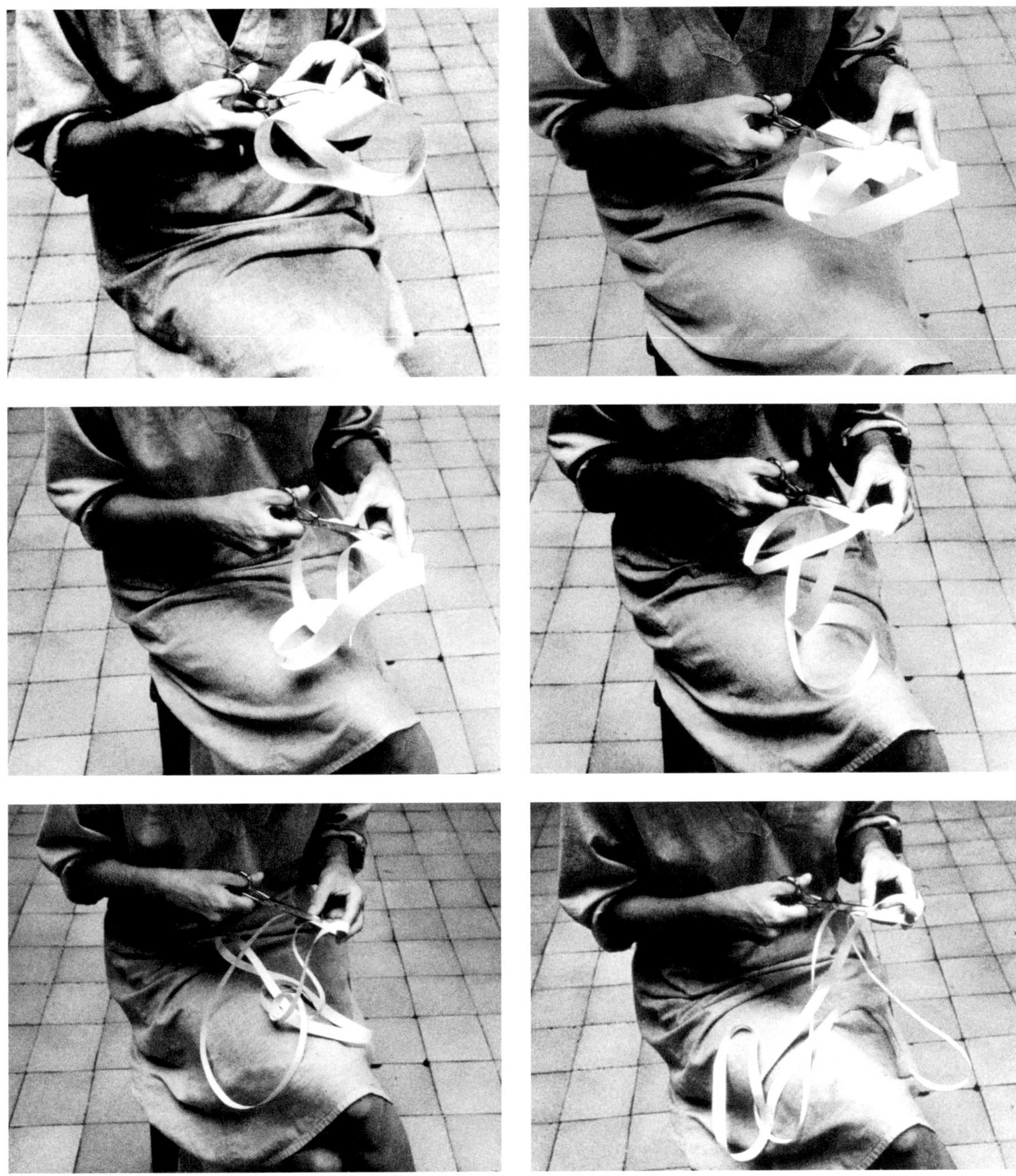

Painting is a criticism of movement, but movement is the criticism of painting.

— Octavio Paz, in a reading of Marcel Duchamp, 1968

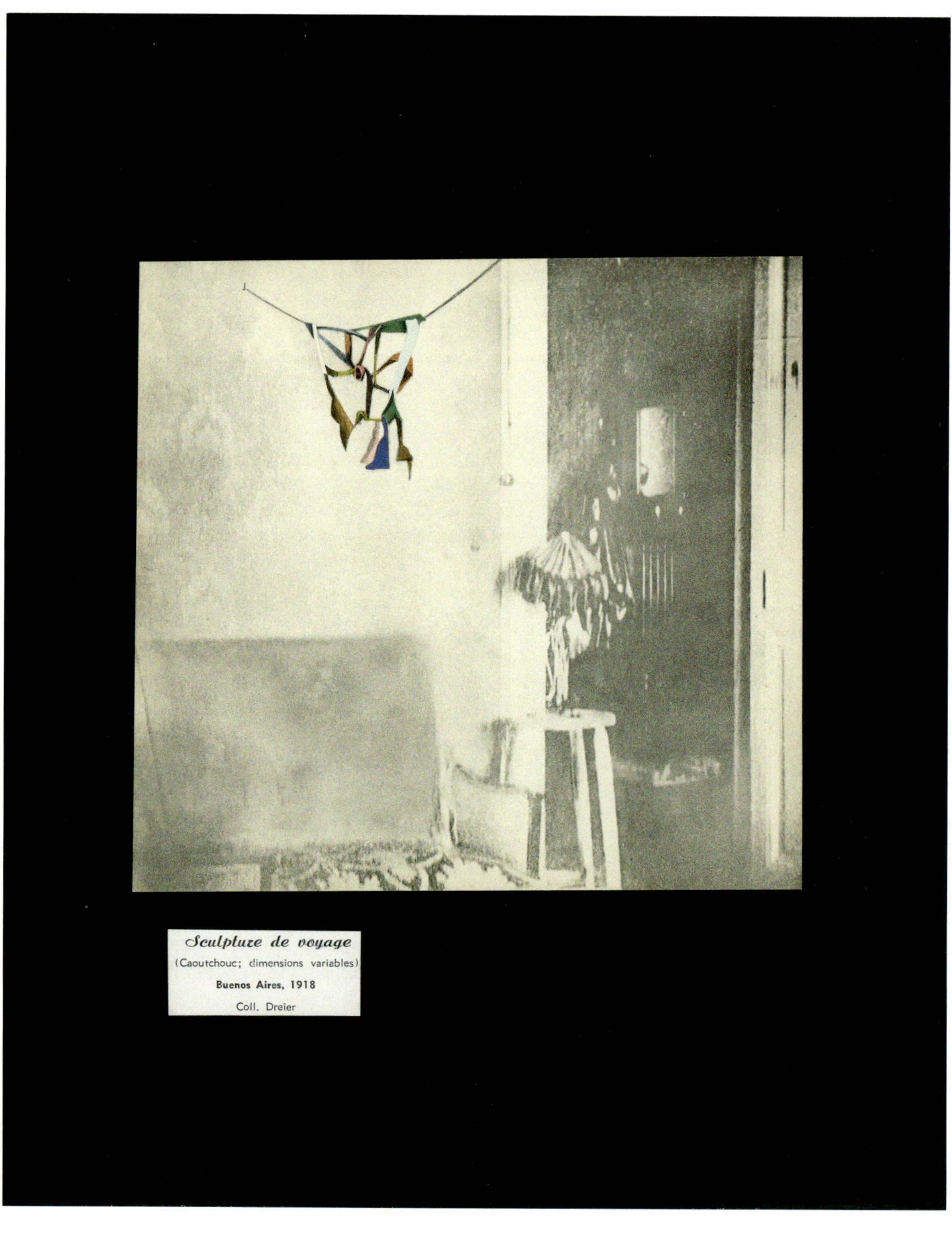

PREAMBLE

One of the great discourses of the last century, meandering yet persistent, is that between dance and drawing. If movement, as Marcel Duchamp believed, may be understood as a critique of painting,[1] and if in the twentieth century drawing often functioned as a critique of painting also, then movement and the lines of drawing are linked in a fundamental embrace, an ebb and flow, a confusion of meaning informed by the evanescence of real life in the space of representation. An eccentric and perhaps unlikely narrative can be traced in parsing the specific moments at which dance and line respectively aspired to the status of art — that is, at which each moved away from a contingent relationship to other art forms and struck out, attempting freedom or release from the discourses of media specificity and a direct engagement with the space of the real, with the everyday, and with life itself.

It might be said that the history of dance in the twentieth century is one of movement aspiring to be art in ways separate from the mimetic function assigned to it in the classical ballet of the eighteenth and nineteenth centuries. The equivalent might be said of drawing. In key moments spanning the century, avant-garde artists can be found writing on line, sometimes in ways more adventurous than can be tracked in their work. These thoughts are often inspired and provoked by direct observation of physical movement in the real world or, in its various modern forms, of dance. Writing during his years as a teacher at the Bauhaus, Vasily Kandinsky described line as a point in motion.[2] Paul Klee too was inspired by the idea of walking and movement in his *Pädagogisches Skizzenbuch* (Pedagogical sketchbook), published by the Bauhaus in 1925. At what moment does point become line rather than a mark? Klee's treatise opens with an exploration of point as it shifts into line: "An active line on a walk, moving freely, without a goal. A walk for a walk's sake. The mobility agent is a point, shifting its position forward."[3] In her introduction to a later edition of the book Sibyl Moholy-Nagy would describe what she calls "Klee's deepest wisdom: To Stand Despite all possibilities to Fall!"[4] Indeed the body's relationship to the ground — the spiraling duel between the vertical and the horizontal — would motivate the discourse of modern dance until the 1960s, when the collapse of spatial hierarchies led to the reinvention of form in defiance of gravity itself. Right up to the present moment, whether in the exteriorized, unbroken line of the classical ballerina or the corporal realignment of the postmodern performer, the glyphic mark made with or by the body has made a lively contribution to the discourse of visual art.

It can be argued that the current period — the end of the first decade of the twenty-first century — is a moment of drawing and dance. Drawing is firmly situated in the expanded field of contemporary practice, as artists embrace its conceptual discursiveness, its formal possibilities, and its economy of means. After a period when drawing occupied a position of status in the art market, many artists today are interested in revisiting its oppositional and ephemeral status as a political and intellectual center for their work. Dance too has emerged as central for a younger generation of artists whose training is often in performance and whose production seeks out a place of in-betweenness, the performative and the productive merging as one.

Among the many moments of rupture in the twentieth century, there were several at which dance and drawing inspired both formal invention and a conceptual liberation in artists' minds. Through inspired musing on line and movement — often in private notes, or in pedagogical texts, rather than through more public statements and writings — artists found in the less canonical media of paper and performance a freedom often absent in other areas of their production. The first such moment was roughly the period from 1910 into the 1920s in Europe, bracketed by Futurism in Italy and the Bauhaus in Germany. Another nexus occurred half a century later, in the 1960s, in New York and in Rio de Janeiro, center of Brazil's avant-garde. For our purposes here, this network of occurrences maps not so much a specific history as an alternative framework for understanding the transformation in drawing over the

140. Marcel Duchamp
(American, born France, 1887–1968)
Sculpture de Voyage (*Sculpture for Traveling*) (1918) as reproduced in *Boîte-en-valise (de ou par Marcel Duchamp ou Rrose Sélavy)* (*Box in a Valise [From or by Marcel Duchamp or Rrose Sélavy]*). 1935–41
Collotype with pochoir, from a leather valise containing 80 miniature replicas, color reproductions, and photographs of works by Duchamp
12 5/8 x 9 3/4" (32.1 x 24.8 cm)

last hundred years through an examination of its intersection with dance and movement-based performance. These moments and geographies provide the conceptual and spiritual centers of *On Line: Drawing through the Twentieth Century*, moments when the drawn line moves from mimesis literally off the page into space, into the realms of three-dimensional form and particularly of the body in motion. If the central questions of the postmodern dance that coalesced in New York with the founding of the Judson Dance Theater, in 1962, had to do with the relationship between dance, as a set of formal enactments, and the body's range of movements and gestures — that is, with a conceptual understanding of the meanings of the body's articulations in both their theatrical and their everyday dimensions — then drawing's attempt to make the graphic mark capture and materialize the movement of the body in the 1910s and '20s is an analogous preoccupation. The arcs of drawing and dance in the twentieth century might be described as dance moving beyond the image or readable gesture and as drawing transcending bodily form or trace.

In a discursive history of drawing and dance, one figure who must loom large is Henri Matisse, whose enormous innovations ranged from the Fauvist period through the radical formal experiments in abstraction and decoration of 1908–13, embodied in the painted movement of *The Dance* (1909), to the spatiotemporal experiments seen in the glorious paper cutouts of the artist's final years (1943–54).[5] Dance was an ongoing subject for Matisse, not only as a carrier for expressive mythologies associated with primitive cultures, and for ultimately essentializing notions of female sexuality and its association with earth and ritual, but as a twentieth-century emblem of movement and freedom. In 1948, Matisse declared, "At last I no longer know how to draw,"[6] thus situating his late works — drawings made of paper

141. Alex Hay
(American, born 1930)
Ground Drawing. 1968
Pencil on paper
68 1/4 x 38" (173.4 x 96.5 cm)

142. Trisha Brown
(American, born 1936)
Floor of the Forest. 1970
Performance, with installation.
Shown here performed by Brown (top) and Carmen Beuchat in the 1970s

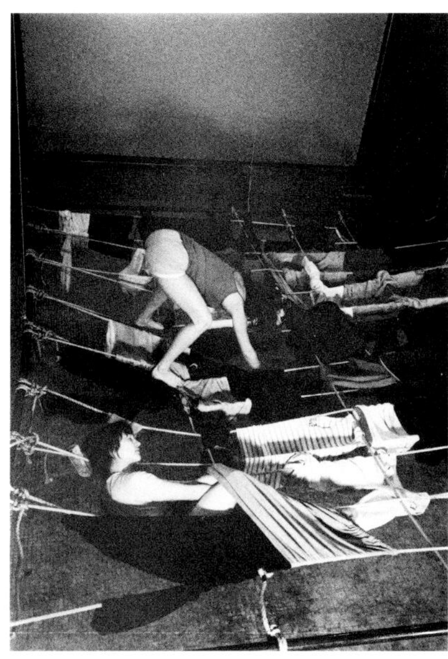

cut with scissors — as a critique both of painting and of *disegno*, the Renaissance notion of the contingency of drawing to painting and to representation that burdened its evolution through the late twentieth century. Over twenty years earlier, in 1922, he had declared, "My drawing and my painting are coming apart."[7] With this vivid image of the unhinging of two practices whose concomitance had previously been unchallenged, Matisse upended the history to which he had made such an instrumental contribution. In celebrating the moment of undoing, of breaking the constraints of technique and training, he constructed an argument for "deskilling," the intentional embrace of process over form and the privileging of means over ends, that situates him in a lineage looking back in time to Duchamp and forward to postmodern dance and its embrace of non-dance-based movement.

Given the year of Matisse's death — 1954 — it is easy to imagine that the sense of permission engendered by his late work would have permeated the neo-avant-garde of the late 1950s, not just in Europe and Latin America but in the United States, where activities in the territory of art — including practices in dance, sculpture, and performance — were beginning a various reaction against Abstract Expressionism and the doctrines of Clement Greenberg. It was at this moment that the international experiments in space, form, and performativity that locate the spiritual and intellectual core of *On Line* began to coalesce. As early as the mid-1950s, working in San Francisco, Anna Halprin had introduced what she called "task-oriented movement" to dance; by 1961, in New York, Simone Forti was working on "dance constructions," hybrids of dance and sculpture. In an intense if brief period of exquisitely low-fi production, the Judson Dance Theater's series of dance works and performances at Manhattan's Judson Church in 1962–64 formalized the shift from expressive modernist choreography to experimental, antihierarchical, radically boiled-down movement, as in Yvonne Rainer's *We Shall Run* (1963), in which twelve performers — both trained dancers and nondancers — run in demarcated patterns. These activities, as well as those of Judson participants Trisha Brown (plate 142), Lucinda Childs, Bill Davis, Judith and Robert Dunn, Ruth Emerson, Alex Hay, Deborah Hay, Fred Herko, Steve Paxton, Carolee Schneemann, and others, were articulated in workshops such as "A Concert of Dance" in 1962.[8]

For dance historian Sally Banes, this cross-media ethos of radical exchanges among disciplines, anticipating much of the foment around dance and performance today, consistently emphasized the aleatory and embraced whatever lay outside "choreotypic codes," in Halprin's phrase:

> Perhaps even more important than the individual dances given at a Judson concert was the attitude that anything might be called a dance and looked at as a dance; the work of a visual artist, a filmmaker, a musician might be considered a dance, just as activities done by a dancer, although not recognizable as theatrical dance, might be reexamined and "made strange" because they were framed as art.[9]

Alex Hay's mysterious *Ground Drawing* (1968; plate 141), though executed later in the decade, is emblematic of the kind of instructional, process-based activities hatched at the Judson. With links to the process art of the later 1960s (an impulse, emerging from Post-Minimalist sculpture, that itself had strong ties to the performative), Hay's drawing tracks incidental bumps and deformations left in the paper when it was wetted, then laid on the ground to dry. As in Brown's and Rainer's dance notations from this period, there is a tautological playfulness here: arrows and lines that Hay drew in pencil are vectors tracing the movement of the paper, but they were created by the hand tracking that movement. Paper and body confuse, as though the paper itself were a body recording the memory of action.

This making strange of everyday activities and movements finds a correspondence in Merce Cunningham's dance work *Walkaround Time* (1968; plate 145), a kind of conceptual collaboration with Duchamp and an homage to that artist's *Large Glass* (1915–23). Cunningham's title beautifully sets up notions that figure into this mapping of drawing and dance: in the early computer workplace, he writes, "walkaround

Man Walking Down the Side of a Building *was exactly like the title — seven stories. A natural activity under the stress of an unnatural setting. Gravity reneged. Vast scale, Clear order. You start at the top, walk straight down, stop at the bottom. All those soupy questions that arise in the process of selecting abstract movement according to the modern dance tradition — what, when, where and how — are solved in collaboration between choreographer and place. If you eliminate all those eccentric possibilities that the choreographic imagination can conjure up and just have a person walk down an aisle, then you see movement as activity.*

— Trisha Brown, 1978

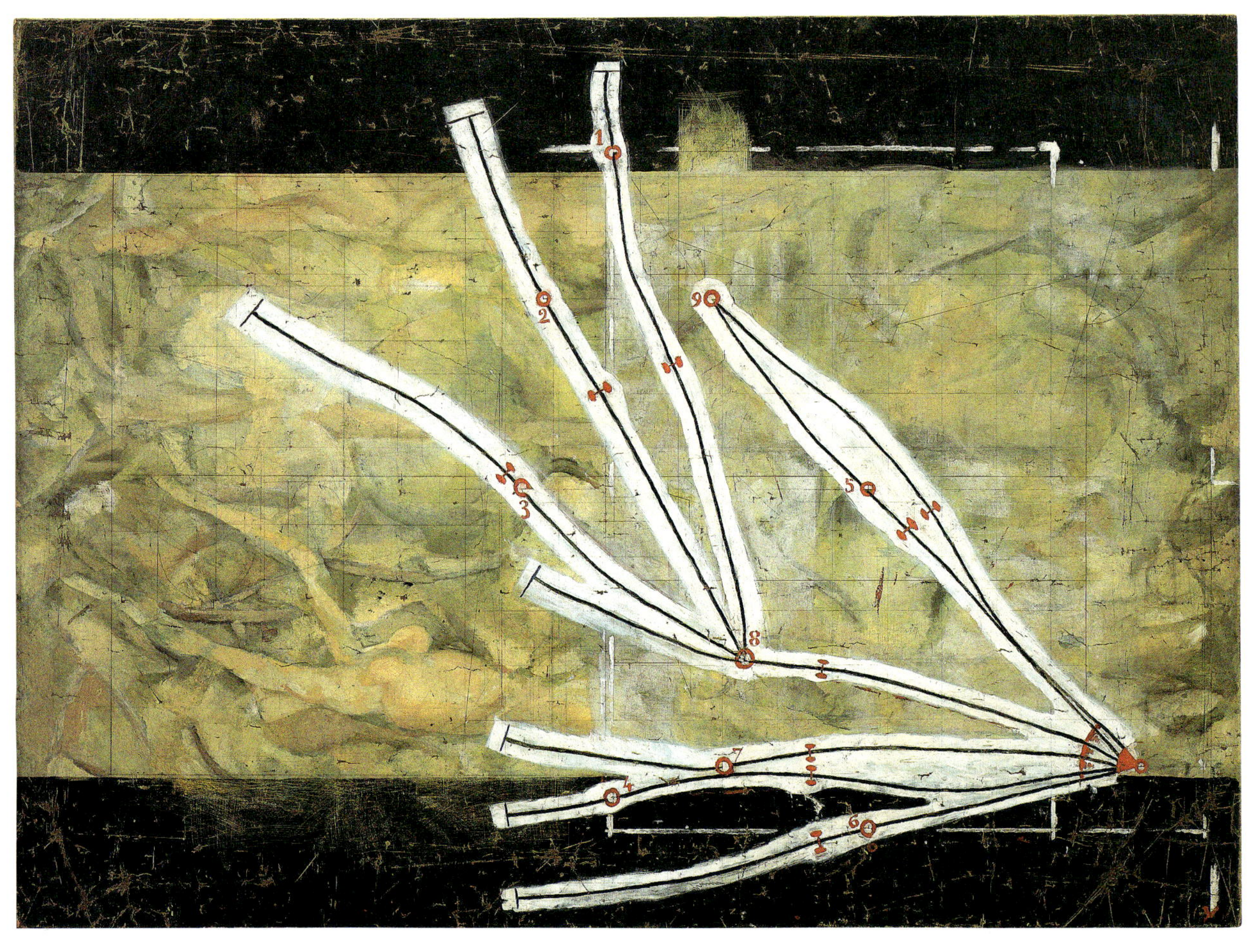

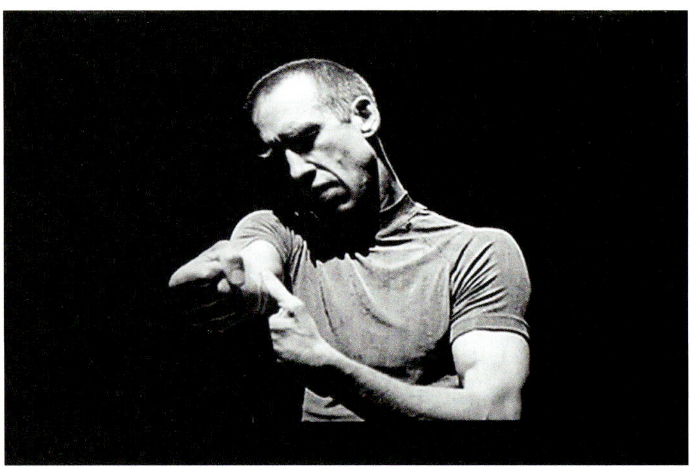

143. Marcel Duchamp
(American, born France, 1887–1968)
Réseaux des stoppages
(*Network of Stoppages*). 1914
Oil and pencil on canvas
58 5/8″ x 6′ 5 5/8″ (148.9 x 197.7 cm)

144. William Forsythe
(American, born 1949)
Solo. 1997
Still from film transferred to video, black and white, sound, 6:40 min. Choreography and performance: Forsythe. Music: Thom Willems, in collaboration with Maxime Franke. Director: Thomas Lovell Balogh. Camera: Jess Hall

145. Merce Cunningham
(American, 1919–2009)
Walkaround Time. 1968
Performance view, left to right: Carolyn Brown, Valda Setterfield, Meg Harper, Gus Solomons, Jr., and Cunningham

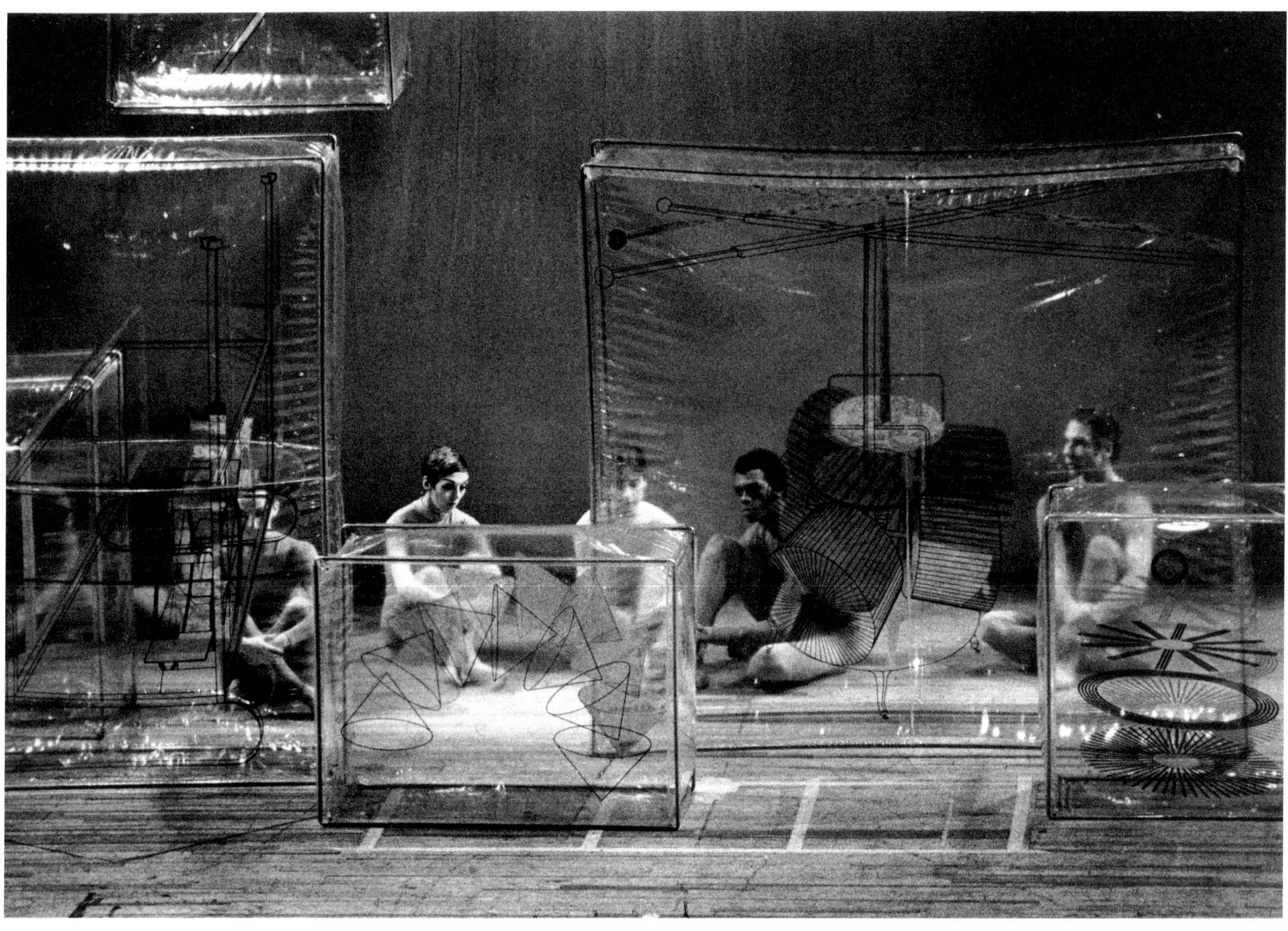

time" was a term for a space/time activity that programmers would engage in when, having input data into a mainframe, no doubt at that point a cumbersome, boxlike, slow-functioning object sitting in the middle of a room somewhere, they would then pace around for a while to span the boredom while the computer digested and processed.[10] In the performance, dancers mingled with large rectangular inflatables, which stood in for early mainframes but were silkscreened with images of the *Large Glass*. The literal marking of time through movement, through walking around to get to the other side of waiting, is a useful metaphor for drawing as an activity both intimate and quotidian, related to artistic processes and gestures close to the studio and to the daily practice of drawing and dance.

Cunningham was not directly involved with a discourse on line; his contribution to art and to postmodern dance was an interrogation of the hierarchies of movement, music, and the space of the stage, for example in his repurposing of the Duchampian idea of the found object by deploying generic pedestrian activities within the choreographic text.[11] In his essay "Space, Time and Dance," written in 1952, Cunningham described what is essentially a move from the vertical consideration of the body in motion against gravity — a frequent trope of classical and early-modern forms of dance — to the postmodern attention to the body cued by its experience of weight and mass, and to movement emanating from the body in response to its own kinesthetic parameters:

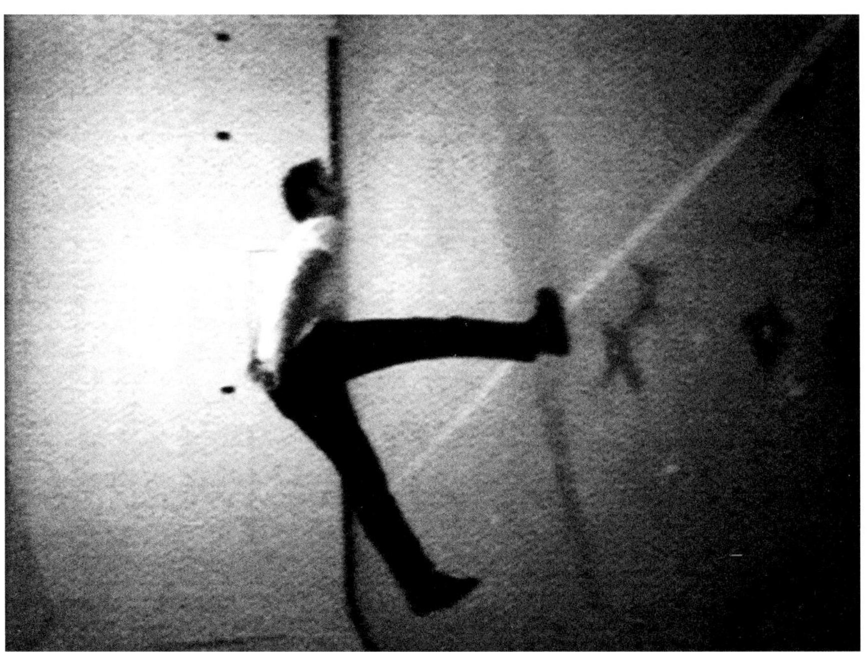

> One of the best discoveries the modern dance has made use of is the gravity of the body in weight, that is, as opposite from denying (and thus affirming) gravity by ascent into the air, the weight of the body in going with gravity, down.... By its nature this kind of moving would make the space seem a series of unconnected spots, along with the lack of clear-connecting movements in the modern dance.[12]

This idea of the vertical versus the horizontal (Klee's standing despite all possibilities to fall), of gravity as one force among others acting on the body or form, parallels experiments in sculpture by American artists of the 1960s and '70s such as Lynda Benglis, Robert Morris, Bruce Nauman, Richard Serra, Richard Tuttle (plate 147), and others. In 1968, the same year as Cunningham's *Walkaround Time*, Nauman made a number of works involving movement, either his own or a dancer's, and by 1970 he was collaborating with Cunningham, designing a set comprising standing industrial fans for a work called *Tread* (1970). Nauman's sculptural practice had merged with his video experiments and performative studio investigations by this point, and his drawings and writings from these years evince a strong relationship not only between sculpture and performance but between sculpture and dance as forms that exist in, indeed require, time and space. For Nauman, whose finished drawings often come after a work is complete, the relationships among performance, video, drawing, and language fundamentally involve reiteration, a productive, almost onomatopoeic conceptual stuttering.[13] His *Performance (Slightly Crouched)* (1968) calls for hiring a dancer, as he explains in the instructional sheet accompanying the work: "It is necessary to have a dancer or person of some professional anonymous presence."[14] By requiring a trained dancer to "perform" the work's completely pedestrian actions, Nauman both articulates the generic body as theatrical and renders the theatrical body generic.

In studio-based exercises recorded with a 16mm camera, such as *Dance or Exercise on the Perimeter of a Square* (1967–68), *Walk with Contrapposto* (1968), and *Slow Angle Walk (Beckett Walk)* (1968; plate 146), Nauman executed dance works that constitute a kind of tracing of space, an inscription of the space of the studio with the body. His description of the mechanics of *Slow Angle Walk (Beckett Walk)* is as uninflected as its execution:

> In the diagrams the squares indicate the length of a step. These steps are made by raising the leg, without bending the knee, until it is at a right angle to the body, then

146. Bruce Nauman
(American, born 1941)
Slow Angle Walk (Beckett Walk). 1968
Still from video, black and white, sound, 60 min.

147. Richard Tuttle
(American, born 1941)
Ten Kinds of Memory and Memory Itself. 1973
Installation view of the exhibition *Richard Tuttle*, Galerie Yvon Lambert, Paris, 1974

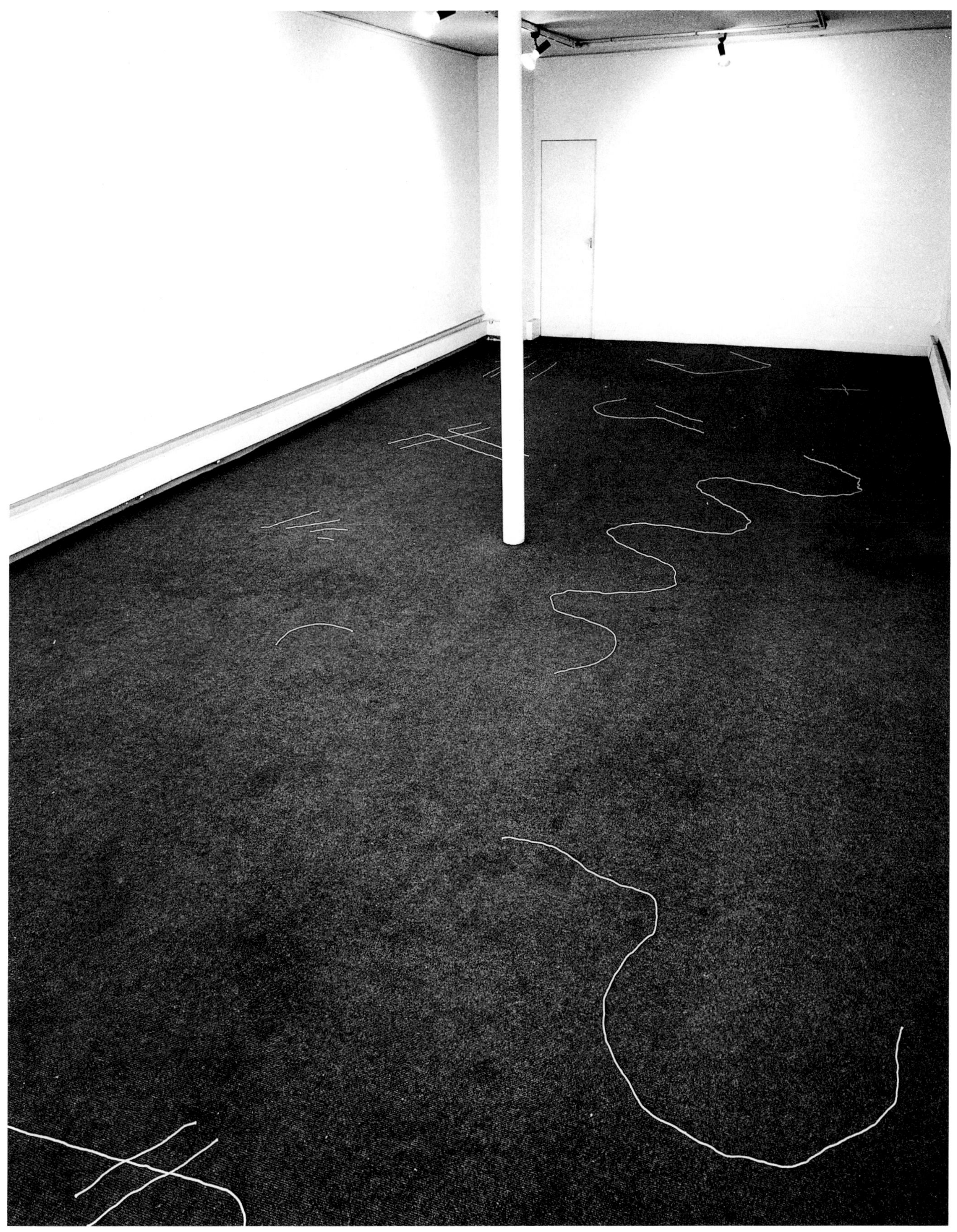

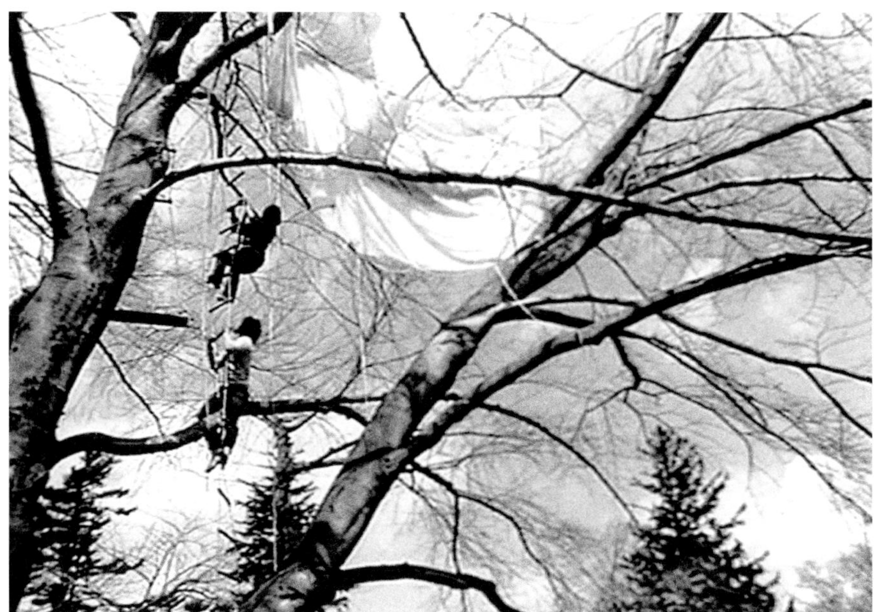

swinging 90 degrees in the direction indicated in the diagram. . . . The body then falls forward onto the raised foot and the other leg is lifted to again make a straight line with the body (which now forms a T over the support leg). The body swings upright with the nonsupport leg swinging through the vertical and into the 90-degree position, as at the beginning. Three step-turns to the right and then three step-turns to the left will advance you two paces — each three steps advances you one step.[15]

Drawings for this simple set of instructions look like dance notation: simple lines at right angles, extended with arrows.[16] Nauman attributes his deployment of amateur movement to Cunningham and other performers, such as Meredith Monk, whom he knew at the time.[17]

In the early 1960s, as dance in the United States and Europe was being revolutionized by a movement-based performance that was the site of an emerging postmodernism in the realm of the body, avant-garde artists in Brazil (many of them involved in the Neo-Concretist movement founded in 1957 in Rio de Janeiro) were engaged in a discourse of rupture from a European strain of abstract painting. In 1963, early in a career that would come to involve a radical break not just with painting but with object-making itself, Lygia Clark made an emblematic work that marks a transition of her production from painting into both sculpture and movement, from line into form and endlessly back again, and from line and form into the everyday and, eventually, into the body itself. Titled *Caminhando*, or "Walking" (plates 134–39), the work is a Möbius strip, and as such a perceptual contradiction, both infinite and nonexistent. Made of paper cut into ever thinner lines by the artist, in a process recorded in a series of photographs, it is both present and absent, standing in direct material opposition to the tradition and artifice of abstract painting and to the Neo-Concretist movement that Clark had helped to found.

Caminhando is directly connected to lived experience, and Clark's writing about this experiment or "proposition," as she called it, connects the act of making it to the poetics of unlearning, linking it to the deskilling of her North American contemporaries working in dance and sculpture at precisely the same moment:

I ask myself whether after the experience of the *Caminhando* we do not become more aware of the gestures we make.

This may become impossible, because it demands us to a priori cast aside all the practical and immediate significance of these gestures. The first time I cut the

148. Gordon Matta-Clark
(American, 1945–1978)
Tree Dance. 1971
Still from 16mm film transferred to video, black and white, silent, 9:32 min.

149 and **150. Ellsworth Kelly**
(American, born 1923)
Automatic Drawing: Pine Branches V and . . . *VI*. 1950
Each: pencil on paper
Each: 16 1/2 x 20 1/4" (41.9 x 51.4 cm)

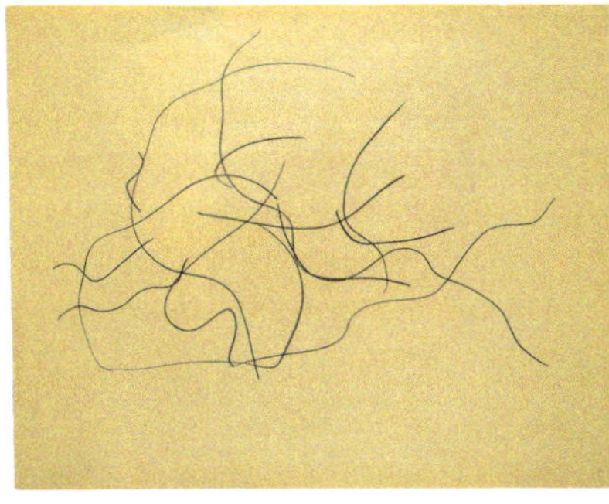

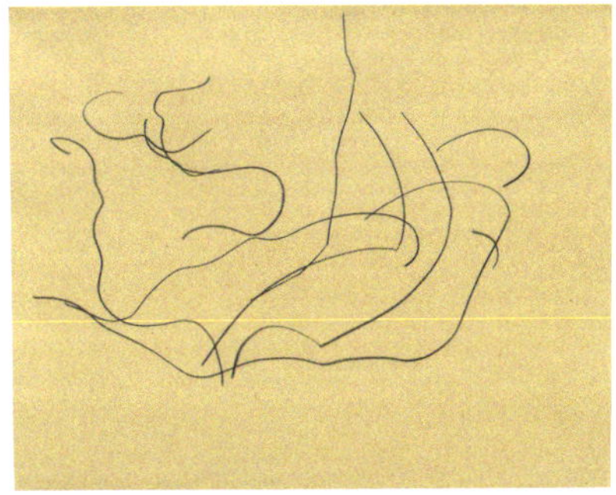

> *Caminhando*, I lived out a ritual which was very significant in itself. And I wished for this same action to be lived out with the greatest possible intensity by the future participants: it is necessary for it to be purely gratuitous and for you not to try to know — while you are cutting — what you are going to cut and what you have already cut.[18]

Walking and the everyday, walking and drawing — these terms commingle throughout the century with startling consistency. The entanglement of line in the body, in space, and on the page populates the avant-garde moments of the teens, the 1960s, and the current moment — from Klee taking his line for a walk to Clark's *Caminhando* to contemporary artists such as William Forsythe, or Marie Cool and Fabio Balducci, who engage with the current discourse of performance and participation through an antitheatrical, deeply kinesthetic engagement with audience and who variously describe their performative work as based in both movement and drawing. Contemporary artists such as Tino Sehgal, who has said that "no work is not participatory at all," are indebted to the work of the Judson artists in New York and to projects such as Clark's in Brazil, which led to a radical transformation of the art object in the direction of performativity.[19]

At the start of the 1970s, Brown and Gordon Matta-Clark created two works that emblematize the art/life, dance/draw equation. In Brown's seminal dance work *Floor of the Forest* (1970; plates 133, 142), two dancers, dressed for the street or for rehearsal, climb into a slinglike structure made of limply hanging items of clothing, as if dragged from a secondhand store. The clothes are knotted together to form a relaxed grid suspended at eye level by the armature of a simple square of metal pipe. In Brown's very unscientific instructions for the work, the performers interact with the clothing, putting on and taking off the various garments and allowing their body weight to sag into each and to be supported by the sling. As they inhabit each garment, legs may go into armholes, waistbands may be occupied by thighs, heads may be cupped in pant legs — over about ten minutes, a slow yet methodical peopling of the grid unfolds. Their configurations are vignettes, sometimes poetic and introspective, sometimes awkward and unlovely in ways that the dancers can't always anticipate: a leg gets stuck, a rear rises in the air, an arm drops limply through an unanticipated gap. What is moving about this work is its deep connection with the everyday, which is literally represented by the used clothes, shed like skin from our bodies over time, and by the direct address of the dancers to the makeshift jungle gym and the ordinary task at hand. Moving in and out of the lines of the grid, they map it with their bodies.

In Matta-Clark's *Tree Dance* (1971; plate 148), a performance that survives as a 16mm film, the artist and dancers hung from ropes and nets in a tree on the campus of Vassar College, Poughkeepsie, New York. The work advanced from earlier linear structures such as *Museum* (1970), an installation at the Bykert Gallery, New York, that included various organic materials suspended on vines, like clotheslines in space. Matta-Clark's practice was involved on other occasions with the life and mysticism of trees, for example in a body of so-called Tree Form drawings, from the early 1970s, constructed of arrows and vectors whose forceful movement nearly jumps off the page. Whether living or dead, upside-down or inhabited, trees seem to have represented for Matta-Clark a generative force — as perhaps they did for other artists across the century who mused on them, including Matisse; Ellsworth Kelly, in his Pine Branches drawings (1950; plates 149, 150); Agnes Martin, in the ethereal painting *The Tree* (1964; plate 80); Giuseppe Penone, in many works including the wall drawing *Propagazione* (Propagation, 1995–2009; plate 227); and Vera Molnar, in her *Arbres et collines géométriques* (Geometric trees and hills, 1946; plate 205), all represented in this exhibition. If Matisse said the line of his tree and plant drawings at Vence had "to grow inside me like a plant in the earth,"[20] Matta-Clark was more literally concerned with alchemy, and the organic materials and processes of decay and regeneration. But in his drawings he used lines of motion and circulation to anthropomorphize the tree form, and it is clear that the idea of the dancing tree had as much to do with the animated humans as with the tree's own life force.

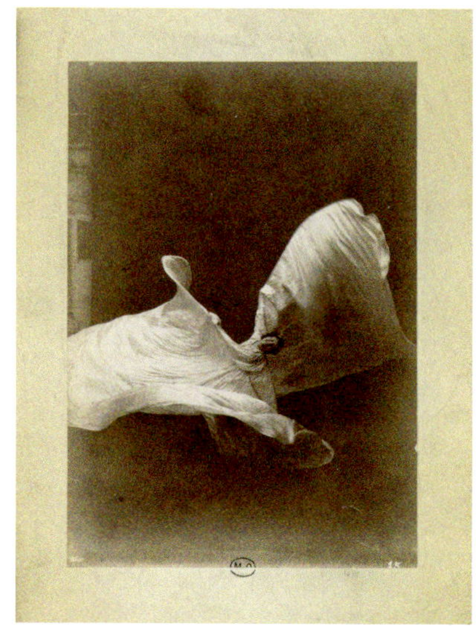

One of the opening cadences of twentieth-century art was the eruption of modern dance out of its devotion to classical forms and into dialogue with the other arts. Having moved in and out of the periphery of avant-garde art practice for most of the century, dance — the poetics and mechanics of the movement of the body in space — now seems clearly to have titillated the visual arts with its adventurous sense of permission and its apparent connection to deep aesthetic impulses codified in the body. Innovators in movement research included Rudolf Steiner, who began to develop the movement practice eurythmy in 1912; Isadora Duncan, who introduced improvisation into her ballet-based choreography; the influential teacher Mary Wigman; and Vaslav Nijinsky, who dominated Sergei Diaghilev's Ballets Russes in the years before World War I.

Between the turn of the nineteenth century and the early 1920s, however, three dancers in particular, all women, turn up repeatedly at the margins of advanced art, appealing to the Futurists' fascination with speed and motion, the Cubists' concern with light and with a quasi-cinematic representation of form, and the Bauhaus desire to integrate all of the arts. Valentine de Saint-Point, a poet and Symbolist dancer, wrote a manifesto of Futurist movement and invented a kind of cross-media performance she called "metachory," or "beyond dance"; Loie Fuller, or "La Loie," as she was known, twirled and whirled on stages in Paris (plates 3, 13, 151), beginning at the Folies Bergère in 1892; and Gret Palucca performed at the Bauhaus and was a muse for Kandinsky in his exploration of line. (In 1911, as if predicting that dance, through its connection with life, would transcend mimesis and lead the charge toward an abstract language, Kandinsky had called for an abstract form of dance.)[21] Of the three, Fuller was perhaps the most influential for visual artists, who paid serious attention to her inventive choreography and innovative use of light.[22] For dance historian Laurence Louppe her work was the central antecedent of contemporary dance: "It is as if the letter, the diffuse textuality inscribed in life, had immediately — and since time immemorial — impressed its seal on the heart of the destiny of dance, an invisible sign which movement and its projection in space will little by little decipher, transcending the mark."[23] All of these women were vivid characters who manipulated their sexuality in various and provocative ways in their performances. Yet in their self-fashioning as "modern" women, their deployment of the everyday through improvisation, their use of technological advances, and their interest in collaborating with visual artists, they clearly inspired both artists and dancers and changed the course of dance and its relationship to cultural production.

The response of drawing to dance in the early part of the century seems generally to have taken two forms: either an attempt to mimic the body's movement, creating a mark as a record of the observed, or a kind of mark-making that sought to move beyond the page to a space of suspension and animation. Convinced by Fuller's use of electric light, which she projected onto the filmy fabric in which she wrapped her body, Filippo Tommaso Marinetti sought a renovation of dance through technology, investing subjectivity in modern machinery and energy.[24] (A full discussion of the relationship of early modern dance to innovations in technology lies beyond the scope of this text.) The attempt to imitate the visual blurring of the body introduced by the new speed and mobility of the urban environment is common in Futurist drawings and paintings. In Umberto Boccioni's three drawings titled *Stati d'animo* (States of mind, 1911), with individual subtitles *Quelli che vanno* (Those who go), *Quelli che restano* (Those who stay), and *Gli addii* (The farewells; plates 1, 152), undulating in and out of what appear to be waves of motion are figures that seem perforated by movement, as through their bodies were at once part of the atmosphere and undone by the swoops and dips of charcoal and chalk. Boccioni was surely familiar with Fuller's choreography; she was invited to perform in conjunction with several Futurist exhibitions beginning in 1910.[25] Her most famous works, *Butterfly Dance* (1892) and *Fire Dance* (1895), which she performed at the World's Fair of 1900 and at the Folies Bergère, merged form with immaterial color through

151. Isaiah West Taber
(American, 1830–1912)
Loie Fuller dancing with her veil. 1897
Gelatin silver printing-out paper print pasted on cardboard
4 7/16 x 6 1/2″ (11.3 x 16.7 cm)

152. Umberto Boccioni
(Italian, 1882–1916)
Stati d'animo. Gli addii
(States of mind: the farewells). 1911
Charcoal and chalk on paper
23 x 34″ (58.4 x 86.4 cm)

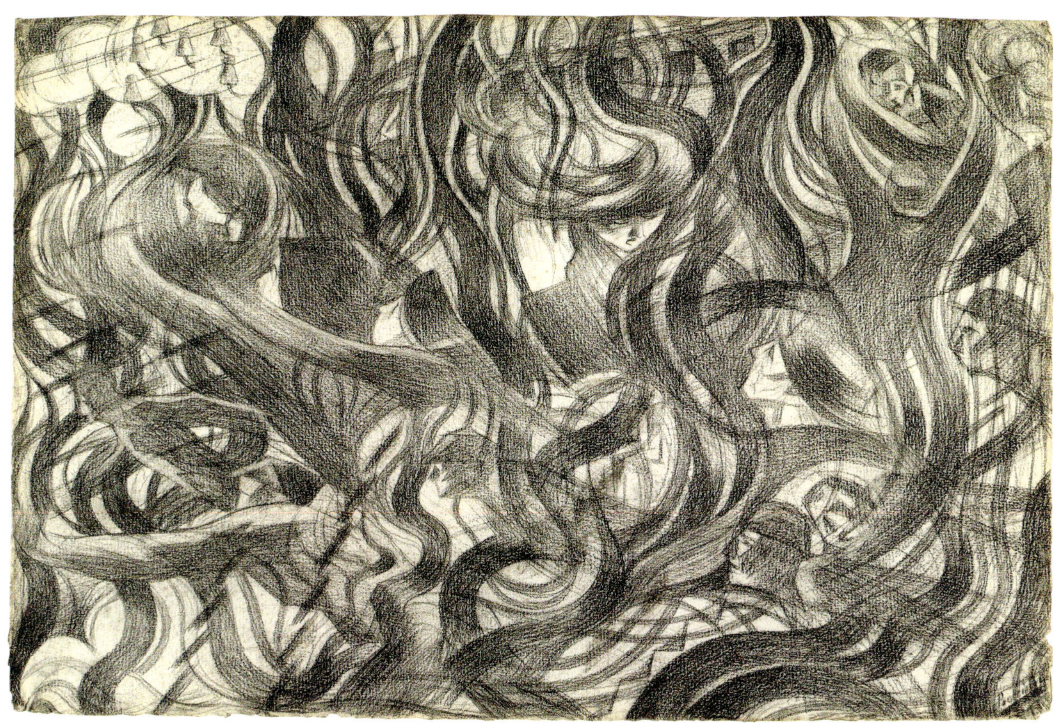

Dance of the Shrapnel
Movement 1: With the feet mark the boom-boom of the projectile coming from the cannon's mouth.
Movement 2: With arms spread apart describe at moderate speed the long whistling parabola of the shrapnel as it passes over the soldier's head and explodes too high or behind him. The danseuse will hold up a sign printed in blue: Short to the right.
Movement 3: With the hands (wearing very long silver thimbles) raised and open, as high as possible, give the proud, blessed, silvery explosion of the shrapnel in its paaaak. The danseuse will hold up a sign printed in blue....
Movement 4: With the whole body vibrating, the hips weaving, and the arms making swimming motions, give the waves and flux and reflux and concentric or eccentric motions of echoes in ravines, in open fields and up the slopes of mountains.

—Filippo Tommaso Marinetti, *Manifesto of Futurist Dance*, 1917

the advanced use of light—indeed she called her dancers "instruments of light."[26] With both artists—Fuller wearing flowing silk, awash in color from projected light, and Boccioni drawing ghostly figures fragmented by the vectors of their own hurried movement through space—the subject is the rush of modern perception. The bodies appearing literally to dissolve into line in Boccioni's drawings seem to be an attempt to depict Marinetti's invocation of technology as an extension of the body.

In the Futurist Manifesto, Marinetti conflates machinery with dance: "We must imitate with gestures the movements of motors, pay assiduous court to steering gear, wheels, pistons, prepare the fusion of man and the machine, and thus arrive at the metallization of the Futurist dance."[27] What is interesting is the writer's very literal descriptive shift from the movements of machines to the gestures the dancer makes to "imitate" those movements, "the fusion of man and the machine." Marinetti wanted a dance independent of music, which he considered nostalgic, irrelevant to technology's revolutionary advances into the future. Inspired by Fuller's use of highly visual (if by our terms low-tech) projection techniques to create a dizzying blur of motion, he perceived a modern spirit in dance and imagined the emergence of a new art form. Yet where Fuller, through her fluttering movements and the smoke and mirrors of her silk costume and projected light, seemed to dissolve the body into a sequence of lines and planes much like those in the drawings of Boccioni and others, many of those drawings remained rather literal attempts to capture or imitate movement with line.

Images of the body in motion occur in the very earliest art, and the avant-garde artists of the first decades of the twentieth century contributed their own renditions of the subject. Many addressed the legacy of the nineteenth-century representation of the pagan dance in the pastoral setting, as in Matisse's *Bonheur de vivre* of 1905–6 and *Dance* paintings of 1909–10. We often see images of a dancer, vertical, swirling in space, the figure undone by its own swooping, undulating line. Gino Severini's painting *Dynamic Hieroglyphic of the Bal Tabarin* (1912; plate 12) is a visually rich if ultimately awkward attempt both to represent dance and to supply some visceral sense of its eroticism and sensuousness. The title equates the dynamism of the human form with the hieroglyph, the graphic mark, and the gyrations of figures engaged in different types of dance are punctuated by text identifying their filmic gyrations—*valse, tango, polka.* A careful smattering of sequins sprayed throughout enlivens the picture, but also reflects the artist's struggle to move it into the realm of the real. Like Boccioni's drawings, Giacomo

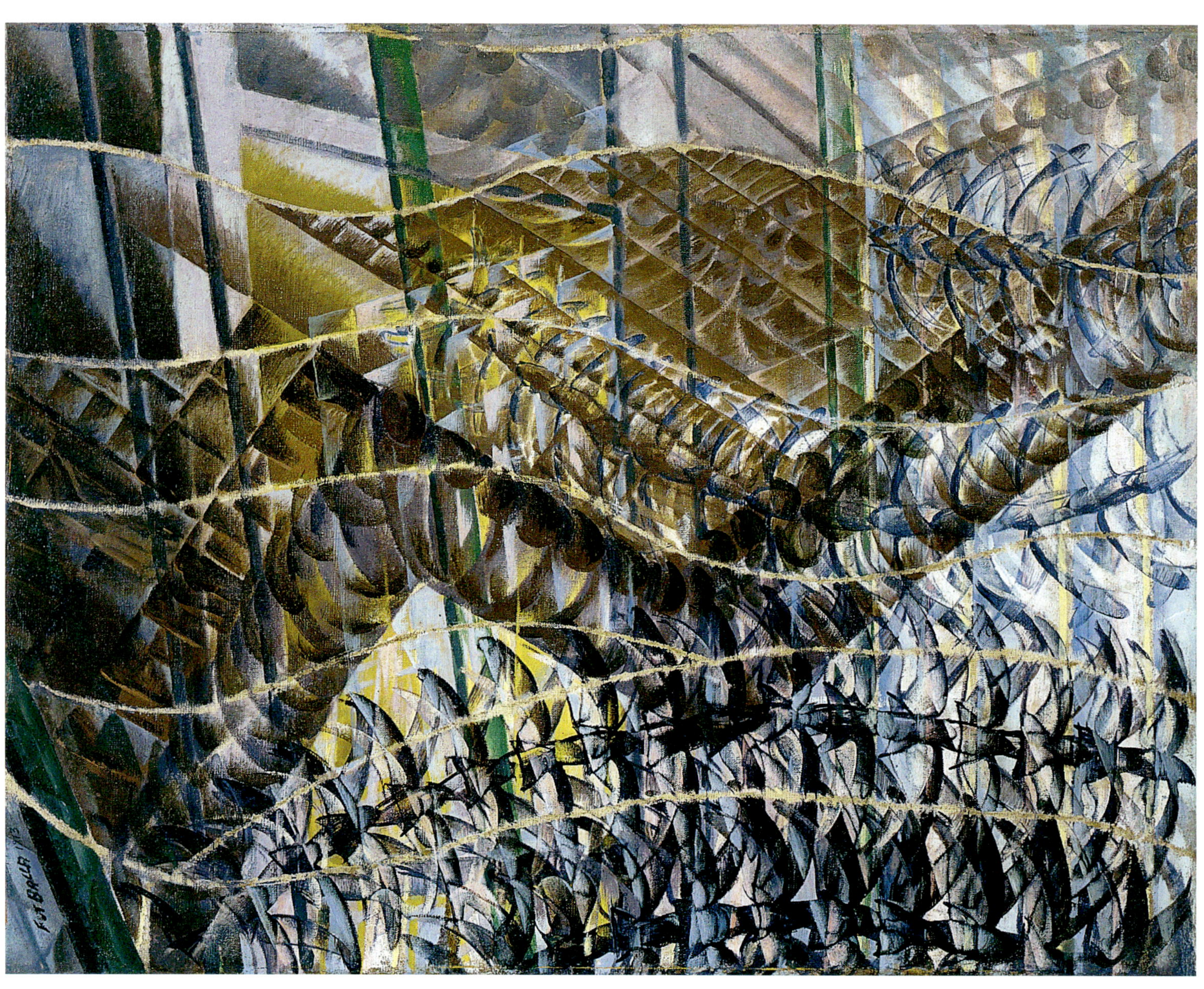

Balla's quite linear painting *Linee andamentali + successioni dinamiche — Volo di rondini* (*Swifts: Paths of Movement + Dynamic Sequences*, 1913; plate 153) allows the lines of motion to disrupt and multiply the figure in space. Advancing the dynamism of Duchamp's *Nude Descending a Staircase, No. 2* (1912), and anticipating much later digital technologies that track movement with line and light, as in Forsythe's *Improvisation Technologies* (1999; plate 218), Balla's lyrical painting is a sea of vectors and lines. Near abstract, it allows enough spatial indication to suggest a sense of a figure and ground generated by the fractured shifting of line and plane. Finally the painting is as serial as cinema, each frame building the dynamism of the whole.

Like Duchamp, Man Ray, too, employed various modes of painting to express his disposition toward the confinement that painting imposed, and was inspired at various points by dance and by studies of motion. In his *Rope Dancer Accompanies Herself with Her Shadows* (1916; plate 18), the little figure of the dancer, hovering Tinkerbell-like at the painting's top, is multiplied by patterned shapes that fill the area below — presumably the shadows of the title, which she casts as she balances to adapt to the motion of the linear rope that animates the picture. Inspired by the composition made by pieces of cut paper dropped on the floor, this enigmatic abstraction gestures toward the automatic collage techniques of Dada. What's fascinating here is the presence of the dancing figure, a small figurative glyph, in the same space as the much larger, abstract but anthropomorphic shapes or shadows. As a line cutting through space, animated by the form of a single figure, the tightrope dancer's rope would turn up across the century.

Recalling photographic images of Fuller performing amid a flurry of fabric, Nijinsky's *Tänzerin* (Dancer, 1917–18; plate 154) and Severini's *Dancer* (1912; plate 155) also show a single central figure undone by the vectors swirling around her. Severini made a number of paintings and drawings of dancers and wrote of one such, *Mer = Danseuse* (Sea = dancer, 1914), "The Sea dancing, its zigzag movements and contrasting scintillations of silver and emerald, evokes within my plastic sensibility the distant vision of a dancer covered in dazzling sequins in her world of light, noise and sound." He elsewhere wrote, "The linking of citizens' bodies in dance appeared to be an effective antidote to the menacing industrial advance of machines that . . . have the power to unite forces without uniting hearts."[28] While Severini's and Nijinsky's representations are lyrical and even a bit decorative in their rendering, they are thoroughly unprecious and modern in their attempt to capture the motion and spirit of the new abstract dance.

Though Nijinsky's drawings are mostly rather conventional figure studies, they support the general thesis that drawing, in its immediacy and informality, was well suited to recording the body in time and space. Like Fuller's body, concealed by the folds of her flapping silks, both Nijinsky's and Severini's dancers stand upright and face forward while line and color swirl around them. Severini's composition is clearly influenced by Cubism, its planes of color seeming to represent every angle of the dancer's body simultaneously. Seen alongside Nijinsky's, it suggests the tension in the representation of movement at the time: one mode flat, lyrical, and fundamentally illustrative, the other a tautological picture that wants to break free of two dimensions.

De Saint-Point, Fuller, and Palucca — along with such figures as Sophie Taeuber-Arp, who emerged in the context of Dada — were powerful icons of the idea of the "new woman" formulated during these years in intellectual circles such as the Bauhaus. As the most recognized dancer of the Weimar Republic, Palucca was seen as the model of this type.[29] A former student of Wigman's, she performed at the Bauhaus in 1925, the same year Kandinsky made a series of highly schematized drawings of her based on photographs of her dancing (plates 30, 156). Performing solo, like Fuller, but sporting short hair and dressed in snug-fitting clothes to expose her toned body, Palucca was athletic and fully modern, and the movements of her body in space were clear and graphic. Kandinsky could record them in clean linear marks that contrast starkly with Nijinsky's and Severini's drawings, where Fuller-like dancing forms peer out from ephemeral abstractions of folds and drapery.

153. Giacomo Balla
(Italian, 1871–1958)
Linee andamentali + successioni dinamiche — Volo di rondini (*Swifts: Paths of Movement + Dynamic Sequences*). 1913
Oil on canvas
38 1/8 x 47 1/4" (96.8 x 120 cm)

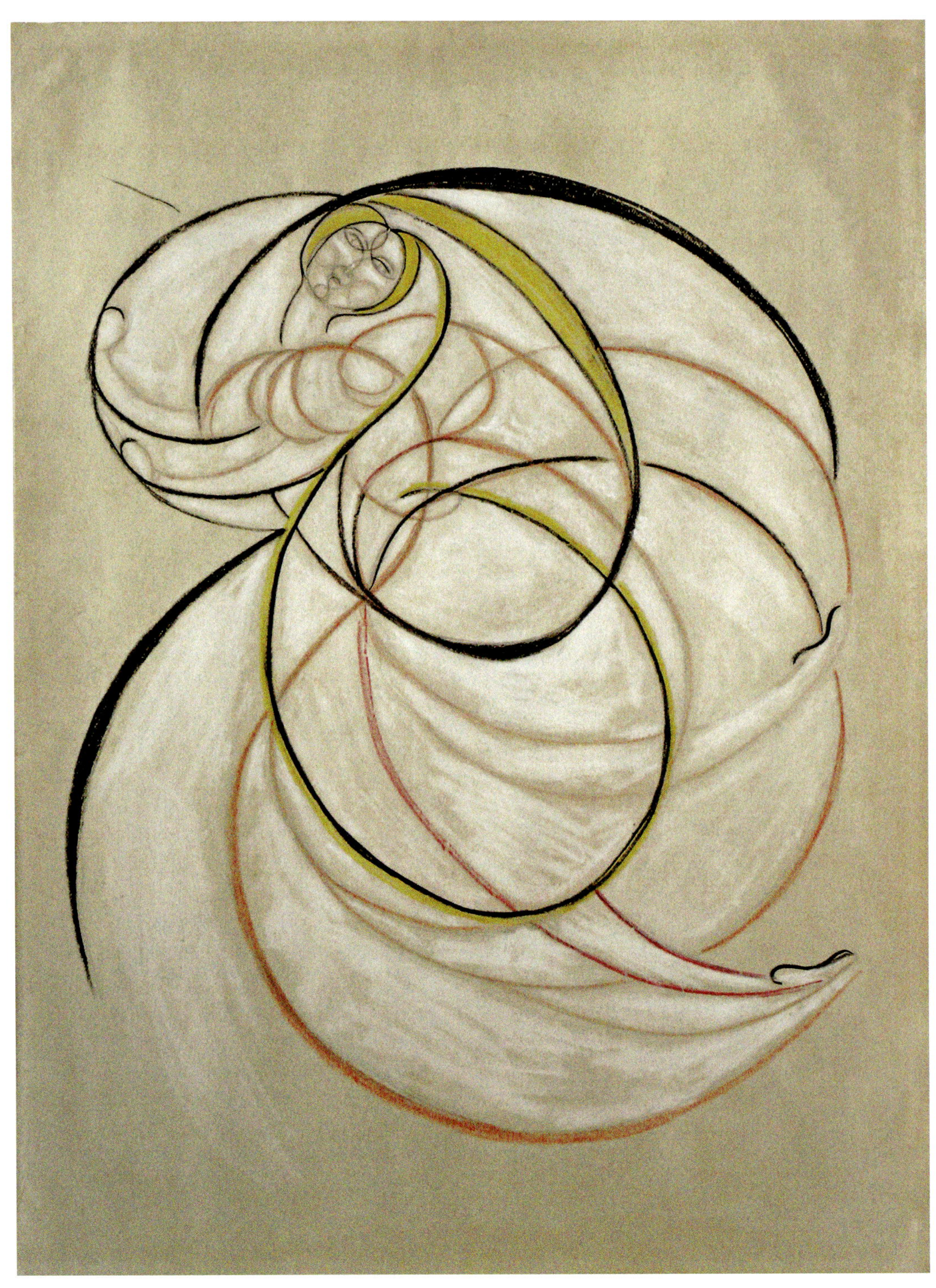

154. Vaslaw Nijinsky
(Russian, 1890–1950)
Tänzerin (Dancer). 1917–18
Chalk, pastel, and pencil on paper
13 3/4 x 9 13/16″ (35 x 25 cm)

155. Gino Severini
(Italian, 1883–1966)
Dancer. 1912
Pastel on paper
19 1/4 x 12 1/2″ (49 x 32 cm)

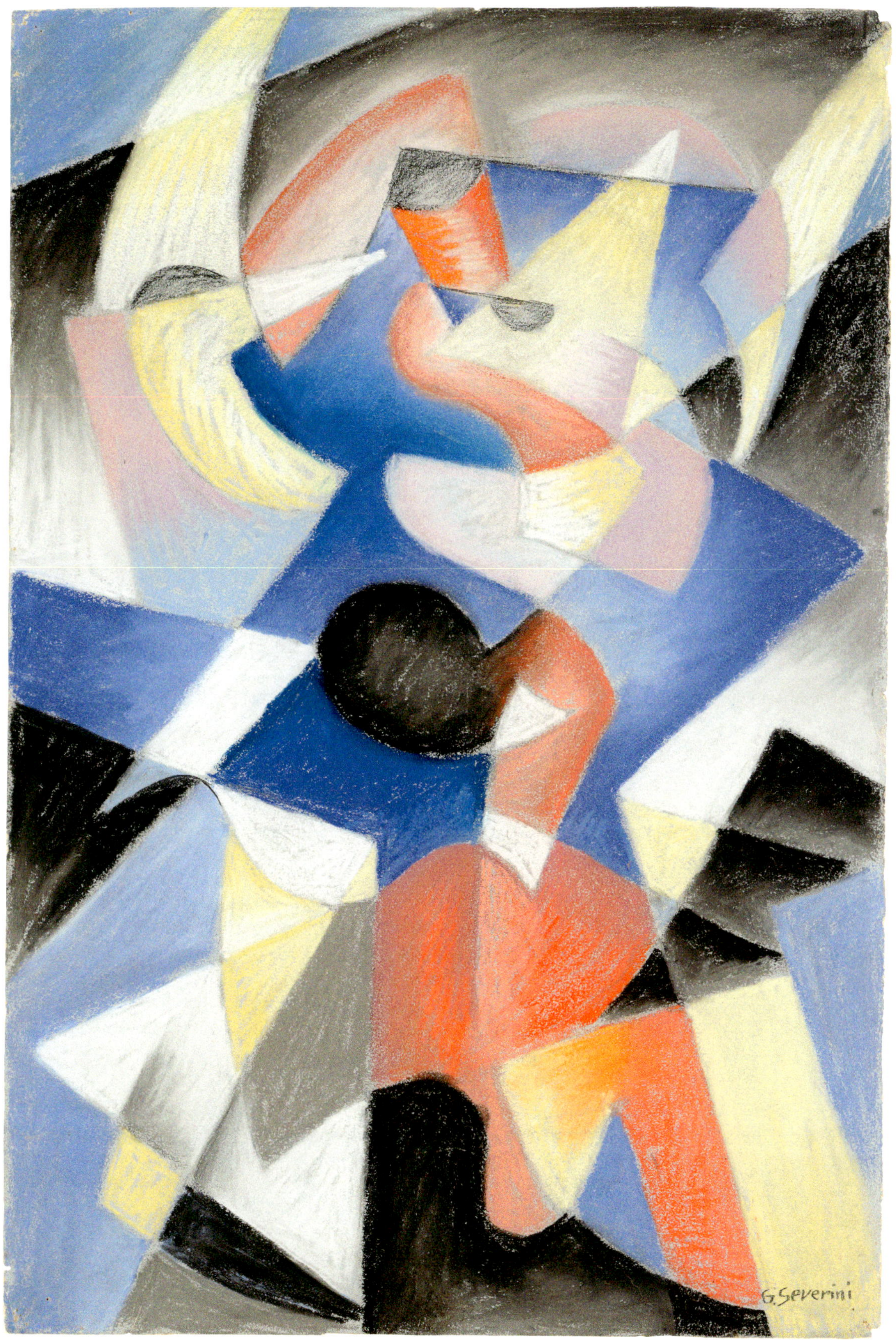
G. Severini

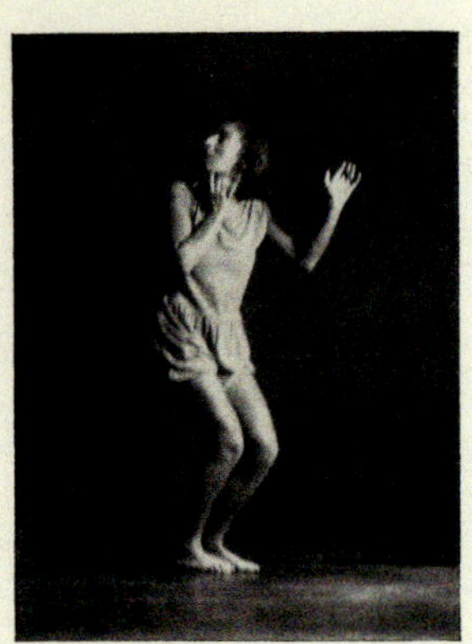

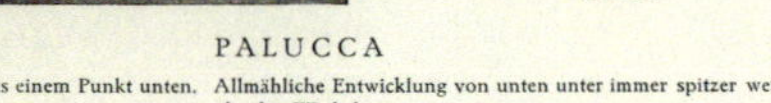

PALUCCA

Paralleler Aufbau aus einem Punkt unten. Allmähliche Entwicklung von unten unter immer spitzer werdenden Winkeln.

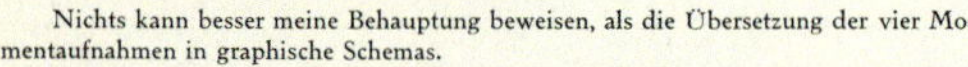

Nichts kann besser meine Behauptung beweisen, als die Übersetzung der vier Momentaufnahmen in graphische Schemas.

Die Exaktheit reißt auch die Falten und Zipfel der Kleidung mit. Auch die „tote Materie“ unterordnet sich dem großen Aufbau.

Die Momentaufnahme bietet abgerissene starre Formen, die einmal der Anfang einer Entwicklung ist, einmal der Schlußpunkt. Das organische langsame Entstehen der Form, die Übergangsstadien bleiben aus und können nur durch Zeitlupe erreicht werden, die das Feld der Beobachtungen in einer überraschenden Weise erweitert.

Der Tanz Paluccas sollte unbedingt mit Zeitlupe aufgenommen werden, wodurch eine exakte Prüfung dieses exakten Tanzes ermöglicht würde.

Ich möchte nicht mißverstanden werden — ich habe hier nur eine Seite der Kunst Paluccas beleuchtet. Aber gerade diese eine Seite ist gerade heute von einer besonderen Wichtigkeit: wir stehen unter dem Zeichen einer aufgehenden Kunstwissenschaft. Ich hoffe mit Sicherheit, daß Palucca auch auf diesem Gebiete Wertvolles beitragen wird.

118

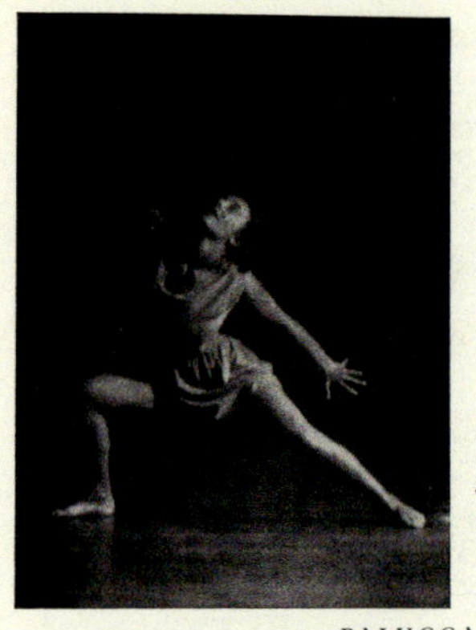

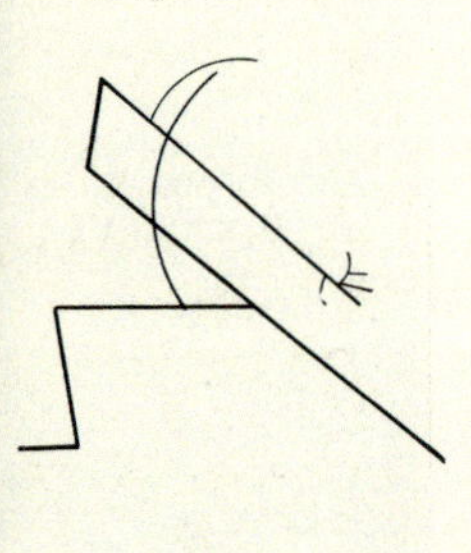

PALUCCA

Zwei große parallellaufende Linien auf einen geraden Winkel gestützt. Energische Entwicklung der Diagonale. Genauer Aufbau der Finger als Beispiel für Exaktheit in jeder Einzelheit.

UMSCHAU

BRIEF AUS WIEN

Schon lange war an dieser Stelle nicht mehr von Wien die Rede. Was sollte man auch von dem Kunstleben dieser Stadt berichten, das sich in diesem Herbst noch uninteressanter gestaltete, als in den vergangenen Jahren. Die Ausstellungen der drei offiziellen Künstlervereinigungen, Künstlerhaus, Sezession und Hagenbund, sind auf einem Niveau angelangt, das mit bestem Willen nicht mehr den Namen eines solchen verdient. Das Künstlerhaus, das heute die einzigen von der Wiener Gesellschaft voll anerkannten Ausstellungen Wiens zeigt, bringt Jahr für Jahr eine Unmenge handwerklich gekonnter Arbeiten, die das Entzücken der zahlreichen Besucher (die gibt es dort wirklich!) hervorrufen, und im führenden Blatt Wiens, der »Neuen Freien Presse«, unter Aufzählung der Namen sämtlicher Künstler in spaltenlangen Artikeln des Hauskritikers A. F. S. lobend Erwähnung finden. Ist im Künstlerhaus wenigstens noch eine gewisse Tradition der Technik zu finden, so fehlt diese seit Jahren völlig in der Sezession, die, sich gewollt modern gebärdend, in den Bahnen von Klimt bis Schiele wandelnd, diese in allen Möglichkeiten abwandelt, bar jedes Könnens und jeder Idee. Der Hagenbund, noch vor kurzem die einzige Gruppe, die wenigstens über einige Qualität und einiges Streben verfügte, ist heute, teils infolge der Unheizbarkeit und Verlotterung seiner Räume, teils infolge eigener Schwäche und interner Vorgänge im Stadium der Auflösung, und wenn auch

119

In dance the whole body, in modern dance every finger, draws lines with a very precise expression. The "modern" dancer moves across the stage in exact lines, which he incorporates as an essential element into the composition of his dance. Apart from which, the dancer's entire body, right down to the fingertips, is at every moment a continuous linear composition.

—Vasily Kandinsky, *Punkt und Linie zu Fläche* (Point and line to plane), 1926

"The Kandinsky Palucca drawings," writes Susan Laikin Funkenstein, "elucidate the fluidity of interchanges between the arts and modernism's openness to seeming antithesis in physical culture and women's culture, thereby contesting the binaries of high art/popular culture, masculine/feminine, and mind/body."[30] The drawings themselves are static, and the zigzags describing the dancer's body are anchored to the bottom of the page. Palucca, the body in question, is shown as a series of straight lines intersecting with curves, a two-dimensional stick figure animated by the ABC's of dance. Gender and indeed expression are evacuated from the image of the young dancer. This androgyny not only aligns Kandinsky and Palucca with representations of modernity and the "new woman" but echoes contemporary writings on other avant-garde dancers. Nijinsky, for example, had also been lauded for the asexuality of his onstage presence, and Fuller's ambiguous form was compared to the sea.[31]

A year after making the Palucca drawings, which he called *Tanzkurven*, or "dance curves," Kandinsky published *Punkt und Linie zu Fläche* (Point and line to plane), a distillation of his thoughts not only on abstraction but, pursuing an idea of aesthetic interconnection that was fundamental to the Bauhaus, on the possible relationship of dance to the other art forms.[32] Next to the rigid geometry of the Palucca drawings, the twenty-nine sheets with which Kandinsky illustrated *Punkt und Linie zu Fläche* are remarkably liberated (plates 157, 158). Here line moves freely across the page—indeed, in striking contrast to the *Tanzkurven*, most of the drawings are horizontal—as if animated by its own invention.

It seems no accident that Rudolf von Laban's creation of the system of dance notation still primarily used today ran parallel to the pedagogical notes of Kandinsky and Klee during their Bauhaus years. Kandinsky speaks of line as "the imprint of energy—the visible trace of the invisible" on the page, while Laban, a founding figure in German modern dance, regarded his linear recordings of dancers'

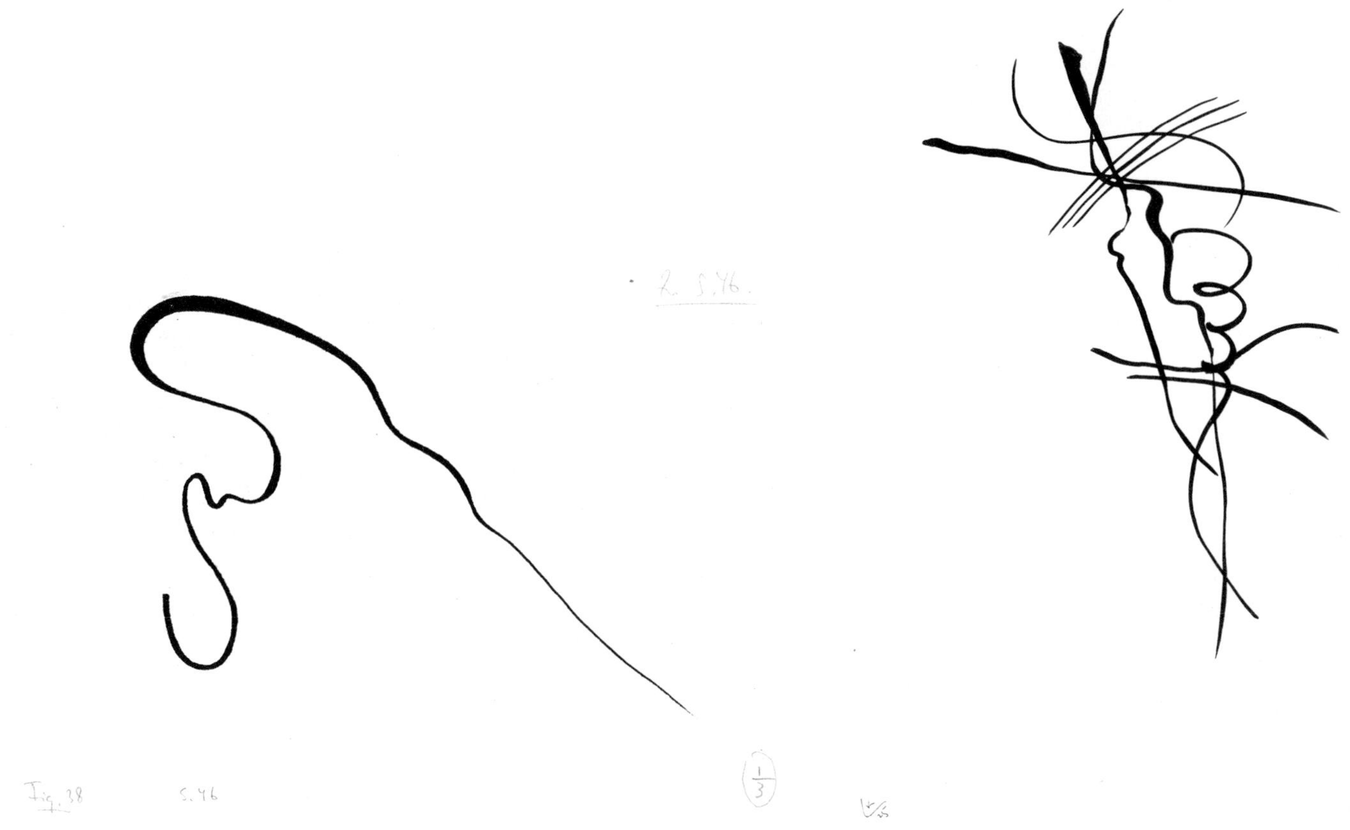

156. **Vasily Kandinsky**
(French, born Russia, 1866–1944)
Spread from Kandinsky's article "*Tanzkurven: Zu den Tänzen der Palucca*" (Dance curves: The dances of Palucca), *Das Kunstblatt*, 1926, juxtaposing the artist's drawings with photographs of Gret Palucca dancing

157. **Vasily Kandinsky**
(French, born Russia, 1866–1944)
Ligne courbe librement ondulée (Curved line undulating freely). 1925. Illustration for Kandinsky's book *Punkt und Linie zu Fläche* (Point and line to plane), 1926
Ink and gouache on paper
7 5/16 x 10 1/16" (18.5 x 25.6 cm)

158. **Vasily Kandinsky**
(French, born Russia, 1866–1944)
Ligne (Line). 1925. Illustration for Kandinsky's book *Punkt und Linie zu Fläche* (Point and line to plane), 1926
Ink on paper
15 1/8 x 9 3/4" (38.4 x 24.8 cm)

gestures as "trace forms" in "the land of silence."[33] Louppe remarks on the proliferation of dance notation in the twentieth century, and indeed, once Laban published his system in 1928, it almost immediately became a widespread discipline, answering the practical needs of dancers to record a work for reperformance and the development of a repertoire. Visual artists similarly may be inspired by "trace forms," images of a line expressed in the body or otherwise liberated in the visible world, to think in ways that go beyond the formal innovations evident in their work. With Klee, for example, for all his wonderful invention, his work with line as a driving compositional force seldom reflects the playfulness and radicality of his thoughts in the *Pädagogisches Skizzenbuch*. "When a point moves and becomes a line, it requires time," he wrote there;[34] the idea of line taking its time, unparalleled in its loveliness, anticipates the notion of a slowed-down or analog experience of time and space that would follow later in the century and in the contemporary moment.

Both Klee's *Artistenbildnis* (Portrait of an artiste, 1927; plate 159) and Francis Picabia's *Tabac-Rat* (Rat tobacco, 1919/1949; plate 160) can be seen as self-portraits, and both are inspired by a kind of dance. Picabia's picture frame with string stretched across it, and small labels erratically affixed, frames the artist's face in an often reproduced photograph and is almost as well-known empty. Also known as *Danse de Saint Guy* (Saint Guy's dance), the work was intended to be shown freestanding in space, where it would have choreographed its viewers to move so that their faces were framed by it and bisected by the strings running across it. String—line in three dimensions—functioned in multiple ways for Picabia, here functioning like Severini's sequins as a collage element leaving the page, if not the frame. It played similarly wide roles for Duchamp and Man Ray, whether as the unbound tethers of the tightrope dancer (plate 18), the bound object (plate 19), or traveling through space (plate 167).

The formal elements of graphic art are: points, linear, planar, and spatial energies. A simple planar element is, for example, the energy produced by the broad unmodulated stroke of a thick crayon. An example of a spatial element is a moist, vaporous spot of varying intensity made by a full brush. . . .

The dead point must be overcome with the first act of movement (line). . . .

When a point moves and becomes a line, it requires time. Also when a line becomes a plane. The same is true of the movement of planes into spaces. Does a picture come into being all at once? No, it is constructed piece by piece, just like a house.

— Paul Klee, *Schöpferische Konfession* (Creative credo), 1919

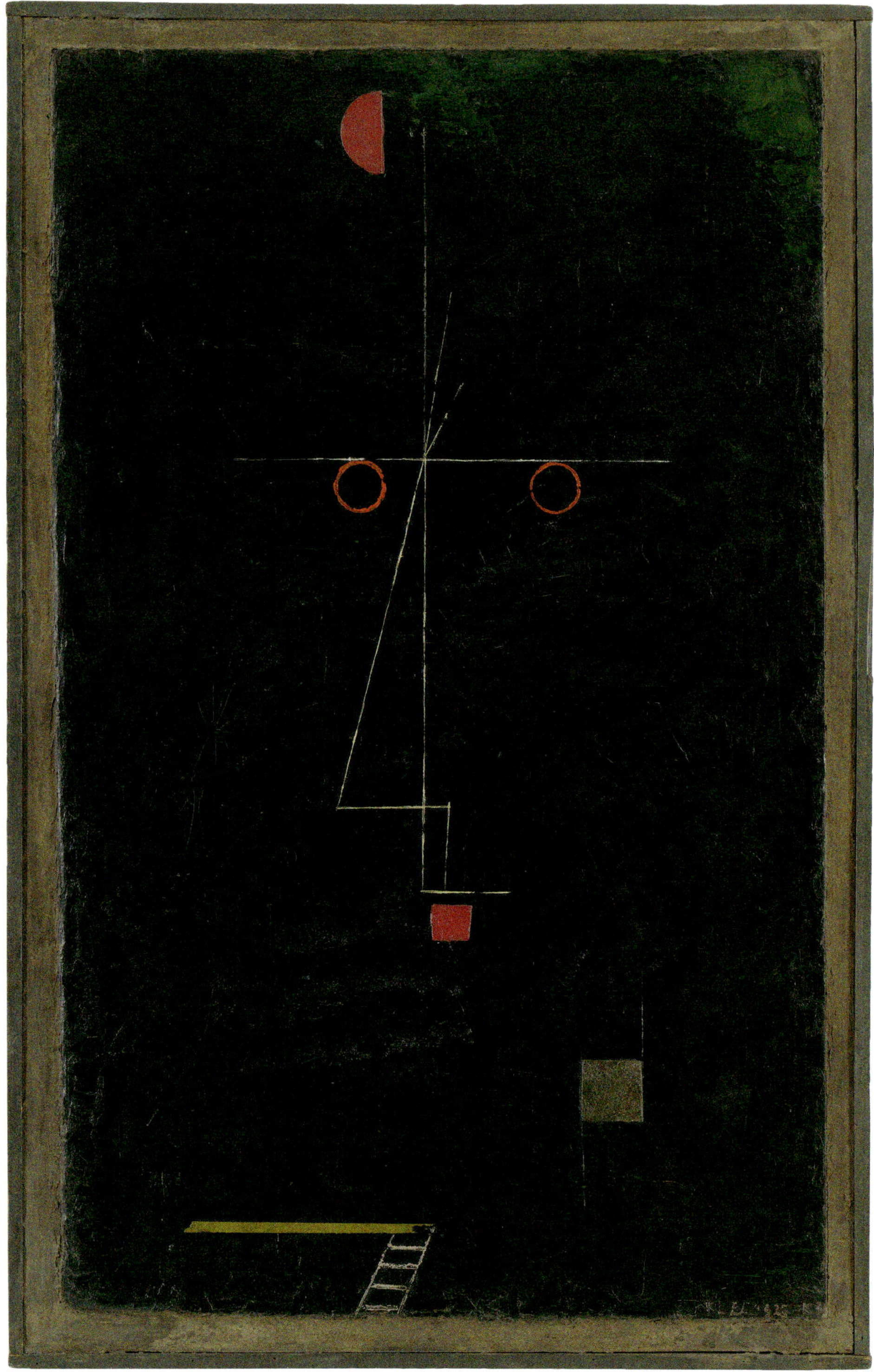

159. Paul Klee
(German, born Switzerland, 1879–1940)
Artistenbildnis (Portrait of an artiste). 1927
Oil and collage on cardboard over wood with painted plaster border
24 7/8 x 15 3/4″ (63.2 x 40 cm)

160. Francis Picabia
(French, 1879–1953)
Tabac-Rat (Rat tobacco; formerly titled *Danse de Saint Guy* [Saint Guy's dance]). 1919/1949
Cardboard, ink and string in a frame
41 1/8 x 33 3/8″ (104.4 x 84.7 cm)

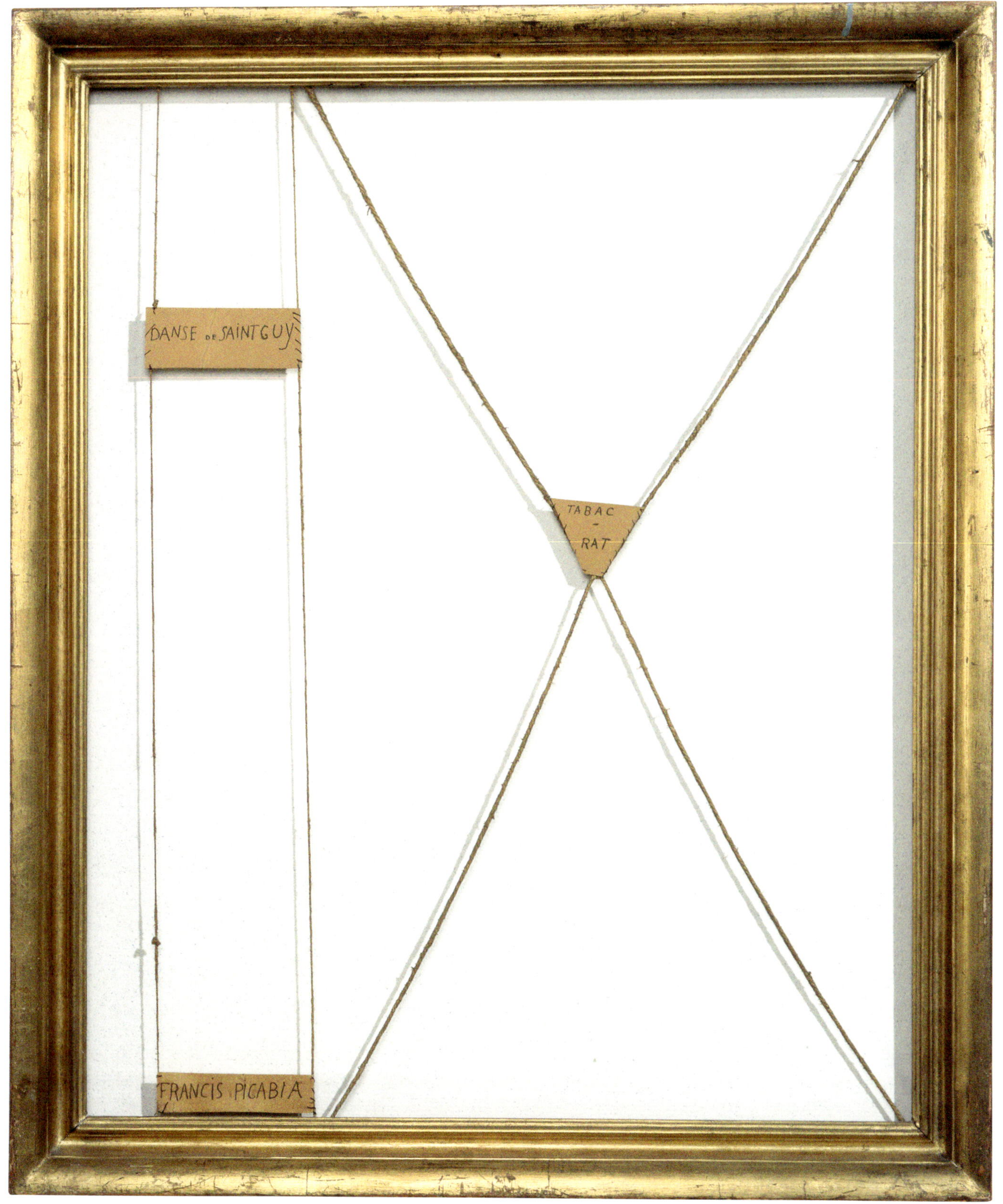
DANSE DE SAINT GUY
TABAC
-
RAT
FRANCIS PICABIA

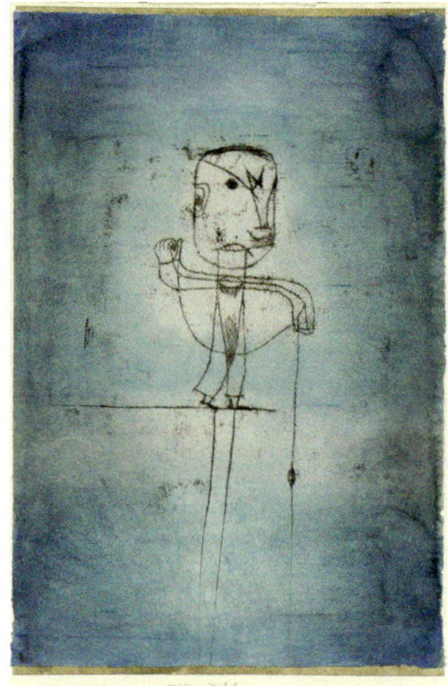

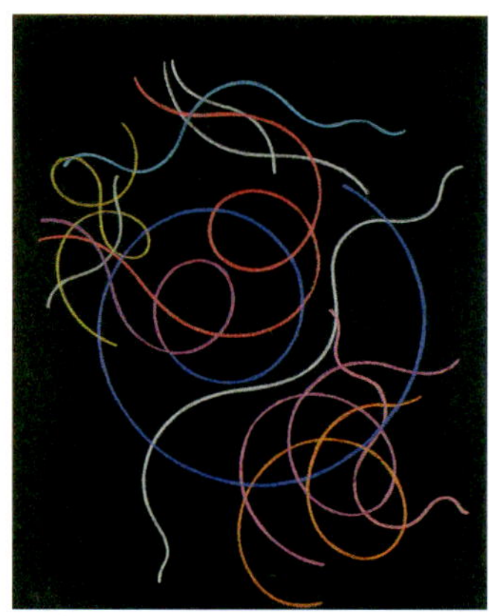

Klee's portrait shows a face constructed out of a series of shapes, rhyming with the voids shaped by Picabia's strings. A simple geometry barely holds the features together. At the bottom, a small ladder implies that the line it climbs up to is a tightrope—that the "artiste" of the title is a circus performer—and the darkness surrounding the figure recalls the yawning upper regions of the circus tent, where lines, cables, ropes, and the bodies of performers dance together. Klee's *Angler* (1921; plate 161) and his well-known *Zwitscher-Maschine* (Twittering machine, 1922; plate 29) display a different kind of line from the rather static geometry of the portrait. Describing a truly useless and fantastical piece of technology, *Die Zwitscher-Maschine* is an iconic Dada image. All motion, noise, and futility, the composition is a mass of lines that accumulate to form the skeletal suggestions of mechanical birds. *Der Angler* is more poignant and solitary, with its small but profoundly suggestive fisherman's line dropping into space and dangling vertically yet indeterminately from its own weight. The line looks as if it could meander off the page on its own, away from its owner and of its own volition. How tempting to pair the freedom implied for line here to contemporary works in which a string or delicate line has great political, social, or aesthetic implications. I am thinking here of Cecilia Vicuña's many works using lines of string, fabric, or even liquid (plates 163, 226), or of Francis Alÿs's poignant *Leak* (2002) and *The Green Line (SOMETIMES DOING SOMETHING POETIC CAN BECOME POLITICAL AND SOMETIMES DOING SOMETHING POLITICAL CAN BECOME POETIC)* (2007; plate 231), each a filament of drizzled paint moving through social and urban space.

Picabia's *Tabac-Rat* aligns with a contemporaneous work by his friend Duchamp, the *Sculpture for Traveling* (1918; plates 5, 140), an ephemeral work today best known through a murky but evocative hand-colored photograph included in the *Boîte-en-valise* (*Box in a Valise*) of 1935–41. This transient net of rubber has profound implications for later projects such as Clark's *Caminhando*, the collapsed frames of Gyula Kosice (of the Argentine Madí group; plate 175), Tuttle's Wire Pieces of 1972 (plate 184), and a range of recent works that engage with notions of an embodied or even nomadic sculptural practice. Dangling from a string across a domestically scaled space, Duchamp's collapsed form also incarnates, as does *Tabac-Rat*, the trope of the collapsed armature of painting deployed by avant-garde artists throughout the century. While *Tabac-Rat* interrogates painting's frontality, artifice, and representational capacity by referencing its physical components of stretcher and frame, *Sculpture for Traveling* undoes that physicality by creating what is essentially a limp grid made out of repurposed rubber bathing caps. Having first made *Sculpture for Traveling* in his studio in New York, Duchamp took it with him when he moved to Buenos Aires, where he reinstalled it, again tethered between floor and ceiling. He initially intended it to be a network of lines extending across the entire space, an idea he later realized with his contribution to the *First Papers of Surrealism* exhibition in New York in 1942, the installation known as *Sixteen Miles of String* (plate 167).

In 1917, at the opening of the first Dada exhibition to take place in Zurich, Sophie Tauber danced, signifying a new focus on dance in Dada activities. A student of Laban, who taught and fostered experimental dance in the city, Tauber believed in integrating all the art forms and incorporated dance into her investigations of abstraction. Her dance at the opening was seen as a delirious breakthrough, prompting the Dadaist Hugo Ball, whose costume she was wearing, to declare,

> Abstract dances: a gong beat is enough to stimulate the dancer's body to make the most fantastic movements. . . . The nervous system exhausts all the vibrations of the sound, and perhaps all the hidden emotion of the gong beater too, and turns them into an image. Here in this special case, a poetic sequence of sounds was enough to make each of the individual word particles produce the strangest visible effect on the hundred-jointed body of the dancer.[35]

Taeuber—or, after marrying Jean Arp in 1922, Taeuber-Arp—later gave up performing and focused on the production of crafts, design objects, paintings, and drawings. But the dynamism of the

161. Paul Klee
(German, born Switzerland, 1879–1940)
Der Angler (The angler). 1921
Oil transfer drawing, watercolor, and ink on paper with watercolor and ink borders on board
19 7/8 x 12 1/2" (50.5 x 31.8 cm)

162. Sophie Taeuber-Arp
(Swiss, 1889–1943)
Mouvement de lignes en couleurs (Movement of colored lines). 1940
Colored pencil on cardboard
14 1/8 x 11" (35.9 x 28 cm)

163. Cecilia Vicuña
(Chilean, born 1948)
Hilacha (Loose thread). 1994
Performance view, New York

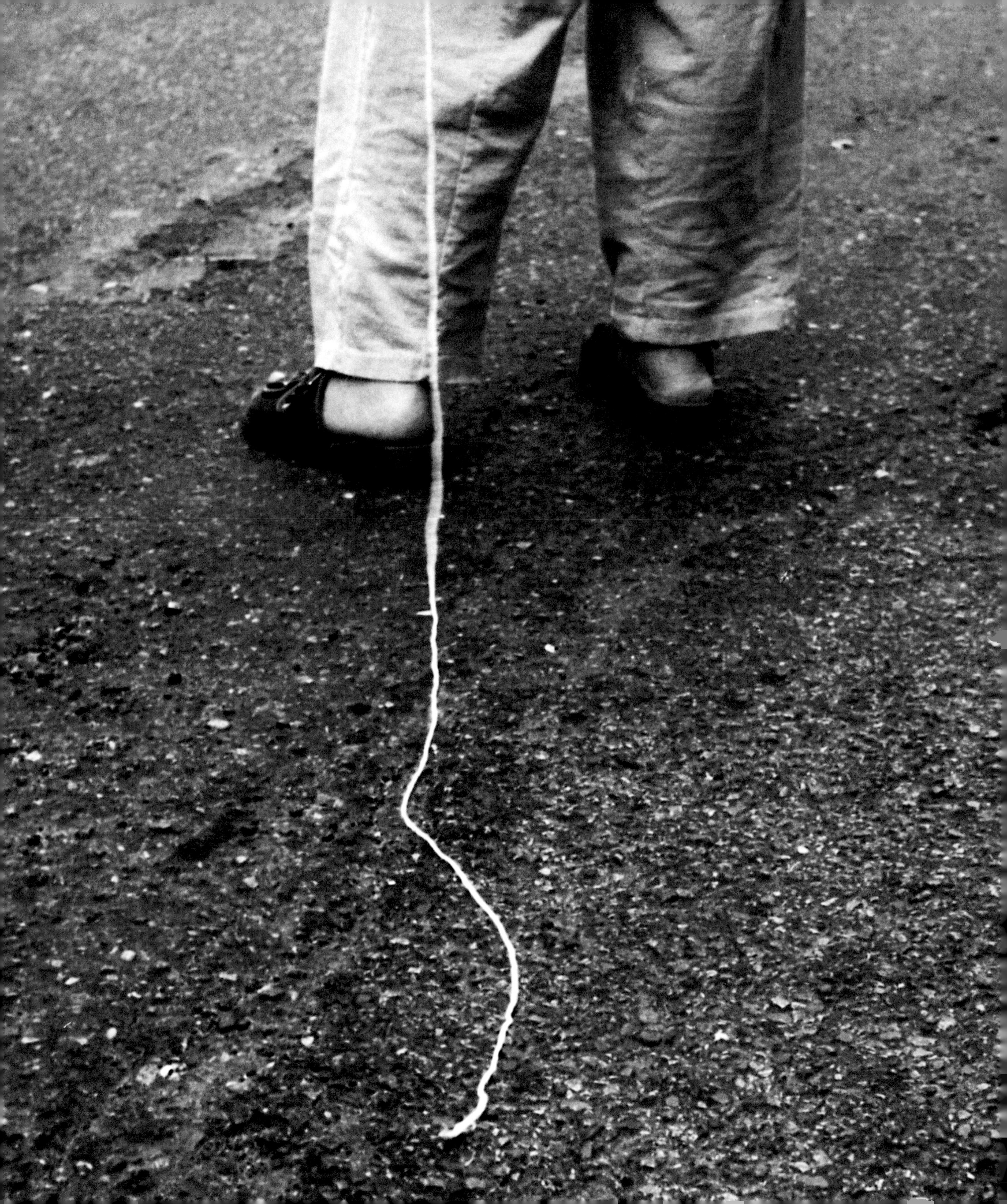

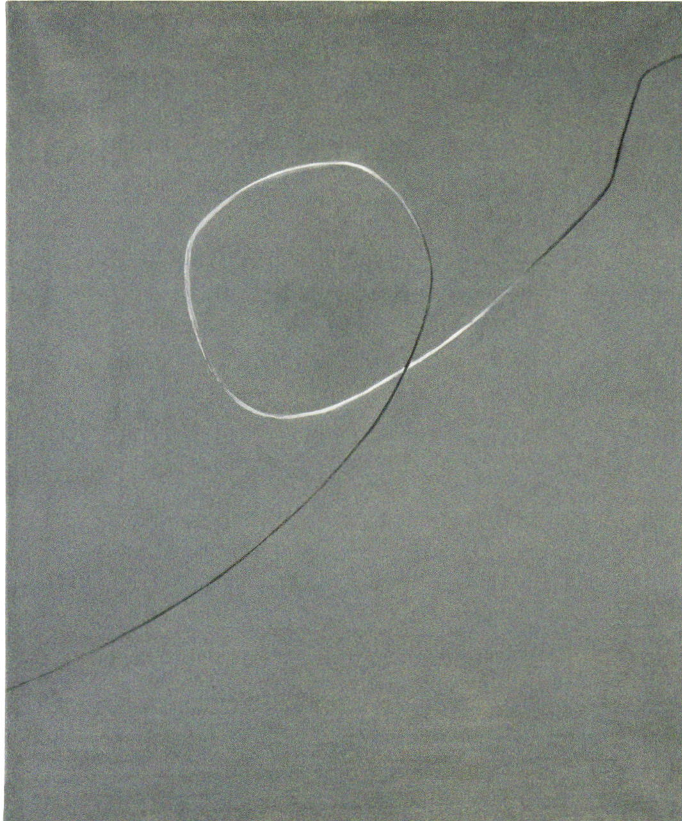

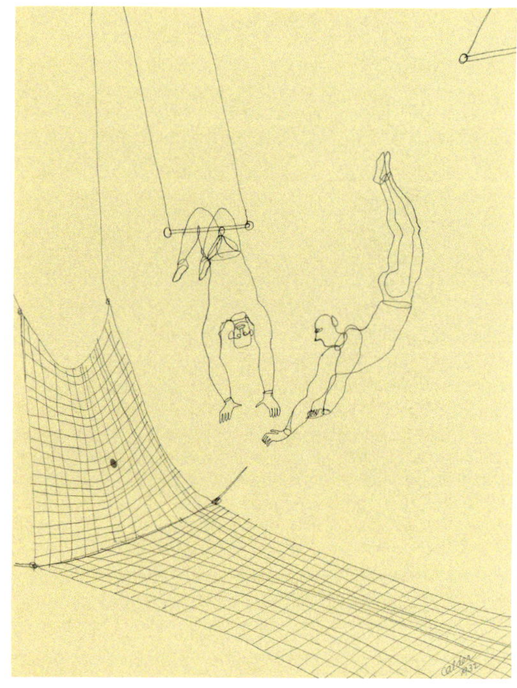

moving form still inhabited her compositions, lending a lively electricity to abstract works such as *Mouvement de lignes en couleurs* (Movement of colored lines, 1940; plates 8, 162). In related drawings, such as *Lignes géométriques et ondoyantes* (Geometric and undulating lines, 1941; plate 49), Taeuber-Arp juxtaposes the grid — a part of her field of vision through the warp and woof of fabric and craft materials — with dancing lines that animate the geometry they bump up against.

In thinking about line and movement, drawing and dance, across the twentieth century, a handful of artists seem essential. Taeuber-Arp is one such; another is Alexander Calder, whose work on the theme of the circus is one of the great instances of a preoccupation with the movement of line in space. While not quite dance, the practices of acrobats and other circus performers epitomize corporeal free spirit, the ambition to defy gravity and perform feats that animate and contort the body, abstracting its usual form. Calder became an aficionado of the circus while working as a sketch artist for a New York weekly in the mid-1920s; in 1926, having moved to Paris, he began the work today known as *Calder's Circus*, which he finished in 1931. This and the extraordinary body of abstract paintings and kinetic sculptures that immediately followed evidence an ongoing dialogue between the static and the animated line. The simple arabesque of Untitled (1930; plate 164) finds human form in the flying acrobats who lunge across the page of *The Catch II* (1932; plate 165).

As well as the antics of the performers, the lovely transparency of the wirelike contours describing their bodies, and those contours' moments of intersection with the tracings of gear and equipment, what is interesting in these drawings is the architecture of the tent as it is defined by the lines of ladders and rigging (plate 224). This preoccupation with structuring space through a connective network of lines and vectors appears not only in Calder's kinetic sculpture, which begins during this same period with works such as *Croisière* (Cruise, 1931) and *A Universe* (1934), but also in the work of other artists working in Paris at this time. In 1936, Maria Helena Vieira da Silva, a Portuguese-born artist who spent much of her life in Paris, made an entirely abstract composition titled *Les Lignes* (The lines, plate 166) in which a black

164. Alexander Calder
(American, 1898–1976)
Untitled. 1930
Oil on canvas
28 3/4 x 23 3/4" (73 x 60.3 cm)

165. Alexander Calder
(American, 1898–1976)
The Catch II. 1932
Ink on paper
19 1/8 x 14 1/8" (48.4 x 35.8 cm)

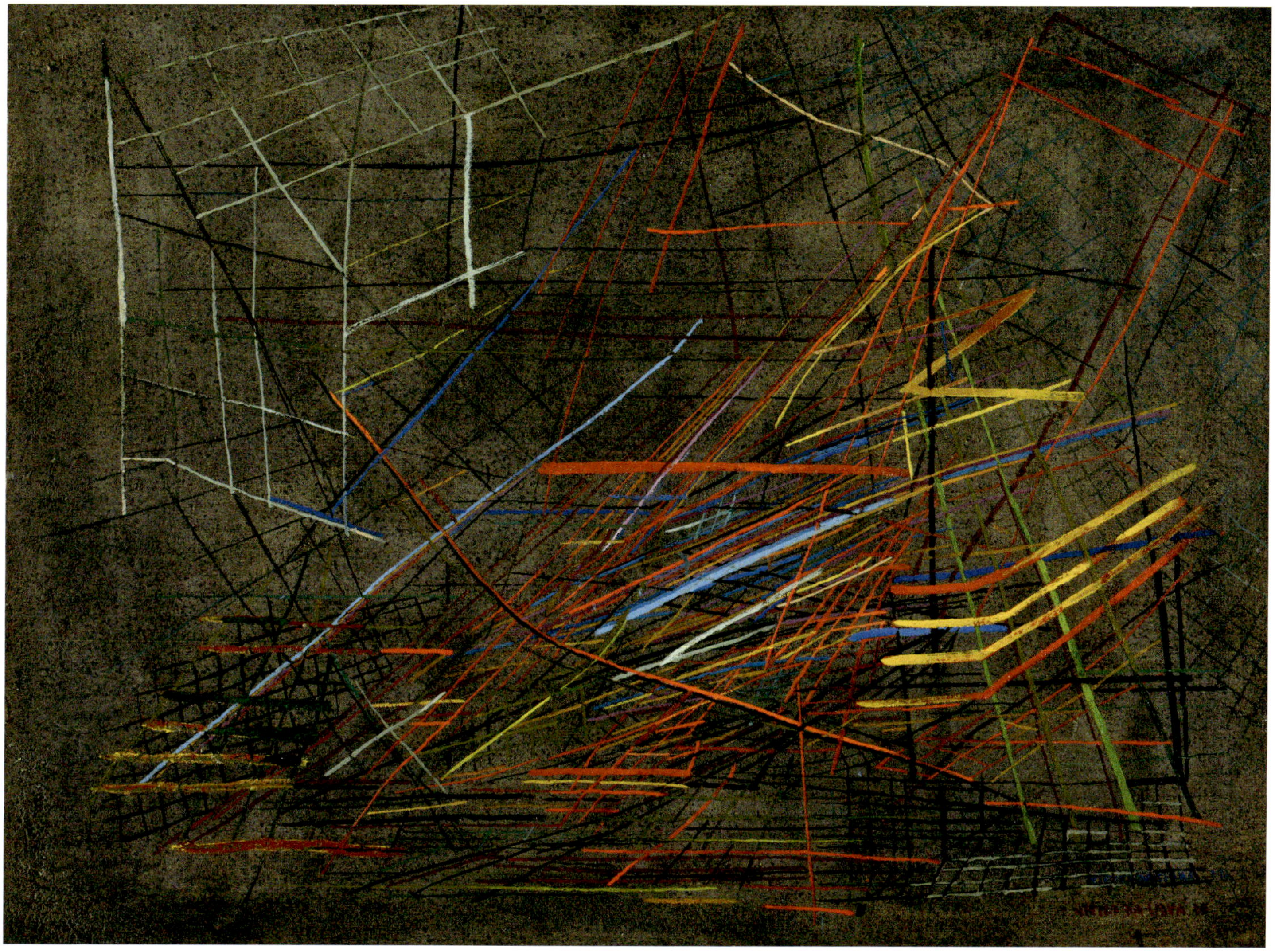

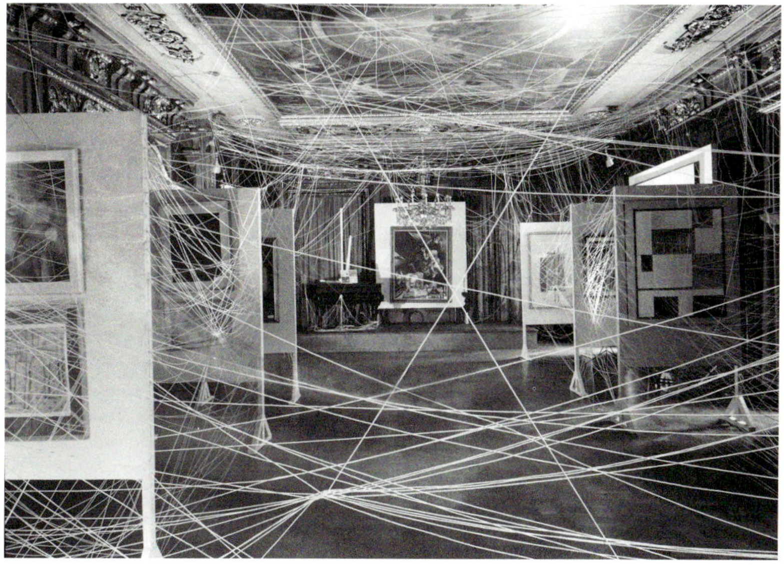

166. Maria Helena Vieira da Silva
(French, born Portugal, 1908–1992)
Les Lignes (The lines). 1936
Oil on canvas
27 9/16 x 36 1/4″ (70 x 92 cm)

167. John D. Schiff
(American, born Germany, 1907–1976)
Gallery view of exhibition *First Papers of Surrealism*, with Marcel Duchamp's installation known as *Sixteen Miles of String*. 1942
Gelatin silver print
7 5/8 x 10″ (19.4 x 25.4 cm)

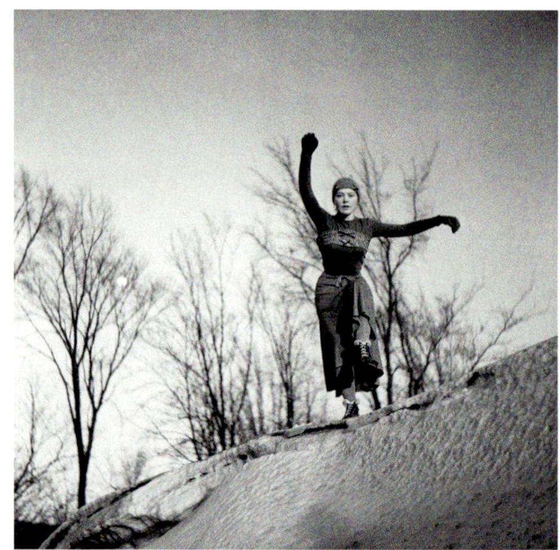

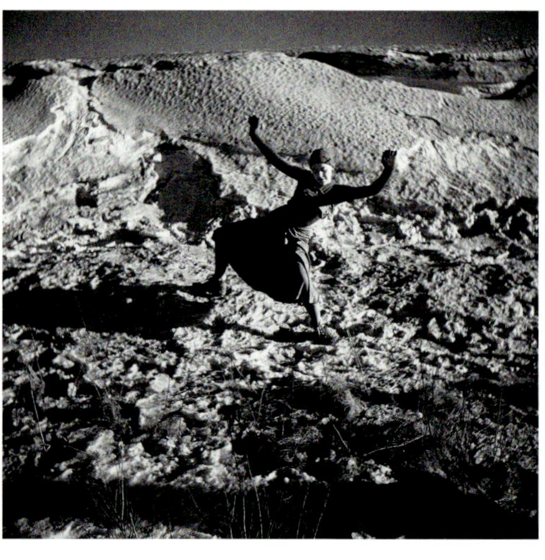

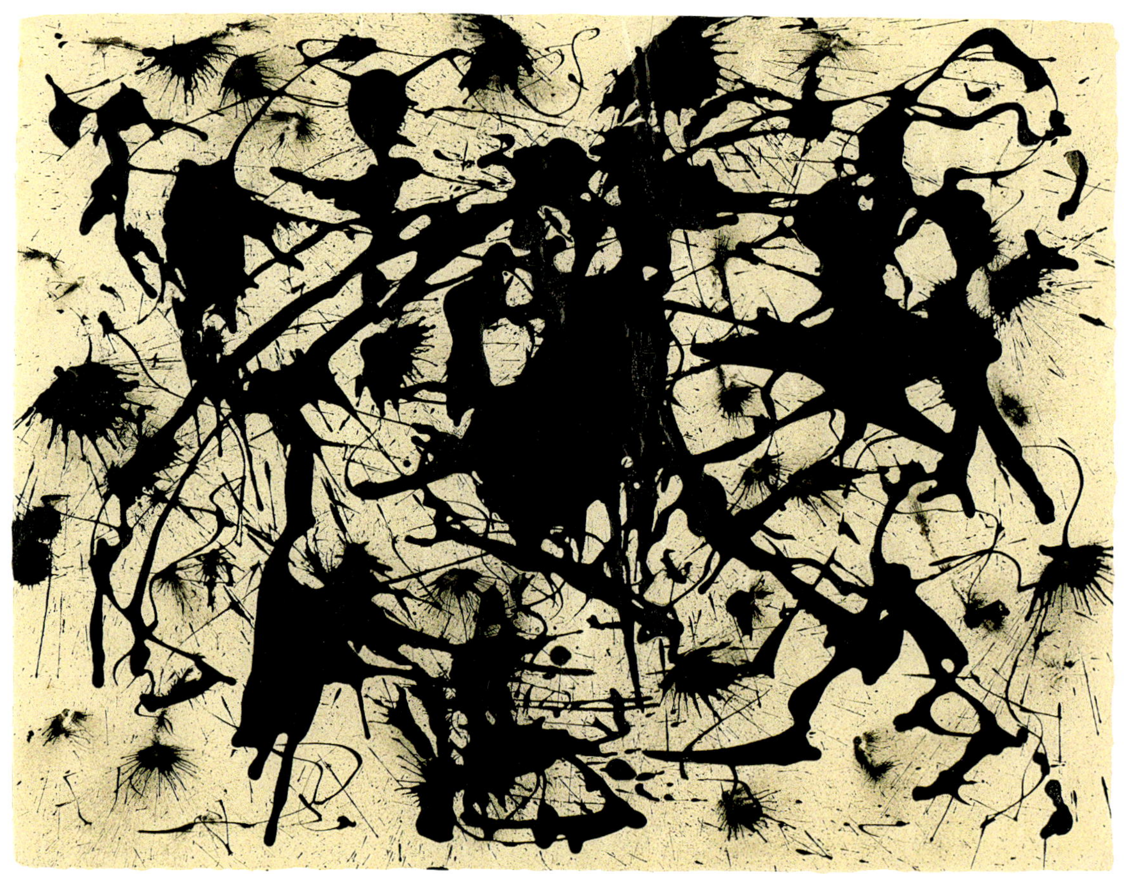

168 (left)**. Jackson Pollock**
(American, 1912–1956)
Untitled. c. 1950
Ink on paper
$17\ 1/2 \times 22\ 1/4''$ (44.5 x 56.6 cm)

169–73 (above)**. Françoise Sullivan**
(Canadian, born 1925)
Danse dans la neige (Dance in the snow)
nos. 3, 6, 12, 13, 15. 1948
5 of 17 gelatin silver prints
(photographs: Maurice Perron)
mounted on Masonite mounted on wood
Each: $15\ 3/8 \times 15\ 3/8''$ (39 x 39 cm)

174. Page from the journal *Arte madí universal* no. 0 (detail), showing Madí dance by **Paulina Ossona**. 1947

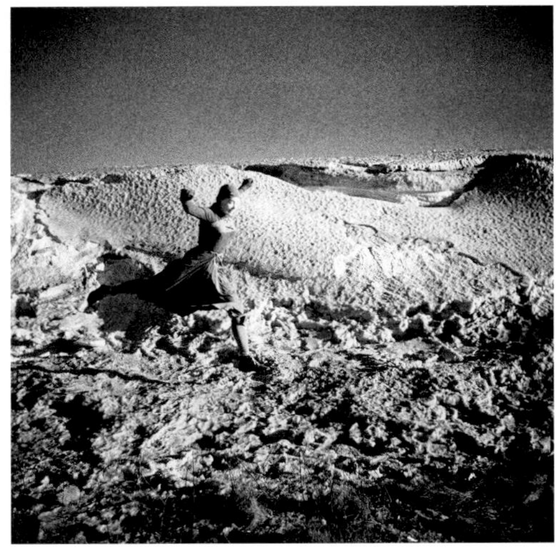

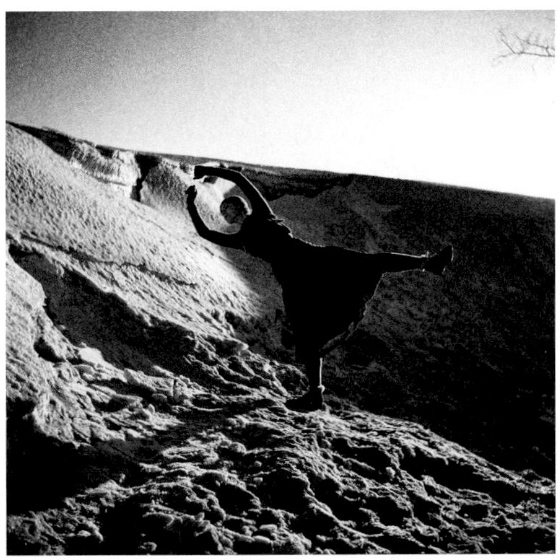

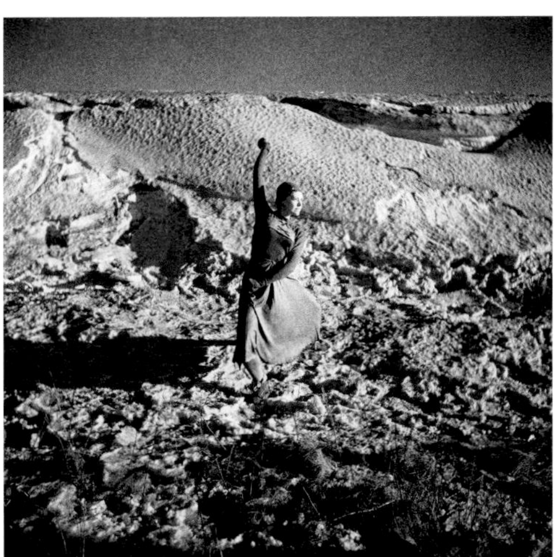

and white geometry in the top register of the picture suggests an architecture that, however, dissolves in a cascade of falling colored lines and marks toward the bottom. Da Silva's work is primarily nonrepresentational, participating in the *tachiste* investigation of the gesture that would characterize Art Informel in Europe after World War II. Compositions such as *La Ville* (The city, 1950–51; plate 86), however, anticipate Guy Debord's ideas of the *dérive*, the drifting urban stroll, and of the psychogeography of the city that would soon emerge in the thinking of the Situationists. Recalling Klee "taking a line for a walk," and the poetic potential of the dangling, gravity-bound line of his *Angler*, the *dérive* was imagined as an experience of the city through a series of walks, a passing through, a spatializing of consciousness literally through and around the urban geography.[36] This finding of a path, a traverse, a line through, would become important for artists of the 1960s in whose work line becomes a way of inscribing space.

In North America after World War II, the discourse of the gesture that was evolving in Abstract Expressionism, and particularly in the work of Jackson Pollock (plates 56, 168), had parallels in modernist dance. The Canadian artist Françoise Sullivan, for example, was making experiments with movement that she considered absolutely related to her painting practice. Beginning in 1947, partly to exploit the possibilities of a 16mm film camera that she owned, Sullivan made four dances responding to the seasons in the landscape around her native Quebec. Akin in spirit to the notion of the wandering *dérive*, and to Pollock's movements as documented in Hans Namuth's film of him at work (which, however, she would only have seen later, since Namuth made it in 1950), Sullivan's improvisations in the winter landscape left traces of her gestures in the snow (plates 169–73). The work also has a place in a broader context, the Canadian awareness of the North — the vast Canadian landmass, and the traversal and claiming of that land both by people and by systems of travel and communication.[37] Sullivan marked the land with her dancing body much as the contemporary Canadian artist Mimi Gellman moves through the snowy expanse in an attempt to map or mark it (plates 209, 228).

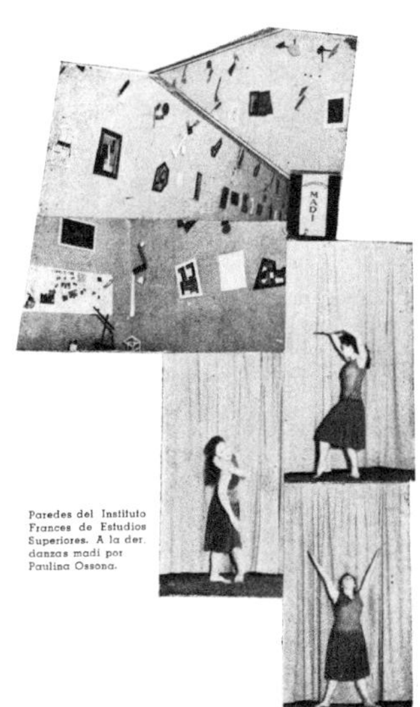

After World War II, allegiances to abstraction, and to modernism in general, were reshaped internationally, in part as an effect of the diaspora of European artists brought about by the war. Concurrent with the advent of Abstract Expressionism in New York, Latin America harbored a new spirit of invention. In Argentina, a center of avant-garde activity, the artists' groups Arte Concreto-Invención and the more experimental Madí group formed in 1945 and 1946 respectively; each would have a presence in Paris, exhibiting in the Salon des Réalités Nouvelles.[38] The Madí group experimented with shaped canvases and with the use of neon and kinetic forms. Kosice's *Escultura Movil Articulada* (Mobile articulated sculpture, 1948; plate 175) is emblematic of the group's way of collapsing frame and surface: as its title suggests, the work is literally a mobile, hanging free in space, and a sculpture rather than the painting that its limp dimensions might imply. The Madí group was a mercurial consortium but the role of Arte

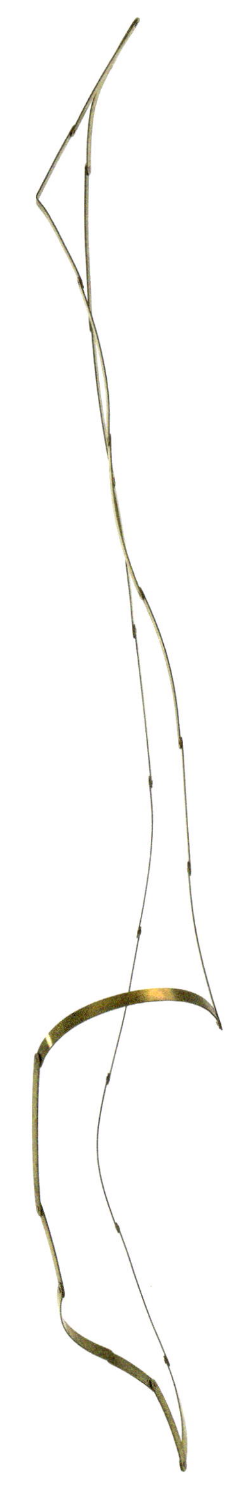

Concreto-Invención as a kind of counter to it is an indication of its strength, and of the vigor of artistic discourse in Buenos Aires at the time. The Arte Concreto-Invención artists remained committed to the two-dimensional surface of painting but created highly inventive abstract compositions, such as Tomás Maldonado's lyrical *Desarrollo de 14 temas* (Development of *14* themes, 1951–52; plate 176), in which broken lines disrupt the field, as in Piet Mondrian's compositions of the 1920s (plate 61), but remain secure within the compositional frame.

Kosice was the primary spokesperson for the Madí group and carried on its legacy long after the group itself disbanded. The group's ambition was international, and it made contacts with artists in art centers as distant as Tokyo by producing a journal, *Arte madí universal*, which included writings and reproductions from beyond Argentina—although many of the artists involved merely corresponded with the group, sending texts and images to be published in the magazine. Even so, the desire for an international presence remains striking. Images of dance appear on occasion, including a series in a 1947 issue of the journal showing the Argentine modern dancer and choreographer Paulina Ossona (plate 174). Like the Madí artists, Ossona clearly welcomed a discourse that included performative activity in an ongoing interrogation of abstraction and painting.

175. Gyula Kosice
(Fernando Fallik; Argentine, born Czechoslovakia [now Slovakia] 1924)
Escultura Movil Articulada (Mobile articulated sculpture). 1948
Brass
Dimensions variable, c. 65 x 12 x 1/2″ (165.1 x 30.5 x 1.3 cm)

176. Tomás Maldonado
(Argentine, born 1922)
Desarrollo de 14 temas
(Development of 14 themes). 1951–52
Oil on canvas
6′ 6 7/8″ x 6′ 10 3/4″ (200.3 x 210.2 cm)

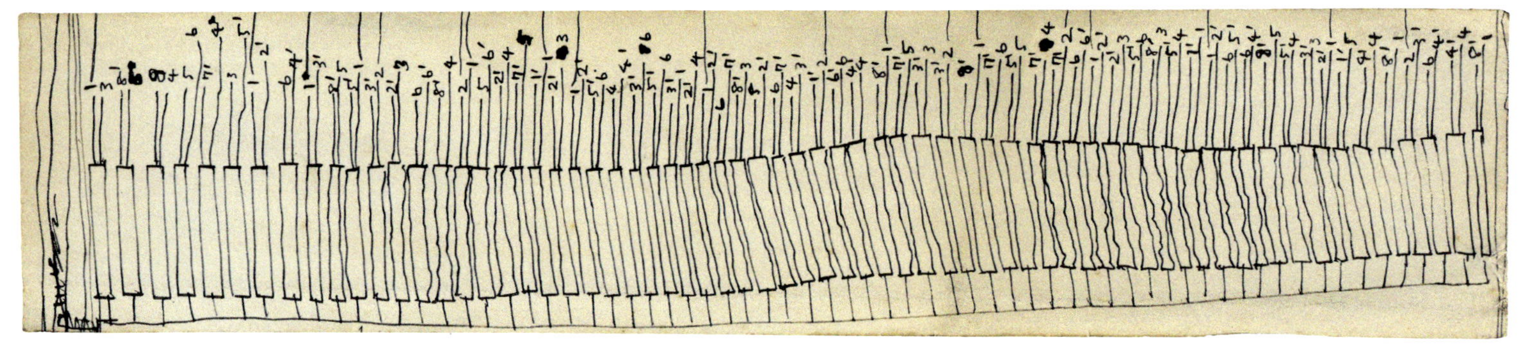

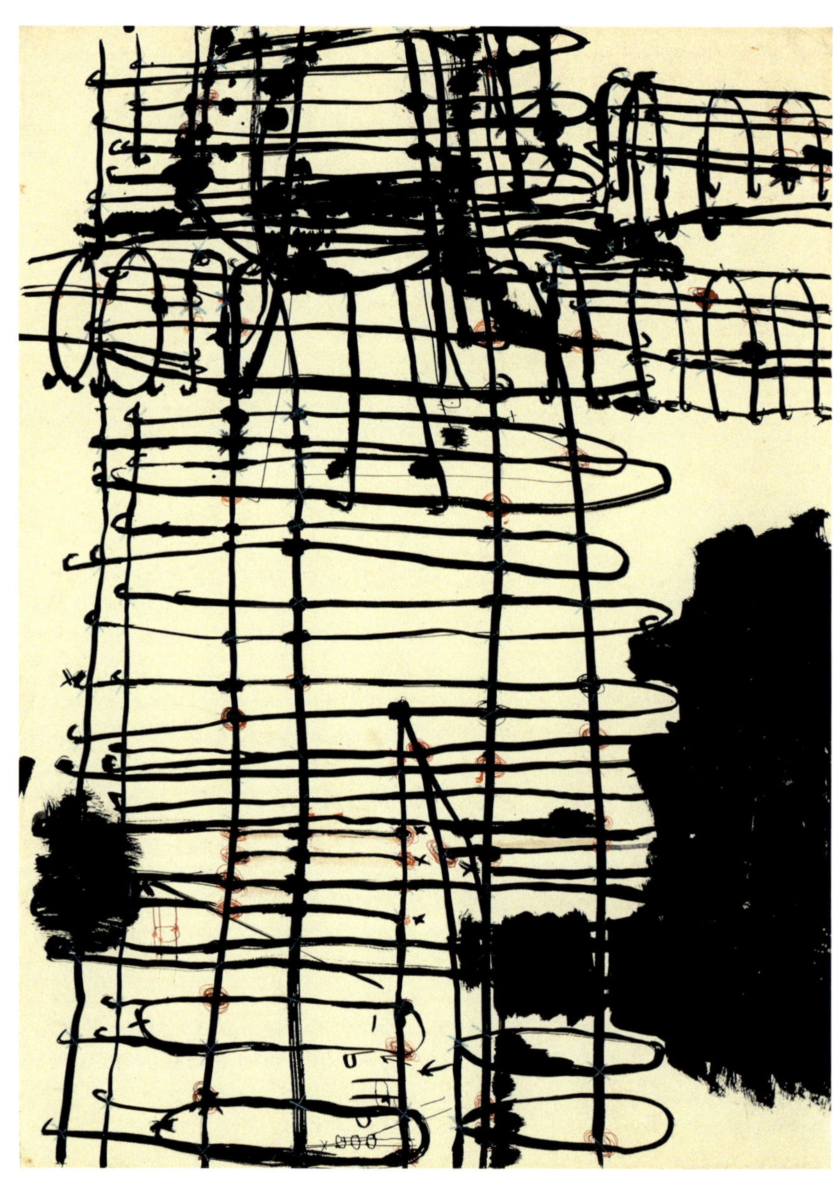

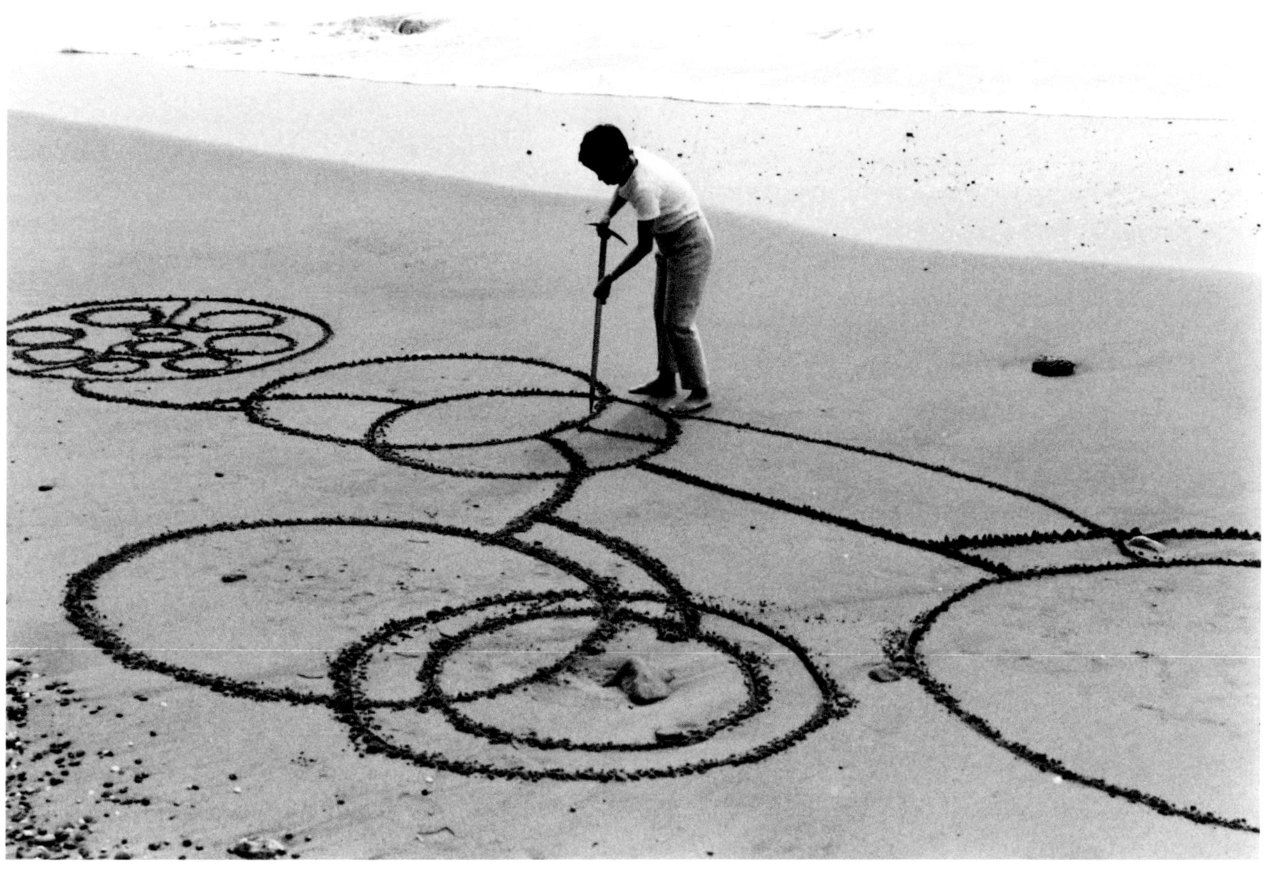

A similar development occurred in Osaka, Japan, in 1954, when the Gutai group came together to experiment with gestural abstract painting. The Japanese word *gutai* is roughly translatable as "concrete," "tangible," or "material," and the spirit of the association was one of creation through destruction. Among the artists who participated in the group's founding and early activities were Jiro Yoshihara (whose name appears as the author of the Gutai Manifesto of 1956), Sadamasa Motonaga, Saburo Murakami, Shozo Shimamoto, and two women, Toshiko Kinoshita and Atsuko Tanaka.[39] Tanaka's *Electric Dress* (1956), mentioned in the manifesto, is a network of electric lights that the artist could wear, or perform, like a kind of coat. In documentary photographs of her in the *Electric Dress*, her small frame seems barely to be able to support what is simultaneously a heavy garment and a colorful, visually engaging work of sculpture — she is swallowed by the lights, her head peering out like Nijinsky's dancer engulfed in fabric and movement. Tanaka's drawings for and after the dress (plates 177, 178) make clear that its circuitry was for her a sign for the circulatory systems of the body.

A public component of the Gutai group's activities is documented in films of its members' performances, including Murakami's famous *Breaking through Many Sheets of Paper* (1956), in which he pushed his way through a sequence of large paper panels to open the first Gutai exhibition, an action of violence and release echoing the performativity of Pollock's drip paintings and anticipating Yves Klein's notorious *Leap into the Void* of 1960. In Tanaka's film *Round on Sand* (1968; plate 179), created during the later years of Gutai activity and one of a number of works she made outdoors, the artist deploys her vocabulary of circular forms to make a drawing in the sand of a beach. Viewed from above, like the large Nazca line drawings in the stones of a desert in Peru, this drawing in nature, a line in the sand, implies the use of action to reach toward the infinite.

177. Atsuko Tanaka
(Japanese, 1932–2005)
Preparatory sketch for *Electric Dress*. c. 1956
Ink on paper
2 3/16 x 10˝ (5.6 x 25.4 cm)

178. Atsuko Tanaka
(Japanese, 1932–2005)
Drawing after *Electric Dress*. 1956
India ink, ink, pencil, and crayon on paper
30 5/16 x 21 5/8˝ (77 x 55 cm)

179. Atsuko Tanaka
(Japanese, 1932–2005)
Round on Sand. 1968
Performance view

A WALK FOR A WALK'S SAKE (1960–1980)

"You'll see I'm going to hold on to the *Guitar*," Pablo Picasso once told his friend André Salmon, "but I shall sell its plan. Everyone will be able to make it for himself."[40] Picasso's desire that his cardboard *Guitar* of 1912 (plates 2, 15) be re-makable by the public sets the stage for an interpretation of the Cubist collage as a move into the real. The emergence of collage as an advanced art form marked a new engagement with the architectonic structure not only of vision but of three-dimensional space.

In three articles written for *Artforum* magazine, New York, in 1976, Brian O'Doherty tracked the evolution of what he called the "white cube" — the supposedly neutral gallery space — toward an engagement with context, and the eventual merging of the contextual with the object itself. Anchored early in the century, his discussion hinges on the Cubist collage:

> The moment a collage was attached to that unruly Cubist surface there was an instantaneous switch. No longer able to pin a subject together in a space too shallow for it, the multiple vanishing points of the Analytic Cubist picture shower out into the room with the spectator. His point of view ricochets among them. The surface of the picture is made opaque by collage. Behind it is simply a wall, or a void. In front is an open space in which the viewer's sense of his own presence becomes an increasingly palpable shadow.[41]

The frontality of the Cubist picture, and that showering out into the room, are visible in Picasso's and Georges Braque's extraordinary experiments of 1912–13 (plate 180), which point toward Picasso's magnificent cardboard *Guitar* and ultimately the sheet metal *Guitar* of 1914. All front, with its flat back subsuming the support of the paper, pregnant with its own possible unmaking, the cardboard *Guitar* virtually moves off the wall into the space of the viewer. The artist's steps through his unruly surface toward the realization of multiple vanishing points in three dimensions are visible in works that begin with the eloquent line drawing *Guitar* (1912; plate 14) and culminate with the pair of three-dimensional guitars. Between these two Picasso had traversed a great distance, extending the act of collage and the rupture of the surface and moving form, plane, and line into the real.

The extension of the plane of painting into the space of experience beyond the visual, and the deployment of line as the instrument of spatiality, would be a recurring concern throughout the century. Many of Eva Hesse's experiments of the mid-1960s, for example, show her disrupting geometric constraints through an almost whimsical series of material provocations: in works on paper, she may make small tendrils of filament emanate from rings of black and white circles, while in biomorphic abstractions she pries and loosens extensions of rope and latex from the unforgiving flatness of the compositional plane. In its sheer ambition and its aggressive graphic and sculptural presence, Hesse's great *Hang Up* (1966; plate 182) is her masterpiece of this period, operating equally as plane, grid, and picture frame while simultaneously and humorously seeking the status of sculpture. The line created by an acrylic-and-cord-coated steel tube moves suggestively out from the frame — which circumscribes only the wall, O'Doherty's void — then circles back to it, creating an embodied zone for the implied viewer.

What Hesse accomplished in this anthropomorphized "painting" — a painting performing as a sculpture enervated through the extension of line — Fred Sandback rehearsed a year later in an untitled string sculpture that is both anchored to the wall and implies a plane at an angle to it (plate 183). Beginning with the wall, Sandback constructs a minimal geometry that is both concrete and dematerialized. His string installations are both drawings in space and spatial constructions made with line. Add to this grouping Robert Ryman's *Impex* of 1968 (plate 66) and Tuttle's Wire Pieces (plate 184) and it is clear that in the wake of Abstract Expressionism, and its vertical optical field, an energetic critique of painting was going on.

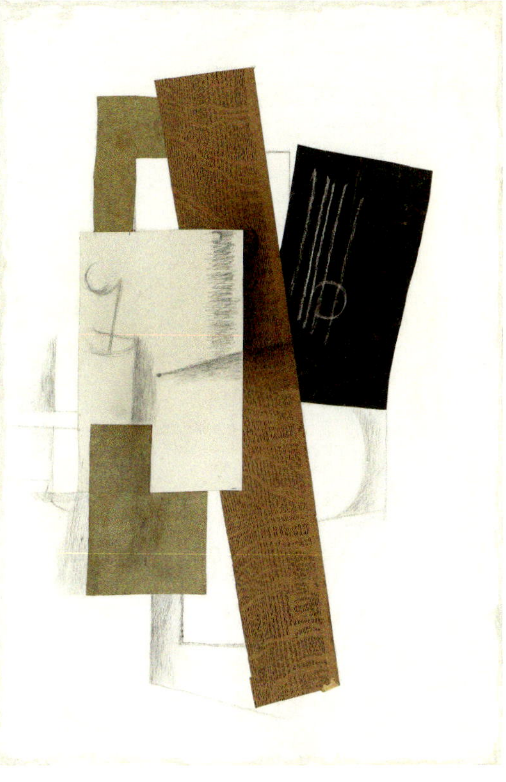

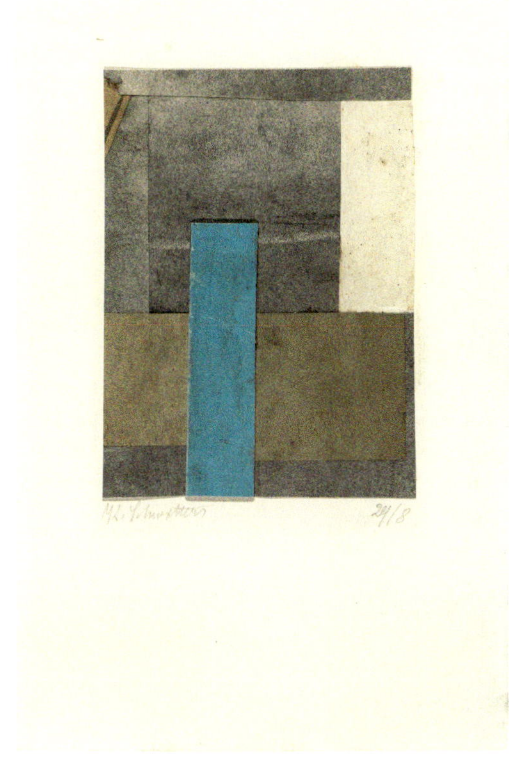

The incursion of real space, the space of the viewer, into the physical perimeter of sculpture, and thus the notion of installation that emerged in the 1960s both in sculpture and in movement-based works such as those at the Judson, had another important antecedent earlier in the century, around 1923, when Kurt Schwitters began construction of his Merzbau, the environment he made out of his home in Hannover. Schwitters initially conceived of modulating the space through a three-dimensional drawing made of string. Always insisting that he was a painter, he spent his career working toward an idea of the house as body, the body as house — the Merzbau, an installation as a kind of sculptural collage. Jaleh Mansoor has called Schwitters's method the "production of the process of production."[42] Even before he began the Merzbau he made wall-based works, the Merz collages (plate 181), that manifest the invention of an architectonic language in two dimensions. What we see in these works is akin to the operation of the Cubist collage: the articulation of space, the grinding through the surface of the paper to get to something tangible and sensorial. In dialogue with Constructivism and in particular with El Lissitzky, Schwitters layered planes of color to the point of the physical disruption of the plane, altogether obliterating the figure/ground duality and setting in motion a delirious mix of color and form.

One way of reading the Merzbau is as the production of space through line, which literally disrupts and opens up the spatiotemporal plane of architecture. As such, the Merzbau was a direct precursor not only to the spatial explorations of Hesse, Sandback, and Ryman in the 1960s in New York but to Clark's work during the same period in Rio de Janeiro, where she struggled to find the language to describe her own radical investigations of the picture plane. In the early 1960s, Clark formulated the idea of what she called the "organic line," a space in the surface that is visible in the progression from her abstract paintings of the 1950s, through her experiments on and with paper in the *Espaços modulados* (Modulated surfaces)

180. Georges Braque
(French, 1882–1963)
Guitar. 1913
Cut-and-pasted printed and painted paper, charcoal, pencil, and gouache on gessoed canvas
39 1/4 x 25 5/8″ (99.7 x 65.1 cm)

181. Kurt Schwitters
(German, 1887–1948)
29/8. 1929
Cut-and-pasted colored paper on paper
9 5/8 x 6 1/4″ (24.5 x 15.9 cm)

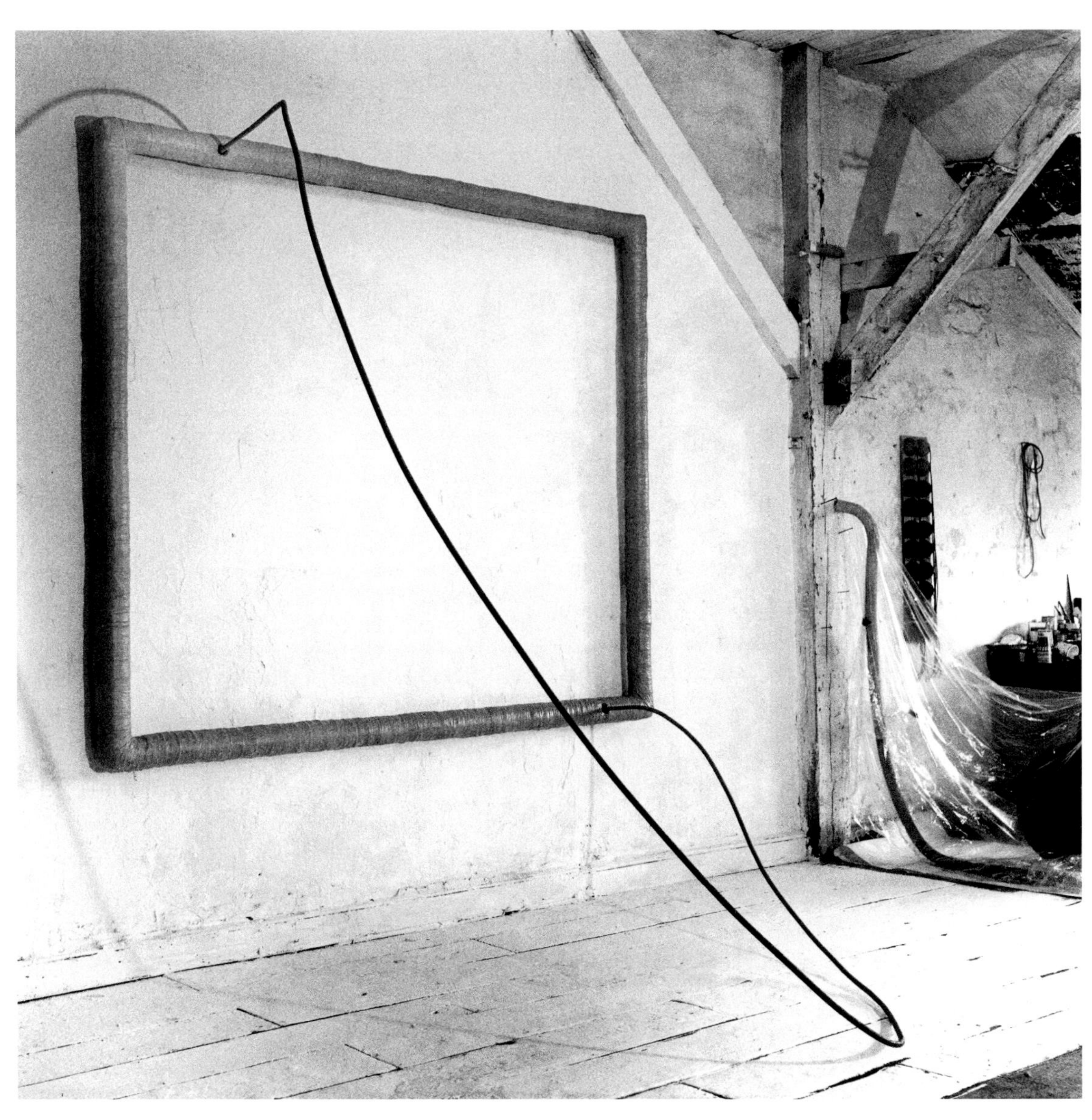

182. Studio of **Eva Hesse**
(American, born Germany, 1936–1970),
New York, 1966, showing *Hang Up* (1966)
Acrylic on cloth over wood, acrylic on
cord over steel tube
6´ x 7´ x 6´ 6˝ (182.9 x 213.4 x 198.1 cm)

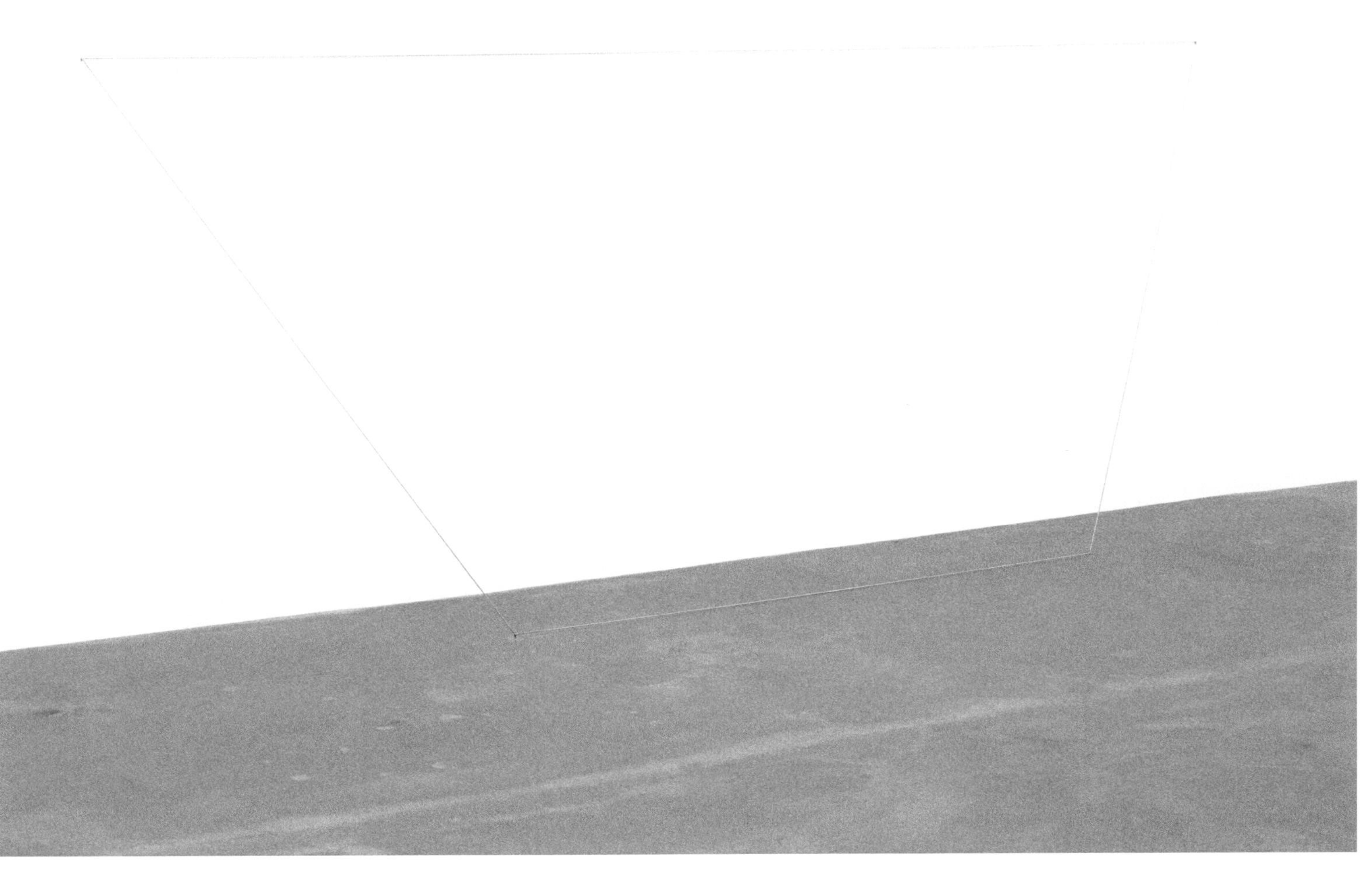

183. Fred Sandback
(American, 1943–2003)
Untitled. 1967
Painted elastic rayon cord and
metal sleeve clamps
69˝ x 14´ x 24˝ (175.2 x 426.7 x 60.9 cm)

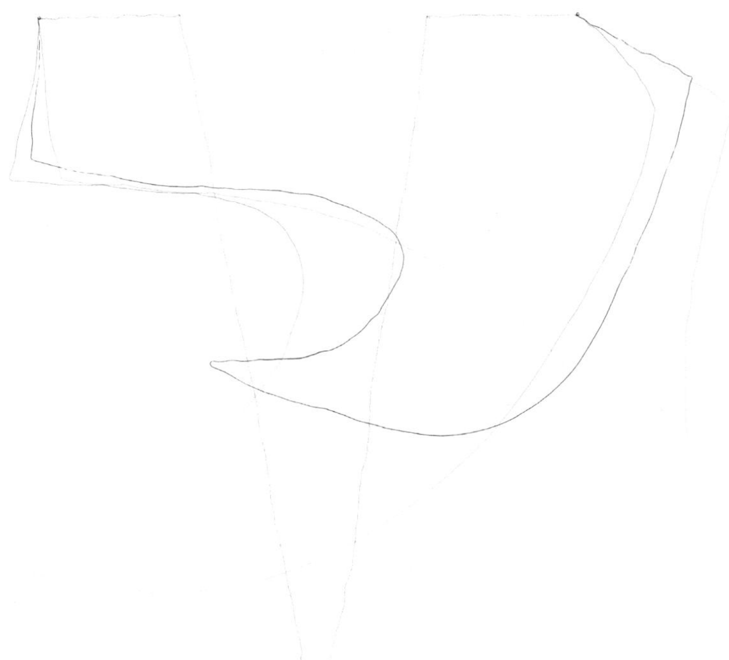

of 1957–58 (plate 60), to the three-dimensional constructions called *Bichos* (Animals, 1960–64). Clark's "organic line" claims a kind of in-between status for line as it moves from two dimensions into three. A line becomes a cut, which in turn becomes a space and metaphor for movement within abstract form. Writing in 1958, Clark spoke of realizing an "*espaço-tempo*," or space-time, and an *idéia-espaço*, or idea-space:

> The idea is the abstract space
> The realization is a space-time
> The modulated surface is the materialization of the idea-space
> The idea-space must be realized in its own time[43]

This text, from a small catalogue of Clark's, is illustrated with paintings and maquettes from the series *Quebra de moldura* (Modulated surfaces), abstract works from 1954–58. Also reproduced are four three-dimensional, quasi-architectural models containing small apertures, spatial incursions anticipating the manipulations of paper and board that at the end of the 1950s would take Clark fully into three dimensions: the *Bichos*; the beautiful, human-scaled *Trepantes* (Climbers, 1964–65), such as *O dentro é o fora* (The inside is the outside, 1963; plate 185); and *Caminhando*, one of her most important topological investigations (plate 134–39). The line is in a sense liberated from its image, both originating inside the picture plane and reaching out of its limiting flatness. The *Trepantes* illustrate this tension in their existence both in a dormant state of presignification, when not activated by the viewer, and then in dynamic movement when manipulated in space and time. For Clark and indeed for Brazilian art generally, this was an emancipatory move: "I started calling it the 'organic line,' as it was real, it existed in itself, organizing space. It was a space line, a fact which I would only come to understand later on."[44] From the moment of this revelation until 1966, when Clark gave up object-making for what she called sensorial works and later for participatory actions such as *Baba antropofágica* (Cannibalistic slobber, 1973; plate 186), her work is about movement, or is in some sense set in motion by a line whose genealogy is abstract but whose legacy is social.

In the mid-1960s, in Brazil as in Europe and the United States, art discourse and the legacy of Neo-Concretism in particular were deeply impacted by the writings of Maurice Merleau-Ponty. Clark certainly

184. Richard Tuttle
(American, born 1941)
21st Wire Piece. 1972
Florist wire, nails, and graphite
Dimensions variable

185. Lygia Clark
(Brazilian, 1920–1988)
O dentro é o fora
(The inside is the outside). 1963
Stainless steel
Dimensions variable, 16 x 17 1/2 x 14 3/4"
(40.6 x 44.5 x 37.5 cm) static

186. Lygia Clark
(Brazilian, 1920–1988)
Baba antropofágica
(Cannibalistic slobber). 1973
Performance view, probably as
Clark worked with her class at
the Sorbonne, Paris

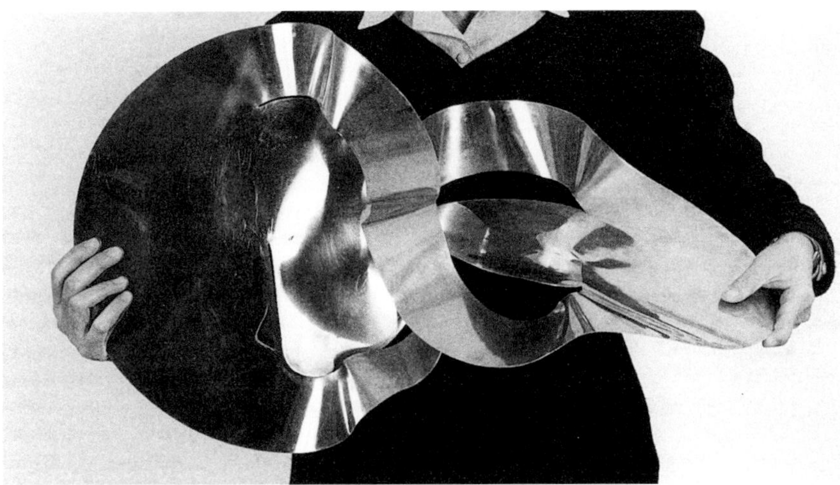

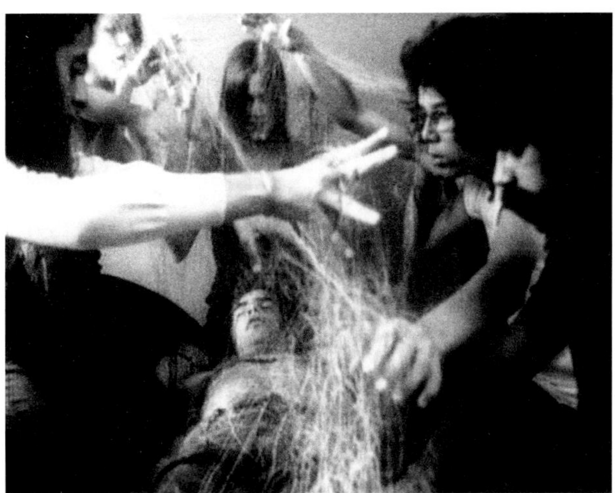

read this French philosopher's hypotheses about overcoming the duality of space and body, which run parallel to her own instincts as reflected in her notes on line, and on the situation of the body in the world and in relationship to the viewer/participant in her work. While Clark postulates a body that "sees" through physical experience of and with materials, Merleau-Ponty's eye and mind are an extension of

> that body which is an intertwining of vision and movement. . . . vision is attached to movement. We see only what we look at. . . . The visible world and the world of my motor projects are each total parts of the same Being. . . . My movement is. . . . the natural consequence and maturation of my vision. I say of a thing that it is moved; but my body moves itself, my movement deploys itself. . . . The enigma is that my body simultaneously sees and is seen. . . . it sees itself seeing; it touches itself touching. . . . the world is made of the same stuff as the body.[45]

Clark's contemporaries Hélio Oiticica and Lygia Pape also experimented with performative interactions of the body with materials, though they were less concerned with using line to make a generative space than with the possibilities of form and color. Pape's *Ballet Neoconcreto* (Neo-Concrete ballet, 1958), for example, performed in 1959, the same year as the first Rio exhibition of Neo-Concrete painting, has interesting points of comparison with the experiments of the Judson Church group in New York. Like Clark, Pape easily transgressed the usual taxonomic boundaries of media and methodology. In the ballet, dancers were hidden, replaced, by geometric solids of color, which moved silently and gracefully, dramatizing, in Guy Brett's words, "the dichotomy between geometry and the organic."[46] The merging of form and background, abstraction and life, art space and world, was a driving force in art of the 1960s internationally but found acute expression in the work of these artists in Brazil.

Another time, contemplating the smoke from my cigarette, I felt as if time incessantly made its own pathway, annihilating itself and remaking itself in a continuous rhythm. . . . I had experienced this in love, in my gestures. And each time the expression "walking" comes up in conversation, a true space is born within me and I become integrated within the world. I feel I am safe.

— Lygia Clark, "Livro-obra," 1983

Experiments in sculpture and dance, and the conjunction of material with the body, were also part of the program of the New York avant-garde by the end of the 1950s. The influence of Duchamp and John Cage on the dismantling of modern dance was already underway in the early 1960s, when Rainer's and Brown's choreography was beginning to take shape. Writing on this moment over a decade later, in 1975, Morris described the collapse of the hierarchies between media:

> I believe there are "forms" to be found within the activity of making as much as within the end products. . . . What the hand and arm motion can do in relation to flat surfaces is different from what hand, arms and body movement can do in relation to objects in three dimensions. Such differences of engagement (and their extensions with technological means) amount to different forms of behavior. In this light the artificiality of media-based distinctions (painting, sculpture, dance, etc.) falls away.[47]

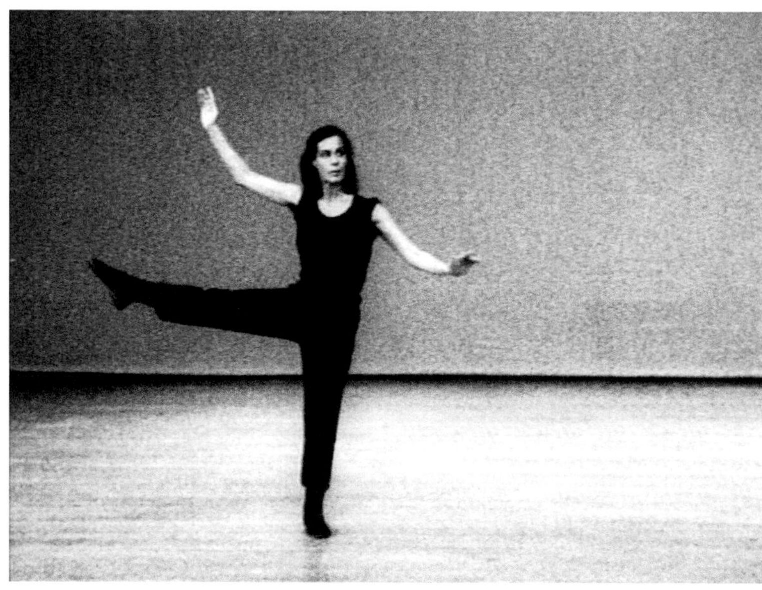

When media-based distinctions begin to fall away, contingent art forms, such as drawing and dance, can move forward as sites of artistic rupture. As Morris elaborated elsewhere, "The subsequent passage of relevant making strategies from painting to sculpture in the mid-1960s had primarily to do with the expansion of this making behavior into the increased possibilities offered to the body in three dimensions. The move from virtual into actual space involved also the annexation of a number of ready-made technological forming processes to replace hand forming."[48]

The first text of Morris's above is from the essay "Some Notes on the Phenomenology of Making," which on its publication, in *Artforum* in 1970, Morris illustrated with photographs of Pollock at work; stonework at Machu Picchu, Peru; and Duchamp's *Sculpture for Traveling*. Lateral movement, a kinesthetics of drawing, an interest in the nomadic potentials of form — these linking ideas among Morris's images are manifest in various ways in avant-garde practices of the 1960s in New York and elsewhere. The desire to interrogate the hierarchies of the body in relationship to architectural space leaves its trace not only in the drawing and sculpture of the time but also on the choreography, which exploits the move from vertical to lateral movement, as in Rainer's use of the floor in dances such as her groundbreaking *Trio A* (1966; plate 187). In Banes's and Robert Alexander's 16mm film of Rainer performing the work in 1978, she performs it from beginning to end, then repeats phrases from it, "details" (her word) from the choreography. In the dozen years since its making, *Trio A* had been performed in many configurations and the artist herself had shifted to a primary focus on filmmaking. Her decision to excerpt fragments of the dance underlies her insistence on it as mutable: like exploratory marks, or the line fragments characteristic of process-based drawings of the period, Rainer's "details" are conceived as components, borrowing the notion, and even the term, from visual art.

When Rainer conceived *Trio A* she was interested in the device of reversal, literally performing sequences in reverse as a way of both generating and complicating the forms and methods of her choreography through a methodological rupture of self-consciousness. The backward version of *Trio A* immediately and seamlessly follows the forward version in the choreographic progression. In part to maintain focus, the dancer's attention is drawn completely away from the audience, at which she never looks directly, creating a kind of flat performance persona that viewers have often experienced as drained of identity.[49] Performed first by Rainer, Paxton, and David Gordon, the work is a trio in name only, since the steps of the dancers, moving independently and without music, inevitably fall in and out of sync. This destabilizing of the unison usually staged by groups of dancers is another source both of discomfort for the viewer and of lack of affect on the part of the performers, who can no longer rely on muscle memory to complete the movement phrases. Rainer's dancers and others, some not trained as dancers, who have

Walking is something you can't tamper with. If you say "ordinary walking," you get a wide range of materials. And the more you tamper with it, the less it has the quality of being just the thing. It starts to look like somebody with a problem on their mind or somebody with an infirmity instead of just someone walking. I tried not to tamper with it too much, so that it wasn't too special and it just occurred.

— Steve Paxton, 1980

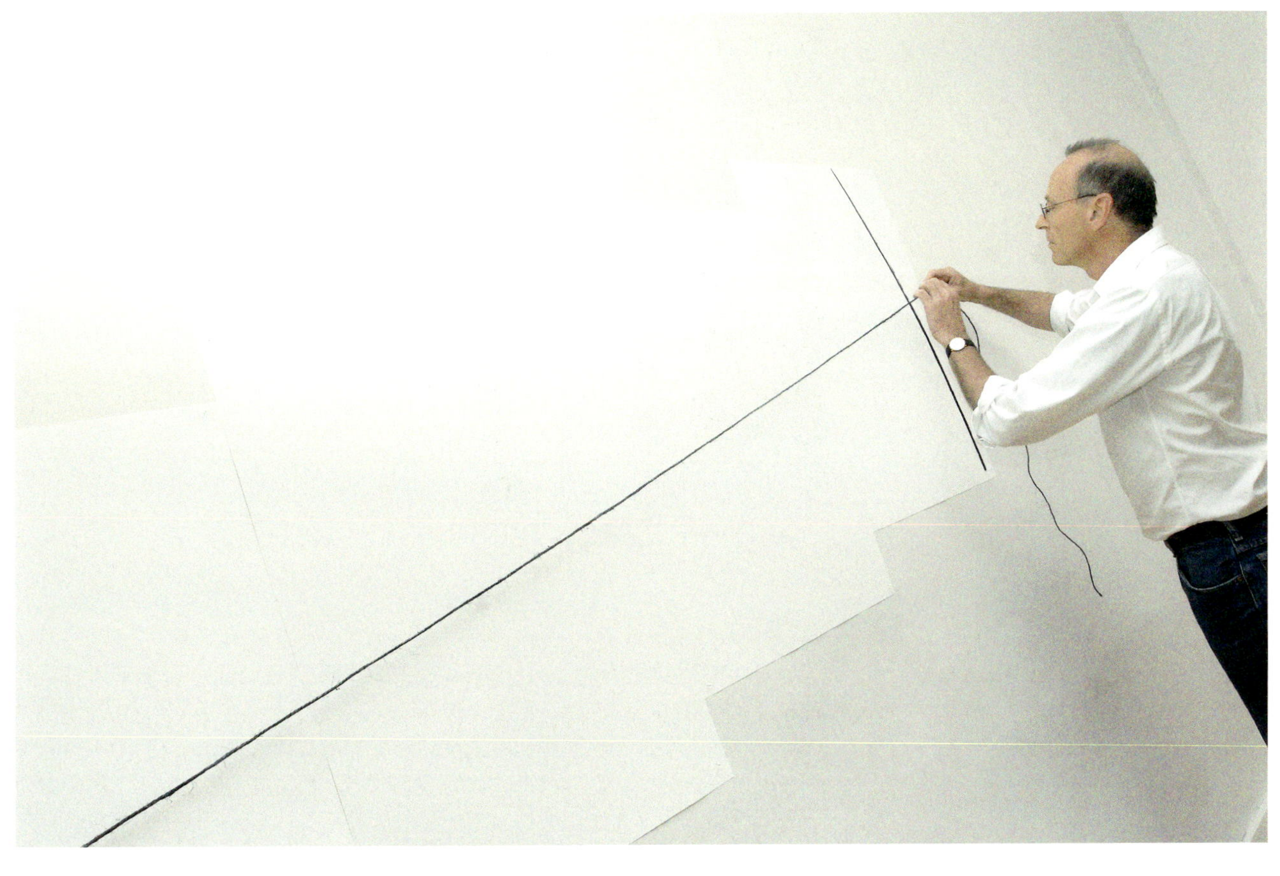

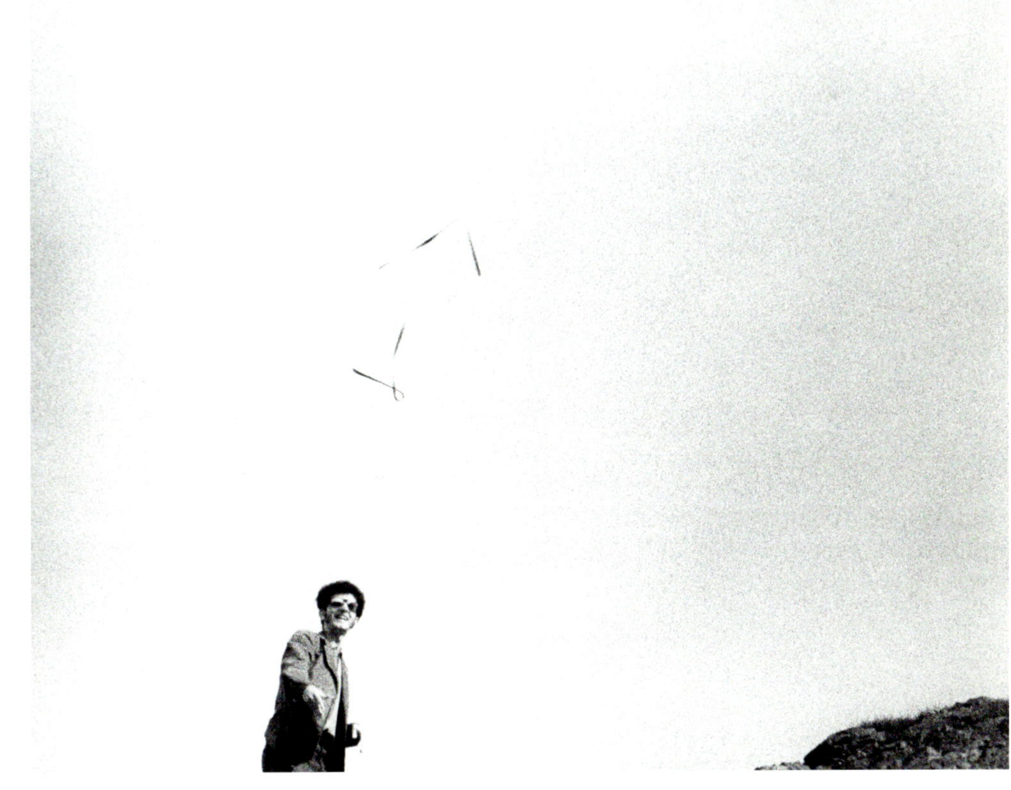

187. Yvonne Rainer
(American, born 1934)
Trio A. 1966
Still from 16mm film by Sally Banes and Robert Alexander, 1978, black and white, silent, 10:12 min.

188. Anthony McCall
(American, born England 1946)
Five Minute Drawing. 1974/2007
Performance view, Musée de Rochechouart, 2007. Original performance at Art Meeting Place, London, June 18, 1974

189. Tom Marioni
(American, born 1937)
One Second Sculpture. 1969
Black and white photograph
31 x 36″ (78.7 x 91.4 cm)

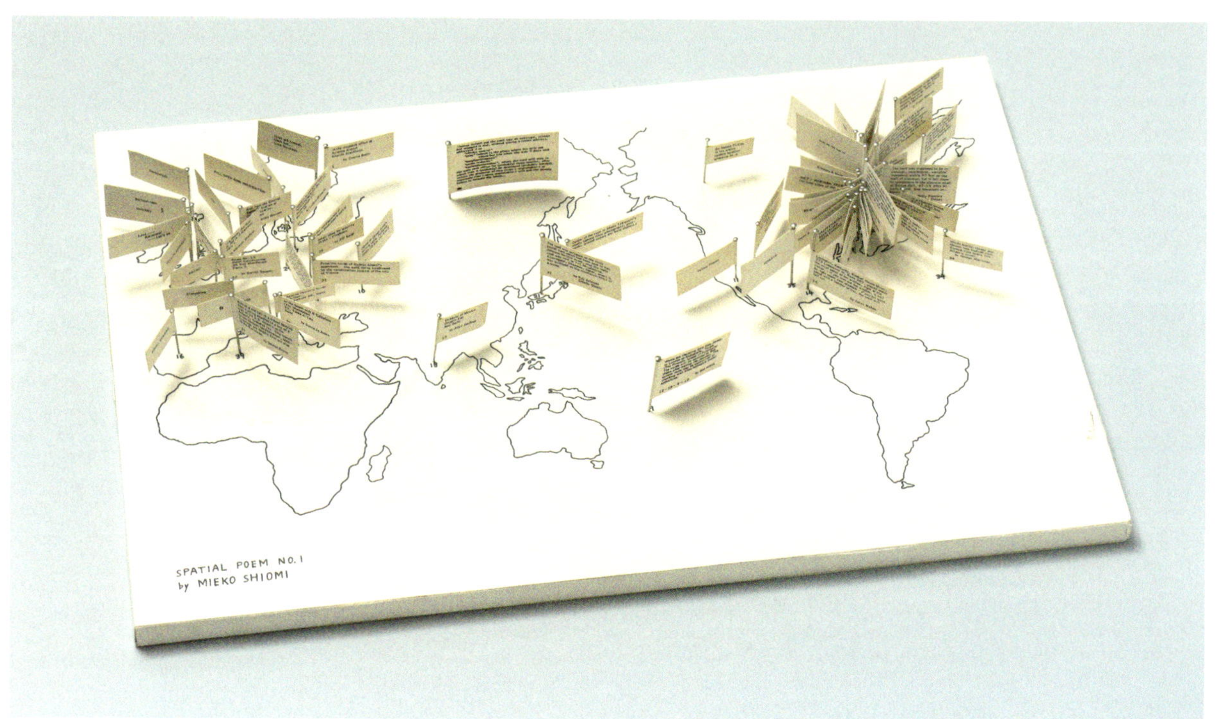

190. Mieko Shiomi
(Japanese, born 1938)
Spatial Poem No. 1. 1965
Stenciled black map on white-painted composition board, 69 printed cards mounted on pins, assembled by George Maciunas
11 15/16 x 18 x 7/8″ (30.3 x 45.7 x 2.2 cm)

191. La Monte Young
(American, born 1935)
Compositions 1961. 1963
Artist's book
Page: 3 9/16 x 3 5/8″ (9 x 9.2 cm)

192. La Monte Young
(American, born 1935)
Composition 1960 #10 (to Bob Morris). 1960
Performance view, showing Nam June Paik as Zen for Head, at Fluxus Internationale Festspiele Neuester Musik, Städtisches Museum Auditorium, Wiesbaden, September 1962
Gelatin silver print
8 1/4 x 6 5/16″ (21 x 16 cm)

continued to perform the work have said that she conceived of *Trio A* as creating a community lasting through time as it is retaught and reperformed.[50] Today it carries with it the memory of each body onto which it is written, creating a network of inhabitances.

Two artists whose conceptual and graphic investigations of line have led them to performative experiments incorporating the body, and working off its dimensions, are Anthony McCall and Tom Marioni. McCall's *Five Minute Drawing* (1974; plate 188) is a line drawing elaborated over six sheets of paper. Standing in front of a wall, the artist snaps a string to make a line, adapting a simple architectural and engineering tool to make a long diagonal that approximates the dimensions of his own body. When McCall first made this work he was involved in film, and what is perhaps his best-known work, *Line Describing a Cone* (1973), is a filmic investigation of line and space. The work exists as a tautology: it is a line that describes a conical form and at the same time carves in space a conical shaft of light that the viewer can penetrate.

Working in San Francisco during the period of Conceptual art's emergence, Marioni made a group of works using the scale and limits of his own body. In *One Second Sculpture* (1969; plate 189) he had himself photographed throwing a metal measuring tape into the air: the tape made a curved line as it left his hands, an arc in midair, and a straight line when it fell to the ground. The gesture combined humor and lightness of touch with a sense of the seductiveness of infinite space, supplied through the broad backdrop of sky and a summarily sketched mountain landscape. It was also in dialogue with the many Conceptual works addressing the idea of measurement, as a construction both of art history and of Western thought more generally. As with Rainer, Tuttle, and others, Marioni's body is fully engaged and visible in a very specific documentary photograph that records the instant of the activity. The stricture of measure becomes a deflated, offhand line in the sky, signifying abandon and the precariousness of empirical knowledge.

Notable among the line projects of the 1960s are works by members of the Fluxus group, including Mieko Shiomi (plate 190), Stanley Brouwn, and many others. Seeking ways to generate their activities from materials at hand, and influenced by Cage's theories of indeterminacy, this international network of artists often turned to investigations of elemental forms. Inheritors of the antiart impulses of Dada, the Fluxus community created many ephemeral objects, physically slight but politically and socially ambitious.

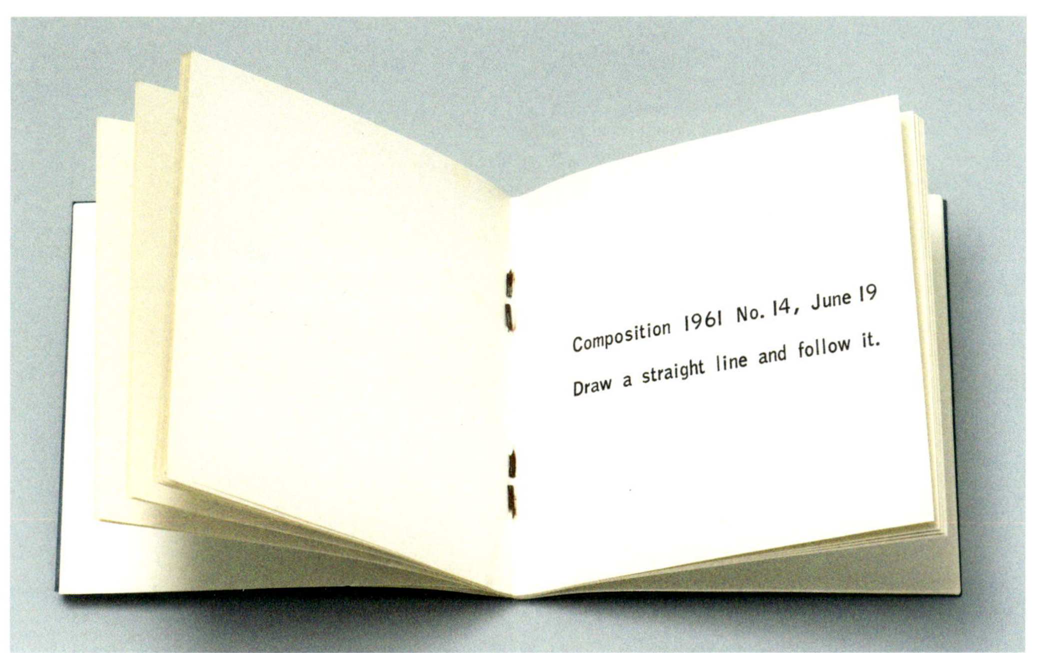

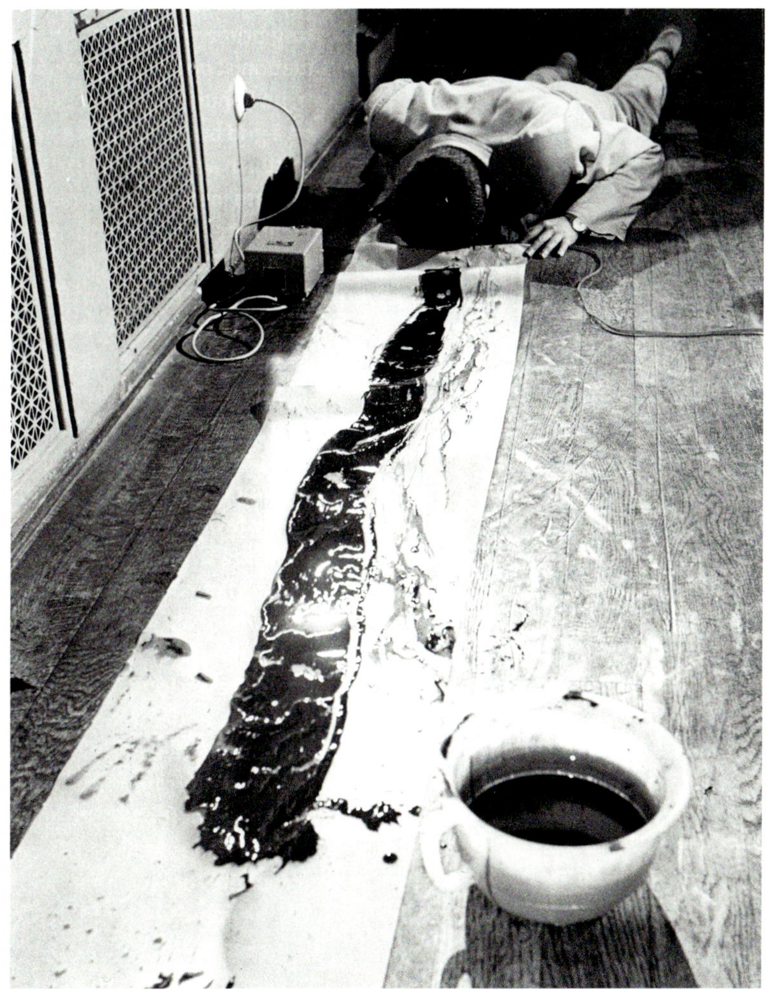

I felt that a line was one of the more sparse, singular expressions of oneness, although it is certainly not the final expression. Somebody might choose a point. However, the line was interesting because it was continuous—it existed in time. A line is a potential of existing in time. In graphs and scores one designates time as one dimension. Nonetheless, the actual drawing of the line did involve time and it did involve a singular event—"Draw a straight line and follow it."

—La Monte Young, "*Draw a Straight Line and Follow It,*" 1968

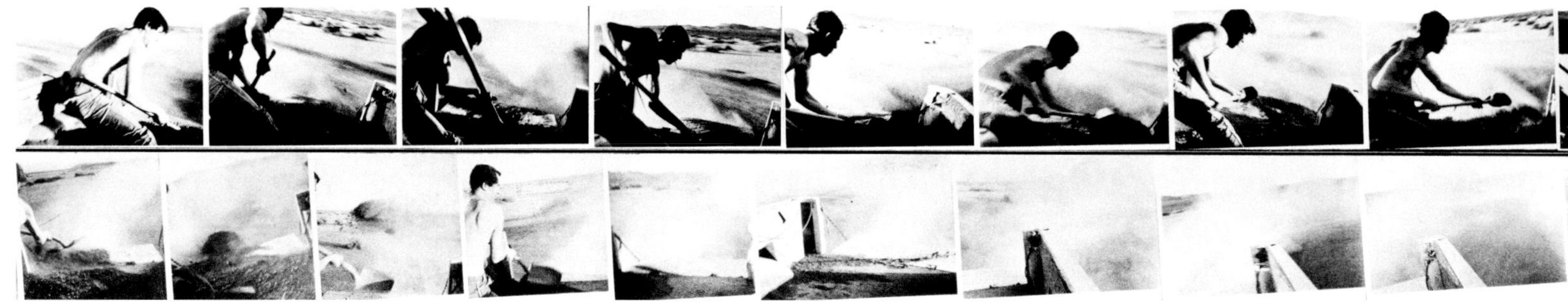

American composer and sound artist La Monte Young, an active Fluxus practitioner, drew on Cage in deploying chance operations as a way to destroy what Yve-Alain Bois has called "traditional authorial models of invention."[51] In 1960, Young began to create numbered compositions in the format of a series of instructions printed in a small book (plate 191), easily mass distributed in keeping with the Fluxus interrogation of the systems by which art reaches its public. Each of the twenty-nine compositions in *Compositions 1961* read "Draw a Straight Line and Follow It." The same sentence had appeared earlier in *Composition 1960 #10 (to Bob Morris)* (1960; plate 192), which Nam June Paik would perform at the first international Fluxus festival in Wiesbaden in 1962, dipping his head in paint and then dragging his body across the floor to leave behind him a line, a more literal version of Pollock-style action painting with the floor as support.

Working primarily in Amsterdam, Brouwn has used line in an ongoing mapping project that extends the Situationist notion of the *dérive*. His works are ephemeral, surviving only in documentation — which, however, he stipulates can be exhibited but not published or otherwise reproduced. Amsterdam is laid out not on a grid but shaped by a meandering series of concentric canals and avenues eddying out from the city center. In a series of walks through the city, Brouwn economically deploys his own body in motion to trace a path in space and time. *Steps* (1970) documents one such walk: a map provides a skeletal indication of the line he has followed, winding through urban space.

In the United States and Canada during roughly the same period, but outside the urban centers, artists were taking a different approach to the mapping of territory, most famously in the open spaces of the American West but elsewhere as well. American artists Michael Heizer and Michelle Stuart, and the Canadian duo calling themselves N.E Thing Co. Ltd. (plate 100), were among the many interested in Peru's Nazca lines, archaic images variously legible as abstractions and as figurative images, such as one evocative drawing of an enormous hand. The Nazca lines were among the visual sources for the large-scale artworks that began to be made outdoors in the late 1960s by artists who shared with the Fluxus group a desire to work outside the institutional or commercial spaces of museums or galleries. Stuart, one of the relatively few women involved in this kind of work, made *Niagara Gorge Path Relocated* (1975; plate 132) by unrolling a 460-foot-long sheet of paper over a steep hillside and then accepting the imprint of the rocks, dirt, and other bits of nature it encountered on the way down as a drawing.

Heizer's *Circular Surface Planar Displacement Drawing* (1970; plates 104, 194, 195) is a drawing executed by a man on a motorcycle driving in circular patterns, scoring lines in the earth of a dry Nevada lake. Heizer documented the performance from a ladder a short distance away, his heightened eye level allowing the tire tracks to be understood as a visual composition. While aerial photographs of the work were also taken, and are seductive in their shadowy portrayal of the vastness of both the drawing and the empty desert, Heizer prefers his own, closer-to-the-ground view, which foregrounds process and conveys a feeling of the earth and of the texture of the tracks. Heizer also makes more conventional drawings, often to work out technical issues of his earthwork projects, but *Circular Surface Planar Displacement Drawing* fully embodies his desire for large scale and for construction with the land as both medium and backdrop.

In 1970, the impulse toward the dematerialization of the art object, and the desire to merge art and life, were surveyed in the Tenth Tokyo Biennial, also titled *Between Man and Matter*. Featuring many

193. Michael Heizer
(American, born 1944)
Circular Surface Drawing, Rotary Photograph. 1968
Showing the making of *Circular Land Drawing*, 1968, three-ton dispersement, 60´ diam., El Mirage Dry Lake, Mojave Desert, California

194. Michael Heizer
(American, born 1944)
Circular Surface Planar Displacement Drawing/90° Vertical Planar Rotary. 1970
Fifty black-and-white photographs
Dimensions variable

195. Michael Heizer
(American, born 1944)
Circular Surface Planar Displacement Drawing (deteriorated, detail). 1970
Tire markings on playa surface
900 x 500´ area, Jean Dry Lake, Nevada

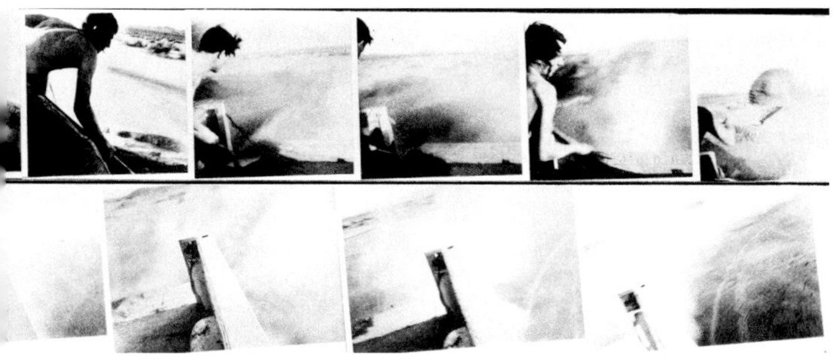

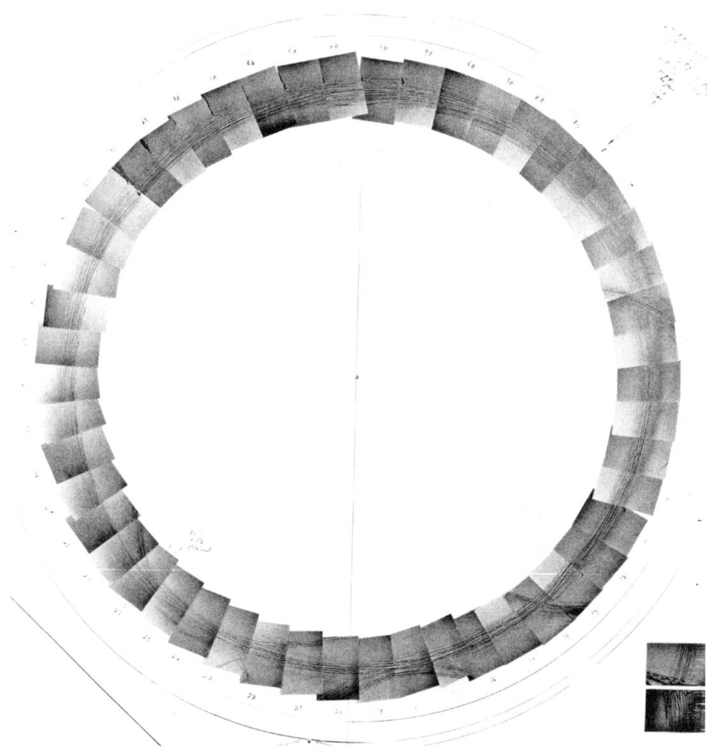

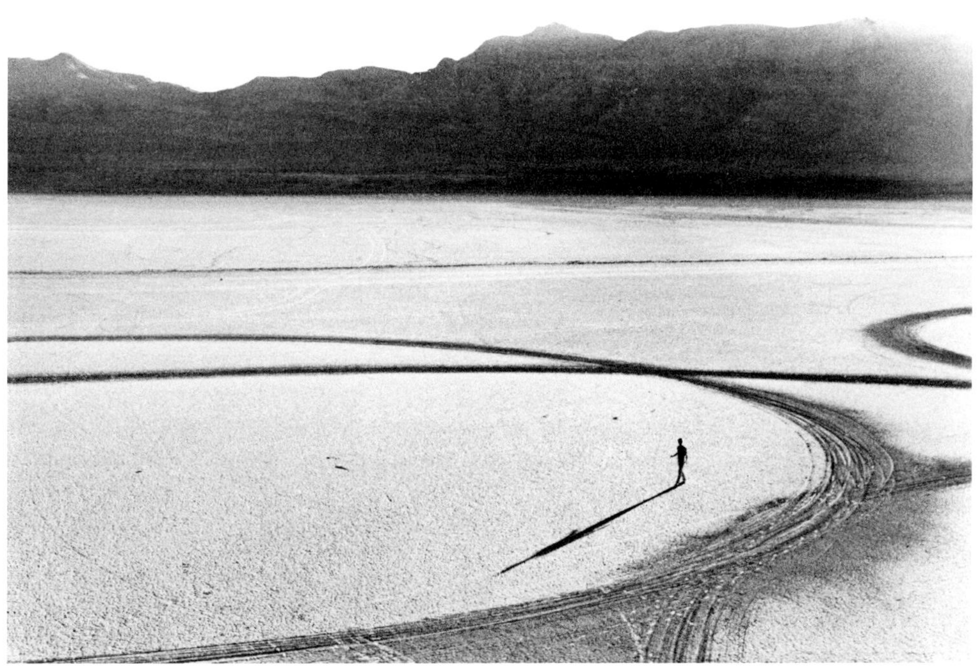

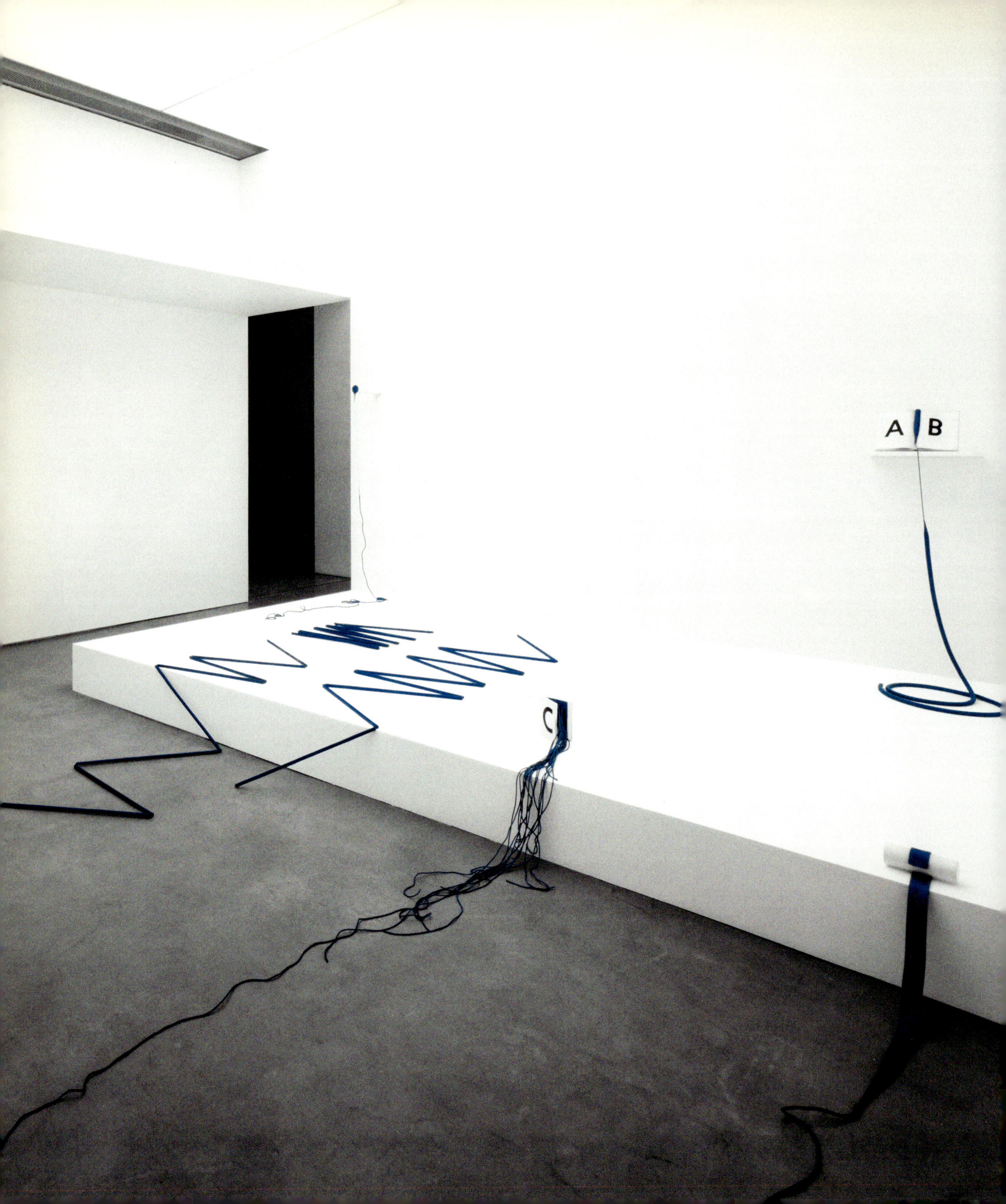
A B
C

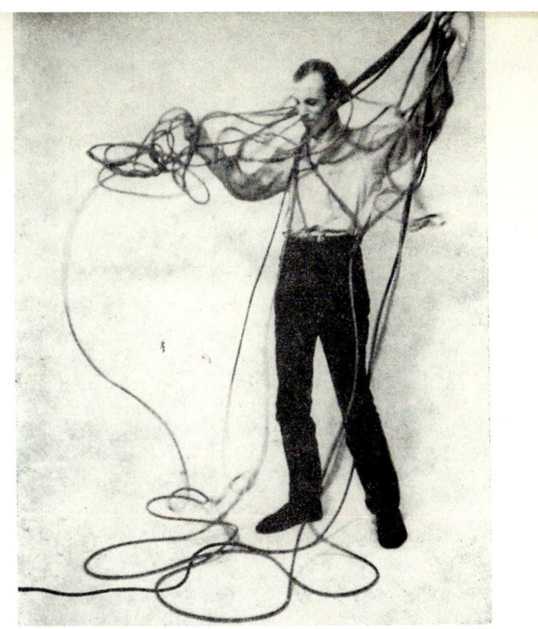

bleu mince longlonglonglonglonglonglonglonglonglonglonglonglonglonglonglonglonglo
nglonglonglonglonglonglonglonglonglonglonglonglonglong...

J'AI PERDU LA FIN!!!

Je la cherche!
Qui la trouvera
est priè d'ECRIRE! de TELEPHONER!
de TELEGRAPHIER!
à l'adresse suivante: Edward Krasiński
Galeria Foksal PSP, Varsovie, rue
Foksal 1/4, tel. 27 62 43

publié par la Galerie Foksal PSP Varsovie, avril 1969

196. Edward Krasiński
(Polish, 1925–2004)
Reconstruction of Krasiński's installation at the 1970 Tokyo Biennial in the exhibition *Edward Krasiński: Les mises en scène*, Generali Foundation, Vienna, 2006

197. Edward Krasiński
(Polish, 1925–2004)
J'AI PERDU LA FIN!!! (I LOST THE END!!!). 1969
Leaflet distributed during the exhibition *Assemblage d'hiver*, Galeria Foksal, Warsaw, 1969
$9^{7}/_{8} \times 6^{3}/_{4}$″ (25 x 17.1 cm)

projects that were site related or ephemeral in nature, the biennial included a handful of members of the Fluxus group as well as such artists as Penone, Serra, Carl Andre, and the Polish artist Edward Krasiński, with a line project emblematic of the desire to move the practices of drawing and scupture out of the gallery and into the street. Krasiński's installation (plate 196) comprised painted domestic objects standing in for sculptures and paintings and extending into space through an appended blue cord. His elliptical denial of the grid had political implications in keeping with the social desires of the moment. This period's shifts in technologies and industrial materials would have direct implications for the impulse toward the analog today.

In 1995, Alÿs walked through the cities of São Paulo, Brazil, and Gent, in his native Belgium, holding a leaking can of paint that left behind a dripped line of color. Linking to both Pollock's action painting and the lines of the Fluxus artists, the work was more importantly a discursive move into the social space of the city. Repeated in Minneapolis in 2001 and Paris in 2002, this work, *The Leak*, initiated a group of works including *The Loop* (1997), an action addressing the trauma of cultural translation and immigration signified by the Tijuana/San Diego border, and *The Green Line* (plate 231), a paint-can walk through Jerusalem along the line drawn on a map in 1949 to divide up territory after the 1948–49 Arab-Israeli War, and essentially demarcating land newly seized by Israel. Alÿs's walks, or *paseos*, shift the meaning of Baudelaire's flaneur strolling through the city, and of the Situationist *dérive*: his movements, Cuauhtémoc Medina writes, are those of a "planetary pedestrian.... For Alÿs, the elaboration of displacements represents a way of inserting himself in the fluidity of the organism in order to invent a working method,... a way of thinking, a way of working flush with the urban tissue and its speed."[52] In fact the question of speed functions in Alÿs's work as a way of creating a line of inquiry — a line in space — that bumps up against the speed of his subject, conflating history, memory, and real time.

A LINE IN THE SAND: THE POLITICAL LINE AND THE EXTREME ANALOG OF THE PRESENT (1980–2010)

Many dance- and line-based works of art since the 1980s involve a notion of line as political — a deployment of line in the space of the political and social. Through the mapping of both abstract and everyday lines, stories are told and social space is narrated and inscribed. For Michel de Certeau, "A space exists when one takes into consideration vectors of direction, velocities, and time variables. Thus space is composed in intersections of mobile elements. . . . In short, *space is a practiced place*."[53] The space charted by those linear vectors is the communal space in which we live.

One place to begin a narrative of line, dance, and drawing since the 1980s is with a realignment of line. In the deserts of Australia's Northern Territory in 1988–89, a group of indigenous women — their oral tradition a strong art form, embedded in everyday narration of their lived experience — began to use paint to record stories and designs that they had already been inscribing through the dyed-cloth batik technique and that they would earlier have drawn as networks of lines on the desert floor. Almost uniquely, their practice of painting, as it evolved, became both performance and drawing. The making of these designs, translated first into luscious nets of batik, then into paint, is both a telling and an enacting of the nomadic, itinerant existence in and of the desert that was traditionally the Aboriginal way of life.

The Aboriginal tradition makes no distinction between work and play. When Emily Kam Kngwarray, a leading figure in this group of women, began to paint, she was eighty years old and had never learned to read or write. The lines she made in batik as part of the Utopia group, who worked collectively from 1977 to 1988, and the later nets of painted lines, also made working flat on the ground, represent a kind of nonverbal representation of experience outside of language. Streams of consciousness are expressed through the marking of the body and the painting of abstract lines, symbolizing networks of tubers and other plants as well as lines of life. The phenomenological and performing body are one. Marks and lines etched into the sand of the desert and painted on the body, folded and dyed into batik cloth, and finally traced in paint on canvas are records of Aboriginal dreaming. Kngwarray's work is her story, her dreaming, her connection to the world. This is her one subject.

The two paintings in the exhibition, *Ankerr* (Emu, 1990; plate 198) and *Anaty* (Wild potato, 1989; plate 200), represent two different dreamings. The weblike pattern in the earlier painting, one of the artist's first, stands for the yam — elementary to both the Aboriginal diet and the desert ecosystem. "The yam's rhizome," Margo Neale writes, "spreading outward like a net, is a symbol of life and a symbol of the earth that nurtures one and one's clan."[54] Kngwarray and her fellow artists developed a technique of making a line or a sequence of dots, then dragging paint out from it — hence the style we see, its evanescent skeins recalling Pollock's tangles of paint, Brice Marden's webs of icy gray and blue, even Kandinsky's symphonies of dancing color. That Kngwarray made paintings is merely a consequence of the materials given to her. What is clear from the image of the women dancing the Awelye ceremony (plate 199), with painted lines visible on their bare chests, is that the lines she executed in paint were just one manifestation of a lived practice that included sand drawing, storytelling, painting, and dancing.

Given the contested history of land rights, citizenship, and nationhood common to Aboriginal and many other indigenous artists, the role of the body as a political site often takes on a heightened significance for them. The contestation over land and identity is played out both symbolically and actually through the physical bodies of a country's or territory's inhabitants. When the women dance, creating tracks, lifelines, in the ground, they are also singing — "singing Country."[55] The body decoration of the Maori people of New Zealand is an analogous exteriorizing of identity, merging body and line, resistance and heritage. The lines in Kngwarray's paintings extend over the edges of the stretched canvas, beyond

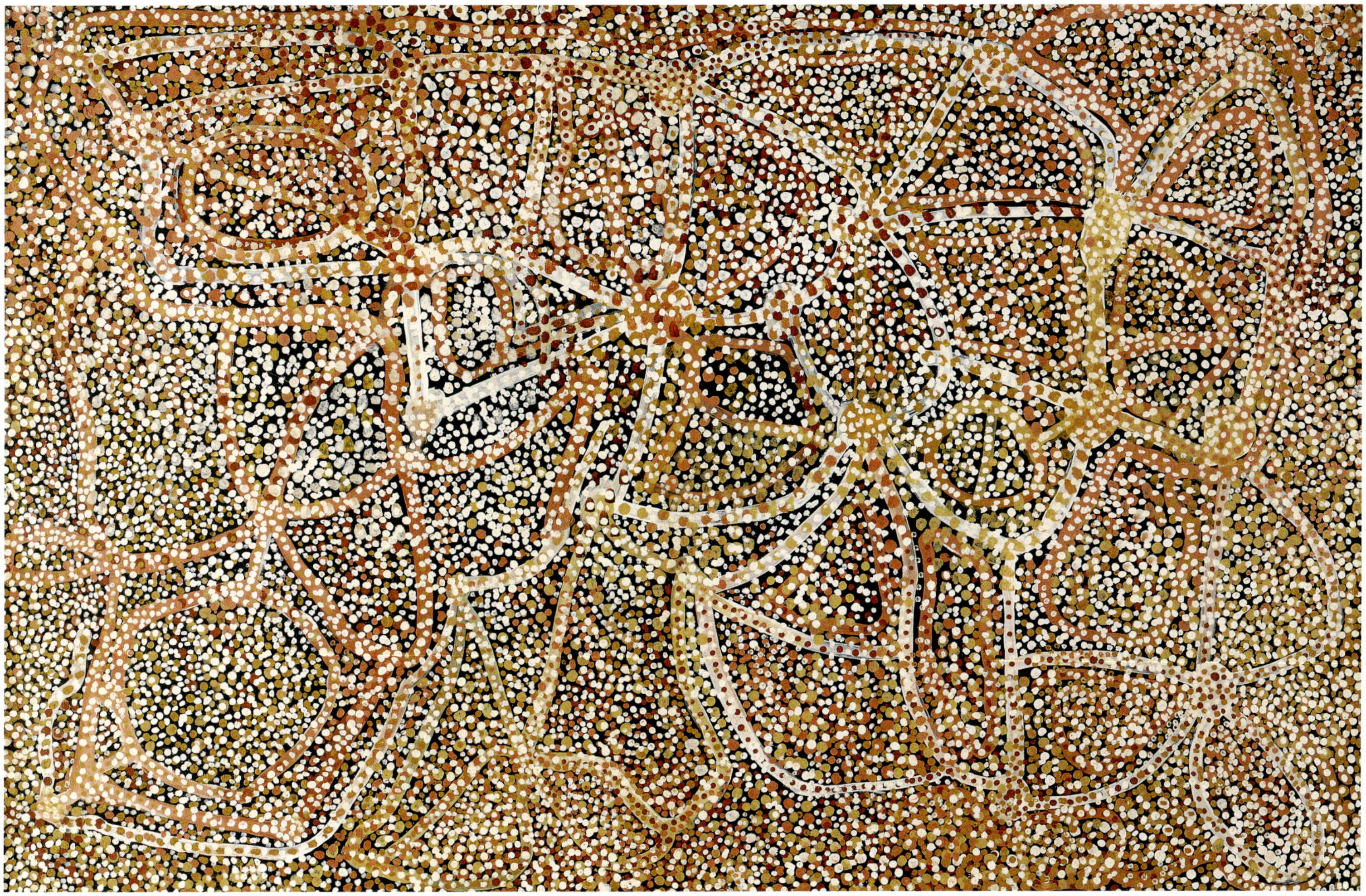

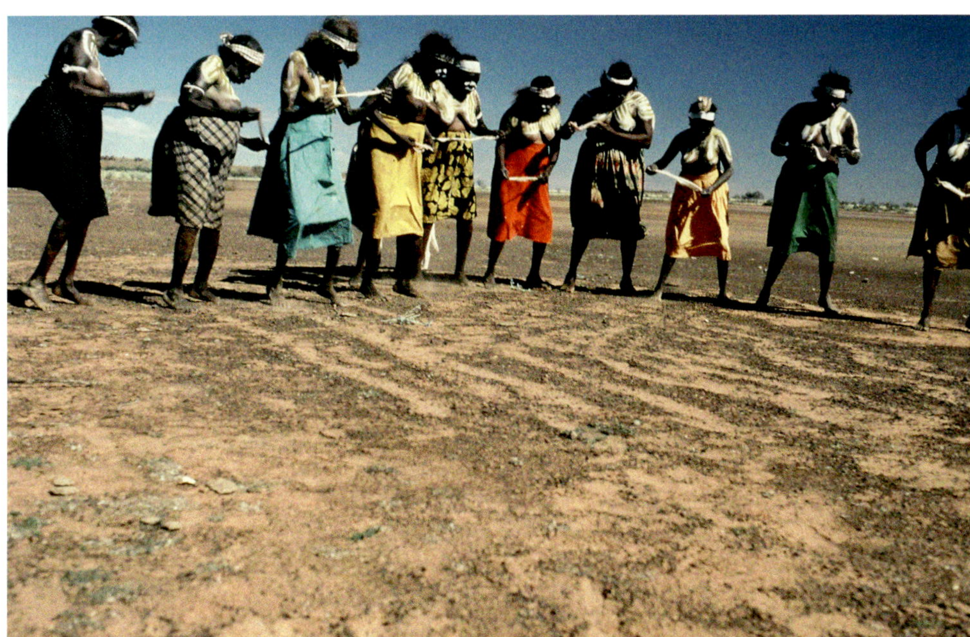

198. Emily Kam Kngwarray
(Anmatyerr [Australian], c. 1910–1996)
Ankerr (Emu). 1990
Synthetic polymer paint on canvas
47 1/4 x 70 1/2" (120 x 179.1 cm)

199. Ngarti and Kukatja women
dancing at Kurnakulu in the Great
Sandy Desert, Western Australia, 1997

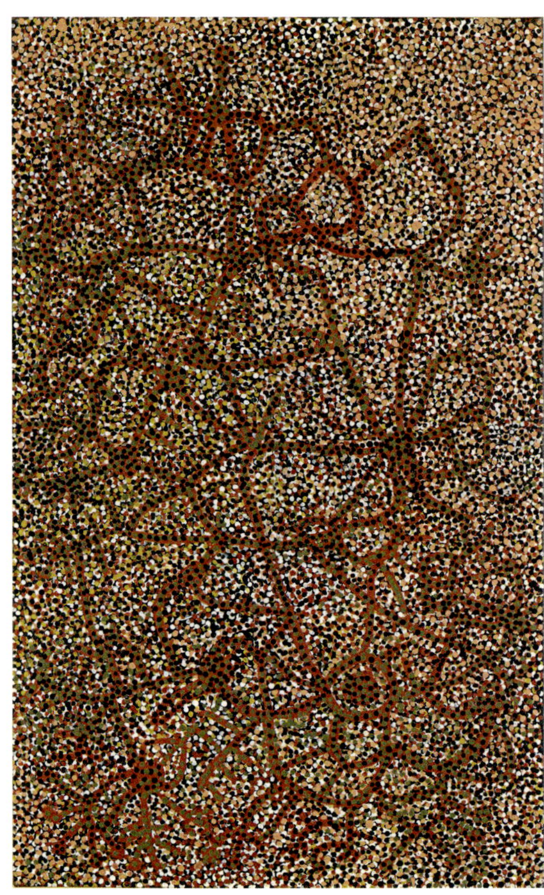

the frame of the composition. This extension of lines into the space beyond the canvas can be read not only as a representation of the cracked earth of the arid desert but as a kind of reaching out into the world beyond representation. Certainly the Aboriginal concept of dreaming functions as a hybridization of the practice of life and the channeling of consciousness.

The hybridity of this practice of life-into-art-into-life, and its navigation through the politics of land and body, has parallels in a history of post-1960s artists whose social and political engagement takes the form of the disruption of social circuits and institutions of various kinds. One such is the Brazilian artist Cildo Meireles, who, in 1976, extended his work in drawing — or "doodling," as he called it at the time — into the realm of sculpture. Each of his three works titled *Malhas da Liberdade* (Meshes of freedom, 1976–77) is in some way an abstraction of earlier works, including the *Ocupações* (Occupations, 1968–69) series of spatial explorations and the *Inserções em Circuitos Ideológicos. Projeto Coca-Cola* and . . . *Projeto cédula* (Insertions into ideological circuits. Coca-Cola project and . . . Banknote project, 1970), which Brett has characterized as "a work about potential, on a tension point between repression and release."[56] All of these works refer to the grid, which Meireles seems to want to spread out into space:

200. Emily Kam Kngwarray
(Anmatyerr [Australian], c. 1910–1996)
Anaty (Wild potato). 1989
Synthetic polymer paint on canvas
59 1/2 x 35 7/8″ (151.2 x 91.1 cm)

> In the 1960s I was always doodling, like anyone who is bored. First I'd draw a line, then another that intersects it, and so on, until I'd made a grid. In 1976 I decided to do the same with more rigid materials. Then it was no longer a matter of lines over lines; the second line was on an altogether different plane. This is the origin of *Meshes of Freedom*, of which the grid is just one manifestation. . . . The composition creates a grid, which spreads over a plane, but it also starts to grow in space, to create a volume. . . . It has no formal limitations, but allows rather the passage from one part of the structure to another, at any point of the structure.[57]

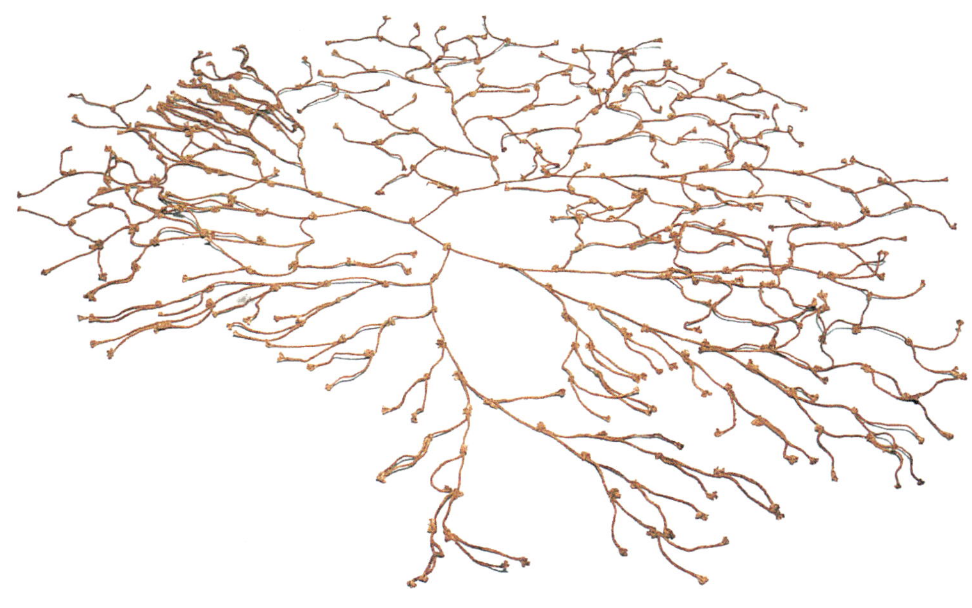

Meireles's first *Malhas* sculpture (plate 201) was indeed not a grid but rather a spray of limp ropes, knotted together and shown on the floor, as though tossed according to the whim of chance action. Inscribed in the work is a notion of freedom: the ropes seem broken, the web loosened, the grid unbound. Metaphorically this tangle invokes the shackles of repressive political regimes, such as the military dictatorship that had ruled Brazil since the mid-1960s. Meireles's magnificent installation *La Bruja* (The witch, 1979–81; plate 125) is a drawing in string that explodes into space, disrupting the geometry of the gallery and short-circuiting the hierarchy implicit in its architecture. Meireles has often made use of the poetics of chance; he has spoken of gesturing toward Duchamp's *3 Standard Stoppages* (1913–14; plate 17),[58] and *La Bruja*, in the weblike reach of its tentacles spreading through the museum, across the terrain of other artworks and other histories, also recalls Duchamp's *Sixteen Miles of String* (plate 167), the installation he contributed to the *First Papers of Surrealism* exhibition in New York in 1942. This mixture of humor and pathos, repression and release, recurs in Meireles's work, along with a deep connection to the political and social gestures of the historical past.For the third *Malhas* (1977; plate 95) Meireles literally built up one line of wire after another until he had constructed a grid, though a disrupted one, since each unit is slightly off register. A leaf of glass inserted into the composition creates the effect of a layered drawing and echoes the artist's earlier use of shadow and light in his *Espaços virtuais: cantos* (Virtual spaces: corners, 1967–68) and *Volumes Virtuais* (Virtual volumes, 1968–69). It is from the slippage of the grid and its expansion into space that these works draw their political potential, appearing to interrogate the codes of perspective and thus the very regimes of Western representation.

Referring to network and early communication theory as influencing his thinking at this time, when his contemporaries Clark and Oiticica were making related experiments, Meireles used line to move from gesture to web to grids implying an interface with the world. Meanwhile, in France, concurrent with these Brazilian artists' work with networks of form, color, and the performative body, Molnar and Pierrette Bloch were responding in very different material ways to the problems of connectivity and form. In a body of work that comprises collages, works on paper, and "drawings" made on the wall with horsehair, but that is essentially an investigation of drawing, Bloch has explored the drift between form, measure, and line. Lines accrue and stratify in her work like sediment, creating an almost filmic record of process over time. A close friend of the French painter Pierre Soulages, Bloch was influenced by his practice of an abstraction that unfolded over time in gestural drawings and films. Her own work seems to move rather seamlessly

201. Cildo Meireles
(Brazilian, born 1948)
Malhas da Liberdade I
(Meshes of freedom I). 1976
Cotton rope
Dimensions variable, c. 47 1/4 x 47 1/4"
(120 x 120 cm)

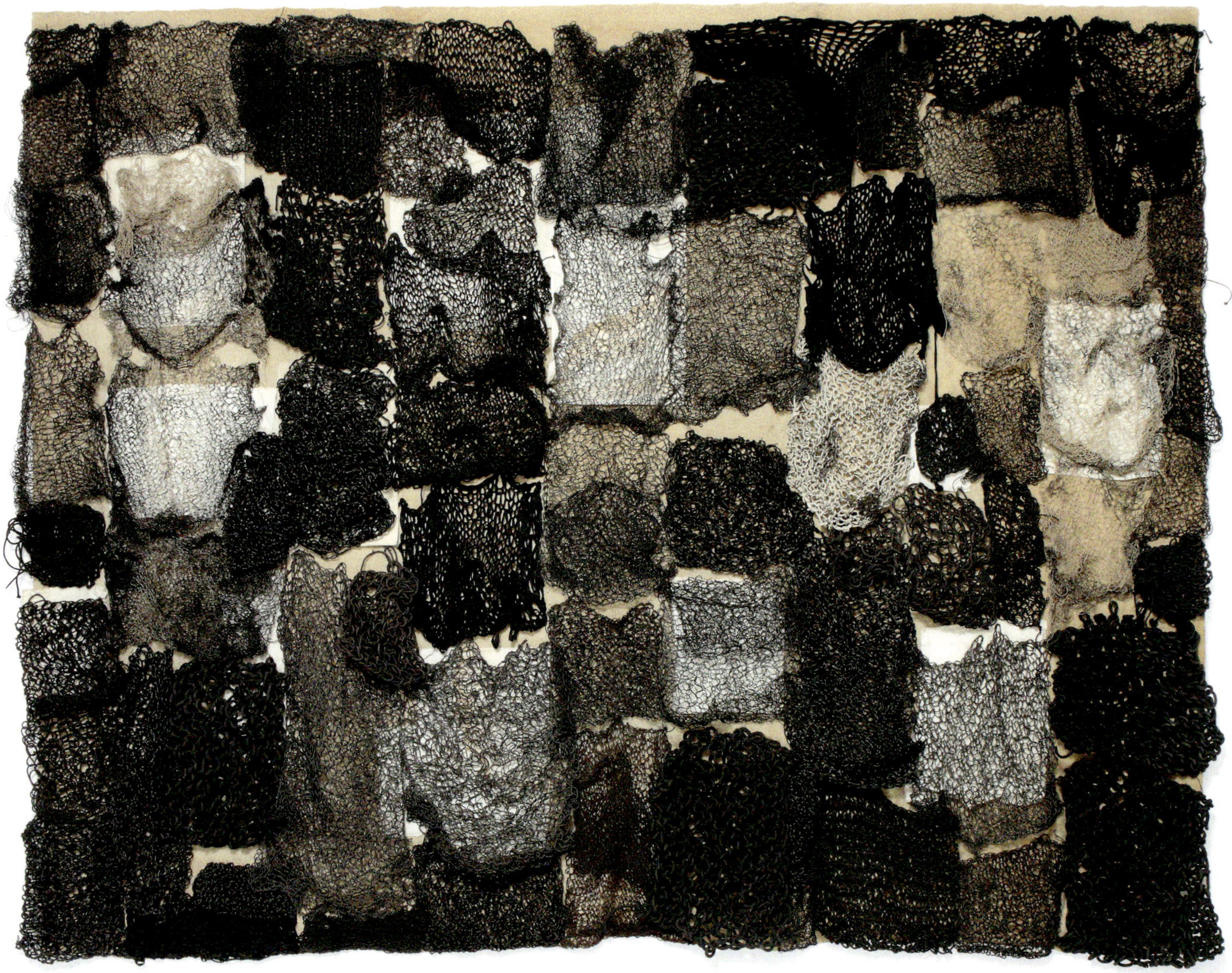

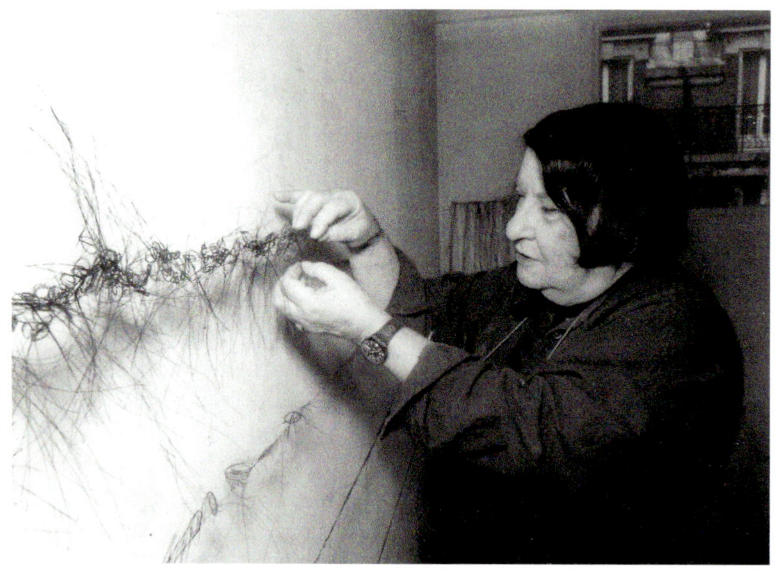

I love the tools that make lines. I know lines, I frequent them, their lack of a conclusion, their lack of an ending, their returns, their accidents, their apparent speed, their tenacious duration, their persistence, their urgency.

— Pierrette Bloch, "Line," 2002

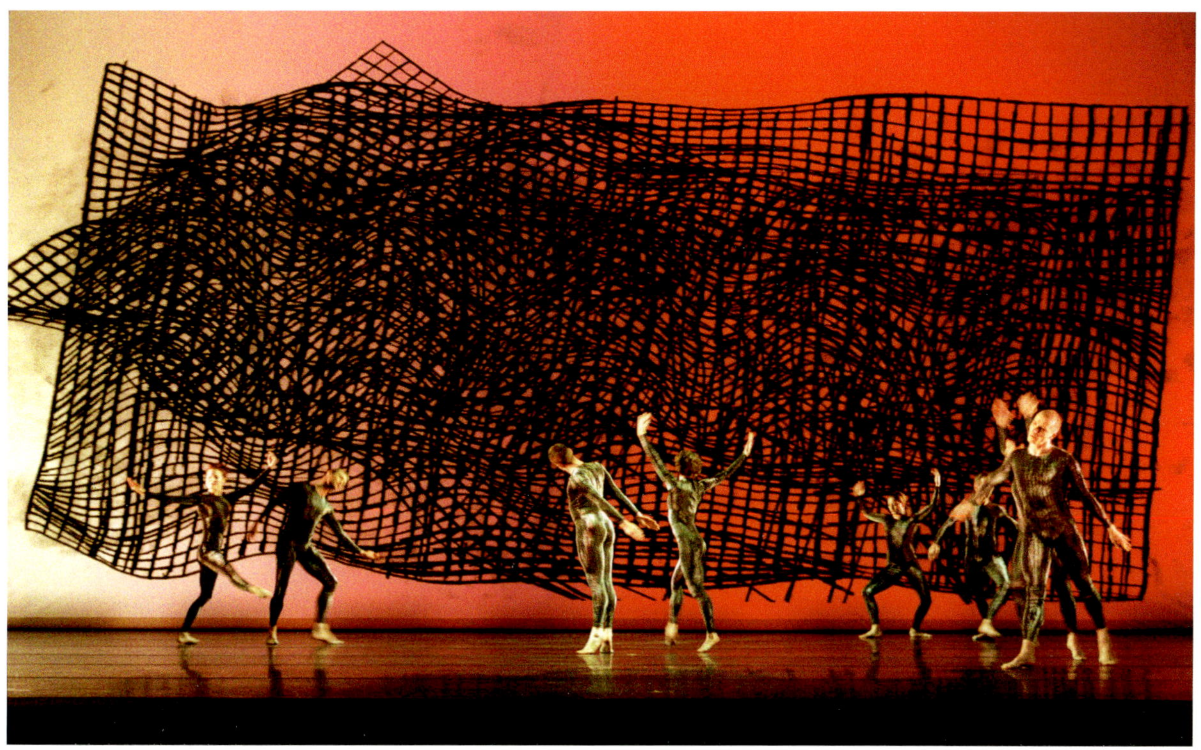

between painting, drawing on paper, and weaving with hair in space and on the wall (plates 202, 203). She also makes reference to the mescaline-influenced drawings of Henri Michaux and the "automatic" collages of Arp, supposedly created through chance operations.[59] The collages she made from roughly the early 1950s into the 1970s explore the implications of illusionistic space through the line of torn shards of paper, each fold and groove suggesting a network or web.

The pursuit of connectivity, of an order, a network, organizing experience and information, has been a preoccupation of the American artist Terry Winters throughout his career. In paintings and works on paper, and in the set and costumes he designed for the Cunningham work *Loose Time* in 2002 (plate 204) — a title signifying Cunningham's interest in describing a territory mapped by the bodies of the dancers moving in front of and through it — Winters has expanded on the idea of imaginary or virtual and real or experiential space through his exploration of the grid and its structure. In *Location Plan* (1999), for example, a group of thirty drawings, Winters synthesizes lines and grid, employing one to undo the weave of the other.

Winters's drawings, and their implication of a virtual space, recall Gego's late wire works, the *Dibujos sin papel* (Drawings without paper; plate 207), and Molnar's mappings before she began to use computers. In works such as *Arbres et collines géométriques* (plate 205) and *Interruptions à recouvrements* (Disturbances through overlappings, 1969; plate 206) Molnar constructs a visual language of abstraction using only lines. *Arbres et collines géométriques*, essentially a landscape traced economically with one meandering line, reads like a diagram of a heartbeat, or a seismographic reading of the earth. The tremors and incidental movements of the otherwise steadily progressing horizon are both indices of the hand and an attempt to remove authorship completely. In two black and white drawings made in homage to one of her most important artistic mentors, *A la recherche de Paul Klee* (Searching for Paul Klee, 1970 and 1971), executed by hand and with the aid of a primitive computer, Molnar links her own breaking apart of the image to the shimmering planes of color that characterize Klee's drawings from the 1920s.

These operations on the grid can be related to the performative projects of artists and choreographers of a younger generation who understand the grid as an architecture imposed on the body by such forms as classical ballet, and indeed by Western ideas of artmaking more generally. One of a generation of choreographers who acknowledge Cunningham and Rainer as their antecedents, Ralph Lemon

202. Pierrette Bloch
(French, born 1928)
Grande maille (Large mesh). 1976
Rope, string, and ribbon
10´x 12´4 7/16˝ (305 x 377 cm)

203. Pierrette Bloch at work
in her studio, 1995

204. Merce Cunningham
(American, 1919–2009)
Loose Time. 2002
Performance view, Zellerbach Hall, University of California, Berkeley, 2002.
Set and costumes: Terry Winters.
Music: Christian Wolff. Lighting: Aaron Copp

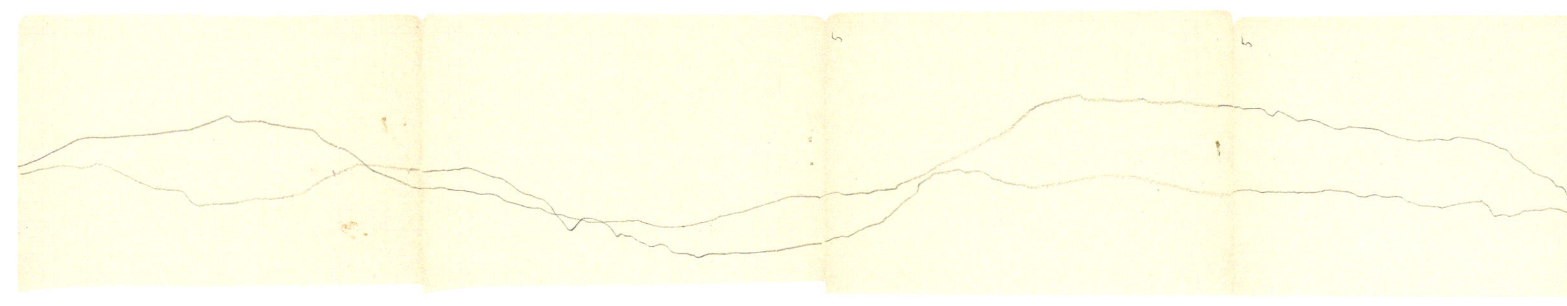

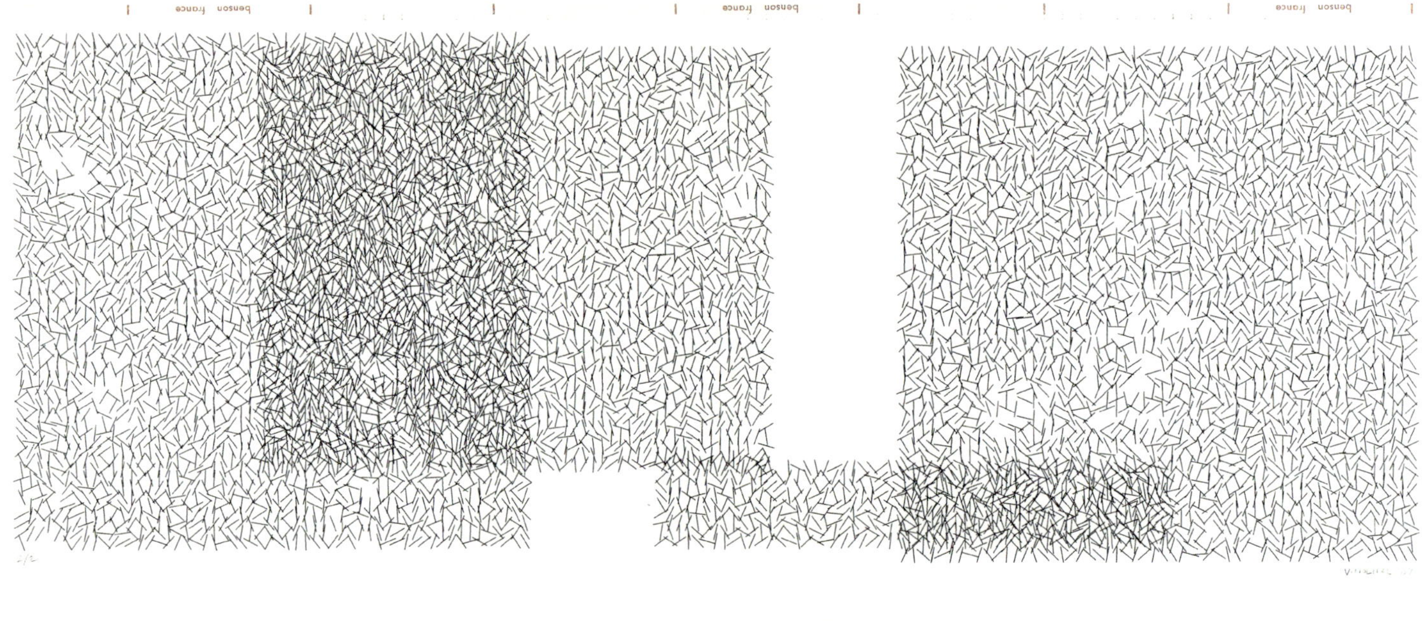

produces extreme works of endurance, shock, and unlearning to arrive at a history told through the body, which is viewed as the site through and on which history is enacted, performed, and played out. Like Rainer, Lemon strives for a radical realignment of the body in order to reclaim it from oppressive or dualistic ways of thinking.[60] In 1995, having developed a deep ambivalence toward performing and the audience, he disbanded his dance company and began to explore the history of the American civil rights movement. The result, ten years later, was *The Geography Trilogy*, a series of works, studies, and what he calls "research events" — combinations of performance, movement, travel, drawing, and actual engagement with his subject through interviews and diaristic photographs, together constituting a self-critical project of historical memory and subjective experience.[61] Lemon's "desire to present history as open-ended, incomplete, unresolved — instead of known, finished, and thus not worth consideration," Katherine Profeta writes, "meant he needed to avoid all ways of talking about the past that felt too familiar."[62] Working with trauma and memory by mining the geography of the civil rights movement — locations such as Selma, Alabama, a flashpoint of the movement, or Jackson, Mississippi, the site of the assassination of Medgar Evers — and through readings of writers such as James Baldwin, Lemon reclaimed history and its residual traces in the present.

Lemon has often collaborated with performance artist Okwui Okpokwasili, for example in *Come Home Charley Patton* (2004; plate 208), a section of *The Geography Trilogy* in which, among other things, she played Lemon's Uncle William and performed a monologue about the first time she was

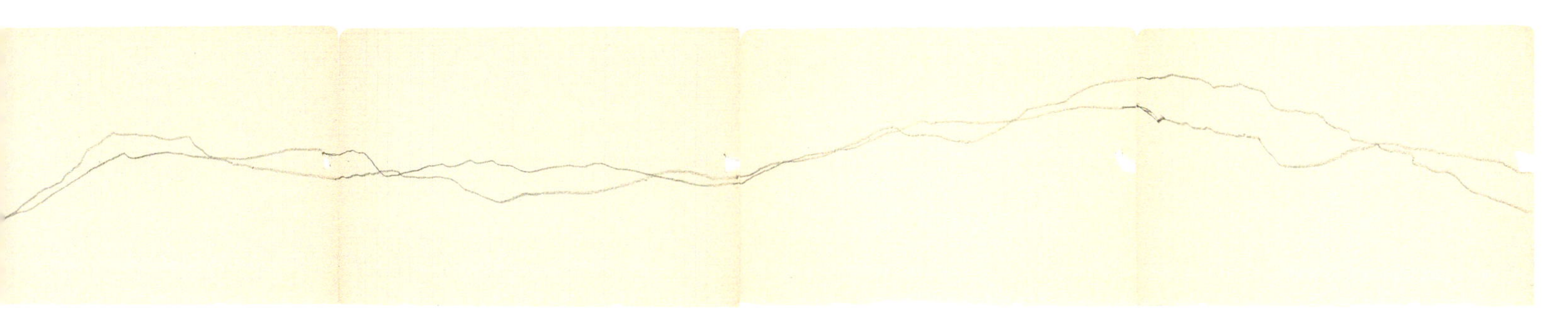

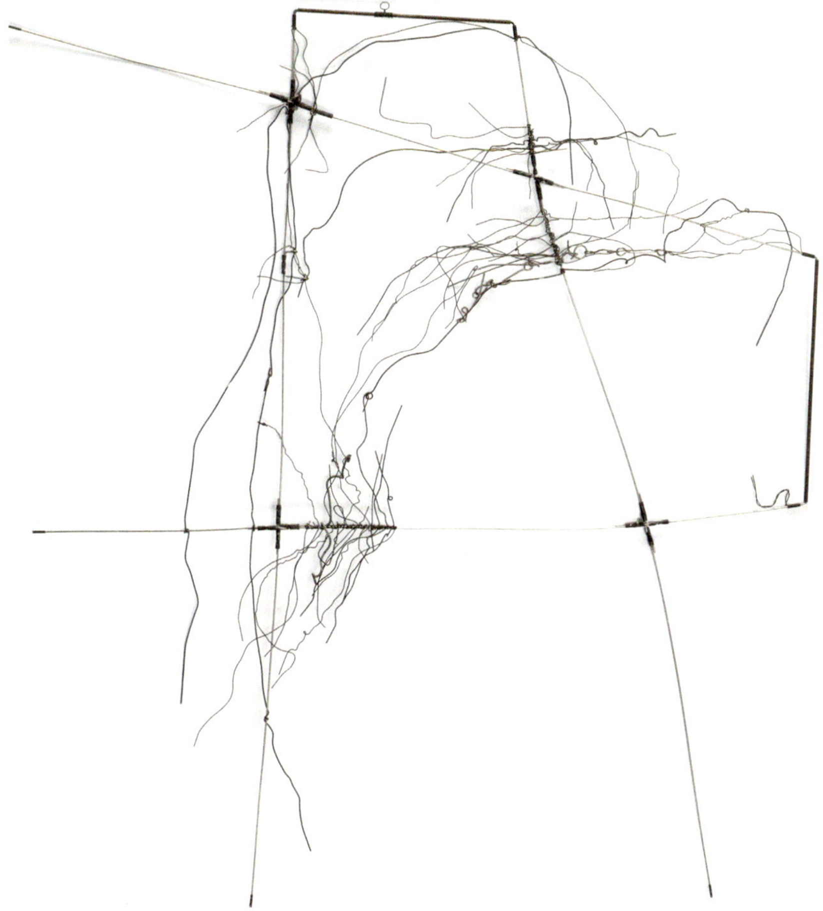

205. Vera Molnar
(French, born Hungary 1924)
Arbres et collines géométriques
(Geometric trees and hills). 1946
Crayon on paper
8 sheets, overall: 6 5/16 x 70 7/8″
(16 x 180 cm)

206. Vera Molnar
(French, born Hungary 1924)
Interruptions à recouvrements
(Disturbances through overlappings).
1969
Ink on paper
11 7/16 x 30 5/16″ (29 x 77 cm)

207. Gego
(Gertrud Goldschmidt; Venezuelan,
born Germany, 1912–1994)
Dibujo sin papel 85/16
(Drawing without
paper 85/16). 1985
Stainless steel and iron
22 x 21 x 5″ (55.9 x 53.3 x 12.7 cm)

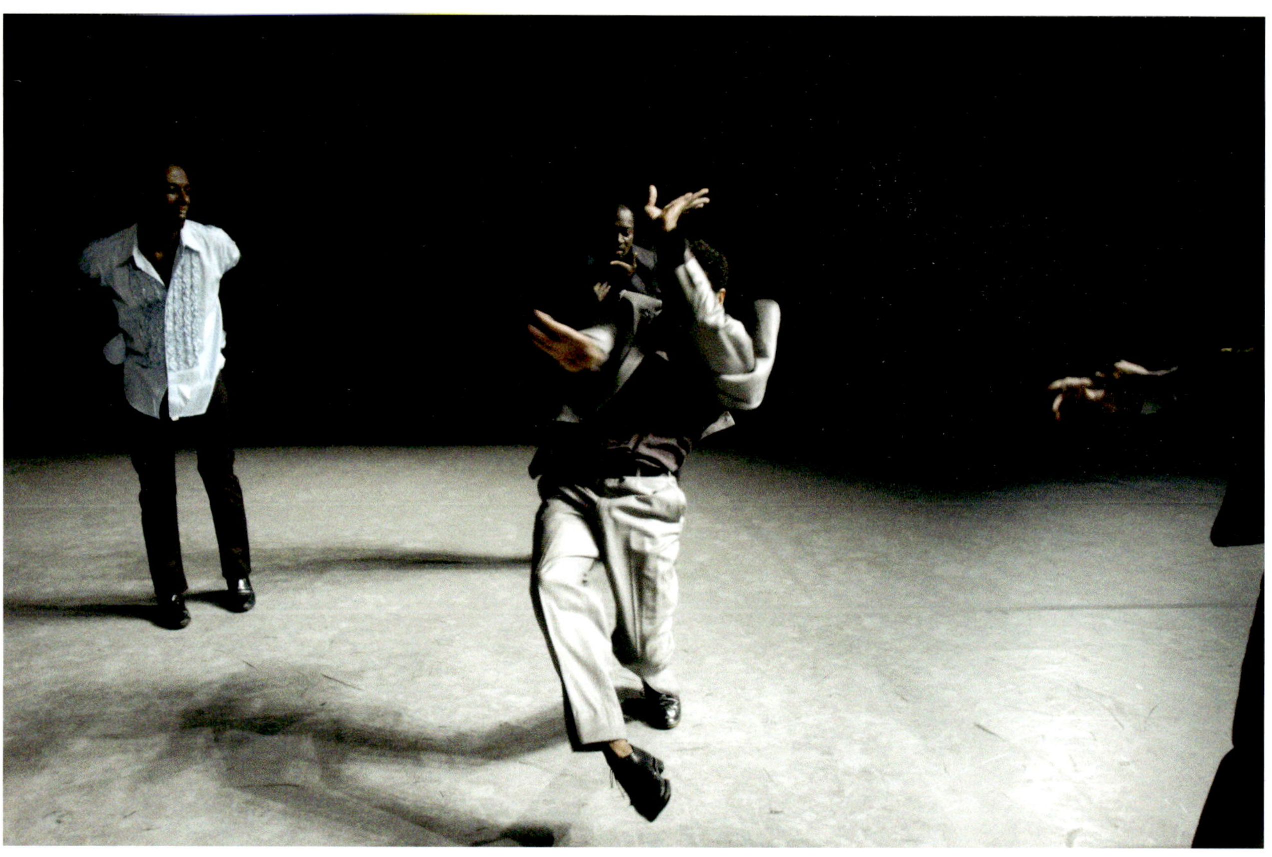

For me, I think in terms of "lines" in my performance work as physical (human) positioning, movements of connection and division (of some kind of partnership?), in space and in the body, bodies, lines of emotions, lines of states, of appearances, appearing and disappearing... sometimes becoming pure sensation, lineless!

—Ralph Lemon, 2010

called "nigger."[63] In an untitled work of 2008 that Lemon created for himself and Okpokwasili, he uses improvisation to explore the body's ability to push beyond the parameters of technique and training, exhaustion and exhilaration, to a point of kinesthetic unknowing. Breaking down the lines of the body to a kind of electric current that animates limbs and form, Lemon strives for an antichoreography, though deeply grounded in the body's impulses, and for a radical reworking of everyday experience and identity.

Gellman describes an ongoing drawing project, *Between the Dreamtime and the GPS* (2008; plates 209, 228), as a place of drift: "In between Terra Firma and Terra Incognita there is another place, a place in which we actually dwell. This place has no name and is part of the geography of the imagination."[64] An artist of Canada's First Nations, Gellman refers to dreaming as a kind of travel or mapping. Having input several drawings into a GPS navigational system, she gave the resulting map the coordinates of a field near her home in Toronto, then proceeded, on a snowy night,

> to enact this series of walk/drawings through the interface of my GPS tracking system that led me to move from place to place according to the map-drawing within.... these photos exemplify the marriage of psychogeography and the physical re-tracing of the walk, with their powerful impact resonating from the disorienting orientation of their location and position in space. Like the Peruvian Nazca lines, the "nightdrawings" position the walker in an in-between place.[65]

Echoing Sullivan's lines in the snow of the Canadian North, and similarly repurposing the Situationist *dérive*, Gellman exploits the notion of the in-between, drifting and dipping her way through a hallucinatory white landscape.

Among the proclivities of recent art history and curatorial practice is a return to, even an obsession with, so-called "professional marginals." As Pierre Bal-Blanc has said of Krasiński and others,

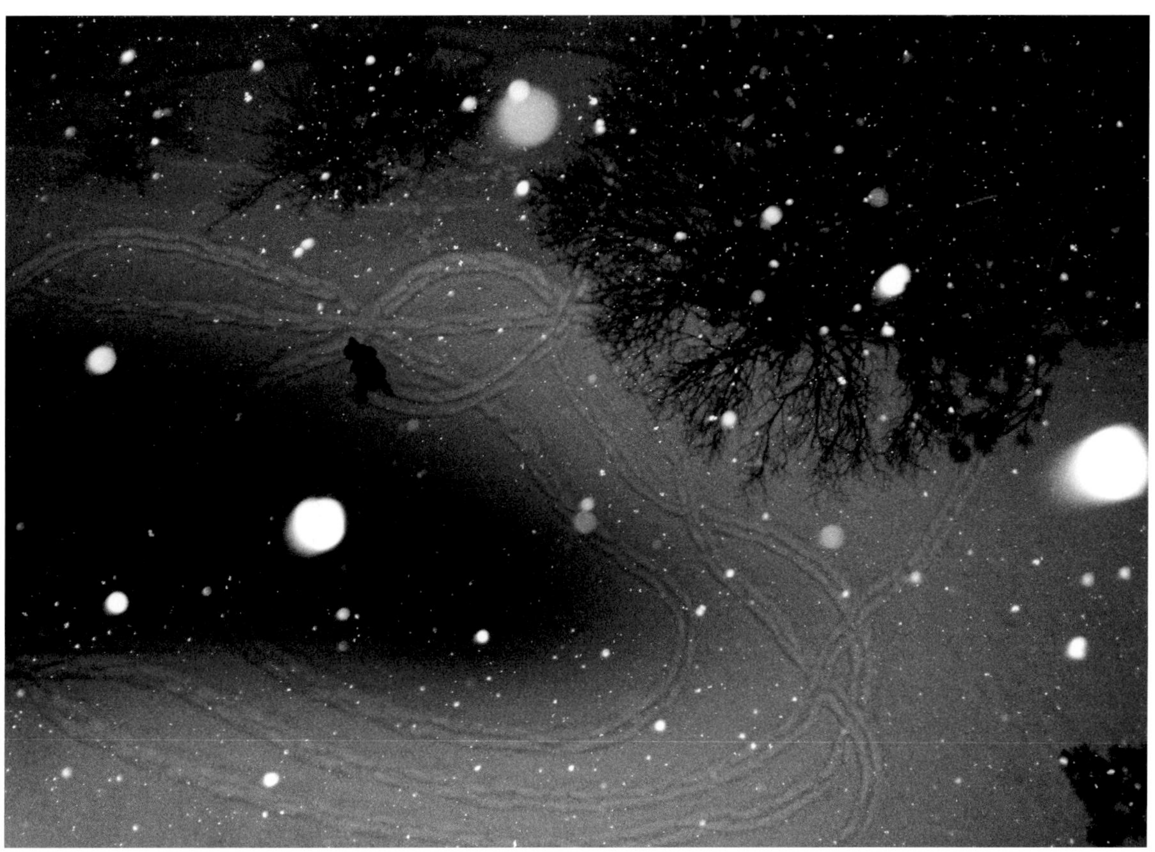

“These are artists who were for the most part left out of the dominant history, and whose work involved a practice of the everyday and a reflection on shared common space, from the intimate to the monumental.... [they] have each given priority to a form of art as a critical, concrete, daily practice.”[66] I want to propose a notion of what I’m calling the extreme analog of the present as a way to understand a return to line in current practices of both drawing and dance. Reflecting on practices of drawing, dance, and movement-based performance since the 1960s, one can draw a loose genealogy of works that engage with the idea of the ordinary, the plane/plain, and the analog as a transgressive methodology and a means of generating form. Though not directly reacting to digital-age attention deficits, these artists are formulating a practice of the everyday that refigures the consciousness of the viewer, focusing on line, time, space — a radical return.

Trisha Brown began to make drawings on paper as extensions of her body and of her work in dance. In a description of trying to draw a perfect square, she remarks,

> I like the fact that in dance you try to be organized in what you are doing, but the biology of the body just doesn’t permit that kind of precision. And especially if it’s covering ground and engaged with speed and variety. It reminds me of how difficult it is to perform; that you try for a perfect form, you have an ideal form in mind and it’s always a little bit different because you are breathing... because you’re exhaling this time when you approach it and you were inhaling the last time. There’s this little throb of variation that goes on which often shows up at the edges.[67]

Before the advent of video, drawing often functioned for dancers as a way of inscribing their work into memory, usually the historical memory of a company or troupe of dancers who would then imitate the original choreography as best they could. Brown’s notations on paper began as distractions, made to pass downtime in rehearsal and performance (recalling Cunningham’s inspiration for the title

208. Ralph Lemon
(American, born 1952)
Come Home Charley Patton from *The Geography Trilogy*. 2004
Performance view, Krannert Center for Performing Arts, University of Illinois, Urbana-Champaign, 2004. Left to right: David Thomson, Djédjé Djédjé Gervais, and Lemon, of Cross Performance Inc.

209. Mimi Gellman
(Canadian, born 1955)
nightdrawing 1. 2009
Black and white photograph
20 x 30˝ (50.8 x 76.2 cm)

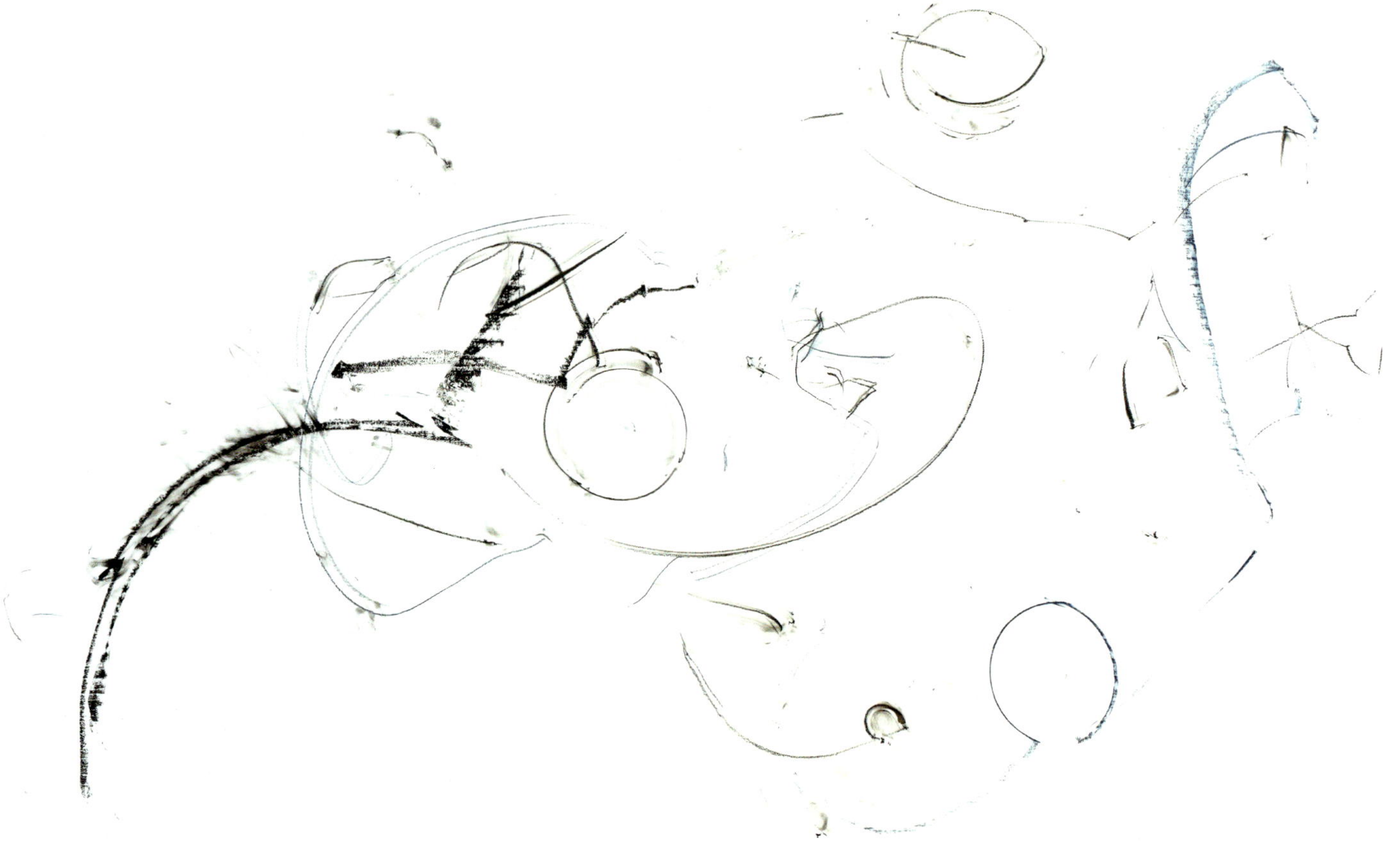

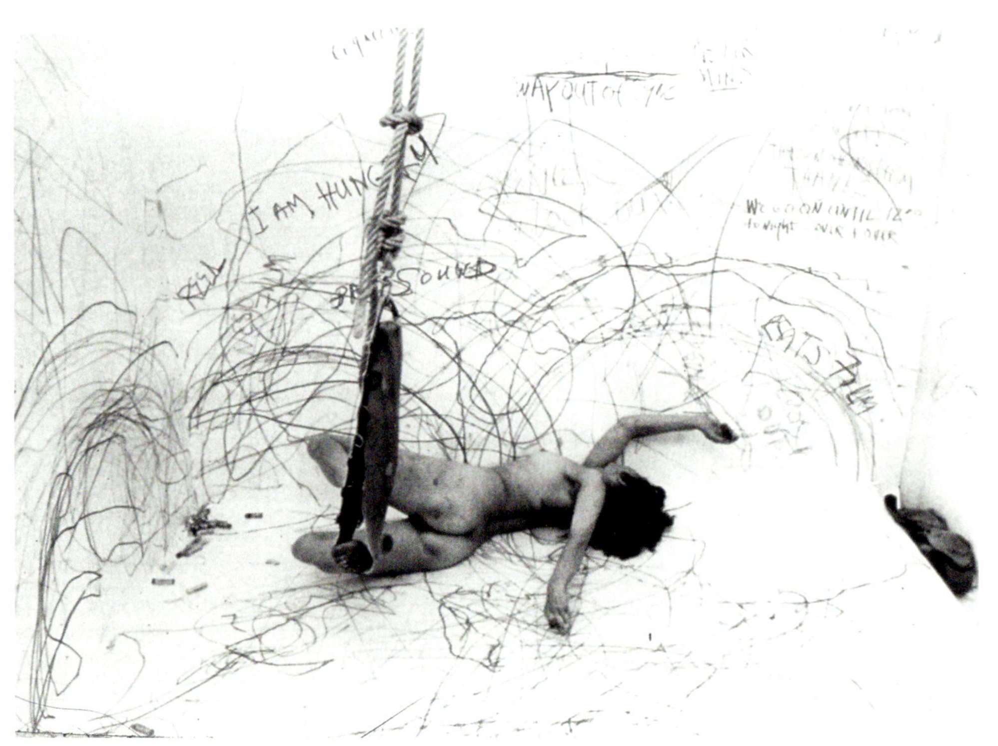

Up To And Including Her Limits *was the direct result of [Jackson] Pollock's physicalized painting process. . . . My entire body becomes the agency of visual traces, vestige of the body's energy in motion.*

— Carolee Schneemann, 1999

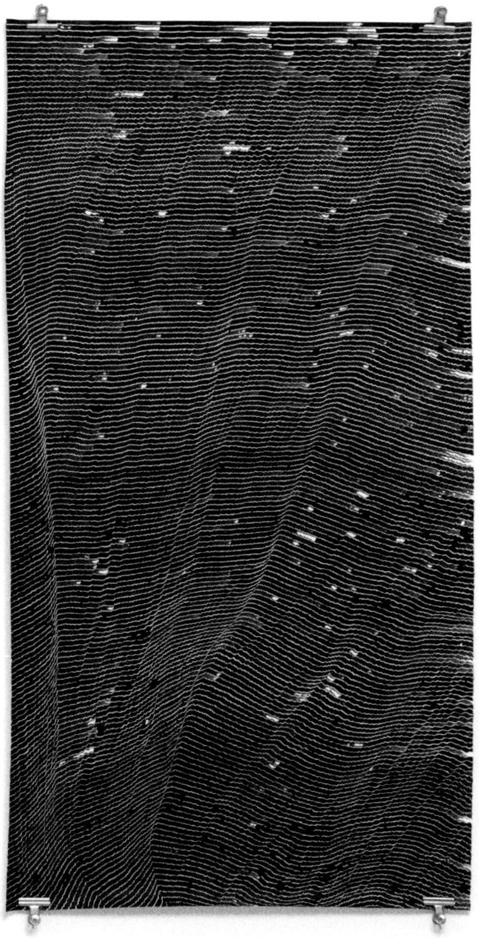

210. Trisha Brown
(American, born 1936)
Untitled. 2007
Charcoal on paper
6´8˝ x 9´9˝ (203.2 x 297.2 cm)

211. Carolee Schneemann
(American, born 1939)
Up To And Including Her Limits. 1973–76
Performance, with crayon on paper and rope and harness suspended from ceiling

212 and **213. Sophie Tottie**
(Swedish, born 1964)
Written Language (line drawings) #V and… *#VI*. 2008
Each: ink on paper
Each: 7´1˝ x 44 3/4˝ (215.9 x 113.7 cm)

Walkaround Time), and evolved into a practice separate from her dance work but parallel with it and originating kinesthetically in the same place: her body. Her early notebook drawings began with a figure in the center of a square, a conjunction of body and space represented by a simple continuous line. This exploration of the conjunction of body and page grew in scale as Brown developed a kind of drawing made using her body to push charcoal around on large sheets (actions she shot on video, initially for her own private records). The almost crude or primitive coupling of body against and on paper, the use of the limbs literally as tools, is both romantic, in its desire to give mark-making a status of authenticity, and oddly transgressive, yielding a visual object that is genetically part drawing, part performance.

Describing the hybridity of these works, the critic and curator Klaus Kertess writes, "Trisha Brown's drawings…are about the body in the mind exploring grammar, syntax, and semantics: about the hand as body and the body as hand, about drawing gesture as dance gesture as writing gesture, about page space as stage space."[68] A large-scale, untitled drawing of Brown's from 2007 (plate 210) recalls Schneemann's *Up To And Including Her Limits* (1973–76; plates 128, 211), in which the artist harnessed herself hanging in the air and used her swinging body to make marks on paper covering the walls and floor of the room, as well as Matta-Clark's cuts into buildings, which functioned like drawings in space and

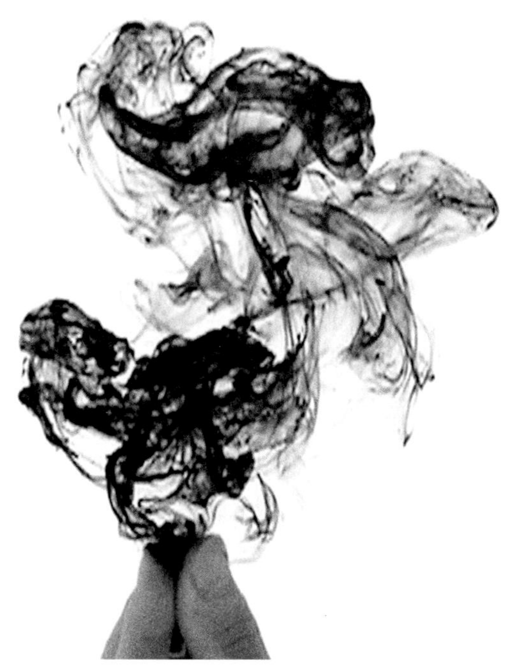

which the artist often suspended himself in midair to make. If Schneemann, in a critique of the heroic, hypermasculine image of the action painter dancing over his canvas, used the harness to erase her own controlling hand and its connotations of authorship, Brown achieves a similarly automated quality by applying her charcoal with virtually all parts of her body — not just hands but heels, toes, an elbow, losing the sense of signature as traditionally understood yet leaving indications of her own weight, mass, and movement over the page. (Matisse likened his work in the Vence chapel to flying, saying, "It's like being on a flying trapeze, doing these drawings on the walls.")[69] If Brown's work is to be taken as an automatic drawing of sorts, it raises the question of whether the awkward quality of the gesture somehow constitutes a signature mark or line. How do we know that the work was made, not conventionally with the hand, but with the whole body, or at least in some unfamiliar way? The idea of the signature mark, appropriated from the discourses of attribution and connoisseurship, here broadens out into the question of whether one's entire body contains a unique language of mark-making — what Tuttle has described as an electric current that flows from the body into the hand.[70]

In some of my works there is a coupling to the drawing as a visual skeleton which is, in itself, an expression of system. One of the driving forces is the tension between the signifying and nonsignifying line. The ability of the grid effectively to flatten or . . . to create a hole in the surface is another.

— Sophie Tottie, 2007

Both Sophie Tottie and Edith Dekyndt deal with line, chance, and the abstraction that can be extracted from the everyday. Since her emergence in the 1990s, Tottie has been experimenting with different ways of generating abstraction while holding on to some system or conceptual content that gives meaning to her subtle, quiet work. Creating a kind of visual white noise, this Swedish artist's installations, canvases, and paper works all involve drawing. Like Bloch, whose horsehair lines are subject to the whim of the material, like Martin, whose subtle manipulations of the grid bear witness to the idiosyncrasies of the hand, and like Tuttle, whose Wire Pieces find their own form in space, Tottie deploys the trope of chance operations, implying a language that yet remains elusive. Her monumental drawings *Written Language (line drawings) #V* and *#VI* (2008; plates 212, 213) suggest at once the automated codes of the digital world and deeply mysterious rubbings, made by hand and harking back to the process art of the 1960s.

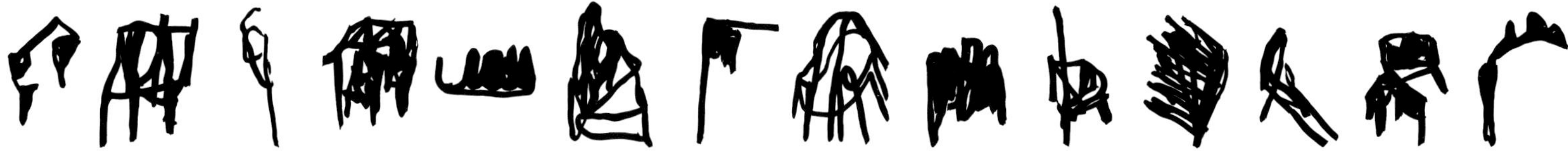

The obdurate silence of these works stems in part from the fact that they are line and only line. Repeated horizontal bands of ink applied to the paper create a visual static; accidents are allowed to remain, and generate the composition. Each drawing, Tottie writes, "starts with a handdrawn line. Materials are a dip pen, pigmented ink, and paper. Every successive line is attempting to incorporate each previous line's deviation. In this way the drawing proceeds by way of the first barely visible, then more and more extreme shifts produced by the previous line."[71] Made both within and out of line, Tottie's abstractions, which she calls "rooms" and "spaces," often evoke moments in the world of information overload, to the point of unintelligibility or distraction: the bar code, the late-night screen of television, whether analog or digital, gone unprogrammed or dead. Subtly referencing memory and preconscious states, these works confuse the terms of contemporary images of boredom, surveillance, recall, and attention generated or constructed by the analog.

The understanding of drawing as an integrated part of an artist's practice, with no dependence on other media, is both liberating and reflective of a desire to slow down, to clarify or isolate perception and attention. The ensuing visual vocabulary, in both visual art and dance, is boiled down to the essentials — or rather, in an almost primitivistic way, it isolates gesture and visual language, reducing them to a precognitive elementary. Dekyndt, in videos such as *Slow Object 04* (1997; plate 123) and *A Is Hotter Than B* (2005; plate 214), lets materials find their own way. A hand, or part of a hand, is seen performing a series of simple actions: tossing a rubber band, releasing a pinch of ink from finger and thumb into water. Recalling the rayographs of Man Ray, the experimental films that Stefan and Franciszka Themerson began to make in Poland in the 1930s, the dancing lines in Len Lye's films starting around the same time, and the earlier motion-efficiency studies of the American management consultant Frank Gilbreth, Dekyndt's videos are experiments in process and reflection. Employing strategies of chance and allowing a very elementary function of film and video technology — the slowing down of action — to alter her subjects slightly, this Belgian artist creates works that recall explorations of the properties of film in the last century yet lie closer to early, process-based video experiments with feedback loops and other low-tech manipulations.

The hand of the artist becomes important here. In Serra's seminal and crude 1968 film *Hand Catching Lead*, the artist repeatedly and silently performs the action of the title, catching and releasing shards of the soft metal dropped from off camera above. Serra has spoken of being inspired by Rainer's film *Hand Movie* (1966), in which her hands form shapes over and over, and disembodied images of hands appear in other experimental and process-based films of the same period.[72] It is as if, at the same moment that the signature becomes conceptual fodder for an investigation of authorship, the hand that makes that signature — anonymous, yet presumed to be that of the artist — becomes part of a postmodern deconstruction of movement and intentionality. We can think, in no scientific order, of a constellation we might call *Sleight of Hand*: Clark's sculptural proposal *Caminhando*, Bruno Munari's poetic outdoor performance *Making Air Visible* (1969), Serrra's *Hand Catching Lead*, Rainer's *Hand Movie*, Stuart Sherman's tabletop spectacles, and so on. As Munari instructed in 1969, "You've got hands. Try it."[73] Whether playful or conceptual, the gesture is markedly isolated. These works seek a transformation of the ordinary gesture, a practice of the everyday.

The title that Arturo Herrera gave to *Walk/14 parts* (2009; plate 215) situates it in a lineage of this Venezuelan artist's works that refer to the everyday, and again to Klee's evocative idea of "taking the line for a walk." *Walk/14 Parts* is inspired by the doodle, the idle wandering of hand and line on paper. Asked how he might address the digital realm in the context of this exhibition, Herrera answered by making

214. Edith Dekyndt
(Belgian, born 1960)
A Is Hotter than B. 2005
DVD projection, color, silent, 9-minute loop

215. Arturo Herrera
(Venezuelan, born 1959)
Walk/14 parts. 2009
Ink on paper
Dimensions variable

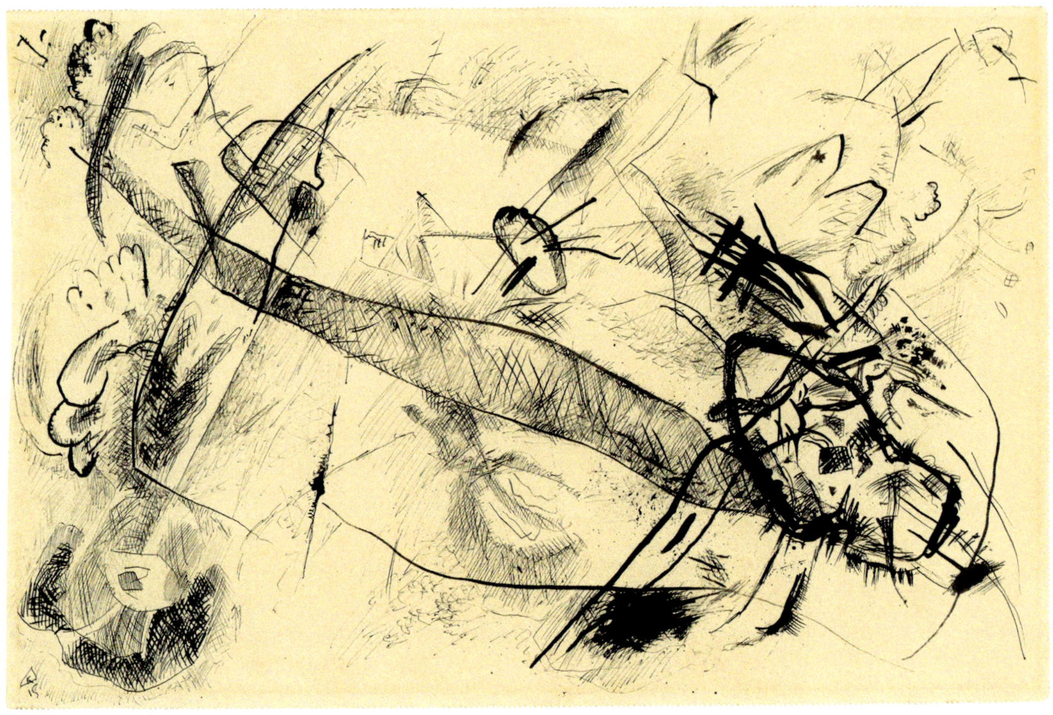

not an interactive work but a digitally projected version of an extremely analog, very basic group of rather banal marks. An artist who elsewhere draws with collage, pushing and exploiting the meandering cut line to an extreme of abstraction and nearly cartoony form, he became interested in revisiting a progression of thirteen marks he had made with ink, and, by enlarging the lines' contours, extracted a series of glyphic marks that hover between the hand drawn and the digitally enhanced. (During the classic period of the New York School, Franz Kline had developed a low-tech version of this technique, making drawings that he used an overhead projector to enlarge, then painting the enlargements.) Both projected in sequence and randomly shuffled on the nine flat video screens permanently set in MoMA's lobby — a space of distraction and disorientation — the artist's "hand," his signature if idly drawn mark, appears larger than life, or at least than expected by the surprising number of museum viewers who today prefer capturing the *Demoiselles d'Avignon* in their camera phones to actually looking at it. Herrera restores the all-but-lost painted gesture to a place of isolation and contemplation. It becomes, in fact, a lure, a sign for what might be experienced within.

Herrera is part of a lineage of artists whose work lies beyond the scope of this exhibition but is worth mentioning here. Over more than half a century, such painters as Hans Hartung, Jonathan Lasker, Albert Oehlen, and others have taken up the history of the mark in all its variations, in practices that some read as one aspect of the modernist preoccupation with formalism but that may also be taken as an intellectual investigation of mark-making. For the purposes of *On Line*, one might situate Kandinsky at the beginning of that lineage. In his early drawings, such as an untitled work from 1915 (plate 216), the autonomy of the individual lines and gestures clearly threatens to pull the entire composition apart. To keep these elements in tension was evidently a concern for Kandinsky, who was interested in a formal and spiritual harmony between elements, an idea he later honed into more structured, more geometrically balanced compositions. But the disharmony of his line during the period of the untitled drawing is perhaps what's most prescient and useful today for the generation of artists currently attempting to move forward the interrogation of painting that has taken place in the intervening century. While a mix of marks may appear in Braque's and Picasso's Analytical Cubist works of 1908–12, they are still used either to break up or to indicate form, always remaining contingent on observation of the three-dimensional subject. The marks in the drawings and paintings of 1909–14 that Kandinsky called "Improvisations," on the other hand,

216. Vasily Kandinsky
(French, born Russia, 1866–1944)
Untitled. 1915
Ink on paper
$8^{7}/_{8} \times 13^{1}/_{4}$″ (22.5 x 33.7 cm)

217. Zilvinas Kempinas
(Lithuanian, born 1969)
Serpentine. 2010
Magnetic tape, fan
Dimensions variable

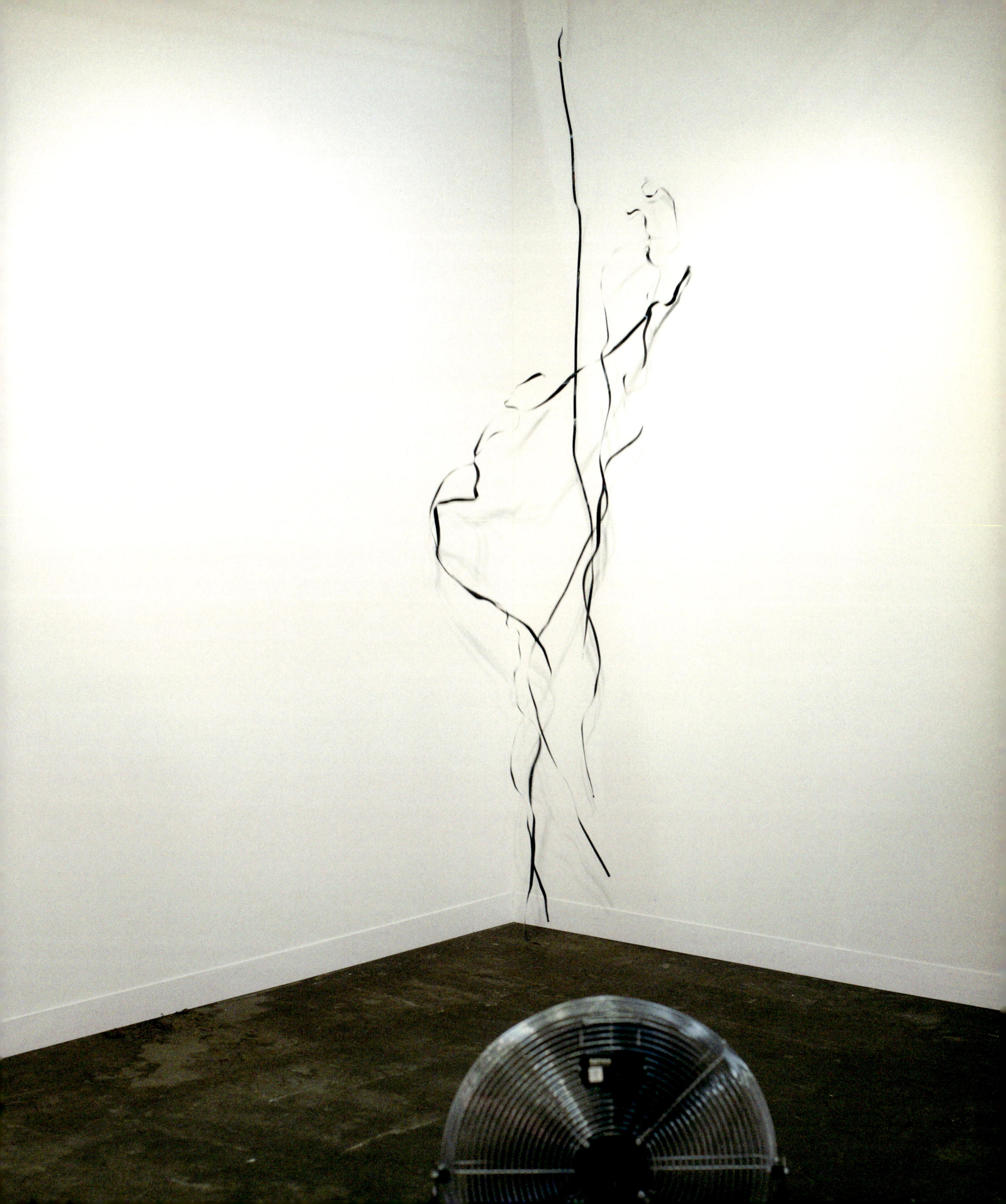

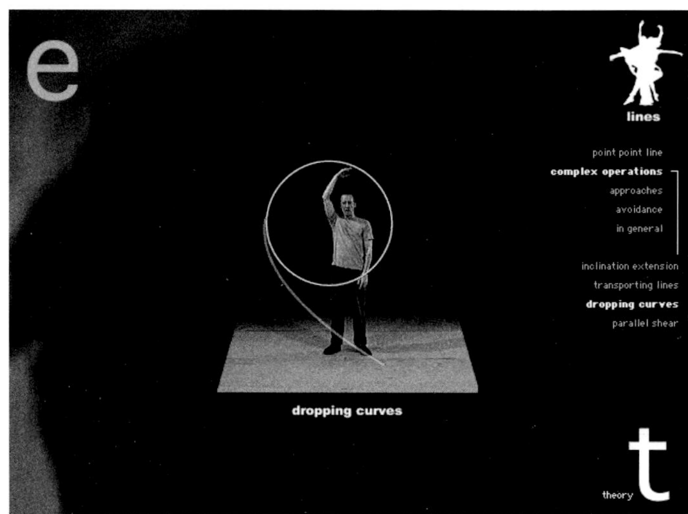

Your kinesphere functions as a memory — say, for example, your hands are near your knee, and you remember that that is where the movement sequence "A" begins or ends. You then perform "A" no longer in its original orientation, as it is prescribed in the movement vocabulary. This unoriginal orientation puts your body into yet another orientation accessing some other sequence of movements; but you keep trying to re-adjust yourself back and forth between states of dis- and re-orientation.

— William Forsythe, program notes for *Eidos: Telos*, 1995

not only construct the prime real estate, the focal point of the composition, but spread across the page as indexical jostling. And Kandinsky sometimes allowed this dance to veer toward the out-of-bounds, courting an almost palpable imbalance in many of his pre-Bauhaus drawings.The contemporary Lithuanian artist Zilvinas Kempinas has made works of extraordinary ethereality and economy out of fans and strips of magnetic tape. Positioning the fans either in groups or in proximity to the architecture of the space, he isolates the uncontrolled movement of the tape as it is set aflight by the movements of the air, which keep it in constant motion. In works where the tape follows vertical air currents (plate 217), the lines it forms maintain integrity as a kind of drawing in space. Elsewhere, held aloft by fans opposing one another, the tape floats horizontally, forming a closed circle, a void. When the tape is graphic in quality, it crystallizes the conceptual isolation of the mark. Made without the artist's active control, these marks rhyme visually with Kandinsky's emotive, melodic linearity and with his attempts to marry line and movement in his studies for *Punkt und Linie zu Fläche* (plates 157, 158). The tapes bump up against each other, throw one another off, then find their way back to the jumping, weaving vertical axis, skittish but never more than a few inches above the ground.

The notion of divorcing line from ground, orientation, and support leads us toward corollaries in contemporary dance such as Forsythe's 1994 work *Alie/nA(c)tion*, in which dancers moving through the piece repeat the phrase "They will never remember where/they always forgot which/they never remember how/they always forgot where."[74] A choreographer and dancer deeply involved with the application of linguistic theory to the body and its movements, Forsythe has used the vocabulary of classical ballet to open a space for a refiguring of movement and for what Gabriele Brandstetter calls "the mise en abyme of the dance — which Forsythe again and again stages in his works, literally, in the destabilizing of the foundation of the movement."[75] He has said that all his work is involved with drawing, indeed functions as drawing, and has made a number of large-scale installations that physicalize the line in space.[76] In *Improvisation Technologies* (plate 218), a lecture/demonstration made as a teaching tool to be viewed on the computer screen, whether as a DVD or downloaded from the Internet, Forsythe stands alone in the "black box" theater of postmodern dance, which doubles, however, as the edgeless universe of virtual space. As he takes the viewer through his choreographic ideas, tracing and gesturing in space, a technology of wiring his body (also used by Cunningham in collaborations with the OpenEnded Group) allows his movements to be exteriorized as onscreen shapes and forms. One screen of the DVD bears the heading "Line," and a series of subsections — "point line point," "complications," "approaches," "avoidance," "in general," "transporting lines," "parallel shear" — break down the movement phrases into choreographic ideas.[77]

The evocative notion of movement "en abyme" suggests the opening up of a space for inversion and reversal, for the horizontal to intercede with the vertical. Perhaps Forsythe's best-known work is *Solo*

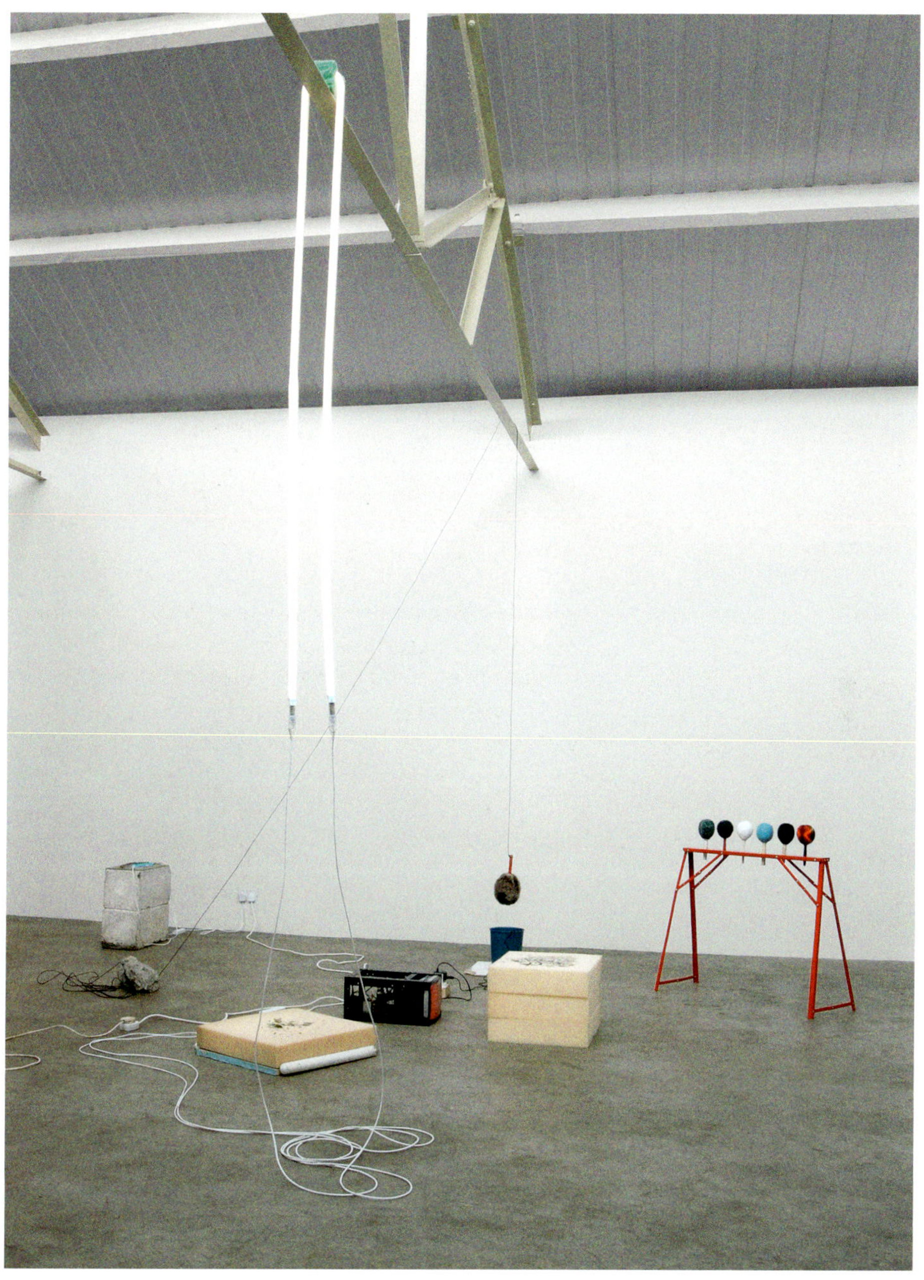

218. William Forsythe
(American, born 1949)
William Forsythe: Improvisation Technologies. A Tool for the Analytical Dance Eye. 1999
Screen shot from CD-ROM, realized by Forsythe with Nik Haffner, Volker Kuchelmeister, and Christian Ziegler. Performance: Forsythe

219. Nina Canell
(Swedish, born 1979)
Slight Heat of the Eyelid exhibition, mother's tankstation, Dublin, 2008. Installation view, showing works including *Dead Heat* (2008; far left), concrete, stick, neon, cable, and 1,000 volts, and *Beam Hang* (2008; center left, from ceiling), house beam, neon, cable, foam, and 3,000 volts

(1997; plate 144), which he performs himself. In this startling masterpiece—as canonical as Rainer's *Trio A*, Cunningham's *Walkaround Time*, and Pina Bausch's *Rite of Spring* (1975), works that arguably altered the course of modern dance—it is as though a force entering Forsythe's body had undone the techniques and expectations of kinesthetic possibility. The viewer witnesses a dismantling of classical dance, through movement and form that were at the time revolutionary. While Forsythe is at the forefront of choreographic experiments with video and digital technologies, he understands that dance's primary medium is the body. In undoing a classical language of dance, *Solo* is conceptually complex, yet it is also a work of extreme simplicity and physical exertion. *Solo* seems deeply subversive in its demand for attention and responsibility on the part of the viewer.

Discussing the notion of the extreme analog of the present in relationship to their work and thought, Cool and Balducci have said,

> In analog, there is the relationship to the real and its infinite combinations, a notion of space which is not defined by the absence (a cancellation of the part that does not conform) but by the presence (noises . . . which are, which belong to density) (for example the question of the vinyl record and the CD in music). And thus in the analogical interval is the richness of the real, in a continuous relationship to memory. A difference in which we lose the depth of the material, and finally space in its reality.[78]

Cool and Balducci, like the Swedish artist Nina Canell, are interested in simple, reductive forms and in an inventory of gestures initiated by the physical properties of the materials with which they work. Canell's sculptural practice brings the idea of truth to materials to the exhaustion point: each object is the residue of some exertion or manipulation that yields a reframing or shifted perception. Asked to name artists she thinks about, Canell mentions a text by Claes Oldenburg, "I Am for an Art." Originally published in the catalogue for *Environments, Situations, Spaces*, an exhibition at the Martha Jackson Gallery, New York, in 1961, and republished in 1967 in conjunction with Oldenburg's installation *The Store*, for which the artist made sculptures of everyday household objects and sold them to pay for groceries, the text is an ode to art as life:

> I am for an art that is political-erotical-mystical, that does something other than sit on its ass in a museum.
>
> I am for an art that grows up not knowing it is art at all, an art given the chance of having a starting point of zero.
>
> I am for an art that embroils itself with the everyday crap & still comes out on top.
>
> I am for an art that imitates the human, that is comic, if necessary, or violent, or whatever is necessary.
>
> I am for an art that takes its form from the lines of life itself, that twists and extends and accumulates and spits and drips, and is heavy and coarse and blunt and sweet and stupid as life itself.[79]

This call to arms for an art practice comprising "the lines of life," and as "stupid as life," is the point from which Canell begins. Culled from fragments of existing objects, natural and not, each of her installations is fashioned as a kind of low-tech laboratory in which materials entropically find their comfort zone. Those materials range from the scientific to the mundane — a work might include cement block, neon, half a watermelon, a walking stick, dry ice, a fan organ, and a contact microphone. The list of mediums for *Beam Hang* (2008; plate 219), like the work's title, not only describes the work but instructs its form: house beam, neon, cable, foam. Resurrecting neon, that favorite of *arte povera* and Post-Minimal artists of the 1960s and '70s, Canell both invokes established art tropes and empties out that history by hanging the neon over a beam, and in natural light. Like an elongated punctuation mark, or Nauman's neon work *My Name as though It Were Written on the Surface of the Moon* (1968) drained and gone limp, it claims a new territory by claiming nothing but its own linearity.

Writing in 1997 about Tuttle, Rob Storr called the art of the 1990s "physically modest and anti-rhetorical."[80] Canell's economy of means has something in common with Tuttle's. Unlike other versions of the antiheroic, her work permits no irony to creep into the selection of materials; rather, like Cool and Balducci, she derives her deflation of theatricality from a form of truth to materials. Cool and Balducci say that their work occupies a territory between drawing, painting, and sculpture but lies closest to drawing. Given that Cool was trained as a dancer, and that the pair's work was initially seen in the context of contemporary dance, an inquiry into the language of the body must be added to their roster of interrogations.

220–23. Marie Cool
(French, born 1961)
and
Fabio Balducci
(Italian, born 1964)
Untitled. 2006
Performance views. Performance: Cool

But now, drawing back to the edge of the table, gradually lower your eye (thus bringing yourself more and more into the condition of the inhabitants of Flatland), and you will find the penny becoming more and more oval to your view; and at last when you have placed your eye exactly on the edge of the table (so that you are, as it were, actually a Flatlander) the penny will then have ceased to appear oval at all, and will have become, so far as you can see, a straight line.

— Edwin A. Abbott, *Flatland: A Romance of Many Dimensions*, 1884

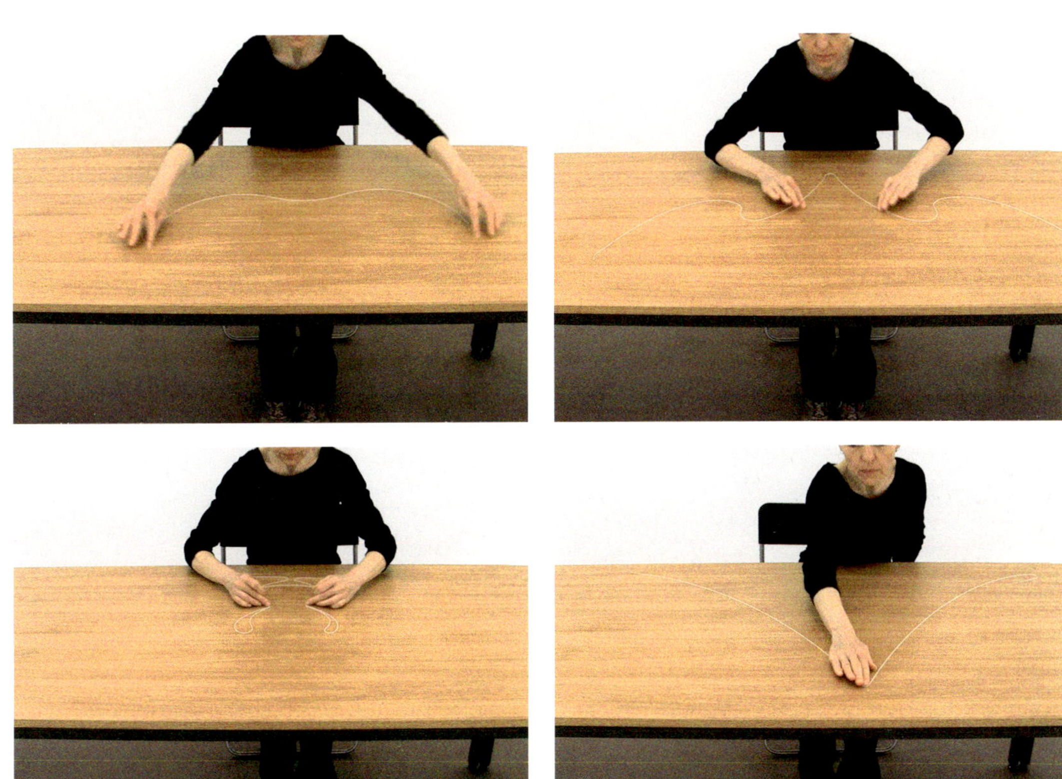

Tino Sehgal, whose work takes the form of encounters with the audience, has rightly said that there is "no work that is not participatory at all,"[81] but in the current discourse of participation the work of Cool and Balducci reaches back more specifically to antecedents such as Tuttle's Wire Pieces, or Clark's cultivation of the inherent power of everyday objects to heal and incite a social participation. It insists on the viewer's attention — indeed, in watching their work (plates 220–23), it is impossible to move a muscle. Part object, part sculpture, part drawing, part action, Cool and Balducci's art found form when out of necessity they turned to everyday found materials and an interest in the potential of the elemental. Although they insist that their work is not performance, it takes the form of a presented moment, a choreographed encounter with moments comprised of ordinary things — a string, two sheets of paper, small piles of rice poured onto a generic tabletop, adhesive tape suspended across the edges of a room. Like Vermeer's crystalline image of the woman with the pearl earring, Cool brings into our space a moment of complete absorption and aloneness, she with the materials and we with our experience of any variation in her precisely articulated actions. In a way, failure or imperfection is both the form and the meaning of the work.

Cool and Balducci gave their 2005 exhibition at the South London Gallery the subtitle *Prayers*, an ambitious call for the viewer's attention and involvement. For Laurent Goumarre, their work is "utterly literal, without a trace of metaphor," and the absorbed, antitheatrical quality of Cool's persona and presence have a willful flatness that recalls Rainer's deliberate refusal of inflection or acknowledgment of audience. "It is not a matter of temporal construction but of waiting," Goumarre writes, "that makes it possible to recognize things: not to witness the reappearance of what we already knew, but to 'keep an eye out' for the appearance of obvious, simple things that we recognize but have never seen before. There is no doubting the tautology of these performances: the action/image functions like an empty commemoration."[82]

Keeping an eye out for the appearance of the obvious — in some way this is what drawing, in its execution and consumption, is all about. When Oldenburg spoke about the lines of life itself, he identified something fundamental about drawing and its alignment with lived experience that is also captured, throughout the twentieth century and into the twenty-first, in drawing and in dance.

NOTES

1. See Octavio Paz, *Marcel Duchamp: Appearance Stripped Bare* (New York: Seaver Books, 1978), p. 2.
2. Vasily Kandinsky, "Point and Line to Plane: A Contribution to the Analysis of Pictorial Elements," 1926, in *Kandinsky: Complete Writings on Art*, ed. Kenneth C. Lindsay and Peter Vergo (New York: G. K. Hall & Co., 1982), 2:542.
3. Paul Klee, *Pedagogical Sketchbook*, 1925 (Eng. trans. New York: Frederick A. Praeger, 1953), p. 16.
4. Sibyl Moholy-Nagy, in ibid., p. 11.
5. See John Elderfield, *The Drawings of Henri Matisse* (London: Arts Council of Great Britain, 1984).
6. Henri Matisse, quoted in Elderfield, "Drawings at an Exhibition," *Matisse* (Brisbane: Queensland Art Gallery and Art Exhibitions Australia Limited, 1995), p. 55.
7. Matisse, quoted in John Hallmark Neff, "Matisse, His Cut-Outs and the Ultimate Method," in Jack Cowart, Jack D. Flam, Dominique Fourcade, et al., *Henri Matisse: Paper Cut-Outs* (St. Louis: St. Louis Art Museum, and Detroit: The Detroit Institute for the Arts, 1977), p. 22.
8. See Sally Banes, *Democracy's Body: Judson Dance Theater, 1962–1964* (Ann Arbor: UMI Research Press, 1980). An excellent and more theoretical treatment of the Judson activities appears in Nick Kaye, "The Collapse of Hierarchies and Postmodern Dance," *Postmodernism and Performance* (New York: St. Martin's Press, 1994).
9. Banes, *Democracy's Body*, p. 3. Elsewhere Ramsay Burt has argued, "One of the legacies of Judson Dance Theater has been a rejection of the idea that a dancer is someone whose specialized training and rarefied artistic sensibilities separate them from ordinary life." Burt, *Judson Dance Theater: Performative Traces* (London: Routledge, 2006), p. 170. Anna Halprin refers to "choreotypic codes" in "Anna Halprin à l'origine de la performance," *Artpress* no. 321 (March 2006):12.
10. See Merce Cunningham's description in David Vaughan, *Merce Cunningham: Fifty Years* (New York: Aperture, 1997), pp. 163–66.
11. See Vaughan, "'Then I thought about Marcel…' Merce Cunningham's *Walkaround Time* (1982)," in Richard Kostelanetz, ed., *Merce Cunningham: Dancing in Space and Time* (Chicago: Chicago Review Press, 1992), pp. 66–70.
12. Cunningham, "Space, Time and Dance," in ibid., p. 38.
13. I thank Janet Kraynak for this observation, the basis of her forthcoming book *Reiterating Nauman*.
14. Kathy Halbreich, Neal Benezra, and Joan Simon, eds., *Bruce Nauman* (Minneapolis: Walker Art Center, 1994), p. 133.
15. Nauman, in Coosje van Bruggen, *Bruce Nauman* (New York: Rizzoli, 1988), p. 115. The relationship between dance and the camera was recently surveyed in the exhibition and book *Dance with Camera* (Philadelphia: Institute of Contemporary Art, University of Pennsylvania, 2009).
16. For an example of this kind of drawing see Halbreich, Benezra, and Simon, p. 137.
17. See Paul Schimmel, "Into the Void: Performance and the Object," *Out of Actions: Between Performance and the Object 1949–1979* (Los Angeles: The Museum of Contemporary Art, 1998), p. 91.
18. Lygia Clark, "On the Magic of the Object," from "Livro-Obra," 1983, in *Lygia Clark* (Barcelona: Fundació Antoni Tàpies, 1997), pp. 152–53.
19. Tino Sehgal, speaking at a performance-art workshop on participation, The Museum of Modern Art, February 25, 2010. Writers such as Claire Bishop and Laurent Goumarre have theorized contemporary performance and dance, making important distinctions from the discourse of relational aesthetics. See Goumarre, "La Vacance du spectateur," *artpress* 331 (February 2007):60–64 and "La Dance. Lieu frontière," *artpress* 270 (July/August 2001):3–38
20. Matisse, quoted in Pierre Schneider, *Matisse*, trans. Michael Taylor and Bridget Strevens Romer (New York: Rizzoli, 1984), p. 595.
21. "Here, too, conventional 'beauty' of movement must be thrown overboard, and the 'natural' progress of the narrative (narrative = the literary element) explained as unnecessary and ultimately distracting." Kandinsky, *On the Spiritual in Art*, 1911, reprinted and trans. in *Kandinsky: Complete Writings on Art*, ed. Lindsay and Vergo, 1:205.
22. See, e.g., Bernice Rose, *Picasso, Braque and Early Film in Cubism* (New York: Pace Wildenstein, 2007), and Rhonda K. Garelick, *Electric Salome: Loie Fuller's Performance of Modernism* (Princeton: at the University Press, 2007).
23. Laurence Louppe, ed., *Traces of Dance: Drawings and Notations of Choreographers*, trans. Brian Holmes and Peter Carrier (Paris: Editions Dis Voir, 1994), p. 14.
24. See Ted Merwin, "Loie Fuller's Influence on F. T. Marinetti's Futurist Dance," *Dance Chronicle* 21, no. 1 (1998):73–92. Merwin writes on p. 86, "While Fuller transcended the physical limitations of her body by putting it on technologically enhanced display, Marinetti projected physical illness onto the world, and proposed technology as the remedy."
25. Garelick, "Radical Mechanicity," in *Electric Salome*, pp. 200–203 .
26. Merwin, "Loie Fuller's Influence," p. 82. Fuller danced solo until c. 1900, when she performed at the World's Fair. She subsequently choreographed for, and often performed with, a group of dancers. In 1908 she organized a school, and many photographs show her with a group of young women who emulate her mode of dress and appearance. Fuller's later works, from the 1920s on, were more ambitiously theatrical and were performed with groups of these women.
27. Filippo Tommaso Marinetti, quoted in ibid., p. 78.
28. Gino Severini, in *Gino Severini, The Dance 1909–1916* (New York: Solomon R. Guggenheim Foundation, New York, 2001), pp. 37, 44.
29. See Susan Laikin Funkenstein, "Engendering Abstraction: Wassily Kandinsky, Gret Palucca, and 'Dance Curves,'" in *Modernism/modernity* 14, no. 3 (September 2007):389. Funkenstein writes on p. 391, "Palucca presented herself as a modernist dancer concerned with abstraction, but combined with an image, on and off stage, that was simultaneously youthfully feminine, New Woman androgynous, and powerfully masculine."
30. Ibid., p. 390.
31. See Garelick, *Electric Salome*, pp. 38–39. *La Mer* (The sea), perhaps Fuller's best-known large-scale work, was choreographed in 1925 and performed in 1930 with a troupe of young dancers who moved beneath an enormous swath of shimmering silk, creating a watery landscape of undulating patterns. Fuller also experimented with phosphorescent salts in combination with the colored dyes applied to her fabric costumes.
32. See Leah Dickerman, "Bauhaus Fundaments," in Barry Bergdoll and Dickerman, *Bauhaus 1919–1933: Workshops for Modernity* (New York: The Museum of Modern Art, 2009), p. 18.
33. Rudolf von Laban, quoted in Louppe, ed., *Traces of Dance*, p. 120. For a survey of more recent dance-notational drawings and a discussion of their relationship to choreographic process, see Ellen Schwartz's exhibition catalogue *Movement Drawings* (New York: Pratt Institute, 1982).
34. Klee, "Schöpferische Konfession (Opinions on Creation)," in Alfred H. Barr, Jr., Julia and Lyonel Feininger, and James Johnson Sweeney, *Paul Klee*, ed. Margaret Miller (New York: The Museum of Modern Art, 1946), p. 11.

35. Hugo Ball, entry for March 29, 1917, in *Flight Out of Time: A Dada Diary*, quoted here from Dickerman, "Zurich," in *Dada* (Washington, D.C.: National Gallery of Art, 2006), p. 36. I am grateful to Dickerman for her insight and counsel.
36. See Guy Debord, "Théorie de la dérive," in *Les Lèvres nues* no. 9 (November 1956), republished in *Internationale Situationiste* no. 2 (December 1958) and more recently in *Art and Theory 1900–1990: An Anthology of Changing Ideas*, ed. Charles Harrison and Paul Wood (London: Blackwell Publishing, 2003), pp. 696–97.
37. See Robert Enright, "A Woman for All Seasons: An Interview with Françoise Sullivan," *Border Crossings* 27, no. 2 (January 2008):48–61.
38. See Gyula Kosice, *Arte Madí* (Buenos Aires: Ediciones de Arte Gaglioannone, 1982) and Maria Lluisa Borras, ed., *Arte Madí* (Madrid: Museo Nacional Centro de Arte Reina Sofía and Museo Extremeño e Iberoamericano de Arte Contemporáneo, 1997). For two U.S. exhibitions surveying Concretism and Neo-Concretism in Latin America and as an international phenomenon see Mari Carmen Ramírez, *Inverted Utopias: Avant-Garde Art in Latin America* (Houston: Museum of Fine Arts, and New Haven: Yale University Press, 2004), and Lynn Zelevansky, *Beyond Geometry: Experiments in Form, 1940s–1970s* (Los Angeles: Los Angeles County Museum of Art, and Cambridge, Mass.: The MIT Press, 2004).
39. See the Gutai Manifesto, 1956. An English translation of the manifesto appears on the website of the Ashiya Museum, which houses Japan's largest collection of Gutai works: http://www.ashiya-web.or.jp/museum en/103education/nyumon_us/manifest_us.htm.
40. Pablo Picasso, quoted in André Salmon, *L'Air de la Butte*, 1945, quoted here from John Richardson, *A Life of Picasso: The Cubist Rebel, 1907–1916* (New York: Alfred A. Knopf, 2007), p. 256. I am grateful to Anne Umland for her insights into Picasso's *Guitar* and papier collé works; see her *Picasso: Guitars 1912–1914* (New York: The Museum of Modern Art, 2010).
41. Brian O'Doherty, *Inside the White Cube: The Ideology of the Gallery Space*, 1976 (reprint ed. Berkeley, Los Angeles, and London: University of California Press, 1996), p. 38.
42. Jaleh Mansoor, "Kurt Schwitters' *Merzbau*: The Desiring House," in *Invisible Culture: An Electronic Journal for Visual Culture* no. 5 (2002), at http://www.rochester.edu/in_visible_culture/Issue4-IVC/Mansoor.html.
43. "A idéia e o espaço abstrato/A realização é um espaço-tempo/A superficie modulada é a materialização da idéia-espaço/A idéia-espaço deve ser realizada dentro do seu próprio tempo." Clark, in Ferreira Gullar, *Lygia Clark. Uma experiencia radical (1954–1958)* (Rio de Janeiro: Departamento de Imprensa Nacional, 1958), n. p.
44. Clark, "Lygia Clark and the Concrete Expressional Space," in *Lygia Clark* (Fundació Antoni Tàpies), p. 83. Originally published as "Lygia Clark e o espaço concreto expressional" in *Jornal do Brasil*, July 2, 1959. Clark writes of the origin of the organic line, "I began to explore this line, making paintings (still then using canvas and frame) in which the concern was that of bursting the nucleus of the painting (canvas) bringing its color into the frame. The very thickness of the frame now began to enter also as a plastic element (in certain points it was painted in relation to the formal composition of the painting itself)."
45. Maurice Merleau-Ponty, "Eye and Mind," *Primacy of Perception* (Evanston: Northwestern University Press, 1964), pp. 162–63.
46. Guy Brett, "The Logic of the Web," *Lygia Pape Gavea de Tocaia* (São Paulo: Cosac Naify, 2000), p. 307. Brett's long commitment to Brazilian artists and his landmark exhibitions, including *Force Fields: Phases of the Kinetic* (2000) in London and Barcelona, were critical in laying the groundwork for exhibitions such as *On Line*.
47. Robert Morris, "Some Notes on the Phenomenology of Making," 1970, in *Continuous Project Altered Daily: The Writings of Robert Morris* (Cambridge, Mass.: The MIT Press, 1993), pp. 73, 75. Other writers who were important in theorizing the work in dance and sculpture done at the Judson and elsewhere in New York include Annette Michelson, Jill Johnston, and Phil Lieder.
48. Morris, ibid., p. 73.
49. See Burt, *Performative Traces*, p. 77.
50. Pat Catterson, who has performed Yvonne Rainer's work for many years, discussed this notion of community at a performance art workshop at The Museum of Modern Art, March 7, 2009.
51. See Yves-Alain Bois, "Chance Encounters: Kelly, Morellet, Cage," *The Anarchy of Silence: John Cage and Experimental Art* (Barcelona: Museu d'Art Contemporani de Barcelona, 2010), pp. 188–203.
52. Cuauhtémoc Medina, "Action/Fiction," in *Francis Alÿs* (Antibes: Musée Picasso, 2001), p. 48.
53. Michel de Certeau, *The Practice of Everyday Life* (Berkeley, Los Angeles, and London: University of California Press, 1984), p. 117.
54. Margo Neale, "Marks of Meaning: The Genius of Emily Kngwarray," in *Utopia: The Genius of Emily Kame Kngwarray* (Canberra: National Museum of Australia Press, 2008), p. 35.
55. Ibid., p. 37.
56. Brett, "Let There Be Light," in Brett, ed., *Cildo Meireles* (London: Tate Publishing, 2008), p. 89.
57. Meireles, in ibid., p. 90.
58. Ibid., p. 164.
59. Umland has convincingly questioned the role of chance in Hans Arp's collages of the 1910s in Umland and Adrian Sudhalter, *Dada in the Collection of The Museum of Modern Art* (New York: The Museum of Modern Art, 2008), pp. 44–49. See also Scott Gerson's "Conservation Notes" in the same entry.
60. See Burt, *Performative Traces*, pp. 32–33, 72–75, and Jeff Friedman, "'Muscle Memory': Performing Oral History," *Oral History* 33, no 2 (Autumn 2005):35–47.
61. For a longer discussion of Ralph Lemon's choreographic work see Katherine Profeta, "The Geography of Inspiration," *Performance Art Journal*, 81 (2005): p. 23–28, and Nicholas Birns, "Ritualizing the Past: Ralph Lemon's Counter-Memorials," *Performance Art Journal*, 81 (2005): pp. 18–22.)
62. Profeta, "The Geography of Inspiration," p. 26.
63. Ibid., p. 27.
64. Mimi Gellman, unpublished artist's statement, 2009.
65. Ibid.
66. Pierre Bal-Blanc, in Elisabeth Lebovici, "The Death of the Audience: A Conversation with Pierre Bal-Blanc," *e-flux journal* no. 13, online at http://www.e-flux.com/journal/view/113.
67. Trisha Brown, in an interview with Hendel Teicher, "Danse et Dessin," *Danse, précis de liberte* (Marseille: Musées de Marseille, 1998), p. 20.
68. Klaus Kertess, "Feet Dancing, Hand Drawing," in ibid., p. 127.
69. Matisse, quoted in Schneider, *Matisse*, p. 571.
70. Richard Tuttle, conversation with the author, June 25, 2010. I am indebted to Tuttle for conversations with him over the years that have deeply informed my thinking about drawing. In a conversation of June 22, 2010, Tuttle spoke of the writings of art historian Richard Offner, a scholar of Florentine painting and a founder of the Institute of Fine Arts in New York, and his work on the study of attribution and its relationship to mark-making and authorship.
71. Sophie Tottie, statement for the press release announcing the exhibition *Written Language (Line Drawings)*, Galerie Konrad Fischer, Berlin, March 13–April 25, 2009.
72. In a recent conversation Rainer recalled her friendship and close artistic dialogue with Richard Serra at the time. In particular she remembered both of them laughing at an early screening of *Hand Movie* and in general discussing the qualities of humor and critique in minimalist dance. Rainer, conversation with the author, August 28, 2010.
73. Bruno Munari, quoted in Claude Lichtenstein and Alfredo W. Haberli, *Far vedere l'aria, Making Air Visible: A Visual Reader on Bruno Munari* (Zurich: Museum für Gestaltung Zürich, 2000), p. 41.
74. Gabriele Brandstetter, "Defigurative Choreography: From Marcel Duchamp to William Forsythe," *The Drama Review* 42, no. 4 (Winter 1988):52.
75. Ibid., p. 43. Other artists and contemporaries of William Forsythe's who emerged in the early 1990s include French choreographers Jerome Bell and Xavier Le Roy, whose contribution to the current discourse around dance and performativity is the creation of a conceptual framework for choreography. Le Roy will perform his landmark work *Self Unfinished* (1998) as part of the dance program in conjunction with *On Line: Drawing Through the Twentieth Century*.
76. Conversation with the artist, March 2010, and also The Forsythe Company website, www.theforsythecompany.com, where a section titled "Choreographic Objects" includes some of the artist's writings.
77. See the "Choreographic Objects" category of The Forsythe Company website.
78. Marie Cool and Fabio Balducci, e-mail to the author, June 4, 2010.
79. Claes Oldenburg, "I am for an Art," in *Environments, Situations, Spaces* (New York: Martha Jackson Gallery, 1961), reprinted in an expanded version in Oldenburg and Emmett Williams, eds., *Store Days: Documents from The Store (1961) and Ray Fun Theater (1962)* (New York: Something Else Press, 1967), pp. 39–42.
80. Robert Storr, "Just Exquisite? The Art of Richard Tuttle," *Artforum* 36, no. 3 (November 1997):87.
81. Sehgal, at the performance-art workshop on participation, The Museum of Modern Art.
82. Goumarre, "La Vacance du Spectateur," p. 63.

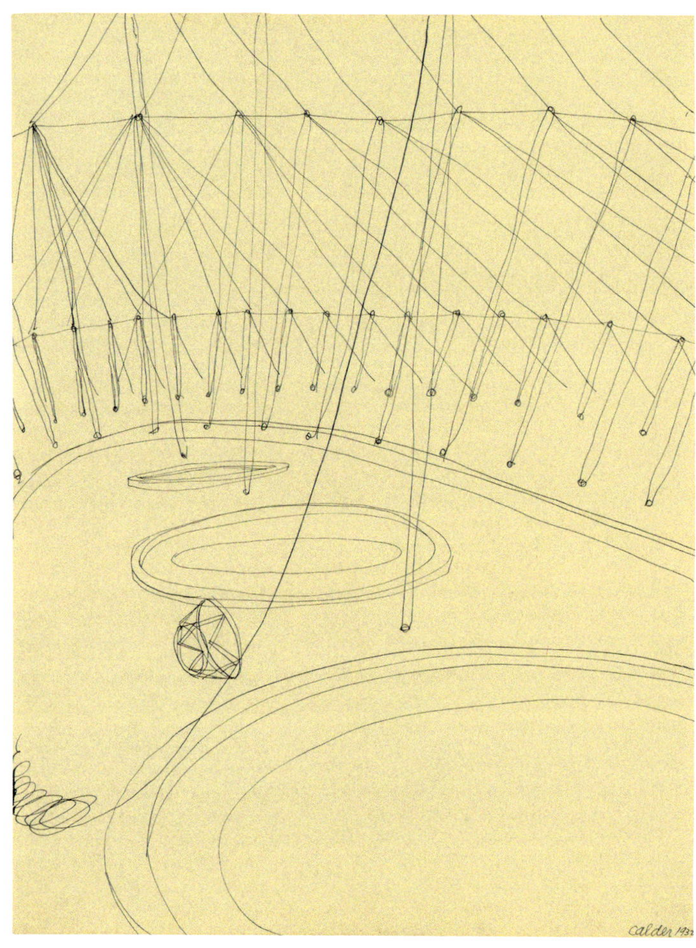

224. Alexander Calder
(American, 1898–1976)
Circus Interior. 1932
Ink on paper
19 x 14″ (48.1 x 35.5 cm)

CONFLUENCE

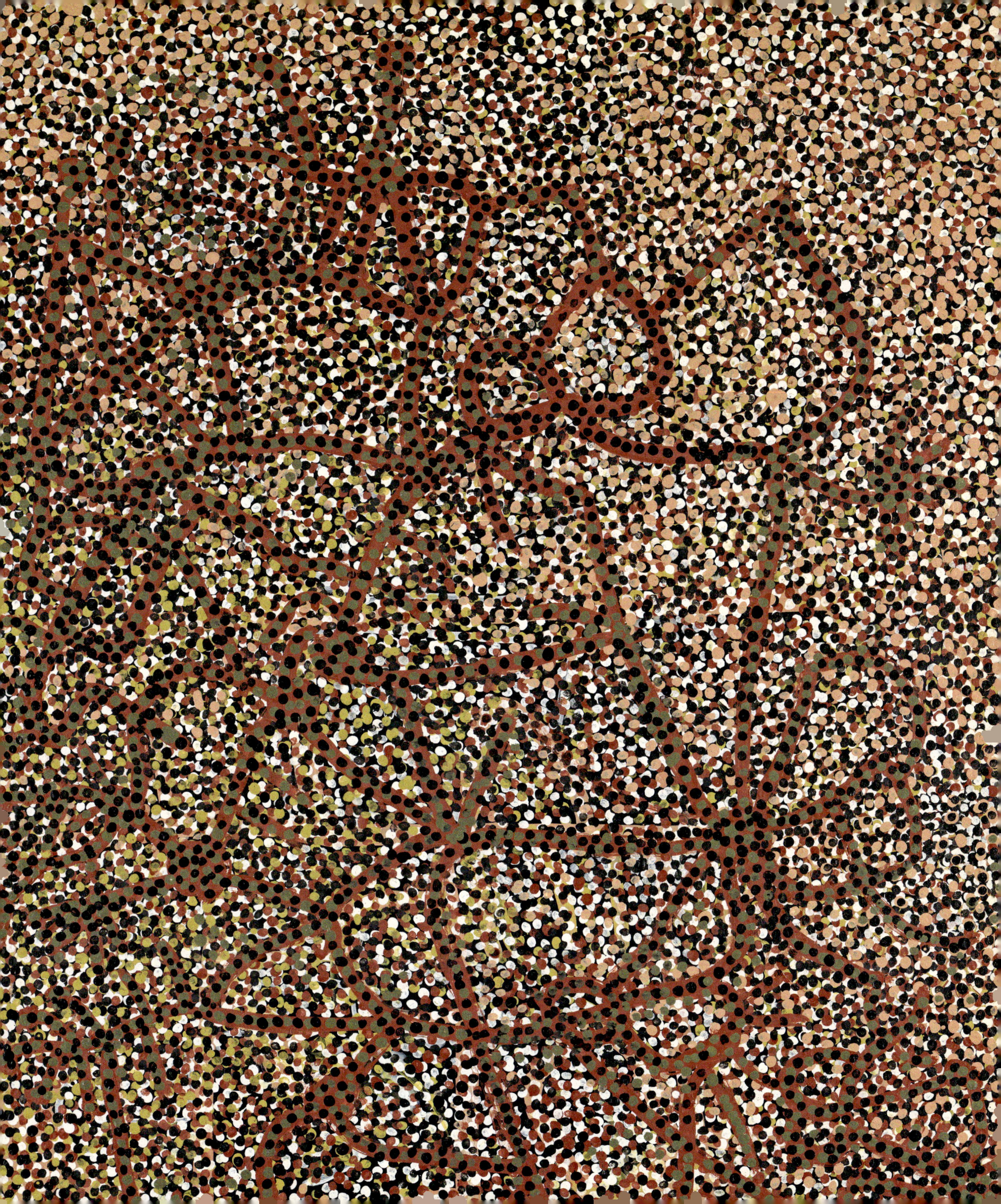

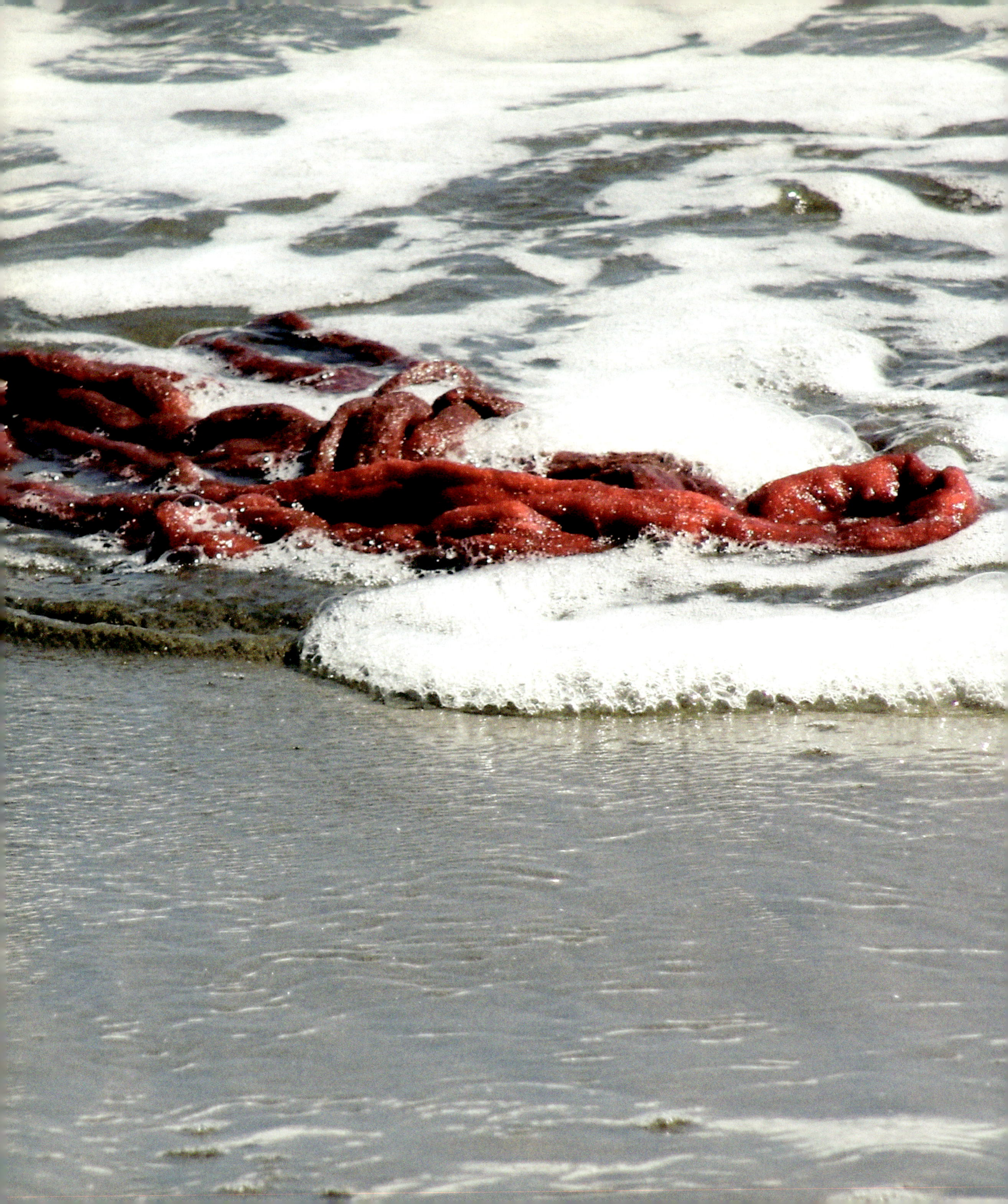

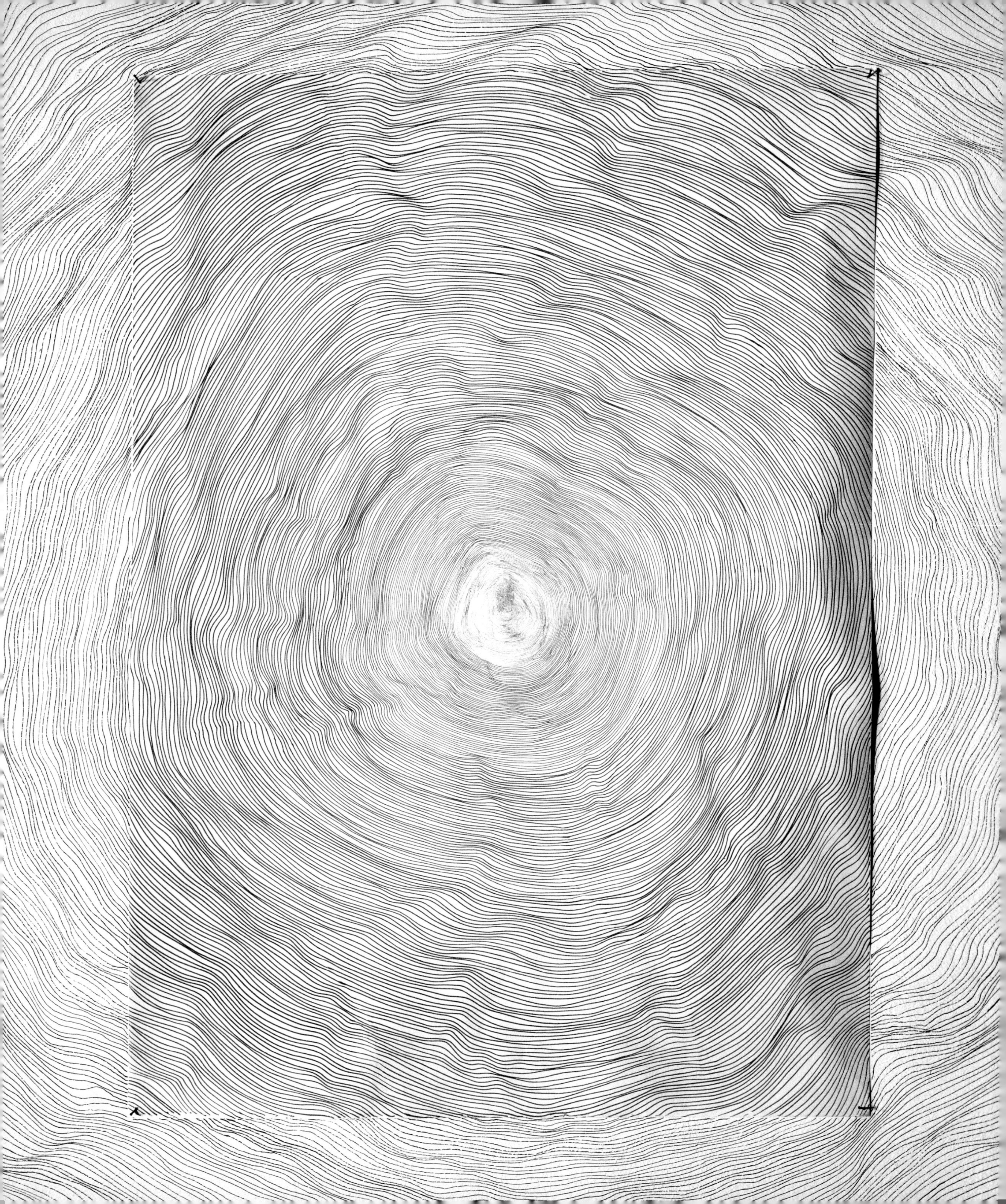

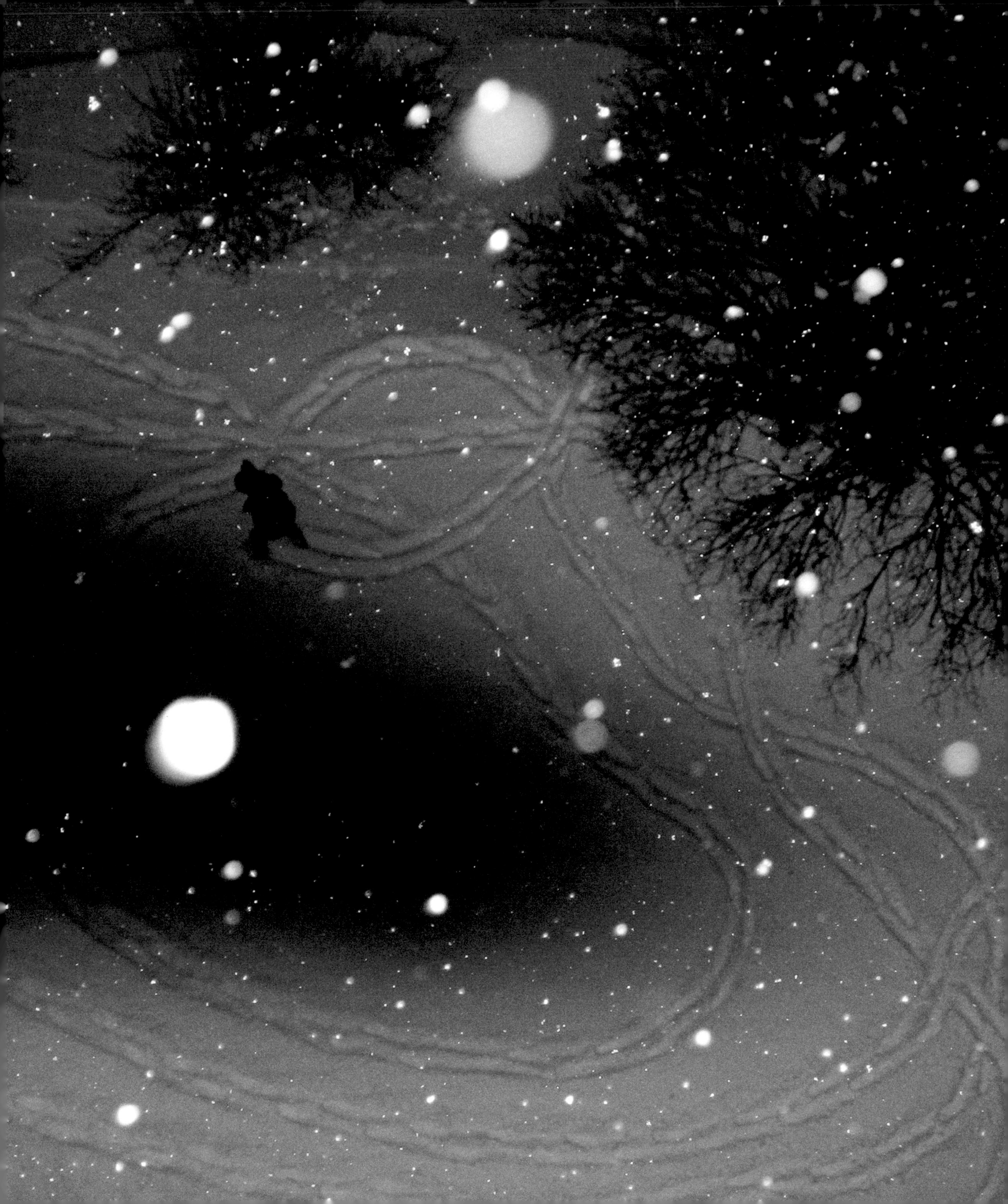

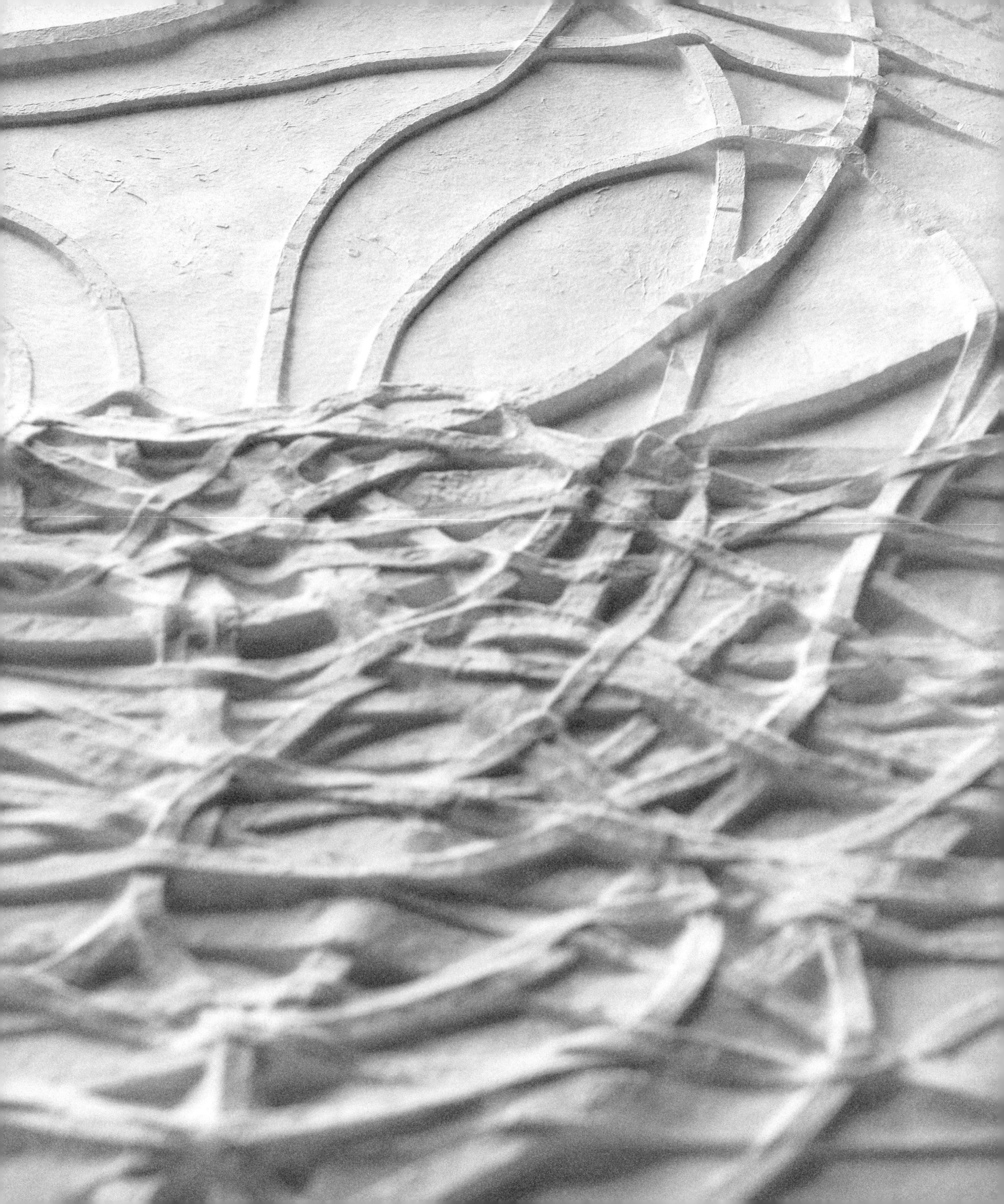

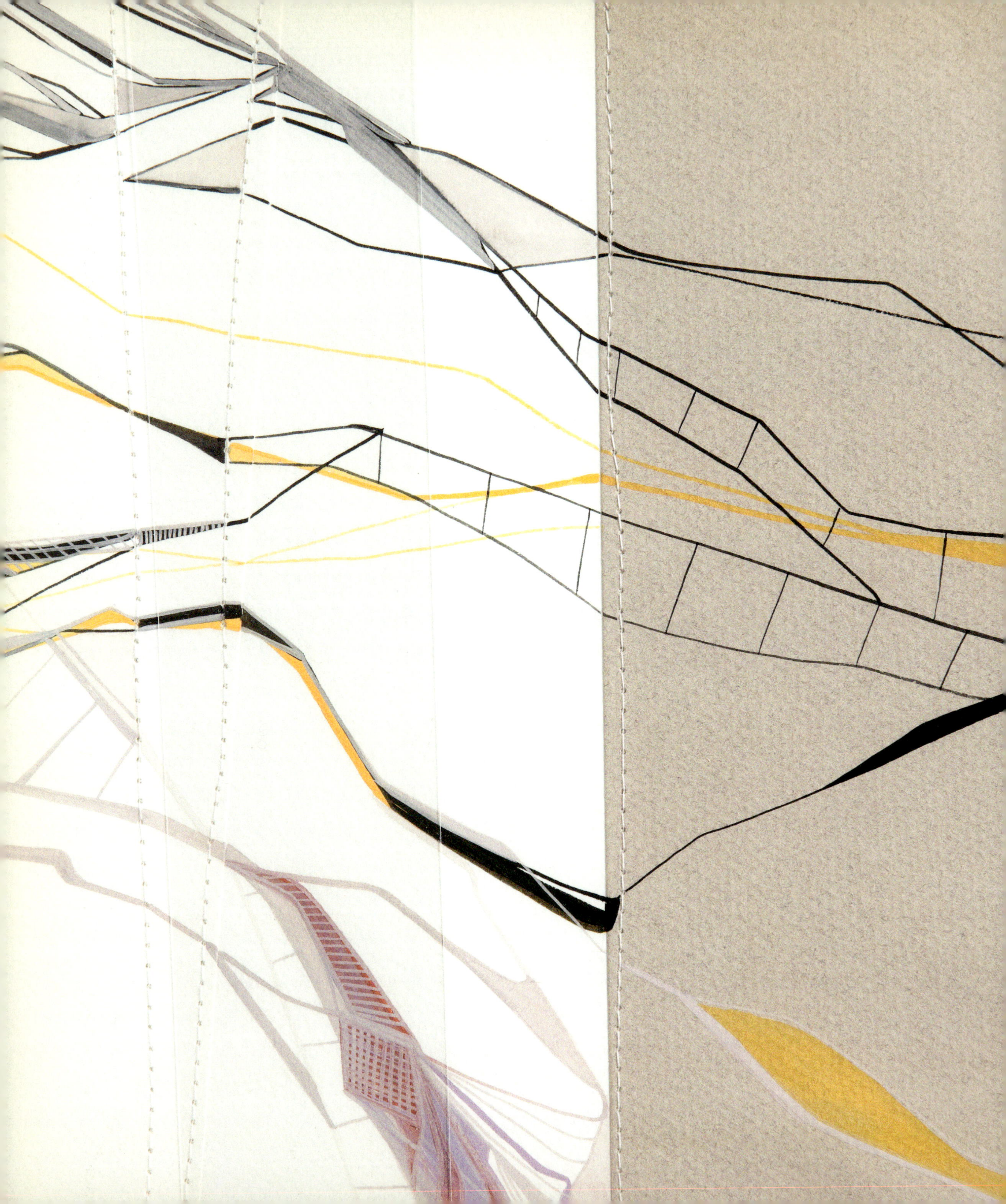

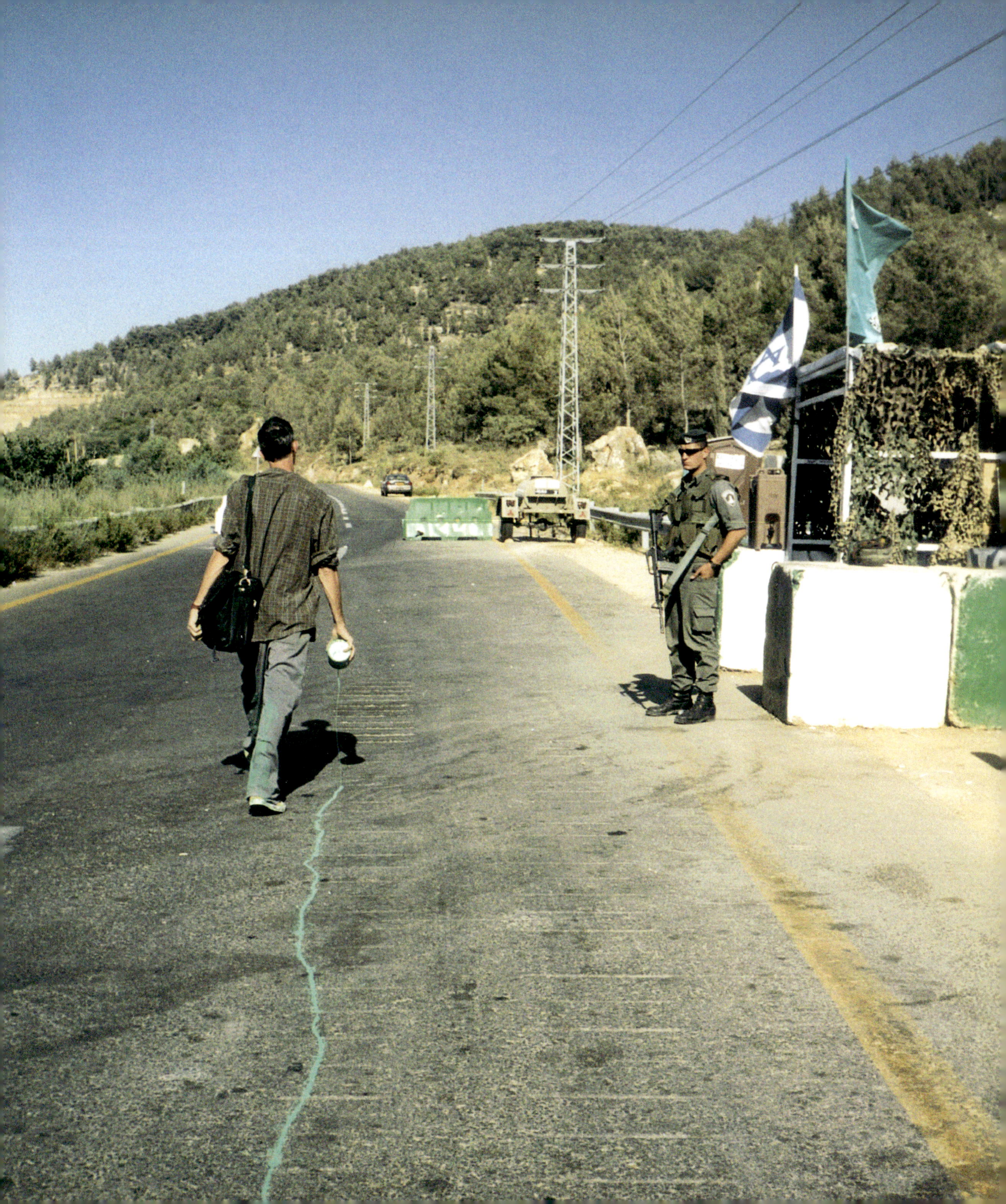

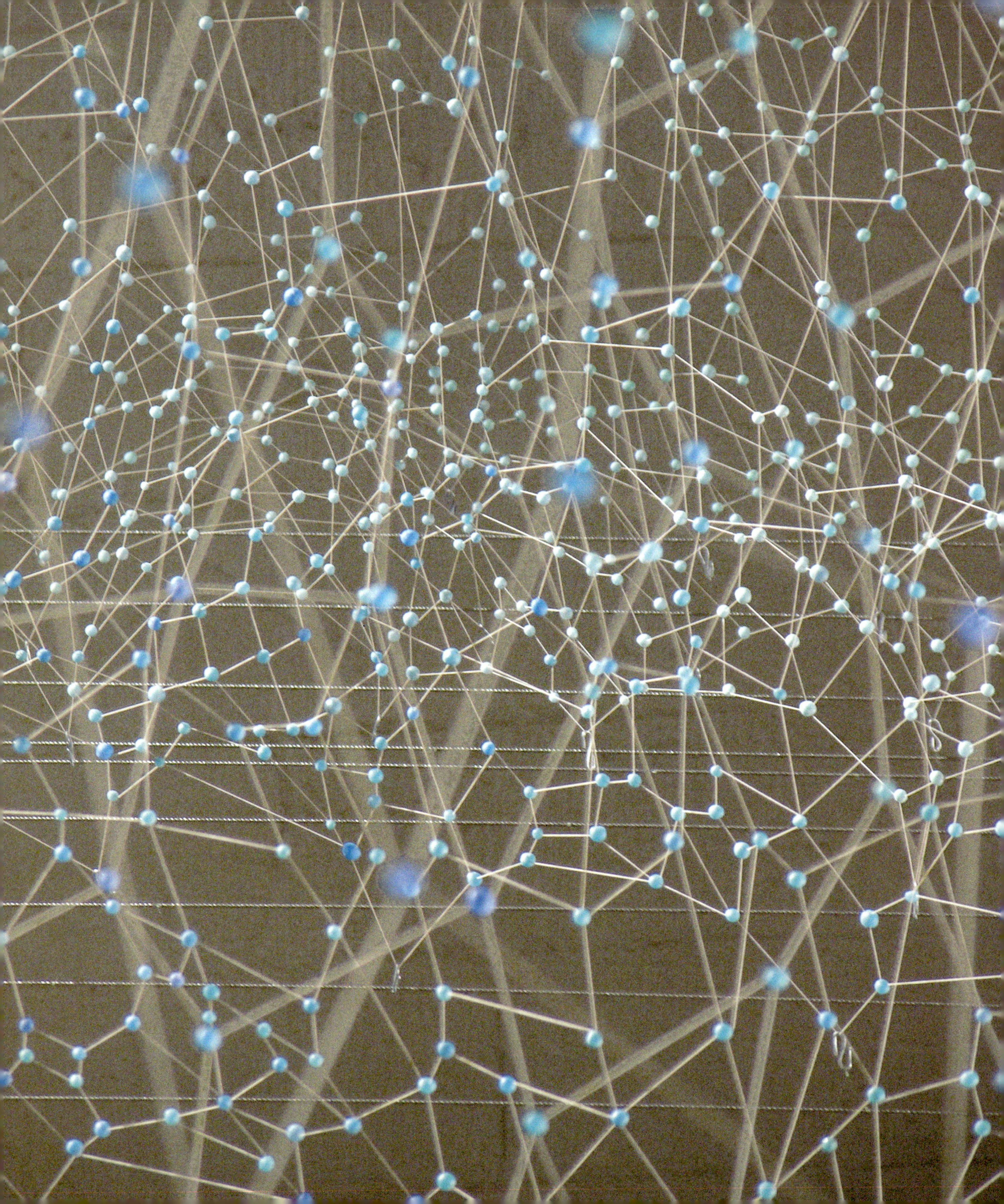

225. Emily Kam Kngwarray
(Anmatyerr [Australian], c. 1910–1996)
Anaty (Wild potato; detail;
see plate 200). 1989
Synthetic polymer paint on canvas
59 1/2 x 35 7/8" (151.2 x 91.1 cm)

226. Cecilia Vicuña
(Chilean, born 1948)
Kon Kon Pi. 2010
Detail of still from video, color,
sound, 13:23 mins.

227. Giuseppe Penone
(Italian, born 1947)
Propagazione (Propagation). 1995–2009
Typographic ink and graphite on
paper, felt pen on wall
Dimensions variable. Installation view,
Tucci Russo Studio per l'arte contem-
poranea, Torre Pellice, Turin, 2009

228. Mimi Gellman
(Canadian, born 1955)
nightdrawing 1 (detail; see plate 209).
2009
Black and white photograph
20 x 30" (50.8 x 76.2 cm)

229. Monika Grzymala
(German, born Poland 1970)
Sequence #3 (detail). 2010
Handmade washi paper
Two sheets, each: 6' 7/8" x 9' 4 1/4"
(185 x 285 cm)

230. Sheila Makhijani
(Indian, born 1962)
Take a leap → (detail; see plate 117). 2009
Gouache and thread on paper and
plastic sheets
12 1/2 x 25" (31.8 x 63.5 cm)

231. Francis Alÿs
(Belgian, born 1959)
*The Green Line: SOMETIMES DOING
SOMETHING POETIC CAN BECOME
POLITICAL AND SOMETIMES DOING
SOMETHING POLITICAL CAN BECOME
POETIC*. 2007
Still from video installation with various
components

232. Ranjani Shettar
(Indian, born 1977)
Just a bit more (detail). 2005–6
Hand-molded beeswax, pigments,
and thread dyed in tea
36 x 24 x 12' (1097.3 x 731.5 x 365.8 cm)

233. Hans Haacke
(German, born 1936)
Circulation. 1969
Vinyl tubes, Y-connectors, water, air,
and electric circulating pump
Dimensions variable

CHECKLIST OF THE EXHIBITION

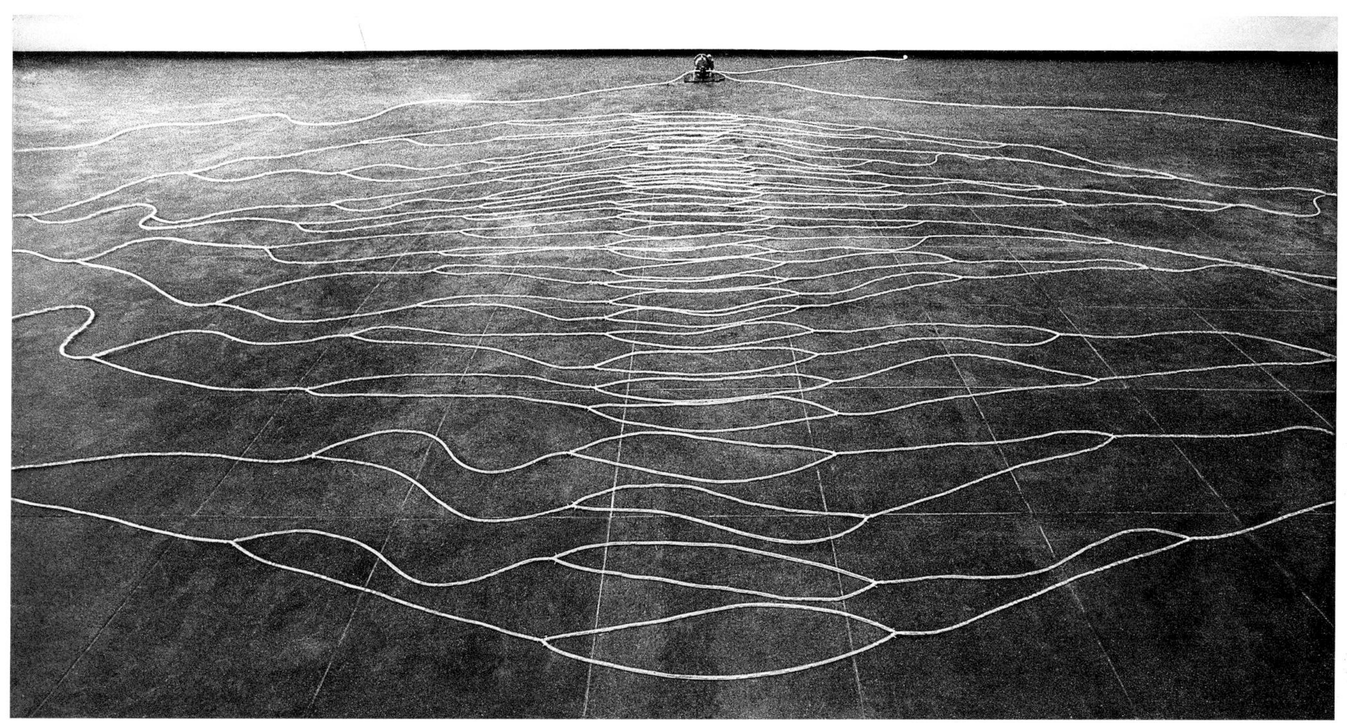

Anni Albers (American, born Germany, 1899–1994)

Line Involvement II, IV, V, VI from *Line Involvements*. 1964
Four from a portfolio of seven lithographs
14 3/4 x 19 13/16″ (37.5 x 50.3 cm) (plates II, IV, horizontal, plates V, VI, vertical)
Edition: 20
The Museum of Modern Art, New York. Gift of Kleiner, Bell & Co.

Francis Alÿs (Belgian, born 1959)

The Loop. Tijuana–San Diego, 1997
Ephemera of an action
Courtesy the artist and David Zwirner, New York

Giovanni Anselmo (Italian, born 1934)

Untitled. 1966
Iron rod and wood
8′ 8 5/16″ x 5 7/8″ x 5 7/8″ (265 x 15 x 15 cm)
Collection Liliane and Michel Durand-Dessert, Paris

Untitled. 1966
Iron, wood, polystyrene, and oil paint
8′ 7/16″ x 4 3/4″ x 4 3/4″ (245 x 12 x 12 cm)
Collection the artist

Untitled. 1967 (plate 63)
Transparent acrylic and iron wire
6′ 5 11/16″ x 47 3/8″ (197.3 x 120.3 cm)
Collection the artist

Jean (Hans) Arp (French, born Germany [Alsace], 1886–1966)

Untitled (Collage with Squares Arranged according to the Laws of Chance). 1916–17 (plate 23)
Torn-and-pasted paper and colored paper on colored paper
19 1/8 x 13 5/8″ (48.5 x 34.6 cm)
The Museum of Modern Art, New York. Purchase

Untitled (Squares Arranged according to the Laws of Chance). 1917
Cut-and-pasted colored paper on colored paper
13 1/8 x 10 1/4″ (33.2 x 25.9 cm)
The Museum of Modern Art, New York. Gift of Philip Johnson

Two Heads. 1927 (plate 46)
Oil and cord on canvas
13 3/4 x 10 5/8″ (35 x 27 cm)
The Museum of Modern Art, New York. Purchase

Leaves and Navels. 1929 (plate 47)
Oil and cord on canvas
13 3/4 x 10 3/4″ (35 x 27.3 cm)
The Museum of Modern Art, New York. Purchase

A. Balasubramaniam (Indian, born 1971)

Rest in Resistance. 2007 (plate 9)
Fiberglass, acrylic, fishing hooks, and elastic
37 x 40 x 15″ (94 x 101.6 x 38.1 cm)
Courtesy the artist and Talwar Gallery, New York/New Delhi

Pierrette Bloch (French, born 1928)

Fil de crin (Horsehair line). 1985
Horsehair and nylon
7′ 3″ (221 cm) long
The Museum of Modern Art, New York. Gift of Pierre Soulages

Fil de crin (Horsehair line). 1986
Horsehair and nylon
13′ 4″ (406.4 cm) long
The Museum of Modern Art, New York. Gift of Sheila Hicks

Fil de crin (Horsehair line). 1986
Horsehair and nylon
8′ 4 1/2″ (255.3 cm) long
The Museum of Modern Art, New York. Gift of Alvin Epstein

Fil de crin (Horsehair line). 1988 (plate 73)
Horsehair and nylon
7′ 1 7/16″ (217 cm) long
Courtesy Haim Chanin Fine Arts, New York

Fil de crin (Horsehair line). 1989
Horsehair and nylon
33 7/16″ (85 cm) long
Courtesy Haim Chanin Fine Arts, New York

Fil de crin (Horsehair line). 1989 (plate 73)
Horsehair and nylon
10′ 7 15/16″ (325 cm) long
Courtesy Haim Chanin Fine Arts, New York

Fil de crin (Horsehair line). 1997 (plate 73)
Horsehair and nylon
8′ 6 3/4″ (261 cm) long
Courtesy Haim Chanin Fine Arts, New York

Umberto Boccioni (Italian, 1882–1916)

Stati d'animo. Gli addii (States of mind: the farewells). 1911 (plates 1, 152)
Charcoal and chalk on paper
23 x 34″ (58.4 x 86.4 cm)
The Museum of Modern Art, New York. Gift of Vico Baer

Stati d'animo. Quelli che vanno (States of mind: those who go). 1911
Charcoal and chalk on paper
23 x 34″ (58.4 x 86.3 cm)
The Museum of Modern Art, New York. Gift of Vico Baer

Stati d'animo. Quelli che restano (States of mind: those who stay). 1911
Charcoal and chalk on paper
23 x 34″ (58.4 x 86.3 cm)
The Museum of Modern Art, New York. Gift of Vico Baer

Georges Braque (French, 1882–1963)

Guitar. 1913 (plate 180)
Cut-and-pasted printed and painted paper, charcoal, pencil, and gouache on gessoed canvas
39 1/4 x 25 5/8″ (99.7 x 65.1 cm)
The Museum of Modern Art, New York. Acquired through the Lillie P. Bliss Bequest

Stanley Brouwn

Steps of Pedestrians on Paper. 1960
Street dust on ten pieces of paper
9 5/8 x 12 5/8″ (24.5 x 32 cm) each
The Museum of Modern Art, New York. Art & Project/Depot VBVR Gift

Steps. 1970
Typewritten text on adhesive labels on gelatin silver print, 27 5/8 x 40″ (70.1 x 101.6 cm)
Typewritten text on paper and seven gelatin silver prints mounted on paperboard with ballpoint pen, 27 1/2 x 40″ (69.9 x 101.6 cm)
Felt-tip pen on map, 26 3/8 x 62 1/2″ (67 x 158.8 cm)
The Museum of Modern Art, New York. Art & Project/Depot VBVR Gift

Trisha Brown (American, born 1936)

Man Walking Down the Side of a Building. 1970 (plate 111)
16mm film transferred to video, black and white, silent, 2 min.
The Museum of Modern Art, New York. Gift of Jerry I. Speyer and Katherine G. Farley, Anna Marie and Robert F. Shapiro, and Marie-Josée and Henry R. Kravis

Untitled. 2007 (plate 210)
Charcoal on paper
6′ 8″ x 9′ 9″ (203.2 x 297.2 cm)
Courtesy the artist and Sikkema Jenkins & Co.

Alexander Calder (American, 1898–1976)

Untitled. 1930 (plate 164)
Oil on canvas
28 3/4 x 23 3/4″ (73 x 60.3 cm)
Calder Foundation, New York

Croisière (Cruise). 1931
Wire, wood, and paint
37 x 23 x 23″ (95.3 x 81.3 x 35.6 cm)
Calder Foundation, New York

Many. 1931
Ink on paper
19 5/8 x 25 1/2″ (49.7 x 64.8 cm)
The Museum of Modern Art, New York. Gift of Mr. and Mrs. Klaus G. Perls

Sphérique I (Spherical I). 1931
Wire and brass with painted wood base
39 1/8 x 13 1/2 x 11 3/4″ (99.4 x 34.3 x 29.8 cm)
Whitney Museum of American Art, New York. Purchase, with funds from the Howard and Jean Lipman Foundation, Inc.

Circus Interior. 1932 (plate 224)
Ink on paper
19 x 14″ (48.1 x 35.5 cm)
The Museum of Modern Art, New York. Gift of Mr. and Mrs. Peter A. Rübel

Cowboy and Rope Ladder. 1932
Ink on paper
19 x 14 1/8″ (48.3 x 35.7 cm)
The Museum of Modern Art, New York. Gift of Mr. and Mrs. Peter A. Rübel

The Catch II. 1932 (plate 165)
Ink on paper
19 1/8 x 14 1/8″ (48.4 x 35.8 cm)
The Museum of Modern Art, New York. Gift of Mr. and Mrs. Peter A. Rübel

A Universe. 1934 (plate 48)
Painted iron pipe, steel wire, motor, and wood with string
40 1/2 x 30″ (102.9 x 76.2 cm)
The Museum of Modern Art, New York. Gift of Abby Aldrich Rockefeller (by exchange)

Swizzle Sticks. 1936
Painted wood panel with steel wire, wood, and lead
56 3/8 x 45 5/8 x 48 1/2″ (143.2 x 115.8 x 123.1 cm)
The Museum of Modern Art, New York. James Thrall Soby Bequest

Luis Camnitzer (Uruguayan, born 1937)

The Instrument and Its Work. 1976 (plates 108, 129)
Wood, glass, and metal
11 13/16 x 10 1/16 x 1 15/16″ (30 x 25.5 x 5 cm)
Collection Reto Ehrbar, Zurich

Two Parallel Lines. 1976–2010 (plate 11)
Mixed media and pencil on wall
Dimensions variable
Courtesy the artist and Alexander Gray Associates

Nina Canell (Swedish, born 1979)

Beam Hang. 2008 (plate 219)
House beam, neon, cable, foam, and 3,000 volts
6′ 6 3/4″ x 1 3/16″ x 3 15/16″ (200 x 3 x 10 cm)
Collection Eileen and Michael Cohen

Dead Heat. 2008 (plate 219)
Concrete, stick, neon, cable, and 1,000 volts
18 1/2 x 17 5/16 x 8 1/4″ (47 x 44 x 21 cm)
AmC Collezione Coppola

Break of Day (N, S, E, W). 2009
White cane and nails
17 11/16 x 23 5/8 x 3/8″ (45 x 60 x 1 cm)
Dohmen Collection, Aachen

Lygia Clark (Brazilian, 1920–1988)

Superfície modulada II (Modulated surface II). 1957
Cut-and-pasted colored cardstock on colored cardstock
11 3/4 x 3 7/8″ (29.9 x 9.9 cm)
The Museum of Modern Art, New York. Purchased with funds provided by The Edward John Noble Foundation and purchase

Superfície modulada III (Modulated surface III). 1957
Cut-and-pasted colored cardstock on colored cardstock
11 3/4 x 3 7/8″ (29.9 x 9.9 cm)
The Museum of Modern Art, New York. Purchased with funds provided by The Edward John Noble Foundation and purchase

Superfície modulada IV (Modulated surface IV). 1957
Cut-and-pasted colored cardstock on colored cardstock
11 3/4 x 3 7/8″ (29.9 x 9.9 cm)
The Museum of Modern Art, New York. Purchased with funds provided by The Edward John Noble Foundation and purchase

Superfície modulada V (Modulated surface V). 1957
Cut-and-pasted colored cardstock on colored cardstock
11 3/4 x 3 7/8″ (29.9 x 9.9 cm)
The Museum of Modern Art, New York. Purchased with funds provided by The Edward John Noble Foundation and purchase

Espaço modulado I (Modulated space I). 1958
Cut-and-pasted colored cardstock on cardstock
11 5/8 x 3 7/8″ (29.5 x 9.8 cm)
The Museum of Modern Art, New York. Purchased with funds provided by The Edward John Noble Foundation and purchase

Espaço modulado II (Modulated space II). 1958 (plate 60)
Cut-and-pasted colored cardstock on cardstock
11 3/4 x 3 7/8″ (29.9 x 9.9 cm)
The Museum of Modern Art, New York. Purchased with funds provided by The Edward John Noble Foundation and purchase

Caminhando (Walking). 1963–64 (plates 134–39)
Performance views. Six black and white exhibition prints
Each: 16 x 20″ (40.6 x 50.8 cm)
Courtesy ″The World of Lygia Clark″ Cultural Association

O dentro é o fora (The inside is the outside). 1963 (plate 185)
Stainless steel
16 x 17 1/2 x 14 3/4" (40.6 x 44.5 x 37.5 cm)
Colección Patricia Phelps de Cisneros

O dentro é o fora (The inside is the outside). 1963 (plate 185)
Black-and-white exhibition print
16 x 20" (40.6 x 50.8 cm)
Courtesy "The World of Lygia Clark" Cultural Association

Marie Cool (French, born 1961) and **Fabio Balducci** (Italian, born 1964)

Untitled. 2004
Video, color, silent, 1:37 min.
Courtesy the artists and gb agency, Paris

Untitled. 2006
Video, color, silent, 2:16 min.
Courtesy the artists and gb agency, Paris

Untitled. 2006 (plates 220–23)
Video, color, silent, 2:19 min.
Courtesy the artists and gb agency, Paris

Untitled. 2009
Video, color, silent, 1:02 min.
Courtesy the artists and gb agency, Paris

Anne Teresa De Keersmaeker (Belgian, born 1960) and **Thierry De Mey** (Belgian, born 1956)

Top Shot. 2002 (plates 88-93)
Video, color, sound, 16:04 min. Choreography and performance: De Keersmaeker. Director: De Mey. Music: Steve Reich. Violin: George Alexander van Dam
Courtesy Thierry De Mey and Rosas

Edith Dekyndt (Belgian, born 1960)

Slow Object 04. 1997 (plate 123)
DVD projection, color, silent, 9:15-minute loop
Courtesy Parker's Box, New York

A Is Hotter than B. 2005 (plate 214)
DVD projection, color, silent, 9-minute loop
Courtesy Parker's Box, New York

XY 02. 2008
DVD projection, color, silent, 7:17-minute loop
Courtesy Parker's Box, New York

Marcel Duchamp (American, born France, 1887–1968)

3 Stoppages Etalon (3 Standard Stoppages). 1913–14 (plate 17)
Wood box, 11 1/8 x 50 7/8 x 9" (28.2 x 129.2 x 22.7 cm), holding three meter-long threads, each glued to a painted canvas strip, each strip mounted on a glass panel, 7 1/4 x 49 3/8 x 1/4" (18.4 x 125.4 x 0.6 cm); and three wood slats 2 1/2 x 43 x 1/8" (6.2 x 109.2 x 0.2 cm), each shaped along one edge to match the curves of the threads
The Museum of Modern Art, New York. Katherine S. Dreier Bequest

Sixteen Miles of String. 1942 (plate 167)
Installation view of *First Papers of Surrealism* exhibition, New York. Photograph: John D. Schiff
Gelatin silver print
7 5/8 x 10" (19.4 x 25.4 cm)
Philadelphia Museum of Art, Archives, Alexina and Marcel Duchamp Papers. Gift of Jacqueline, Paul and Peter Matisse in memory of their mother Alexina Duchamp

Luciano Fabro (Italian, 1936–2007)

Ruota (Wheel). 1964/2001
Stainless steel
Edition: 8 of 8
20 1/16 x 60 5/8 x 3/8" (51 x 154 x 1 cm)
Collection the estate of the artist, Milan

Contatto-Tautologia (Contact-Tautology). 1967/2001 (plate 62)
Stainless steel
Edition: 8 of 8
1" x 9' 10 1/8" x 3/16" (2.5 x 300 x 0.4 cm)
Collection the estate of the artist, Milan

León Ferrari (Argentine, born 1920)

Reflexiones (Reflections). 1963 (plate 106)
Ink on gessoed wood, copper wire, and ink on glass, in artist's painted wood frame
34 1/8 x 28 x 2" (86.7 x 71.1 x 5.1 cm)
The Museum of Modern Art, New York. Latin American and Caribbean Fund

Lucio Fontana (Italian, born Argentina, 1899–1968)

Concetto spaziale (Spatial concept). 1957 (plate 54)
Ink and pencil on paper on canvas
55" x 6' 6 7/8" (139.7 x 200.4 cm)
The Museum of Modern Art, New York. Gift of Morton G. Neumann

Concetto spaziale. Attese (Spatial concept: expectations). 1959 (plate 55)
Synthetic polymer paint on slashed burlap
39 3/8 x 32" (100 x 81.5 cm)
The Museum of Modern Art, New York. Philip Johnson Fund

William Forsythe (American, born 1949)

Solo. 1997 (plate 144)
Film transferred to video, black and white, sound, 6:40 min. Choreography and performance: Forsythe. Music: Thom Willems, in collaboration with Maxime Franke. Director: Thomas Lovell Balogh. Camera: Jess Hall
Courtesy The Forsythe Company

Loie Fuller (American, 1862–1928)

Danse Serpentine (II) (Serpentine dance II). 1897–99 (plate 13)
Film by Société Lumière transferred to video, color, silent, 44 seconds

Ellen Gallagher (American, born 1965)

They Could Still Serve. 2001 (plate 81)
Pigment and synthetic polymer on paper mounted on canvas
10 x 8' (304.8 x 243.8 cm)
The Museum of Modern Art, New York. Emily and Jerry Spiegel and Anna Marie and Robert F. Shapiro Funds and gift of Agnes Gund

Mimi Gellman (Canadian, born 1955)

nightdrawing 1. 2009 (plates 209, 228)
Black and white photograph
20 x 30" (50.8 x 76.2 cm)
Collection the artist. Courtesy The David Kaye Gallery, Toronto

nightdrawing 2. 2009
Black and white photograph
20 x 30" (50.8 x 76.2 cm)
Collection the artist. Courtesy The David Kaye Gallery, Toronto

Gego (Gertrud Goldschmidt. Venezuelan, born Germany, 1912–1994)

Reticulárea cuadrada 71/6 (Square reticularea 71/6). 1971
Stainless steel and copper
6' 8 11/16" x 55 1/8" x 21 5/8" (205 x 140 x 55 cm)
Colección Patricia Phelps de Cisneros

Dibujo sin papel 83/16 (Drawing without paper 83/16). 1983
Iron and steel rods, billet, steel wires, steel-chrome-plated tubes, and metal clasps
17 11/16 x 13 9/16 x 3 3/8" (45 x 34.5 x 8.5 cm)
Fundación Gego Collection at the Museum of Fine Arts, Houston

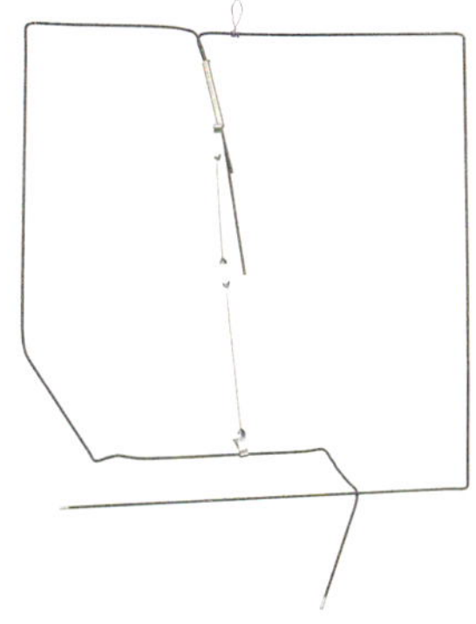

Dibujo sin papel 83/18 (Drawing without paper 83/18). 1983
Painted saw blades and washers with nuts and bolts
13 7/8 x 12 3/8 x 3/8" (35.2 x 31.5 x 1 cm)
Fundación Gego Collection at the Museum of Fine Arts, Houston

Dibujo sin papel (Drawing without paper). 1984
Stainless steel and copper
9 13/16 x 9 13/16 x 7 7/8" (25 x 25 x 20 cm)
Colección Patricia Phelps de Cisneros

Dibujo sin papel 86/13 (Drawing without paper 86/13). 1986
Iron, aluminum, plastic, and wire
38 1/2 x 25 1/2 x 3" (97.8 x 64.8 x 7.6 cm)
Colección Patricia Phelps de Cisneros

Dibujo sin papel 88/33 (Drawing without paper 88/33). 1988
Copper and iron rods, iron, copper and steel wires, and polythene tube
9 13/16 x 8 11/16 x 1 3/4" (25 x 22 x 4.5 cm)
Fundación Gego Collection at the Museum of Fine Arts, Houston

Dibujo sin papel 88/35 (Drawing without paper 88/35). 1988
Iron and steel wires, copper, aluminum and iron rods, aluminum and plastic tubes, rubber gaskets, and paint
13 3/4 x 11 13/16 x 13/16" (35 x 30 x 2 cm)
Fundación Gego Collection at the Museum of Fine Arts, Houston

Monika Grzymala (German, born Poland 1970)

Untitled (skeleton of a drawing). 2010
Site-specific sculpture, sixth floor, The Museum of Modern Art, New York
Paperclay
Installation commissioned by The Museum of Modern Art, New York

Mona Hatoum (British of Palestinian origin, born Beirut, Lebanon, 1952)

Cube (9 x 9 x 9). 2008 (plate 96)
Black finished steel
71 x 71 1/2 x 71 1/2" (180.3 x 181.6 x 181.6 cm)
The Minneapolis Institute of Arts. The Ethel Van Derlip Fund

Alex Hay (American, born 1930)

Ground Drawing. 1968 (plates 130, 141)
Pencil on paper
68 1/4 x 38" (173.4 x 96.5 cm)
The Museum of Modern Art, New York. Committee on Drawings Funds

Susan Hefuna (German, born 1962)

Building. 2008 (plate 120)
Pencil and embroidery on tracing paper
Nine drawings, each 21 1/16 x 27 3/16" (53.5 x 69 cm)
A. Huda and Samia Farouki, FIIC

Michael Heizer (American, born 1944)

Circular Surface Planar Displacement Drawing/90° Vertical Planar Rotary. 1970 (plate 194)
Fifty black-and-white photographs
Dimensions variable
Private collection

Arturo Herrera (Venezuelan, born 1959)

Walk/14 Parts. 2009 (plate 215)
Digital images derived from ink-on-paper drawings
Courtesy the artist and Sikkema Jenkins & Co.

Eva Hesse (American, born Germany, 1936–1970)

Hang Up. 1966 (plate 182)
Acrylic on cloth over wood, acrylic on cord over steel tube
6' x 7' x 6' 6" (182.9 x 213.4 x 198.1 cm)
The Art Institute of Chicago. Through prior gifts of Arthur Keating and Mr. and Mrs. Edward Morris

Vasily Kandinsky (French, born Russia, 1866–1944)

Schwarze Beziehung (Black relationship). (plate 31) 1924
Watercolor and ink on paper
14 1/2 x 14 1/4" (36.9 x 36.2 cm)
The Museum of Modern Art, New York. Acquired through the Lillie P. Bliss Bequest

38 drawings for Kandinsky's book *Punkt und Linie zu Fläche* (Point and line to plane). 1925 (frontispiece, plates 157, 158)
Variously ink, ink wash, gouache, pencil, crayon, and chalk on paper and tracing paper
Ranging from 3 3/4" (9.6 cm) to 15 3/16" (38.6) high and from 3 7/8" (9.8 cm) to 27 3/16" (69 cm) wide
Centre Pompidou, Paris. Musée national d'art moderne/Centre de création industrielle. Bequest of Nina Kandinsky

Untitled. 1930
Ink and watercolor on paper
14 3/8 x 14 3/4" (36.5 x 37.5 cm)
Centre Pompidou, Paris. Musée national d'art moderne/Centre de création industrielle. Bequest of Nina Kandinsky

Ellsworth Kelly (American, born 1923)

Automatic Drawing: Pine Branches I–VII. 1950 (plates 149, 150)
All: pencil on paper
All: 16 1/2 x 20 1/4″ (41.9 x 51.4 cm)
All: collection the artist, except no. VI: The Museum of Modern Art, New York. Gift of the artist

Gate-Board. 1950
Oil on wood with string
26 3/4 x 35 1/4″ (67.9 x 89.5 cm)
Collection the artist

Brushstrokes Cut into Forty-Nine Squares and Arranged by Chance. 1951
Cut-and-pasted paper and ink
13 3/4 x 14″ (34.9 x 35.6 cm)
The Museum of Modern Art, New York. Purchased with funds given by Agnes Gund

Zilvinas Kempinas (Lithuanian, born 1969)

Double O. 2008
Magnetic tape, fans
Dimensions variable
Courtesy the artist, Yvon Lambert Paris and New York, and Galerija Vartai, Vilnius

Paul Klee (German, born Switzerland, 1879–1940)

Der Angler (The angler). 1921 (plate 161)
Oil transfer drawing, watercolor and ink on paper with watercolor and ink borders on board
19 7/8 x 12 1/2″ (50.5 x 31.8 cm)
The Museum of Modern Art, New York. John S. Newberry Collection

Die Zwitscher-Maschine (Twittering machine). 1922 (plate 29)
Oil transfer drawing, watercolor and ink on paper with gouache and ink borders on board
25 1/4 x 19″ (64.1 x 48.3 cm)
The Museum of Modern Art, New York. Purchase

Artistenbildnis (Portrait of an artiste). 1927 (plate 159)
Oil and collage on cardboard over wood with painted plaster border
24 7/8 x 15 3/4″ (63.2 x 40 cm)
The Museum of Modern Art, New York. Mrs. Simon Guggenheim Fund

Emily Kam Kngwarray (Anmatyerr [Australian], c. 1910–1996)

Anaty (Wild potato). 1989 (plates 200, 225)
Synthetic polymer paint on canvas
59 1/2 x 35 7/8″ (151.2 x 91.1 cm)
National Gallery of Victoria, Melbourne. Purchased from Admission Funds, 1990

Ankerr (Emu). 1990 (plate 198)
Synthetic polymer paint on canvas
47 1/4 x 70 1/2″ (120 x 179.1 cm)
Kluge-Ruhe Aboriginal Art Collection, University of Virginia

Gyula Kosice (Fernando Fallik; Argentine, born Czechoslovakia [now Slovakia] 1924)

Escultura Movil Articulada (Mobile articulated sculpture). 1948 (plate 175)
Brass
Dimensions variable, c. 65 x 12 x 1/2″ (165.1 x 30.5 x 1.3 cm)
The Museum of Modern Art, New York. Gift of Patricia Phelps de Cisneros in honor of Jay Levenson

Arte madí universal (plate 174)
Journals nos. 0–8 (1947–54)
The Museum of Modern Art Library

Edward Krasiński (Polish, 1925–2004)

K 3. 1968
Canvas, wood, cable, wire, plaster, and paint
Canvas: 21 5/8 x 18 1/8 x 13/16″ (55 x 46 x 2 cm), cable: c. 14′ 9″ (450 cm) long
Muzeum Sztuki, Lódz

K 5. 1968
Wood, cable, and paint
61 x 6 5/16 x 4 3/4″ (155 x 16 x 12 cm)
Muzeum Sztuki, Lódz

K 6. 1968
Wood, cable, rubber, and paint
9′ 10 1/8″ x 4 3/4″ x 10 1/4″ (300 x 12 x 26 cm)
Muzeum Sztuki, Lódz

Kompozycja z książką (Composition with book). 1969
Two books, wood, cables, and paint
Books: 4 3/4 x 6 5/16 x 11 13/16″ (12 x 16 x 30 cm), cables: c. 47 1/4″ (120 cm) and 13′ 9 3/8″ (420 cm) long
The National Museum in Poznań

Kompozycja z walcem (Composition with cylinder). 1969 (plate 196)
Wood cylinder , rubber, cables, and paint
Cylinder: 2 9/16 x 6 5/16″ (6.5 x 16 cm), cable: c. 15′ 5″ (470 cm) long
The National Museum in Poznań

K. 1969 (plate 196)
Cardboard tube, plastic, cord, cable, adhesive tape, and paint
Tube: 12 3/16″ (31 cm) long, 2 3/4″ (7 cm) diam., cord and cable: together c. 82 5/8″ (210 cm) long
Generali Foundation Collection, Vienna

L. 1969 (plate 196)
Book, plaster, cable, tube, and paint
Book: 8 11/16 x 13 9/16 x 1 3/16″ (22 x 34.5 x 3 cm), cable: c. 11′ 11″ (363 cm) long
Muzeum Sztuki, Lódz

L 3. 1969 (plate 196)
Book, cables, and paint
6 7/8 x 5 5/16 x 3 9/16″ (17.5 x 13.5 x 9 cm), cables: c. 39 3/8–118″ (100–300 cm) long
The National Gallery in Prague

N… (Interwencja 4, Zyg-Zag) (Intervention 4, Zigzag). 1969 (plate 196)
3 parts, of 11, 10, and 9 wooden sticks respectively, and plastic hinges
Each: 25′ 3 1/8″ (770 cm), 22′ 11 5/8″ (700 cm), and 20′ 8″ (630 cm) long respectively
Generali Foundation Collection, Vienna

Design for an exhibition of works at the 10th Tokyo Biennial. 1970
Ink, felt-tip pen, and pasted numbers on paper
10 1/8 x 9 13/16″ (25.7 x 24.9 cm)
Courtesy Paulina Krasińska and Foksal Gallery Foundation, Warsaw

Design for an exhibition of works at the 10th Tokyo Biennial. 1970
Pencil, ink, felt-tip pen, and ballpoint pen on paper
9 x 9 13/16″ (22.8 x 24.9 cm)
Courtesy Paulina Krasińska and Foksal Gallery Foundation, Warsaw

Design for an exhibition of works at the 10th Tokyo Biennial. 1970
Ink on paper
9 x 12 11/16″ (22.9 x 32.2 cm)
Courtesy Paulina Krasińska and Foksal Gallery Foundation, Warsaw

Fragment of telex related to an exhibition of works at the 10th Tokyo Biennial. 1970
Punched paper strip
11/16 x 3/16″ (1.7 x 3 cm)
Courtesy Paulina Krasińska and Foksal Gallery Foundation, Warsaw

František Kupka (Czech, 1871–1957)

Amorpha. Fugue à deux couleurs (Amorpha: Fugue in two colors). 1912
Gouache, ink, and pencil on paper
16 3/8 x 18 5/8″ (41.6 x 47.3 cm)
The Museum of Modern Art, New York. Gift of Mr. and Mrs. František Kupka

Amorpha. Fugue à deux couleurs (Amorpha: Fugue in two colors). 1912
Gouache, ink, and pencil on paper
11 1/8 x 11 5/8″ (28.3 x 29.5 cm)
The Museum of Modern Art, New York. Gift of Mr. and Mrs. František Kupka

Amorpha. Fugue à deux couleurs (Amorpha: Fugue in two colors). 1912
Gouache and ink on paper
11 1/2 x 11 5/8″ (29.2 x 29.5 cm)
The Museum of Modern Art, New York. Gift of Mr. and Mrs. František Kupka

Amorpha. Fugue à deux couleurs (Amorpha: Fugue in two colors). 1912 (plate 75)
Gouache, ink, and pencil on paper
8 1/2 x 9″ (21.6 x 22.9 cm)
The Museum of Modern Art, New York. Gift of Mr. and Mrs. František Kupka

Amorpha. Fugue à deux couleurs (Amorpha: Fugue in two colors). 1912
Gouache and pencil on paper
8 3/8 x 9″ (21.3 x 22.9 cm)
The Museum of Modern Art, New York. Gift of Mr. and Mrs. František Kupka

Amorpha. Fugue à deux couleurs (Amorpha: Fugue in two colors). 1912
Gouache, ink, and pencil on paper
8 1/2 x 8 7/8″ (21.6 x 22.5 cm)
The Museum of Modern Art, New York. Gift of Mr. and Mrs. František Kupka

Amorpha. Fugue à deux couleurs (Amorpha: Fugue in two colors). 1912 (plate 74)
Gouache and ink on paper
8 1/4 x 8 7/8″ (21 x 22.5 cm)
The Museum of Modern Art, New York. Gift of Mr. and Mrs. František Kupka

Sol LeWitt (American, 1928–2007)

From Serial Project, I, A5 (small). 1969
Baked enamel on steel rods, mounted on painted steel plate
8 1/8 x 32 x 32″ (20.6 x 81.3 x 81.3 cm) including steel plate
The Museum of Modern Art, New York. Ruth Vollmer Bequest

Cubic Construction: Diagonal 4, Opposite Corners 1 and 4 Units. 1971 (plate 78)
Painted wood
24 1/4 x 24 1/4 x 24 1/4″ (61.6 x 61.6 x 61.6 cm)
The Museum of Modern Art, New York. The Riklis Collection of McCrory Corporation

Untitled. 1971 (p. 5)
Folded colored paper
10 3/4 x 21 3/4″ (27.3 x 55.2 cm)
The Museum of Modern Art, New York. The Judith Rothschild Foundation Contemporary Drawings Collection Gift (purchase, and gift, in part, of The Eileen and Michael Cohen Collection)

Rip Drawing. 1973
Torn paper
13 1/2 x 13 3/8″ (34.3 x 34.2 cm)
The Museum of Modern Art, New York. Ruth Vollmer Bequest

From the Upper Left and the Lower Right Comes toward the Center of the Page. 1975
Pencil on torn colored paper
19 3/4 x 19 3/4″ (50.2 x 50.2 cm)
The Museum of Modern Art, New York. Art & Project/Depot VBVR Gift

El Lissitzky (Russian, 1890–1941)

Proun 19D. c. 1922 (plate 41)
Gesso, oil, paper, and cardboard on plywood
38 3/8 x 38 1/4″ (97.5 x 97.2 cm)
The Museum of Modern Art, New York. Katherine S. Dreier Bequest

Prounenraum (Proun room). 1923 (plate 40)
Reconstruction for the exhibition
9′ 10 1/8″ x 9′ 10 1/8″ x 8′ 6 3/8″ (300 x 300 x 260 cm)

Mark Lombardi (American, 1951–2000)

Banco Nazionale del Lavoro, Reagan, Bush, Thatcher, and the Arming of Iraq, c. 1979–1990 (4th version). 1998 (plate 99)
Colored pencil and pencil on paper
50″ x 10′ (127 x 304.8 cm)
The Museum of Modern Art, New York. Gift of Shirley and Donald Lombardi

Richard Long (British, born 1945)

Walking a Straight 10-Mile Line, Dartmoor, England. 1970
Typewriting on cut-and-pasted paper, cut-and-pasted printed map, and gelatin silver print on board
8 7/8 x 39 1/2″ (22.5 x 100.3 cm)
The Museum of Modern Art, New York. Charles Simon Fund

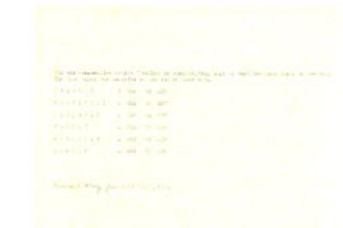

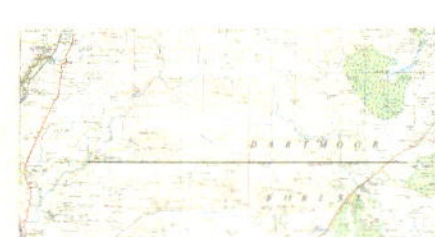

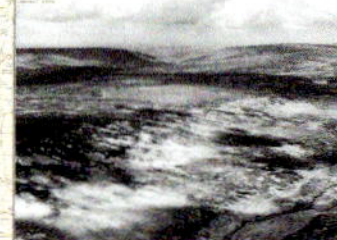

Anna Maria Maiolino (Brazilian, born Italy 1942)

Escape Point. 1971
Etching and transfer letters on paper
Edition: 11 of 30
24 3/16 x 18 5/16" (61.5 x 46.5 cm)
Collection the artist

Entre os dois (Between the two) from the series *Projetos construídos* (Constructed projects). 1972 (plate 131)
Paper in wooden box with glass
Artist's proof
18 7/8 x 11 13/16 x 2 3/8" (48 x 30 x 6 cm)
Collection the artist

Untitled from the series *Projetos construídos* (Constructed projects). 1972
Ink and thread on paper in wooden box
Edition: 2 of 5
14 9/16 x 14 9/16 x 1 15/16" (37 x 37 x 5 cm)
Collection the artist

Untitled from the series *Projetos construídos* (Constructed projects). 1972 (plate 70)
Acrylic and transfer letters on paper in wooden box, with Styrofoam backing
Edition: 4 of 5
17 11/16 x 17 11/16 x 4 15/16" (45 x 45 x 12.5 cm)
Collection the artist

Desde A até M (From A to M) from the series *Mapas mentais* (Mental maps). 1972–99 (plate 69)
Thread, synthetic polymer paint, ink, transfer type, and pencil on paper
19 5/8 x 19 1/2" (49.8 x 49.5 cm)
The Museum of Modern Art, New York. Purchase

Espiral (Spiral) from the series *Desenhos objetos* (Drawing objects). 1975
Acrylic on paper in wooden box
Edition: impression outside the edition of 3 and 1 artist's proof
28 1/8 x 28 1/8 x 2 15/16" (71.5 x 71.5 x 7.5 cm)
Collection the artist

Untitled from the series *Desenhos objetos* (Drawing Objects). 1975–2001 (plate 71)
Thread on paper in wooden box
Edition: 2 of 5
9 13/16 x 13 3/8 x 2 9/16" (25 x 34 x 6.5 cm)
Collection the artist

Untitled from the series *Indícios* (Indices). 2000
Black thread sewn to paper
12 x 8 1/2" (30.5 x 21.6 cm)
The Museum of Modern Art, New York. Gift of Michael Maiolino in memoriam of Sofia Gegner

Untitled from the series *Vestígios I* (Vestiges I). 2000
Ink on paper
12 x 9" (30.5 x 22.9 cm)
The Museum of Modern Art, New York. Purchase

Untitled from the series *Indícios* (Indices). 2005 (plate 72)
Thread on paper
13 3/4 x 10 1/16" (35 x 25.5 cm)
Collection the artist

Untitled from the series *Indícios* (Indices). 2005
Thread on paper
13 3/4 x 10 1/16" (35 x 25.5 cm)
Collection the artist

Sheila Makhijani (Indian, born 1962)

Like this you mean. 2009
Gouache and thread on paper and plastic sheets
17 1/2 x 15 1/2" (44.5 x 39.4 cm)
Courtesy the artist and Talwar Gallery, New York/New Delhi

Moving around a lot. 2009
Gouache and thread on paper and plastic sheets
15 1/4 x 22 3/4" (38.7 x 57.8 cm)
Courtesy the artist and Talwar Gallery, New York/New Delhi

So now move it! 2009
Gouache and thread on paper and plastic sheets
17 1/4 x 25 1/4" (43.8 x 64.1 cm)
Courtesy the artist and Talwar Gallery, New York/New Delhi

Start getting used to it! 2009
Gouache and thread on paper and plastic sheets
14 1/2 x 27" (36.8 x 68.6 cm)
Courtesy the artist and Talwar Gallery, New York/New Delhi

Take a leap →. 2009 (plates 117, 230)
Gouache and thread on paper and plastic sheets
12 1/2 x 25" (31.8 x 63.5 cm)
Courtesy the artist and Talwar Gallery, New York/New Delhi

Tomás Maldonado (Argentine, born 1922)

Desarrollo de 14 temas (Development of 14 themes). 1951–52 (plate 176)
Oil on canvas
6' 6 7/8 x 6' 10 3/4" (200.3 x 210.2 cm)
Colección Patricia Phelps de Cisneros

Kazimir Malevich (Russian, born Ukraine, 1878–1935)

Reservist of the First Division. 1914 (plate 25)
Oil on canvas with collage of printed paper, postage stamp, and thermometer
21 1/8 x 17 5/8" (53.7 x 44.8 cm)
The Museum of Modern Art, New York. 1935 acquisition confirmed in 1999 by agreement with the Estate of Kazimir Malevich and made possible with funds from the Mrs. John Hay Whitney Bequest (by exchange)

Suprematist Drawing. c. 1916–17 (plate 26)
Pencil on paper
4 3/4 x 6 7/8" (12 x 17.5 cm)
The Museum of Modern Art, New York. The Riklis Collection of McCrory Corporation

Suprematist Drawing. c. 1916–17 (plate 27)
Pencil on paper
4 3/4 x 6 7/8" (12 x 17.5 cm)
The Museum of Modern Art, New York. The Riklis Collection of McCrory Corporation

Suprematist Diagonal Construction 79. 1917
Pencil on paper
13 7/8 x 20 3/8" (35.2 x 51.8 cm)
The Museum of Modern Art, New York. 1935 acquisition confirmed in 1999 by agreement with the Estate of Kazimir Malevich and made possible with funds from the Mrs. John Hay Whitney Bequest (by exchange)

Karel Malich (Czech, born 1924)

Odpoutaná krajina IV (a) (Untitled landscape IV [a]). 1973–74 (plate 76)
Galvanized iron wire, thread, and paint
6' 2 3/8" x 59" x 40 1/8" (188.9 x 149.9 x 101.9 cm)
Courtesy Marian Goodman Gallery, New York

Krajina (Energie) (Landscape [energy]). 1974
Galvanized iron wire, aluminum, thread, and paint
60 1/2 x 37 3/8 x 55 1/8" (153.7 x 94.9 x 140 cm)
Courtesy Marian Goodman Gallery, New York

Krajina II (Landscape II). 1974
Galvanized iron wire, thread, aluminum netting, and paint
66 7/8 x 55 1/8 x 51 1/8" (169.9 x 140 x 129.9 cm)
Courtesy Marian Goodman Gallery, New York

Energie I (Energy I). 1974–75
Galvanized iron wire and thread
66 7/8 x 63 x 49 1/4" (169.9 x 160 x 125.1 cm)
Courtesy Marian Goodman Gallery, New York

Man Ray (American, 1890–1976)

The Rope Dancer Accompanies Herself with Her Shadows. 1916 (plate 18)
Oil on canvas
52" x 6' 1 3/8" (132.1 x 186.4 cm)
The Museum of Modern Art, New York. Gift of G. David Thompson

Piero Manzoni (Italian, 1933–1963)

Linea m 1000 (1000 meter line). 1961 (plate 58)
Chrome-plated metal drum containing a roll of paper with an ink line drawn along its 1,000-meter length
20 1/4 x 15 3/8" diam. (51.2 x 38.8 cm diam.)
The Museum of Modern Art, New York. Gift of Fratelli Fabbri Editori and purchase

Tom Marioni (American, born 1937)

One Second Sculpture. 1969 (plate 189)
Black and white photograph
Edition: 1 of 3
31 x 36" (78.7 x 91.4 cm)
Collection the artist

Agnes Martin (American, born Canada, 1912–2004)

Untitled. 1960 (plate 82)
Ink on paper
11 7/8 x 12 1/8" (30.2 x 30.6 cm)
The Museum of Modern Art, New York. Acquired with matching funds from The Lauder Foundation and the National Endowment for the Arts

Tremolo. 1962
Ink on paper
10 x 11" (25.5 x 28 cm)
The Museum of Modern Art, New York. The Riklis Collection of McCrory Corporation

Wood I. 1963
Watercolor and pencil on paper
15 x 15 1/2" (38.1 x 39.4 cm)
The Museum of Modern Art, New York. Fractional and promised gift of Sally and Wynn Kramarsky

Stone. 1964
Ink on paper
10 7/8 x 10 7/8" (27.7 x 27.7 cm)
The Museum of Modern Art, New York. Eugene and Clare Thaw Fund

The Tree. 1964 (plate 80)
Oil and pencil on canvas
6 x 6' (182.8 x 182.8 cm)
The Museum of Modern Art, New York. Larry Aldrich Foundation Fund

Orchards of Lightning. 1966
Ink on paper
11 3/4 x 9 3/8" (29.8 x 23.8 cm)
The Museum of Modern Art, New York. The William S. Paley Collection

André Masson (French, 1896–1987)

Combat de poissons (Battle of fishes). 1926 (plate 44)
Sand, gesso, oil, pencil, and charcoal on canvas
14 1/4 x 28 3/4" (36.2 x 73 cm)
The Museum of Modern Art, New York. Purchase

Gordon Matta-Clark (American, 1945–1978)

Tree Dance. 1971 (plate 148)
16mm film transferred to video, black and white, silent, 9:32 min.
The Museum of Modern Art, New York. Gift of Jerry I. Speyer and Katherine G. Farley, Anna Marie and Robert F. Shapiro, and Marie-Josée and Henry R. Kravis

Untitled. 1973
Stack of gessoed paper, cut, mounted on cardboard
27 1/2 x 39 3/4" (69.9 x 101 cm)
Collection Gail and Tony Ganz

Splitting. 1974
Super 8 film transferred to video, black and white and color, silent, 10:50 min.
The Museum of Modern Art, New York. Committee on Media Funds

Day's End. 1975
Super 8 film transferred to video, color, silent, 23:10 min.
The Museum of Modern Art, New York. Committee on Media Funds

Untitled (Cut Drawing). 1976–77 (plate 112)
Pencil on layers of cut paper
22 1/2 x 29 1/2 x 1/2" (57 x 74 x 1.3 cm)
The Museum of Modern Art, New York. Purchase through the Vincent D'Aquila and Harry Soviak Bequest Fund, The Judith Rothschild Foundation, and Purchase Fund

Anthony McCall (American, born England 1946)

Five Minute Drawing. 1974/2010 (plate 188)
Charcoal on paper
Six sheets, each 31 1/2 x 21 5/8" (80 x 55 cm)
Courtesy the artist and Sean Kelly Gallery, New York

Julie Mehretu (American, born Ethiopia 1970)

Rising Down. 2008 (plate 115)
Ink and synthetic polymer paint on canvas
8′ x 12′ (243.8 x 365.8 cm)
Collection Jeanne Greenberg Rohatyn, New York

Cildo Meireles (Brazilian, born 1948)

Malhas da Liberdade I (Meshes of freedom I). 1976 (plate 201)
Cotton rope
Dimensions variable, c. 47 1/4 x 47 1/4″ (120 x 120 cm)
Collection the artist. Courtesy Galerie Lelong and Galeria Luisa Strina

Malhas da Liberdade III (Meshes of freedom III). 1977 (plate 95)
Iron, glass sheet
47 1/4 x 47 1/4″ (120 x 120 cm)
Collection the artist. Courtesy Galerie Lelong and Galeria Luisa Strina

Marisa Merz (Italian, born 1931)

Untitled (Stave). 1993 (plate 87)
Copper wire, gold leaf on clay, and steel
Dimensions variable
The Museum of Modern Art, New York. Marcia Riklis Fund

Joan Miró (Spanish, 1893–1983)

Spanish Dancer. 1928 (plate 45)
Sandpaper, paper, string, nails, linoleum, drafting triangle, hair, cork, and paint on flocked paper mounted on wood boards
43 1/8 x 28″ (109.5 x 71.1 cm)
Private collection

Nasreen Mohamedi (Indian, 1937–1990)

Untitled. c. 1970
Graphite and ink on paper
18 11/16 x 18 11/16″ (47.5 x 47.5 cm)
Courtesy Talwar Gallery, New York/New Delhi

Untitled. c. 1970
Graphite and ink on paper
18 11/16 x 18 11/16″ (47.5 x 47.5 cm)
Courtesy Talwar Gallery, New York/New Delhi

Untitled. c. 1970
Graphite and ink on paper
18 11/16 x 18 11/16″ (47.5 x 47.5 cm)
Courtesy Talwar Gallery, New York/New Delhi

Untitled. c. 1970
Graphite and ink on paper
18 11/16 x 18 11/16″ (47.5 x 47.5 cm)
Courtesy Talwar Gallery, New York/New Delhi

Untitled. c. 1970 (plate 83)
Graphite and ink on paper
18 11/16 x 18 11/16″ (47.5 x 47.5 cm)
Private collection. Courtesy Talwar Gallery, New York/New Delhi

Untitled. c. 1970
Graphite and ink on paper
18 11/16 x 18 11/16″ (47.5 x 47.5 cm)
Courtesy Talwar Gallery, New York/New Delhi

Vera Molnar (French, born Hungary 1924)

Arbres et collines géométriques (Geometric trees and hills). 1946 (plate 205)
Crayon on paper
8 sheets, overall: 6 5/16 x 70 7/8″ (16 x 180 cm)
Collection the artist. Courtesy Gallery [DAM], Berlin

Interruptions à recouvrements (Disturbances through overlappings). 1969 (plate 206)
Ink on paper
Edition: 2 of 2
11 7/16 x 30 5/16″ (29 x 77 cm)
Collection Anne and Michael Spalter

A la recherche de Paul Klee (Searching for Paul Klee). 1970
Ink on paper
26 3/4 x 26 3/4″ (68 x 68 cm)
Collection the artist. Courtesy Gallery [DAM], Berlin

A la recherche de Paul Klee (Searching for Paul Klee). 1971
Felt-tip pen on paper
17 5/16 x 19 11/16″ (44 x 50 cm)
Collection the artist. Courtesy Gallery [DAM] Berlin

Piet Mondrian (Dutch, 1872–1944)

Composition in Brown and Gray. 1913
Oil on canvas
33 3/4 x 29 3/4″ (85.7 x 75.6 cm)
The Museum of Modern Art, New York. Purchase

Compositie No. 5, with color planes 5 (Composition no. 5, with color planes 5). 1917 (plate 24)
Oil on canvas
19 3/8 x 24 1/8″ (49 x 61.2 cm)
The Museum of Modern Art, New York. The Sidney and Harriet Janis Collection

Tableau I: Lozenge with Four Lines and Gray. 1926 (plate 61)
Oil on canvas
44 3/4 x 44″ (113.7 x 111.8 cm)
The Museum of Modern Art, New York. Katherine S. Dreier Bequest

Composition (Unfinished). 1938 or 1939 (plate 77)
Charcoal on canvas
27 5/8 x 28 3/8″ (70 x 72.3 cm)
Collection Caroll and Donna Janis, New York

Bruce Nauman (American, born 1941)

Slow Angle Walk (Beckett Walk). 1968 (plate 146)
Video, black and white, sound, 60 min.
The Museum of Modern Art, New York. Gift of Jerry I. Speyer and Katherine G. Farley, Anna Marie and Robert F. Shapiro, and Marie-Josée and Henry R. Kravis.

N.E. Thing Co. Ltd. (Iain Baxter&, Canadian, born England 1936, and **Ingrid Baxter**, Canadian, born the United States 1938)

Act #76 — Crop Configurations, Chili, S. Am., and Anywhere Else. 1968
Gelatin silver print mounted on board
12 1/2 x 19 1/4″ (31.8 x 48.9 cm)
Courtesy the artist and Corkin Gallery, Toronto

Act #80 — World's Most Productive Open Pit Copper Mine, Chuquicamata, Atacama Desert, Chili, S. Am. Crater is 2 miles long, 1200′ deep (structure only). 1968
Gelatin silver print mounted on board
12 1/2 x 19 1/4″ (31.8 x 48.9 cm)
Courtesy the artist and Corkin Gallery, Toronto

Act #89 — Crop Stakes, N. California. 1968
Gelatin silver print mounted on board
27 1/2 x 39 1/2″ (69.9 x 100.3 cm)
Private collection. Courtesy Corkin Gallery, Toronto

Act #106 — Irrigation Field, Arizona, U.S.A. 1968
Gelatin silver print mounted on board
12 1/2 x 19 1/4″ (31.8 x 48.9 cm)
Courtesy the artist and Corkin Gallery, Toronto

One Mile Skied Line—1968. 1968 (plate 100)
Gelatin silver print collaged on paper with seal and felt-pen handwriting
18 x 24″ (45.7 x 61 cm)
Courtesy the artist and Corkin Gallery, Toronto

Avis Newman (British, born 1946)

Configuration of no-thing. 2007–9 (plate 114)
Acrylic and chalk on linen and cotton duck, paper, and metal
Six parts: 11 13/16 x 9 13/16″ (30 x 25 cm), 11 13/16 x 9 13/16″ (30 x 25 cm), 6′ 1/16″ x 6′ 1/16″ (183 x 183 cm), 39 3/8 x 55 1/8″ (100 x 140 cm), 6′10 11/16″ x 68 7/8″ (210 x 175 cm), 11 13/16 x 11 13/16″ (30 x 30 cm)
Collection the artist

Vaslaw Nijinsky (Russian, 1890–1950)

Tänzerin (Dancer). 1917–18 (plate 154)
Chalk, pastel, and pencil on paper
13 3/4 x 9 13/16″ (35 x 25 cm)
Stiftung John Neumeier, Dance Collection

Cornelia Parker (British, born 1956)

Bullet Drawing. 2009 (plate 97)
Lead from a bullet drawn into wire
24 7/8 x 24 7/8″ (63.2 x 63.2 cm)
Private collection, New York

Bullet Drawing. 2009
Lead from a bullet drawn into wire
24 7/8 x 24 7/8″ (63.2 x 63.2 cm)
Collection Joanne Gold and Andrew Stern

Bullet Drawing. 2009
Lead from a bullet drawn into wire
24 7/8 x 24 7/8″ (63.2 x 63.2 cm)
Collection Judith and Bruce Eissner

Bullet Drawing. 2009
Lead from a bullet drawn into wire
24 7/8 x 24 7/8″ (63.2 x 63.2 cm)
Private collection, New York

Giuseppe Penone (Italian, born 1947)

Propagazione (Propagation). 1995–2010 (plate 227)
Typographic ink and graphite on paper, felt pen on wall
Dimensions variable, site-specific
Courtesy the artist and Marian Goodman Gallery, New York

Pablo Picasso (Spanish, 1881–1973)

Guitar. 1912 (plate 14)
Charcoal on paper
18 1/2 x 24 3/8″ (47 x 61.9 cm)
The Museum of Modern Art, New York. Gift of Donald B. Marron

Maquette for Guitar. 1912
Cardboard, string, and wire (restored)
25 3/4 x 13 x 7 1/2″ (65.1 x 33 x 19 cm)
The Museum of Modern Art, New York. Gift of the artist

Guitar. 1913 (plate 16)
Cut-and-pasted paper and printed paper, charcoal, ink, and chalk on colored paper on board
26 1/8 x 19 1/2″ (66.4 x 49.6 cm)
The Museum of Modern Art, New York. Nelson A. Rockefeller Bequest

Head. 1913
Cut-and-pasted colored and printed paper, ink, and pencil on paper
17 7/8 x 11 3/8″ (42.9 x 28.7 cm)
The Museum of Modern Art, New York. The Sidney and Harriet Janis Collection

Jackson Pollock (American, 1912–1956)

Untitled. c. 1950 (plate 168)
Ink on paper
17 1/2 x 22 1/4″ (44.5 x 56.6 cm)
The Museum of Modern Art, New York. Gift of Jo Carole and Ronald S. Lauder in honor of Eliza Parkinson Cobb

White Light. 1954
Oil, enamel, and aluminum paint on canvas
48 1/4 x 38 1/4″ (122.4 x 96.9 cm)
The Museum of Modern Art, New York. The Sidney and Harriet Janis Collection

Lyubov Popova (Russian, 1889–1924)

Space-Force Construction. 1921 (plate 37)
Oil with wood dust on plywood
28 x 25 5/16″ (71.1 x 64.3 cm)
Greek State Museum of Contemporary Art, Thessaloníki—Costakis Collection

Study for Space-Force Construction. c. 1921 (plate 36)
Crayon on paper
10 7/8 x 8 3/16″ (27.6 x 20.8 cm)
Greek State Museum of Contemporary Art, Thessaloníki — Costakis Collection

Study for "Space-Force Construction No. 80". c. 1921
Gouache on paper
13 7/8 x 10 1/2″ (35.2 x 26.6 cm)
Greek State Museum of Contemporary Art, Thessaloníki — Costakis Collection

Untitled (From the INKHUK Portfolio). 1921
Crayon on paper
10 7/8 x 8 1/8″ (27.6 x 20.6 cm)
Greek State Museum of Contemporary Art, Thessaloníki — Costakis Collection

Drawing in *5 x 5 = 25: An Exhibition of Painting* catalogue. 1921
Crayon on paper
Page: 7 x 4 5/8″ (17.8 x 11.7 cm)
The Museum of Modern Art, New York. Gift of Mrs. Alfred H. Barr, Jr.

Textile design. 1923–24
Gouache on paper
6 5/16 x 12 7/16″ (16 x 31.6 cm)
Greek State Museum of Contemporary Art, Thessaloníki — Costakis Collection

Textile design. 1923–24 (plate 38)
Gouache, ink, and pencil on paper
13 3/4 x 11 1/8″ (34.9 x 28.2 cm)
Greek State Museum of Contemporary Art, Thessaloníki — Costakis Collection

Textile design. 1923–24
Gouache and ink on paper
9 5/16 x 5 5/8″ (23.6 x 14.3 cm)
Greek State Museum of Contemporary Art, Thessaloníki — Costakis Collection

Jean Pougny (Ivan Puni; Russian, born Finland, 1892–1956)

Relief. 1915 (plate 28)
Wood mounted on canvas, painted in oil
25 3/8 x 31 7/8″ (64.5 x 81 cm)
Centre Pompidou, Paris. Musée national d'art moderne/Centre de création industrielle. Gift of Xénia Pougny

Yvonne Rainer (American, born 1934)

Trio A. 1966, filmed 1978 (plate 187)
16mm film transferred to video, black and white, silent, 10:12 min.
The Museum of Modern Art, New York

Selection from *Five Easy Pieces*. 1966-69
Film transferred to video, black and white, silent
Courtesy Video Databank, Chicago

Robert Rauschenberg (American, 1925–2008)

Automobile Tire Print. 1953 (plate 59)
Black paint on twenty sheets of paper, mounted on fabric
16 1/2″ x 22′ 1/2″ (41.9 x 671.8 cm)
San Francisco Museum of Modern Art. Purchase through a gift of Phyllis Wattis

Dorothea Rockburne (American, born Canada 1932)

Drawing Which Makes Itself. 1972
Carbon, carbon transfer, and pencil on paper
22 1/2 x 30″ (57.2 x 76.2 cm)
The Museum of Modern Art, New York. The Riklis Collection of McCrory Corporation

Drawing Which Makes Itself: FPI 16. 1973
Folded paper and ink
30 x 40″ (76.2 x 101.5 cm)
The Museum of Modern Art, New York. Blanchette Hooker Rockefeller Fund

Aleksandr Rodchenko (Russian, 1891–1956)

Non-Objective Painting. 1919
Oil on canvas
33 x 28″ (84.5 x 71.1 cm)
The Museum of Modern Art, New York. Gift of the artist, through Jay Leyda

Construction. 1920 (plate 35)
Ink and colored ink on paper
12 3/4 x 7 3/4″ (32.4 x 19.7 cm)
The Museum of Modern Art, New York. Given anonymously

Construction no. 104. 1920 (plate 34)
Oil on canvas
40 3/8 x 27 7/16″ (102.5 x 69.7 cm)
Greek State Museum of Contemporary Art, Thessaloníki — Costakis Collection

Line Construction. 1920
Ink and gouache on paper
14 3/4 x 9″ (37.5 x 23 cm)
The Museum of Modern Art, New York. The Riklis Collection of McCrory Corporation

Linear Construction. 1920
Ink, colored ink, and pencil on paper
12 1/2 x 8″ (31.8 x 20.3 cm)
The Museum of Modern Art, New York. Gift of an anonymous donor

Spatial Construction no. 12. c. 1920 (plate 32)
Plywood, partly painted with aluminum paint, and wire
24 x 33 x 18 1/2″ (61 x 83.7 x 47 cm)
The Museum of Modern Art, New York. Acquisition made possible through the extraordinary efforts of George and Zinaida Costakis, and through the Nate B. and Frances Spingold, Matthew H. and Erna Futter, and Enid A. Haupt Funds

Untitled. c. 1920 (plate 7)
Pencil on colored paper
12 1/4 x 8 1/4″ (31.1 x 21 cm)
The Museum of Modern Art, New York. Gift of an anonymous donor

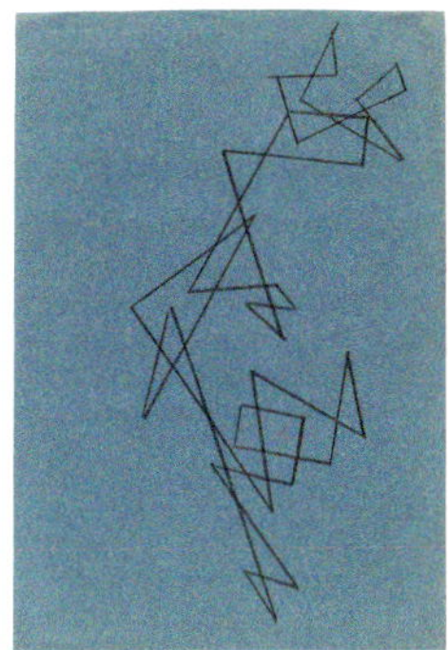

Lotty Rosenfeld (Chilean, born 1943)

Una milla de cruces sobre el pavimento (A mile of crosses on the pavement). 1979 (plate 101)
Video, color, silent, 4:45 mins.
FRAC Lorraine, Metz

Robert Ryman (American, born 1930)

Stretched Drawing (Red). c. 1963
Colored pencil on stretched sized cotton canvas
16 x 15 3/4″ (40.6 x 40 cm)
Private collection

Impex. 1968 (plate 66)
Oil on unstretched linen canvas, and blue chalk line on wall
Canvas: 8′1″ x 8′1″ (246.4 x 246.4 cm); overall dimensions variable
Solomon R. Guggenheim Museum, New York. Panza Collection, 1991

Bent Line Drawing. c. 1970
Ballpoint pen on stretched polyester fabric over foamcore
12 x 12″ (30.5 x 30.5 cm)
Private collection

Fred Sandback (American, 1943–2003)

Untitled. 1967 (plate 183)
Painted elastic rayon cord and metal sleeve clamps
69″ x 14′ x 24″ (175.2 x 426.7 x 60.9 cm)
The Museum of Modern Art, New York. Gift of Philip Johnson

Mira Schendel (Brazilian, born Switzerland, 1919–1988)

Untitled from the series *Droguinhas* (Little nothings). c. 1964–66 (plate 107)
Paper
Dimensions variable, c. 35 1/2″ (90 cm) long fully extended
The Museum of Modern Art, New York. Scott Burton Fund

Carolee Schneemann (American, born 1939)

Up To And Including Her Limits. 1973–76 (plates 128, 211)
Crayon on paper, rope, harness, and two-channel analog video, with audio, transferred to digital video
Two wall drawings, 8 x 8′ (243.8 x 243.8 cm) each, and one floor drawing, 8 x 8′ (243.8 x 243.8 cm) with rounded edge
Courtesy the artist and P·P·O·W Gallery, New York

Kurt Schwitters (German, 1887–1948)

Revolving. 1919 (plate 21)
Wood, metal, cord, cardboard, wool, wire, leather, and oil on canvas
48 3/8 x 35″ (122.7 x 88.7 cm)
The Museum of Modern Art, New York. Advisory Committee Fund

Mz. 252. Colored Squares. 1921
Cut-and-pasted colored and printed paper with pencil on paper with cardstock border
10 7/8 x 8 1/4″ (27.4 x 21 cm)
The Museum of Modern Art, New York. The Sidney and Harriet Janis Collection

Merz 1926 17. Lissitzky. 1926 (plate 22)
Cut-and-pasted colored paper on cardstock
11 5/8 x 8 1/8″ (29.5 x 20.6 cm)
The Museum of Modern Art, New York. Katherine S. Dreier Bequest

29/8. 1929 (plate 181)
Cut-and-pasted colored paper on paper
9 5/8 x 6 1/4″ (24.5 x 15.9 cm)
The Museum of Modern Art, New York. Katherine S. Dreier Bequest

29/32. 1929
Cut-and-pasted gelatin silver prints on paper on cardstock
5 x 3 3/4″ (12.7 x 9.5 cm)
The Museum of Modern Art, New York. Katherine S. Dreier Bequest

Gino Severini (Italian, 1883–1966)

Dancer. 1912 (plate 155)
Pastel on paper
19 1/4 x 12 1/2″ (49 x 32 cm)
The Museum of Modern Art, New York. The Riklis Collection of McCrory Corporation

Dynamic Hieroglyphic of the Bal Tabarin. 1912 (plate 12)
Oil on canvas with sequins
63 5/8 x 61 1/2″ (161.6 x 156.2 cm)
The Museum of Modern Art, New York. Acquired through the Lillie P. Bliss Bequest

Ranjani Shettar (Indian, born 1977)

Just a bit more. 2005–6 (plate 232)
Hand-molded beeswax, pigments, and thread dyed in tea
36 x 24 x 12′ (1097.3 x 731.5 x 365.8 cm)
Courtesy the artist and Talwar Gallery, New York/New Delhi

Mieko Shiomi (Japanese, born 1938)

Spatial Poem No. 1. 1965 (plate 190)
Stenciled black map on white-painted composition board, 69 printed cards mounted on pins, assembled by George Maciunas
11 15/16 x 18 x 7/8″ (30.3 x 45.7 x 2.2 cm)
The Museum of Modern Art, New York. The Gilbert and Lila Silverman Fluxus Collection Gift

Michael Snow (Canadian, born 1929)

A Man with a Line. 1953–54 (plate 65)
Mixed media on canvas
16 x 18″ (40.6 x 45.7 cm)
Art Gallery of Ontario, Toronto. Gift of Mrs. Nora E. Vaughan, Toronto, 1993

Jesús Rafael Soto (Venezuelan, 1923–2005)

Oliva y negro (Olive and black). 1966 (plate 84)
Flexible mobile of metal strips suspended in front of two plywood panels painted with synthetic polymer paint and mounted on composition board
61 1/2 x 42 1/4 x 12 1/2″ (156.1 x 107.1 x 31.7 cm)
The Museum of Modern Art, New York. Inter-American Fund

Michelle Stuart (American, born 1938)

Niagara Gorge Path Relocated. 1975 (plate 132)
Video, black and white, silent, 36 min.
Courtesy the artist and Leslie Tonkonow Artworks + Projects

Nazca Lines Star Chart. Nazca Lines Southern Hemisphere Constellation Chart Correlation. 1981–82
Earth from Nazca Plateau, Peru, rubbed into paper
10′ 1/4″ x 14′ 1/2″ (305.3 x 428 cm) and 17 x 22″ (43.2 x 55.9 cm)
The Museum of Modern Art, New York. Gift of William S. Paley

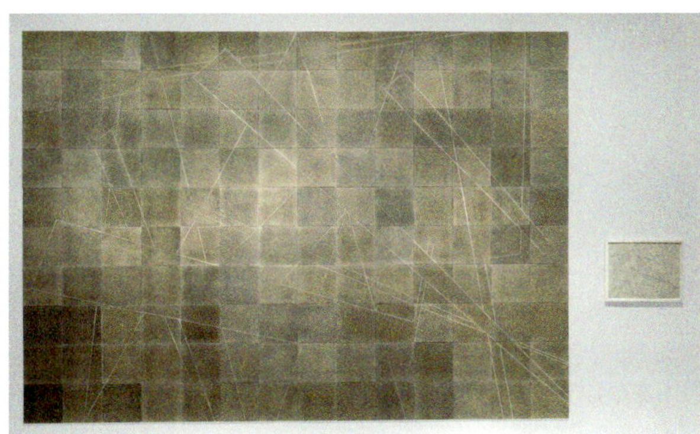

Françoise Sullivan (Canadian, born 1925)

Danse dans la neige (Dance in the snow) nos. 1–17. 1948 (plates 169–73)
Seventeen gelatin silver prints (photographs: Maurice Perron) mounted on Masonite mounted on wood
Each: 15 3/8 x 15 3/8" (39 x 39 cm)
Collection Vivian and David Campbell, Promised Gift to The Art Gallery of Ontario, Toronto

Alia Syed (British, born 1964)

Priya. 2007–8
16mm film transferred to DVD, color, silent, 11:30 min.
Courtesy the artist and Talwar Gallery, New York/New Delhi

Sophie Taeuber-Arp (Swiss, 1889–1943)

Lignes ondoyantes (Undulating lines). 1940
Colored pencil on paper
13 5/8 x 10 3/8" (34.6 x 26.3 cm)
Stiftung Hans Arp und Sophie Taeuber-Arp e.V., Rolandswerth

Mouvement de lignes en couleurs (Movement of colored lines). 1940 (plates 8, 162)
Colored pencil on cardboard
14 1/8 x 11" (35.9 x 28 cm)
Stiftung Hans Arp und Sophie Taeuber-Arp e.V., Rolandswerth

Mouvement de lignes en couleurs (Movement of colored lines). 1940
Colored pencil on paper
10 7/16 x 13 9/16" (26.5 x 34.5 cm)
Stiftung Hans Arp und Sophie Taeuber-Arp e.V., Rolandswerth

Mouvement de lignes en couleurs (Movement of colored lines). 1940
Colored pencil on paper
10 7/16 x 13 11/16" (26.5 x 34.8 cm)
Stiftung Hans Arp und Sophie Taeuber-Arp e.V., Rolandswerth

Lignes géométriques et ondoyantes (Geometric and undulating lines). 1941 (plate 50)
Colored pencil on paper
8 7/16 x 5 1/4" (21.5 x 13.4 cm)
Stiftung Hans Arp und Sophie Taeuber-Arp e.V., Rolandswerth

Lignes géométriques et ondoyantes (Geometric and undulating lines). 1941 (plate 49)
Colored pencil on paper
8 3/4 x 5 1/2" (22.2 x 13.9 cm)
Stiftung Hans Arp und Sophie Taeuber-Arp e.V., Rolandswerth

Atsuko Tanaka (Japanese, 1932–2005)

Preparatory sketch for *Electric Dress*. c. 1956 (plate 177)
Ink on paper
2 3/16 x 10" (5.6 x 25.4 cm)
Private collection

Drawing after *Electric Dress*. 1956 (plate 178)
India ink, ink, pencil, and crayon on paper
30 5/16 x 21 5/8" (77 x 55 cm)
Deutsche Bank Collection

Drawing after *Electric Dress*. 1956
Crayon on paper
30 5/16 x 21 5/8" (77 x 55 cm)
Deutsche Bank Collection

Round on Sand. 1968 (plate 179)
16mm film, color, silent, 9:50 min.
Private collection

Sophie Tottie (Swedish, born 1964)

Written Language (line drawings) #V. 2008 (plate 212)
Ink on paper
7' 1" x 44 3/4" (215.9 x 113.7 cm)
The Museum of Modern Art, New York. Fund for the Twenty-First Century

Written Language (line drawings) # VI. 2008 (plate 213)
Ink on paper
7' 1" x 44 3/4" (215.9 x 113.7 cm)
The Museum of Modern Art, New York. Fund for the Twenty-First Century

Joëlle Tuerlinckx (Belgian, born 1958)

Room of Volume of Air—13 Elements. 1993–2004 (plates 116, 119, 120)
Iron, copper, wood, and found floor materials
Overall dimensions variable
The Museum of Modern Art, New York. Gift of Clarissa and Edgar Bronfman, Jr., Kathy and Richard S. Fuld, Jr., Agnes Gund, Mimi Haas, and Marie-Josée and Henry Kravis

Richard Tuttle (American, born 1941)

Wire Pieces. 1972/2010 (plate 184)
Florist wire, nails, and graphite
Dimensions variable
Courtesy the artist and The Pace Gallery, New York

Cy Twombly (American, born 1928)

Untitled. 1955 (plate 127)
Pencil on paper
24 3/8 x 36 1/8" (62 x 91.7 cm)
The Museum of Modern Art, New York. Gift of Jo Carole and Ronald S. Lauder

Georges Vantongerloo (Belgian, 1886–1965)

Relation de lignes et couleurs (Relation of lines and colors). 1939
Oil on composition board
28 5/8 x 21" (72.6 x 53.3 cm)
The Museum of Modern Art, New York. The Riklis Collection of McCrory Corporation

Etendue (ligne dans l'espace) (Stretching [line in space]). 1945
Steel wire
46 7/16 x 38 3/16 x 27 9/16" (118 x 97 x 70 cm)
Chantal and Jakob Bill Collection, Switzerland

Noyau (Nucleus). 1946
Painted wood and nickel alloy
7 7/8" (20 cm) diam.
Chantal and Jakob Bill Collection, Switzerland

Cocon, chrysalide, embryonnaire (Cocoon, chrysalis, embryonic). 1950 (plate 53)
Plexiglas
3 15/16 x 5 1/8 x 3 1/8" (10 x 13 x 8 cm)
Chantal and Jakob Bill Collection, Switzerland

Des éléments (ligne fermée) (Elements [closed line]). 1954
Plastic and pigments
13 3/4 x 13 3/4 x 11 13/16" (35 x 35 x 30 cm)
Chantal and Jakob Bill Collection, Switzerland

Espace et couleur (Space and color). 1956 (plate 52)
Plastic
9 13/16 x 11 7/16 x 3 15/16" (25 x 29 x 10 cm)
Chantal and Jakob Bill Collection, Switzerland

Ondes transparentes (Translucent waves). 1958
Plastic
11 13/16" (30 cm) diam.
Chantal and Jakob Bill Collection, Switzerland

Anneau et elliptique (Ring and elliptical). 1959
Plexiglas
22 7/16 x 7 7/8 x 3 1/8" (57 x 20 x 8 cm)
Chantal and Jakob Bill Collection, Switzerland

Cecilia Vicuña (Chilean, born 1948)

Kon Kon Pi. 2010 (plate 226)
Video, color, sound, 13:23 min.
Courtesy the artist

Maria Helena Vieira da Silva (French, born Portugal, 1908–1992)

Les Lignes (The lines). 1936 (plate 166)
Oil on canvas
27 9/16 x 36 1/4" (70 x 92 cm)
Centre Pompidou, Paris. Musée national d'art moderne/Centre de création industrielle. Conferment

La Ville (The city). 1950–51 (plate 86)
Oil on canvas
38 3/8 x 51" (97.3 x 129.4 cm)
The Museum of Modern Art, New York. Gift of Mrs. Gilbert W. Chapman

Jacques de la Villeglé (French, born 1926)

bleu O noir (blue O black). 1955 (plate 98)
Torn-and-pasted paper on canvas
12 x 20 7/8" (30.5 x 53 cm)
The Museum of Modern Art, New York. General Drawings Fund

Terry Winters (American, born 1949)

Location Plan. 1999
Ink and felt-tip pen on thirty pieces of transparentized paper
11 5/8 x 16 3/8" (29.5 x 41.6 cm)
The Museum of Modern Art, New York. The Judith Rothschild Foundation Contemporary Drawings Collection Gift

La Monte Young (American, born 1935)

Composition 1960 #10 (to Bob Morris). 1960 (plate 192)
Performance view, showing Nam Jun Paik as Zen for Head, at Fluxus Internationale Festspiele Neuester Musik, Städtisches Museum Auditorium, Wiesbaden, September 1962
Gelatin silver print
8 1/4 x 6 5/16" (21 x 16 cm)
The Museum of Modern Art, New York. The Gilbert and Lila Silverman Fluxus Collection Gift

Compositions 1961. 1963 (plate 191)
Artist's book
Page: 3 9/16 x 3 5/8" (9 x 9.2 cm)
The Museum of Modern Art, New York. The Gilbert and Lila Silverman Fluxus Collection Gift

INDEX OF PLATES NOT INCLUDED IN THE CHECKLIST

Photograph Credits

Individual works of art appearing herein may be protected by copyright in the United States of America, or elsewhere, and may not be reproduced in any form without the permission of the rights holders. In reproducing the images contained in this publication, the Museum obtained the permission of the rights holders whenever possible. Should the Museum have been unable to locate the rights holder, notwithstanding good-faith efforts, it requests that any contact information concerning such rights holders be forwarded so that they may be contacted for future editions.

Unless otherwise noted, credits are cited by plate number.

© 2010 The Josef and Anni Albers Foundation/Artists Rights Society (ARS), New York. Courtesy The Museum of Modern Art, New York, Department of Imaging Services: 68 (work collection The Museum of Modern Art, New York. Gift of Kleiner, Bell & Co.). Copy photo David Allison: 6, 33.
© 2010 Francis Alÿs. Courtesy David Zwirner, New York: 231 (work collection the Los Angeles County Museum of Art. Purchased with funds provided by the Bernard and Edith Lewin Collection of Mexican Art Deaccession Fund and the Michael and Dorothy Blankfort Bequest by exchange).
© 2010 Giovanni Anselmo. Courtesy Archivio Anselmo, photo © 2010 Paolo Mussat Sartor: 63.
© 2010 Artists Rights Society (ARS), New York: 66.
© 2010 Artists Rights Society (ARS), New York/ADAGP, Paris: 73, 203. Photo Adam Rzepka: 202 (work collection the artist). Courtesy CNAC/MNAM/Dist. Réunion des Musées Nationaux/Art Resource, NY: frontispiece, 28, 157, 158. Courtesy CNAC/MNAM/Dist. Réunion des Musées Nationaux/Art Resource, NY, photo Jacques Faujour: 160 (work collection Centre Pompidou, Paris, Musée national d'art moderne/Centre de création industrielle. Purchase). Courtesy Kupferstich-Kabinett, Staatliche Kunstsammlungen Dresden, photo Herbert Boswank: 30. Courtesy The Museum of Modern Art, New York, Department of Imaging Services: 98, 156, 181, 206. Courtesy The Museum of Modern Art, New York, Department of Imaging Services, photo Robert Gerhardt: 31. Courtesy The Museum of Modern Art, New York, Department of Imaging Services, photo Robert Gerhardt: 10 (work collection The Museum of Modern Art, New York. Katharine S. Dreier Bequest). Courtesy The Museum of Modern Art, New York, Department of Imaging Services, photo Robert Gerhardt: 216 (work collection The Museum of Modern Art, New York. Purchase). Courtesy The Museum of Modern Art, New York, Department of Imaging Services, photo Thomas Griesel: 180. Courtesy The Museum of Modern Art, New York, Department of Imaging Services, photo Kate Keller: 75. Courtesy The Museum of Modern Art, New York, Department of Imaging Services, photo Mali Olatunji: 74. Courtesy The Museum of Modern Art, New York, Department of Imaging Services, photos John Wronn: 44, 84. Courtesy The Museum of Modern Art, New York, Department of Imaging Services, photos John Wronn: 42, 43 (works collection The Museum of Modern Art, New York. Abby Aldrich Rockefeller Fund). Photo © Foundation Claudine and Jean-Marc Salomon, photo Marc Domage: 205. Photo Rémi Villaggi: 110 (work collection FRAC Lorraine, Metz).
© 2010 Artists Rights Society (ARS), New York/ADAGP, Paris/Estate of Marcel Duchamp: 19 (work collection the Philadelphia Museum of Art. The Louise and Walter Arensberg Collection). Courtesy The Museum of Modern Art, New York, Department of Imaging Services: 5, 140 (collection The Museum of Modern Art, New York. Gift of the artist). Courtesy The Museum of Modern Art, New York, Department of Imaging Services, photo Thomas Griesel: 143 (collection The Museum of Modern Art, New York. Abby Aldrich Rockefeller Fund and gift of Mrs. William Sisler). Courtesy The Museum of Modern Art, New York, Department of Imaging Services, photo John Wronn: 17. Courtesy the Philadelphia Museum of Art: 167.
© 2010 Artists Rights Society (ARS), New York/BUS, Stockholm. Photo Bernd Borchardt: 212, 213.
© 2010 Artists Rights Society (ARS), New York/IVARO, Dublin. Courtesy the artist and mother's tankstation, Dublin: 219.
© 2010 Artists Rights Society (ARS), New York/SIAE, Rome. Courtesy The Museum of Modern Art, New York, Department of Imaging Services: 58. Courtesy The Museum of Modern Art, New York, Department of Imaging Services, photo Kate Keller: 153 (work collection The Museum of Modern Art, New York. Purchase).
© 2010 Artists Rights Society (ARS), New York/SODRAC, Montreal. Copy photo © Art Gallery of Ontario, courtesy the artist and Corkin Gallery, Toronto: 169–73, back cover.
© 2010 Artists Rights Society (ARS), New York/VG Bild-Kunst, Bonn. Photos Wolfgang Morell: 8, 49, 50, 162. Courtesy The Museum of Modern Art, New York, Department of Imaging Services: 41. Courtesy The Museum of Modern Art, New York, Department of Imaging Services, photos Robert Gerhardt: 29, 161. Courtesy The Museum of Modern Art, New York, Department of Imaging Services, photos Thomas Griesel: 46, 47, 159. Courtesy The Museum of Modern Art, New York, Department of Imaging Services, photo Thomas Griesel: 40 (work collection The Museum of Modern Art, New York. Gift of Elaine Lustig Cohen). Courtesy The Museum of Modern Art, New York, Department of Imaging Services, photo Kate Keller: 23. Courtesy The Museum of Modern Art, New York, Department of Imaging Services, photo John Wronn: 21. Courtesy The Museum of Modern Art, New York, Department of Imaging Services, photo Jonathan Muzikar: 22. Original photo Wilhelm Redemann, Hannover, copy photo Michael Herling/Aline Gwose, courtesy Kurt Schwitters Archives at the Sprengel Museum Hannover: 4.
© 2010 Artists Rights Society (ARS), New York/VISCOPY, Australia: 198, 200, 225.
© 2010 A. Balasubramaniam: 9. Courtesy Talwar Gallery New York/New Delhi: 124 (work collection FRAC Lorraine, Metz).
© 2010 Iain Baxter&. Courtesy Corkin Gallery, Toronto: 100.
© 2010 Trisha Brown. Courtesy Sikkema Jenkins & Co., photo Jason Wyche: 210.
© 2010 Calder Foundation, New York/Artists Rights Society (ARS), New York. Courtesy Calder Foundation, New York/Art Resource, NY, photo Robert Grove: 164. Courtesy The Museum of Modern Art, New York, Department of Imaging Services, photo Thomas Griesel: 165. Courtesy The Museum of Modern Art, New York, Department of Imaging Services, photo Jonathan Muzikar: 224. Courtesy The Museum of Modern Art, New York, Department of Imaging Services, photo Mali Olatunji: 48.
© 2010 Luis Camnitzer. Photos David Allison: 108, 129. Courtesy The Museum of Modern Art, New York, Department of Imaging Services, photo Thomas Griesel: 11.
© 2010 "The World of Lygia Clark" Cultural Association: 134, 185, 186. Courtesy The Museum of Modern Art, New York, Department of Imaging Services: 60.
© 2010 Marie Cool and Fabio Balducci. Photo courtesy GB agency, Paris: 220–23.
Courtesy Merce Cunningham Dance Company, photo Oscar Bailey: 145.
© 2010 Edith Dekyndt: 122, 123, 214.
© 2010 Tony Dougherty, photo Tony Dougherty: 204.
© 2010 The estate of Luciano Fabro. Photos © 2010 Giorgio Colombo, Milan: 62, 64. Photo © 2010 Ph_Giovanni Ricci, Milan: 79.
© 1986 Harun Farocki: 103.
© 2010 León Ferrari. Courtesy The Museum of Modern Art, New York, Department of Imaging Services, photo John Wronn: 106.
© 2010 Fondation Lucio Fontana. Courtesy The Museum of Modern Art, New York, Department of Imaging Service, photo Jonathan Muzikar: 54. Courtesy The Museum of Modern Art, New York, Department of Imaging Service, photo Thomas Griesel: 55.
Courtesy The Forsythe Company: 144.
© Association frères Lumière: 13.
© 2010 Ellen Gallagher. Courtesy The Museum of Modern Art, New York, Department of Imaging Services, photo Paige Knight: 81.
© 2010 Fundación Gego: p. 219. Photo Reinaldo Armas: 85 (work Colección Fundación de Museos Nacionales–Museo de Bellas Artes, Caracas). Colección Patricia Phelps de Cisneros: 207.
© 2010 Mimi Gellman: 209, 228.
© 2010 Carol Goodden: 111, 142.
© 2010 Monika Grzymala. Courtesy the artist: 121, 229.
© Hans Haacke/Artists Rights Society (ARS), New York/VG Bild-Kunst, Bonn. Photo the artist, courtesy the artist: p. 217.
© 2010 Mona Hatoum. Courtesy Alexander and Bonin, New York, and Galerie Max Hetzler Berlin, photo Jörg von Bruchhausen: 96.
© 2010 Alex Hay. Courtesy The Museum of Modern Art, New York, Department of Imaging Services, photos Thomas Griesel: 130, 141.
© 2010 Susan Hefuna: 118.
© 2010 Michael Heizer: 193, 194. Photos © Gianfranco Gorgoni, courtesy the photographer and Galleria Repetto, Acqui Terme: 104, 195.
© 2010 Arturo Herrera: 215.
© 2010 Estate of Eva Hesse, Galerie Hauser & Wirth, Zurich. Courtesy Galerie Hauser & Wirth, Zurich: 182. Courtesy Galerie Hauser & Wirth, Zurich, photo Ed Glenndinning: 67 (work collection Gail and Tony Ganz).
© 2010 Ryoji Ito: 178. Courtesy Ashiya City Museum of Art & History: 177.
© 2010 Ryoji Ito and Takehiro Nabekura. Courtesy Ashiya City Museum of Art & History, photo Takehiro Nabekura: front endpapers, 179.
© 2010 Amar Kanwar. Courtesy Amar Kanwar and Galerie Marian Goodman, Paris/New York: 102.
© 2010 Anne Teresa De Keersmaeker. Courtesy Rosas archive: 94.
© 2010 Ellsworth Kelly: 149. Courtesy The Museum of Modern Art, New York, Department of Imaging Services, photo John Wronn: 150.
© 2010 Zilvinas Kempinas. Courtesy the artist: 217.
© 2010 Hilma af Klint Foundation, Stockholm. Photo Cathy Carver: 20.
© 2010 Gyula Kosice. Courtesy The Museum of Modern Art, New York, Department of Imaging Services: 174. Courtesy The Museum of Modern Art, New York, Department of Imaging Services, photo Jonathan Muzikar: 175.
© 2010 Estate of Edward Krasiński. © Galeria Foksal MCKiS: 197. Photo © Generali Foundation, Vienna, photo Werner Kaligofsky: 196.
© 2010 Sol LeWitt/Artists Rights Society (ARS), New York. Courtesy The Museum of Modern Art, New York, Department of Imaging Services: 78. Courtesy The Museum of Modern Art, New York, Department of Imaging Services, photo David Allison: contents page.
© 1997 Pamela Lofts. Photograph by Pamela Lofts, from *YARRTJI—Six Women's Stories from the Great Sandy Desert*, Aboriginal Studies Press, Canberra, 1997: 199.
© 2010 Estate of Mark Lombardi. Courtesy The Museum of Modern Art, New York, Department of Imaging Services: 99.
© 2010 Richard Long: p. 220.
© 2010 Anna Maria Maiolino: 70–72, 131, p. 221 (right). Courtesy The Museum of Modern Art, New York, Department of Imaging Services: 69.
© 2010 Sheila Makhijani. Photo David Allison: 117, 230.
© 2010 Tomás Maldonado: 176.
© 2010 Karel Malich. Photo Cathy Carver: 76.
© 2010 Man Ray Trust/Artists Rights Society (ARS), New York/ADAGP, Paris. Courtesy The Museum of Modern Art, New York, Department of Imaging Services: 18.
© 2010 Tom Marioni: 189.
© 2010 Estate of Agnes Martin/Artists Rights Society (ARS), New York. Courtesy The Museum of Modern Art, New York, Department of Imaging Services, photo John Wronn: 80. Courtesy The Museum of Modern Art, New York, Department of Imaging Services, photo Thomas Griesel: 82.
© 2010 Estate of Gordon Matta-Clark/Artists Rights Society (ARS), New York. Courtesy Electronic Arts Intermix (EAI), New York: 148. Courtesy The Museum of Modern Art, New York, Department of Imaging Services, photo Thomas Griesel: 112. Courtesy The Museum of Modern Art, New York, Department of Imaging Services, photo John Wronn: 113 (work collection The Museum of Modern Art, New York. Acquired through the generosity of The Junior Associates of The Museum of Modern Art, with contributions from Robert Beyer, Ellen R. Herman, Scott J. Lorinsky, Steven T. Mnuchin and Muffy Perlbinder).
© 2010 Anthony McCall. Photo Bruno Barlier: 188.
© 2010 Julie Mehretu. Photo Ellen Page Wilson Photography, 2010: cover. Photo Tim Thayer, courtesy the artist and Marian Goodman Gallery: 115.
© 2010 Cildo Meireles. Courtesy Galerie Lelong, New York: 125. Photo Regina Bittencourt: 95. Photo Wilton Montenegro: 201.
© 2010 Dan Merlo. Photo Dan Merlo: 208.
© 2010 Marisa Merz. Courtesy The Museum of Modern Art, New York, Department of Imaging Services, photo John Wronn: 87.
© 2010 Thierry De Mey: 88–93.
© 2010 Successió Miró/Artists Rights Society (ARS), New York/ADAGP, Paris: 45.
© 2010 Estate of Nasreen Mohamedi: 83.
© 2010 Mondrian/Holtzman Trust c/o HCR International Virginia. Photo Otto E. Nelson: 77. Courtesy The Museum of Modern Art, New York, Department of Imaging Services: 61. Courtesy The Museum of Modern Art, New York, Department of Imaging Services, photos Thomas Griesel: 1, 24, 26, 27, 152. Courtesy The Museum of Modern Art, New York, Department of Imaging Services, photo John Wronn: 25.
© 2010 Bruce Nauman/Artists Rights Society (ARS). Courtesy Electronic Arts Intermix (EAI), New York: 146.
© 2010 Neue Zürcher Zeitung. Photo Ernst Scheidegger: 51.
© 2010 Stiftung John Neumeier–Dance Collection: 154.
© 2010 Avis Newman. FXP Photography, London: 114.
© 2010 Cornelia Parker. Courtesy the artist, D'Amelio Terras, New York, and Frith Street Gallery, London, photo Adam Reich: 97.
© 2010 Giuseppe Penone/Artists Rights Society (ARS), New York/ADAGP, Paris. Photo © Paolo Mussat Sartor: 227.
© 2010 Estate of Pablo Picasso/Artists Rights Society (ARS), New York. Réunion des Musées Nationaux/Art Resource, NY: 2, 15 (work collection Musée Picasso, Paris). Courtesy The Museum of Modern Art, New York, Department of Imaging Services, photo John Wronn: 14. Courtesy The Museum of Modern Art, New York, Department of Imaging Services, photo Jonathan Muzikar: 16.
© 2010 Pollock-Krasner Foundation/Artists Rights Society (ARS), New York. Courtesy The Museum of Modern Art, New York, Department of Imaging Services: 56 (work collection The Museum of Modern Art, New York. Purchase), 168.
© 2010 Yvonne Rainer. Courtesy Video Data Bank (www.vdb.org): 187.
© 2010 Estate of Robert Rauschenberg/Licensed by VAGA, New York, NY: 59.
Courtesy Réunion des Musées Nationaux/Art Resource, NY, copy photo Michèle Bellot: 3, 151 (work collection the Musée d'Orsay, Paris).
© 2010 Dorothea Rockburne/Artists Rights Society (ARS), New York. Courtesy The Museum of Modern Art, New York, Department of Imaging Services, photo Kate Keller: 109 (work collection The Museum of Modern Art, New York. Gift of J. Frederic Byers III).
© Estate of Alexander Rodchenko/RAO, Moscow/VAGA, New York: 34, 39. Courtesy The Museum of Modern Art, New York, Department of Imaging Services: 32, 35. Courtesy The Museum of Modern Art, New York, Department of Imaging Services, photo John Wronn: 7, p. 223 (left).
© 2010 Lotty Rosenfeld. Photo Rony Goldschmit: 101.
© 2010 Estate of Fred Sandback. Courtesy The Museum of Modern Art, New York, Department of Imaging Services: 183.
© 2010 Estate of Mira Schendel. Courtesy The Museum of Modern Art, New York, Department of Imaging Services, photo John Wronn: 107.
© 2010 Carolee Schneemann/Artists Rights Society (ARS), New York. Photo Henrik Gaard: 128, 211.
Courtesy Jiří Ševčík: 126.
© 2010 Gino Severini/Artists Rights Society (ARS), New York/ADAGP, Paris. Courtesy The Museum of Modern Art, New York, Department of Imaging Services, photos John Wronn: 12, 155.
© 2010 Ranjani Shettar: 232.
© 2010 Mieko Shiomi. Courtesy The Museum of Modern Art, New York, Department of Imaging Services: 190.
© 2010 Michael Snow. Photo © 2010 Art Gallery of Ontario: 65.
© 2010 Eva Sørensen, Verbania, Italy. Photo Eva Sørensen, Herning, Denmark, 1960: 57.
© 2010 Michelle Stuart: 132. Courtesy The Museum of Modern Art, New York, Department of Imaging Services, photo John Wronn: p. 223 (right), back endpapers.
© 2010 Joëlle Tuerlinckx. Courtesy Marian Goodman Gallery, photo Cathy Carver: 116, 120. Courtesy the artist and Stella Lohaus Gallery, Antwerp: 119.
© 2010 Richard Tuttle. Photo Andre Morain: 147. Collection Judith Neisser, Chicago, photo Ben Blackwell: 184.
© 2010 Cy Twombly. Courtesy The Museum of Modern Art, New York, Department of Imaging Services, photo Thomas Griesel: 127, p. 224.
© 2010 max, binia and jakob bill foundation/Georges Vantongerloo/Artists Rights Society (ARS), New York/ProLitteris, Switzerland. Photo Theres Bütler, Lucerne: 52, 53.
© 2010 Cecilia Vicuña: 226. Photo César Paternosto: 163.
© 2010 Maria Helena Vieira da Silva/Artists Rights Society (ARS), New York/ADAGP, Paris. Courtesy The Museum of Modern Art, New York, Department of Imaging Services: 86. Courtesy CNAC/MNAM/Dist. Réunion des Musées Nationaux/Art Resource, NY, photo Philippe Migeat: 166.
Photo Isabel Winarsch: 133.
© 2006 Steven Yazzie. Photo Nicole Haas: 105.
© 2010 La Monte Young. Courtesy The Museum of Modern Art, New York, Department of Imaging Services: 191, 192.
© ZKM | Zentrum für Kunst und Medientechnologie Karlsruhe: 218.

FILM PROGRAM

Intersections between the world and line, as both a visual element and a rich metaphor, appear in countless films. Cinematic animation techniques originally sprang directly from drawing — they activated the drawn line — and despite technical advances, some artists continue to work in the territory between the two mediums. Film history includes many examples of the film strip itself being painted, scratched, and otherwise manipulated to create moving lines and patterns, which in some films stand alone as moving drawings and in others combine with the camera's record of the actual world, a backdrop for artistic intervention. In yet other films line functions symbolically, evoking life's various trajectories through travel, the passage of time, the marks left in the landscape, the lines drawn both to join and to separate us from each other.

On Line includes a program of films, drawn mainly from The Museum of Modern Art's extensive film collection, to be screened in the Museum's theaters. Among the filmmakers included in the program are:

Yann Beauvais (French, born 1953)
Stan Brakhage (American, 1933–2003)
Robert Breer (American, born 1926)
Mary Ellen Bute (American, 1906–1983)
Doris Chase (American, 1923–2008)
Jim Capobianco (American, born 1969)
Walt Disney (American, 1901–1966)
Ed Emshwiller (American, 1925–1990)
VALIE EXPORT (Austrian, born 1940)
Harun Farocki (German, born Czechoslovakia [present-day Czech Republic] 1944)
Emily Hubley (American, born 1958)
Amar Kanwar (Indian, born 1964)
Bernard Longpre (Canadian, 1937–2002)
Len Lye (New Zealander, 1901–1980)
Norman McLaren (Canadian, born Scotland, 1914–1987)
Bill Morrison (American, born 1965)
David Piel (American, 1926–2004)
Yvonne Rainer (American, born 1934)
Randy Rotheisler (Canadian, born 1953)
Carolee Schneemann (American, born 1939)
Zdenek Smetana (Czech, born 1925)
Stuart Sherman (American, 1945–2001)
Steven Yazzie (American, born 1970)

Organized by Anne Morra, Associate Curator, Department of Film, and Esther Adler, Curatorial Assistant, Department of Drawings.

PERFORMANCE PROGRAM

The dancing body has long been a subject matter for drawing, as seen in a variety of works included in this exhibition. These documentations show dance in two dimensions, allowing it to be seen in a gallery setting. But if one considers line as the trace of a point in motion — an idea at the core of this project — the act of dance itself becomes a drawing, an insertion of drawing into the time and three-dimensional space of our lived world.

On Line includes a program of live performance and dance as an extension of the exhibition, to take place in The Museum of Modern Art's Donald B. and Catherine C. Marron Atrium in January 2011.

Trisha Brown Dance Company
Relay Re-Laid. 2011. Based on *Roof Piece*. 1971
Sticks. 1973
Scallops. 1973
Locus Solo. 1975

Cool Balducci
Selected untitled works. 2004–9

Anne Teresa De Keersmaeker
Violin Phase from *Fase: Four movements to the Music of Steve Reich*. 1982
Line. 2009. In collaboration with Ann Veronica Janssens and Michel François

Ralph Lemon
Untitled. 2008. With Ralph Lemon and Okwui Okpokwasili

Xavier Le Roy
Self Unfinished. 1998. A collaboration with Laurent Golding. Music by Diana Ross

Organized by Cornelia H. Butler and Catherine de Zegher with Jenny Schlenzka, Assistant Curator for Performance, Department of Media and Performance Art.

LENDERS TO THE EXHIBITION

Francis Alÿs
AmC Collezione Coppola
Giovanni Anselmo
Stiftung Hans Arp und
Sophie Taeuber-Arp e.V., Rolandswerth
Art Gallery of Ontario, Toronto
The Art Institute of Chicago
A. Balasubramaniam
Iain Baxter&
Chantal and Jakob Bill Collection, Switzerland
Trisha Brown
Calder Foundation, New York
Luis Camnitzer
Vivian and David Campbell
Haim Chanin Fine Arts, New York
Colección Patricia Phelps de Cisneros
"The World of Lygia Clark" Cultural Association
Eileen and Michael Cohen
Marie Cool and Fabio Balducci
Corkin Gallery, Toronto
Gallery [DAM] Berlin
Thierry de Mey
Deutsche Bank Collection
Dohmen Collection, Aachen
Liliane and Michel Durand-Dessert, Paris
Reto Ehrbar, Zurich
Judith and Bruce Eissner
The estate of Luciano Fabro
A. Huda and Samia Farouki, FIIC
Foksal Gallery Foundation, Warsaw
The Forsythe Company
FRAC Lorraine, Metz
Gail and Tony Ganz
gb agency, Paris
Fundación Gego
Mimi Gellman
Generali Foundation Collection, Vienna
Joanne Gold and Andrew Stern
Marian Goodman Gallery, New York
Alexander Gray Associates, New York
Greek State Museum of Contemporary Art,
Thessaloníki—Costakis Collection
Monika Grzymala
Solomon R. Guggenheim Museum, New York
Arturo Herrera
Carroll and Donna Janis, New York
The David Kaye Gallery, Toronto
Sean Kelly Gallery, New York
Zilvinas Kempinas
Kluge-Ruhe Aboriginal Art Collection,
University of Virginia, Charlottesville
Paulina Krasińska
Yvon Lambert, Paris, New York
Galerie Lelong, New York
Anna Maria Maiolino
Sheila Makhijani
Tom Marioni
Anthony McCall
Cildo Meireles
The Minneapolis Institute of Arts
Vera Molnar
Museum of Fine Arts, Houston
The Museum of Modern Art, New York
Muzeum Sztuki, Lódz
The National Gallery in Prague
National Gallery of Victoria, Melbourne, Australia
The National Museum in Poznań
Stiftung John Neumeier, Dance Collection
Avis Newman
Parker's Box, New York
The Pace Gallery, New York
Giuseppe Penone
Philadelphia Museum of Art
Centre Pompidou, Paris. Musée national d'art moderne/
Centre de création industrielle
P·P·O·W Gallery, New York
Private collections
Jeanne Greenberg Rohatyn
Rosas, Belgium
San Francisco Museum of Modern Art
Carolee Schneemann
Ranjani Shettar
Sikkema Jenkins & Co.
Anne and Michael Spalter
Galeria Luisa Strina, São Paulo
Michelle Stuart
Alia Syed
Talwar Gallery, New York/New Delhi
Leslie Tonkonow Artworks + Projects
Richard Tuttle
Galerija Vartai, Vilnius
Cecilia Vicuña
Video Databank, Chicago
Whitney Museum of American Art, New York
David Zwirner, New York

TRUSTEES OF THE MUSEUM OF MODERN ART

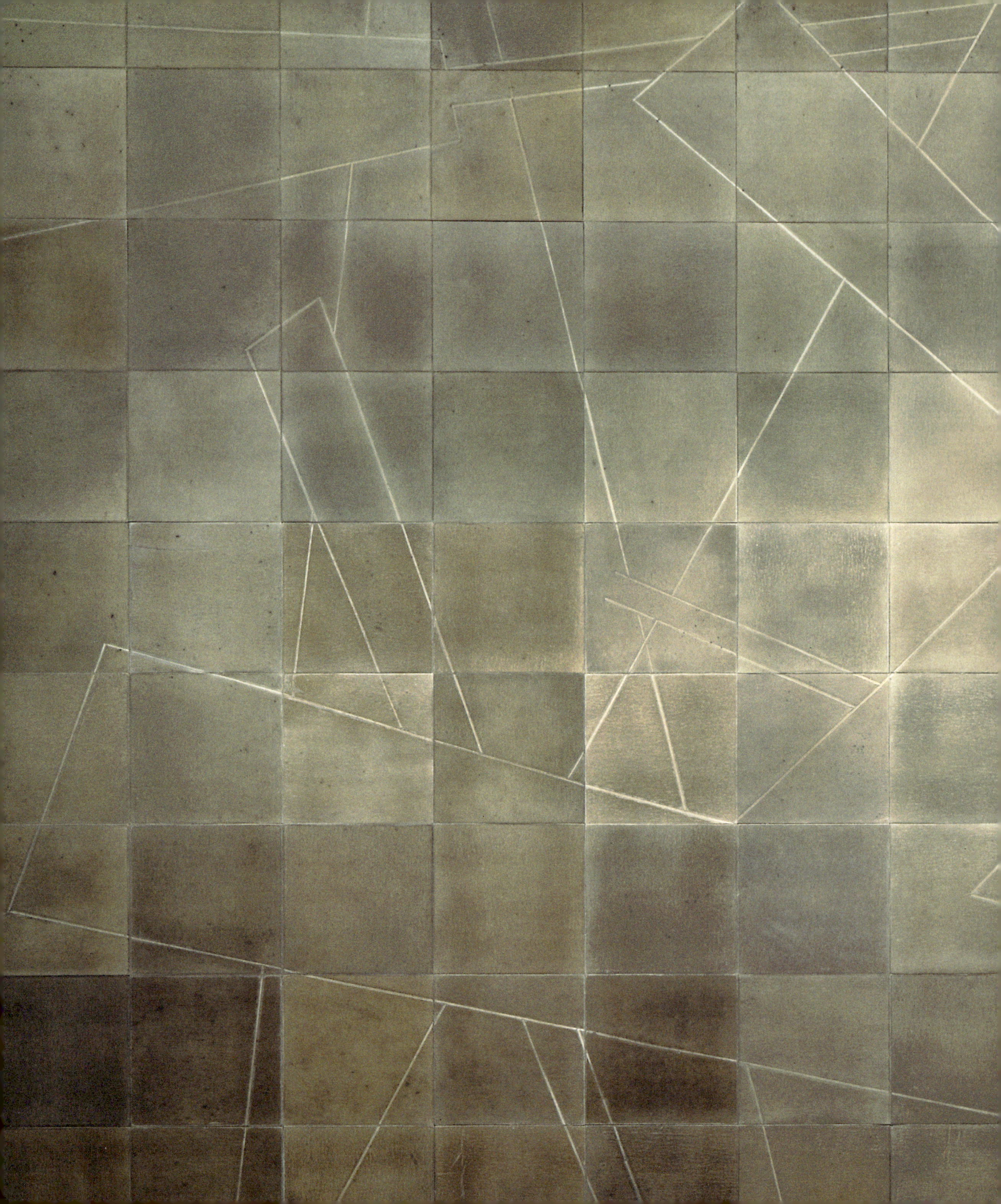